Lecture Notes in Computer Science

Lecture Notes in Artificial Intelligence   14735

Founding Editor

Jörg Siekmann

Series Editors

Randy Goebel, *University of Alberta, Edmonton, Canada*
Wolfgang Wahlster, *DFKI, Berlin, Germany*
Zhi-Hua Zhou, *Nanjing University, Nanjing, China*

The series Lecture Notes in Artificial Intelligence (LNAI) was established in 1988 as a topical subseries of LNCS devoted to artificial intelligence.

The series publishes state-of-the-art research results at a high level. As with the LNCS mother series, the mission of the series is to serve the international R & D community by providing an invaluable service, mainly focused on the publication of conference and workshop proceedings and postproceedings.

Helmut Degen · Stavroula Ntoa
Editors

Artificial Intelligence in HCI

5th International Conference, AI-HCI 2024
Held as Part of the 26th HCI International Conference, HCII 2024
Washington, DC, USA, June 29 – July 4, 2024
Proceedings, Part II

Springer

Editors
Helmut Degen
Siemens Corporation
Princeton, NJ, USA

Stavroula Ntoa
Foundation for Research
and Technology – Hellas (FORTH)
Heraklion, Crete, Greece

ISSN 0302-9743   ISSN 1611-3349 (electronic)
Lecture Notes in Artificial Intelligence
ISBN 978-3-031-60613-7   ISBN 978-3-031-60611-3 (eBook)
https://doi.org/10.1007/978-3-031-60611-3

LNCS Sublibrary: SL7 – Artificial Intelligence

© The Editor(s) (if applicable) and The Author(s), under exclusive license
to Springer Nature Switzerland AG 2024

This work is subject to copyright. All rights are solely and exclusively licensed by the Publisher, whether
the whole or part of the material is concerned, specifically the rights of translation, reprinting, reuse of
illustrations, recitation, broadcasting, reproduction on microfilms or in any other physical way, and transmission
or information storage and retrieval, electronic adaptation, computer software, or by similar or dissimilar
methodology now known or hereafter developed.
The use of general descriptive names, registered names, trademarks, service marks, etc. in this publication
does not imply, even in the absence of a specific statement, that such names are exempt from the relevant
protective laws and regulations and therefore free for general use.
The publisher, the authors and the editors are safe to assume that the advice and information in this book
are believed to be true and accurate at the date of publication. Neither the publisher nor the authors or the
editors give a warranty, expressed or implied, with respect to the material contained herein or for any errors
or omissions that may have been made. The publisher remains neutral with regard to jurisdictional claims in
published maps and institutional affiliations.

This Springer imprint is published by the registered company Springer Nature Switzerland AG
The registered company address is: Gewerbestrasse 11, 6330 Cham, Switzerland

If disposing of this product, please recycle the paper.

Foreword

This year we celebrate 40 years since the establishment of the HCI International (HCII) Conference, which has been a hub for presenting groundbreaking research and novel ideas and collaboration for people from all over the world.

The HCII conference was founded in 1984 by Prof. Gavriel Salvendy (Purdue University, USA, Tsinghua University, P.R. China, and University of Central Florida, USA) and the first event of the series, "1st USA-Japan Conference on Human-Computer Interaction", was held in Honolulu, Hawaii, USA, 18–20 August. Since then, HCI International is held jointly with several Thematic Areas and Affiliated Conferences, with each one under the auspices of a distinguished international Program Board and under one management and one registration. Twenty-six HCI International Conferences have been organized so far (every two years until 2013, and annually thereafter).

Over the years, this conference has served as a platform for scholars, researchers, industry experts and students to exchange ideas, connect, and address challenges in the ever-evolving HCI field. Throughout these 40 years, the conference has evolved itself, adapting to new technologies and emerging trends, while staying committed to its core mission of advancing knowledge and driving change.

As we celebrate this milestone anniversary, we reflect on the contributions of its founding members and appreciate the commitment of its current and past Affiliated Conference Program Board Chairs and members. We are also thankful to all past conference attendees who have shaped this community into what it is today.

The 26th International Conference on Human-Computer Interaction, HCI International 2024 (HCII 2024), was held as a 'hybrid' event at the Washington Hilton Hotel, Washington, DC, USA, during 29 June – 4 July 2024. It incorporated the 21 thematic areas and affiliated conferences listed below.

A total of 5108 individuals from academia, research institutes, industry, and government agencies from 85 countries submitted contributions, and 1271 papers and 309 posters were included in the volumes of the proceedings that were published just before the start of the conference, these are listed below. The contributions thoroughly cover the entire field of human-computer interaction, addressing major advances in knowledge and effective use of computers in a variety of application areas. These papers provide academics, researchers, engineers, scientists, practitioners and students with state-of-the-art information on the most recent advances in HCI.

The HCI International (HCII) conference also offers the option of presenting 'Late Breaking Work', and this applies both for papers and posters, with corresponding volumes of proceedings that will be published after the conference. Full papers will be included in the 'HCII 2024 - Late Breaking Papers' volumes of the proceedings to be published in the Springer LNCS series, while 'Poster Extended Abstracts' will be included as short research papers in the 'HCII 2024 - Late Breaking Posters' volumes to be published in the Springer CCIS series.

I would like to thank the Program Board Chairs and the members of the Program Boards of all thematic areas and affiliated conferences for their contribution towards the high scientific quality and overall success of the HCI International 2024 conference. Their manifold support in terms of paper reviewing (single-blind review process, with a minimum of two reviews per submission), session organization and their willingness to act as goodwill ambassadors for the conference is most highly appreciated.

This conference would not have been possible without the continuous and unwavering support and advice of Gavriel Salvendy, founder, General Chair Emeritus, and Scientific Advisor. For his outstanding efforts, I would like to express my sincere appreciation to Abbas Moallem, Communications Chair and Editor of HCI International News.

July 2024   Constantine Stephanidis

HCI International 2024 Thematic Areas and Affiliated Conferences

- HCI: Human-Computer Interaction Thematic Area
- HIMI: Human Interface and the Management of Information Thematic Area
- EPCE: 21st International Conference on Engineering Psychology and Cognitive Ergonomics
- AC: 18th International Conference on Augmented Cognition
- UAHCI: 18th International Conference on Universal Access in Human-Computer Interaction
- CCD: 16th International Conference on Cross-Cultural Design
- SCSM: 16th International Conference on Social Computing and Social Media
- VAMR: 16th International Conference on Virtual, Augmented and Mixed Reality
- DHM: 15th International Conference on Digital Human Modeling & Applications in Health, Safety, Ergonomics & Risk Management
- DUXU: 13th International Conference on Design, User Experience and Usability
- C&C: 12th International Conference on Culture and Computing
- DAPI: 12th International Conference on Distributed, Ambient and Pervasive Interactions
- HCIBGO: 11th International Conference on HCI in Business, Government and Organizations
- LCT: 11th International Conference on Learning and Collaboration Technologies
- ITAP: 10th International Conference on Human Aspects of IT for the Aged Population
- AIS: 6th International Conference on Adaptive Instructional Systems
- HCI-CPT: 6th International Conference on HCI for Cybersecurity, Privacy and Trust
- HCI-Games: 6th International Conference on HCI in Games
- MobiTAS: 6th International Conference on HCI in Mobility, Transport and Automotive Systems
- AI-HCI: 5th International Conference on Artificial Intelligence in HCI
- MOBILE: 5th International Conference on Human-Centered Design, Operation and Evaluation of Mobile Communications

List of Conference Proceedings Volumes Appearing Before the Conference

1. LNCS 14684, Human-Computer Interaction: Part I, edited by Masaaki Kurosu and Ayako Hashizume
2. LNCS 14685, Human-Computer Interaction: Part II, edited by Masaaki Kurosu and Ayako Hashizume
3. LNCS 14686, Human-Computer Interaction: Part III, edited by Masaaki Kurosu and Ayako Hashizume
4. LNCS 14687, Human-Computer Interaction: Part IV, edited by Masaaki Kurosu and Ayako Hashizume
5. LNCS 14688, Human-Computer Interaction: Part V, edited by Masaaki Kurosu and Ayako Hashizume
6. LNCS 14689, Human Interface and the Management of Information: Part I, edited by Hirohiko Mori and Yumi Asahi
7. LNCS 14690, Human Interface and the Management of Information: Part II, edited by Hirohiko Mori and Yumi Asahi
8. LNCS 14691, Human Interface and the Management of Information: Part III, edited by Hirohiko Mori and Yumi Asahi
9. LNAI 14692, Engineering Psychology and Cognitive Ergonomics: Part I, edited by Don Harris and Wen-Chin Li
10. LNAI 14693, Engineering Psychology and Cognitive Ergonomics: Part II, edited by Don Harris and Wen-Chin Li
11. LNAI 14694, Augmented Cognition, Part I, edited by Dylan D. Schmorrow and Cali M. Fidopiastis
12. LNAI 14695, Augmented Cognition, Part II, edited by Dylan D. Schmorrow and Cali M. Fidopiastis
13. LNCS 14696, Universal Access in Human-Computer Interaction: Part I, edited by Margherita Antona and Constantine Stephanidis
14. LNCS 14697, Universal Access in Human-Computer Interaction: Part II, edited by Margherita Antona and Constantine Stephanidis
15. LNCS 14698, Universal Access in Human-Computer Interaction: Part III, edited by Margherita Antona and Constantine Stephanidis
16. LNCS 14699, Cross-Cultural Design: Part I, edited by Pei-Luen Patrick Rau
17. LNCS 14700, Cross-Cultural Design: Part II, edited by Pei-Luen Patrick Rau
18. LNCS 14701, Cross-Cultural Design: Part III, edited by Pei-Luen Patrick Rau
19. LNCS 14702, Cross-Cultural Design: Part IV, edited by Pei-Luen Patrick Rau
20. LNCS 14703, Social Computing and Social Media: Part I, edited by Adela Coman and Simona Vasilache
21. LNCS 14704, Social Computing and Social Media: Part II, edited by Adela Coman and Simona Vasilache
22. LNCS 14705, Social Computing and Social Media: Part III, edited by Adela Coman and Simona Vasilache

https://2024.hci.international/proceedings

Preface

The 5th International Conference on Artificial Intelligence in HCI (AI-HCI 2024), an affiliated conference of the HCI International conference, aimed to bring together academics, practitioners, and students to exchange results from academic and industrial research, as well as industrial experiences, on the use of artificial intelligence (AI) technologies to enhance human-computer interaction (HCI).

The rapid progress of AI, witnessing advancements across numerous domains, has transformed it from a research and academic field to a service available to the wide public, a landmark which has been recently achieved. In this rapidly evolving context, Human-Centered Artificial Intelligence has garnered the interest of researchers and scholars, emphasizing the seamless integration of AI technologies into human activities through well-planned design and development, and the prioritization of human values and well-being. Submissions explored user requirements and perceptions of AI systems, discussed evaluation aspects, and proposed frameworks to foster user participation in AI decision-making. Furthermore, papers delved into issues related to explainability and transparency, encompassing user studies, design principles, frameworks for explainable AI, and approaches to explanations of neural networks. Trust in AI and ethical considerations have constituted inspiring avenues of research, with contributions investigating issues related to fair representations, bias identification, responsible AI and the role of designers, ethical constraints, as well as trust formation and repair. Further, contributions included in the proceedings also addressed the role of AI systems in HCI. From methods to design AI systems to the use of AI tools in design, authors have illuminated the interplay between these two fields offering rich insights into aspects such as co-creation, interaction design, evaluation, but also information uncertainty, human annotation, emotion recognition, and gamification. Finally, numerous papers have explored application domains within the realm of AI in HCI across various contexts, such as immersive environments, industrial AI, e-Commerce, cultural heritage and learning. As editors of the proceedings of AI-HCI 2024, we are proud to present this outstanding collection of research contributions, which demonstrate the intricate interplay between AI and HCI and how they are shaping our future technological environments.

Three volumes of the HCII 2024 proceedings are dedicated to this year's edition of the AI-HCI conference. The first focuses on topics related to Human-Centered Artificial Intelligence, Explainability and Transparency, and AI Systems and Frameworks in HCI. The second focuses on topics related to Ethical Considerations and Trust in AI, Enhancing User Experience Through AI-Driven Technologies, and AI in Industry and Operations. Finally, the third focuses on topics related to Large Language Models for Enhanced Interaction, Advancing Human-Robot Interaction Through AI, and AI Applications for Social Impact and Human Wellbeing.

The papers in the AI-HCI 2024 volumes were accepted for publication after a minimum of two single-blind reviews from the members of the AI-HCI Program Board or, in some cases, from members of the Program Boards of other affiliated conferences. We would like to thank all of them for their invaluable contribution, support, and efforts.

July 2024

Helmut Degen
Stavroula Ntoa

5th International Conference on Artificial Intelligence in HCI (AI-HCI 2024)

Program Board Chairs: **Helmut Degen,** *Siemens Corporation, USA,* and **Stavroula Ntoa,** *Foundation for Research and Technology – Hellas (FORTH), Greece*

- Silvio Barra, *Università degli Studi di Napoli, Italy*
- Joerg Beringer, *ProContext, USA*
- Luis A. Castro, *Sonora Institute of Technology (ITSON), Mexico*
- Gennaro Costagliola, *Università di Salerno, Italy*
- Ahmad Esmaeili, *Purdue University, USA*
- Ozlem Ozmen Garibay, *University of Central Florida, USA*
- Julian Grigera, *LIFIA, UNLP, Argentina*
- Thomas Herrmann, *Ruhr-University of Bochum, Germany*
- Pei-Hsuan Hsieh, *National Chengchi University, Taiwan*
- Aimee Kendall Roundtree, *Texas State University, USA*
- Sandeep Kaur Kuttal, *North Carolina State University, USA*
- Carsten Lanquillon, *Hochschule Heilbronn, Germany*
- Madhu Marur, *Independent Researcher, Switzerland*
- Rafal Michalski, *Wroclaw University of Science and Technology, Poland*
- Mahnaz Moallem, *Towson University, USA*
- Deshen Moodley, *University of Cape Town, South Africa*
- Jennifer Moosbrugger, *Siemens, Germany*
- Adina Panchea, *Université de Sherbrooke, Canada*
- Ming Qian, *Charles River Analytics, USA*
- Adrienne Raglin, *Army Research Lab, USA*
- Robert G. Reynolds, *Wayne State University, USA*
- Marco Romano, *Università degli Studi Internazionali di Roma - UNINT, Italy*
- Brian C. Stanton, *National Institute of Standards and Technology (NIST), USA*
- Gabriele Trovato, *Shibaura Institute of Technology, Japan*
- Benjamin Van Giffen, *University of St. Gallen, Switzerland*
- Giuliana Vitiello, *University of Salerno, Italy*
- Xi Wang, *Zhengzhou University, P.R. China*
- Brent Winslow, *Google, USA*
- Carsten Wittenberg, *Heilbronn University of Applied Sciences, Germany*

The full list with the Program Board Chairs and the members of the Program Boards of all thematic areas and affiliated conferences of HCII 2024 is available online at:

http://www.hci.international/board-members-2024.php

HCI International 2025 Conference

The 27th International Conference on Human-Computer Interaction, HCI International 2025, will be held jointly with the affiliated conferences at the Swedish Exhibition & Congress Centre and Gothia Towers Hotel, Gothenburg, Sweden, June 22–27, 2025. It will cover a broad spectrum of themes related to Human-Computer Interaction, including theoretical issues, methods, tools, processes, and case studies in HCI design, as well as novel interaction techniques, interfaces, and applications. The proceedings will be published by Springer. More information will become available on the conference website: https://2025.hci.international/.

General Chair
Prof. Constantine Stephanidis
University of Crete and ICS-FORTH
Heraklion, Crete, Greece
Email: general_chair@2025.hci.international

https://2025.hci.international/

Contents – Part II

Enhancing User Experience Through AI-Driven Technologies

AI in Industry and Operations

Ethical Considerations and Trust in AI

Effects of Explanations by Robots on Trust Repair in Human-Robot Collaborations

Zhangyunfan Bai and Ke Chen(✉)

Department of Psychology and Behavioral Sciences, Zhejiang University, Hangzhou, China
kechen@zju.edu.cn

Abstract. Trust can be undermined when robots deviate from human expectations in human-robot collaborations (HRC), whereas proactive trust repair strategies can be employed by robots to mitigate the negative impacts of trust violations. Drawing from the attribution theory, the current study investigated the effects of four types of explanation strategies on trust repair, namely internal-low integrity attribution, internal-low ability attribution, external attribution, and no repair. This study involved 149 university students in an online, between-subjects experiment scenario to simulate a situation in which a robot violates integrity-based trust in HRC. Participants' trust in the robot was measured before and after the trust violation across four time points. The results showed that external attribution outperforms internal-low ability attribution, internal-low integrity attribution, and no repair to restore trust. The explanatory strategies that induce individuals to attribute low integrity have the most negative impact on trust repair.

Keywords: Ethical and Trustworthy AI · Trust Repair · Human-Robot Collaboration

1 Introduction

Humans and robots are increasingly engaging in collaborative work arrangements [1]. A fundamental premise of human-robot collaboration (HRC) is that robots possess some degree of autonomy or agency, enabling them to act on and adapt to novel constraints in the complex task environment [2]. Therefore, human trust in robots is vital for fostering collaboration and ensuring task success in HRC [3]. Trust is defined as the attitude that robots will help achieve human goals in a situation characterized by uncertainty and vulnerability [4], and it influences how humans perceive and interact with robots as teammates. When robots inevitably make mistakes (i.e., trust violations), human trust in the robots is anticipated to decrease dramatically [3]. Consequently, the HRC performance may be adversely affected, including excessive scrutiny of completed tasks and an imbalance allocation of teamwork, which would result in a loss of collaboration efficiency and quality [5].

Trust violations by robots can be categorized into ability-based, integrity-based, and benevolence-based violations, which correspond to three dimensions of trustworthiness,

© The Author(s), under exclusive license to Springer Nature Switzerland AG 2024
H. Degen and S. Ntoa (Eds.): HCII 2024, LNAI 14735, pp. 3–14, 2024.
https://doi.org/10.1007/978-3-031-60611-3_1

namely ability (i.e., competency and performance), integrity (i.e., honesty), and benevolence (i.e., concern for the trustor) [3]. Any of the three types of trust violations can erode the trust relationship between humans and robots. Extant literature on human-robot trust violations has predominantly focused on ability-based violations, ignoring the other two types [6]. However, with the rapid development of robot technologies and artificial intelligence, the abilities and autonomy of robots have significantly advanced. This trajectory may raise more concerns about the moral aspects of robots, with the idea that robots are capable of engaging in cheating behavior or making unethical decisions. As a result, trust violations grounded in integrity and benevolence have become increasingly important in HRC, necessitating a thorough investigation.

Proactive trust repair strategies can be employed by robots to restore trust, mitigate the adverse impacts of trust violations, and ensure the continuous workflow of HRC. Researchers have put forward that trust repair abilities should be a fundamental component of intelligent robots [7]. Common strategies for repairing trust in human-robot interactions include apology, denial, promise, and explanation [3]. Previous research has found that apology, denial, and promise can effectively repair trust [2]. Although most current studies have focused on apology [3], a recent study discovered that explanation is also useful in repairing trust in HRC [2]. Explanations can enhance the transparency of robot behavior [8] and can help maintain situational awareness by improving understanding of the robot's intentions, processes, and performance [9]. Additionally, explanations often involve explicit clarifications behind the robot's behavior, thereby aiding the process of attribution and trust repair. Even though explanations may be effective in repairing trust, the specific content and strategies of robots' explanations are diverse and still underexplored.

Previous literature has theoretically suggested various explanatory approaches, such as decision-theory-based explanation, contrastive explanation, counterfactual explanation, example-based explanation, and attribution-theory-based explanation [10]. Among these, attribution theory posits that an individual's trustworthiness determines trustworthy behavior [11], and trust repair is strengthened when the trustor understands the causal attributions of an event [12]. According to Weiner's attribution theory [13], people assign causal attributions for outcomes in three dimensions: locus (i.e., the extent to which the perceived causes are related to the trustee's internal qualities or external situational factors), stability (i.e., the extent to which the causes are perceived to be either fluctuate or remain constant), and controllability (i.e., the degree to which the perceived control of reinforcement is external or internal). For example, if the trustor attributes a trust violation to factors that the trustee cannot control, it is more conducive to trust repair. It is anticipated that explanations that influence any one of the three attribution dimensions may have an impact on a robot's trustworthiness and perceived trust.

Trust in robots represents a dynamic calibration process encompassing the stages of trust formation, maintenance, and may involve fluctuations over time due to moment-to-moment human-robot interactions [7]. In order to assess and compare the effectiveness of trust repair strategies, human trust in robot teammates needs to be measured before and after trust repair. For instance, certain trust repair strategies may lead to a faster recovery than others. Additionally, in cases where the robot doesn't make any trust repair efforts, human trust may naturally revert to baseline levels based on prior interaction experiences

[14]. However, most of the previous research on trust repair in HRC has only used a single time assessment of trust state following trust violation or repair, making it impossible to determine how long the trust repair strategies can be sustained [7]. Longitudinal measurements of trust in robots can fill the gap and complement the understanding of dynamic trust changes after repair.

This study investigated the longitudinal effects of four types of explanation strategies on trust repair after an integrity-based trust violation in HRC. Drawing from attribution theory, the four explanation types were internal-low integrity attribution, internal-low ability attribution, external attribution, and no repair. According to attribution theory, external attributions may be more effective in repairing trust than internal attributions. People tend to perceive low integrity as more stable compared to low ability, making it less amenable to repair [12]. This means that the robot's choice to guide humans to attribute negative outcomes to its low ability rather than directly to low integrity may result in a better trust-repair effect. In this regard, this study hypothesized that:

After an integrity-based trust violation, the external attribution explanation strategy is expected to be the most effective in trust repair. This is followed by internal-low ability attribution, no repair, and internal-low integrity attribution.

2 Method

2.1 Participants

The study was approved by the ethics committee of Zhejiang University. A total of 161 participants were recruited from universities in China after signing an informed consent form, and 12 of them failed attention check, resulting in a sample of 149 participants (mean age = 21.36, standard deviation = 2.55, 97 women).

2.2 Design and Procedure

This study employed an online scenario-based experimental approach using textual materials as stimuli. The experiment utilized a 4 × 4 mixed design with time point (T1, T2, T3, & T4) as a repeated-measures variable and explanation type (internal-low integrity attribution, internal-low ability attribution, external attribution, & no repair) as a between-groups variable. Participants were randomly assigned to one of the four explanation strategies.

Participants read a textual description that introduced an intelligent driving robot equipped with a high-definition camera for road navigation and photography. It was capable of independently planning and executing tasks without human intervention, as well as interacting with users. Participants were instructed to collaborate with this robot to complete an urban landscape photography task in four different cities (T1 to T4). In each city, the robot generated three visual routes for participants to choose for the photography task (an example is shown in Fig. 1), and subsequently committed to complete the task. In T1, T3, and T4, the robot would follow the route chosen by participants. In the T2, the robot violated integrity-based trust by deviating from the intended route in the middle of the mission, but still met the task requirement. Following the violation, the robot reported task completion and provided an explanation for the deviation. There were four explanation types. For internal-low integrity attribution, the robot stated, *"Task completed; deviating from the chosen route midway was because I could drive not following your route"*. For internal-low ability attribution, the robot stated, *"Task completed; deviating from the chosen route midway was because I made a scene misjudgment at the deviation point"*. For external attribution, the robot stated, *"Task completed; deviating from the chosen route midway was because temporary road control set at the deviation point"*. For no repair, the robot stated, *"Task completed"*. The experimental procedure is illustrated in Fig. 2.

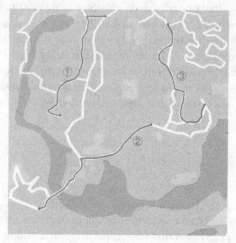

Fig. 1. The sample visual routes provided by the robot

2.3 Measures and Analyses

Participants' trust in the robot was measured at the end of each round using a 12-item human-robot trust scale [15]. Additionally, two dimensions of the robot's trustworthiness were measured (6 items for ability and 6 items for integrity) at the end of T2 [16]. All items were rated using a 7-point Likert scale ranging from strongly disagree to strongly agree.

The total trust score ranges from 12 to 84, with higher scores indicating higher levels of trust. This human-robot trust scale exhibits satisfactory internal consistency (T1: Cronbach's $\alpha = 0.89$; T2: Cronbach's $\alpha = 0.91$; T3: Cronbach's $\alpha = 0.92$; T4: Cronbach's $\alpha = 0.94$). The trustworthiness scale also demonstrates good internal consistency (ability: Cronbach's $\alpha = 0.90$; integrity: Cronbach's $\alpha = 0.80$).

All statistical analyses were conducted using SPSS 24.0, with the statistical significance threshold set at $p < 0.05$. A repeated-measures ANOVA was conducted on trust.

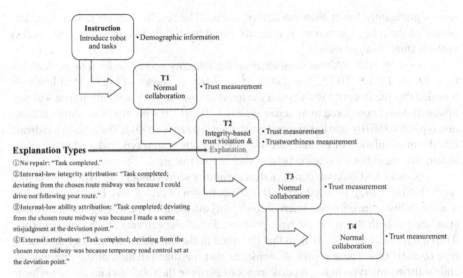

Fig. 2. Experiment flowchart

3 Results

The means and standard deviations of participants' trust and trustworthiness perception toward the robot under the four explanation types are presented in Table 1.

Table 1. Means and standard deviations of trust and trustworthiness perception under four explanation types

Explanation Types	n = 149	Trustworthiness		Trust			
		Ability	Integrity	T1	T2	T3	T4
No Repair	n = 36	27.25 (5.08)	22.00 (5.13)	61.72 (10.19)	47.36 (9.45)	60.17 (10.80)	61.36 (11.41)
Integrity Attribution	n = 36	26.61 (6.96)	17.72 (5.28)	60.14 (10.86)	39.72 (11.89)	56.53 (12.37)	58.14 (11.39)
Ability Attribution	n = 37	23.84 (7.10)	20.97 (6.02)	64.46 (9.63)	46.16 (10.17)	62.32 (9.06)	66.70 (9.08)
External Attribution	n = 40	29.50 (6.11)	24.60 (4.85)	60.83 (10.27)	50.95 (10.01)	62.15 (10.67)	62.15 (10.84)

3.1 Perceptions of Trustworthiness

A paired-sample t-test was conducted on the ability and integrity scores under the no repair type (t (35) = 6.10, d = 1.02, $p < 0.001$), indicating that the integrity scores were significantly lower than the ability scores. The results suggest that participants perceived the robot's action as an integrity-based trust violation, indicating the success of the textual manipulation.

A one-way ANOVA was conducted on the integrity scores under four explanation types (F (3, 145) $\doteq$ 10.75, $p < 0.001$, $\eta_p^2 = 0.18$), as shown in Fig. 3. Post hoc tests revealed that the integrity score under the internal-low integrity attribution type was significantly lower compared to no repair type ($p = 0.001$), the internal-low ability attribution type ($p = 0.010$), and the external attribution type ($p < 0.001$). These results indicate that the manipulation of the internal-low integrity attribution type induced participants to attribute the robot's violation behavior to its low integrity.

A one-way ANOVA was conducted on the ability scores under four explanation types (F (3, 145) = 5.14, $p = 0.002$, $\eta_p^2 = 0.096$), as shown in Fig. 3. Post hoc tests indicated that the ability score under the internal-low ability attribution type was significantly lower compared to both the no repair type ($p = 0.023$) and the external attribution type ($p < 0.001$), but marginally lower than that observed in the internal-low integrity attribution type ($p = 0.065$). These results demonstrate that the manipulation of the internal-low ability attribution type induced participants to attribute the robot's violation behavior to its low ability.

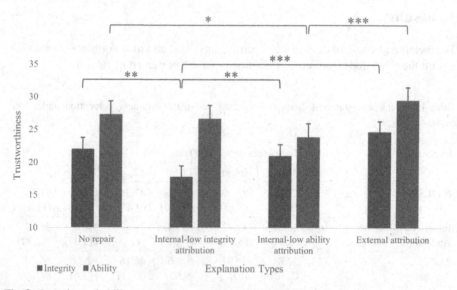

Fig. 3. Integrity and ability perceptions under four explanation types (error bars represent 95% confidence intervals)

3.2 Effects of Explanations on Trust Repair

A one-way ANOVA was conducted on the trust scores at T1 (F (3, 145) = 1.27, $p = 0.29$, $\eta_p^2 = 0.026$), indicating a nonsignificant difference at T1 under four explanation types.

A repeated-measures ANOVA was conducted on trust, considering both the explanation type (between-subjects) and time point (within-subjects). The main effects of explanation type (F (3, 145) = 3.89, $p = 0.010$, $\eta_p^2 = 0.075$) and time point (F (3, 435) = 171.54, $p < 0.001$, $\eta_p^2 = 0.54$) were significant. There was a significant interaction between explanation type and time point (F (9, 435) = 3.56, $p < 0.001$, $\eta_p^2 = 0.069$). The trust scores under four explanation types at different time points are illustrated in Fig. 4. In terms of demographic information, gender did not have an impact on trust. Age was correlated with trust at T3 ($p = 0.005$) and T4 ($p < 0.001$). When age was used as a covariate, the results remained unchanged, hence age was excluded from further analysis.

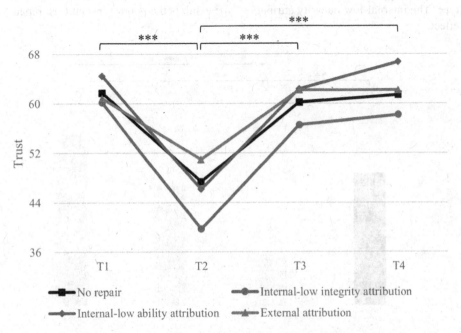

Fig. 4. Trust across four time-points under four explanation types

Further post hoc tests were conducted to examine trust changes across four time points. Trust at T2 significantly decreased compared to T1 ($d = 1.49$, $p < 0.001$), indicating a drop in trust when the robot behaved unexpectedly. Under the internal-low integrity attribution type, trust at T3 was significantly lower than that at T1 ($d = 0.34$, $p = 0.027$). Under the other three explanation types, trust did not exhibit significant differences between T3 and T1 (no repair: $d = 0.15$, $p = 0.34$; internal-low ability attribution: $d = 0.20$, $p = 0.18$; external attribution: $d = 0.12$, $p = 0.39$). These findings suggest that participants' trust had returned to baseline levels following the robot's first normal action at T3, except for those under the internal-low integrity attribution. Trust at T4 did not differ significantly from T1 ($d = 0.029$, $p = 0.68$), and this pattern was consistent across four explanation types (no repair: $d = 0.034$, $p = 0.81$; internal-low integrity attribution: $d = 0.19$, $p = 0.18$; internal-low ability attribution: $d = 0.21$, $p = $

0.13; external attribution: d = 0.13, p = 0.35). These results indicate that trust in the robot had fully recovered to baseline levels at T4, following two regular human-robot interactions after trust violation.

Post hoc tests were conducted to examine trust at T2 under four explanation types, as shown in Fig. 5. Trust was significantly lower under the internal-low integrity attribution type compared to the other three explanation types (no repair: d = 0.73, p = 0.002; internal-low ability attribution: d = 0.61, p = 0.009; external attribution: d = 1.07, p < 0.001). Trust under the internal-low ability attribution type was significantly lower than that under the external attribution type (d = 0.45, p = 0.046). These results suggest that among the four explanation types, external attribution proves to be the most effective explanation type for trust repair, followed by no repair and internal-low ability attribution type. The internal-low integrity attribution type exhibits the poorest instant trust repair effect.

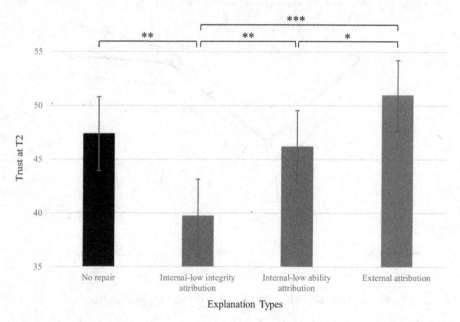

Fig. 5. Trust at T2 under four explanation types (error bars represent 95% confidence intervals)

4   Discussion

Based on attribution theory, this study investigated the effects of four types of explanation strategies on trust repair after a robot teammate's integrity-based trust violation through a textual-based online experiment. The results showed that external attribution outperformed internal-low ability attribution, internal-low integrity attribution, and no repair to restore trust. The explanation that induces individuals to attribute low integrity has the most negative impact on trust repair. Not only does it have the poorest instant trust repair effect, but it also has the slowest repair rate.

This study extends previous research threefold. First, we demonstrated the effectiveness of designing explanations for trust repair based on attribution theory. The attribution process helps people understand the factors that caused the negative outcome and predict the likelihood of recurrence. According to attribution theory [13], people evaluate causes based on three primary, continuous attribution dimensions (i.e., locus, controllability, and stability). This analytical framework enables individuals to make informed decisions regarding the extent of trust in subsequent HRC. In the realm of interpersonal trust, it has been clarified that external attribution is more effective for trust repair compared to internal attribution [12]. The rationale for this is that an external locus of causality indicates that the trustee had no role in causing the outcome, which precludes any need to impugn the trustee's ability, integrity, or benevolence. Additionally, the locus dimension is considered to have a greater advantage in trust repair compared to the other two dimensions of attribution theory [12]. This aligns with the viewpoint proposed by Kim et al. [17] that "the transgressor should prove their innocence at the first level." In this study, we found that the external attribution type was more successful in repairing trust than the two different internal attribution types. These results indicate that prioritizing the locus dimension and the utility of external attribution are applicable in the field of human-robot trust as well. The attribution theory, which originated from the human-human trust domain, has demonstrated its effectiveness in the human-robot trust interaction. With the rapid development of robotics in the current era, people are increasingly attributing intentions and integrity to robots, and the human-robot relationships mirror human-human relationships. In such situations, trust in robots goes beyond conventional ability-based trust and becomes more closely related to relational-based trust (i.e., integrity and benevolence), which is comparable to human-human trust. Our results confirm this and show that a robot's integrity-based trust violation leads to a decrease in perceived integrity, and the internal-low integrity attribution explanation exhibits the lowest effectiveness. Our findings of human-robot interactions are consistent with those from the interpersonal field [12, 18].

Second, we unexpectedly found that no repair, which served as the control group, was less effective than the external explanation but outperformed two other internal explanations in trust repair. In other words, internal-low integrity and ability attribution types were rated even worse for restoring trust than no repair. This is in contrast to the extant belief in previous research that largely suggested that robots should employ proactive trust repair strategies to rebuild trust [1]. Even if these efforts yield little effect in inappropriate circumstances, they will not be worse than taking no action at all. For example, Kox et al.'s study suggested that a mere acknowledgment absent any notion of explanation or regret could have been an ineffective strategy for repairing trust [19]. Similarly, Lyons et al. found that acknowledging or providing goal-oriented explanations offered no benefit compared to no repair [2]. However, there is little research suggesting that proactive trust repairing actions may have adverse effects on trust. Zhang et al. pointed out that in human-robot interaction, taking an inappropriate and unpleasant action may have a negative impact on trust repair than doing nothing [6]. All of these emphasize the importance of being cautious when designing trust repair modules for robots, as an inappropriate trust repair strategy can be even worse than taking no action.

Third, the overall rate of trust recovery appeared to be faster than expected in this study, as trust under three explanation types, except internal-low integrity attribution, had already restored to baseline levels at T3. Furthermore, trust had fully recovered under all four explanation types at T4, corresponding to the second regular human-robot collaboration after trust violation. According to de Visser et al., the rate of trust restoration may be influenced by the type of behavioral violation and the method used for trust repair [7]. The relatively rapid trust recovery observed in this study could be attributed to the robot's violation behavior. In our experiment, the robot only exhibited unexpected behavior rather than making errors (i.e., despite the deviation, the task was successfully completed), implying that task performance remained unaffected. Given that the severity of trust violation is a key indicator of trust in HRC [5], trust is likely to rebound more quickly in situations characterized by milder or no adverse consequences. The results may differ in cases where the trust violation creates serious consequences in individuals and collaboration performance.

4.1 Limitations and Future Work

This study also has limitations. First, the scenario-experimental approach is feasible to implement, but the participants receive no exposure or direct interaction with the robot. These findings are limited when it comes to generalizability with real-time human-robot interactions. Second, the experimental vignettes were highly specific, such as "scene misjudgment" and "temporary road control", which may raise concerns about the replication of the results in different scenarios. Furthermore, while these descriptions effectively manipulated independent variable, they did not rule out the possibility of confounding factors influencing the results or alternative explanations. Therefore, to enhance the persuasiveness of the hypothesized effect, it would be beneficial to create multiple descriptions for the same explanation type across parallel experiments, or to include discriminant manipulation checks to exclude alternative explanations. Third, although this study measured trust multiple times, it is still limited to self-report measures of trust. Future research could combine objective measures of trust, such as behavioral (e.g., eye gaze, body gesture, and decision time) and physiological indicators (e.g., electrodermal activity, and heart rate change) with self-report measures. Fourth, the effectiveness of trust repair strategies may be moderated by other factors, such as the severity of trust violation and the timing of the explanation [3], but this study did not consider those moderators. Future work is needed to incorporate potential moderating factors into their theoretical models.

5 Conclusion and Implications

As robots are increasingly deployed as intelligent teammates, it appears useful to incorporate social abilities into their design, such as trust repair. Our findings can potentially benefit robot developers and designers in identifying human-centered trust repair strategies in HRC. Our results suggest that the design of robots' explanations should prioritize inducing external attribution while carefully considering the option of inducing internal attribution, which may be less effective than maintaining silence. Furthermore, when robots violate trust based on integrity, the best approach for trust repair is to avoid or divert information related to low integrity. However, while we recommend that robots adopt suitable trust repair strategies, this should not be misconstrued as endorsing the use of deceptive tactics or the creation of an innocent image to avoid accountability for the purpose of repairing human trust. In particular, our findings highlight the importance of establishing a robot's integrity. Beyond the advancements in machine intelligence, autonomy, and learning capabilities, robots must be regarded as having integrity and benevolence, whether intrinsic or cultivated by developers. In practical applications, trust repair in HRC should be guided by principles akin to human relationships, adhering to ethical, moral, and legal constraints. Establishing and repairing trust also requires robot developers to enhance the explainability and transparency of algorithms and decision-making processes. Additionally, governments and relevant organizations should promptly strengthen regulations and oversight in this regard.

Acknowledgments. This study was funded by the Humanity and Social Science Youth Foundation of the Ministry of Education of China (22YJC840004)).

Disclosure of Interests.   The authors have no competing interests.

References

1. Esterwood, C., Robert, L.P.: Do you still trust me? human-robot trust repair strategies. In: 2021 30th IEEE International Conference on Robot & Human Interactive Communication (RO-MAN), pp. 183–188 (2021)
2. Lyons, J.B., Hamdan, I.A., Vo, T.Q.: Explanations and trust: what happens to trust when a robot partner does something unexpected? Comput. Hum. Behav. **138**, 107473 (2023)
3. Esterwood, C., Robert, L.P.: A literature review of trust repair in HRI. In: 2022 31st IEEE International Conference on Robot and Human Interactive Communication (RO-MAN), pp. 1641–1646 (2022)
4. Lee, J.D., See, K.A.: Trust in automation: designing for appropriate reliance. Hum. Factors **46**(1), 50–80 (2004)
5. Baker, A.L., Phillips, E.K., Ullman, D., Keebler, J.R.: Toward an understanding of trust repair in human-robot interaction: current research and future directions. ACM Trans. Interact. Intell. Syst. **8**(4), 1–30 (2018)
6. Zhang, X., Lee, S.K., Kim, W., Hahn, S.: "Sorry, it was my fault": repairing trust in human-robot interactions. Int. J. Hum. Comput. Stud. **175**, 103031 (2023)
7. de Visser, E.J., Pak, R., Shaw, T.H.: From 'automation' to 'autonomy': the importance of trust repair in human-machine interaction. Ergonomics **61**(10), 1409–1427 (2018)
8. Floyd, M.W., Aha, D.W.: Using explanations to provide transparency during trust-guided behavior adaptation. AI Commun. **30**, 281–294 (2017)
9. Chiou, E.K., Demir, M., Buchanan, V., Corral, C.C., Endsley, M.R., Lematta, G.L., et al.: Toward human-robot teaming: tradeoffs of explanation-based communication strategies in a virtual search and rescue task. Int. J. Soc. Robot. **14**(5), 1117–1136 (2021)
10. Kim, S., et al.: Designing an XAI interface for BCI experts: a contextual design for pragmatic explanation interface based on domain knowledge in a specific context. Int. J. Hum. Comput. Stud. **174**, 103009 (2023)

11. Yao, Q., Yue, G.-A., Lai, K.-S., Zhang, C., Xue, T.: Trust repair: present research and challenges. Adv. Psychol. Sci. **20**(6), 902–909 (2013)
12. Tomlinson, E.C., Mayer, R.C.: The role of causal attribution dimensions in trust repair. Acad. Manag. Rev. **34**(1), 85–104 (2009)
13. Weiner, B.: An attributional theory of achievement motivation and emotion. Psychol. Rev. **92**(4), 548–573 (1985)
14. Schilke, O., Reimann, M., Cook, K.S.: Effect of relationship experience on trust recovery following a breach. Proc. Natl. Acad. Sci. - PNAS **110**(38), 15236–15241 (2013)
15. Jian, J., Bisantz, A.M., Drury, C.G.: Foundations for an empirically determined scale of trust in automated systems. Int. J. Cogn. Ergon. **4**(1), 53–71 (2000)
16. Mayer, R.C., Davis, J.H.: The effect of the performance appraisal system on trust for management: a field quasi-experiment. J. Appl. Psychol. **84**(1), 123–136 (1999)
17. Kim, P.H., Dirks, K.T., Cooper, C.D.: The repair of trust: a dynamic bilateral perspective and multilevel conceptualization. Acad. Manag. Rev. **34**(3), 401–422 (2009)
18. Deng, H., Wang, W., Lim, K.: Repairing integrity-based trust violations in ascription disputes for potential E-commerce customers. MIS Q. **46**(4), 1983–2014 (2022)
19. Kox, E.S., Kerstholt, J.H., Hueting, T.F., de Vries, P.W.: Trust repair in human-agent teams: the effectiveness of explanations and expressing regret. Auton. Agent. Multi-Agent Syst. **35**, 30 (2021)

Do You Trust AI? Examining AI Trustworthiness Perceptions Among the General Public

Aria Batut, Lina Prudhomme, Martijn van Sambeek, and Weiqin Chen(✉) iD

Oslo Metropolitan University, St. Olavs Plass, P.O. Box 4, NO-0130 Oslo, Norway
weiche@oslomet.no

Abstract. Societal acceptance and successful adoption of artificial intelligence (AI) hinge critically on our trust in AI technology. Trust becomes particularly crucial in human-AI interaction due to perceived risks arising from AI behaviors' complexity and the technology's nondeterministic nature. While several studies have examined trust in AI within specific domains and have focused on particular types of AI technology, this study aims to investigate trust in AI among the general public. Through an analysis of questionnaire data collected from 120 respondents, we have gained insights into the factors that the general public associates with trust in AI. This research potentially can contribute to improving the trustworthiness of AI technology and promoting confidence in AI applications, ultimately enhancing public trust in AI.

Keywords: Artificial Intelligence (AI) · Trust · Trustworthy AI

1 Introduction

Artificial intelligence (AI) technology is transforming every facet of our lives, but its rapid development and application have also raised many concerns. For example, AI systems have the potential to inflict harm or perpetuate unfairness. Furthermore, AI behaviors' complexity and nondeterministic nature may hinder understanding of the reasoning behind decisions. These possibilities decrease people's trust in AI.

As indicated in previous research [1, 2], the trust placed in AI is pivotal for ensuring societal acceptance and successful integration of AI technologies, products, and services. Establishing and sustaining trust in AI depends on various factors, encompassing users' characteristics and expectations, as well as AI properties. The literature has identified and discussed many AI factors – including explainability, transparency, fairness, accountability, accuracy, and reliability [3, 4] – that play a crucial role in shaping AI's perceived trustworthiness. Trustworthiness perceptions impact AI, influencing people's decisions and behaviors toward AI technologies, products, and services [5].

Trust in AI has also been examined across various domains, including health, management and business, as well as different types of AI technology, such as robotic, virtual, and embedded AI [6]. However, few studies have focused on trust in AI from the general public's perspective.

© The Author(s), under exclusive license to Springer Nature Switzerland AG 2024
H. Degen and S. Ntoa (Eds.): HCII 2024, LNAI 14735, pp. 15–26, 2024.
https://doi.org/10.1007/978-3-031-60611-3_2

Trust has been defined differently among various disciplines [7]. In everyday life, it is used intuitively, but in this paper, we view trust as a person's belief in AI's characteristics under conditions of risk and uncertainty. The goal of this study is to understand the general public's trust in AI and the factors or aspects of AI that they view as important in attaining their trust.

2 Related Work

In recent years, with the rapid development and widespread applications of AI technology, research on trust in relation to AI acceptance and adoption has been proliferating. For example, Bedué and Fritzsche [8] conducted a qualitative study on trust requirements and their significance in AI adoption by interviewing experts from various companies. The study employed Mayer et al.'s [9] Ability, Benevolence, and Integrity (ABI) model as a foundational framework and then identified subcategories for the three main trust dimensions. The study revealed that access to knowledge, transparency, explainability, certification, and self-imposed standards and guidelines are key determinants of trust in AI. Omrani et al. [10] analyzed survey data collected in 2019 from over 30,000 individuals from European member states regarding attitudes toward *"the obligations to inform users when digital services or mobile applications use AI."* The results from the analysis indicated that AI trust is linked to concerns related to AI use, such as discrimination/bias, responsibility, accountability, and lack of an interlocutor in the case of complaints. To enhance trust, the authors proposed that practitioners can optimize AI systems' technological features.

AI trustworthiness has gained significant attention in recent years, both within the research community and international bodies overseeing regulation and standards. The increase in research publications dedicated to AI trustworthiness reflects a growing awareness of its importance, and many factors have been identified in various studies. Toreini et al. [5] proposed to classify trustworthy technologies based on Fair, Explainable, Auditable, and Safe Technologies (FEAS) framework. Approaching the topic from a computational perspective, Liu et al. [11] presented a comprehensive evaluation of trustworthy AI that focused on six dimensions: Safety and Robustness; Nondiscrimination and Fairness; Explainability; Privacy; Accountability & Auditability; and Environmental Well-being. Li et al. [3] categorized the representative principles related to practical AI applications' trustworthiness into two main groups: technical aspects – including robustness, explainability, transparency, reproducibility, and generalization – and ethical aspects, including fairness, privacy, and accountability. This comprehensive examination of these dimensions has contributed to a more nuanced understanding of AI trustworthiness.

Furthermore, numerous guidelines have been established to direct the design, development, and deployment of trustworthy AI. According to EU guidelines [12], trustworthy AI should adhere to lawfulness, ethics, and robustness principles. The guidelines further specified seven key requirements that AI systems should fulfill to be viewed as trustworthy: human agency and oversight; technical robustness and safety; privacy and data governance; transparency; diversity, nondiscrimination, and fairness; societal and environmental well-being; and accountability. The International Organization for Standardization (ISO) and the International Electrotechnical Commission (IEC) have recommended approaches to establish trust and assess and achieve availability, resiliency, reliability, accuracy, safety, security, and privacy in AI systems based on their analysis of the factors influencing AI trustworthiness, such as transparency, explainability, and controllability [13]. The Organization for Economic Cooperation and Development (OECD) has identified five principles for cultivating trustworthy AI: 1) inclusive growth, sustainable development, and well-being; 2) human-centered values and fairness; 3) transparency and explainability; 4) robustness, security, and safety; and 5) accountability [14]. Moreover, methods and approaches for assessing and evaluating user trust in AI systems have also been proposed. In the United States, the National Institute of Standards and Technology (NIST) [15] has put forth nine factors that influence a human's potential trust in an AI system, namely accuracy, reliability, resiliency, objectivity, security, explainability, safety, accountability, and privacy. These guidelines, principles, and factors provide valuable frameworks for understanding and ensuring trustworthiness in AI systems, thereby helping to enhance user trust in AI.

In light of these various guidelines, principles, and factors pertaining to AI trustworthiness, researchers have attempted to analyze them and identify common themes. Fjeld et al. [16] conducted an analysis of existing principled AI frameworks from diverse sources, such as industry, governments, the general public, civil societies, and academic bodies. They identified eight key themes, namely privacy, accountability, safety and security, transparency and explainability, fairness and nondiscrimination, human control, professional responsibility, and promotion of human values. Jobin et al. [4] identified a global convergence around five ethical AI principles: transparency; justice and fairness; nonmaleficence; responsibility; and privacy. After analyzing 22 guidelines, Hagendorff [17] found that six aspects – privacy protection; fairness, nondiscrimination, and justice; accountability; transparency and openness; safety and cybersecurity; and common good, sustainability, and well-being – appeared in over 72% of the guidelines.

3 Method

Building on the literature analysis on AI trust and trustworthiness aspects, and incorporating the requirements outlined in the guidelines and principles, we formulated 27 questions that reflect the 12 aspects related to trust in AI and AI trustworthiness: Autonomy; Beneficence; Explainability and transparency; Justice and fairness; Non-maleficence; Responsibility; Privacy; Robustness; Safety; Security; Solidarity; and Sustainability. A comprehensive explanation of these aspects can be found in Li et al. [3] and Jobin et al. [4].

The questionnaire begins with a brief introduction to the study, providing an overview and clarification of what AI entails. This ensures that all participants, particularly those unfamiliar with AI, possess a somewhat similar understanding of the concept before responding to the questionnaire, which comprised three sections:

- Demographic information: The first section gathers participants' demographic details, including gender, age, education level, academic background, and knowledge about AI.

- AI Trust and Trustworthiness: The second section starts with the question *"To what degree do you trust AI?"* Following this, participants respond to 27 questions addressing the 12 aspects of AI trust and trustworthiness.
- Rating of importance: The third section asks participants to rate the five most and least important aspects concerning their trust in AI. Furthermore, an open-ended question allows participants to specify any other aspects that they deem significant. The questionnaire concludes by reiterating the question *"To what degree do you trust AI?"* This repetition aims to assess whether participants adjust their responses after considering the various aspects covered in the questionnaire.

A pilot test of the questionnaire was conducted on three groups of participants, each of which provided valuable feedback on various aspects. The objectives were to assess the questions' clarity and understandability, identify any necessary or missing elements, evaluate the questionnaire's length, examine the order of the questions, and obtain general comments. Below is an overview of the three groups:

1. Group 1 comprised three engineering students, all of whom had some knowledge about AI and provided feedback on the questions' relevance, clarity, and understandability.
2. Group 2 comprised three journalism students, all of whom had minimal knowledge about AI and evaluated the questions' precision and whether examples were necessary for better comprehension.
3. Group 3 comprised two professors with extensive experience in qualitative and quantitative research who primarily assessed the survey design.

The feedback from the pilot test was discussed carefully among the authors, and adjustments were made accordingly. For example, we added an explanation of what AI entails to the questionnaire's introduction based on feedback from the pilot test. We also added real-life examples to certain questions to enhance participants' comprehension.

Information about the study and online questionnaire was distributed through the authors' social and professional networks, as well as the department newsletter. The questionnaire data were analyzed using statistical methods, and the responses to the open-ended question were analyzed using lightweight content analysis.

4 Results

The questionnaire received responses from 120 participants, and their demographic details are presented in Table 1. Key observations include a slight female majority, with five more female respondents than males. Half the participants (n = 60) fell within the 18–24 age group, with no respondents aged 65 or older. A diverse range of backgrounds was represented among the respondents, with technology being predominant (n = 44). Other respondents came from many different backgrounds and professions, including literature, film, design, journalism, economics, human resources, business, accounting, and sales.

Table 1. Demographic details on the study participants

Characteristics	Value	%
Gender		
Female	62	51.7%
Male	57	47.5%
Non-binary	1	0.8%
Prefer not to answer	0	0.0%
Age		
18–24	60	50.0%
25–34	15	12.5%
35–44	9	7.5%
45–54	33	27.5%
55–64	3	2.5%
65 +	0	0.0%
Background		
Education	12	10%
Medicine	3	2.5%
Social sciences	2	1.7%
Technology	44	36.7%
Law	3	2.5%
Other	31	25.8%
Only specified in note	25	20.8%

As presented in Table 2, nearly half the respondents reported having basic knowledge about AI (n = 51). The primary sources through which they acquired this knowledge were reading articles or watching documentaries.

Table 2. Self-reported knowledge about AI

Knowledge status	Value	%
I don't know anything about it	8	6.7%
I have basic knowledge	51	42.5%
I learned about it during my studies	11	9.2%
I am learning about it by reading articles or watching documentaries	36	30.0%
I am very familiar with it	7	5.8%
I am an expert user; I use AI in my job	7	5.8%

4.1 The Most and Least Important Aspects that Influence Trust in AI

As presented in the left-hand pie chart in Fig. 1, the most important aspects that influence trust in AI are Explainability and Transparency (15.4%), Security (13.9%), and Privacy (12%), with Beneficence (5.49%), Autonomy (5.32%), and Solidarity (2.74%) registering the lowest percentages. The right-hand pie chart in Fig. 1 indicates that the least important aspects are Autonomy (14%), Solidarity (13.4%), and Robustness (11.2%), with Safety (5.33%), Explainability and Transparency (4.6%), and Security (3.13%) registering the lowest percentages. In considering both charts, the respondents consistently identified Explainability & Transparency and Security as the most important aspects, while Autonomy and Solidarity emerged as the least important aspects affecting their trust in AI.

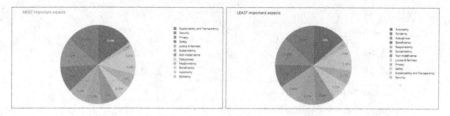

Fig. 1. The most and least important aspects that respondents selected.

4.2 Changes in Trust at the Beginning and End of the Questionnaire

We asked the participants *"To what degree do you trust AI?"* at the beginning and end of the questionnaire to observe any changes in responses after completion of the questionnaire. As depicted in Fig. 2, the histograms exhibited different patterns. Initially, 47 participants (39.1%) selected a response less than 5, while 73 (60.8%) opted for a response greater than 5. By the end of the questionnaire, 77 participants chose a response greater than 5. The mean increased only marginally, from 6.0 (SD: 1.94) to 6.1 (SD: 2.09).

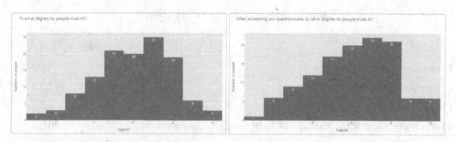

Fig. 2. Histograms illustrating the distribution of participants who selected different trust levels at the beginning and end of the questionnaire.

Table 3 presents changes in trust based on gender. The data indicate that male respondents had higher trust in AI than females. Both male and female participants exhibited increased trust by the end of the questionnaire.

Table 3. Changes in trust based on gender

Gender	Beginning (mean ± SD)	End (mean ± SD)	Mean Difference	N
Female	5.56 ± 1.74	5.68 ± 1.73	0.12	62
Male	6.54 ± 1.99	6.65 ± 2.26	0.11	57
Non-binary	5.00 ± 0.00	2.00 ± 0.00	3.00	1

Table 4. Changes in trust based on age group

Age group	Beginning (mean ± SD)	End (mean ± SD)	Mean Difference	N
18–24	6.25 ± 1.55	6.36 ± 1.95	0.11	60
25–34	6.33 ± 2.26	6.27 ± 2.25	-0.06	15
35–44	5.89 ± 2.47	6.67 ± 2.23	0.78	9
45–54	5.52 ± 2.18	5.36 ± 2.10	-0.16	33
55–64	5.00 ± 2.64	5.33 ± 3.05	0.33	3

Table 5. Changes in trust based on knowledge of AI

Knowledge status	Beginning (mean ± SD)	End (mean ± SD)	Mean difference	N
I don't know anything about it	4.88 ± 2.99	5.12 ± 1.81	0.24	8
I have basic knowledge	5.53 ± 1.54	5.49 ± 1.84	-0.04	51
I learned about it during my studies	7.0 ± 1.41	7.18 ± 1.66	0.18	11
I am learning about it by reading articles or watching documentaries	5.97 ± 1.87	5.86 ± 2.00	-0.11	36
I am very familiar with it	6.71 ± 2.36	7.71 ± 2.36	1.00	7
I am an expert user; I use AI in my job	8.57 ± 0.97	9.14 ± 0.90	0.57	7

Table 4 illustrates changes in trust across age groups. The 18–24 age group, comprising 60 participants, registered an increase in mean trust, from 6.25 to 6.36, with a lower standard deviation than other age groups. In contrast, the 45–54 age group (33 participants) experienced a decrease in mean trust, from 5.52 to 5.36, coupled with a higher standard deviation.

Table 5 outlines changes in trust based on participants' knowledge of AI. Those with expertise in AI consistently exhibited higher trust levels at both the beginning and end of the questionnaire than those with no knowledge of AI. Notably, the group with basic knowledge (51 participants) registered a slight decrease in mean trust.

4.3   Results from Analysis of the Open-Ended Question

The open-ended question prompted the respondents to specify additional aspects that they viewed as important to their trust in AI. The results from the analysis are organized based on the themes identified through the lightweight thematic analysis.

Who Creates AI and Who Manages AI? This theme emerged prominently in responses to the open-ended question, with 15 respondents emphasizing the significance of individuals, companies, or organizations involved in creating or managing AI. The respondents highlighted the importance of creators and managers' motivations, technical competence to ensure reliability and accuracy, ethical standards, and ability to anticipate negative consequences of AI technologies and products. In essence, the respondents viewed the trustworthiness of "*AI creators/owners/distributors*" as crucial to their trust in AI. Below are some statements from respondents:

> *The qualifications of the team that developed it and the accuracy of the test.*
>
> *Who controls it to know if it is an ethical AI.*
>
> *I trust AI to do its computation. Whether I trust that this computation is useful depends very much on the field of use and the company behind the AI.*
>
> *I think the question of whether we can trust AI is synonymous with whether we can trust its designers, what data is used for the AI, and how they handle that data to design the AI.*

Explainability and Transparency. Although Explainability and Transparency are already included in the questionnaire as one of the aspects of trustworthy AI, 12 respondents reiterated its importance in their responses to the open-ended question, emphasizing the significance of AI having the "*capability to justify all decisions*" and providing transparency in "*how the data collected will be used*," "*the training/development process*," and an explanation of "*the process of making decisions*." The respondents expressed a desire to understand the algorithm behind AI and wished for those who develop or manage AI to create a "*user manual*" that "*explains in detail how it was designed and how it works.*"

This indicates how crucial the respondents view this aspect for their trust in AI. It also supports the findings presented in the previous section, highlighting that this aspect is ranked within the top three important aspects of AI trustworthiness.

Human Control. While AI's autonomy is already included in the questionnaire as one of the aspects in trustworthy AI, 11 respondents emphasized the need for human control in their responses to the open-ended question. They highlighted the importance of "*human oversight*," the opportunity to "*control AI in decision making*," and the option to halt AI processes "*at any point.*" One respondent expressed the need for humans to have the capacity to intervene in AI functions effectively. Below are some statements from respondents on this theme:

"Objectives associated with algorithms must be controlled by human intelligence to account for the complexity of our world."

"AI should always be challenged by a human."

These comments align with the findings presented in the previous section, in which autonomy is ranked as one of the least important aspects of trustworthy AI. The respondents emphasized a preference for humans maintaining control over granting AI a high level of autonomy.

Comments Pertaining to Social and Economic Aspects. Although Privacy, Beneficence, Fairness, and Solidarity have already been addressed in the questionnaire, several respondents provided additional comments related to these aspects. For example, some emphasized the importance of AI being able to *"delete information if the user asks for it,"* demonstrating *"respect for personal data,"* and conducting *"ethical evaluations."* Others stressed that AI's objectives should not focus solely on economic or political gains and should actively avoid *"discrimination in training data"*.

Furthermore, six respondents advocated for the clear governance and regulation of AI through laws. This perspective is consistent with the responses to the question *"To what extent do you think the current laws/regulations protect personal data when using it for AI development?"* Over half of the respondents answered negatively. Below are some statements from respondents on this theme:

Manage its power through safeguards.

Most important for me would be to trust the corporations making and using the AI and have these regulated by state laws.

Regulations on AI matter the most, and that should be the main focus before trying to implement AI.

5   Discussion

Our study supports the finding in [10] that men tend to trust AI more than women, but unlike [10], we discovered that individuals aged 55 and older exhibit a lower level of trust in AI compared with their younger counterparts.

Furthermore, our study confirms the significance of explainability and transparency in influencing people's trust in AI. This aligns with the extensive body of ongoing research dedicated to AI explainability and transparency, which seeks to disclose information through effective communication about the intrinsic mechanisms of an AI system's data, parameters, procedures, and outcomes, as well as the entire AI life cycle, including design purposes, data sources, hardware requirements, configurations, working conditions, expected usage, and system performance [3]. AI systems face vulnerabilities to various security threats throughout their whole life cycles, spanning from initial data collection and preparation to training, inference, and final deployment [18]. Being able to address potential security threats is a crucial aspect in trustworthy AI, as our study confirmed, in which participants viewed AI systems capable of protecting their data from malicious attacks as important for establishing and sustaining trust.

The respondents in our study emphasized the importance of trustworthiness of individuals, companies, and organizations involved in the development and management of AI. Previous studies have highlighted that corporate credibility plays a vital role in establishing and sustaining customer trust [19]. In the context of AI systems, these individuals, companies, and organizations are essential to ensuring AI accountability and its impact on users and society. Our study's respondents stressed the responsibility of these individuals, companies, and organizations in shaping their trust in AI. This aligns with the notion that certifications are viewed as important indicators of an AI system's overall trustworthiness [8, 20].

Merely responding to the questionnaire evidently impacted respondents' trust in AI somewhat, as indicated by the differences in trust scores between the beginning and end of the survey. However, the average trust score across all respondents remained unchanged, suggesting that while some respondents registered higher trust scores, others reported lower ones. One plausible explanation could be that the questionnaire prompted respondents to reflect, leading to changes in their trust in AI.

The level of knowledge about AI was identified as a significant factor in influencing people's trust in AI. The respondents who had no knowledge about AI expressed lower levels of trust compared with those with basic knowledge and those who were familiar with AI. Some respondents answered the open-ended question by indicating how they lacked sufficient knowledge to determine whether or not they trusted AI. This highlights the potential for increasing knowledge about AI through education, training, and enhancing AI explainability and transparency to empower people to make informed decisions about their trust in AI.

One limitation in our study is the absence of respondents aged 65 or older. This gap is addressed partially in another study [21] that focused on AI literacy among older adults, in which 30% (57 out of 183) of respondents indicated that they trusted AI, and that their trust likely would increase as they learned more about it.

Trust is viewed as an ongoing relationship, rather than a static concept, subject to strengthening or weakening over time [5]. In our study, we did not account for the time-sensitive nature of trust, while collecting data at a specific point in time, although we observed changes in trust scores between the beginning and end of the questionnaire. Future research could consider collecting data over time to identify factors influencing changes in people's trust in AI. Furthermore, our study was conducted right before the release of ChatGPT, and given its increased popularity among the general public, trust in AI may have evolved since its release. Comparing trust in AI before and after the introduction of ChatGPT could be an interesting avenue for future research.

6   Conclusion and Future Work

This paper presents a study aimed at understanding what the general public deems important to their trust in AI. The research identifies explainability, transparency, and security as the most crucial aspects in trustworthy AI. Moreover, the credibility of individuals, companies, and organizations involved in AI development and management was found to be pivotal in shaping the general public's trust in AI. The findings suggest that people are more likely to trust AI when they have acquired more knowledge about it and gained a better understanding of how it works.

This study has contributed to the literature by enhancing our understanding of trust in AI and shedding light on crucial aspects related to AI trustworthiness. Furthermore, it has raised awareness and generated reflection on AI trust among the respondents based on the observed differences in trust scores between the beginning and end of the questionnaire. Future research can build on these findings to examine trust's dynamic nature and its further evolution over time by conducting comparative studies that follow significant AI developments in particular, such as the release of ChatGPT.

Acknowledgments. The authors would like to thank all the respondents for generously dedicating their time to respond to the questionnaire. Special thanks to the participants in the pilot study for their valuable feedback that contributed to the improvement of the questionnaire.

References

1. Choung, H., David, P., Ross, A.: Trust in AI and its role in the acceptance of AI technologies. Int. J. Hum.-Comput. Inter. **39**, 1727–1739 (2023)
2. Kelly, S., Kaye, S.-A., Oviedo-Trespalacios, O.: What factors contribute to the acceptance of artificial intelligence? a systematic review. Telematics Inf. **77** (2023)
3. Li, B., et al.: Trustworthy AI: from principles to practices. ACM Comput. Surv. **55**, Article 177 (2023)
4. Jobin, A., Ienca, M., Vayena, E.: The global landscape of AI ethics guidelines. Nature Mach. Intell. **1**, 389–399 (2019)
5. Toreini, E., Aitken, M., Coopamootoo, K., Elliott, K., Zelaya, C.G., Moorsel, A.V.: The relationship between trust in AI and trustworthy machine learning technologies. Proceedings of the 2020 Conference on Fairness, Accountability, and Transparency, pp. 272–283. Association for Computing Machinery, Barcelona (2020)
6. Glikson, E., Woolley, A.W.: Human Trust in Artificial Intelligence: Review of Empirical Research. Academy of Management Annals 14 (2020)
7. Andras, P., et al.: Trusting intelligent machines: deepening trust within socio-technical systems. IEEE Technol. Soc. Mag. **37** (2018)
8. Bedué, P., Fritzsche, A.: Can we trust AI? an empirical investigation of trust requirements and guide to successful AI adoption. J. Enterp. Inf. Manag.Enterp. Inf. Manag. **35**, 530–549 (2022)
9. Mayer, R.C., Davis, J.H., Schoorman, F.D.: An integrative model of organizational trust. Acad. Manag. Rev.Manag. Rev. **20**, 709–734 (1995)
10. Omrani, N., Rivieccio, G., Fiore, U., Schiavone, F., Agreda, S.G.: To trust or not to trust? an assessment of trust in AI-based systems: concerns, ethics and contexts. In: Technological Forecasting and Social Change Technological Forecasting and Social Change (2022)
11. Liu, H., et al.: Trustworthy AI: a computational perspective. ACM Trans. Intell. Syst. Technol. 14, Article 4 (2022)
12. EU Commission: Ethics Guidelines for Trustworthy AI. High-Level Expert Group on Artificial Intelligence (2019)
13. ISO 24028:2020: Information Technology–Artificial Intelligence–Overview of Trustworthiness in Artificial Intelligence, p. 43. International Organization for Standardization (2020)
14. OECD: Recommendation of the Council on Artificial Intelligence. Organization for Economic Co-operation and Development (2023)

15. NIST: Measuring Trust in AI Systems. Standards National Institute of and Technology (NIST) (2021)

16. Fjeld, J., Achten, N., Hilligoss, H., Nagy, A., Srikumar, M.: Principled Artificial Intelligence: Mapping Consensus in Ethical and Rights-Based Approaches to Principles for AI. Berkman Klein Center for Internet & Society (2020)

17. Hagendorff, T.: The ethics of AI ethics: an evaluation of guidelines. Minds Mach. **30**, 99–120 (2020)

18. Hu, Y., et al.: Artificial intelligence security: threats and countermeasures. ACM Comput. Surv. **55**, Article 20 (2021)

19. Nguyen, N., Leclerc, A., LeBlanc, G.: The mediating role of customer trust on customer loyalty. J. Serv. Sci. Manag.Manag. **6**, 96–109 (2013)

20. Shneiderman, B.: Bridging the Gap Between Ethics and Practice: Guidelines for Reliable, Safe, and Trustworthy Human-centered AI Systems. ACM Trans. Interact. Intell. Syst. **10**, Article 26 (2020)

21. Kaur, A., Chen, W.: Exploring AI Literacy Among Older Adults. Assistive Technology: Shaping a Sustainable and Inclusive World, vol. 306, pp. 9–16. IOS Press (2023)

Factors of Trust Building in Conversational AI Systems: A Literature Review

Cornelia Becker and Mahsa Fischer(✉)

Department of Information Systems, Heilbronn University of Applied Sciences, Heilbronn,
Germany
mahsa.fischer@hs-heilbronn.de

Abstract. Trust is essential for successful human-machine interaction. It is particularly important for conversational artificial intelligence (AI) systems in the
service sector of the online world. This paper focuses on trust-building factors
in conversational AI systems and explores strategies to strengthen trust. First, an
overview of trust, AI, conversational AI systems, and related literature is provided
before discussing related literature on the concept of trust and factors influencing
user trust in human-computer interactions. Through a structured literature review,
a concept matrix of several trust factors from the existing literature is presented.
The findings highlight trust-building factors such as controllability, adaptability,
transparency, intelligence, intimacy, empathy, engagement, anthropomorphism,
security, brand perception, organizational trust, risk perception, personality traits,
and expertise. Each factor has its importance and limitations in building user trust.
For example, transparency enables a better understanding of users, but complex
AI systems cannot be fully transparent, which leads to mistrust. Best practices
from different domains highlight context-specific approaches that are essential
for building trust in conversational AI systems. In addition, best practices, such as
keeping control over the decision-making process and careful handling of sensitive
data, were offered. The study highlights the importance of user trust in functionality, reliability, and security for the successful development and deployment of
this technologies. Understanding user concerns and overcoming these barriers will
lead the way for further development and innovation in this area.

Keywords: Conversational AI System · Trust · Literature Review

1 Introduction

In recent years, advances in artificial intelligence (AI) methods and conversational AI
systems, such as chatbots and virtual assistants, have revolutionized human-computer
interactions. These systems simulate natural conversations and provide users with seamless access to information, services, and support. However, building trust between users
and these technological interfaces is critical to the successful adoption and sustainable
use of conversational AI systems. The integration of conversational interfaces represents
a transition to a more interactive and user-centered design philosophy and will become

© The Author(s), under exclusive license to Springer Nature Switzerland AG 2024
H. Degen and S. Ntoa (Eds.): HCII 2024, LNAI 14735, pp. 27–44, 2024.
https://doi.org/10.1007/978-3-031-60611-3_3

ubiquitous in the coming years. This trend challenges designers to move beyond traditional design frameworks and venture into a domain where conversations are prioritized as the primary mode of interaction [1].

Governments are exploring AI projects to better serve the public and efficiently man-age resources. AI tools aim to streamline public sector processes, engage citizens in service design, and enable agile, personalized interactions with government. Successfully implemented, AI could be integrated into policymaking, support reforms, and increase public sector productivity. Some governments are deploying AI in social welfare programs, using machine learning for accurate stock forecasting in health and social service centers. This improves forecasting and informs policy development [2].

The purpose of this paper is to explore the role of trust in conversational AI systems (e.g., chatbots such as ChatGPT that appear increasingly human). It examines the multiple aspects of trust, including factors that influence its development and effective strategies for enhancing it, to uncover the complex dynamics that influence user trust in these technological interfaces.

The paper begins with a brief overview of the background of trust, of artificial intelligence, and of conversational AI systems. It then reviews related literature on the concept of trust, key challenges in trusting AI, and factors that influence user trust in human-computer interaction. The paper then outlines the research question, methodology and results. The results include factors that build trust in conversational AI systems, strategies for building and enhancing trust and recommended best practices. The paper concludes with a discussion of the findings. Limitations and future research efforts are suggested.

2 Background

2.1 Trust

The American Psychological Association [3] defines trust as confidence in the reliability of someone or something. Specifically, the basis of trust is the degree to which each party feels they can rely on the other to deliver on their promises. Predictability is the key factor. According to Corritore et al. [4], trust is a person's willingness to be vulnerable in relation to a particular issue, context, or information. Trust is not synonymous with belief. Trust involves reasoning because it implies making a strategic decision to take a risk under uncertainty. In conversational AI systems, information is exchanged between the user of the system and the AI technology, there is no communication with other parties. Users have to trust the virtual AI assistants to solve their problem without human intervention or supervision [5]. In the context of human-computer interaction (HCI), trust is the belief that a system will perform as expected [4].

2.2 Artificial Intelligence

In the absence of a universally accepted definition of AI, in November 2018, the OECD AI Expert Group (AIGO) asked a subgroup to develop a description. The result is the following definition of an AI system [2, p. 23–24]: *"An AI system is a machine-system that, for a given set of human-defined goals, can make predictions, recommendations, or decisions that affect real or virtual environments."* An AI system uses machine learning (ML) techniques that allow machines to learn on their own by recognizing patterns and drawing conclusions, rather than relying on specific instructions [2].

2.3 Conversational AI Systems

Conversational agents (CA) are dialog systems, also known as chatbots, digital assistants, or virtual agents. They understand and simulate human-like conversations, either through text-based or speech-based interactions, using artificial intelligence and natural language processing (NLP) [6–8]. The goal of these systems is to enhance the user experience, facilitate goal attainment, and provide accessibility to services. For effective functionality, most solutions require the integration of essential components such as text-to-speech or speech-to-text capabilities, natural language processing, understanding, generation, and image recognition when image and video analysis is required [8]. To improve user comfort and engagement, chatbots are designed to use human language features such as idioms and emoticons. This conversational approach aims to build trust by leveraging the familiarity of natural language interactions often associated with human intelligence [9].

3 Related Work

3.1 Concept of Trust

The concept of trust and relationships is the subject of research in a variety of disciplines [4, 10–15]. Corritore et al. [4] examined the viability of technological artifacts as potential recipients of trust and the validity of attributing human-like characteristics to these entities [10]. Trust reduces risk, fear, and complexity in offline environments. Since trust is the basis for cooperation and coordination, it is also of great importance in the online environment. The authors concluded that it is to be expected that the social rules of interaction between people will have the same effect in the online world and that the results of trust research from the real world can be transferred to the online world. Referring to this, Corritore et al. [4] refer to websites as objects of trust and draw on Nass et al.'s CASA (Computers are social Actors) paradigm [15], where it has been empirically demonstrated that users interact socially with computers and assign them human characteristics (e.g., motivation, integrity, and personality). Without trust, a stable and interactive online environment would not be possible. Establishing and maintaining trust is critical to the success of any system or service, especially in areas where user confidence is fundamental, such as healthcare, finance, and government services [4].

According to trust theory, trust is characterized by competence (the ability to work effectively in a certain area), benevolence (the trust-giver acts in the user's best interest), and integrity (adherence to principles such as keeping promises) [10, 11] and is necessary in situations of vulnerability and risk, such as trusting an online environment like an AI system [4, 14]. Corritore et al.'s model [4] also addresses user trust in online technologies, which depends on the factors of usability, risk, and credibility. Technology acceptance is facilitated by user-friendly technologies. Risk and credibility refer to the user's perception of the probability of an undesired outcome by the user.

3.2 Key Challenges in Trusting an AI System

AI systems are usually based on machine learning methods that are not explainable due to their complexity and are therefore often referred to as "black boxes" [16]. As a result, user remain unaware of the inner working of these systems, including where data comes from and how it works. Trust will be improved by increasing the transparency of AI applications [14]. User trust in AI systems can be fostered by knowing how an AI system works and achieves its final output. Also, reliability is fundamental to building trust, with accuracy as a key component. Trust in AI systems depends on their accuracy, while resilience to traditional and emerging attacks is critical. In addition, the outcomes of AI-enabled systems must be both accurate and fair, without bias or discrimination [17, 18]. Like any other software, AI-powered systems and software are subject to various types of attacks [18]. AI often relies on vast amounts of data, raising concerns about the privacy and security of personal information. One of the most important challenges for trust in AI systems is securing the systems against security threats and protecting private data. Some AI systems require extensive training data to work correctly. A lack of available data can, in the worst case, cause a critical safety issue, e.g. in AI for driverless cars, where a lack of sufficient real-world data to prepare for unforeseen scenarios can lead to critical situations [2].

3.3 Factors Affecting Trust in Human-Computer Interaction

Trust building factors can vary depending on the context and the specific user-system interaction. Current literature provides insight into the factors that play a role in user trust in human-computer interaction. It is important to understand and consider these factors when designing and implementing a trust-building system. Establishing and increasing user trust is fundamental to creating a positive user environment, increasing user satisfaction, and encouraging continued use and engagement with technological systems, ultimately leading to their success and sustainability.

In his study on smart systems, Michler et al. [19] identified the following trust-building factors: control, transparency, safety and security, product performance, product handling (user-friendly interface), brand reputation, onboarding and information. Drawing on Park et al. [20] and subject matter expert guidance, Hancock et al. [21] categorize factors of trust development into external or environmental factors, system-related factors, and human-related factors. Regarding environmental factors, Hancock et al. [21] subdivide into team collaboration (e.g. communication and culture) and tasking (task type, complexity, etc.). System-related factors include performance-related characteristics such as behavior, system reliability, failure rates, transparency, and predictability, as well as characteristics such as the adaptability of the system, the degree of humanization and the "personality" of the agent. For human-related factors, Hancock et al. [21] distinguishes between skill-based characteristics of the system user, such as expertise, workload, prior experience or competency, and character-based characteristics, such as attitude and comfort in dealing with dialog agents, tendency to trust or personality traits. In other studies, such as Corritore et al. [4], the system-based factors include expertise, predictability, and humanization. In contrast to Hancock et al. [21], Corritore et al. [4] relate environment-based factors to risk or users' perception of the likelihood of an undesirable outcome and the reputation of the system than to team collaboration and tasking. Similar to Hancock et al. [21]., Corritore et al. [4] consider user-related factors to include technology trust, referring to individual differences in a user's general propensity to establish a relationship of trust with an interactive system. Følstad et al. [13] found that trust in customer service chatbots is influenced by two main factors: chatbot-specific aspects (such as its accuracy and human-like characteristics) and service context elements (including brand perception and security). Building on this, Nordheim et al. [22] proposed a trust model for customer service chatbots that considers factors such as chatbot expertise, environmental risk, brand perception, and users' propensity to trust technology.

Table 1. Factors of trust development in Human-Computer Interaction

Group	Factor	Reference
system-based factors	- Expertise (failure rates)	[4, 21, 22]
	- Predictability	[4, 21]
	- Humanization	[4, 13, 21]
	- Behavior	[21]
	- System reliability	[21]
	- Transparency	[19, 21]
	- Adaptability of the system	[21]
	- Accuracy	[13]
	- Product performance	[19]
	- Product handling (user-friendly interface)	[19]
	- Control	[13, 19]
	- Safety and security	
external or environmental factors	- Team collaboration (*e.g., culture*)	[21]
	- Tasking (*task type, complexity, etc.*)	[21]
	- Risk (*likelihood of undesirable outcome*)	[4, 22]
		[4]
		[13, 19, 22]
	- Reputation of the system	[19]
	- Brand perception	
	- Onboarding and information	
human-related or user-related factors	- Expertise (*amount of training*)	[21]
	- Technology trust	[4, 22]
	- Competency	[21]
	- Workload	[21]
	- Personality traits	[21]
	- Attitudes towards dialog agents	[4, 21]
	- Comfort with dialog agents	[4, 21]
	- Tendency to trust	[4, 21]

4   Methodology

The goal of this study is to identify and investigate factors, that influence user trust in conversational AI systems. The literature presented in Sect. 3 discusses some relevant factors. However, these factors are not limited to conversational AI systems and represent a gap in current knowledge that this paper addresses. The research questions are:

- What are the factors impacting user trust in a conversational AI-based system and what strategies can be employed to improve trust?
- What best practices can be identified for conversational AI-based systems?

To answer this questions, a structured literature review based on the search process recommendations of vom Brocke et al. [23] is conducted. These recommendations cover the identification of the relevant literature to be reviewed (journals, conferences, scientific databases), the methodology to be used (keywords, search term, forward and backward search), and the systematic analysis of the literature. The results obtained are structured and evaluated using a concept matrix developed by Webster and Watson [24] and can serve as guidelines for the design and development of conversational AI systems.

5   Results

5.1   Trust-Building Factors in Conversational AI-Based Systems

Based on Table 1, the structured literature review in this study analyzed the trust building factors in relevant published studies and classified them in a concept matrix. As can be seen from Table 2, the group of system-related factors forms the largest group in the literature analyzed. Some factors mentioned theoretically in Table 1, such as product performance, user friendly interface, tasking, workload, and comfort with the agent, were not mentioned in the analyzed studies and were therefore not considered further.

The environmental and user-related factors were significantly less represented in the results. Environmental factors include risk perception, i.e., the risk of an undesired outcome when using a chatbot, or brand perception, which refers to the reputation and trust in a brand. The group of user-relevant factors, such as user education, refers to the expertise or amount of training that the chatbot user can demonstrate and has been grouped with the competence factor. Technology trust or tendency to trust has received little attention in the literature, as it does not have a significant impact on the establishment of a trust relationship. Personality traits have only been touched on in one study.

5.2   How to Build and Improve Trust

Controllability. To improve trust, the agent should give access to history data or information to ensure that users can see what personal information they have told to the agent [25]. User are often concerned about how to delete personal information after using a chatbot [26] and don't want the conversational agent to make independent decisions [5]. In addition, Perez Garcia and Saffon Lopez [5] suggest that users prefer to be consulted before the chatbot makes autonomous changes in order to maintain control over the decision-making process.

Adaptability & Proactivity. Adaptability of the system means that users should be able to update their provided information during conversations for refinement and accuracy. In addition, a reliable agent should detect user errors and proactively remind the user. This minimizes the user's self-correction effort [25]. It is also important for the participants in the study by Perez Garcia and Saffon Lopez [5] and Kraus, Seldschopf et al. [27] that the agent acts proactively. Users prefer a proactive and accurate agent, that can make intelligent suggestions and show them how to get the most out of the service. Pizzi, Scarpi et al. [28] found that an auto-activated non-humanized digital assistant resulted in higher user satisfaction than a human-like, consumer-activated digital assistant. Based on their findings on the impact of prior experience, Law, van As et al. [29] found that both prior usage preference and prior chatbot satisfaction have a significant impact on trust in customer service chatbots. This means that users with prior experience with chatbots may be treated differently. For example, a welcome message that asks users if this is their first experience with a chatbot can be used to gather prior user experience and preferences, allowing the AI to personalize interactions accordingly.

Transparency. Explainability of AI processes and functionality of conversational AI agents is important for building trust. For better usage, a clear articulation of chatbot operations, outcomes, and contributions supports user understanding [30, 31]. Transparency, or honesty about the bot's capabilities and limitations, fosters trust by aligning user expectations and improving the user experience [30]. Conversational agents should indicate the ongoing process or operational status so that users can track the progress of the activity [25]. In addition, when a user is in a critical situation, such as confirming an order or making a payment, the chatbot should provide a clear and specific prompt to confirm [25].

Intelligence & Reliability. Reliability is key to building trust in the technology. When a conversational agent's behavior matches the user's expectations and provides useful responses, it builds cognitive trust for continued use [32]. Most respondents said they trust customer service chatbots most when they act intelligently, meaning they accurately interpret queries and provide helpful responses [13]. Belen Saglam, Nurse et al. [26] found that study participants have a notable preference for technical quality in chatbots, such as grammatical correctness and response quality, over social factors such as the perceived gender of the agent or friendliness. In addition, fast and efficient response [30] and data processing, such as information visualization, are effective ways to enhance the image of a trustworthy, intelligent chatbot and demonstrate its expertise [25]. Guo, Wang et al. [25] also suggest the use of symbols and images to communicate with users when initiating a request or providing a service, to reflect security and increase user trust and comfort.

Intimacy & Empathy. Trust can be improved through the creation of intimacy and engagement with users through interactions that are attentive and empathetic. To achieve intimacy, the conversational agent acts as a caring assistant, demonstrating an understanding of the user's context and personal information. For example, it provides reminders, recommendations, and explanations based on the user's needs and preferences. In addition, the agent assesses the user's emotions and expresses empathy and goodwill, promoting a friend-like relationship by using emoticons for a positive and relaxed user experience [25]. Making small talk and showing empathy does not always help build trust. Especially in industries dealing with very personal and sensitive issues like health, the opposite can be the case. This could be because users are concerned about privacy [27]. In addition, chatbots require thoughtful design to minimize bias, ensure inclusivity, and align with user norms and values [30]. However, in addition to encouragement, the provision of critical feedback and the prevention of users from making poor decisions also increases trust [33].

Engagement & Accuracy. Trust between user and conversational agent can also be built up by encouraging or rewarding users for commendable actions. It also strengthens the relationship when users are actively involved and encouraged by the chatbot to make suggestions or develop an action plan together [25]. Clear communication from the chatbot about its capabilities and an explanation of where it can (and cannot) help was cited by study participants as a trust builder [13].

Anthropomorphism. Anthropomorphism is the attribution of human-like qualities to technology. A visual, human-like presence of a conversational agent encourages users to form a personal relationship and address it by name. It also encourages the user to share the responsibility for the outcome, rather than directly blaming the bot [34]. Folstad, Nordheim et al. [13] noted, that approximately half of the participants associated a chatbot's character with a more personal or relational tone of communication to potentially increase trust. They highlighted the benefits of humor, a human-like communication style, and polite interactions as elements that contribute to fostering trust. In addition, Adam, Wessel et al. [35] observed that users tend to attribute human-like characteristics to nonhuman agents, and that anthropomorphism positively influences users' compliance with the CA's request. No differences in trust were found based on the perceived gender of a chatbot. Bastiansen, Kroon et al. [36] and Law, van As et al. [29] discovered no significant effect on the hypothesis, that female chatbots would be assigned more trustworthiness and male chatbots more competence. The study also found that age had no effect on trust level [29]. Hill, Randolph Ford et al. [37] found that people adapt their language to the language of the chatbot, so the conversation between human and chatbot is shorter and clearer. In contrast, Xie, Qu et al. [38] noted that conversation speed can generally increase trustworthiness, with faster speeds increasing persuasiveness due to the correlation with extraversion and dominance. However, a chatbot that is too human-like may decrease trust in certain situations due to the uncanny valley effect, where a robot's excessive human resemblance may cause discomfort [13].

Safety & Security. In service chatbots, trust is highly dependent on privacy and data handling [13, 30, 39]. Users value the ability to oversee and control the collection, usage, and storage of their personal data by the chatbot, emphasizing transparency and minimal data [13] and to opt out before sharing personal information if they wish [30]. Privacy and security are especially important in industries that deal with sensitive and personal information, such as healthcare, insurance, and banking [40]. A low level of trust can be a barrier to the use of these chatbots or to the sharing of personal information with them.

Privacy concerns of users who may be anxious about technology can be addressed by providing guidance on privacy and data protection efforts [31, 40]. To convince users with significant privacy concerns to use conversational agents, companies should improve environmental factors such as brand awareness and reduce the perceived risk of using chatbots [39]. The General Data Protection Regulation (GDPR) establishes essential legal guidelines for chatbot providers and companies operating in the European Union, including privacy considerations such as privacy by design and users' right to erasure [41].

Brand Perception. About half of the respondents in the study by Folstad, Nordheim et al. [13] emphasized the importance of the brand associated with the chatbot in building trust. The perception of the brand represented by the chatbot and accessible through the website was highlighted by customers as an important trust factor. Perez Garcia and Saffon Lopez [5] noted that in terms of privacy and personal data security, it is important that the operator of the conversational agent is a trustworthy company with a good brand reputation. A company that cannot build trust with its customers cannot operate a trustworthy chatbot.

Organizational Trust. Users also show trust in the organization and in their colleagues. They rely on the conversational agent based on peer recommendations or its status as an internal tool, which indicates trust in the organization as well as trust in the chatbot [32].

Risk Perception. The perceived risk of using a chatbot involves user concerns about potential negative outcomes like data security, privacy issues, incorrect information, or unsatisfactory service. Participants emphasized that the perceived risk had a significant impact on their level of trust in using the chatbot [13, 39].

Information & Service Quality. The study by Tisland, Sodefjed et al. [42] shows that information and service quality have a significant impact on citizens' trust in e-government chatbots, with service quality having the most influence. This highlights that citizens' trust is formed based on their perceptions of these chatbots. Consequently, improving the quality of e-government chatbots can strengthen citizens' trust in such services.

Technology Trust. Lv, Hu et al. [39] found no significant effect of trust in technology factor on user trust in their study. In contrast, Nordheim, Følstad et al. [22] reported that some study participants were skeptical about chatbot technology and said they would prefer to contact human customer service. Dekkal, Arcand et al. [40] recommend focusing on reducing the uncanny factor for technology anxious users to build trust in chatbots.

Education. Weitz, Schlagowski et al. [43] observed that higher levels of education among their study participants correlated with greater trust in the presented AI system, indicating a linear relationship; the factors age and gender showed no significant effect. In comparison, Belem Saglam, Nurse et al. [26] found no significant effect from the participants' education level.

Personality Traits. According to Dekkal, Arcand et al. [40], operators of conversational agents should not ignore the different personality traits of customers, as these can provide insights into customer behavior in conjunction with CRM platforms, adding significant value to chatbots with personalized services.

5.3 Best Practices of Conversational AI Systems

The landscape of AI-driven assistants in various domains has evolved rapidly, particularly in the areas of telecommunications, mental health, and fashion. The following best practices highlight the importance of trust-building features and user empowerment in shaping the relationship between users and AI-driven assistants in a variety of domains.

Mental Health Chatbot. Kraus, Seldschopf et al. [27] present a mental health chatbot that focuses on daily mood checks to build trust for improved utilization. In the study conducted, users value different types of social language, such as small talk and empathy, to build trust. The results show that small talk helps to deepen relationships, but that excessive relational dialogue strategies can reduce personal engagement with the chatbot. One possible reason may be that users are cautious about disclosing sensitive information. This suggests that privacy concerns arise when interacting with chatbots, especially in personal contexts such as mental health. Proactive chatbots, with features such as push notifications and guided conversations, increase trust and perceived competence, and seem to be beneficial for mental health applications.

Telecoms Data Driven Virtual Assistant. Perez Garcia and Saffon Lopez [5] conducted a study to identify the qualities necessary for a Telecom Data Driven Virtual Assistant (DDVA) to emotionally engage users. Users preferred a robotic character for the DDVA, prioritizing precision in information delivery. They wanted creativity and proactive assistance but were cautious about giving the AI full decision-making power. Interviews revealed users' initial hesitation but eventual preference for DDVA-enhanced customer service. Users preferred human backup support alongside DDVA, indicating an inclination toward a hybrid human-AI approach. They expressed interest in a proactive DDVA that educated them about its capabilities but insisted on retaining control over the decision-making process. The study also explored users' initial discomfort with the amount of personal data. However, users gained confidence when they realized that their data was being handled responsibly by service providers, fostering a sense of acceptance and trust in data management.

PSBot – The Personal Stylist Chatbot. Vaccaro, Agarwalla et al. [33] investigate common fashion problems in online environments by building and releasing a chatbot that facilitates personalized sessions with a stylist. This fashion-related chatbot aims to build trust by incorporating features and language consistent with human trust-building techniques into its design, as well as providing critical feedback and preventing users from making poor decisions by employing strategies to politely decline suggestions. These tactics included humor, hedging, and offering explanations and alternatives. They learned from the results that online and in-person styling sessions have comparable goals, but online sessions tend to address smaller issues that can be resolved more quickly.

Table 2. Results of the Literature Research

	System-related factors							Environmental factors					User-related factors		
	Controllability	Adaptability & Proactivity	Transparency	Intelligence & Reliability	Intimacy & Empathy	Engagement & Accuracy	Anthropomorphism	Safety & Security	Brand Perception	Organizational Trust	Risk Perception	Information & Service Quality	Technology Trust	Education	Personality Traits
Pizzi, Scarpi et al. [28]		●					●								
Guo, Wang et al. [25]	●	●	●	●	●	●		●							
Perez Garcia, Saffon Lopez [5]	●	●		●		●			●						
Dekkal, Arcand et al. [40]		●				●							●		●
Gkinko, Elbanna et al. [32]		●	●	●			●			●					
Kraus, Seldschopf et al. [27]					●		●								
Bastiansen, Kroon et al. [36]							●								
Xie, Qu et al. [38]			●	●	●										
Hartikainen, Väänänen et al. [30]													●		
Lv, Hu et al. [39]	●	●		●				●	●	●	●				

(continued)

Table 2. (continued)

	System-related factors			Environmental factors								User-related factors	
Law, van As et al. [29]		•					•						
Adam, Wessel et al. [35]							•						
Shin [31]			•					•					
Vaccaro, Agarwalla et al. [33]					•								
Weitz, Schlagowski et al. [43]													•
Belen Saglam, Nurse et al. [26]	•			•			•	•					•
Ng, Coopamootoo et al. [9]								•					
Tisland, Sodefjed et al. [42]											•		
Folstad, Nordheim et al. [13]				•		•	•	•	•	•			
Nordheim, Folstad et al. [22]				•			•		•	•		•	

6 Discussion

The rise of conversational AI agents as service chatbots presents several design challenges in terms of user trust. The use of this systems can make users feel insecure and question whether they can trust the conversational agent. Especially in the public sector, such as healthcare or finance, private data is exchanged that is particularly worthy of protection and requires trust.

The results of the literature review show that the successful deployment and long-term use of these systems depends on users gaining confidence in their functionality, reliability, and security. Therefore, it is necessary to identify relevant trust building factors and to evaluate their pros and cons for a critical assessment of their impact on the development and use of such technologies.

The study identifies various factors that influence trust in conversational AI systems and provides a differentiated understanding of their importance. Factors examined include controllability, proactivity, transparency, expertise, empathy, engagement, anthropomorphism, safety, brand perception, organizational trust, risk perception, personality traits, tendency to trust, education, and service quality.

These factors are critical to building user trust. For example, transparency is an important element that allows users to understand how the system works and its limitations. This helps to manage expectations and improve the user experience. Users also want to be able to track the collection, use, and storage of their personal information and to opt out. Controllability means that users can control the information they receive and the decisions they make. The expertise and reliability of AI agents have a significant impact on user confidence, ensuring accurate responses and expert-level assistance. Engagement, proactivity, and empathetic interactions are key to building relationships and user trust.

However, each of these factors has its limitations. It is not possible to provide as much transparency as possible in complex AI systems such as machine learning models. AI systems are often seen as "black boxes", as the exact process of how these results are achieved remains hidden from the user and can lead to mistrust. The reliability of AI systems can also be affected by biases, errors, and a lack of sufficient training data. Anthropomorphism fosters personal relationships but can cause discomfort due to excessive resemblance to humans (uncanny valley effect). Overly proactive systems can violate user autonomy, leading to discomfort or a sense of being overwhelmed. Privacy and security concerns and the resulting perceived risk of using a chatbot can also reduce user trust. A good brand reputation, on the other hand, increases user trust in data processing and service quality. Certain factors like intimacy and empathy are less effective at building trust than others, especially when privacy concerns overshadow the benefits.

The identified best practices highlight the importance of context-specific approaches in the development of conversational AI systems. For example, Telekom's data-driven virtual assistant focuses on accuracy, creativity, and proactive support while maintaining user control. Mental health chatbots should balance relational dialogue strategies to deepen relationships without compromising privacy. Fashion chatbots can use humor and critical feedback to build trust and prevent users from making poor decisions.

7 Conclusion

Trust remains a fundamental element of user interaction with conversational AI systems. In summary, there are many different factors for building trust in conversational AI systems. Each factor brings its own benefits and challenges. It is important to find the right balance between transparency, reliability, adaptability, humanization, security, and brand perception. Handling user data responsibly, mitigating bias, and ensuring user privacy and security emerge as critical issues in fostering user trust. The findings highlight the difficult balance required in the design and implementation of conversational agents. It requires a good understanding of the target audience, the system environment, and data-specific requirements to develop effective and trustworthy conversational AI agents in different domains. Finally, this thesis contributes to the broader discourse on trust in AI systems by encouraging critical reflection and guiding ethical and user-centered developments in this emerging technology area.

8 Limitations and Future Research

This study is based on a literature review, which has certain limitations. A structured approach using multiple research databases and iterative refinement of search terms was used to avoid bias. As conversational AI agents are a very young field of research, the inclusion criteria focused on recent conference papers from the last five years, which may have missed some relevant studies. In addition, language barriers and limited access to certain databases or publications could affect the inclusivity of the review. The scope and breadth of the review may be limited by the amount of available literature, potentially resulting in overlooked perspectives or gaps in coverage. Consideration of these limitations may guide future research and improve the rigor and depth of subsequent investigations in this area.

Another limitation and opportunity for future research is the investigation of trust building factors in conversational AI systems. The referenced studies may be limited by the selection of participants in terms of demographic characteristics or industry context. This may affect the generalizability of the study results. The subjective perception of trust on the part of the study participants may also lead to bias. Future studies should use different samples for broader applicability and develop standardized measures of trust.

Study results may also vary depending on the context. For example, trust factors such as intimacy and empathy may be more important in healthcare than in retail. Trust in the use of chatbots can also be affected by cultural differences and social norms. Chatbots may need to adapt their language, tone, use of emoticons, or formality to cultural communication norms. Failure to meet these expectations can lead to a lack of trust or misunderstanding of the bot's intent.

Another approach is to study long-term observations of repeated user interactions and the impact of personalization features in AI systems on user trust. Interdisciplinary research from psychology, sociology, and computer science could help here. Research efforts could focus on reducing bias, ensuring fairness, and developing ethical guidelines for AI systems to make AI systems more robust, user-friendly, and trustworthy.

Disclosure of Interests. The authors have no competing interests to declare that are relevant to the content of this article.

References

1. Ramlochan, S.: How AI is Transforming User Interfaces - The Conversation (2023). https://promptengineering.org/how-ai-is-transforming-user-interfaces-the-conversation/ . Accessed 30 Nov 2023
2. OECD: Artificial Intelligence in Society. OECD Publishing, Paris (2019)
3. American Psychological Association: trust. https://dictionary.apa.org/trust. Accessed 13 Nov 2023
4. Corritore, C.L., Kracher, B., Wiedenbeck, S.: On-line trust: concepts, evolving themes, a model. Int. J. Hum. Comput. Stud.Comput. Stud. (2003). https://doi.org/10.1016/S1071-581 9(03)00041-7
5. Perez Garcia, M., Saffon Lopez, S.: Building trust between users and telecommunications data driven virtual assistants. In: Iliadis, L., Maglogiannis, I., Plagianakos, V. (eds.) Artificial Intelligence Applications and Innovations, vol. 519. IFIP Advances in Information and Communication Technology, pp. 628–637. Springer, Cham (2018)
6. Radziwill, N.M., Benton, M.C.: Evaluating Quality of Chatbots and Intelligent Conversational Agents (2017)
7. Müller, L., Mattke, J., Maier, C., Weitzel, T., Graser, H.: Chatbot acceptance. In: Joseph, D. (ed.) Proceedings of the 2019 on Computers and People Research Conference. SIGMIS-CPR '19: 2019 Computers and People Research Conference, Nashville TN USA, 20 06 2019 22 06 2019, pp. 35–42. Association for Computing Machinery, New York (2019). https://doi.org/10.1145/3322385.3322392
8. Carter, R.: Conversational Interfaces: What Are They? UC Today, 23 December 2020. https://www.uctoday.com/collaboration/conversational-interfaces-what-are-they/. Accessed 4 Dec 2023
9. Ng, M., Coopamootoo, K.P., Toreini, E., Aitken, M., Elliot, K., van Moorsel, A.: Simulating the effects of social presence on trust, privacy concerns & usage intentions in automated bots for finance. In: 2020 IEEE European Symposium on Security and Privacy Workshops (EuroS&PW), Genoa, Italy, 07.09.2020 - 11.09.2020, pp. 190–199. IEEE (2020). https://doi.org/10.1109/EuroSPW51379.2020.00034
10. Benbasat, I., Wang, W.: Trust in and adoption of online recommendation agents. JAIS (2005). https://doi.org/10.17705/1jais.00065
11. Johnson, D., Grayson, K.: Cognitive and affective trust in service relationships. J. Bus. Res. (2005). https://doi.org/10.1016/S0148-2963(03)00140-1
12. Nass, C., Moon, Y., Fogg, B.J., Reeves, B., Dryer, C.: Can computer personalities be human personalities? In: Miller, J. (ed.) Conference Companion on Human Factors in Computing Systems. Conference companion, Denver, Colorado, United States, 5/7/1995 - 5/11/1995, pp. 228–229. ACM, New York (1995). https://doi.org/10.1145/223355.223538
13. Følstad, A., Nordheim, C.B., Bjørkli, C.A.: What makes users trust a chatbot for customer service? an exploratory interview study. In: Bodrunova, S.S. (ed.) Internet science. 5th International Conference, INSCI 2018, St. Petersburg, Russia, October 24–26, 2018: proceedings, vol. 11193. LNCS, vol. 11193, pp. 194–208. Springer, Cham (2018)
14. Lockey, S., Gillespie, N., Holm, D., Someh, I.A.: A review of trust in artificial intelligence: challenges, vulnerabilities and future directions. In: Hawaii International Conference on System Sciences 2021 (HICSS-54) (2021)

15. Nass, C., Steuer, J., Tauber, E.R.: Computers are social actors. In: Plaisant, C. (ed.) Conference Companion on Human Factors in Computing Systems. Conference companion, Boston, Massachusetts, United States, 4/24/1994 - 4/28/1994, pp. 204. ACM, New York (1994). https://doi.org/10.1145/259963.260288

16. Wischmeyer, T.: Artificial intelligence and transparency: opening the black box. In: Wischmeyer, T., Rademacher, T. (eds.) Regulating artificial intelligence, pp. 75–101. Springer, Cham (op. 2020)

17. Zhang, C., Zhou, R., Zhang, Y., Sun, Y., Zou, L., Zhao, M.: How to design the expression ways of conversational agents based on affective experience. In: Kurosu, M. (ed.) Human-Computer Interaction. Multimodal and Natural Interaction. Thematic, vol. 12182. LNCS, pp. 302–320. Springer, [S.l.] (2020)

18. Zhang, T., Qin, Y., Li, Q.: Trusted artificial intelligence: technique requirements and best practices. In: International Conference on Cyberworlds (CW). 2021 International Conference on Cyberworlds (CW), Caen, France, 9/28/2021 - 9/30/2021, pp. 303–306. IEEE (2021). https://doi.org/10.1109/CW52790.2021.00058

19. Michler, O., Decker, R., Stummer, C.: To trust or not to trust smart consumer products: a literature review of trust-building factors. Manag. Rev. Q (2020). https://doi.org/10.1007/s11301-019-00171-8

20. Park, E., Jenkins, Q., Jiang, X.: Measuring trust of Human operations in new generation rescue robots. Proceedings of the JFPS International Symposium on Fluid Power (2008). https://doi.org/10.5739/isfp.2008.489

21. Hancock, P.A., Billings, D.R., Schaefer, K.E., Chen, J.Y.C., de Visser, E.J., Parasuraman, R.: A meta-analysis of factors affecting trust in human-robot interaction. Hum. Factors (2011). https://doi.org/10.1177/0018720811417254

22. Nordheim, C.B., Følstad, A., Bjørkli, C.A.: An initial model of trust in chatbots for customer service—findings from a questionnaire study. Interact. Comput.Comput. (2019). https://doi.org/10.1093/iwc/iwz022

23. vom Brocke, J., Simons, S., Niehaves, B., Riemer, K., Plattfaut, R., Cleven, A.: Reconstructing the giant: on the importance of rigour in documenting the literature search process. In: European Conference on Information Systems (2009)

24. Webster, J., Watson, R.T.: Analyzing the past to prepare for the future: writing a literature review. MIS Quart. **26**, xiii–xxiii (2002)

25. Guo, Y., Wang, J., Wu, R., Li, Z., Sun, L.: Designing for trust: a set of design principles to increase trust in chatbot. CCF Trans. Pervasive Comp. Interact. (2022). https://doi.org/10.1007/s42486-022-00106-5

26. Belen Saglam, R., Nurse, J.R.C., Hodges, D.: Privacy concerns in chatbot interactions: when to trust and when to worry. In: Stephanidis, C., Antona, M., Ntoa, S. (eds.) HCI International 2021 - Posters, vol. 1420. Communications in Computer and Information Science, pp. 391–399. Springer, Cham (2021)

27. Kraus, M., Seldschopf, P., Minker, W.: Towards the Development of a Trustworthy Chatbot for Mental Health Applications. In: Lokoč, J., Skopal, T., Schoeffmann, K., Mezaris, V., Li, X., Vrochidis, S., Patras, I. (eds.) MultiMedia Modeling. 27th International Conference, MMM 2021, Prague, Czech Republic, June 22–24, 2021, Proceedings, Part II, vol. 12573. Information Systems and Applications, incl. Internet/Web, and HCI, vol. 12573, 1st edn., pp. 354–366. Springer, Cham (2021)

28. Pizzi, G., Scarpi, D., Pantano, E.: Artificial intelligence and the new forms of interaction: who has the control when interacting with a chatbot? J. Bus. Res. (2021). https://doi.org/10.1016/j.jbusres.2020.11.006

29. Law, E.L.-C., van As, N., Følstad, A.: Effects of prior experience, gender, and age on trust in a banking chatbot with(Out) breakdown and repair. In: Abdelnour Nocera, J., Kristín Lárusdóttir, M., Petrie, H., Piccinno, A., Winckler, M. (eds.) Human-Computer Interaction – INTERACT 2023, vol. 14143. Lecture notes in computer science, pp. 277–296. Springer, Cham (2023). Doi: https://doi.org/10.1007/978-3-031-42283-6_16

30. Hartikainen, M., Väänänen, K.: Towards human-centered design of AI service chatbots: defining the building blocks. In: Degen, H., Ntoa, S. (eds.) HCI 2023, vol. 14051. LNCS, vol. 14051, 1st edn., pp. 68–87. Springer, Cham (2023). Doi: https://doi.org/10.1007/978-3-031-35894-4_5

31. Shin, D.: The effects of explainability and causability on perception, trust, and acceptance: implications for explainable AI. Int. J. Hum. Comput. Stud.Comput. Stud. (2021). https://doi.org/10.1016/j.ijhcs.2020.102551

32. Gkinko, L., Elbanna, A.: Good morning chatbot, do i have any meetings today? investigating trust in AI chatbots in a digital workplace. In: Elbanna, A., McLoughlin, S., Dwivedi, Y.K., Donnellan, B., Wastell, D. (eds.) Co-creating for Context in the Transfer and Diffusion of IT. IFIP WG 8.6 International Working Conference on Transfer and Diffusion of IT, TDIT 2022, Maynooth, Ireland, June 15–16, 2022, Proceedings, vol. 660. IFIP Advances in Information and Communication Technology, vol. 660, 1st edn., pp. 105–117. Springer, Cham (2022). Doi: https://doi.org/10.1007/978-3-031-17968-6_7

33. Vaccaro, K., Agarwalla, T., Shivakumar, S., Kumar, R.: Designing the future of personal fashion. In: Mandryk, R., Hancock, M., Perry, M., Cox, A. (eds.) Proceedings of the 2018 CHI Conference on Human Factors in Computing Systems. CHI '18: CHI Conference on Human Factors in Computing Systems, Montreal QC Canada, 21 04 2018 26 04 2018, pp. 1–11. ACM, New York (2018). https://doi.org/10.1145/3173574.3174201

34. McAllister, D.J.: Affect- and cognition-based trust formations for interpersonal cooperation in organizations. Acad. Manag. J.Manag. J. (1995). https://doi.org/10.2307/256727

35. Adam, M., Wessel, M., Benlian, A.: AI-based chatbots in customer service and their effects on user compliance. Electron Markets (2021). https://doi.org/10.1007/s12525-020-00414-7

36. Bastiansen, M.H.A., Kroon, A.C., Araujo, T.: Female chatbots are helpful, male chatbots are competent? Publizistik (2022). https://doi.org/10.1007/s11616-022-00762-8

37. Hill, J., Randolph Ford, W., Farreras, I.G.: Real conversations with artificial intelligence: a comparison between human–human online conversations and human–chatbot conversations. Comput. Hum. Behav.. Hum. Behav. (2015). https://doi.org/10.1016/j.chb.2015.02.026

38. Xie, Y., Qu, J., Zhang, Y., Zhou, R., Chan, A.H.S.: Speaking, fast or slow: how conversational agents' rate of speech influences user experience. Univ. Access Inf. Soc. (2023). https://doi.org/10.1007/s10209-023-01000-2

39. Lv, Y., Hu, S., Liu, F., Qi, J.: Research on users' trust in customer service chatbots based on human-computer interaction. In: Meng, X., Xuan, Q., Yang, Y., Yue, Y., Zhang, Z.-K. (eds.) Big Data and Social Computing. BDSC 2022, vol. 1640. Communications in Computer and Information Science, vol. 1640, pp. 291–306. Springer, Singapore (2022)

40. Dekkal, M., Arcand, M., Prom Tep, S., Rajaobelina, L., Ricard, L.: Factors affecting user trust and intention in adopting chatbots: the moderating role of technology anxiety in insurtech. J. Financ. Serv. Mark (2023). https://doi.org/10.1057/s41264-023-00230-y

41. Sartor, G.: The impact of the General Data Protection Regulation (GDPR) on artificial intelligence. Study. European Parliament, Brussels (2020)

42. Tisland, I., Sodefjed, M.L., Vassilakopoulou, P., Pappas, I.O.: the role of quality, trust, and empowerment in explaining satisfaction and use of chatbots in e-government. In: Papagianni-dis, S., Alamanos, E., Gupta, S., Dwivedi, Y.K., Mäntymäki, M., Pappas, I.O. (eds.) The Role of Digital Technologies in Shaping the Post-Pandemic World, vol. 13454. LNCS, pp. 279–291. Springer, Cham (2022). Doi: https://doi.org/10.1007/978-3-031-15342-6_22

43. Weitz, K., Schlagowski, R., André, E.: Demystifying artificial intelligence for end-users: findings from a participatory machine learning show. In: Edelkamp, S., Möller, R., Rueckert, E. (eds.) KI 2021: Advances in Artificial Intelligence. LNCS, vol. 12873, pp. 257–270. Springer, Cham (2021)

BlocklyBias: A Visual Programming Language for Bias Identification in AI Data

Claudio De Martino[1]([✉]), Tommaso Turchi[2][iD], and Alessio Malizia[2,3][iD]

[1] CNR-ISTI, Pisa, Italy
claudio.demartino@isti.cnr.it
[2] Department of Computer Science, University of Pisa, Pisa, Italy
{tommaso.turchi,alessio.malizia}@unipi.it
[3] Molde University College, Molde, Norway
alessio.malizia@himolde.no

Abstract. In the current landscape of Artificial Intelligence (AI), bias has emerged as a central concern in both public discourse and scientific inquiry. In today's rapidly evolving landscape, marked by increasing complexity and challenges, there is a growing need to address the issue of biases and discrimination that can be exacerbated by algorithms. Biases can infiltrate data collection, whether conducted by humans or systems they design, highlighting the multifaceted nature of this challenge. Consequently, addressing this issue from diverse perspectives is imperative, extending its reach beyond technical domains to include stakeholders from various backgrounds.

This paper aims to illustrate how the democratization of the data analysis process – specifically regarding intersectional biases – can be achieved through the use of Visual Programming Languages (VPLs). By reducing the technical entry barrier, fostering an understanding of bias, and providing mitigation strategies, this research introduces BlocklyBias, a platform founded on VPL principles. BlocklyBias serves as a foundational stepping stone for future improvements, as a tool to explore and resolve bias-related challenges in data analysis. Through this study, we seek to bridge the gap between technical and non-technical stakeholders, fostering a collaborative approach to bias mitigation in AI.

Keywords: Bias · Visual Programming Languages · Data Analysis

1 Introduction

The advent of Artificial Intelligence (AI) in various sectors has been one of the most significant technological advancements in recent years. However, this rapid development brings forth critical challenges, particularly concerning inherent biases in AI systems. These biases, if left unchecked, can lead to skewed data interpretations and compromised decision-making, resulting in serious real-world

© The Author(s), under exclusive license to Springer Nature Switzerland AG 2024
H. Degen and S. Ntoa (Eds.): HCII 2024, LNAI 14735, pp. 45–59, 2024.
https://doi.org/10.1007/978-3-031-60611-3_4

consequences. Addressing these biases requires a collaborative effort between technical experts and stakeholders from various non-technical domains to ensure solutions are effectively tailored to specific needs [1, 2].

One of the primary challenges in this collaborative endeavour is the communication gap that exists between non-technical professionals and data analysts. Bridging this gap is crucial for effective mitigation of biases in AI. To address this problem, our research introduces BlocklyBias, a platform built upon a Visual Programming Language (VPL), specifically a block-based interface using Blockly[1]. This platform enables non-experts to manage data and inspect biases through visual blocks within a Visual Programming Environment (VPE), which is then translated into and actionable Python notebook for data analysts. This facilitates a continuous dialogue and collaborative process between various stakeholders.

The central research question of this study is: "How can Visual Languages enhance collaboration between technical and non-technical stakeholders, particularly in the context of identifying and mitigating biases in AI data?" The objectives of BlocklyBias include democratizing the data analysis process by providing an intuitive platform for non-experts to contribute their insights, strengthening the analytical foundation through the integration of diverse domain-specific insights, and facilitating effective collaborative engagements for continuous improvement and feedback.

This paper also delves into the concept of bias in data interpretation, defined as a deviation or prejudice in representing reality, and how Machine Learning (ML) algorithms can inadvertently amplify these biases, leading to disparities [3]. We focus on intersectional bias, a nuanced form of bias derived from intersecting dataset features, which is difficult to spot due to its multi-faceted nature. Exploiting Blockly's capabilities, we developed custom blocks for BlocklyBias to analyze such intersectional biases and translate these into Python-executable ML algorithms using BlocklyML[2], an extension of Blockly supporting ML operations.

A preliminary evaluation study with different experts in usability and data analysis was conducted, inspired by the cognitive walkthrough model. This qualitative experiment simulated real-world user interactions with BlocklyBias, gathering valuable feedback from participants. This feedback was instrumental in iterative enhancements of the prototype, particularly in refining the user interface and minimize adoption barriers.

The contributions of this paper are threefold: (1) we propose an extension of a block-based VPL for analyzing and mitigating dataset biases, (2) we introduce a system that enables the generation and execution of Python notebooks for diverse user groups, and (3) we report on a preliminary evaluation of the prototype with expert feedback.

---

[1] https://developers.google.com/blockly.
[2] https://github.com/chekoduadarsh/BlocklyML.

2   Related Works

The foundation of our study lies at the intersection of two critical domains: bias in data and Visual Languages. This section delves into the historical and contemporary perspectives of bias, its various forms, and the role of Visual Programming Languages in mitigating these biases.

The term "bias" has a rich historical evolution, originating from the French term "biais" in the 1520 s, meaning "slant" or "oblique line". While its exact origin is uncertain, it may be derived from the ancient Provençal language. In later centuries, the term found its way into the game of bowls, symbolizing balls with uneven weight that curved obliquely. Figuratively, it expressed the "unilateral tendency of the mind" [4].

More recently, Kahneman and Tversky published a study [5] examining how people evaluate the probability of future events using the representativeness heuristic, a cognitive bias which causes people to apply long-term odds to short-term sequences. The well-known "Linda problem" exemplifies the tendency to overestimate probabilities based on stereotypes, revealing intricate aspects of human decision-making.

A 2005 study [6] claims that cognitive biases, influencing perception, memory, reasoning, and decisions, are evolutionary adaptations aimed at solving survival and reproductive problems. However, these biases persist in modern society, affecting various aspects of human behaviour [6]. The advent of Artificial Intelligence introduces new challenges as these systems learn and assimilate information from diverse datasets. Biases may infiltrate the data during collection, leading to unfair, unbalanced, or disproportionate outcomes. The consequences of such biases, amplified by algorithms, can have profound social, psychological, and economic implications [7].

The criticality of bias in AI is underscored by instances like ProPublica's investigation into software predicting criminal activities [8]. The study revealed biases against people of colour, impacting risk assessments. Monitoring algorithmic development and ensuring transparency in formulae and parameters are highlighted as crucial to addressing these disparities and promoting fair treatment.

Amongst the main types of biases reported in the literature, it's worth mentioning the following.

Measurement Bias. These biases are introduced through errors or personal/professional biases [9].

Representation Bias. This occurs when collected data under-represents parts of the population, hindering accurate generalization [10].

Aggregation Bias. Incorrect assumptions about individuals based on observations made on the entire population, neglecting specificities and variety within the population [11].

Anchoring Bias. Influences decision-making choices based on an erroneous perception, often tied to initial choices [12].

Intersectional Bias. A form of discrimination or inequality observed through the intersection of multiple fields in a structured dataset [12]. For instance, a study [13] highlights intersectional bias in error rates related to gender and ethnicity.

Machine Learning methods play a role in detecting and analyzing intersectional bias. Lack of representativeness in reference datasets contributes to bias in ML outcomes. Digital systems reflect the biases present in the data they receive as input, emphasizing the human responsibility in addressing and mitigating bias [1]. The amplification of bias in Machine Learning results serves as a societal warning, prompting increased awareness and strategies to address social problems.

Our prototype initially implements strategies to identify and mitigate Intersectional Bias, as it's one of the trickiest types to diagnose.

2.1   Visual Languages in Data Analysis

In this paper, we argue that addressing the challenges of bias in computing could be done by allowing experts and non-experts to appropriate and analyse datasets, integrating domain-specific knowledge and computing methodologies. To allow this, non-experts need to be supported in overcoming the barrier of textual programming languages, a traditional approach to algorithm design. In recent decades, there has been a notable surge in the development of programming languages based on visual representation and interaction techniques, aiming to make the algorithm design process more intuitive and accessible.

A visual language, encompassing visual syntax and semantics, incorporates various visual elements such as lines, shapes, and points, each characterized by attributes like direction, movement, scale, and orientation. The term "visual language" holds diverse meanings, ranging from languages where handled objects are visual to languages where the language itself is visual. This diversity is acknowledged by Chang's definition [14], emphasizing the multifaceted nature of visual languages.

Visual Programming Languages (VPLs) inherit the challenge of multiple definitions associated with visual languages. Regardless of the varying definitions, VPLs encompass syntax, semantics, and pragmatics. The overarching objective of VPLs is to enhance the design of programming languages without necessarily eliminating text. Burnett [15] defines visual programming as multidimensional programming used to communicate semantics. VPLs introduce visual expressions like icons and diagrams into programming languages, constituting a Visual Programming Language (VPL). When used to generate code with the same or different syntax for code modification, it is termed a visual programming environment (VPE).

The advantages of using VPLs over textual languages include the elimination of entry barriers in computer programming, enhanced intuitiveness through visual coding, applicability in educational settings for teaching and personal development, and effectiveness in children's learning [16]. The choice between flow-based and block-based VPLs depends on the application's needs. Flow-based VPLs, employing flow diagrams or data flows, find applications in diverse fields, including system simulation, automation, and IT for structured data aggregation. On the other hand, block-based VPLs, using block logic, are prevalent in educational and corporate contexts. This paper focuses on the block-based typology, considering it more suitable for the intended application.

Blockly, a block-based framework chosen for this paper, is frequently employed in educational projects like MIT App Inventor[3] and Microsoft Make-Code[4]. Developed by Google, Blockly is a JavaScript framework that combines visual and textual programming. It features an editor where programming concepts are represented as blocks that can be assembled to create a syntactically correct program. Blockly is compatible with major browsers, operates locally, and can be seamlessly integrated into web pages or run as an app in a browser.

In parallel with the development of Visual Programming Languages (VPLs), which aim to democratize computing by making programming more accessible through visual elements, Interactive Machine Learning (IML) offers a complementary approach by leveraging human input to enhance ML algorithms. This collaborative paradigm empowers users to interactively contribute to the learning process, facilitating the creation of machine-learning-based systems tailored to their specific needs. IML integrates feedback interactively from users to help machines learn faster or more effectively, thereby improving algorithmic transparency, explainability, and fairness [17–20]. Moreover, IML provides a mechanism through visualization to allow users to understand and interact with the learning process [21], and as the field matures, more consideration is being put into possible defects in human-machine interaction [22]. IML's application across various domains such as computer science, biology, sociology, and linguistics demonstrates its versatility and potential impact across different fields [23]. This synergy between VPLs and IML underscores a broader movement towards more user-friendly and interactive technologies, aligning with the goal of democratizing technology and making it more inclusive [15,16].

In conclusion, the exploration of Visual Programming Languages and Interactive Machine Learning highlights a significant shift towards more accessible, intuitive, and collaborative approaches in computing. These innovations not only promise to democratize the field of computer science by reducing entry barriers but also play a crucial role in addressing biases within computing. Through the integration of visual elements and interactive learning processes, these technologies empower users to engage more deeply with data analysis and algorithm design, fostering a more inclusive and transparent technological landscape.

3   BlocklyBias

The main objective of this application is to address the main research question posed in the Introduction, seeking to explore the role of Visual Languages in

---

[3] https://appinventor.mit.edu/.
[4] https://www.microsoft.com/en-us/makecode.

fostering cooperative engagement between technical and non-technical participants, especially regarding the identification and reduction of biases within AI
datasets.

This section reports the design requirements and implementation choices of
BlocklyBias.

3.1   Design

The goal of our application is to go beyond simple programs that output results
without practical use. The outputs should be easy to understand for users who
may not have strong computer or math skills. We aimed for a design that is
neither too simple nor too difficult to understand.

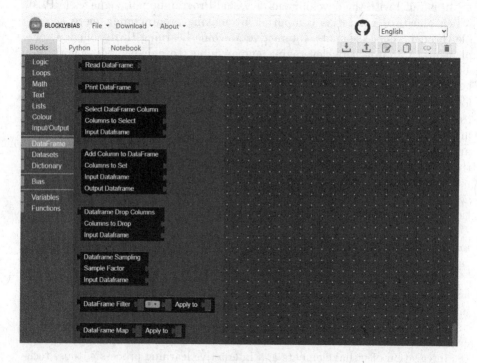

Fig. 1. The BlocklyBias User Interface.

Additionally, the application showcases bias mitigation strategies to its users;
in fact, this effort was inspired by the MiniCoDe project, which developed a multidisciplinary method with the dual objective of highlighting bias and thinking
about mitigation strategies [1,2]. However, it's important to recognize that some
datasets cannot be fully or partially freed from bias: an example of a dataset
containing biases that cannot be removed by the program could be one concerning nurses – a profession historically associated with the female figure and which

for this reason can natively contain prejudices that affect the representativeness of the populations.

The system is designed to be modular, allowing for the addition of new features to analyze different types of bias in the future.

We aim to reach a wide audience, including both people with technical backgrounds like computer science and mathematics, as well as those without such expertise who are interested in using the tool to understand and address bias. While Blockly is generally aimed at children, BlocklyBias is intended for a more mature audience due to the complex nature of bias analysis.

The User Interface (depicted in Fig. 1) was mostly inherited by BlocklyML, adding the extra blocks needed for the bias detection and different UI elements needed to interact with other functionalities that will be discussed later.

3.2 Development

The application was built on the foundation of BlocklyML, a Blockly version tailored for Machine Learning, designed to simplify data analysis involving ML algorithms in Python. We selected BlocklyML as our starting point due to its existing data analysis blocks, such as those for reading and manipulating DataFrames, and the opportunity to apply the Blockly library in a practical scenario. In BlocklyBias, we corrected several bugs found in the latest BlocklyML version available at the start of 2023, updated the user interface, and revised the block collection by removing some and adding others.

A significant addition to the block set is the intersectional bias analysis block, which incorporates a comprehensive suite of functions, variables, and commands utilizing statistical fairness metrics and an AI computation library (see Fig. 2). This block, alongside others for printing, filtering, managing data structures, and aggregating values within a DataFrame, enriches the application's analytical capabilities.

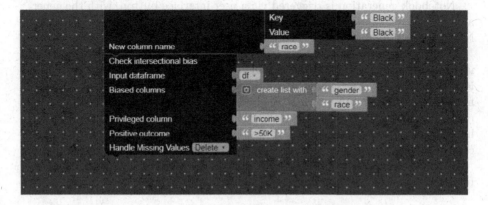

Fig. 2. The block for the analysis of intersectional bias.

The intersectional bias block requires a DataFrame as its primary input, followed by two strings identifying the fields of interest for bias intersection analysis. Additional inputs include one for the privilege variable, indicating the feature linked to discrimination, and another for the positive outcome, representing the favorable condition in a dataset's binary column for a subset of the reference population.

We integrated a customized Jupyter Notebook version to enable users to execute and adjust the generated code locally, avoiding the need for external platforms and facilitating code reuse. BlocklyBias automatically formats notebooks for ease of use by the intended audience. The local execution of notebooks offers several benefits, including independence from internet connectivity, encouragement of tool retention over platform migration, and a user-friendly, immediate alternative without additional resource demands on the user's device.

To the best of our knowledge, no prior projects have merged a Jupyter Notebook environment with a block-based visual language, enhancing the project's accessibility regarding skills, resources, and usability, acting as a communication bridge between non-experts and expert users.

BlocklyBias runs on both Windows and Linux, tested specifically on Windows 10 and 11, Ubuntu 20.04 on WSL, and Debian version 11.7.0 64-bit.

The supported workflow includes:

- Building with the visual language, including dataset loading, optional preprocessing, and bias analysis;
- Notebook generation and code execution;
- Results viewing and interpretation;
- Optional saving of the work.

Starting with dataset loading, preprocessing is recommended to ensure data accuracy and reliability. The application provides various blocks for DataFrame management to facilitate this phase. After preparing the dataset, the bias analysis block can be added.

Notebook generation is triggered via a user interface button, with the generated file accessible in the notebook management tab, which mirrors the Jupyter Notebook's original interface, facilitating code execution (see Fig. 3).

The output from the analysis is segmented into various sections, each addressing different dimensions and metrics of the bias analysis [24], including calculations on the Effective Difference Frequency (EDF), disparity measures, and metrics on individual input variables and their intersections, supplemented by ratios, frequent patterns, and a correlation matrix graph for easy understanding. The application is presented in English to ensure global accessibility and comprehensibility.

Finally, users can save their work status via a button, allowing them to resume their tasks without starting over upon reopening the application.

3.3   Testing

We tested our application on three different datasets: one with demographic, social, and economic information [25], another with hepatitis patient data [26], and a third with information from a fictional company's employees [27].

The first dataset was the main focus for developing our code because it was the largest, with 15 columns and 48,842 entries. The smaller datasets helped us check that our program worked well in different situations and with datasets of different sizes without crashing or making errors.

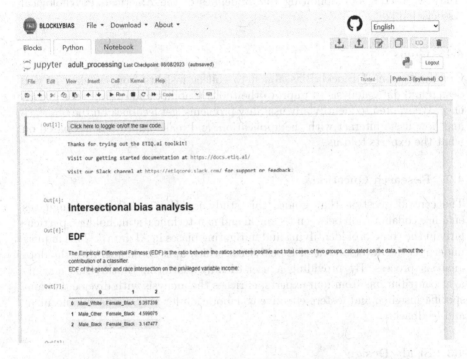

Fig. 3. A Jupyter Notebook generated and visualised in BlocklyBias.

During testing with the hepatitis dataset, an unexpected and interesting use case for the bias analysis algorithm emerged: we explored the use of the bias analysis algorithm to investigate causal intersectionality, which involves identifying causal links by intersecting different factors or categories. For this purpose, we aggregated the "age" field into 20-year intervals and then analyzed the intersection of "age" and "sex" as bias dimensions with "class" as the privilege dimension. While the results were preliminary and not fully refined, the program successfully processed the dataset without any issues. This approach highlights the algorithm's capacity to not only identify biases but also to potentially uncover cause-effect relationships in scenarios like medical datasets where identifying risk factors for diseases is crucial. It should be noted that this type of use is secondary to the purposes for which the code was designed, and the results might not be reliable yet.

Finally, by analysing these datasets, we were able to see how well BlocklyBias works with various types of data. This shows that BlocklyBias is a flexible tool that can be useful for studying biases.

4   Evaluation

This section presents the goals, hypotheses, and description of the evaluation study we carried out, following the guidelines of the American Psychological Association [28].

4.1   Goals

Our evaluation of BlocklyBias aimed to collect insights from experts in web design and data analysis to improve the tool's usability and overall user experience. We wanted to identify any usability problems, get feedback on the interface and how users interact with the application, and make improvements based on what the experts told us.

4.2   Research Question

The central question that guides this study is: "How can Visual Languages enhance collaboration between technical and non-technical stakeholders, particularly in the context of identifying and mitigating biases in AI data?". This inquiry underpins the development of BlocklyBias, which aims to democratize the data analysis process. By providing a user-friendly platform, BlocklyBias encourages contributions from non-experts, enriches the analysis with diverse domain-specific insights, and fosters effective collaboration for continuous enhancement and feedback.

4.3   Study Design

This study was designed as an expert evaluation, inspired by the cognitive walk-through model [29,30]. It was a qualitative experiment that simulated how real users would interact with BlocklyBias, allowing us to gather valuable feedback from our participants. The evaluation was split into two main stages: a demo of the application showcasing a real-world example of use, followed by a discussion with the experts to gather their feedback following a set of predefined questions.

4.4   Participants

We selected four experts (2 women, 2 men) with 5+ years of experience in Web Design and data analysis for the evaluation. These experts were chosen for their background knowledge, which would provide detailed insights into the interface and how users might interact with BlocklyBias.

4.5 Settings and Tasks

The meeting with the experts was held online using Microsoft Teams and lasted about 70 min. It was divided into two parts. The first part gave an overview of the theoretical context of the project and the goals of BlocklyBias, supported by a short PowerPoint presentation. This was followed by a live demo of BlocklyBias, showing how it works. The second part of the meeting was based on the cognitive walkthrough method published by the Nielsen Norman Group. This method involves evaluating each crucial step of the workflow with a set of questions [31]. These questions were adapted during the meeting to better fit the flow of the discussion, turning the session into semi-structured interviews that focused on the cognitive walkthrough method.

4.6 Procedure

During the meeting, participants had the chance to interact with BlocklyBias through a live demonstration. They shared their first impressions, provided deeper insights, and pointed out aspects that might not have been caught in an individual review. After initially responding on their own, the evaluators engaged in group discussions about their ideas and feedback, offering deeper insights and highlighting issues that might not have come up in individual discussions.

Acting on the roles suggested by the Nielsen Norman Group, one author served as the facilitator, presenter, and recorder. To ensure the privacy of the participants and to allow for a thorough review of the discussions, the session was recorded and kept private.

4.7 Findings

From the evaluation of BlocklyBias we gathered rich insights from the experts, which guided a further refinement of the tool. Through the discussions, several themes emerged that were pivotal to enhancing BlocklyBias's usability and functionality. Here we delve into the key findings as well as the modifications inspired by expert feedback.

Experts unanimously highlighted the necessity of a user guide for newcomers to navigate BlocklyBias effectively. They pointed out that first-time users might struggle with initializing the application, particularly during the initial dataset upload and variable declaration phase. The variety of blocks available in the Blockly toolbox, while providing flexibility, was also seen as potentially overwhelming. One evaluator remarked on the dual-edged nature of this flexibility – offering users a wealth of options but at the risk of confusion when searching for the right block. To address this, a comprehensive user guide was introduced, outlining step-by-step instructions for composing visual programs for bias identification and analysis, with additional tips on generating and executing notebook files.

Another critical area for improvement identified by the experts was the visual distinction and accessibility of essential functions within the application. The notebook generation button, deemed the most crucial feature by the evaluators, was relocated to a more prominent position at the top of the toolbar and highlighted to underscore its significance. This modification aimed to facilitate easier access and highlight the button's importance for the application's core functionality.

The need to differentiate between basic and advanced functionalities emerged from the experts' recommendations, suggesting the creation of a visual filter to separate these feature sets. This approach intended to streamline the user experience by preventing non-expert users from feeling overwhelmed or intimidated by advanced features they might not need.

Visual feedback in response to user inputs was another area where experts saw room for enhancement. They recommended introducing visual cues that clarify the types of errors users might encounter, especially during the assembly of the VPL. For instance, highlighting incompatible block connections could help alleviate user frustrations attributed to perceived application misbehaviours. In line with this, visual elements were proposed to guide users on which blocks could be interconnected, serving as an intuitive alternative to the suggested user guide.

Furthermore, the introduction of a toggle button for switching between parallel and individual views of the "Blocks" and "Python" tabs was suggested to cater to diverse user preferences. This feature aimed to provide users with the flexibility to customize their interface based on their expertise level and specific needs, addressing the inefficient use of visual space noted in the Python code view, especially on desktop screens.

Enhancements to the notebook generation process were also recommended, including the ability to open the generated notebook in a new browser tab and to execute notebook cells automatically. These improvements sought to streamline the workflow, reducing the operational burden on users.

Lastly, experts called for clearer tooltips and descriptions for the principal blocks used in visual program creation. For example, specifying that the "Read DataFrame" block requires a string input containing the file name was suggested to enhance user understanding and ease of use.

These findings underscore the importance of user-centered design considerations in developing tools like BlocklyBias. By incorporating expert feedback, the tool was significantly improved, making it more intuitive, accessible, and effective in empowering users to identify and mitigate biases in AI data.

5   Discussion

The development and refinement of BlocklyBias highlight its potential as a novel bridge in the dialogue between technical and non-technical stakeholders tackling bias in AI data analysis. Unlike complex platforms such as KNIME[5] and Rapidminer[6], BlocklyBias demystifies data analysis, enabling users with varying levels

---

[5] https://www.knime.com.

[6] https://altair.com/altair-rapidminer.

of expertise to contribute meaningfully to the process. This inclusivity is further supported by a user-friendly interface and access to detailed documentation, enhancing its usability and appeal.

Key improvements – such as the introduction of a user guide, enhanced visual feedback, and clearer block tooltips – directly respond to the challenges of making a sophisticated tool accessible to a wider audience. These changes not only make the application more intuitive but also reinforce the principle of user-centered design. By streamlining the user experience, BlocklyBias allows individuals to focus on analytical exploration rather than navigational hurdles.

Crucially, BlocklyBias serves as a communication tool, facilitating collaboration between non-experts and experts. Non-experts are supported in analyzing datasets through a VPL, while experts can seamlessly incorporate the results into their workflows via the produced Jupyter Notebooks. This functionality underscores BlocklyBias's role in democratizing data analysis – bridging the gap between initial data exploration and advanced analytical processes.

The balance between offering flexibility and ensuring usability emerges as a pivotal consideration. The application's design, which now distinguishes between basic and advanced functionalities, reflects a nuanced understanding of user needs – accommodating both novice users and those seeking deeper analytical capabilities.

In essence, the validation phase was critical not just for enhancing Blockly-Bias's interface, but for realizing its vision as a collaborative platform. By prioritizing feedback and fostering a collaborative development process, BlocklyBias is poised to become an essential tool in the collective effort to identify and mitigate biases in AI data. This approach not only improves the tool's functionality but also contributes to a more inclusive and equitable field of data analysis.

6   Conclusions

This paper presented BlocklyBias, a block-based system with the ability to generate and execute Jupyter Notebooks locally, evaluating it through feedback from experts. Its design choices focused on making data analysis accessible to a wider audience and integrating complex analytical processes for users regardless of their technical background.

A major feature of BlocklyBias is enabling users to customize and reuse code more easily. Users can modify code locally and run it immediately for visual feedback, taking full advantage of the Jupyter Notebook environment. This feature highlights BlocklyBias's role in making data analysis more inclusive, serving as a practical tool for identifying and addressing biases in AI data.

The evaluation of BlocklyBias's performance with existing datasets showcases its capability to produce results consistent with established benchmarks. However, the challenge of generating complete results with smaller datasets points to an area for improvement, prompting for the need of better data handling.

Looking ahead, BlocklyBias offers ample opportunities for further development. The adaptability of Blockly's VPL and the wide range of biases yet to be explored open up new avenues for enhancement. Adding features to analyze different types of biases, such as anchoring bias, is a viable direction for future updates. Overcoming the current limitation of incomplete results with small datasets, potentially by integrating different algorithms or libraries, is a key goal for making it more effective.

Additionally, the feedback from the expert evaluation suggests several paths for ongoing refinement. Paying close attention to user feedback and adopting an iterative approach to design will be essential in making BlocklyBias a more user-friendly and comprehensive tool for collaborative data analysis.

In conclusion, BlocklyBias marks an initial step in the effort to make AI data analysis more collaborative and accessible, providing a platform that bridges the gap between users with different levels of expertise. This study lays a solid foundation for future enhancements that will further enable users to contribute to the field of AI data analysis actively.

Acknowledgments. Research partly funded by PNRR - M4C2 - Investimento 1.3, Partenariato Esteso PE00000013 - "FAIR - Future Artificial Intelligence Research" - Spoke 1 "Human- centered AI", funded by the European Commission under the NextGeneration EU programme.

Disclosure of Interests. The authors have no competing interests to declare that are relevant to the content of this article.

References

1. Malizia, A., Carta, S., Turchi, T., Crivellaro, C.: Minicode workshops: minimise algorithmic bias in collaborative decision making with design fiction. In: Proceedings of the Hybrid Human Artificial Intelligence Conference (2022)
2. Turchi, T., Malizia, A., Borsci, S.: Reflecting on algorithmic bias with design fiction: the minicode workshops. IEEE Intell. Syst. (01), 1–13 (jan 5555)
3. Barocas, S., Selbst, A.D.: Big data's disparate impact. California law review, pp. 671–732 (2016)
4. Dictionary, O.E.: bias (n.). https://www.etymonline.com/word/bias
5. Kahneman, D., Tversky, A.: Subjective probability: a judgment of representativeness. Cogn. Psychol. **3**(3), 430–454 (1972)
6. Haselton, M.G., Nettle, D., Andrews, P.W.: The evolution of cognitive bias. In: Buss, D.M. (ed.) The Handbook of Evolutionary Psychology, chap. 25, pp. 724–746. John Wiley & Sons (2005)
7. Rovatsos, M., Mittelstadt, B., Koene, A.: Landscape summary: Bias in algorithmic decision-making: what is bias in algorithmic decision-making, how can we identify it, and how can we mitigate it? (2019)
8. Angwin, J., Larson, J., Mattu, S., Kirchner, L.: Machine bias (2016). https://www.propublica.org/article/machine-bias-risk-assessments-in-criminal-sentencing
9. Srinivasan, R., Chander, A.: Biases in AI systems. Commun. ACM **64**(8), 44–49 (2021)
10. Shahbazi, N., Lin, Y., Asudeh, A.: Representation bias in data: a survey on identification and resolution techniques. ACM Comput. Surv. (CSUR) **55**(13, art. n. 293), 1–39 (2023)

11. Clark, W.A.V., Avery, K.L.: The effects of data aggregation in statistical analysis. Geograph. Anal. **VIII**, 428–438 (1976)
12. Cole, E.R.: Intersectionality and research in psychology. Am. Psychol. **64**, 170–180 (2009)
13. Buolamwini, J., Gebru, T.: Gender shades: intersectional accuracy disparities in commercial gender classification. In: Conference on Fairness, Accountability and Transparency, pp. 77–91. PMLR (2018)
14. Chang, S.K.: Introduction: visual languages and iconic languages. In: Chang, S.K., Ichikawa, T., Ligomenides, P. (eds.) Visual Languages, chap. 1, pp. 1–7. Springer (2005)
15. Burnett, M.M.: Visual programming. In: Webster, J.G. (ed.) Encyclopedia of Electrical and Electronics Engineering, pp. 275–283. John Wiley & Sons, New York (1999)
16. Weintrop, D., Wilensky, U.: Comparing block-based and text-based programming in high school computer science classrooms. ACM Trans. Comput. Educ. **18**(1, art. n. 3), 1–25 (2017)
17. Holzinger, A., et al.: Interactive machine learning: experimental evidence for the human in the algorithmic loop. Applied Intelligence (2018)
18. Amershi, S., Çakmak, M., Knox, W.B., Kulesza, T.: Power to the people: the role of humans in interactive machine learning. Ai Mag. (2014)
19. Rahwan, I.: Society-in-the-loop: programming the algorithmic social contract. Ethics and Information Technology (2017)
20. Ribeiro, M.T., Singh, S., Guestrin, C.: "Why should i trust you?": Explaining the predictions of any classifier (2016)
21. Li, H., Fang, S., Mukhopadhyay, S., Saykin, A.J., Shen, L.: Interactive machine learning by visualization: a small data solution (2018)
22. Holzinger, A.: Interactive machine learning for health informatics: when do we need the human-in-the-loop? Brain Informatics (2016)
23. Upstill-Goddard, R., Eccles, D., Fliege, J., Collins, A.: Machine learning approaches for the discovery of gene-gene interactions in disease data. Briefings in Bioinformatics (2012)
24. Mehrabi, N., Morstatter, F., Saxena, N., Lerman, K., Galstyan, A.: A survey on bias and fairness in machine learning. ACM Comput. Surv. (CSUR) **54**(6), 1–35 (2021)
25. Becker, B., Kohavi, R.: Adult. UCI Machine Learning Repository (1996). https://doi.org/10.24432/C5XW20
26. Hepatitis. UCI Machine Learning Repository (1988). https://doi.org/10.24432/C5Q59J
27. Patalano, D.C.: Human resources data set (2020). https://www.kaggle.com/dsv/1572001
28. Wohlin, C., Runeson, P., Höst, M., Ohlsson, M.C., Regnell, B., Wesslén, A.: Experimentation in Software Engineering: An Introduction. Kluwer Academic Publishers, Norwell (2000)
29. https://www.nngroup.com/articles/cognitive-walkthroughs (2022). Accessed 22 Jan 2024
30. https://www.nngroup.com/articles/cognitive-walkthrough-workshop (2022). Accessed 22 Jan 2024
31. Salazar, K.: Evaluate interface learnability with cognitive walkthroughs (2022). https://www.nngroup.com/articles/cognitive-walkthroughs/

Comparing Socio-technical Design Principles with Guidelines for Human-Centered AI

Thomas Herrmann[✉] [iD]

Institut für Arbeitswissenschaft, Ruhr-University Bochum, Bochum, Germany
Thomas.Herrmann@ruhr-uni-bochum.de

Abstract. Human-centered AI (HCAI) refers to guidelines or principles that aim on ethically oriented design of systems. We compare HCAI-guidelines with principles of socio-technical systems that emerged in the context of conventional information technology. The comparison leads to a revision of socio-technical heuristics by including aspects of AI-usage. The comparison reveals that continuous evolution is a basic characteristic of socio-technical systems, and that human oversight or interventions and the subsequent appropriation of AI-systems lead to continuous adaptation and re-design of the systems, if autonomy is collaboratively exercised. From a socio-technical point of view, the crucial requirement of transparency has not only to be fulfilled with technical features, but also by contributions of the whole system including human actors. It will be promising for using AI, if not only technical features, but organizational and social practices are socio-technically designed in a way that compensates shortcomings of AI.

Keywords: Artificial Intelligence · socio-technical design · ethical guidelines · design principles

1 Introduction

A considerable number of different guidelines and principles have been developed in the field of human-centered AI (HCAI) [1, 2]. They focus ethical questions about the effects – such as biases – of AI-outcome on people who use it or about whom decisions are made. Additionally, there is an increasing discussion about the future role of humans who work to accomplish tasks while AI is included. The relation between human work and AI will develop within organizational practices and is a matter of socio-technical design and evaluation. Thus, questions arise of how principles of socio-technical design can be adapted with respect to AI (RQ1) and how a comparison between them and guidelines for HCAI can result into a scientific benefit (RQ2). RQ1 has to take the specific characteristics of AI into account such as "AI offers a higher level of automation and self-direction, requiring less human input" [3, p. 1]. We propose that HCAI should deal with a wide variety of different roles AI can take over such as serving as a tool, running automatized processes, providing decision making, or being a member of hybrid teams [4].

In what follows, we provide background on HCAI-related and socio-technical principles and guidelines (Sect. 2), we describe the process of the systematic literature research

© The Author(s), under exclusive license to Springer Nature Switzerland AG 2024
H. Degen and S. Ntoa (Eds.): HCII 2024, LNAI 14735, pp. 60–74, 2024.
https://doi.org/10.1007/978-3-031-60611-3_5

(Sect. 3), present the most relevant aspects of guidelines and principles found within the HCAI discourse (Sect. 4), provide a revision of socio-technical heuristic (RQ1) (Sect. 5) and a conclusion by comparing the sociotechnical and the HCAI principles (Sect. 6).

2 Background

One quickly can identify basic contributions that give an overview of ethical principles and guidelines in the context of HCAI. For example, Bingley et al. [5] refer to the European Commission, to national initiatives as well as to contribution of companies and research institutions. They give examples like "... fairness, inclusiveness, reliability, safety, transparency, privacy, security, and accountability ...". An appropriate starting point is provided by an European Commission's expert group [6] who require respect for human autonomy, prevention of harm, fairness and explicability, and focus on:

1. human agency and oversight,
2. technical robustness and safety,
3. privacy and data governance,
4. transparency,
5. diversity, non-discrimination and fairness,
6. environmental and societal well-being and
7. accountability.

A recent paper of an expert group [3] outlines six challenges in the context of applying AI and HCAI: Governance and independent oversight; human well-being, human-AI interaction, responsible design of AI, Privacy, and Design and Evaluation framework. These challenges are not directly elaborated as guidelines but include a wide spectrum of them. Examples are – in the context of human well-being – avoidance of harm, multi-optimization of benefits, agency, trust, accountability, and minimizing frustration, stress, anxiety etc. during human-AI interaction. With respect to privacy, not only secrecy and the protection of one's personality are mentioned but also limitation of reachability. Also relevant are preserving human dignity, safety, and agency. The discussion of governance adds the aspects of integrity and resilience.

Weisz et al. [7] add to the discussion that explainability should be extended by possibilities for exploration. Furthermore, they emphasize variability to make clear that a certain AI-output might only be one variant in the context of several appropriate solutions. Variability should and include multiple outputs and imperfection and become part of users' mental models of AI.

Although the paper on the six challenges values the relevance of the socio-technical perspective, it does not refer to basic socio-technical principles as described for example by Cherns [8, 9] or Mumford [10], and summarized by Clegg [11]. Recently, Herrmann et al. [12] give an updated overview by distilling eight socio-technical evaluation heuristics. They use the term "heuristics" since in the field of rapidly developing IT, principles can only have tentative validity and serve more as rule of thumb. Their heuristics are derived not only from the conventional socio-technical principles, but additionally from five further, closely related fields: human-computer interaction, computer supported cooperative work, process design, privacy, and job design. A total of 17 papers from these six areas were analyzed and 173 items were derived that represent aspects of socio-technical principles. These items were grouped into 13 categories. These categories were contrasted against an empirical data base of 306 socio-technical problems in 13 different cases, such as health care, manufacturing industries, or education. The relevance and external validity of the categories were checked by attempting to assign them to the problems in the data base and to identify unassignable problems, overlaps between the categories, or the necessity for new aspects. As a result, eight heuristics were derived (see Table 1, left column). Only one of the cases that were analyzed by Herrmann et al. [13] refers to problems with using AI. Thus, there is a need to update the proposed socio-technical heuristics with regard to AI.

3   Method

To extend the scope of relevant principles and guidelines presented in the background section, we conducted a systematic literature research. Table 1 displays the search terms we have applied and the number of hits as well as the steps of filtering. We used Google Scholar to include a wide scope of interdisciplinary research. From our experience, Google Scholar usually covers what can be found with Web of Science, Scopus, IEEE Explore or the ACM digital library. The search term for the combined result is "Human-centered Artificial Intelligence" AND ("ethical guidelines" OR "ethical principles" OR "design guidelines" OR "design principles"). The search was limited to the years 2014 to 2024 since HCAI is a relatively new field. One could criticize that the focus on "HCAI" represents an inappropriate narrowing of potentially relevant work. However, we realized that at least some authors in the field of HCAI who deal with reviews of guidelines and principles have found relevant papers that were not directly related to HCAI, such as [6, 14–17].

Table 1. Sorting out relevant literature.

Step	Filtering strategy	Papers
1	"human-centered artificial intelligence" "ethical guidelines"	219
	"human-centered artificial intelligence" "design principles"	333
	"human-centered artificial intelligence" "design guidelines"	163
	"human-centered artificial intelligence" "ethical principles"	351
2	Without duplets	795
3	Of general relevance	576
4	Titles point to an overview over guidelines and principles	46
5	Content contributes to the elaboration of guidelines and principles	13
6	Further papers found by analyzing the 13 papers	5
	Number of papers analyzed	**18**

To filter the 795 hits (without duplets), we firstly excluded those entries that are not in English, or havw less than 2 citations per year although they were published before 2023. In a further step 3), we removed all those whose title does not suggest that an overview of guidelines or principles is given or which only refer to only single principles or guidelines (like Fairness). We then (step 5) filtered out all entries that use lists of guidelines and principles for specific research questions without expanding or critically reflecting these lists. We also removed entries that refer to a specific domain, take a meta-perspective or focus only on processes for applying guidelines or principles. We carefully analyzed the remaining 13 papers; by checking their reference lists we identified five further relevant papers. We extracted 44 aspects and grouped them into 8 categories to allow for an overview.

4   Findings

The results of the grouping procedure are presented with Table 2. An important decision was to find the appropriate level of abstraction. We decided to introduce eight main categories since this level allows a comparison with the socio-technical heuristics. The sub-aspects of each category serve two purposes: On the one hand, they are intended as a reference that shows how the analyzed papers characterize the respective main category. On the other hand, they represent examples for requirements that refer to the specific characteristics of AI.

Transparency and autonomy, in particular human agency, are aspects that are highly relevant in the context of AI but were also discussed since years in the context of automation, e.g. the requirement of keeping the human in the loop. The concept of "human agency" has become particularly important in the context of the new AI capabilities. It emphasizes that humans are not restricted to the role of passive recipients of AI-generated outcomes, but can influence and shape the results of AI as active agents [18, p. 2]. The aspect of fairness is of particular relevance in the context of autonomy, as it is addressed to people who are not directly involved in the socio-technical processes of AI usage, e.g. as customers, and are therefore limited to a passive role. Trust could have been an own category. Trustworthiness can be considered as a very general requirement [6] – we assigned it to accountability since we are interested in the features that support trustability – and which similarly accountability requirements.

Table 2 also covers contradictory requirements. For example, safety might not be compatible with variance when requiring accuracy and correctness. Variance is offered as a way to handle imperfectness of AI-outcome and to offer the user diverse options between which they can choose on the basis of their own capabilities for decision-making. This example mirrors the general tension between the idea that AI has to be designed and supervised in a way that it provides always appropriate results and the insight that AI might be possibly fallible.

Table 2. Eight groups of HCAI-related aspects of guidelines and principles

Identified aspects of guidelines and principles	
Transparency • Awareness of misuse [14, 19] • Comprehensible AI [20] • Workspace awareness [21] • Transparency and explicability [6, 16, 22]… • Awareness and literacy: [23] • Explainability and exploration [7] • Design for Mental Models, … [7] • Traceability [6]	**Fairness** • Non-discrimination and fairness, e.g. avoidance of unfair has bias [6, 17, 19] (Bingley et al., 2023 • Promotion of human values [17, 19] • Justice, fairness and equity [16, 22] • Dignity [16, 22] • Solidarity [16, 22] • Diversity, [6] • Professional responsibility [17, 19] • Inclusiveness [5]
Autonomy • Human agency [3] • Human autonomy and oversight, e.g. capability for intervention [6, 15] • Freedom and autonomy [16, 22] • Human-in-the-loop e.g. a stop-button [24] • Human control of technology [7, 17, 19]	**Privacy** • Secrecy [3] • Protection of one's personality [3] • Limitation of reachability [3] • Privacy and data governance (e.g. access to data [6])
Accountability • Accountability [3, 6, 25] • Responsibility and accountability [16, 21] • Trust [3, 26]	**Variance** • Variability [7] • Multiple outputs and visualizing differences [7] • Imperfection [7]
Benefits and well-being • Multi-optimization of benefits [3] • Minimizing frustration, stress, anxiety[3] • Environmental well-being [6] • Sustainable development [25]	**Safety** • Avoidance and prevention of harm [3, 6, 7] • Non-maleficence [16, 22] • Technical robustness and safety [6] • Reliability [5] • Accuracy [24] • Data quality, integrity and access [24]

Table 3 represents the socio-technical heuristics (left column) and relates them to the aspects of AI principles and guidelines (right column) which are relevant for the AI-related revision of these heuristics.

5   AI-Related Revision of Sociotechnical Heuristics

In what follows we use the findings of Sect. 4 to revise the socio-technical heuristics as they have been documented more explicitly with the English version of https://hi4.iaw. rub.de/#!/manual (retrieved on 02/04/2024). We include the AI-related aspects in the description of the heuristics and mark them in italics.

Table 3. Extending socio-technical heuristics by considering AI

No.	Socio-technical heuristics according to Herrmann et al. [12]	Related aspect of AI-related principles and guidelines
1	Visibility about task handling and feedback about its success	Transparency, Accountability, Privacy
2	Flexibility for variable task handling leading to ... evolution of the system	Autonomy, Variance
3	Communication support for task handling and social interaction	Benefits and wellbeing, accountability, selected aspects of privacy: limited reachability,
4	Purpose-orientated information exchange for facilitating mental work	Privacy and data governance, selected aspects of safety: data quality, integrity and access;
5	Balance of effort and experienced benefit by organizational structuring of tasks	Benefits and wellbeing, selected aspects of fairness, such as promotion of human values
6	Compatibility between requirements, development of competencies, and the system's features	Selected aspects of fairness: avoidance of biases
7	Efficiency-oriented allocation of tasks for pursuing holistic goals	Benefits and wellbeing
8	Supportive technology and resources for productive and flawless work	Safety

1. Visibility about task handling and feedback about its success

The status and progress of workflows and technical procedures *into which AI is integrated* are visible and actively explorable as far as it is relevant for task processing and permissible from a privacy point of view. *AI can help to support this visibility. AI-outcome is also a subject of explainability and explorability where users can experimentally research the behavior of AI, e.g. by interventions. Not only the AI-system itself but also other human actors should contribute to explaining the behavior of AI.* Visibility also includes explainability of the background of the socio-technical system, so that one understands why certain events or outcome occur or not, whether certain effects can be expected or not, and how they affect people within and outside the socio-technical system – *also with respect to fairness. This includes an understanding of the data basis being used for the training of machine learning components.* Visibility also applies to possible further collaborative work steps and *to the options for individually and collaboratively adapting AI-outcome,* and for further developing and adapting the system, *including AI components.* One can see what one is contributing and what others are contributing, *and – with respect to accountability – which of others' contributions result from employing AI.* The representation of the information for the purpose of visibility must be well understandable *and comprehensible* [20]. Accordingly, one can individually and purposefully select and adapt the extent as well as the degree of abstraction of this information. *This adaptation and person-alization of visibility can be supported by AI.* Awareness for the behavior of other agents – *human as well as AI* – serves as a basis for giving appropriate feedback on collaborative work. *Understanding the background includes knowledge about which interests have been involved in the design, training and selection of a system that might include AI-components. Thus, possible interests in misuse or in causing bias are detectable.*

Regular and timely feedback helps to understand how far one has met the expec-tations of others and *what has been contributed in addition to AI-outcome. Feedback and Visibility have to serve as a prerequisite for AI-related trust building.*

2. Flexibility for variable task handling leading to a participatory evolution of the system

One can vary manifold options of task handling and can flexibly decide about technology usage, time management, sharing of tasks etc. *This includes autonomy for teams of human actors who possibly control AI-based processes – such as autonomous driving – and decide whether or how an AI-outcome is included in subsequent work-flows.* Consequently, human actors can develop a wide range of competences that support their participation in the ongoing evolution of the whole socio-technical system.

Flexibility, freedom of decision and room for a broad scope of actions open the way to the evolution of the overall system, *e.g. by interactive machine learning* [27]. By minimizing strict rules for how to run tasks, different ways of *decision making* [28] and task handling become possible; this concerns methods, tools, the exchange of information, time management, sequences of action, etc. *For example, people should be able to choose between different AI-systems to be included and they should be able to decide when in the steps of task handling AI is employed* [29]. Groups can flexibly share tasks among themselves *particularly whether an AI-agent is included or not.* The way of using technology can also be varied and includes its adaptability. Workload and stress – *e.g. through the need for oversight of complex AI-processes* – can be mitigated by having different approaches on a team's disposal. *Possibilities for intervention* [30] *have to be provided that allows for interruptions and phases of fine-grained control without terminating or manipulating all facets of an AI-process.*

By exploiting flexibility, competences are simultaneously developed in a holistic way that promotes participation in the further development of the system. *Conse-quently, AI has to offer modes of usage that promotes the development of human competencies and capabilities* [13]. The coupling of flexibility with participation in this further development is realized in such a way that one can react to systemic interactions, *imperfection* [7], incompleteness, contingency, social dynamics and con-textual changes such as renewal of technologies. This includes the development of people's personality to enable them to process tasks more efficiently or to take on new tasks, *or to specify new ways of task sharing between humans and AI.*

With respect to employing AI-generated outputs, users as well as indirectly affected members of the socio-technical system should not remain passive recipients [18] *but active participants who can influence and shape the outcomes of AI interac-tions or even veto them* [31]. *Offering a variance of different outcomes between which the participants can choose or that can be adapted, contributes to flexible usage of AI. Interactive usage of AI allows for exploring the capacities and reliability of a systems and thus helps to build trust* [32] *in the context of possible imperfectness and continuous evolution.*

3. Communication support for task handling and social interaction

By technical and spatial support for communication one can be reached for purposes of task handling and coordination. Furthermore, this support is inevitably intertwined with building social relations that include negotiating the duties and rights of roles, or conversation about values, so that reciprocal reliability can be developed. *Opportunities for communication between people is an aspect of well-being that must not be disturbed by AI that mimics human beings.* Opportunities for communication can be established by organizational practices, technical media and spatial arrangements. *AI can help to find communication partners and channels on the one hand and can be used to replace human communicators, e.g. with chatbots, on the other hand. As a prerequisite of accountability, the difference between both options has to be crystal clear. The role an AI-agent might take over as a teammate must be negotiable by communicational means.*

Informal communication has to be maintained and promoted. It is less task-related but more relevant for building social relations and it contributes to the bridging of hierarchies, preservation of confidentiality and trust building. *Informal communication is relevant for trust calibration in the case of employing AI, since trust arises in network relationships (e.g., A trusts an AI system, if A trusts B and B trusts the system).* The extent of reachability is relevant for people's privacy and must be controllable in order to avoid interruptions of communication and task handling. *AI can serve as a gatekeeper to help regulate reachability. Integrating AI into teams and into organizational practices requires new social relations between humans and between humans and AI* [33]. These relationships have to be negotiated, established and maintained via communication between the involved stakeholders.

4. Information exchange for facilitating mental work

To support task handling, information is purposefully exchanged via technical means, updated, kept available and minimized. This implies that information items are technically linked with each other, and new information can be derived that possibly violates privacy rights, e.g. in the case of personal profiles. *AI can help to trace the origin of information, and the information from which AI-generated output is derived has also to be traceable. At least, AI has to provide documents and information that back its outcome.*

In order to complete tasks, the necessary information is made available systematically, comprehensibly and situation-related (right time, right place) with the help of technology. *AI can be employed to analyze contextual clues that indicate when which information should be provided.* Thus, no one has to memorize data or struggle with information over-load. People have access to the data they need or have created. The quality, security and accountability of information is technically supported, e.g. by regular archiving, updating and deletion; the conversion of data for the purpose of transfer between different media types is avoided. *Documentation activities and increasing data quality can be supported and automated by AI.*

The availability of information must not violate privacy or confidentiality. *Personal data must not be hidden in large language models or foundation models* [34]. *AI has to be employed to detect and eliminate personal data, e.g. in pictures made in the public.* For those affected, the processing of their personal data or their virtual image is transparent and traceable. Minimization of data and of their accessibility ensures privacy and protects trust, as does self-determination about the information that is transmitted, processed and linked, *or used for the training of machine learning systems.*

5. Balance between effort and experienced benefit

Tasks are assigned to people, pooled, and technically supported in a way that make sense and provide fun for people. Thus, a sustaining balancing of efforts and personal benefits is pursued by organizational practices and technical artefacts *including AI-components.*

The handling of tasks is pooled in appropriate task bundles that are meaningful for the work force and is distributed in such a way between persons and technical support that a balanced relationship between benefit and effort can be experienced. *This applies particularly to the task sharing between humans and AI and to the integration of AI-teammates. In accordance with the concept of hybrid intelligence systems* [2], *the strengths of humans and of AI have to be optimally combined, not only to achieve the best possible results but also to improve beneficial experience during work.* Motivation and sense of fun are also promoted by the fact that the challenges of the task accomplishment correspond to the individual mental, physical and social abilities. The degree of beneficial experience might be technically measured – *possibly with AI-components* – to provide feedback to those who are affected or responsible. Individual preferences, goals, values, and interests are taken into account to achieve the balance; health impairments and unsolicited stress are avoided. *AI helps to reduce stress by offering the interaction-free usage of automated processes or by taking over tasks of routinized documentation. However, the need for oversight and being in control can cause additional effort and stress that have to be balanced.* The complete competence spectrum of a person or team and their different communication needs are considered. The balance must also be experienced at the level of groups and organizations. Effort and benefit are not only balanced in everyday work, but also when employees participate in the further development of the system. *The effort of exercising autonomy when dealing with AI must be balanced by the experienceable benefits; this applies also when people participate in the continuous evolution of AI.*

6. Compatibility between requirements, development of competences and the system's features

Technical and organizational features of the system are continuously adjusted to each other. They have to meet – within in clarified limits – the requirements from outside in a way that is based on the development of competencies and proactive help for dealing with changing challenges. People's tasks must comply with their technical, social and physical competences and skills. *This is specifically true for AI-related requirements such as using transparency, exercising autonomy, providing accountability, or ensuring fairness. Not only technical, but also organizational practices must support people in meeting these requirements.*

Through continuous adaptation of the socio-technical system and continuous individual and organizational learning, the characteristics of the system fit into the direct organizational environment and meet the requirements imposed on an organization from outside. This fit concerns the language used, legal and ethical aspects – *such as fairness and avoidance of bias in the case of AI* –, social dynamics, goals, processes, physical and technical conditions, etc.

The request to achieve compatibility in order to fulfill external requirements can only be fulfilled within reasonable limits, which must be clarified and comprehensible. In order to achieve compatibility with external requests, corresponding internal compatibility must be maintained: The various components of the overall socio-technical system must support each other consistently and expectably. *For example, AI must transparently reflect the values and goals of the actors involved, e.g. for decision-making or the execution of autonomous processes.* This includes, for example, mutual assistance, instructions and hints (prompting) as a contribution to holistic skills development. The skills are required in order to be prepared for upcoming and future tasks as well as regular changes in conditions and challenges. *According to the concept of hybrid intelligence, the reciprocal, interactive learning of both sides, AI and humans, must contribute to the necessary compatibility of skills.*

7. Efficiency-oriented allocation of tasks for pursuing holistic goals

By appropriate sequencing, integration and distribution of tasks – between humans and technology – seamless collaboration is supported. Unnecessary steps or waste of resources are avoided. If needed, an increase of efficiency can be realized.

People are supported so that they can efficiently manage their tasks and workflows without obstacles, health risks, etc. This is achieved through an efficient organization of workflows, for example through a suitable sequence, division or grouping of tasks. *AI can help – e.g. via process monitoring – to optimize workflows that include human work.* Tasks are bundled in such a way that the achievement of holistic goals can be experienced. *AI must not be integrated into workflows in a way that prevents people from understanding the key objectives to be achieved.* Unnecessary tasks or inflexible processes must not be enforced. Waste of resources and the involvement of unnecessary persons or departments are avoided. *AI can be employed to optimize the use of resources.* This includes assistance and quality controls to avoid mistakes or their consequences. For example, tasks are not continued if intermediate results are faulty and unusable. Thus, resources are used sparingly, and tasks are shared between people and distributed between people and technology – *e.g. AI-agents* – in such a way that efficiency is achieved. An increase in performance is made possible by the continuous further development of organization and technology, *e.g. retraining of machine learning components. When comparing the efficiency between conventional technology and AI, the whole AI-lifecycle has to be taken into account, including design, training, organizational integration and retraining as well as the effort of exercising control.*

8. Supportive technology and resources for productive and flawless work

Technology and further resources support work and collaboration and consider the intertwining of criteria such as technology acceptance, usability and accessibility for different users, avoiding consequences of mistakes or of misuse, security, and constant updating.

Technology and additional resources are available at the right time and are being further developed according to current possibilities so that task processing is simple and robust against errors. Accordingly, access to the resources is uncomplicated and reliable; they are easy and quick to use (usability) and allow to accelerate the use with increasing experience. Individual human limitations are taken into account and acceptance barriers are reduced. *AI can help to optimize the adaptability of human-computer interfaces.*

The loss or non-availability of data as well as unnecessary waiting times are example of most striking problems to be avoided. Reliability and robustness prevent individually or jointly caused errors as well as unintentional misconduct and prevent deliberate misuse. The entire system can quickly return to an error-free state or revise unwanted effects. *For AI-interfaces, it is important that automated processes can be temporarily interrupted, e.g. to allow users to take over control. Interactive tools are needed to deal with imperfect results* [32]. *User-driven possibilities for retraining must be offered* [27], *and within training material, the data included that has caused erroneous results must be detectable.*

6 Discussion and Conclusion

The question (RQ1) of how principles of socio-technical design can be adapted with respect to AI is answered by Sect. 5. The second research question (RQ2) asks how a comparison between them and guidelines for HCAI can result into a scientific benefit.

There are clear overlaps between socio-technical heuristics for evaluating conventional information technology and for AI usage. The relation between visibility and transparency (see Table 3) is a highly relevant example. In the study of Herrmann et al. [13], visibility proved to be the most important recommendation since it got the highest number of assignments (>20%). The black box character of AI increases the problems of invisibility. From a socio-technical point of view, visibility has not only to be provided for the direct users but also for indirectly affected people such as patients in health care [35, 36]. Visibility or transparency have to take privacy concerns into account and are a crucial prerequisite for trustability and trust calibration [37]. This influence of visibility has been given greater emphasis with the emergence of HCAI. AI can not only decrease but also increase the possibilities for visibility by providing explainability and personalization of explanations by taking mental models into account. However, from a socio-technical point of view, visibility is a requirement that has not only to be fulfilled with technical features but also by contributions of the whole system including human actors. If users do not comprehend the output of an AI-system, they also must have the possibility to ask human experts, such as data analysts, AI-developers or domain experts, for explanations. This example points towards a general recommendation that is neglected in the HCAI discourse: It will be promising for using AI if not only technical features, but organizational and social practices are socio-technically designed in a way that compensates shortcomings of AI.

Similarly, promoting autonomy and human control that allows for flexible, autonomous task handling and AI usage is a requirement that has to be addressed by the whole socio-technical system. It is not sufficient to address this requirement with interface design and functionality of AI. By contrast, organizational practices that promote humans capabilities and readiness for collaboratively staying in control are most crucial to guarantee autonomy [38]. Comparing the socio-technical approaches with HCAI regarding autonomy or flexibility reveals further insights:

- The relation between control, interactive usage and exploration on the one hand and trust building on the other hand is not sufficiently present in the discussion on socio-technical systems and should be given more attention.
- Completely stopping an autonomous process or decision-making workflows that include AI can be risky, especially if not everyone involved is aware of the stop [39]. Temporary interventions are more appropriate as they allow for limited interruptions or have restricted effects, support a "what-if" exploration, and can be easily revised or canceled.
- Continuous evolution is a basic characteristic of socio-technical systems. Human oversight and interventions and the subsequent appropriation of AI-systems [40] lead to continuous adaptation and re-design of the systems when autonomy is collaboratively exercised. This interrelationship should be taken into account more rigorously in the context of HCAI.

The heuristics of Herrmann et al. [12] differentiate between communication and information exchange to emphasize that informal communication is crucial to support building of social relationships as well as the negotiation of rights and duties. Since trust building is embedded in social relationships, a sufficient amount of human communication is necessary, in which the communicators cannot be replaced by AI agents. Furthermore, the difference between the heuristic 'balance of effort and experienced benefit' and the heuristic 'efficiency-oriented allocation of tasks' is important for the HCAI discussion: On the one hand, people may be willing to exercise control and oversight – even if this causes inefficiencies – as long as the invested efforts supports the feeling of being in control and allows for freedom of decision. Autonomy and exercising control can be a value for its own. On the other hand, efficiency is an important aspect where AI can help to reduce the waste of resources and lead to economic benefits.

Methods and criteria that support the design and evaluation of socio-technical systems are widely focused on the interests and wellbeing of those people who are part of the system. The aspect of fairness is therefore underestimated in conventional socio-technical discourses insofar as it addresses those being affected outside the socio-technical system. Only if fairness is reflected in the values of the actors within the socio-technical system and becomes part of their responsibility will it be sufficiently taken into account. Consequently, an additional socio-technical principle or heuristic such as 'value implantation' could be relevant.

Concludingly, HCAI might expand research of how social and organizational practices contribute to mitigate AI-related problems. A continuous evolution of socio-technical systems that include AI has to be promoted as a means to deal with the general imperfectness and fallibility of AI. For research that pursues the socio-technical perspective in HCAI, the relevance of fairness and accountability, particularly of traceability has to be given more attention. It has to be realized that socio-technical requirements are not only meant to regulate AI or to inform its design and usage, but also that AI can help to meet these requirements as a valuable component within socio-technical processes.

References

1. Shneiderman, B.: Human-Centered AI. Oxford University Press, Oxford (2022)
2. Dellermann, D., Calma, A., Lipusch, N., Weber, T., Weigel, S., Ebel, P.: The future of human-AI collaboration: a taxonomy of design knowledge for hybrid intelligence systems. In: Proceedings of the 52nd Hawaii International Conference on System Sciences (HICSS) (2019)
3. Garibay, O.O., et al.: Six human-centered artificial intelligence grand challenges. Int. J. Hum.-Compute. Interact. **39**(3), 391–437 (2023). https://doi.org/10.1080/10447318.2022.2153320
4. Dwivedi, Y.K., et al.: Opinion paper: 'so what if ChatGPT wrote it?' Multidisciplinary perspectives on opportunities, challenges and implications of generative conversational AI for research, practice and policy. Int. J. Inf. Manag. **71**, 102642 (2023). https://doi.org/10.1016/j.ijinfomgt.2023.102642
5. Bingley, W.J., et al.: Where is the human in human-centered AI? Insights from developer priorities and user experiences. Comput. Hum. Behav. **141**, 107617 (2023). https://doi.org/10.1016/j.chb.2022.107617
6. European Commission, Directorate-General for Communications Networks, Content and Technology, Ethics guidelines for trustworthy AI (2019). https://data.europa.eu/doi/10.2759/346720. Accessed 23 May 2021
7. Weisz, J.D., Muller, M., He, J., Houde, S.: Toward general design principles for generative AI applications. arXiv, 13 January 2023. http://arxiv.org/abs/2301.05578. Accessed 26 Oct 2023.
8. Cherns, A.: Principles of sociotechnical design revisited. Hum. Relat. **40**(3), 153–162 (1987)
9. Cherns, A.: The principles of sociotechnical design. Hum. Relat. **29**(8), 783–792 (1976)
10. Mumford, E.: Designing Human Systems for New Technology: The ETHICS Method. Manchester Business School (1983). https://books.google.de/books?id=JTjxIwAACAAJ
11. Clegg, C.W.: Sociotechnical principles for system design. Appl. Ergon. **31**(5), 463–477 (2000). https://doi.org/10.1016/S0003-6870(00)00009-0
12. Herrmann, T., Jahnke, I., Nolte, A.: A problem-based approach to the advancement of heuristics for socio-technical evaluation. Behav. Inf. Technol. **41**(14), 3087–3109 (2022). https://doi.org/10.1080/0144929X.2021.1972157
13. Herrmann, T.: Promoting human competences by appropriate modes of interaction for human-centered-AI. In: Degen, H., Ntoa, S. (eds.) HCII 2022. LNCS, vol. 13336, pp. 35–50. Springer, Cham (2022). https://doi.org/10.1007/978-3-031-05643-7_3
14. Chatila, R., Havens, J.C.: The IEEE global initiative on ethics of autonomous and intelligent systems. In: Aldinhas Ferreira, M.I., Silva Sequeira, J., Virk, G.S., Tokhi, M.O., Kadar, E.E. (eds.) Robotics and Well-Being. ISCASE, vol. 95, pp. 11–16. Springer, Cham (2019). https://doi.org/10.1007/978-3-030-12524-0_2
15. De Visser, E.J., Pak, R., Shaw, T.H.: From 'automation' to 'autonomy': the importance of trust repair in human–machine interaction. Ergonomics **61**(10), 1409–1427 (2018). https://doi.org/10.1080/00140139.2018.1457725
16. Jobin, A., Ienca, M., Vayena, E.: The global landscape of AI ethics guidelines. Nat. Mach. Intell. **1**(9), 389–399 (2019). https://doi.org/10.1038/s42256-019-0088-2
17. Fjeld, J., Achten, N., Hilligoss, H., Nagy, A., Srikumar, M.: Principled artificial intelligence: mapping consensus in ethical and rights-based approaches to principles for AI. SSRN J. (2020). https://doi.org/10.2139/ssrn.3518482
18. Usmani, U.A., Happonen, A., Watada, J.: Human-centered artificial intelligence: designing for user empowerment and ethical considerations. In: 2023 5th International Congress on Human-Computer Interaction, Optimization and Robotic Applications (HORA). IEEE, Istanbul, Turkiye, June 2023, pp. 1–7 (2023). https://doi.org/10.1109/HORA58378.2023.10156761

19. Shneiderman, B.: Bridging the gap between ethics and practice: guidelines for reliable, safe, and trustworthy human-centered ai systems. ACM Trans. Interact. Intell. Syst. **10**(4), 1–31 (2020). https://doi.org/10.1145/3419764

20. Shneiderman, B.: Responsible AI: bridging from ethics to practice. Commun. ACM **64**(8), 32–35 (2021). https://doi.org/10.1145/3445973

21. Hofeditz, L., Mirbabaie, M., Ortmann, M.: Ethical challenges for human–agent interaction in virtual collaboration at work. Int. J. Hum.–Comput. Interact. 1–17 (2023). https://doi.org/10.1080/10447318.2023.2279400

22. Kieslich, K., Keller, B., Starke, C.: Artificial intelligence ethics by design. Evaluating public perception on the importance of ethical design principles of artificial intelligence. Big Data Soc. **9**(1), 205395172210929 (2022). https://doi.org/10.1177/20539517221092956

23. Díaz-Rodríguez, N., Del Ser, J., Coeckelbergh, M., López De Prado, M., Herrera-Viedma, E., Herrera, F.: Connecting the dots in trustworthy artificial intelligence: from AI principles, ethics, and key requirements to responsible AI systems and regulation. Inf. Fusion **99**, 101896 (2023). https://doi.org/10.1016/j.inffus.2023.101896

24. Georgieva, I., Lazo, C., Timan, T., Van Veenstra, A.F.: From AI ethics principles to data science practice: a reflection and a gap analysis based on recent frameworks and practical experience. AI Ethics **2**(4), 697–711 (2022). https://doi.org/10.1007/s43681-021-00127-3

25. Noble, S.M., Dubljević, V.: Ethics of AI in organizations. In: Human-Centered Artificial Intelligence, pp. 221–239. Elsevier, Amsterdam (2022). https://doi.org/10.1016/B978-0-323-85648-5.00019-0

26. Reinhardt, K.: Trust and trustworthiness in AI ethics. AI Ethics **3**(3), 735–744 (2023). https://doi.org/10.1007/s43681-022-00200-5

27. Amershi, S., Cakmak, M., Knox, W.B., Kulesza, T.: Power to the people: the role of humans in interactive machine learning. AI Mag. **35**(4), 105–120 (2014)

28. Jarrahi, M.H.: Artificial intelligence and the future of work: human-AI symbiosis in organizational decision making. Bus. Horiz. **61**(4), 577–586 (2018)

29. Fogliato, R., et al.: Who goes first? Influences of human-AI workflow on decision making in clinical imaging. arXiv, 19 May 2022. http://arxiv.org/abs/2205.09696. Accessed 03 June 2022

30. Schmidt, A., Herrmann, T.: Intervention user interfaces: a new interaction paradigm for automated systems. Interactions **24**(5), 40–45 (2017)

31. Rakova, B., Yang, J., Cramer, H., Chowdhury, R.: Where responsible AI meets reality: practitioner perspectives on enablers for shifting organizational practices. Proc. ACM Hum.-Comput. Interact. **5**(CSCW1), 1–23 (2021)

32. Cai, C.J., et al.: Human-centered tools for coping with imperfect algorithms during medical decision-making. In: Proceedings of the 2019 CHI Conference on Human Factors in Computing Systems, pp. 1–14 (2019)

33. Cai, C.J., Winter, S., Steiner, D., Wilcox, L., Terry, M.: 'Hello AI': uncovering the onboarding needs of medical practitioners for human-AI collaborative decision-making. Proc. ACM Hum.-Comput. Interact. **3**(CSCW), 1–24 (2019). https://doi.org/10.1145/3359206

34. Schneider, J., Meske, C., Kuss, P.: Foundation models: a new paradigm for artificial intelligence. Bus. Inf. Syst. Eng. (2024). https://doi.org/10.1007/s12599-024-00851-0

35. Herrmann, T., Pfeiffer, S.: Keeping the organization in the loop as a general concept for human-centered AI: the example of medical imaging. In: Proceedings of the 56th Hawaii International Conference on System Sciences (HICSS), pp. 5272–5281 (2023)

36. Ackermann, M.S., Goggins, S.P., Herrmann, T., Prilla, M., Stary, C.: Designing Healthcare That Works – A Socio-technical Approach. Academic Press, United Kingdom, United States (2018)

37. Okamura, K., Yamada, S.: Adaptive trust calibration for human-AI collaboration. PLoS ONE **15**(2), e0229132 (2020). https://doi.org/10.1371/journal.pone.0229132

38. Herrmann, T., Pfeiffer, S.: Keeping the organization in the loop: a socio-technical extension of human-centered artificial intelligence. AI Soc. **38**, 1523–1542 (2023). https://doi.org/10.1007/s00146-022-01391-5

39. Herrmann, T., Lentzsch, C., Degeling, M.: Intervention and EUD. In: Malizia, A., Valtolina, S., Morch, A., Serrano, A., Stratton, A. (eds.) IS-EUD 2019. LNCS, vol. 11553, pp. 67–82. Springer, Cham (2019). https://doi.org/10.1007/978-3-030-24781-2_5

40. Herrmann, T.: Collaborative appropriation of AI in the context of interacting with AI. In: Degen, H., Ntoa, S. (eds.) HCII 2023. LNCS, vol. 14051, pp. 249–260. Springer, Cham (2023). https://doi.org/10.1007/978-3-031-35894-4_18

Negative Emotions Towards Artificial Intelligence in the Workplace – Motivation and Method for Designing Demonstrators

Jennifer Link(✉) [iD] and Sascha Stowasser

ifaa - Institute of Applied Industrial Engineering and Ergonomics, Uerdinger Str. 56,
40474 Düsseldorf, Germany
j.link@wirksam.nrw

Abstract. Artificial Intelligence (AI) in the workplace can boost company productivity and reduce employee workload. Workers may especially benefit from higher workplace standards, such as fewer monotonous tasks and greater physical safety. Nevertheless, companies in the manufacturing sector in Germany see employee fears as one of the three main barriers to the use of AI. Against this backdrop, we present the results of a survey of manufacturing employees on their feelings about AI in the workplace. The results show that non-managerial employees in particular express negative feelings such as fear, insecurity, or concern about the use of AI in the workplace. In contrast managers have a positive attitude toward AI. According to the survey, the main reasons for negative feelings are loss of control over AI, fear of job loss, dependence on technology, and unreliability of technology. Finally, after considering approaches to address the feelings, a method for developing a demonstrator that addresses negative feelings related to AI in the workplace is proposed. The method includes a mixed methods approach, incorporating literature review and interviews. This approach aims to define the requirements for demonstrators in general and specifically in the context of AI in the workplace.

Keywords: Artificial Intelligence · Emotions · Workplace · Demonstrators

1 Introduction

Artificial intelligence (AI) has become ubiquitous in our daily lives. ChatGPT, in particular, has made significant inroads into the professional lives of many individuals [1]. The use of AI in the workplace can enhance productivity [2, 3]. It also enables faster and more accurate decision-making [3, 4] and provides various opportunities to alleviate employees in different ways [5]. AI can effectively support a variety of tasks and improve job quality [6]. It also allows employees to focus on activities where human skills are particularly in demand [7]. Additionally, AI can reduce tedious aspects of work, making daily tasks less monotonous [8, 9]. Moreover, the use of AI can improve physical safety in the workplace [9].

© The Author(s), under exclusive license to Springer Nature Switzerland AG 2024
H. Degen and S. Ntoa (Eds.): HCII 2024, LNAI 14735, pp. 75–86, 2024.
https://doi.org/10.1007/978-3-031-60611-3_6

In the production sector, AI has the potential to improve working conditions and increase employee satisfaction [10]. However, in Germany's manufacturing sector, companies cite employees' fear of AI as a major obstacle to its introduction. According to a survey of 332 respondents, 39% consider fear a major obstacle and 12% consider it a very major obstacle [11]. But where do negative feelings about AI in the workplace originate? What does current scientific literature reveal about employees' emotions when using AI at work? What methods exist to alleviate negative emotions, such as worries or fears, among employees?

This article presents current scientific findings on employees' feelings regarding AI in the workplace and contributes to expand the field of research by conducting an empirical survey. The study allows a detailed analysis of employee emotions and their reasons in the manufacturing industry regarding AI at work. In this article, we discuss various approaches to increase the acceptance and trustworthiness of AI applications, which are crucial for the successful implementation of AI technologies. One such approach is the use of demonstrators. Therefore, we conclude the article by presenting a specific method for developing a demonstrator that can help reduce negative emotions caused by the introduction of AI in the work environment. The purpose of the demonstrator is to encourage employees to have a positive attitude towards AI, thereby facilitating its effective and integrated use in the workplace.

2   Negative Emotions Related to AI in the Workplace

Research on negative emotions related to AI in the workplace is a significant and growing area of study. For instance, a survey of 13,000 people from 18 countries found that 30% of respondents were concerned about the impact of AI on their work [12]. Additionally, more than half of the manufacturing companies in Germany cite employees' fears of AI as an obstacle to the technology's introduction [11]. Several sources mention concerns about job losses [6, 13–16]. In companies that do not currently use AI fear of job loss is greater than in those that already use AI [11]. A study by the Boston Consulting Group confirms that people who have little or no contact with AI systems are more concerned about AI. According to this study, only 22% of regular users of generative AI report feeling concerns about the technology, while 42% of non-users express concerns [12]. Regarding generative AI, 4% of respondents reported feeling very afraid, 12% reported feeling more afraid than enthusiastic about the technology, and 35% reported having a mixture of fear and enthusiasm [17]. Another concern highlighted in the studies is the fear of a lack of AI skills. In a 2022 study conducted by PwC, 39% of respondents expressed concern about inadequate training in digital and technological skills from their employer [18]. Additionally, respondents in this study expressed apprehension about having to learn AI skills that they are not confident they can acquire [18]. Further potential concerns regarding AI usage include its possible negative impact on work [18, 19]. Other apprehensions encompass fears of increased employee surveillance through AI [20], data security risks [21], dependence on technology [22], loss of control [23], discrimination [24] and increased work intensity [25]. However, none of the sources found provide quantitative analysis of the reasons for these concerns or the context in which they arise.

3   Empirical Survey: Employee Reactions to AI in the Workplace in Manufacturing Industry

An empirical study is presented below based on the results of Harlacher's 2023 survey, which showed significant fears of artificial intelligence hindering its use, mainly in the manufacturing industry [11]. Despite available research, no survey has yet been conducted on feelings in the manufacturing industry regarding the use of AI in the workplace. This study explores participants' perceptions of AI's impact on work, emotional responses to AI in the workplace, and reasons for negative sentiments toward this technology.

3.1   Research Design

The study presented here examines the manufacturing industry in Germany. A total of 531 participants were surveyed between end of October and beginning of December 2023. The participants were recruited by a panel company and completed an anonymous online questionnaire to ensure data protection. Prior to participating, the participants were fully informed about the objectives, methods, and potential benefits of the study and gave their informed consent. The study included 90 employees from small companies (up to 99 employees), 173 individuals from medium-sized companies (100–499 employees), and 268 individuals from large companies (500 employees and more). Of the 531 participants, 389 held management positions, while 142 did not. The questions below are part of a trend barometer that assesses ergonomic and organizational topics. Additionally, questions were asked about AI and sustainability, as well as the use of AI in the company and associated sentiments. The questions regarding feelings about AI in the workplace are based on the current state of research described above and consist of closed questions, some with multiple choice. The evaluation of the data is quantitative and is linked to the results of current research by interpreting the results below.

3.2   Results of the Survey

The following survey results provide an in-depth analysis of participants' emotional reactions and concerns regarding the use of AI in the workplace. The focus is on the diversity of feelings and underlying reasons for negative emotions.

Figure 1 illustrates respondents' answers to the question of how AI will change their work. The data was filtered to display the current implementation of AI within the company (left), planned implementation of AI (center), or lack of planned implementation of AI (right). Upon closer analysis of the results, 86% of respondents in AI-using companies see more benefits than drawbacks. Only 2% of participants see predominantly negative effects on their work, while 12% remain undecided. These findings suggest that individuals whose companies have experience with AI have had mainly positive experiences with the technology in the workplace. Similar results have been reported in other studies [11, 12].

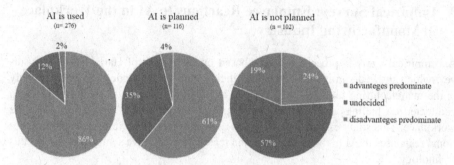

Fig. 1. The use of artificial intelligence is changing the world of work. How do you personally see this affecting you and your work? (filtered according to the use of AI in the company)

The percentage of individuals employed by companies that intend to implement AI and believe that its benefits outweigh its drawbacks is lower. In this case, the percentage of individuals who are undecided is higher than that of participants whose companies have already implemented AI (35% vs. 12%). This may suggest that there is optimism regarding the advantages of AI, but there are also uncertainties about its specific impact on their own workplace. In companies without AI plans, most people are undecided (57%), while 24% state that the advantages outweigh the disadvantages resulting from the use of AI, compared to 19%. Overall, this shows that people in companies with AI deployment or planning have a positive outlook on the impact of AI on their workplace. In contrast those in companies without AI plans are generally more undecided.

Filtering the same question based on whether the respondent holds a management position or not reveals a distinct pattern. It becomes apparent that employees without a management position are even more indifferent to the use of AI in their workplace. In this case, 59% state that they are undecided about the change, and 16% expect it to have a negative impact (refer to Fig. 2).

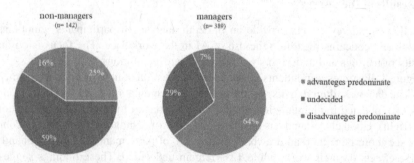

Fig. 2. The use of artificial intelligence is changing the world of work. How do you personally see this affecting you and your work? (filtered by people with a management position and people without a management position)

In contrast, 64% of individuals in management positions believe that the benefits of utilizing AI outweigh the drawbacks for their work. The percentage of managers who perceive disadvantages with the use of AI at work is lower than that of employees (7% vs. 16%).

When asked what they feel most when thinking about the use of artificial intelligence (AI) in the workplace, the results are similar (see Fig. 3). Some 77% of managers surveyed expressed positive feelings (anticipation, satisfaction, curiosity) about AI in the workplace. In contrast, only 38% of non-managerial employees reported similarly positive associations. Interestingly, the number of people experiencing curiosity is higher among non-managers (25%) than among managers (18%). It should be noted, however, that the proportion of non-managers who feel curious when thinking about AI in the workplace (25%) is similar to the proportion who feel worried or concerned (26%).

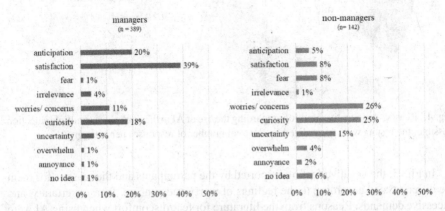

Fig. 3. What do you feel most strongly when you think about the use of AI in your workplace? (Single selection, filtered by employees with and without a management position)

However, more than half of non-leadership respondents (55%) experience one of the negative emotions (fear, worry and anxiety, uncertainty, overwhelm, and annoyance). In comparison only 18% of leadership respondents experience negative emotions related to the use of AI in the workplace. Most non-managerial employees who experience negative feelings cite concern or worry (26%), followed by uncertainty (15%), fear (8%), being overwhelmed (4%), and annoyance (2%). Among managers, the order is similar but less pronounced: 11% cite worry, 5% uncertainty, 1% fear, 1% annoyance, and 1% overwhelm. Neutral feelings such as "no idea" or "irrelevant" are rarely mentioned by either managers or employees. Overall, non-managerial employees are more likely to react negatively to the use of artificial intelligence in the workplace, particularly through concerns, worries and uncertainty. In contrast, managers show a comparatively more positive attitude, with a dominant share of positive feelings such as anticipation, satisfaction, and curiosity. Other literature comes to similar conclusions [26, 27].

A holistic view of negative emotions and their underlying causes, as shown in Fig. 4, reveals that these emotions vary individually. There can no single emotion be identified as predominant. Nevertheless, it is possible to draw conclusions about the concerns that need to be addressed when implementing artificial intelligence in the workplace. These include loss of control over AI, dependence on the technology, fear of job loss, and unreliability of the technology. Issues such as increased control over work, lack of data security, and potentially increased work intensity are also identified as relevant concerns.

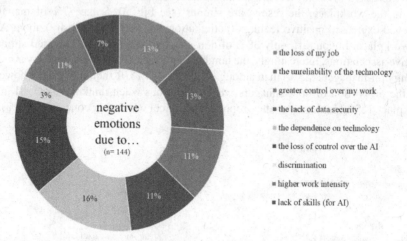

Fig. 4. Reasons for negative emotions regarding the use of AI in the workplace (multiple selection possible, the results were normalized by the total number of responses per category)

In Fig. 5, the negative feelings reported by the participants and the reasons for them are differentiated according to the feelings of worry and concern, fear, uncertainty, and excessive demands. Reasons from the literature for fear/discomfort when using AI were taken into account [20–25]. In analyzing these responses, it was striking that none of the feelings could be associated with a specific or notably pronounced reason. Instead, a variety of reasons were given, with no one reason standing out, as most reasons were less than 25%. Only among those who reported feeling overwhelmed did dependence on technology stand out at 33%. Discrimination, on the other hand, played a minor role in the overall negative feelings surveyed, particularly in the case of overwhelm (not stated) and worries, uncertainty and fear (only 3 and 2%, respectively). People who expressed fear as their strongest emotion when thinking about AI in the workplace cited fear of losing their job as the main reason (22%). In contrast, fear of losing one's job was less prominent in the context of other reported feelings. This may be due to the fact that fear is classified as the most negative of the emotions mentioned, and job loss is lower on Maslow's hierarchy of needs, in the security category [28]. Interestingly, among those respondents who reported fear as their strongest emotion, the unreliability of technology (20%) and dependence on technology (17%) were also cited as significant reasons, even though fear of job loss is mentioned in many sources [6, 13–16].

Most people worried about higher work intensity (17%), dependence on technology (15%), losing control over AI (14%), unreliable AI and job loss (both 12%). For persons who feel insecure the reasons were similar, but fewer people (7%) feel insecure about more intense work.

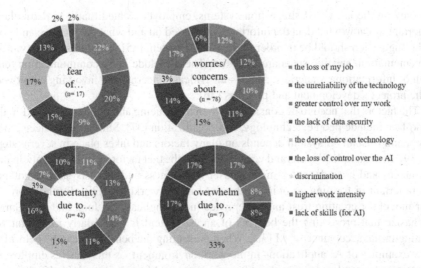

Fig. 5. When using artificial intelligence in the work environment, I have worries / concerns about / am afraid of / feel insecure / feel overwhelmed because of... (multiple selection possible, the results were normalized by the total number of answers per category)

3.3 Conclusions from the Survey

Respondents, especially non-managers, express specific concerns and fears about AI, including loss of control, job loss, dependency on technology, and its unreliability. Compared to other sources, the current study shows that fear is less prevalent than worry and other emotions such as uncertainty. These differences in emotional reactions underscore the need to consider not only technological aspects when introducing AI technologies, but also to understand the individual feelings of employees and to take targeted measures to promote trust and acceptance.

4   Approaches to Create Acceptance and Trust in AI in the Workplace

Acceptance and trust of AI depend on various factors, including generation and AI skills [29]. Additionally, the structure and culture of the organization significantly influence attitudes towards AI in the workplace [30]. The introduction of AI may lead to significant changes in work processes and tasks, which may impact the roles and responsibilities of employees. It is critical to anticipate these changes to ensure a smooth transition from working without AI to working with AI [19].

Companies can address negative emotions and build acceptance through several methods outlined in general AI introduction guidelines [31, 32]. These methods include fostering a positive attitude towards AI [31] and ensuring transparency and employee involvement [32]. It is also important to train employees [10, 33, 34] and to address data protection concerns by protecting personal and sensitive data [34]. In addition, in a survey on the use of AI suggestion systems, employees stated that it is particularly important to know what data the information is based on and what the purpose and goal of the suggestion should be in order to trust an AI system [35]. To address anxiety in AI implementation, specific steps are essential. These include early communication, creation of informational materials, addressing critical concerns, and involving employees in the project's development and progress [36].

The factors that need to be considered when introducing and implementing AI in the workplace include people, technology, and organization [37]. Similarly, the decision to accept and trust an AI system depends on many factors and takes place in several steps [38, 39]. For example, Werens and von Garrel describe that factors such as the anticipated advantages and hazards, assessment of user-friendliness and of costs and advantages are important in forming an opinion about AI in the workplace [39]. Furthermore, in their model for creating trust and acceptance in AI applications, Jung and von Garrel emphasize that presenting the benefits of an AI system is particularly important for creating initial acceptance of AI [38]. When presenting the benefits, it can be helpful to show examples of AI applications in the work environment, as this enables employees to better understand and assess the role and impact of AI on their work [6, 13, 40].

Demonstrators can be used as a tool to make AI applications and their benefits for the work system tangible [41]. Overall, there is little literature dealing with the design of demonstrators [41]. Moultrie for example, defines areas of application for demonstrators in research, such as the presentation of scientific principles, communication within and outside the scientific community, or convincing sponsors and investors [42], while other publications define initial requirements for demonstrators: Furthermore, Bobbe et al. define thirteen design principles for demonstrators, which are categorized into the goal-related topics of "communication", "visitor engagement" and "resources" [43]. In contrast, Altepost et al. define characteristics that a demonstrator should include, such as "intriguing", "useful", and "specific" [41]. However, these publications do not specifically refer to the representation of the change in work through AI by means of demonstrators, which would be necessary to create the attitudinal acceptance mentioned above. They also do not specifically address the reduction of negative emotions related to AI in the work environment with the help of demonstrators.

5 Method for Designing a Demonstrator to Reduce Negative Emotions About AI in the Workplace

The method developed is based on the double diamond model of design thinking (see Fig. 6). This model provides a structured approach to address complex problems and develop creative solutions [44].

It consists of four phases, namely "Discover", "Define", "Develop", and "Elaborate". While in the "Discover" and "Develop" phases the focus is deliberately broad to explore a variety of ideas and perspectives (divergence), in the "Define" and "Elaborate" phases the focus is on selecting and implementing the best ideas (convergence) [45]. The respective phases are designed in such a way that first the topic of AI demonstrators in general is considered, then the topic of AI and work is examined in more detail, and finally the topic of AI, work and negative emotions is considered (see arrow in Fig. 1, left). This three-dimensional approach aims to provide comprehensive insights into the design of demonstrators for AI (in the work environment) that have been lacking in the scientific literature [41]. To keep the innovation funnel open, the last two phases of the method are described rather roughly, while the first two phases are defined in detail (see arrow in Fig. 6 below).

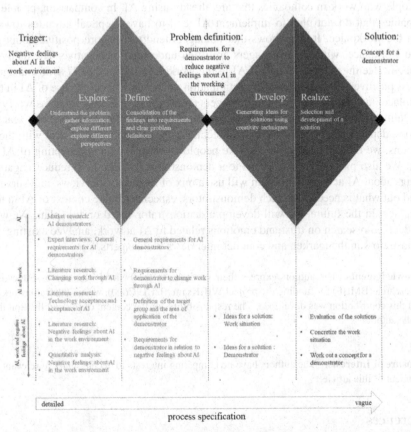

Fig. 6. Method for designing a demonstrator to reduce negative emotions in relation to AI in the workplace (own illustration based on Design Thinking Double Diamond Model [45])

The first phase is to understand the problem of "negative emotions of AI in the workplace" and gather information from different perspectives. To this end, literature and market research will be conducted. On the other hand, expert interviews about the requirements for AI demonstrators in general will be conducted. The survey on emotions when using AI in the work environment was presented in this paper. All this information will be used to generate requirements for demonstrators in the second phase. Based on these requirements, solution ideas for a work situation in which the demonstrator can be integrated and for the design of the demonstrator will be generated in the third phase. The final phase is used to evaluate the ideas and develop the demonstrator concept.

6 Summary and Outlook

This article provides an insight into the current state of research on negative feelings associated with the use of AI in the workplace. As a significant contribution to the research, the article presents a study with findings on the emotional state of employees in the context of AI in the workplace. A key finding of the study is the positive attitude of people who work in companies that are already using AI. In comparison, people in companies that do not plan to implement AI tend to have skeptical attitudes toward AI in the workplace. It also shows that managers tend to be more positive about AI in the workplace, while non-managers are often undecided or negative. The analysis of specific feelings about the use of AI in the workplace shows that 77% of managers express positive associations such as anticipation or curiosity about the use of AI in the workplace. In contrast, 55% of non-managers report negative feelings such as worry or uncertainty. The main causes of negative feelings are loss of control over AI, fear of job loss, dependence on technology, and technology's unreliability. To deal with these emotions, we list different ways to make people more trusting and accepting of AI at work. We also propose a plan to create a demonstrator that can help reduce negative feelings about AI at work. This plan will use a mix of research, interviews, and surveys to find out what is needed for such demonstrators, especially in the context of AI in the workplace. In the future, we will develop a demonstrator based on this plan. We will do a detailed research on trust and emotions related to AI at work, analyze existing AI demonstrators in the market, and conduct interviews with experts.

Acknowledgments. The authors express their gratitude to the Federal Ministry of Education and Research (BMBF) for funding the project WIRKsam (02L19C600), within the framework of which this contribution was developed. The responsibility for the content of this publication lies with the authors.

Disclosure of Interests. The authors have no competing interests to declare that are relevant to the content of this article.

References

1. Oppel, F.: ZEW-Studie: ChatGPT & Co. werden Teil des Arbeitsalltags, Mannheim (2023)
2. Czarnitzki, D., Fernández, G.P., Rammer, C.: Artificial intelligence and firm-level productivity. J. Econ. Behav. Organ. **211**, 188–205 (2023). https://doi.org/10.1016/j.jebo.2023.05.008
3. Plathottam, S.J., Rzonca, A., Lakhnori, R., et al.: A review of artificial intelligence applications in manufacturing operations. J. Adv. Manuf. Process. **5**, e10159 (2023). https://doi.org/10.1002/amp2.10159
4. Dömer, M.: Agilität in Realität: Chancen und Herausforderungen in der digitalen Transformation. Wirtsch Inform. Manag. **15**, 252–259 (2023). https://doi.org/10.1365/s35764-023-00489-9
5. Stowasser, S.: Successful introduction of AI in the company. In: Knappertsbusch, I., Gondlach, K. (eds.) Work and AI 2030, pp. 133–141. Springer Fachmedien Wiesbaden, Wiesbaden (2023). https://doi.org/10.1007/978-3-658-40232-7_15

6. Gamkrelidze, T., Zouinar, M., Barcellini, F.: Artificial Intelligence (AI) in the workplace: a study of stakeholders' views on benefits, issues and challenges of AI systems. In: Black, N.L., Neumann, W.P., Noy, I. (eds.) IEA 2021. LNNS, vol. 223, pp. 628–635. Springer, Cham (2022). https://doi.org/10.1007/978-3-030-74614-8_78

7. Stowasser, S., Neuburger, R.: Führung im Wandel: Herausforderungen und Chancen durch KI (2022)

8. Giering, O.: Künstliche Intelligenz und Arbeit: Betrachtungen zwischen Prognose und betrieblicher Realität. Zeitschrift für Arbeitswissenschaft **76**, 50–64 (2021). https://doi.org/10.1007/s41449-021-00289-0

9. Milanez, A.: The impact of AI on the workplace: evidence from OECD case studies of AI implementation. In: OECD Social, Employment and Migration Working Papers, No, 289, Paris (2023)

10. Lane, M., Williams, M., Broecke, S.: The impact of AI on the workplace: main findings from the OECD AI surveys of employers and workers. In: OECD Social, Employment and Migration Working Papers, vol. 288, Paris (2023)

11. Harlacher, M.: ifaa-Studie: Künstliche Intelligenz in produzierenden Unternehmen (2023). https://www.arbeitswissenschaft.net/ki-studie-ergebnisse. Accessed 09 Jan 2023

12. Beauchene, V., Bellefond, N., Duranton Sylvain et al. (2023). AI at Work: What People Are Saying

13. Lane, M., Williams, M.: Defining and classifying AI in the workplace. Lecture Notes in Networks and Systems (2023)

14. Cheng, K.-T., Chang, K., Tai, H.-W.: AI boosts performance but affects employee emotions. Inf. Resourc. Manag. J. **35**(1) (2022)

15. Grant, A.: Work Trend Index: Annual Report: Will AI Fix Work? (2023)

16. Yadrovskaia, M., Porksheyan, M., Petrova, A., et al.: About the attitude towards artificial intelligence technologies. In: E3S Web of Conference, vol. 376, pp. 5–25 (2023). https://doi.org/10.1051/e3sconf/202337605025

17. Grampp, M., Brandes, D., Laude, D.: Generative AI's fast and furious entry into Switzerland: usage and attitudes of the Swiss workforce towards Generative AI (2023)

18. Sethi, B., Brown, P., Stubbings, C., et al.: Global Workforce Hopes and Fears: Survey 2022 (2022)

19. Mirbabaie, M., Brünker, F., Möllmann Frick, N.R.J., et al.: The rise of artificial intelligence – understanding the AI identity threat at the workplace. Electron Mark. **32**, 73–99 (2022). https://doi.org/10.1007/s12525-021-00496-x

20. Berg, A., Dehmel, S.: Künstliche Intelligenz (2020)

21. Borges, G.: Potenziale von KünstlicherIntelligenz mit Blick auf das Datenschutzrecht (2021)

22. Krüger, S.: Die KI-Entscheidung. Springer Fachmedien Wiesbaden, Wiesbaden (2021). https://doi.org/10.1007/978-3-658-34874-8

23. Wittpahl, V.: Künstliche Intelligenz. Springer, Heidelberg (2019)

24. Gür-Seker, D.: Künstliche Intelligenz und die Zukunft der Arbeit: Die digitale Transformation in den (sozialen) Medien (2021)

25. Badura, B., Ducki, A., Schröder, H., et al. (eds.): Fehlzeiten-Report 2017. Springer, Heidelberg (2017). https://doi.org/10.1007/978-3-662-54632-1

26. Huang, H., Kim, K.-C., Young, M.M., et al.: A matter of perspective: differential evaluations of artificial intelligence between managers and staff in an experimental simulation. Asia Pac. J. Publ. Admin. **44**, 47–65 (2022). https://doi.org/10.1080/23276665.2021.1945468

27. Cardon, P.W., Getchell, K., Carradini, S., et al.: Generative AI in the workplace: employee perspectives of ChatGPT benefits and organizational policies (2023)

28. Maslow, A.H.: A theory of human motivation. Psychol. Rev. **50**, 370–396 (1943). https://doi.org/10.1037/h0054346

29. Chaudhry, I.S., Paquibut, R.Y., Chabchoub, H.: Factors influencing employees trust in AI & its adoption at work: evidence from United Arab Emirates. In: 2022 International Arab Conference on Information Technology (ACIT), pp. 1–7. IEEE (2022)

30. Ambati, L.S., Narukonda, K., Bojja, G., et al.: Factors influencing the adoption of artificial intelligence in organizations - from an employee's perspective (2020)

31. Pokorni, B., Braun, M., Knecht, C.: Menschzentrierte KI-Anwendungen in der Produktion: Praxiserfahrungen und Leitfaden zu betrieblichen Einführungsstrategien (2021)

32. Stowasser, S., Suchy, O.: Wie die Einführung von KI im Unternehmen gelingt. hr journal (2021)

33. Hornung, O., Smolnik, S.: AI invading the workplace: negative emotions towards the organizational use of personal virtual assistants. Electron Mark. **32**, 123–138 (2022). https://doi.org/10.1007/s12525-021-00493-0

34. Lukyanenko, R., Maass, W., Storey, V.C.: Trust in artificial intelligence: from a foundational trust framework to emerging research opportunities. Electron Mark. **32**, 1993–2020 (2022). https://doi.org/10.1007/s12525-022-00605-4

35. Moring, A.: KI im Job: Leitfaden zur erfolgreichen Mensch-Maschine-Zusammenarbeit, 1. Auflage 2021. Springer, Heidelberg (2021). https://doi.org/10.1007/978-3-662-62829-4

36. Ottersböck, N.: Tipps gegen die KI-Angst vor Beschäftigten (2023). https://www.haufe.de/personal/hr-management/tipps-gegen-die-ki-angst-von-beschaeftigten_80_604568.html. Accessed 30 Sept 2023

37. Yu, X., Xu, S., Ashton, M.: Antecedents and outcomes of artificial intelligence adoption and application in the workplace: the socio-technical system theory perspective. ITP **36**, 454–474 (2023). https://doi.org/10.1108/ITP-04-2021-0254

38. Jung, M., von Garrel, J.: Mitarbeiterfreundliche Implementierung von KI -Systemen im Hinblick auf Akzeptanz und Vertrauen. TATuP **30**, 37–43 (2021). https://doi.org/10.14512/tatup.30.3.37

39. Werens, S., von Garrel, J.: Implementation of artificial intelligence at the workplace, considering the work ability of employees. TATuP **32**, 43–49 (2023). https://doi.org/10.14512/tatup.32.2.43

40. Dabbous, A., Aoun Barakat, K., Merhej Sayegh, M.: Enabling organizational use of artificial intelligence: an employee perspective. JABS **16**, 245–266 (2022). https://doi.org/10.1108/JABS-09-2020-0372

41. Altepost, A., Berlin, F., Ferrein, A., et al.: Demonstrativ-aktiv-iterativ: Arbeitssysteme Mit Künstlicher Intelligenz an Demonstratoren im Reallabor vermitteln, erproben und weiterentwickeln (2023)

42. Moultrie, J.: Understanding and classifying the role of design demonstrators in scientific exploration. Technovation **43–44**, 1–16 (2015). https://doi.org/10.1016/j.technovation.2015.05.002

43. Bobbe, T., Opeskin, L., Lüneburg, L.-M., et al.: Design for communication: how do demonstrators demonstrate technology? Des. Sci. (2023). https://doi.org/10.1017/dsj.2023.1

44. Kochanowska, M., Gagliardi, W.R., with reference to Ball, J.: The double diamond model: in pursuit of simplicity and flexibility. In: Raposo, D., Neves, J., Silva, J. (eds.) Perspectives on Design II. Springer Series in Design and Innovation, vol. 16, pp. 19–32. Springer, Cham (2022). https://doi.org/10.1007/978-3-030-79879-6_2

45. Tschimmel, K. (ed.): Design Thinking as an Effective Toolkit for Innovation (2012)

Why Designers Must Contribute
to Responsible AI

Aletta Smits[1]([✉]), Luc van der Zandt[2] [iD], and Koen van Turnhout[1]

[1] HU University of Applied Sciences Utrecht, Utrecht, The Netherlands
aletta.smits@hu.nl
[2] Drillster B.V., Utrecht, The Netherlands

Abstract. In this paper, we argue that the creation of Responsible AI over the past four decades has predominantly relied on two approaches: contextual and technical. While both are indispensable, we contend that a third equally vital approach, focusing on human-AI interaction design, has been relatively neglected, despite the ongoing efforts of pioneers in the field. Through the presentation of four case studies of real-world AI systems, we illustrate, however, how small design choices impact an AI platform's responsibleness independent of the technical or contextual level. We advocate, therefore, for a larger role for design in the creation of Responsible AI, and we call for increased research efforts in this area to advance our understanding of human-AI interaction design in Responsible AI. This includes both smaller case studies, such as those presented in this paper, that replicate or swiftly test earlier findings in different contexts, as well as larger, more comprehensive studies that lay the foundations for a framework.

Keywords: Responsible AI · Interaction Design · Algorithmic Affordances · Human-AI Interaction

1 The Need for Responsible AI

Decisions influenced by artificial intelligence (AI) are increasingly shaping both individual lives and society as a whole. With the rise in AI adoption, concerns regarding potential harmful consequences have also grown [1]. While these concerns may seem contemporary, their roots, in fact, extend back to the previous century. As early as 1985, Bundy and Clutterbuck [2] coined the term *Responsible AI* when advocating for its regulation. In their paper 'Raising the Standards of AI Products', they argued that AI's potential for harm necessitated responsible and cautious implementation to effectively harness its power [2].

Over the years, the criteria for evaluating AI responsibility have expanded. Initially focussing on transparency, fairness, and reliability, they now encompass safety, honesty, trustworthiness, inclusivity, and accountability [1, 3–5]. Additionally, Responsible AI should prioritize human agency and human oversight [1], technical robustness, compliance with data regulations, and protection of human dignity and self-determination [6, 7]. Lastly, Responsible AI should enhance societal and environmental wellbeing [6, 8].

© The Author(s), under exclusive license to Springer Nature Switzerland AG 2024
H. Degen and S. Ntoa (Eds.): HCII 2024, LNAI 14735, pp. 87–104, 2024.
https://doi.org/10.1007/978-3-031-60611-3_7

Over the past four decades, two primary approaches have emerged to advance Responsible AI [6, 9], each representing prolific research domains. The first is a contextual approach involving regulation through legal frameworks (see Fig. 1). The second approach is technical, focusing on embedding responsible values within datasets and algorithms. However, an equally crucial yet underemphasized third approach is the interactional approach. At this level, Responsible AI is promoted through the design of user interfaces and interactions [10–13].

We assert that all three approaches are interconnected and indispensable. Additionally, we also assert that the interactional approach is vital, since interaction design is uniquely equipped to provide users with the control, and therefore the autonomy that is needed to assume responsibility for an AI application outcome [1].

Vital as it may be, however, the interactional approach to Responsible AI has been underemphasized and requires rapid development [9, 14, 15]. Active involvement from professionals within the design community is essential for the advancement of Responsible AI. To facilitate such effective contribution, designers require resources that aid in shaping human-AI interactions [15]. Currently, however, designers feel that that research is lacking in volume, in accessibility and in transferability to their projects at hand [15], despite the ongoing efforts of the pioneer researchers in this domain (see, for instance, [13, 16–21]).

The contributions of this paper are, therefore, threefold:

1. It qualifies the important yet understated role of design in the development of Responsible AI (Sect. 2).
2. It underscores the significance of the interactional level in empirical studies of four real-life AI-applications (Sects. 3–5).
3. It demonstrates the value of small, low-investment studies, such as online surveys demonstrating interaction mechanisms with short videos and screenshots, as a means to rapidly increase both the volume of studies and the diversity of application domains.

2   The Impact of the Interactional Approach

In their original proposal to establish Responsible AI, Bundy and Clutterbuck advocated for the formation of a self-regulating "Professional association" comprising "Responsible AI companies" [2]. This association was tasked with evaluating the reliability, transparency, and fairness of AI products introduced by its members. Companies not affiliated with the association would be prohibited from deploying AI applications for public use. This proposal represents one of the earliest examples of a contextual approach to Responsible AI (see Fig. 1). It has inspired a host of studies with as their most recent tangible outcome the proposed European AI Act [13]. The AI Act, once introduced, will serve as a legal framework regulating the development and deployment of AI applications, ensuring adherence to the principles of Responsible AI.

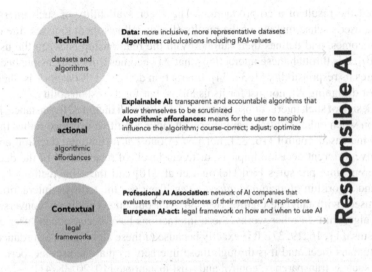

Fig. 1. Three approaches to creating Responsible AI

The contextual level alone is, however, insufficient. Imposing rules, regulations and limitations at this level inherently implies changes at a technical level, as well. For example, when legal frameworks mandate AI platforms to exhibit diversity, the technical approach to Responsible AI may entail evaluating and improving the representativeness of biased historical datasets [22–24], mitigating algorithmic bias by adjusting computational thresholds [25, 26], and integrating human cognitive factors, such as attrition, into calculations [27].

While such techniques demonstrably enhance values such as *diversity* [22, 23, 28], again, another level is required. As long as users cannot assess what is going on inside the AI system's black box, they do not necessarily experience the intended diversity; they do not know how the system defines diversity; and they fail to notice the algorithmic attempts at diversity. They may simply consider the outcomes 'wrong'. As a result, users cannot be expected to feel in control and assume responsibility for the AI outcomes. Responsibility is in such cases solely contextual, where users (if they have a choice) decide to employ an AI, and subsequently (if they have a choice) decide to comply with its outcomes [1, 29, 30].

At the interactional level, this can be remedied by extracting an explanation from the AI, and presenting this explanation in such a way that it is interpretable for users. That invites users to assume at least shared responsibility for an AI's outcomes [4, 13, 31, 32], since they can now understand how these outcomes came about and, therefore, assess their quality. Explainable AI is, therefore, a first example of creating Responsible AI via the interactional level (see Fig. 1).

When, additionally, the application allows not just for explainability and interpretability, but also for exploration through explicit interactions between user and algorithm – such as experimenting with parameters, controlling or inspecting data sources, debugging assumptions, evaluating recommendations – the AI's final outcome can be considered the result of a co-production. The sheer availability of such interactions impacts a user's sense-making of the results already, allows them to assess the quality of the outcomes, and defines their autonomy in the relationship between the user and the AI [10]. It is through these interactions that AI becomes truly responsible because it truly shares its responsibility [1, 33, 34]. Interaction design – UX design – is, therefore, crucial for designing AI, not just for its usability, but for its responsibility.

The design of such interactions is not trivial, however. It includes, for instance, having a grasp on when enhanced transparency results in a cognitive overload rather than the intended increased control [16, 35], not just in one but in multiple decision contexts that involve different decision impacts, different levels of reversibility of the decisions and different time pressures [36] Hekman et al. [10] call these interactions between human and algorithm *algorithmic affordances*. They use the term for interactions that provide users with tangible control over an AI's outcome via direct 'conversations' with the algorithm. In other works, these interactions have been dubbed 'user control mechanisms' [11, 16, 19, 37]. It is exactly because of these algorithmic affordances that AI and humans meet, and it is through these interactions that the user's experience of qualities such as transparency, control and trust instantiate [10, 20, 38–41].

Considering their crucial role, the design of algorithmic affordances including their impact on user experience, deserves, therefore, voluminous, versatile, and systematic research. In a study amongst 200 practitioners worldwide, Smits & Van Turnhout established professionals' need for such research and for other resources to help them navigate the still new design challenges associated with algorithmic affordances [14]. However, while studies on algorithms and datasets abound [9, 42, 43] and while AI is identified as a key technology, the studies on design of the algorithmic affordances are falling behind in volume and attention [9, 18, 42, 43].

For this paper, we carried out an online survey featuring four small real-life case studies of AI applications to reproduce impact of design choices in interface and user interactions in different contexts. The case studies also serve to illustrate to what extent low-investment studies yield valuable insights and valid results [44]. A host of such smaller studies that complement the larger research designs could help accelerate the continued maturing of the interactional approach in Responsible AI.

3   Case Studies

3.1   Design

All case studies in this paper aim to gain insight into how user interface and user interactions affect the experienced responsibleness of AI platforms. In an online survey, participants were introduced to one of four case studies: a digital learning platform (Drillster), a smart website that helps select sustainability measures, a streaming video platform (Netflix), and a professional social network (LinkedIn).

The case studies introduce participants to highly formatted variants of a light cognitive walkthrough, including reflections on if and how their sense of control (Netflix) or trust (sustainability and LinkedIn), or their mental model (Drillster) have been affected by design. The questions in each of the walkthroughs have been tested in cognitive interviews. The formats of the walkthroughs varied per case (see Table 1).

Table 1. Four case studies, their research goals, methods, and participants

Domain	Description	Participants	Age (19–88)
Education Drillster	**Research question**: How is a user's *mental model* affected by design? **Format**: detailed examination of user interface; open questions on UI-elements and mental model	90	mean: 36.6 s.d.: 18.6
Entertainment Netflix	**Research question**: How is a user's sense of *control* affected by design? **Format**: open question on mental model; mix of open and closed questions on *sense of control* based on screenshots of how 'rating content' is design	65	mean: 39.1 s.d.: 17.3
Sustainability Website	**Research question**: How is a user's sense of *trust*, affected by design? **Format**: open and closed question gauging shifts in experienced trust based on short videos demonstrating user interaction	44	mean: 44 s.d.: 11,2
Social Media LinkedIn	**Research questions**: How is the user's *trust* affected by design **Format**: open and closed question gauging shifts in experienced trust based on short videos demonstrating algorithmic affordance 'curating network'	87	mean: 40.8 s.d.: 19.4

For the online learning environment, for instance, we were interested in the formation and evolution of respondents' idea of how the platform's proficiency algorithm worked. We asked participants assigned to this case first how they thought a platform such as this could assess their proficiency (open question). We then presented them with Drillster's user interface and asked them to comment on individual UI-elements (see Fig. 2). We concluded by asking again about their mental model of the progress algorithm, whether it changed and which elements may have contributed to that change.

Alternatively, for the LinkedIn-case, we were interested in how respondents' sense of trust changed during the journey of removing a connection from their network. We presented users with videos demonstrating the 'curating my network-journey in LinkedIn's interface. After each step in that process, we asked to indicate to what extent their level of trust had changed and why.

3.2 Data Collection and Participants

During January 2024, a total of 286 international respondents (average age 39.6, s.d. 16.8. Range 18–88) completed our survey (see Table 1). They were recruited via LinkedIn

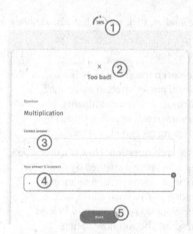

Fig. 2. Prompting users to examine individual elements in Drillster's user interface

and other social media and through a commercial database that paid $10 to participate. The participants were randomly assigned to one of four cases. Their backgrounds are mainly Dutch, British, and American, most of them residing in The Netherlands. Their heritage varies from Asian to North-African, Southern-, Northern (mainly Dutch) and Central European, and again British and American.

We asked the respondents to rate themselves on a scale of 1–5 with regard to their familiarity with algorithms. The scale is not standardized, and the steps on the scale were clarified with behavioral indicators such as '5': 'I can explain exactly what an algorithm is', and '1': 'I have no idea what an algorithm is.' There were no differences in self-reported skills between the four case studies. The backgrounds, too, were evenly distributed over the cases. The respondents to the sustainability case were on average older due to the requirement of living independently in the Netherlands for more than three months. The cases will be discussed in more detail in Sects. 4 (Drillster and Netflix) and 5 (Sustainability and LinkedIn).

3.3 Validating the Online Survey Design

Among other aspects, in these smaller studies we were interested in the formation and development of users' mental model of the AI. We consider a mental model to be a subjective representation of the algorithm, including how it reasons, what its sources are and how it weighs those sources [20, 45]. Mental models are relevant for the user's interaction with an AI system, since a user's trust and willingness to comply with its outcomes, will generally be higher when the outcomes are consistent with a user's mental model [45, 46].

In light of the need for a rapid increase of studies on interaction design in Responsible AI, we chose this light online-survey format of a cognitive walkthrough, in spite of the consideration in, for instance, Ngo et al. [20]. They hold that the elicitation of mental models is necessarily a qualitative type of study including an intensive analysis of interview data, think-aloud protocols, and expressive tasks such as users drawing their mental model of the algorithm.

One of our concerns, therefore, is to what extent this design generates data that can serve to replicate findings from current studies in other contexts. To establish an initial level of confidence, we utilize Ngo et al.'s findings from their investigation into users' perceptions of Netflix as our benchmark [20]. Based on their extensive dataset, they developed a grounded theory on users' understanding of how Netflix's recommender algorithm functions, proposing that this model serves as a general representation of users' perceptions of recommender algorithms [20]. According to this model, users recognize four distinct steps: (1) data acquisition, (2) inference of a virtual user profile, (3) comparison of user profiles or items, and (4) generation of recommendations. The system's data acquisition is driven by three sources: user characteristics (such as age, gender, and location), implicit user behaviour (such as video content consumption), and explicit user behaviour (such as rating video content). The comparison in step (3) could involve comparison against other items or other users.

We will employ this model to template-code the results of the mental models' questions that we collected in a much smaller design, thus assessing the saturation of our own dataset. The cases in which we examined users' mental model were, as was the topic for with Ngo et al., Netflix, and the online learning platform Drillster.

4 Mental Models and Control

4.1 Case 1 Digital Learning: Mental Models

Design. Drillster is an online digital learning platform that provides asynchronous training modules for professional skills. A key feature is the implementation of continuous maintenance of acquired skills and knowledge. Failure to maintain knowledge leads to a decline in proficiency, even after initially achieving 100% proficiency. As a result, various proficiency indicators play a crucial role in Drillster's user interface. This case study investigates participants' mental models regarding how their progress is measured and the extent to which UI elements influence these mental models.

We did not inform respondents about the focus on the proficiency model. Instead, we asked them to explore various elements in the user interface. Participants viewed one of four sets of interfaces, representing different stages in the learning journey: starting out and completing the first assignment (case 1a), receiving feedback on a question (case 1b and 1c), and reaching the completion screen (Fig. 3). In each scenario, the progress indicator was relevant, reflecting changes based on answers or time elapsed since the last study session.

Before and after examining the interface, we questioned participants about their ideas on how the proficiency assessment was carried out (mental model) through open-ended questions. After the second inquiry, we asked participants to indicate if their idea had changed (multiple choice) and, if so, what factors influenced the change (open question).

Results: General Model of Recommenders is Confirmed. Respondents' answers to the two mental model questions were template-coded based on the categories in Ngo et al.'s general mental model of a recommender system. Table 2 presents the results of the first mental model elicitation.

Firstly, we observed that, except for user comparison, all four main aspects of Ngo et al.'s general mental model were present in our respondents' initial mental models

Fig. 3. Progress indicators in Drillster (2023); 3a: proficiency indicator at the top of each screen; 3b: graph visualizing current proficiency at 100% and the journey to that level; 3c: graph visualizing the decline of proficiency from 100% to 86% after time elapsed

Table 2. Initial mental model of level assessment

Case 1.	Participants	Data acquisition			Inference user profile*	Comparison		Result
		User characteristics	Implicit data	Explicit data		Items	Users	
a	22	0	4	18	2			14
b	25	4	2	13	2			13
c	23		1	10	1	2		13
d	20		2	8	3			6

[20]. The aspect of "comparison to other users," absent in the initial model, emerged in the second model, with three respondents suggesting proficiency assessment "using algorithms and data from other users." Secondly, despite the constrained data collection format, respondents presented a surprisingly diverse range of metaphors underlying their models. Table 3 provides an overview of the general metaphors, relevant data sources, and resulting types or outcomes. Thirdly, explicit behaviour appears to be the primary data collection source in respondents' mental models. Fourthly, the two most prominent phases in their minds are the data collection phase and the decision resulting from that data. The analytical steps between data collection and presenting conclusions, such as inferring a profile and comparison, are in many respondents' models either implied or dismissed with phrases like 'with AI' or 'with an algorithm'. Due to the limited data collection format, further probing was not possible. Ghori et al. encountered similar limitations [44].

The Role of Design in the Change of the Mental Model. Upon re-evaluation of their mental model of proficiency assessment after studying the interface more closely, 22 out of 90 respondents reported a change in their understanding, attributing these changes to interface elements. For instance, some noted, "I could see the system changing, depending on if the answer was correct," while others stated, "The visualization at the end cleared up a lot" (see Fig. 3). Some participants transitioned from a survey-model to a test-model and primarily credited the design of proficiency indicators for this shift,

Table 3. Examples of mental models (initial and final model)

Type	Mental model	Examples[*]
Metaphors	**Test-metaphor**: Quality of the answers determines **level** (with **permanently proficient** and **currently proficient** as sub-categories) **Test-metaphor:** Mastery learning – you have to have all mistakes corrected **Survey-metaphor:** Number of answers determines level	- "Maybe by using a **point system** where **correct answers** lead to positive points and wrong answers to negative points" - Based on my faults I will **decline in progress** and have to make new questions until I have **corrected all my mistakes** "**how many questions** they answered before"
Data sources	**Quality** of the answers Response time Time passed since last activity Number of answers (correct or not) Number of correct answers User characteristics	- "If a **question is answered wrong,** their **level will go down,** and if they get it right, the level will go up." - "Based on if they **accurately** answer and maybe **on how long it took them.**" - "on their [**the users'**] education"
Comparisons	Difficulty level of the questions Performance other users	- "[the] change might also be **weighted by how difficult the question is**" "with the use of algorithms **and data from other users**"
Results	Adjust repeat frequency Adjust allotted response time Adjust level	"Quicker reaction means **less often** asking the question" "**Repeat** if you get it wrong. **Speed up** if you're fast and correct"

[*]for the benefit of this paper, answers in Dutch have been translated

stating, "First, I thought it was about the number of questions [survey-model], now I think it is about the level of the questions [test-model]." Others expressed that while they initially lacked understanding, they now "have a better understanding of what e-learning meant/how things are calculated."

Interestingly, of the 68 participants that claimed their model had not changed, an additional 29 respondents in fact did exhibit a changed mental model. These respondents, too, adjusted metaphors ("it is about how much I have corrected, not how much I answered") or primary data sources ("there is no time indicator, so it cannot be about how quickly I answer"), or they let go of mystical models [20], such as "it calculates your level based] on how susceptible you are to fake news and adverts on those platforms."

4.2 Case 2 Streaming Video: Design Affecting Control

Design and Data Collection. Our second case study concerns Netflix and it examines to what extent the design of an algorithmic affordance affects the level of control users feel over the AI's outcome. As a sensitizing question for this case, we elicited respondents' mental model on how Netflix selects content for users (open answer). We then asked how they currently attempt to influence Netflix' suggestions (open answer), whether they desire more influence (scale), and concluded by presenting Netflix's current design of the algorithmic affordance 'rating content.' We asked participants to discuss their reasons for using that option or ignoring it (both open answer).

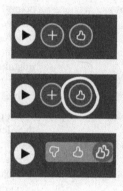

Fig. 4. Feedback in Netflix

Mental Model of Recommendations. Again, template coding revealed correspondence to Ngo et al.'s general mental model of recommenders. In addition to this study replicating this model, we, as did Ngo et al. [20], found respondents expressing their awareness of the various stakeholders in this process. Multiple users made comments along the lines of "I think they just check what they want to sell". This perspective resurfaced later when users explained their intention to use the algorithmic affordance of 'rating content' to communicate not only with the algorithm to influence selections for themselves but also with Netflix's producers: "To provide feedback and hope for Netflix to continue the series in the future."

"Current Sense of Control". When asked about strategies to influence AI outcome users expressed a limited sense of control (average rating: 2.3 on a scale of 1–5). Some felt powerless, stating, "you almost seem not to be able to exert any influence…you always get to see what Netflix wants you to see." Among those aware of available strategies, two main options were cited: 1. mimicking implicit user behaviour by purposefully watching preferred genres, and 2. explicitly indicating preferences by using the 'I liked this content' option. Three users suggested alternative methods: using VPN to access content from different regions, employing specific keywords in search strategies, and removing movies from the viewing history. When asked if they desired more control over Netflix' recommendations (multiple choice), roughly half (36) expressed a desire for more or much more control. Around 27 respondents felt they did not require additional control, while only 2 firmly stated they did not need more control.

The Impact of Design on a Sense of Control. We then explored respondents' opinions on Netflix' content rating feature, an algorithmic affordance that potentially offers more control over recommendations. Currently, Netflix's rating option is represented by a

Table 4. Respondents' assessment of Netflix' matches and their wish to have more influence*.

Reasons to rate	Reasons to not rate
GENUINE ASSESSMENT: If I have really enjoyed it/If it was really good, or really bad/if it was boring	**DISLIKE**: İf l didn't like it. /when it is moderate/if it was ok or not good at all/I don't want to say I like it if I didn't
ALTRUISTIC MOTIVES: Help others decide whether to watch/To save other people time, so they don't have to watch it/I want to support the movie/series/express my appreciation to the makers/To make it popular	**EFFORT**: too much work, especially on the tv/No personal gain/Could not be bothered/Laziness/Too lazy/Not interested enough to make a rating
FEEDING THE ALGORITHM: Trying to influence the algorithm/ to get a show higher on my list/to get better suggestions/I really really disliked something, and they can never send me anything like that again	**FEEDING THE ALGORITHM**: to mess with the algorithm/It would affect your suggestions...
FEEDING NETFLIX: To provide feedback and hope for Netflix to continue the series in the future/To make sure similar shows are made/not made in the future	**PRIVACY**: It is my personal opinion/It is none of their business/I don't want Netflix to collect data about me
DIARY: I want to remember that I liked it if I come across it again/To remember the shows I liked	**DIARY**: If I don't find it worth remembering/If I don't need to know about this show anymore

* for the benefit of this paper some answers in other languages that English have been translated.

thumbs-up icon, with additional options revealed upon mouse-over, including a thumbs-down (see Fig. 4). This survey aimed to assess whether this design choice impacts users' sense of control.

The results in Table 4, depicting respondents' reasons for using or not using the rating option, appear to confirm this hypothesis. The column 'reasons not to rate' prominently features arguments such as 'If I didn't like it'. Additionally, almost all respondents who chose not to rate because they disliked the movie indicated a desire for more influence over recommendations. It can be inferred that the thumbs-up design choice for this algorithmic affordance discourages user engagement, consequently diminishing their sense of control.

When asked how respondents would exert more control over recommendations on Netflix, they made suggestions as outlined in Table 5. These suggestions have been categorized according to Hekman et al.'s classifications of algorithmic affordances [11]. It is noteworthy that these suggestions all advocate for interactions that foster greater autonomy and the ability to define preferences, thereby assuming more responsibility for outcomes: examples include 'being able to browse myself', 'removing viewing history', 'indicating preferences at a more granular level', and 'presenting Netflix with my profile'. Therefore, it can be concluded that design choices significantly influence engagement with algorithmic affordances, and perceived limitations of these affordances impact users' sense of control and their perception of the algorithm's responsibility.

Table 5. Respondents' suggestions for more influence

How to exert influence on Netflix' recommendations
NAVIGATING THE RECOMMENDATION SPACE: I would like to be able to browse myself/If I was able to remove recommendations it gives me/I can remove recommendations I don't think are right
FEEDING THE ALGORITHM: Something on the screen to indicate negative suggestions/By commenting on the suggestions/Actively fill in preferences and enforce it/To select genres I'd like more suggestions of/To give Netflix an overview of what I like/I would like to be able to select categories/have a thumbs down/To select actors I'd like more suggestions of (in films in which they star)/Allow me to specifically exclude or include categories, or actors, or playwrights/Removing watched content from my history
TUNING THE ALGORITHM: Give more weight for likes and dislikes/It will be good if I can manage the settings more in detail/providing me with many options to configure my choice for future referrals as comprehensively as possible
FEEDING NETFLIX: 'I do not want suggestions based on this' button/I think that would be difficult, as large companies tend not to give away any power to users/customers
ACTIVATING RECOMMENDATION CONTEXT: Sometimes I watch dumb stuff, I would like that to be easily stricken from my viewing history

5   Design Choices Affecting Trust

To efficiently examine the impact of design on the quality of trust, we carried out two final small case studies. The first (case 3) studied a sustainability website to elicit how trust is influenced by decisions that affect transparency. The second (case 4) is a small study into LinkedIn's option to remove people from a network. In this case, due to the sensitive nature of explicitly breaking a connection, trust, too, could be affected. We will report on both studies succinctly.

5.1   Case 3: Smart Sustainability Websites

We compare two smart sustainability websites. Both aim to help homeowners select which sustainability-enhancing measures are most effective for their home and both use the same government-owned database with information on all houses in The Netherlands for the initial stage of the user journey. The general user journey is as in Fig. 5: a user is asked to provide postal code and house number (in The Netherlands a combination that uniquely identifies every address), and the next screen presents data on construction year, square meters, and monumental status, including a photo of the house sourced from Google Maps.

An important difference between the two websites is, however, that website 3a presents the data immediately after clicking on the 'start'-button (case 3a: implicit data retrieval). The other website, in contrast, first shows two screens that ask the respondent for their patience, while they are in the process of retrieving data from government-owned databases (case 3b: explicit data retrieval).

Fig. 5. User journey smart sustainability websites (screenshots are from case 3b)

In the online survey, respondents for case 3a and 3b were provided with the same brief description as introduction to the case. They were then asked, based on their limited information, to what extent they would trust a website such as this (scale from 1–5, with 5 being very much). After random assignment to either Case 3a or Case 3b and presented with a videoclip demonstrating the implicit or explicit data retrieval journey, respondents were again asked about the extent of their trust in this website.

The results of Fisher's exact test ($p = .45$) do not indicate a difference regarding initial trust. However, upon second probing, the implicit-data retrieval group exhibited less trust on the website compared to the explicit-data retrieval group ($p = 0.04$). Upon further inquiry, participants attributed a positive change in trust mainly to the explicit data-retrieval. Respondents found it comforting that the data was retrieved from a data based rather than "magically" retrieved from satellites. Not for all respondents, the government-owned data bases installed trust however, with two respondents inquiring in the open-ended questions how they could have their data removed from these data bases.

5.2 Case 4 Professional Social Media

LinkedIn is a networking platform for professionals. Users employ it to share professional success and insights or to curate their career. An important feature is the possibility to build their professional network. However, sometimes, people would like to disconnect from people earlier admitted into their network. That is not always a problem, but it can be when there is still analogue contact with such a person, privately or professionally [47].

In a workshop at Interact 2023 [48], professional designers and researchers analysed the disconnect-flow of LinkedIn with the help of close reading: precisely analysing what each UI element implied. Deemed to be positive aspects in this flow were the clear and succinct help page, that featured not only a how-to guide for various devices but also addressed potential worries ("will the disconnectee be notified?"; answer: no) and future scenarios ("If you ever reconnect, endorsements and other mutual exchanges will remain lost").

Negative aspects were however the immediate execution of the removal request: no pop-up to verify, no final warning, just an immediate removal. Since people transfer

Table 6. Progressive decline in trust during LinkedIn's removal of connection-journey

Level of trust	Reported Initial trust	Change in trust	After help page	After sudden removal	After being recommended to the removed connection
1	1	Much less	0	9	9
2	2	A little less	0	2	31
3	24	Did not affect my trust	59	67	41
4	4	A little more	22	5	2
5	10	Much more	4	0	0

their mental model from other applications, and other applications generally do include such a warning, users' mental model could well be violated by this flow [20]. Finally, LinkedIn's algorithm still calculates the recently removed person to be a good match for the remover. When that person visits their 'my network'-page, the remover features prominently as a possible connection. We hypothesized that that design choice, too, violates trust.

As with the previous case, we asked participants to report on their initial level of trust in LinkedIn and then led them through the removal journey with the help of short videos demonstrating steps in this process. After each phase we asked if and how their level of trust was affected by what they just saw. As Table 6 shows: the level of trust declines progressively, with both the design choices of the removal-without-warning and the suggestion-to-the-removed-connection having a considerable impact.

6 Discussion

In this paper, we have illustrated through four different case studies how design decisions can influence mental models, trust, and sense of control. In the Netflix case, the perceived absence of an algorithmic affordance impacted users' sense of control. In the LinkedIn case, despite an initial increase in trust facilitated by a helpful support page, two subsequent design choices reduced this trust gain. Similarly, in the sustainability case, platforms with varying levels of transparency elicited different levels of trust for otherwise similar algorithms. These findings underscore the significance of design in realizing values such as control and trust, both of which are integral to the principles of Responsible AI. These finding underscore also how the interactional level of Responsible AI is as vital as the other two levels, and, in fact, the three levels intimately work together. Design professionals need to claim, therefore, their rightful place at the table, and be equal partners to engineers and data scientists in the creation of Responsible AI.

In order to be able to do so, however, professionals need increased resources to adequately address AI-related design challenges. They call, for instance, for a systematic overview of algorithmic affordances [15] and of other available design choices, including their impact on the perceived responsibleness of AI [49]. Despite early robust case studies, such as Herlocker, Konstan, and Riedl's research of recommender interface design in 2000 [25], and later course-correcting studies with telling titles such as "Improving recommender systems beyond the algorithm" [26], and despite the pioneering work of, among others, Verbert, Masthoff, Jugovac, Ziegler, Kunkel, Jannach, and Nunes [11, 13, 17, 18, 21, 50, 51], this critical need of the professional community remains as of yet unfulfilled [52–54].

The case studies presented in this paper represent a modest attempt to address this issue. While the online survey studies were limited in their ability to gather detailed responses, and tailored follow-up questions were impossible [44], they still provided valuable insights. Furthermore, the results of the open-ended mental model questions stood up to scrutiny, for instance, when compared to the answers of a more elaborate mental model study [20]. We cautiously assert, therefore, that small studies such as these, despite their methodological limitations, could be used to support the transferability larger studies to a host of other domains, or to verify to what extent results from older studies still hold. Kleemann & Ziegler's recent elaborate study [51] on transparency affecting user control during an online selection process of a new computer, for instance, could then be transferred to different contexts in retail (buying products in different price categories, such as books, or an electric vehicle), or in even in different contexts entirely: enrolling for an elective course.

Acknowledgments. We thank Sia Raak for financing case studies 1 and 3 (file: GOCI.KIEM.02.011).

Disclosure of Interests. Aletta Smits and Koen van Turnhout have no competing interests to declare that are relevant to the content of this article. Luc van der Zandt is currently employed at Drillster.

References

1. Alfrink, K., Keller, I., Kortuem, G., Doorn, N.: Contestable AI by design: towards a framework. Minds Mach (Dordr). (2022). https://doi.org/10.1007/s11023-022-09611-z
2. Bundy, A.; Clutterbuck, R.: Raising the standards of AI products. In: Proceedings of the 9th International Joint Conference on Artificial Intelligence, vol. 2, pp. 1289–1294. Morgan Kaufmann Publishers Inc., San Francisco, CA, USA (1985)
3. Appelo, J.: Accountable Versus Responsible. https://www.forbes.com/sites/jurgenappelo/2016/12/08/accountable-versus-responsible. Accessed 12 Sept 2023
4. Barredo Arrieta, A., et al.: Explainable artificial intelligence (XAI): concepts, taxonomies, opportunities and challenges toward responsible AI. Inf. Fusion **58** (2020). https://doi.org/10.1016/j.inffus.2019.12.012
5. Jobin, A., Ienca, M., Vayena, E.: The global landscape of AI ethics guidelines. Nat. Mach. Intell. **1** (2019). https://doi.org/10.1038/s42256-019-0088-2
6. Kazim, E., et al.: Proposed EU AI act—presidency compromise text: select overview and comment on the changes to the proposed regulation. AI Ethics **3**, 381–387 (2023). https://doi.org/10.1007/s43681-022-00179-z
7. Hildebrandt, M.: Privacy as protection of the incomputable self: agonistic machine learning. SSRN Electron. J. (2017). https://doi.org/10.2139/ssrn.3081776

8. Morley, J., Floridi, L., Kinsey, L., Elhalal, A.: From what to how: an overview of AI ethics tools, methods and research to translate principles into practices. arXiv. abs/1905.0 (2019)

9. Beel, J., Dixon, H.: The "unreasonable" effectiveness of graphical user interfaces for recommender systems. In: UMAP 2021 - Adjunct Publication of the 29th ACM Conference on User Modeling, Adaptation and Personalization (2021). https://doi.org/10.1145/3450614.3461682

10. Hekman, E., Nguyen, D., Stalenhoef, M., Van Turnhout, K.: Towards a pattern library for algorithmic affordances. In: Joint Proceedings of the IUI 2022 Workshops, vol. 3124, pp. 24–33 (2022)

11. Jannach, D., Naveed, S., Jugovac, M.: User control in recommender systems: overview and interaction challenges. In: Bridge, D., Stuckenschmidt, H. (eds.) EC-Web 2016. LNBIP, vol. 278, pp. 21–33. Springer, Cham (2017). https://doi.org/10.1007/978-3-319-53676-7_2

12. Kulesza, T., Stumpf, S., Burnett, M., Yang, S., Kwan, I., Wong, W.K.: Too much, too little, or just right? Ways explanations impact end users' mental models. In: Proceedings of IEEE Symposium on Visual Languages and Human-Centric Computing, VL/HCC (2013). https://doi.org/10.1109/VLHCC.2013.6645235

13. Tintarev, N., Masthoff, J.: Explaining recommendations: design and evaluation. In: Ricci, F., Rokach, L., Shapira, B. (eds.) Recommender Systems Handbook, pp. 353–382. Springer, Boston, MA (2015). https://doi.org/10.1007/978-1-4899-7637-6_10

14. Holmquist, L.E.: intelligence on tap: artificial intelligence as a new design material. Interactions 24 (2017). https://doi.org/10.1145/3085571

15. Smits, A., Van Turnhout, K.: Towards a practice-led research agenda for user interface design of recommender systems. In: Abdelnour Nocera, J., Lárusdóttir, M.K., Petrie, H., Piccinno, A., Winckler, M. (eds.) Human-Computer Interaction – INTERACT 2023. LNCS, vol. 14144, pp. 170–190. Springer, Cham (2023). https://doi.org/10.1007/978-3-031-42286-7_10

16. Jin, Y., Cardoso, B., Verbert, K.: How do different levels of user control affect cognitive load and acceptance of recommendations? In: CEUR Workshop Proceedings (2017)

17. Nunes, I., Jannach, D.: A systematic review and taxonomy of explanations in decision support and recommender systems (2020). https://doi.org/10.1007/s11257-017-9195-0

18. Jugovac, M., Jannach, D.: Interacting with recommenders-overview and research directions. ACM Trans. Interact. Intell. Syst. 7 (2017). https://doi.org/10.1145/3001837

19. Kulesza, T., Burnett, M., Wong, W.K., Stumpf, S.: Principles of explanatory debugging to personalize interactive machine learning. In: International Conference on Intelligent User Interfaces, Proceedings IUI (2015). https://doi.org/10.1145/2678025.2701399

20. Ngo, T., Kunkel, J., Ziegler, J.: Exploring mental models for transparent and controllable recommender systems: a qualitative study. In: UMAP 2020 - Proceedings of the 28th ACM Conference on User Modeling, Adaptation and Personalization (2020). https://doi.org/10.1145/3340631.3394841

21. Verbert, K., Parra, D., Brusilovsky, P., Duval, E.: Visualizing recommendations to support exploration, transparency and controllability. In: International Conference on Intelligent User Interfaces, Proceedings IUI (2013). https://doi.org/10.1145/2449396.2449442

22. Köchling, A., Wehner, M.C.: Discriminated by an algorithm: a systematic review of discrimination and fairness by algorithmic decision-making in the context of HR recruitment and HR development. Bus. Res. 13 (2020). https://doi.org/10.1007/s40685-020-00134-w

23. Hoffmann, A.L.: Where fairness fails: data, algorithms, and the limits of antidiscrimination discourse. Inf. Commun. Soc. 22 (2019). https://doi.org/10.1080/1369118X.2019.1573912

24. Chin, J.Y., Chen, Y., Cong, G.: The datasets dilemma. In: Proceedings of the Fifteenth ACM International Conference on Web Search and Data Mining, pp. 141–149. ACM, New York, NY, USA (2022). https://doi.org/10.1145/3488560.3498519

25. Angwin, J., Larson, J., Mattu, S., Kirchner, L.: Machine Bias: There's software used across the country to predict future criminals. And it's biased against blacks. ProPublica. (2016)

26. Bozdag, E.: Bias in algorithmic filtering and personalization. Ethics Inf. Technol. **15** (2013). https://doi.org/10.1007/s10676-013-9321-6
27. Lex, E., Kowald, D., Seitlinger, P., Tran, T.N.T., Felfernig, A., Schedl, M.: Psychology-informed recommender systems (2021). https://doi.org/10.1561/1500000090
28. Pagano, T.P., et al.: Bias and unfairness in machine learning models: a systematic review on datasets, tools, fairness metrics, and identification and mitigation methods (2023). https://doi.org/10.3390/bdcc7010015
29. Katell, M., et al.: Toward situated interventions for algorithmic equity: lessons from the field. In: FAT* 2020 - Proceedings of the 2020 Conference on Fairness, Accountability, and Transparency (2020). https://doi.org/10.1145/3351095.3372874
30. Franssen, M.: Design for values and operator roles in sociotechnical systems. In: Handbook of Ethics, Values, and Technological Design: Sources, Theory, Values and Application Domains (2015). https://doi.org/10.1007/978-94-007-6970-0_8
31. Simkute, A., Luger, E., Jones, B., Evans, M., Jones, R.: Explainability for experts: a design framework for making algorithms supporting expert decisions more explainable. J. Respons. Technol. 7–8, (2021). https://doi.org/10.1016/j.jrt.2021.100017
32. Ali, S., et al.: Explainable artificial intelligence (XAI): what we know and what is left to attain trustworthy artificial intelligence. Inf. Fusion (2023). https://doi.org/10.1016/j.inffus.2023.101805
33. Februari, M.: Doe zelf eens normaal: Menselijk recht in tijden van datasturing en natuurgeweld. Prometheus, Amsterdam (2023)
34. Aflrink, K., Keller, I., Yurrita Semperena, M., Bulygin, D., Kortuem, G., Doorn, N.: Envisioning contestability loops: evaluating the agonistic arena as a generative metaphor for public AI (2024, submitted)
35. Tsai, C.H., Brusilovsky, P.: Explaining recommendations in an interactive hybrid social recommender. In: International Conference on Intelligent User Interfaces, Proceedings IUI (2019). https://doi.org/10.1145/3301275.3302318
36. Smits, A., et al.: Assessing the Utility of an interaction qualities framework in systematizing the evaluation of user control. In: Bramwell-Dicks, A., Evans, A., Nocera, J., Petrie, H., Winckler, M. (eds.) Submitted to INTERACT2023 Workshop Proceedings Selected Papers. Interact 2023, York (2024)
37. Bartels, E., et al.: Exploring categorisations of algorithmic affordances in graphical user interfaces of recommender systems. In: Bramwell-Dicks, A., Evans, A., Norcera, J., Petrie, H., Winckler, M. (eds.) Submitted to INTERACT2023 Workshop Proceedings Selected Papers. Springer, Cham (2024)
38. Kunkel, J., Donkers, T., Barbu, C.M., Ziegler, J.: Trust-related effects of expertise and similarity cues in human-generated recommendations. In: CEUR Workshop Proceedings (2018)
39. Chiou, E.K., Lee, J.D.: Trusting automation: designing for responsivity and resilience. Hum. Factors **65** (2023). https://doi.org/10.1177/00187208211009995
40. Shneiderman, B.: Human-centered artificial intelligence: reliable, safe & trustworthy. Int. J. Hum. Comput. Interact. **36** (2020). https://doi.org/10.1080/10447318.2020.1741118
41. Smits, A., Bartels, E., Van Turnhout, K.: Tried-and-tested algorithmic affordances: a systematic literature review of user control mechanisms in recommender systems' interfaces. (in preparation)
42. Gunawardana, A., Shani, G., Yogev, S.: Evaluating recommender systems. In: Ricci, F., Rokach, L., Shapira, B. (eds.) Recommender Systems Handbook, pp. 547–601. Springer US, New York, NY (2022). https://doi.org/10.1007/978-1-0716-2197-4_15

43. Murphy-Hill, E., Murphy, G.C.: Recommendation delivery: getting the user interface just right. In: Robillard, M., Maalej, W., Walker, R., Zimmermann, T. (eds.) Recommendation Systems in Software Engineering, pp. 223–242. Springer, Heidelberg (2014). https://doi.org/10.1007/978-3-642-45135-5_9

44. Ghori, M.F., Dehpanah, A., Gemmell, J., Qahri-Saremi, H., Mobasher, B.: Does the user have a theory of the recommender? A pilot study. In: CEUR Workshop Proceedings (2019)

45. Norman, D.: Some observations on mental models. In: Gentner, D. and Stevens, A. (eds.) Mental Models, pp. 7–14. Psychology Press, New York (1983). https://doi.org/10.4324/9781315802725-5

46. Kulesza, T., Stumpf, S., Burnett, M., Kwan, I.: Tell me More? The effects of mental model soundness on personalizing an intelligent agent. https://doi.org/10.1145/2207676.2207678

47. Zhu, Q.: Political implications of disconnective practices on social media: unfriending, unfollowing, and blocking. In: Research Handbook on Social Media and Society, pp. 135–147. Edward Elgar Publishing (2024). https://doi.org/10.4337/9781800377059.00021

48. Smits, A., Bartels, E., Detweiler, C., van Turnhout, K.: Algorithmic affordances in recommender interfaces. In: Interact 2023: Design for equality and justice, pp. 605–609 (2023). https://doi.org/10.1007/978-3-031-42293-5_80

49. Lenz, E., Hassenzahl, M., Diefenbach, S.: Aesthetic interaction as fit between interaction attributes and experiential qualities. New Ideas Psychol. **47** (2017). https://doi.org/10.1016/j.newideapsych.2017.03.010

50. Ooge, J., Kato, S., Verbert, K.: Explaining recommendations in e-learning: effects on adolescents' trust. In: International Conference on Intelligent User Interfaces, Proceedings IUI, pp. 93–105. Association for Computing Machinery (2022). https://doi.org/10.1145/3490099.3511140

51. Kleemann, T., Ziegler, J.: Blending conversational product advisors and faceted filtering in a graph-based approach. In: Abdelnour Nocera, J., Kristín Lárusdóttir, M., Petrie, H., Piccinno, A., Winckler, M. (eds.) INTERACT 2023. LNCS, vol. 14144, pp. 137–159. Springer, Cham (2023). https://doi.org/10.1007/978-3-031-42286-7_8

52. Norman, D.A.: The research-practice gap. Interactions **17**, 9–12 (2010). https://doi.org/10.1145/1806491.1806494

53. Shneiderman, B.: Bridging the gap between ethics and practice: guidelines for reliable, safe, and trustworthy human-centered AI systems. ACM Trans. Interact. Intell. Syst. **10** (2020). https://doi.org/10.1145/3419764

54. Smeenk, W., Zielhuis, M., Van Turnhout, K.: Understanding the research practice gap in design research: a comparison of four perspectives (2023)

Learning Fair Representations: Mitigating Statistical Dependencies

Aida Tayebi[1], Mehdi Yazdani-Jahromi[2], Ali Khodabandeh Yalabadi[1], Niloofar Yousefi[1], and Ozlem Ozmen Garibay[1]([⊠])

[1] Industrial Engineering and Management Systems, University of Central Florida, Orlando, USA
{aida.tayebi,yalabadi,niloofar.yousefi,ozlem}@ucf.edu
[2] Computer Science, University of Central Florida, Orlando, USA
yazdani@ucf.edu

Abstract. The social awareness around the possibility of machine learning algorithms making biased decisions has led to an increase in Responsible AI studies in recent years. Algorithmic fairness is one of the concepts that should be considered when designing responsible AI models. The goal of these studies is to ensure the decisions made by machine learning algorithms in automated decision-making systems are bias-free and not affected by sensitive information that may lead to discrimination and consequences for individuals. Learning a fair representation is an effective approach to mitigate algorithmic bias and has been successfully applied in this domain. The objective of these approaches is to create representations by removing sensitive information while retaining the non-sensitive information that is required. In this paper, we propose a novel fair representation framework to generate fair representation that can be easily adjusted for a range of downstream classification tasks. Our proposed algorithm integrates the β-VAE encoder with a classifier to extract meaningful features. Simultaneously, it leverages the Hilbert-Schmidt independence criterion [24] as a constraint to maintain statistical independence between the representations and the sensitive attribute. Experimental results on three benchmark datasets have demonstrated our model's ability to create fair representations and yield a better fairness-accuracy tradeoff compared to state-of-the-art models.

Keywords: Responsible AI · Fairness in AI · Human-centered AI

1 Introduction

In the past few years, Responsible AI has been developed as a result of the human-centered AI community's growing social awareness and ethical considerations. The concerns surrounding algorithms for social decision-making revolve around the possibility of these algorithms making unfavorable decisions based on an individual's sensitive attribute and impact on the welfare of individuals and society [29]. Responsible AI practices aimed at tackling challenges like

© The Author(s), under exclusive license to Springer Nature Switzerland AG 2024
H. Degen and S. Ntoa (Eds.): HCII 2024, LNAI 14735, pp. 105–115, 2024.
https://doi.org/10.1007/978-3-031-60611-3_8

fairness in machine learning models, fairness, in this context, entails that algorithms produce similar outcomes for groups with different sensitive attributes. Consequently, the field of fair machine learning emerged and grew rapidly, with the primary goal of ensuring algorithmic results remain unaffected by sensitive attributes and other inherent biases that may ultimately lead to discrimination and have substantial consequences for individuals. Recently, representation learning has been successfully applied to eliminate sensitive data and enhance the fairness of machine learning algorithms. Representation learning is employed to convert input data into a concise low-dimensional summary that aligns with different task demands. The encoded representation filters out sensitive data while preserving crucial information necessary for downstream tasks, offering an effective approach to mitigate algorithmic bias and enabling them to produce fair outcomes [10]. Learning fair representation problem has been studied in many different research papers [9,10,14,22,23]. Most of these studies fall into two primary categories: Adversarial Methods [5,9], and Variational Autoencoders (VAE) based methods [22]. Adversarial frameworks consist of two models, one for predicting the target task while the other is dedicated to generating adversarial examples to confuse the first model. The main idea behind these approaches is to force the model to not rely on protected attributes. So, the objective is to predict the sensitive attributes from the representations utilizing an adversarial discriminator network, with the expectation that the predictions will be inaccurate and the loss will be maximized. Adversarial networks struggle to minimize losses in optimization sufficiently [21]. On the other hand, VAE-based approaches exhibit greater efficacy by maintaining a Gaussian distribution of latent representations. Among all VAE-based models, β-VAE has shown its capacity for providing independent and disentangled latent representation by controlling the KL divergence term. Some papers [8–10], including this one, use β-VAE to improve the independence of dimensions of representations z. Although β-VAE has demonstrated its ability to disentangle latent dimensions, identifying which latent features contain sensitive information remains uncertain. To tackle this issue, some studies, such as [10], have added a correlation coefficient to the loss function of β-VAE to keep track of latent features that include sensitive information. They divide the latent representation into two subspaces(sensitive and non-sensitive) by reducing or increasing the correlation between the subspace latent representation and the sensitive attribute while keeping them independent by utilizing β-VAE, respectively. However, two random variables can sometimes possess zero correlation while still exhibiting dependency. Besides, handling two random variables lacking correlation is comparatively more straightforward than achieving true independence.

In this paper, we propose a fair representation learning framework to calculate a concise yet predictive representation or encoding of the dataset, which can be easily adjusted for various downstream classification tasks and result in fair output. We propose integrating the encoder of β-VAE along with a classifier to extract meaningful features from the input data to keep the most crucial information required for predicting the target label while utilizing the Hilbert-

Schmidt independence criterion [24] to keep the statistical independence between the representation z and the sensitive attribute. Our analysis of three benchmark datasets in this domain shows that our representation achieves a better fairness-accuracy tradeoff than state-of-the-art works.

The rest of the paper is organized as follows: In Sect. 2, we provide preliminaries and related works. In Sect. 3, our proposed model is discussed in detail. The experimental settings are provided in Sect. 4. Section 5 provides a discussion of the experimental results, and finally, the conclusion is provided in Sect. 6.

2 Preliminaries

2.1 Fairness Metric

Improving fairness in machine learning algorithms is a challenging task since a natural trade-off exists between accuracy and fairness. Different definitions and metrics have been defined and used to measure fairness in classification problems [32]. They can be categorized into two primary definitions: individual fairness and group fairness. Individual fairness demands that similar individuals receive similar treatment. On the other hand, group fairness aims to ensure that algorithmic outcomes remain consistent regardless of whether an individual is part of a sensitive group or not. In this paper, we employ group fairness. *Demographic Parity*, as utilized in this paper, is a widely used metric in group fairness. Demographic parity aims to maintain an equal proportion of favorable decisions for both privileged and unprivileged groups, ensuring that the likelihood of a favorable outcome is not dependent on an individual's sensitive information [30–32]. If we consider $D = (x, s, y)$ as the input dataset where $s \in \{0, 1\}$ is the binary sensitive attribute, x representing non-sensitive attributes, and $y \in \{0, 1\}$ be the target label. In fair classification, the goal is to learn a classifier $f : (x, s) \rightarrow \hat{y}$, which is predictive of y and achieves certain fairness criteria concerning sensitive attribute s. In this paper, our fairness criterion is demographic parity, which is satisfied when the predicted labels by classifier $\hat{y}$ are independent of the sensitive attributes $\hat{y} \perp s$. Based on this definition, the favorable outcome should ideally be the same for both privileged and unprivileged groups:

$$P(\hat{y} = 1 \mid x, s = 1) = P(\hat{y} = 1 \mid x, s = 0) \tag{1}$$

and the discrimination or absolute demographic parity difference for a binary classification problem is the difference between these two probabilities:

$$DP = |P(\hat{y} = 1 \mid x, s = 1) - P(\hat{y} = 1 \mid x, s = 0)| \tag{2}$$

2.2 Fair Representation Learning

Learning a fair representation is an effective approach to mitigate algorithmic bias [5,9,22]. In this paper, we use z to indicate the latent representations. Let's consider an encoder mapping the input data to the latent representation

$g : (x, s) \rightarrow z$. If the representation z is independent of the sensitive attribute $z \perp s$, then it is very likely that any predictor trained on this representation $h : (z) \rightarrow \hat{y}$ will also be independent of the protected attribute $\hat{y} \perp s$. In fair representation learning, the objective is to remove the sensitive information (reducing the mutual information between z and s) while keeping the essential non-sensitive information (improving the mutual information between z and x) to achieve a representation that is independent of sensitive attributes. So any classifier trained with these representations will achieve the desired demographic parity and leads to a fair decision-making system. As mentioned before, these works can be categorized into *Adversarial approaches* and *Variational-Autoencoder (VAE) approaches* or a combination of both. The adversarial methods [5, 6] in these problems are commonly written in the following form:

$$L_{adv} = \max_{D} \; l_{CE}(D(E(x)), s), \tag{3}$$

where the objective is to maximize the cross entropy loss of l_{CE}, and D is the discriminator that measures how the representation $z = E(x)$ is informative over domain s. Due to the limitations of adversarial approaches, variational autoencoder approaches were utilized.

While numerous research efforts in computer vision have introduced invariant representation learning frameworks [2–4] or disentanglement [7], they often do not specifically address issues of fairness in AI. However, few studies have incorporated elements of these representation learning concepts to tackle fairness concerns.

The vanilla **Variational Autoencoder (VAE)** was proposed by [25] to ensure that the latent representations follow a normal distribution $p(z) = N(0; I)$, and the objective is to maximize the Evidence Lower Bound (ELBO) function:

$$L_{VAE}(p, q) = \mathbb{E}_{q(z|x)}[\log p(x|z)] - D_{KL}[q(z|x) \parallel p(z)] \tag{4}$$

By maximizing ELBO, we ensure the maximization of the decoder's ability to generate new data by $\log p(x|z)$. Also Kullback-Leibler divergence(D_{KL}) calculates the distance of the estimated distribution of encoder $q(z|x)$ and normal prior of $p(z)$ [9].

β-**VAE** proposed by [7] modified the VAE objective function with adding hyperparameter β:

$$L_{\beta VAE}(p, q) = \mathbb{E}_{q(z|x)}[\log p(x|z)] - \beta D_{KL}[q(z|x) \parallel p(z)], \tag{5}$$

To reduce the KL divergence of variational distribution $q(z|x)$ and normal distribution of prior $p(z)$ The authors [7] argue that well-chosen values of this hyperparameter $\beta > 1$, give greater control over the model and lead to higher factorization of the latent representation, thus yields *disentanglement*. In a well-disentangled latent code, every dimension should represent only a single meaningful aspect of variation within the data [9].

3 Methodology

The schematic Fig. 1 shows the proposed fair representation learning framework. To force the representations to include the most crucial information required for predicting the target, we utilize the encoder part of the β-VAE along with a classifier. We incorporate the Hilbert-Schmidt independence criterion [24] to decrease the interdependence between the representation and protected attributes. In this scenario, the representation and the protected attribute are treated as variables, and Hilbert-Schmidt measures their statistical dependence.

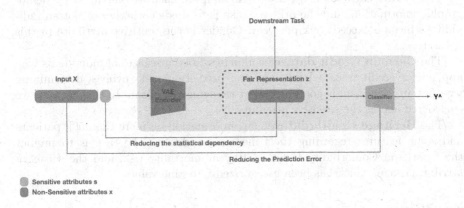

Fig. 1. The schematic diagram of proposed fair representation learning framework

While some fairness studies such as [10] focus on reducing the correlation between the representation and the protected attribute, achieving independence between them should be the ultimate goal. Dealing with two uncorrelated random variables is a simpler task than achieving independence. It's worth noting that two random variables can have zero correlation and still be dependent. We propose integrating the encoder part of β-VAE along with a classifier and Hilbert-Schmidt independence criterion to achieve more fair representations and to maximize the below objective function:

$$L(\theta, \phi; x, y) = \alpha BCE(f(z), y) - \beta \, |D_{KL}(q(z|x) \, \| \, N(0, I)) - C| - \lambda HSIC(z, s)$$
$$(6)$$

where θ, ϕ are the parameters of the encoder and classifier, respectively. $HSIC(\cdot)$ denotes the Hilbert-Schmidt Independence Criterion between the representation and sensitive data, BCE denotes the binary cross entropy, and $f(\cdot)$ denotes the classifier that maps the representation z to the raw output (logits) $\hat{y}$.

4 Experiments

4.1 Dataset

In our experiments, we employed three benchmark datasets in this field: The Adult and German datasets, which are available in the UCI ML repository [1] and the Heritage Health dataset[1].

The **Adult dataset** consists of 48k samples, each accompanied by demographic information, and the primary task is to predict whether or not an individual's income exceeds 50k per year. Gender is the sensitive attribute in this dataset.

The **German Credit dataset** comprises 1,000 instances of individuals who applied for credit from a bank, and the prediction task involves determining whether an individual is good or bad at repaying their loan. In this dataset, we considered age as the sensitive attribute.

The **Heritage Health dataset** has information on more than 50k patients and some features regarding their medical condition. The task is to predict the Charleson Comorbidity Index, a 10-year mortality risk, and the sensitive attribute is age, which has been categorized into nine values.

4.2 Setting

To evaluate our model's performance and fairness, we conduct a fair classification audit. After training our model, we freeze the encoder's parameters. Then, the representations of the train set and test set are extracted from the outputs of the frozen encoder. We train a downstream task classifier $(T : Z \rightarrow Y)$ to predict y given z, with the encoded train set z_{train} and evaluate the accuracy and demographic parity (DP) on the encoded test set z_{test}. We compared these results to a standard MLP classifier trained on the Adult dataset to observe the discrimination and bias without incorporating any fairness measures. Also we implemented linear version of β-VAE [7], suitable for tabular data for a fair comparison. Finally we compared our results with Learning Fair Representations (LFR) [23], Variational Fair Auto-Encoders (VFAE) [22] CORR [17], Fair-scale [15], CFair [16], and FBC [14].

5 Results and Discussion

The trade-off between accuracy and fairness across all datasets is depicted in Figs. 3a, 3c, 3b. As evident from the figures, in the case of the Adult dataset, our model achieves the highest accuracy when the demographic parity (DP) is below 0.02. As DP increases, the accuracy of all models steadily improves.

---

[1] https://foreverdata.org/1015/index.html.

For the German dataset, our model achieves the highest accuracy when DP is less than 0.025. Fair-scale outperforms for DP values greater than 0.075. Our model's accuracy peaks when approximately DP is 0.06, and it does not fall in DP between 0.06–0.14.

On the Health dataset, our model achieves its highest accuracy within the DP range of 0.0041–0.2769. Similar to the Adult dataset, as DP increases, the accuracy of all models steadily improves.

The optimal trade-off results for all models on the three datasets are summarized in Table 1. It's worth noting that for the Adult dataset, β-VAE solely is insufficient in reducing demographic parity compared to Unfair MLP, which is trained on the original dataset (not the representations). Our proposed model achieves comparable accuracy to CORR and VFAE while achieving the lowest demographic parity among them. Except LFR model, our model exhibits the lowest discrimination, indicating its effectiveness in learning fair representations by controlling statistical dependencies. The LFR model achieves the lowest demographic parity among all models but compromises 13% in accuracy compared to MLP, which is a non-negligible trade-off.

On the German dataset, our model excels by simultaneously achieving the lowest demographic parity and the highest accuracy. On the Health dataset, our model demonstrates the lowest demographic parity while maintaining accuracy comparable to FBC and Cfair.

Despite the decoder's role being changed to a classifier, the remainder of our model, including the encoder and training process, remains similar to a standard β-VAE. However, our model distinguishes itself by significantly reducing the demographic parity, which leads to generating fair representation compared to β-VAE. This underscores the significant impact of incorporating HSIC into the loss function, particularly in ensuring fairness, especially when dealing with the Health dataset, which features a non-binary sensitive attribute and a more complex distribution compared to the other datasets.

To demonstrate the significance of the Hilbert-Schmidt independence criterion, we also conducted a comparison between the encoded representations generated by our model (on the test dataset) and those generated by the β-VAE model. We assessed the degree of purification and fairness in these representations by calculating the absolute Pearson correlation coefficient between each dimension of the representation and the sensitive attribute. These analyses are visualized in Fig. 3. Our findings reveal that, across all datasets, our model exhibits a lower correlation with sensitive attributes compared to the β-VAE model. Notably, in the Adult dataset, the β-VAE model successfully disentangled the latent representation, with most of the sensitive information concentrated in the final dimension (z_{10}). However, the identification of which latent features contained the sensitive information was not possible before conducting the correlation experiments and visualizing the correlations. In both the German and

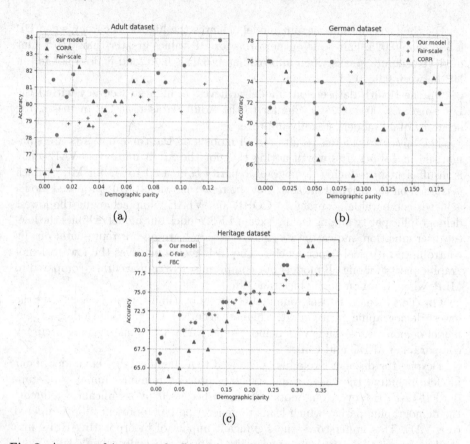

Fig. 2. Accuracy-fairness tradeoff and comparison to state-of-the-art models across three benchmark datasets: (a) Adult, (b) German, and (c) Heritage Health. The optimal region on the graph is the upper left corner, representing high accuracy and low demographic parity. Our model demonstrates a superior fairness-accuracy tradeoff.

Health datasets, the performance of the β-VAE model in disentangling sensitive information was poor. This was particularly evident in the Health dataset, which, as previously noted, features a non-binary sensitive attribute and exhibits a more complicated distribution when compared to the other datasets. These findings once again emphasize the impact of incorporating the Hilbert-Schmidt independence criterion into the β-VAE model, leading to yield consistent representations and its ability to improve fairness in downstream tasks.

Table 1. Best accuracy-fairness tradeoffs on the Adult, German and Health datasets.

	Adult dataset		German dataset		Health dataset	
	Accuracy ↑	DP ↓	Accuracy ↑	DP ↓	Accuracy ↑	DP ↓
Unfair MLP	0.8376	0.1811	0.78	0.2682	0.8268	0.6412
β-VAE [7]	0.8215	0.1876	0.66	0.2009	0.7351	0.3822
LFR [23]	0.7023	0.0006	0.5909	0.0042	–	–
VFAE [22]	0.8129	0.0708	0.727	0.043	–	–
FBC [14]	–	–	–	–	0.7276	0.1184
Fair-scale [15]	0.7874	0.0121	0.75	0.0867	0.7047	0.2011
Cfair [16]	0.75	0.0867	–	–	0.7293	0.156
CORR [17]	0.8157	0.0115	0.75	0.0203	–	–
Our Model	0.8146	0.0061	0.76	0.002	0.7217	0.1121

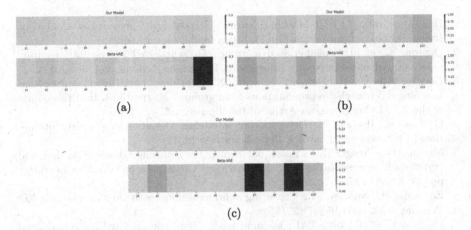

(a)   (b)

(c)

Fig. 3. Correlation Heatmap of Encoded Representations. This heatmap visually depicts the absolute value of Pearson correlation coefficients between each dimension of the encoded representations and the sensitive attribute across our experimental datasets (Adult, German, and Health). Lower correlation values indicate lower independence to sensitive attributes in the encoded representations, emphasizing the effectiveness of our model in achieving fair and unbiased representations.

6 Conclusion

In this paper, we proposed a novel fair representation learning algorithm by incorporating the β-VAE encoder integrated with a classifier to extract useful non-sensitive information, while utilizing the Hilbert-Schmidt independence criterion to remove any sensitive information. The experimental results on three benchmark datasets demonstrated that although our encoder and the training process are similar to standard β-VAE, our model exhibits superior performance compared to β-VAE. Compared to other state-of-the-art models, our proposed model shows a better fairness-accuracy tradeoff.

There are various possible directions for future research. We can delve deeper into the topic by exploring different statistical dependence metrics to tackle this problem and then compare the results with those presented in this paper. Moreover, there are fairness metrics beyond demographic parity, such as Equalized Odds and Equal Opportunity [31], and it is essential to develop fair representations based on these metrics to expand our approach. We are also interested in broadening our research to encompass image datasets. Furthermore, another potential direction for future work is to delve deeper into the interpretability of fairness using causality and conditional dependencies. Although learning fair representations is an ongoing challenging research, this research represents a step towards achieving improved and fair representations.

References

1. Dua, D., Graff, C.: UCI Machine Learning Repository. University of California, Irvine, School of Information (2017). http://archive.ics.uci.edu/ml
2. Denton, E., et al.: Unsupervised learning of disentangled representations from video. In: Advances in Neural Information Processing Systems, vol. 30 (2017)
3. Bouchacourt, D., Tomioka, R., Nowozin, S.: Multi-level variational autoencoder: Learning disentangled representations from grouped observations. In: Proceedings of the AAAI Conference on Artificial Intelligence, vol. 32 (2018)
4. Gabbay, A., Hoshen, Y.: Demystifying Inter-class Disentanglement. In: International Conference on Learning Representations (2019)
5. Madras, D., Creager, E., Pitassi, T., Zemel, R.: Learning adversarially fair and transferable representations. In: International Conference on Machine Learning, pp. 3384–3393 (2018)
6. Edwards, H., Storkey, A.: Censoring representations with an adversary. arXiv Preprint arXiv:1511.05897 (2015)
7. Higgins, I., et al.: beta-VAE: learning basic visual concepts with a constrained variational framework. In: International Conference on Learning Representations (2016)
8. Park, S., Hwang, S., Kim, D., Byun, H.: Learning disentangled representation for fair facial attribute classification via fairness-aware information alignment. In: Proceedings of the AAAI Conference on Artificial Intelligence, vol. 35, pp. 2403–2411 (2021)
9. Creager, E., et al.: Flexibly fair representation learning by disentanglement. In: International Conference on Machine Learning, pp. 1436–1445 (2019)
10. Quan, T., Zhu, F., Ling, X., Liu, Q.: Learning fair representations by separating the relevance of potential information. Inf. Process. Manag. **59**, 103103 (2022)
11. Raff, E., Sylvester, J.: Gradient reversal against discrimination. arXiv Preprint arXiv:1807.00392 (2018)
12. Chen, T., Kornblith, S., Norouzi, M., Hinton, G.: A simple framework for contrastive learning of visual representations. In: International Conference on Machine Learning, pp. 1597–1607 (2020)
13. Hadsell, R., Chopra, S., LeCun, Y.: Dimensionality reduction by learning an invariant mapping. In: 2006 IEEE Computer Society Conference on Computer Vision and Pattern Recognition (CVPR'06), vol. 2, pp. 1735–1742 (2006)

14. Gitiaux, X., Rangwala, H.: Fair representations by compression. In: Proceedings of the AAAI Conference on Artificial Intelligence, vol. 35, pp. 11506–11515 (2021)
15. Petrović, A., Nikolić, M., Radovanović, S., Delibašić, B., Jovanović, M.F.A.I.R.: Fair adversarial instance re-weighting. Neurocomputing **476**, 14–37 (2022)
16. Zhao, H., Coston, A., Adel, T., Gordon, G.: Conditional learning of fair representations. arXiv Preprint arXiv:1910.07162 (2019)
17. Beutel, A., et al.: Putting fairness principles into practice: challenges, metrics, and improvements. In: Proceedings of the 2019 AAAI/ACM Conference on AI, Ethics, and Society, pp. 453–459 (2019)
18. Kim, H., Mnih, A.: Disentangling by factorising. In: International Conference on Machine Learning, pp. 2649–2658 (2018)
19. Chen, R., Li, X., Grosse, R., Duvenaud, D.: Isolating sources of disentanglement in variational autoencoders. In: Advances in Neural Information Processing Systems, vol. 31 (2018)
20. Watanabe, S.: Information theoretical analysis of multivariate correlation. IBM J. Res. Dev. **4**, 66–82 (1960)
21. Kahana, J., Hoshen, Y.: A contrastive objective for learning disentangled representations. In: European Conference on Computer Vision, pp. 579–595 (2022)
22. Louizos, C., Swersky, K., Li, Y., Welling, M., Zemel, R.: The variational fair autoencoder. arXiv Preprint arXiv:1511.00830 (2015)
23. Zemel, R., Wu, Y., Swersky, K., Pitassi, T., Dwork, C.: Learning fair representations. In: International Conference on Machine Learning, pp. 325–333 (2013)
24. Gretton, A., Borgwardt, K., Rasch, M., Schölkopf, B., Smola, A.: A kernel method for the two-sample-problem. In: Advances in Neural Information Processing Systems, vol. 19 (2006)
25. Kingma, D., Welling, M.: Auto-encoding variational Bayes. arXiv Preprint arXiv:1312.6114 (2013)
26. Jaiswal, A., Wu, R., Abd-Almageed, W., Natarajan, P.: Unsupervised adversarial invariance. In: Advances in Neural Information Processing Systems, vol. 31 (2018)
27. Amini, A., Soleimany, A., Schwarting, W., Bhatia, S., Rus, D.: Uncovering and mitigating algorithmic bias through learned latent structure. In: Proceedings of the 2019 AAAI/ACM Conference on AI, Ethics, and Society, pp. 289–295 (2019)
28. Moyer, D., Gao, S., Brekelmans, R., Galstyan, A., Ver Steeg, G.: Invariant representations without adversarial training. In: Advances in Neural Information Processing Systems, vol. 31 (2018)
29. Riedl, M.: Human-centered artificial intelligence and machine learning. Hum. Behav. Emerg. Technol. **1**, 33–36 (2019)
30. Rajabi, A., Garibay, O.: TabfairGAN: fair tabular data generation with generative adversarial networks. Mach. Learn. Knowl. Extract. **4**, 488–501 (2022)
31. Hardt, M., Price, E., Srebro, N.: Equality of opportunity in supervised learning. In: Advances in Neural Information Processing Systems, vol. 29 (2016)
32. Verma, S., Rubin, J.: Fairness definitions explained. In: 2018 IEEE/ACM International Workshop on Software Fairness (Fairware), pp. 1–7 (2018)

Model-Free Motion Planning of Complex Tasks Subject to Ethical Constraints

Shaoping Xiao$^{(\boxtimes)}$, Junchao Li , and Zhaoan Wang

The University of Iowa, Iowa City, IA 52242, USA
shaoping-xiao@uiowa.edu
https://xiao.lab.uiowa.edu

Abstract. Artificial Intelligence (AI) ethics establishes a moral framework to guide responsible AI technology use. This paper introduces a model-free Reinforcement Learning (RL) approach to address ethical constraints in motion planning problems, particularly in complex tasks within partially observable environments. Leveraging the Partially Observable Markov Decision Process (POMDP) for motion planning in environments with incomplete knowledge and Linear Temporal Logic (LTL) for task formulation, ethical norms are categorized as 'hard' and 'soft' constraints. Our approach involves generating a product of POMDP and LTL-induced automaton. An optimal policy is then learned, ensuring task completion while adhering to ethical constraints through model checking. To handle the situations where the agent lacks task awareness, we propose a novel modification to deep Q-learning. This model-free deep RL method employs a neural network architecture with environmental observations and recognized labels as inputs. An illustrative example showcases the applicability of our approach to motion planning problems. The flexibility and generality of this method make it suitable for addressing various ethical decision-making problems.

Keywords: Ethical constraints · Motion planning · Partially observable environments · Reinforcement learning

1 Introduction

Classical ethical theories, such as Utilitarianism [1], Deontology [2], virtue ethics [3], and consequentialism [4], significantly shape our daily lives, guiding ethical decision-making in various contexts. In the evolving landscape of Artificial Intelligence (AI), ethical considerations are paramount, given the potential societal impact on intelligent decision-making [5]. However, as AI technologies rapidly advance, the "black box" nature of their underlying models presents challenges in understanding the decision processes. It becomes necessary for AI systems to incorporate ethical considerations, ensuring their decisions not only meet the technical specifications but also align with social values and norms.

© The Author(s), under exclusive license to Springer Nature Switzerland AG 2024
H. Degen and S. Ntoa (Eds.): HCII 2024, LNAI 14735, pp. 116–129, 2024.
https://doi.org/10.1007/978-3-031-60611-3_9

This paper introduces a model-free Reinforcement Learning (RL) approach to address ethical constraints in motion planning within complex tasks in partially observable environments. Specifically, we employ the Partially Observable Markov Decision Process (POMDP) to model motion planning in environments with incomplete knowledge and use Linear Temporal Logic (LTL) for task formulation. Ethical norms are classified into 'hard' and 'soft' categories. Our approach involves generating a product of POMDP and LTL-induced automaton. An optimal policy is learned, ensuring task completion while adhering to ethical constraints through model checking.

To address situations where agents lack awareness of assigned tasks, we present a novel solution utilizing modified Q-learning to learn optimal policies in partially observable environments. This model-free deep RL method employs a Q network architecture, incorporating Recurrent Neural Networks (RNNs) to process sequences of environmental observations and recognized labels as inputs.

In the following sections of this paper, we will provide a structured presentation. The initial part will cover essential preliminaries, followed by a detailed exploration of methodologies. This includes defining ethical constraints, outlining the process of generating a product POMDP, and presenting the algorithm of our proposed method. Subsequently, we will illustrate our approach through a practical example, demonstrating motion planning under diverse ethical constraints. Finally, we will conclude with a summary of key findings and potential avenues for future research.

2   Preliminary

2.1   Parially Observable Markov Decision Process (POMDP)

When an agent can not fully identify the state of its environment, POMDP [6] is typically employed to model the interaction between the agent and the environment.

Definition 1 (POMDP). *A tuple $\mathcal{P} = (S, A, s_0, T, R, O, \Omega)$ is utilized to denote a POMDP, including*

- *A set of states $S = \{s_1, \ldots, s_n\}$.*
- *A set of actions $A = \{a_1, \ldots, a_m\}$. Specifically, $A(s)$ is a set of available actions the agent can take at the current state s.*
- *An initial state $s_0 \in S$.*
- *A transition probability function $T : S \times A \times S \rightarrow [0,1]$, satisfying $\sum_{s' \in S} T(s, a, s') = 1$. It defines the probability when the agent moves from the current state s to the next state s' after executing an action a.*
- *A reward function $R : S \times A \times S \rightarrow \mathcal{R}$. The reward function can sometimes be written as $R(s)$ or $R(s, a)$.*
- *A set of observations $O = \{o_1, \ldots, o_k\}$.*
- *An observation probability function $\Omega : S \times A \times O \rightarrow [0,1]$, satisfying $\sum_{o \in O(s')} \Omega(s', a, o) = 1$. It represents the probability that the agent can perceive observation o at the next state s' after taking action a at the current state s.*

To address complex tasks, we utilize a set of atomic propositions Π to represent event occurrences. Additionally, we introduce a labeling function $L : S \rightarrow 2^{\Pi}$, where 2^{Π} is the power set of Π, to indicate events associated with individual states. This paper exclusively focuses on static events, meaning no probabilities are assigned to the occurrences of events.

2.2 Linear Temporal Logic (LTL)

Linear Temporal Logic [7], a formal language, is capable of expressing linear-time properties that represent the relation between state labels and sequential executions. In this study, we leverage LTL to articulate complex tasks. The basic operators encompass boolean connectors such as negation ($\neg$) and conjunction ($\wedge$), as well as temporal operators like "next" ($\bigcirc$) and "until" ($\mathcal{U}$). Assuming a word $w = w_0 w_1 \ldots$ with $w_i \in 2^{\Pi}$, where $a \in \Pi$ is an atomic proposition, and ϕ, ϕ_1 and ϕ_2 are single LTL formulas, the grammar for forming an LTL formula and its semantics are expressed below [8].

$$\phi := \text{True} \mid a \mid \phi_1 \wedge \phi_2 \mid \neg\phi \mid \bigcirc\phi \mid \phi_1\mathcal{U}\phi_2 \tag{1}$$

$$
\begin{aligned}
w &\models \text{True} \\
w &\models a & &\Leftrightarrow a \in L(w[0]) \\
w &\models \phi_1 \wedge \phi_2 & &\Leftrightarrow w \models \phi_1 \text{ and } w \models \phi_2 \\
w &\models \neg\phi & &\Leftrightarrow w \not\models \phi \\
w &\models \bigcirc\phi & &\Leftrightarrow w[1 :] \models \phi \\
w &\models \phi_1\mathcal{U}\phi_2 & &\Leftrightarrow \exists t \text{ s.t. } w[t :] \models \phi_2, \forall t' \in [0,t), w[t' :] \models \phi_1
\end{aligned}
\tag{2}
$$

Other commonly-used temporal operators include "eventually" ($\Diamond\phi \equiv \text{True } \mathcal{U}$) and "always" ($\Box\phi \equiv \neg(\Diamond\neg\phi)$).

2.3 Limit-Deterministic Generalized Büchi Automaton (LDGBA)

Once complex tasks are expressed, an LTL formula can be transformed into a finite state automaton. This automaton takes a word as input and verifies temporal properties. In this study, we utilize LDGBA, which involves specific state transitions and allows the evaluation of task and constraint satisfaction through model checking [7].

Definition 2 (LDGBA). *A tuple $\mathcal{A} = (Q, \Sigma, \delta, q_0, \mathcal{F})$ is utilized to represent an LDGBA, which consists of*

- *A finite set of states Q, which can be decomposed into a deterministic set (Q_D) and a non-deterministic one (Q_N). The following relationships are satisfied: $Q_D \cup Q_N = Q$ and $Q_D \cap Q_N = \emptyset$.*
- *A finite alphabet $\Sigma = 2^{\Pi}$ where Π is a set of atomic propositions.*

- A transition function $\delta: Q \times (\Sigma \cup \{\epsilon\}) \to 2^Q$, where ϵ-transitions do not take the input symbols. The state transitions satisfy the following requirements: (1) The transitions in Q_D are restricted, i.e., $\delta(q, \alpha) \subseteq Q_D$, for every state $q \in Q_D$ and $\alpha \in \Sigma$; (a) The state transitions in Q_D are total, i.e., $|\delta(q, \alpha)| = 1$; and (3) The ϵ-transitions are only valid from $q \in Q_N$ to $q' \in Q_D$.
- An initial state $q_0 \in Q$.
- A set of accepting sets $\mathcal{F} = \{\mathcal{F}_1, \mathcal{F}_2, \ldots, \mathcal{F}_f\}$ where $\mathcal{F}_i \subseteq Q$, $\forall i \in \{1, \ldots, f\}$. It shall be noted that the accepting states in each accepting set belong to the deterministic set only, i.e., $\mathcal{F}_i \subseteq Q_D$ for every $\mathcal{F}_i \in \mathcal{F}$.

After taking an input word $\boldsymbol{w} = w_0 w_1 \ldots$ where $w_i \in 2^\Pi$, the LDGBA generates a corresponding run $\boldsymbol{q} = q_0 q_1 \ldots$. This run is a sequence of automaton states determined by the transition function $\delta(q_i, w_i) = q_{i+1}$. The LDGBA accepts this word if the transitioned state eventually belongs to at least one of the accepting sets. Such a satisfaction condition can be mathematically expressed as $\inf(\boldsymbol{q}) \cap \mathcal{F}_i \neq \emptyset$, $\forall i \in \{1, \ldots f\}$ where $\inf(\boldsymbol{q})$ represents the infinite portion of $\boldsymbol{q}$. In other words, we can affirm that the run $\boldsymbol{q}$ satisfies the LDGBA's acceptance condition.

3 Methodologies

3.1 Ethical Constraints

This study categorizes various concepts of ethical norms into 'hard' and 'soft' constraints. Obligations and prohibitions are considered 'hard' ethical constraints and must be satisfied. These constraints can be formulated using LTL with temporal operators $\Box$ ("always"). For instance, expressing the prohibition of event a can be done with the LTL formula $\Box \neg a$, indicating that an acceptable sequence of agent's behaviors shall avoid all the actions leading to the occurrence of event a. Additionally, conditional obligations or prohibitions can be expressed by LTL formulas, such as $\Box(a \to \bigcirc b)$, stating that the agent must take action to ensure event 'b' is true once event 'a' becomes true. It is important to note that LTL was employed to express complex tasks, as discussed above. Therefore, some atomic propositions labeled on POMDP states in this study represent task events, while others are associated with 'hard' ethical constraints.

When ethical norms, such as permission, are not strictly prohibited or obligated for agents, they fall into the 'soft' constraints category, which LTL cannot express. In this study, an additional reward function is introduced as below when the selected actions lead to permissible ethical events.

$$R_s(s, a, s') = \begin{cases} R_s & a \in A, \text{ and } L(s') \in L_p \\ 0 & \text{otherwise.} \end{cases} \tag{3}$$

where L_p denotes the set of labels indicating the permissible ethical events.

The reward R_s is assigned with positive or negative values to distinguish permissions with encouragement from discouragement. Additionally, a large or small positive (negative) reward signifies strong or weak encouragement (discouragement). It is worth noting that there is no necessity to assign a reward to the occurrence of events with simple permissions.

3.2   Product POMDP

We have outlined a POMDP to represent partially observable environments, incorporating an additional reward function for 'soft' ethical constraints and LTL specifications to express complex tasks and 'hard' ethical constraints. Subsequently, the original problem can be reformulated by creating a Cartesian product of the POMDP and the LTL-induced LDGBA, referred to as the product POMDP.

Definition 3 (Product POMDP). *Given a POMDP* $\mathcal{P} = (S, A, s_0, T, R, O, \Omega)$ *and an LDGBA* $\mathcal{A} = (Q, \Sigma, \delta, q_0, \mathcal{F})$, *the generated product POMDP can be represented by a tuple* $\mathcal{P}^\times = \mathcal{P} \times \mathcal{A} = (S^\times, A^\times, s_0^\times, T^\times, R^\times, O, \Omega^\times, \mathcal{F}^\times)$, *consisting of*

- *A finite set of product states,* $S^\times = S \times Q$ *or* $s^\times = \langle s, q \rangle \in S^\times$ *where* $s \in S$ *and* $q \in Q$.
- *A finite set of actions,* $A^\times = A \cup \{\epsilon\}$.
- *An initial product state* $s_0^\times = \langle s_0, q_0 \rangle \in S^\times$ *where* $s_0 \in S$ *and* $q_0 \in Q$.
- *A transition function,* $T^\times = S^\times \times A^\times \times S^\times \to [0, 1]$.
- *A reward function* $R^\times = S^\times \times A^\times \times S^\times \to \mathcal{R}$.
- *An observation function* $\Omega^\times = S^\times \times A^\times \times O \to [0, 1]$.
- *A set of accepting sets* $\mathcal{F}^\times = \left\{\mathcal{F}_1^\times, \mathcal{F}_2^\times, ..., \mathcal{F}_f^\times\right\}$ *where* $\mathcal{F}_i^\times = \{\langle s, q \rangle | s \in S; q \in \mathcal{F}_i\}$ *and* $i = 1, ...f$.

The transition function describes the state transition probabilities on the product POMDP as

$$T^\times \left(s^\times, a^\times, s^{\times'}\right) = \begin{cases} T(s, a^\times, s') & q' = \delta(q, l), l \in L(s'), \text{ and } a^\times \in A \\ 1 & s' = s, a^\times \in \{\epsilon\}, \text{ and } q' \in \delta(q, \epsilon) \\ 0 & \text{otherwise.} \end{cases} \quad (4)$$

where $s^{\times'} = \langle s', q' \rangle$. The reward function in the product POMDP comprises two terms, one for acceptance conditions and the other for 'soft' ethical constraints, defined below.

$$R^\times(s^\times, a^\times, s^{\times'}) = R_a^\times(s^\times, a^\times, s^{\times'}) + R_s^\times(s^\times, a^\times, s^{\times'}), \quad (5)$$

and

$$R_a^\times(s^\times, a^\times, s^{\times'}) = \begin{cases} R(s, a^\times, s') & a^\times \in A, l \in L(s'), q' = \delta(q, l) \in \mathcal{F}_i \\ 0 & \text{otherwise.} \end{cases} \quad (6)$$

$$R_s^\times(s^\times, a^\times, s^{\times'}) = \begin{cases} R_s(s, a^\times, s') & a^\times \in A, l \in L(s'), \text{ and } l \in L_p \\ 0 & \text{otherwise.} \end{cases} \quad (7)$$

The available actions in the product POMDP include the physical actions on POMDP and ϵ-transitions on LDGBA. If the agent takes a physical action $a^\times \in A$, the observation probability is

$$\Omega^\times(s^{\times\prime}, a^\times, o) = \Omega(s', a^\times, o) \tag{8}$$

Otherwise, if ϵ-transitions are selected, the agent stays at the same POMDP state, $s' = s$, although the LDGBA state transitioned, i.e., $q' = \delta(q, \epsilon)$. In this case, no observation is perceived.

In addition, the expected return on the product POMDP can be written as below if an agent starts from the initial state and follows a policy $\xi^\times$.

$$U^{\xi^\times}(s_0^\times) = \mathbb{E}^{\xi^\times}\left[\sum_{t=0}^{\infty} \gamma^t R(s_t^\times, a_t^\times, s_{t+1}^\times) \Big| s_{t=0}^\times = s_0^\times\right] \tag{9}$$

3.3   Problem Definition

If a path $s_0 s_1 \cdots$ exists on the POMDP, the corresponding path $q_0 q_1 \cdots$ on the LDGBA can be derived via the labeling function and then automaton state transitions. Those two paths can be integrated to generate a path on the product POMDP. It can be stated that any feasible path $\sigma^{\xi^\times} = (s_0, q_0)(s_1, q_1) \cdots$ generated by the learned policy $\xi^\times$ on product POMDP $\mathcal{P}^\times$ shares the intersections between an accessible path over the original POMDP $\mathcal{P}$ and a word accepted by the LTL-induced LDGBA $\mathcal{A}$. Furthermore, from an optimal policy $\xi^{\times^*}$ on the product POMDP $\mathcal{P}^\times$, we can derive an optimal policy ξ^* on the POMDP $\mathcal{P}$. Additionally, as the product POMDP includes LTL specifications represented by LDGBA $\mathcal{A}$, the input word that corresponds to a path generated from ξ^* on POMDP is accepted by the LTL-induced LDGBA. In other words, the specifications are satisfied.

In this study, we adopt the strategy for solving MDP problems with LTL specifications [8–12]: generating a product MDP and applying the model-checking technique. Since the generated product POMDP is a type of POMDP, an optimal policy aims to maximize the expected return in (9). In our POMDP setting, the agent receives labels, which are input symbols to the LTL-induced automaton, as part of the feedback. In addition, the agent is unaware of the complex task (i.e., unknown to the automaton transitions). Consequently, the observations and labels can be grouped as the input of the policy $\xi^\times(\mathbf{o}_t, \mathbf{l}_t)$ on the product POMDP $\mathcal{P}^\times$.

Problem 1. A product POMDP $\mathcal{P}^\times = \mathcal{P} \times \mathcal{A}$ is formed by combining a POMDP $\mathcal{P}$ describing a partially observable environment with 'soft' ethical constraints and an LDGBA $\mathcal{A}$ expressing LTL specifications ϕ for a complex task and 'hard' ethical constraints. The objective is to discover an optimal policy $\xi^{\times^*}(\mathbf{o}_t, \mathbf{l}_t)$, where $\mathbf{o}_t$ and $\mathbf{l}_t$ represent the sequences of observations and labels on POMDP states, respectively, on the product POMDP $\mathcal{P}^\times$ for maximizing the expected return of $\mathcal{P}^\times$.

3.4   Q-Learning

This study employs Q-learning [13], a model-free RL method where agents lack knowledge of the transition probability function, observation probability function, and reward function. In MDP problems, an agent learns state-action values or Q values, denoted as $Q(s, a)$, through interactions with the environment. For large or infinite state spaces, deep Q-learning (DQN) [14] is often utilized, where Q values are approximated via Deep Neural Networks (DNNs), referred to as Q networks. Deep Q-learning consists of two Q-networks. One is an evaluation Q-network $Q_e(s, a; \theta_e)$, usually trained and updated at each step. The other is a target Q-network $Q_t(s, a; \theta_t)$ with fixed weights periodically copied from the evaluation Q-network. Note that θ_e and θ_t represent the network weights.

Algorithm 1. Deep Recurrent Q-Network for Product POMDP Problems.

1: Define 'hard' and 'soft' ethical constraints
2: Initialize LTL formula ϕ expressing complex tasks with 'hard' ethical constraints and POMDP $\mathcal{P}$ with 'soft' ethical constraints.
3: Convert ϕ to an LDGBA $\mathcal{A}$.
4: Construct the product POMDP $\mathcal{P}^\times = \mathcal{P} \times \mathcal{A}$.
5: Initialize the evaluation network $Q_E^\times$, the target network $Q_T^\times$, the replay memory D, the length of observation sequence p, the length of label sequence k, the learning rate α, the discount factor γ, the total number of episodes E, the total number of steps N, the batch size M, and the number of steps K to update the target Q network $Q_T^\times$.
6: **while** The current episode e in E **do**
7:      Randomly select a start state $s_0^\times$.
8:      **while** The current step i in N **do**
9:          Select a random action $a_i^\times$ if $i < p$; otherwise, select an action via the ϵ-greedy technique.
10:         Obtain observation and label.
11:         Generate $\mathbf{o}_{i+1}$ and $\mathbf{l}_{i+1}$.
12:         Collect the rewards $r_i^\times$.
13:         Store the experience $\langle \mathbf{o}_i, \mathbf{l}_i, a_i^\times, r_i^\times, \mathbf{o}_{i+1}, \mathbf{l}_{i+1} \rangle$ in D.
14:         **if** $i > 0$ and $i\%M{=}0$ **then**
15:             Randomly select M data samples as $U(D)$ from the replay memory.
16:             Compute $Q_{new}^\times$ for each data sample.
17:             Train $Q_E^\times$ by the batch of samples.
18:         **end if**
19:         **if** $i > 0$ and $i\%K{=}0$ **then**
20:             Pass the weights of $Q_E^\times$ to $Q_T^\times$.
21:         **end if**
22:     **end while**
23: **end while**
24: Training end and save the evaluation network $Q_E^\times$

In a partially observable environment, determining the current state solely from instant observations is not possible for the agent. However, the agent can make informed decisions based on the history of observations. In other words, the policy, representing the agent's function, maps a sequence of observations to the selected action. In such cases, Recurrent Neural Networks (RNNs), including Long Short-Term Memory (LSTM) [16], can replace DNNs in Q-networks to approximate Q values in DQN [15].

To address the problems defined in this study, an agent needs to collect information for decision-making in the product POMDP, encompassing both POMDP and LDGBA. Assuming the agent is unaware of the assigned task, i.e., lacking knowledge of LDGBA's transitions, its decisions rely on the observation and label sequences, serving as inputs to the Q-networks.

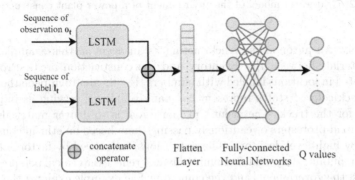

Fig. 1. The architecture of Q networks taking $\mathbf{o}_t$ and $\mathbf{l}_t$ as inputs.

Denoting $\mathbf{o}_t = o_1 \ldots o_p$ as the sequence of observations at time step t and the corresponding sequence of state labels as $\mathbf{l}_t = l_1 \ldots l_k$, it is important to note that the sequence lengths k and p may not the same since not every state is labeled. Therefore, two input sequences are pre-processed by one-hot-encoding before entering LSTMs. The hidden states are then concatenated and flattened into a fully connected neural network to predict Q values. The Q-network architecture in our DQN is illustrated in Fig. 1. We employ two Q networks: the evaluation network $Q_E^{\times}(\mathbf{o}_t, \mathbf{q}_t, a_t^{\times}; \theta_E^{\times})$ and the target network $Q_T^{\times}(\mathbf{o}_t, \mathbf{q}_t, a_t^{\times}; \theta_T^{\times})$ where $a_t^{\times} \in A$. The details of the training process are provided in Algorithm 1.

4 Example

A company is in the process of constructing a nuclear power plant, facing opposition from local residents who are protesting for a permanent closure. The construction site, depicted in Fig. 2, is represented as a 10×10 grid. States 'a' and 'b' denote the inventory of construction materials and plant-building areas,

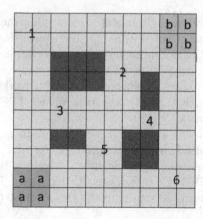

Fig. 2. Grid-world model of the environment of a power-plant construction.

respectively. An autonomous truck, acting as an agent in this example, transports materials between the inventory and the construction areas. Protesters, concentrated in locations labeled with numbers '1'−'6,' aim to impede the truck's route. Black-colored states represent company buildings, serving as impassible obstacles for the truck. The agent's primary goal is to deliver materials, navigating around protesters or cautiously passing them based on ethical constraints dictated by high-level decisions. These decisions, influenced by factors like local legislation, public safety, and economic impacts, reflect the ethical perspectives of protesters, the government, and the company. The example explores the agent's motion planning (pathfinding) in three scenarios with varying ethical constraints.

During the simulations, the agent's observation of the current state is assumed with a probability of 0.9 after taking an action. Alternatively, adjacent states (excluding those colored black) can be observed with a total probability of 0.1 uniformly distributed. Upon the agent's first visit to states 'a' or 'b' during a trip, a reward of 1 is received. In addition, there is an action cost of 0.01. Every simulation consists of 25,000 episodes, each with 800 steps. The observation sequence has a length of $p = 5$, and the label sequence length is $k = 3$. The batch size is set to $M = 32$ for training the evaluation Q-network at every time step. The target Q-network is updated by copying the weights of the evaluation Q-network every 50 time steps. Moreverover, the discount factor $\gamma = 0.95$.

4.1 Scenario 1: Deontological Government and Company but Utilitarian Protesters

This scenario operates under the assumption that both the government and the company strictly adhere to ·local environmental and public safety legislation. According to those regulations, roads must always remain clear for public transportation. However, the protesters hold the opposite view, prioritizing environmental safety over temporary disruptions and economic losses for greater well-being. They have chosen to fully block streets in areas 1 and 2, while keeping areas 3 to 6 clear. To model this situation, we adopt the concept of 'hard' constraints and use the atomic proposition 'c' to represent the agent passing through areas 1 and 2. Consequently, the LTL formula for the request task with ethical constraints can be formulated as follows.

$$\phi_1 = \Box\Diamond(a \wedge \Diamond b) \wedge \Box\neg c \tag{10}$$

The LTL formula described above specifies that the agent is required to visit states 'a' and then 'b' in a repeated manner. Importantly, it also enforces the constraint that the agent should never pass through areas 1 and 2.

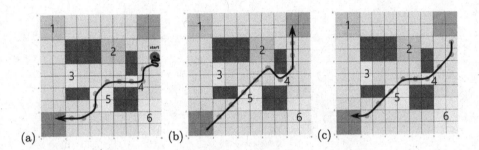

(a)   (b)   (c)

Fig. 3. A path to accomplish task ϕ_1 in case 1.

After the convergence of the learning process is converged and the acquisition of the optimal policy, we generate paths, as depicted in Fig. 3, to visually showcase the agent successfully completing the task. The agent initiates its journey near the construction area, taking random actions in 5 steps before generating the first observation and label sequences. Subsequently, the agent adopts a greedy approach in action selection based on the predicted Q values.

In Fig. 3(a), the agent navigates through areas 4 and 5, highlighted in light beige, where no protesters are present in these particular areas. It then reaches the inventory areas. After loading the materials, the agent follows the path outlined in Fig. 3(b), arriving at the construction areas and unloading the materials. In Fig. 3(c), the agent retraces its steps back to the inventory location for the second round. All paths traverse through areas 4 and 5, minimizing the total cost.

4.2 Scenario 2: Utilitarian Government and Company but Deontological Protesters

In the second scenario, both the government and the company believe that the construction project brings significant benefits to the community, outweighing the limited environmental impact. Consequently, they focus on prioritizing the construction while still permitting a certain degree of lawful protest. Unlike the

first scenario, protesters in this case strictly adhere to the law, avoiding street
blockages but potentially assembling near the company site within areas 3 to
6, prompting the agent to navigate those zones with caution. It is essential to
note that areas 1 and 2 remain clear. As a result, soft constraints come into
play, imposing negative rewards on the agent when passing through areas 3 to 6.
Various reward values are considered for these soft constraints, illustrating permission with different levels of discouragement. Given that only soft constraints
are at play in this scenario, the LTL formula for the assigned task is defined
below.

$$\phi_2 = \Box\Diamond(a \wedge \Diamond b) \tag{11}$$

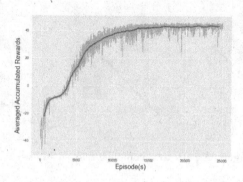

Fig. 4. The evolution of the cumulative reward.

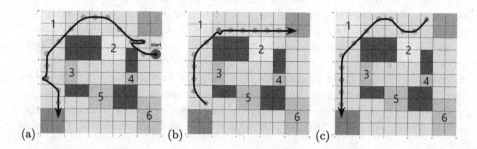

Fig. 5. A path to accomplish task ϕ_2 when permitted with strong encouragement.

In the initial variation, the agent is permitted but strongly discouraged from
entering protest areas 3 through 6. Navigating through these areas incurs a negative reward of -0.3. During the learning process, the progression of accumulated
rewards averaged every 10 episodes is depicted in Fig. 4. The darker color represents the Simple Moving Average (SMA) of rewards computed every 50 episodes.

The optimal policy emerges upon the convergence of cumulative rewards. Then, a path is generated and illustrated in Fig. 5. Commencing from the same location as in case 1, the agent systematically traverses the inventory and construction locations in order through areas 1 and 2, both devoid of protests. Despite the potential efficiency of passing through protest areas, specifically areas 4, 5, and 6, where fewer steps would be required, imposing high penalties steers the agent towards a route through areas 1 and 2. This strategic decision is influenced by the relatively higher costs incurred due to the strong discouragement associated with the occupied protest areas.

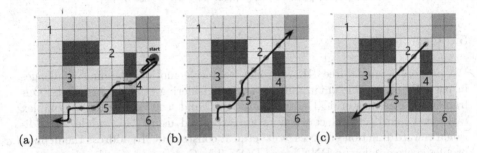

(a)   (b)   (c)

Fig. 6. A path to accomplish task ϕ_2 when permitted with weak encouragement.

When the penalties are reduced to -0.01 in the second variation, the agent experiences only weak discouragement from passing through protest areas 4 and 5. Consequently, prioritizing a considerably shorter route becomes the agent's focus to minimize the total cost, as shown in Fig. 6.

4.3   Scenario 3: Utilitarian Government, Company, and Protesters

In the final scenario, we assume that all stakeholders prioritize social well-being. The protesters attempted to block all the streets across areas 1 to 6. Contrarily, government law enforcement refrains from dispersing them entirely but opts to clear several main streets in areas 3 to 6, engaging in persuasive dialogue to encourage the protesters to disperse voluntarily. Recognizing the situation's complexity, the company requests the agent to avoid areas 1 and 2 and exercise caution when navigating through areas 3 to 6. Consequently, this scenario involves both 'hard' and 'soft' ethical constraints. The LTL formula remains consistent with the expression presented in Eq. (10). Permissions with strong and weak discouragement are implemented, introducing a negative reward of -0.3 when the agent traverses areas 3 to 5, and -0.01 for area 6.

After acquiring the optimal policy, the path generated for the agent to accomplish the task is illustrated in Fig. 7. As area 6 is permitted with weak encouragement, the agent opts to navigate through it to minimize the total cost, even though the path is longer than traversing areas 4 and 5.

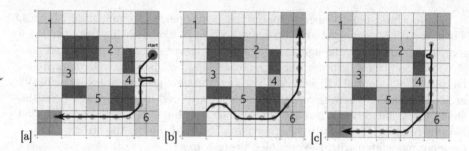

Fig. 7. A path to accomplish task ϕ_1 in case 3.

5   Conclusion

We propose a model-free RL approach to tackle motion planning challenges in partially observable environments while considering ethical constraints. Our framework classifies ethical norms into 'hard' and 'soft' constraints. Complex tasks and 'hard' ethical constraints are expressed using LTL, while an additional reward function enforces 'soft' ethical constraints. To address the defined problems, we employ an RNN-based DQN. The Q networks use the observation history and label sequences as inputs to estimate Q values, enabling the agent to make optimal decisions. We conduct a simulation example to showcase the effectiveness and flexibility of our proposed approach. Future research directions include handling dynamic ethical constraints and exploring multi-objective RL approaches.

Acknowledgments. This study was funded by US Department of Education (ED #P116S210005) and NSF (#2226936).

Disclosure of Interests. The authors have no competing interests to declare that are relevant to the content of this article.

References

1. Mill, J.-S.: Utilitarianism. Crips, Roger (ed.). Oxford University Press, Oxford, England (1998)
2. Davis, N.-A.: Contemporary Deontology. Blackwell, Malden, Massachusetts, United States (1991)
3. Crisp, R., Slote, M.: Virtue Ethics. Oxford University Press, Oxford, England (1997)
4. Sinnott-Armstrong, W.: Consequentialism. Stanford Encyclopedia of Philosophy (2019)
5. Slavkovik, M.: Automating moral reasoning. In: Bourgaux, C., Ozaki, A., Penaloza, R. (eds.) International Research School in Artificial Intelligence in Bergen, Open Access Series in Informatics (OASIcs), vol. 99, pp. 6:1 – 6:13. University of Bergen, Norway (2022)

6. Chadès, I., Pascal, L.-V., Nicol, S., Fletcher, C.-S., Ferrer-Mestres, J.: A primer on partially observable Markov decision processes (POMDPs). Methods Ecol. Evol. **12**, 2058–2072 (2021). https://doi.org/10.1111/2041-210X.13692

7. Baier, C., Katoen, J.-P.: Principles of Model Checking, 1st edn. MIT press, Cambridge, Massachusetts (2008)

8. Bozkurt, A.-K., Wang, Y., Zavlanos, M.-M., Pajic, M.: Control synthesis from linear temporal logic specifications using model-free reinforcement learning. In: Proceedings - IEEE International Conference on Robotics and Automation, pp. 10349–10355. IEEE, Paris, France (2020)

9. Cai, M., Hasanbeig, M., Xiao, S., Abate, A., Kan, Z.: Modular deep reinforcement learning for continuous motion planning with temporal logic. IEEE Robot. Autom. Lett. **6**(4), 7973–7980 (2021). https://doi.org/10.1109/LRA.2021.3101544

10. Cai, M., Xiao, S., Li, B., Li, Z., Kan, Z.: Reinforcement learning based temporal logic control with maximum probabilistic satisfaction. In: Proceedings - IEEE International Conference on Robotics and Automation, pp. 806–812, IEEE, Xi'an, China (2021). https://doi.org/10.1109/ICRA48506.2021.9561903

11. Cai, M., Xiao, S., Li, Z., Kan, Z.: Optimal probabilistic motion planning with potential infeasible LTL constraints. IEEE Trans. Autom. Control **68**(1), 301–316 (2023). https://doi.org/10.1109/TAC.2021.3138704

12. Cai, M., Xiao, S., Li, J., Kan, Z.: Safe reinforcement learning under temporal logic with reward design and quantum action selection. Sci. Rep. **13**, 1925 (2023). https://doi.org/10.1038/s41598-023-28582-4

13. Watkins, C., Dayan, P.: Q-Learning. Mach. Learn. **3**–**4**, 279–292 (1992). https://doi.org/10.1007/bf00992698

14. Mnih, V., et al.: Human-level control through deep reinforcement learning. Nature **7540**, 14764687 (2015). https://doi.org/10.1038/nature14236

15. Hausknecht, M., Stone, P.: Deep recurrent q-learning for partially observable MDPs. In: Technical Report - AAAI Fall Symposium, (2015)

16. Hochreiter, S., Schmidhuber, J.: Long short-term memory. Neural Comput. **9**(8), 08997667 (1997). https://doi.org/10.1162/neco.1997.9.8.1735

Enhancing User Experience Through AI-Driven Technologies

Incorporating Artificial Intelligence into Design Criteria Considerations

Gilbert Drzyzga(✉) ⓘ

Institute for Interactive Systems, Technische Hochschule Lübeck, Lübeck, Germany
gilbert.drzyzga@th-luebeck.de

Abstract. The use of Artificial Intelligence (AI) methods in everyday products is increasing. As AI technologies become more prevalent in interactive software applications and user interfaces (UIs), this study investigates the incorporation of AI into the consideration of design criteria. In particular, it explores the implications for issues that arise between AI and the field and context of Human–Computer Interaction (HCI). Through a two-part literature review (AI & HCI related topics) followed by a multi-stage analysis process, key findings were identified that highlight the need to explore the nature of HCI in AI-based UIs. It was found that there is a need to extend or add new principles to established ones. The findings also highlight the importance of understanding fundamental aspects of human-AI collaboration. However, they also suggest potential avenues for further guidance in the area of human interaction with AI-based outputs, such as comprehensibility, trust, transparency and cultural issues in the design of AI-based UIs.

Keywords: Artificial Intelligence · Human–Computer Interaction · Usability · User Experience · Design Principles · Design Criteria Considerations

1 Introduction and Background

Through the use of Artificial Intelligence (AI) and its underlying methods and algorithms, everyday services and products become "smarter" and could deliver greater user value [72]. For example, the use of such technologies could improve the quality of route planners and provide personalized recommendations for products, movies or music [61, 78, 92, 103]. AI technologies such as Machine Learning (ML) or its subset Deep Learning (DL) [8, 31], and in particular the use of NLP methods could be integrated into such applications to facilitate collaboration between humans and AI [3, 30, 38, 52, 66, 83].

1.1 Improving User Interaction by Understanding User Attention

AI, ML, and DL have the potential to improve the use of interactive systems by providing personalized experiences through understanding user attention and improving accessibility e.g. [11, 15, 18, 64]. The increasing emphasis on integrating AI into user interface (UI) design is driven by a number of key factors that underscore the importance of

© The Author(s), under exclusive license to Springer Nature Switzerland AG 2024
H. Degen and S. Ntoa (Eds.): HCII 2024, LNAI 14735, pp. 133–151, 2024.
https://doi.org/10.1007/978-3-031-60611-3_10

considering various aspects in their design and development [96]. These include changing user expectations, technological advances, and the potential of AI to improve user experience (UX) and personalization. For example, users expect more intelligent, intuitive, and personalized interactions with technology as they become more accustomed to smartphones, voice assistants and other AI-based devices in their daily lives, e.g. [47, 79, 88]. This has created a demand for UIs that seamlessly integrate AI capabilities, enabling natural and efficient communication between humans and machines [88]. As mentioned in several of the references cited, technological advances have also made it possible to harness the strength of ML algorithms, natural language processing (NLP), computer vision and other AI techniques to create more sophisticated and customizable UIs. With these technologies, systems can learn from data, understand contextual information and predict user needs in real time. The integration of AI into UIs has significant potential to improve usability by optimizing interactions based on user behavior and feedback over time [2].

1.2   The Interdisciplinary Approach to the Design of Effective UIs

In the context of the UI design of interactive systems, Human–Computer Interaction (HCI) and related disciplines such as usability, accessibility and UX are addressed to provide solutions that meet the needs of users e.g. [27, 32, 65]. They allow different methods and possibilities to evaluate the UI design of software applications, as discussed for example in [6, 9, 49, 82].

Usability research is here concerned with the design and evaluation of interactive systems (e.g. [28, 32, 33, 36]); its methods play a crucial role in assessing how well an interactive system achieves its intended goals while providing a positive experience for users [1, 12, 60]. The analysis techniques include inspection methods such as heuristic evaluation (e.g. [56]) or cognitive walkthroughs [76], as well as methods in formal usability testing such as user observation (e.g. expert reviews or thinking aloud [19, 46]). Usability emphasizes ease of use, learnability and clear feedback by minimizing errors, reducing cognitive load and providing effective communication [57, 70]. Another important discipline to consider in this context is accessibility,[1] which aims to ensure that these technologies are inclusive and accessible to people with disabilities[2] [51, 60]. UX takes a broader approach than just usability, including a focus on the pre-use ("anticipated use") phase of a product as well as a broader view of user interaction, e.g. [57, 70, 71]. Evaluation methods for UX can include standard questionnaires such as AttrakDiff,[3] User Experience Questionnaire (UEQ),[4] and meCUE[5] [22], interviews, observations, surveys, diaries, storytelling, or prototyping techniques e.g. [5, 29, 71, 91].

---

[1] According to the Web Accessibility Initiative, accessibility is a subset of usability and shares similar goals of minimizing errors and providing clear feedback, https://www.w3.org/WAI/test-evaluate/conformance/wcag-em/, accessed August 12, 2023.

[2] As the World Health Organization (WHO) states: "An estimated 1.3 billion people – about 16% of the global population – currently experience significant disability." https://www.who.int/health-topics/disability#tab=tab_1, accessed August 12, 2023.

[3] AttrakDiff: https://www.attrakdiff.de/index-en.html, accessed August 12, 2023.

[4] UEQ: https://www.ueq-online.org/, accessed August 12, 2023.

[5] meCUE: http://mecue.de/english/index.html, accessed August 12, 2023.

1.3 Assessing AI Integration into Design Criteria for UI Design

By focusing on established UI evaluation criteria that can help to improve user engagement in interactive AI systems [42, 67], three central research questions (RQs) are posed with respect to the investigation of design criteria in AI UIs:

1. How can AI be incorporated into design criteria considerations in the implementation of interactive software systems?
2. What design criteria have been proven and established in the evaluation of UI?
3. Are additional design criteria needed to optimize the UX of AI-based interfaces, and if so, what are the considerations?

Addressing the issues raised in the questions requires a holistic view of human-centered system integration of AI-based UIs due to the multiple aspects that exist in their interaction. The questions aim to explore the integration of AI into the design considerations of interactive software systems, to assess potential areas of conflict between traditional design principles and AI-driven interfaces, and to identify solutions where appropriate.

RQ1 is therefore concerned with incorporating AI into design criteria for interactive software systems in terms of HCI. It involves identifying the strengths, weaknesses and potential impact of AI on the overall UI design. A further goal is to achieve an efficient cooperation and a positive UX between users and AI-based UI. RQ2 aims to identify which traditional design principles remain valid for the evaluation of an AI-based software system, as well as conflicts that may arise when evaluating the UI design of AI-based systems using traditional design principles. Both RQ1 and RQ2 should help to identify where there are shortcomings.

In addition, the aim of RQ3 is to obtain information on whether new design principles should be considered for evaluation in order to address the specific challenges of interactive AI UIs.

2 Method

In order to answer RQs, the following analysis was carried out (Fig. 1).

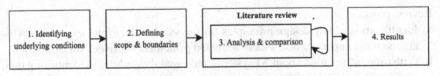

Fig. 1. Process of the analysis

The first step was to identify the underlying conditions that will guide the ongoing review of the literature (Fig. 1, step 1; see section "3 Identifying underlying conditions"). Together with the definition of the scope and boundaries of the literature to be reviewed and any limitations or constraints on the systems to be considered in the review (Fig. 1, step 2; see section "4 Scope & Boundaries"). Both steps are based on a breakdown of each RQ into key concepts and themes. Based on these constraints, a two-part literature review (AI & design criteria topics) was conducted to critically analyze and compare the relevant publications (Fig. 1, step 3; see section "5 Literature review (review process)"). A synthesis of the relevant literature was then carried out (analysis process), which involved organizing and analyzing the identified themes in relation to design criteria and AI-based software systems, identifying key categories and topics based on similarity and relevance, as well as patterns, trends and insights related to usability, UX and HCI (Fig. 1, step 4; see section "6 Comparison (Analysis Process)").

2.1 Identifying Underlying Conditions

To identify the underlying conditions, the RQs were examined for their inherent scope, and research was conducted on the topic of incorporating AI into design criteria considerations, addressing challenges related to human-AI collaboration and traditional design principles. Based on this information, a list of conditions and factors was compiled to enable an informed assessment of design criteria options in this context.

2.2 Defining Scope and Boundaries

The field of HCI is the central area of investigation for defining the scope and boundaries for considering AI in design criteria. In particular, the usability and UX of interactive UIs will be the focus of the research problem.

2.3 Validation Process

Based on the underlying conditions, as well as the scope and boundaries, there are two main steps in conducting the literature review and analysis. The first step is the review process, which involves gathering information from the two areas of (1) established principles in HCI and (2) AI for interactive systems. The second step is the analysis process, in which the data from these literature reviews are integrated to examine the interrelationship of the two fields and to derive considerations for potential conflicts between them. This structured approach also includes specific questions related to the RQs that will guide each step.

1. Review process
    a. Identification of key design principles for the validation of interactive UIs: What are the most important and widely accepted principles/heuristics for evaluation?
    b. Gathering information about AI systems and capabilities through identifying their challenges in HCI: How do AI-based systems work, and what characteristics define their functioning and potential impact?
2. Analysis process
    c. Considerations in the use of established design principles for AI-based systems: What are the theoretical and conceptual implications of these interactions?
    d. Based on the analysis in step 2a, what discrepancies arise between these principles and AI characteristics in interactive system design?

3 Identifying Underlying Conditions

In order to identify the assumptions or contextual factors of the literature review and the subsequent critical analysis and comparison in the validation process, the key aspects and influencing factors for the inclusion of AI in the design criteria of each RQ were derived as shown in Table 1.

Table 1. Summary of the first part of the literature review for established principles/heuristics

#	RQ	Factors/key concepts	Conditions
1	How can AI be incorporated into design criteria considerations in the implementation of interactive software systems?	AI capabilities (e.g. AI/ML/DL methods and algorithms), design criteria considerations, interactive software systems	1. Types of AI technologies to consider 2. Level of implementation 3. Contextual factors
2	What design criteria have been proven and established in the evaluation of UI?	Design criteria, established evaluation methods, user interface (UI) design	1. Proven design criteria in the evaluation of UIs 2. Transferable factors
3	Are additional design criteria needed to optimize the UX of AI-based interfaces, and if so, what are the considerations?	Additional design criteria, Optimizing user experience (UX), AI-based interfaces, Considerations	1. Challenges posed by AI in UI design that require new or modified design criteria

4 Scope and Boundaries

The definition of scope refers to the breadth of the literature review and the boundaries define the limits of the review. These are determined by the following inclusion criteria (IC) and exclusion criteria (EC) based on the research context (Table 2).

Table 2. Inclusion and exclusion criteria for the literature review

#	Inclusion criteria	Exclusion criteria
1	It has to be a final version of the publication	It is not the final version of the publication
2	The publication must have been published and peer-reviewed at a conference, in a journal, or in a book	The publication has not been published and peer-reviewed at a conference, in a journal or in a book
3	The publication was published in English	The publication was not published in English

(continued)

Table 2. (*continued*)

#	Inclusion criteria	Exclusion criteria
4	Thematic relevance (HCI, Usability, UX for AI-based UIs)	Non-thematic relevance (HCI, Usability, UX for AI-based UIs)
5	Technique is applicable, especially for AI-based UIs (no limitations)	Technique is not applicable, especially for AI-based UIs (limitations)

5 Literature Review (Review Process)

The following search terms and combinations were used to conduct the literature review on the incorporation of AI into design criteria considerations as an initial screening, using the extended searches where available (see details below), and taking into account the aforementioned conditions, scope and boundaries.

5.1 Conducting the Literature Review

Initial Keyword Selection. Based on the considerations, the search strategy included terms such as "design", "principle/principles", "heuristics", "criteria", "user", "interface", "human–computer interaction/hci", "usability" and "user experience" to capture design concepts for the evaluation of interactive UIs. For AI-related aspects relevant to the RQs, terms such as "artificial intelligence/AI" were also searched. The overall searches also included terms such as "evaluation/evaluating/assessment".

Expanding the Set of Keywords and Refining the Search. After reviewing the initial results, the keyword set was expanded to include relevant terms from the literature found in this first round of searches. This step allowed for the identification of more specific subtopics related to HCI and AI. The search criteria were extended by an explicit search within the search result or by related documents in relation to the sources found. In addition, snowball sampling was used, a method used to expand the literature base by examining citations and references of the relevant literature found.

Database-Specific Searches. Google Scholar[6] was used as an initial search with keyword combinations using the above terms, with scanning of titles, followed by an extended search/view/read for abstracts (in all databases). For this search, the Scopus[7] database was exclusively searched using appropriate keywords (see below). The reason for this is that a high level of results could be expected due to the objective described in the methodology. The search results were then analyzed electronically using frequencies (see next section for details).

- Scopus (advanced search): ABS (design AND ((principle OR principles OR heuristics OR criteria) AND user AND interface) AND (usability OR (user AND experience))

---

[6] https://scholar.google.com, accessed August 23, 2023.
[7] https://www.scopus.com/, accessed August 23, 2023.

AND (evaluation OR evaluating OR assessment)) AND PUBYEAR > 1971 AND PUBYEAR < 2024
- Number of sources: 791

Analysis and Review of Results and Selection of Relevant HCI-Publications. Careful consideration was given to the focus and relevance of the collected resources to the topic under review. In addition to reviewing the identified resources, the reference lists of these resources were searched for related work on heuristics and UI design principles to ensure a thorough review (see Table 1). The question was therefore which of the heuristics, principles, guidelines or rules were most frequently cited in the literature on this topic area. To streamline the process of counting literature occurrences, the capabilities of Python were used in this systematic approach. The frequency of each cited article was systematically counted using a custom script. By incorporating this technique into the analysis, it was possible to efficiently analyze a large amount of data and accurately identify key trends in the literature, ultimately providing valuable insights for further investigation. Alongside this automation process, the results were manually verified by validating the citations in the relevant literature.

Searching AI-Specific Literature. This part of the literature review is based on an initial exploration of the topic and scope, exploring general concepts related to AI and its applications in different domains (see Table 1, Conditions). The review provided an understanding of how AI is being used in different areas and to identify potential areas where it is impacting on design criteria or practices. This helped to identify possible recurring themes and patterns related to the impact of AI in different domains (e.g. usability, user experience). These themes were used as a starting point for the subsequent focused search, which was then narrowed down to specific aspects within each theme that were relevant to the topic (e.g. the impact of AI on UX). In this way, search terms were generated for the literature review on the intersection of AI and design criteria. This search was extended to two additional literature databases (ACM Digital Library[8] and IEEE Xplore[9]) in order to obtain additional information on techniques and methods in the field of AI/ML/DL in relation to HCI, usability, and UX issues.

- Google Scholar (initial search): Keyword combinations using the above aspects, with extended search/view for abstracts.
- Scopus (advanced search): ABS (("Artificial Intelligence" OR "Machine Learning" OR "Deep Learning") AND (characteristics OR techniques) AND user AND interface* AND human-computer AND interaction) AND PUBYEAR > 2018 AND PUBYEAR < 2024
- Number of sources: 45
- ACM Digital Library (advanced search): [[[Abstract: "artificial intelligence"] OR [Abstract: "machine learning"] OR [Abstract: "deep learning"]] AND [[Abstract: characteristics] OR [Abstract: techniques]] AND [Abstract: user] AND [Abstract: interface*] AND [Abstract: human-computer] AND [Abstract: interaction]] OR [All:))] AND [E-Publication Date: (01/01/2019 TO 12/31/2023)

---

[8] https://dl.acm.org, accessed August 23, 2023.

[9] https://ieeexplore.ieee.org/Xplore/home.jsp, accessed August 23, 2023.

- Number of sources: 36
- IEEE Xplore (advanced search): ("Abstract":"Artificial Intelligence" OR "Abstract":"Machine Learning" OR "Abstract":"Deep Learning") AND ("Abstract":characteristics OR "Abstract":techniques) AND ("Abstract":user) AND ("Abstract":interface*) AND ("Abstract":human-computer) AND ("Abstract":interaction) Filters Applied: 2019 - 2023
- Number of sources: 9

Time Frame. Literature database searches were conducted between August and early September 2023. With a revised search for relevant topics in early 2024.

5.2 Summary of the Results

Traditional Design Principles. As a result of the systematic analysis, both *Nielsen's Ten Heuristics* and *Shneiderman's Eight Golden Rules* were found to be the most cited resources in the literature in terms of thematic relevance, indicating their importance in UI design. A summary of the literature review for the consideration of traditional and thus established design principles in the area of UI creation or validation is shown in Table 3. It shows that Nielsen's heuristic, e.g. [56], is strongly represented in various forms of publications. There is several literature by Nielsen on this topic and he recommends "Enhancing the explanatory power of usability heuristics" for citation.[10] In addition, "The Eight Golden Rules of Interface Design" by Shneiderman, 2016 [82] was identified. This was found as a chapter in the book. They are largely complementary, as the following brief extract from these two sources of principles/heuristics identified in the literature review shows.

Table 3. Summary of the first part of the literature review for established principles/heuristics

#	Principles/Heuristics	Document type
1	Enhancing the explanatory power of usability heuristics [56]	Conference publication
2	Designing the user interface: Strategies for effective human–computer interaction [82], *(The most recent version is quoted here.)*	Book, includes "The Eight Golden Rules of Interface Design (1986)"

"10 Heuristics" by Nielsen, 1994. The analysis identified different publications on heuristics. For further research, the publication from 1994 is used [56]; the use of this publication is also recommended by Nielsen himself10. The heuristics assist in the identification of usability problems through the evaluation of UIs [56]. This are: visibility of system status; match between system and the real world; user control and freedom; consistency and standards; error prevention; recognition rather than recall; flexibility

---

[10] https://www.nngroup.com/articles/ten-usability-heuristics/, accessed September 10, 2023.

and efficiency of use; aesthetic and minimalist design; help users recognize, diagnose, and recover from errors; help and documentation.

"The Eight Golden Rules of Interface Design" by Shneiderman, 2016. The latest version of Shneiderman's "The Eight Golden Rules of Interface Design" [82] was used for further research. Such principles ensure that the system is easy to use, learn and understand by reducing errors, reducing cognitive load and providing clear feedback. These are: strive for consistency; enable frequent users to use shortcuts; offer informative feedback; design dialog to yield closure; offer simple error handling; permit easy reversal of actions; support internal locus of control; reduce short-term memory load.

Standards for the Implementation and Validation of UIs. The review also identified standards for the implementation and validation of usable interfaces. In particular, the 9241 series of ISO standards. In particular, the "EN ISO 9241–110:2020" standard was identified. As it is a standard and therefore an important source of verification in the area of usability, it was included in the list of verifiable principles. First published in 2006, it is an international standard for software design and interaction (see summary in Table 4).

Table 4. Summary of the first part of the literature review for established principles/heuristics

#	Standard	Document type
1	ISO 9241–110:2020 (en) Ergonomics of human-system interaction — Part 110: Interaction principles [23]	Standard

The design principles of ISO 9241–110:2020 are used for validation in the field of HCI and provide recommendations for the implementation of interactive systems. Seven principles and 65 recommendations for designing and interacting with interactive systems are specified in the current standard: suitability for the user's tasks; self-descriptiveness; conformity with user expectations; learnability; controllability; use error robustness; user engagement.

Summary and Findings. By identifying the main sources of usability heuristics and principles in the field, it emphasizes their value in building usable interfaces. They also provide guidance for evaluating existing systems, identifying improvements, and ensuring that they meet users' expectations and goals. Some of the methods for creating and verifying usable interfaces found in the literature have been known since the mid-1980s and are still valid today. By the mid-2000s, many of the usability methodologies established in previous decades, research findings or expert feedback had been formalized into standards. For example, the EN ISO 9241[11] family of standards, in particular as shown the standard ISO EN 9241–110:2020.[12] The various sources deal with topics

---

[11] An overview of the 9241 family in the search result can be found on the ISO website: https://www.iso.org/search.html?q=9241&hPP=10&idx=all_en&p=0&hFR%5Bcategory%5D%5B0%5D=standard, accessed September 10, 2023.

[12] ISO 9241–110:2020 (en) Ergonomics of human-system interaction — Part 110: Interaction principles, https://www.iso.org/standard/75258.html, accessed June 20, 2023.

related to the subject areas and are a widely known and established guide to the creation or verification of UI designs.

AI-Based Software Systems. The review identified aspects related to Table 1 (Conditions) for human-AI UI interaction, which are shown in the following Table 5.

Table 5. Summary of the second part of the literature review for AI-based techniques

#	Technique/Method	Description
1	Deep learning	- Modelling complex interaction patterns [85] - Deep learning-based super-resolution and tracking algorithms [99] - ANN models for predicting visual perception according to the Aesthetics, Complexity and Orderliness scales [7]
2	Deep neural networks	- Improvement of user engagement and usability metrics [90] - A Deep Convolutional Neural Network (DCNN) is proposed to exploit the benefits of recognizing hand gestures [58]
3	NLP	- Chatbot (text) & Voice Agents (verbal) [73]
4	Sentiment Analysis (SA)	- NLP algorithm. For example, analyzing product reviews or answering questions automatically [84]

In addition, themes related to the literature review conducted (e.g. real world, uncertainty, cognition mentioned in e.g. [39]) and sources of the initial themes (AI/ML/DL) were discussed and supplemented by further literature searches to gain a deeper insight into the interrelationships for further discussion.

6 Comparison (Analysis Process)

The following are considerations based on the theoretical findings of the literature review on how to incorporate AI into design criteria considerations, together with additional literature review on topics found in the initial literature review.

6.1 Pre-Considerations Incorporating AI into Design Criteria

Real-World Factors and Unpredictability. This could cause users to lose confidence in AI-based UIs (as seen in works such as [10, 34, 35, 45]). Knowledge-based methods for automatically generating UIs for specific types of applications are important as stated e.g. by [26, 44, 68, 93, 98]. However, when it comes to implementing AI techniques and algorithms, the design of human-centered explanatory interfaces remains a significant challenge. In this context, the ability to convey algorithmic decision-making processes to humans becomes crucial, as demonstrated in studies such as [16, 43, 53, 87]. Another aspect is the cultural background of the users, as mentioned by [41, 50, 62, 63], as well as privacy and security issues, such as those mentioned by [72, 94, 95] and social responsibility in AI-based systems e.g. [13, 14].

Predictions and Historical Data. When it comes to generating predictions or recommendations based on historical data and patterns derived from past user behavior (as discussed in works such as [40]), this aspect presents significant challenges. According to [40] and others, the potential problems arise when study designs do not accurately reflect real-world scenarios, particularly in high-stakes domains where decisions made by AI systems can have significant consequences [54, 98, 100]. It is crucial that users retain control over such decision-making processes and have the right to appeal if they do not fully understand a system's decision (as highlighted in studies such as [54, 98, 100]). Ensuring that human intervention remains possible and that transparent explanations are provided when necessary [4] should address these challenges and support user trust in AI-based UIs [25].

Training Data. When considering the use of training data in AI-based systems, it is important to recognize that changes that occur in the real world can potentially lead to model failure over time. As these technologies continue to evolve and advance (as seen in studies such as [21, 69, 101]), it is crucial to examine how changes in training data and algorithms affect the behavior of AI systems throughout their lifecycle [20]. Monitoring and adapting AI-based systems accordingly is necessary to ensure that they remain effective and reliable e.g. [17, 48].

Mitigating Bias. When discussing bias in ML systems, it is important to consider strategies to mitigate these biases and ensure that predictions and recommendations do not lead to discriminatory outcomes. As shown in studies such as [59, 75, 94, 102], various analysis and optimization techniques have been explored to promote fairness in AI decision making. Implementing these approaches to addressing bias in ML systems should help to ensure that technologies are fairer, more accountable e.g. [55, 80] and more trustworthy for all users e.g. [77, 94].

6.2 Design Criteria to Consider When Integrating AI into UI Design

Based on considerations from the literature review conducted, several components interact to influence the inclusion of AI in UI design criteria and can be summarized and derived as follows:

1. Real World/Uncertainty (e.g. context & human factors)
2. Usage Pattern (e.g. individual behavior & tailored preferences)
3. Design Logic (e.g. AI methods & algorithms, training data)
4. Challenges (e.g. explanation, trust, transparency, fairness, intuitive UIs)

The first is the real world and uncertainty, where context and human factors affect the UI. This is where design logic, AI methods and algorithms come in. When interacting with UIs, there are user usage patterns with individual behavior and tailor-made preferences and challenges that should be considered when generating output.

Reality vs. Assumption. While it may seem logical for a system to make predictions or recommendations based on historical data and patterns, these assumptions may not always match the complexity of real-world scenarios (the "model" is based on different evaluation factors than what should actually be used). For example, an AI-based recommendation system that relies solely on past user behavior may not take into account external influences or personal growth, leading to less relevant suggestions over time.

Real-World Factors vs. Explanatory Interfaces. In the area of AI-based UIs, challenges arise from the uncertainties of the real world and the transparency with which these systems operate, which can potentially reduce user trust in such systems.

Assumption vs. Reality. The results generated by AI systems are not always what users expect, but a logical conclusion based on the available data and the algorithms used in their training. This may be because these systems make decisions or predictions by analyzing patterns from past events and user interactions. While this approach may work well for certain scenarios, it may fail to account for unforeseen circumstances or changes in a user's preferences over time.

Personalization vs. Standardization. One of the factors that distinguishes an AI-based UI from a real-world user is the way in which it follows specific knowledge-based methods and algorithms. While some UIs are designed for personalization, responding to individual preferences and needs, others rely on standardized approaches that may not take into account unique user characteristics. This difference can lead to a mismatch between what a system offers and what an actual user might expect or require from their experience (systems follow the underlying AI methods and algorithms, which may vary from person to person).

Database vs. Diversity. Another concern with AI-driven systems is the potential presence of bias in the data collection and training processes. This can lead to biased results, as algorithms learn from datasets that may not accurately represent the full range of human experiences or perspectives.

7 Conclusion and Outlook

In summary, based on the three RQs presented at the beginning, the research, which is based on a reflection on how to incorporate AI into design considerations, has uncovered issues that there is a need to extend or add new principles to established ones. As AI permeates various aspects of daily life through interactive software applications, it is crucial to develop guidelines or design principles that ensure these systems provide a positive UX, while ensuring reliability, usability, understandability and comprehensibility in line with user needs and preferences. The results highlight the importance of understanding fundamental aspects of human-AI collaboration [97], including the inclusion of trust-building measures such as explainability e.g. [10, 35, 80], transparency e.g. [24, 74, 97] or trustworthiness e.g. [81, 94] in the design criteria of AI systems. By creating intuitive and transparent UIs that explain how AI systems work, it is possible to increase user confidence in these technologies [97].

The need to evaluate system performance from both a quantitative (e.g. accuracy) [86, 97] and qualitative (e.g. perceived ease of use or satisfaction) [54, 79, 90] perspective should also be considered, as this provides a more comprehensive understanding of users' experiences with AI-based systems. The consideration of ethical issues [89] has been identified as an important aspect in the development of AI-based systems, as well as cultural [41, 50, 62], privacy and security concerns e.g. [72, 94, 95], fairness [77, 94], accountable e.g. [55, 80] or social responsibility e.g. [13, 14] and diversity [37]. These are critical for ensuring user rights and values are respected in interactions with these technologies.

7.1 Outlook

The next step is to conduct an in-depth review of the topic, with the aim of applying in particular the established principles to AI-based UIs in order to condense the formulation of the derived considerations into usability design principles. On this basis, the considerations can be refined and optimized.

7.2 Limitations

The focus of the study is mainly on AI systems that involve direct interaction, such as recommendation systems. This may limit the generalizability of the findings to other types of AI-based systems or interactions with users, although it provides a specific context and scope for analysis. There is an inherent subjective element in assessing design criteria based on user experience, usability and UX, as these aspects are highly dependent on individual preferences and contexts. Therefore, it can be difficult to objectively compare different approaches to the development of AI-enabled systems, or to identify clear limitations arising from the above analytical approaches. In addition, due to the rapid development of AI technologies, research focusing on their integration into design criteria needs to be regularly updated to reflect current advances in the field and to ensure that the results remain relevant and applicable. The review was conducted as a theoretical literature review and has a lack of quantitative evidence, which hinders a comprehensive assessment of the limitations of AI integration in design criteria analysis. The list in Sect. 6 with the comparison represents a current state of the discussion based on the literature review and will be iteratively reviewed and possibly expanded in future research, which is why it should not be considered exhaustive.

Disclosure of Interests. The author has no competing interests to declare that are relevant to the content of this article.

References

1. Adebesin, F., et al.: The complementary role of two evaluation methods in the usability and accessibility evaluation of a non-standard system. In: Proceedings of the 2010 Annual Research Conference of the South African Institute of Computer Scientists and Information Technologists, pp. 1–11. ACM, Bela Bela South Africa (2010). https://doi.org/10.1145/189 9503.1899504.

2. Alkatheiri, M.S.: Artificial intelligence assisted improved human-computer interactions for computer systems. Comput. Electr. Eng.. Electr. Eng. **101**, 107950 (2022). https://doi.org/ 10.1016/j.compeleceng.2022.107950

3. Allouch, M., et al.: Conversational agents: goals, technologies, vision and challenges. Sensors **21**(24), 8448 (2021)

4. Almada, M.: Human intervention in automated decision-making: toward the construction of contestable systems. In: Proceedings of the Seventeenth International Conference on Artificial Intelligence and Law, pp. 2–11. ACM, Montreal QC Canada (2019). https://doi.org/10.1145/3322640.3326699.

5. Arhippainen, L., Tähti, M.: Empirical evaluation of user experience in two adaptive mobile application prototypes. In: Proceedings of the 2nd International Conference on Mobile and Ubiquitous Multimedia, pp. 27–34 (2003).

6. Badashian, A.S., et al.: Fundamental usability guidelines for user interface design. In: 2008 International Conference on Computational Sciences and Its Applications, pp. 106–113. IEEE, Perugia (2008). https://doi.org/10.1109/ICCSA.2008.45.

7. Bakaev, M., Heil, S., Chirkov, L., Gaedke, M.: Benchmarking neural networks-based approaches for predicting visual perception of user interfaces. In: Degen, H., Ntoa, S. (eds.) Artificial Intelligence in HCI: 3rd International Conference, AI-HCI 2022, Held as Part of the 24th HCI International Conference, HCII 2022, Virtual Event, June 26 – July 1, 2022, Proceedings, pp. 217–231. Springer International Publishing, Cham (2022). https://doi.org/10.1007/978-3-031-05643-7_14

8. Bavaresco, R., et al.: Conversational agents in business: a systematic literature review and future research directions. Comput. Sci. Rev. **36**, 100239 (2020). https://doi.org/10.1016/j.cosrev.2020.100239

9. Benyon, D.: Designing Interactive Systems: A Comprehensive Guide to HCI and Interaction Design. Pearson, Boston (2013)

10. Bhatt, U., et al.: Uncertainty as a form of transparency: measuring, communicating, and using uncertainty. In: Proceedings of the 2021 AAAI/ACM Conference on AI, Ethics, and Society, pp. 401–413. ACM, Virtual Event USA (2021). https://doi.org/10.1145/3461702.3462571.

11. Borsci, S., et al.: The Chatbot usability scale: the design and pilot of a usability scale for interaction with AI-based conversational agents. Pers. Ubiquit. Comput. Ubiquit. Comput. **26**, 95–119 (2022)

12. Brajnik, G.: Beyond conformance: the role of accessibility evaluation methods. In: Hartmann, S., Zhou, X., Kirchberg, M. (eds.) Web Information Systems Engineering – WISE 2008 Workshops, pp. 63–80. Springer Berlin Heidelberg, Berlin, Heidelberg (2008). https://doi.org/10.1007/978-3-540-85200-1_9

13. Chang, Y.-L., Ke, J.: Socially responsible artificial intelligence empowered people analytics: a novel framework towards sustainability. Hum. Resour. Dev. Rev.Resour. Dev. Rev. **23**(1), 88–120 (2024). https://doi.org/10.1177/15344843231200930

14. Cheng, L., Varshney, K.R., Liu, H.: Socially responsible AI algorithms: issues, purposes, and challenges. J. Artif. Intell. Res.Artif. Intell. Res. **71**, 1137–1181 (2021). https://doi.org/10.1613/jair.1.12814

15. Chew, H.S.J.: The use of artificial intelligence–based conversational agents (Chatbots) for weight loss: scoping review and practical recommendations. JMIR Med. Inf. **10**(4), e32578 (2022)

16. Mark Chignell, L., Wang, A.Z., Li, J.: The evolution of HCI and human factors: integrating human and artificial intelligence. ACM Trans. Comput. Hum. Interact. **30**(2), 1–30 (2023). https://doi.org/10.1145/3557891

17. Davahli, M.R., Karwowski, W., Fiok, K., Wan, T., Parsaei, H.R.: Controlling safety of artificial intelligence-based systems in healthcare. Symmetry **13**(1), 102 (2021). https://doi.org/10.3390/sym13010102

18. Laura, M., et al.: Preliminary results of a systematic review: quality assessment of conversational agents (Chatbots) for people with disabilities or special needs. In: Miesenberger, K., Manduchi, R., Rodriguez, M.C., Peňáz, P. (eds.) Computers Helping People with Special Needs: 17th International Conference, ICCHP 2020, Lecco, Italy, September 9–11, 2020, Proceedings, Part I, pp. 250–257. Springer International Publishing, Cham (2020). https://doi.org/10.1007/978-3-030-58796-3_30

19. De Kock, E., et al.: Usability evaluation methods: mind the gaps. In: Proceedings of the 2009 Annual Research Conference of the South African Institute of Computer Scientists and Information Technologists, pp. 122–131. ACM, Vanderbijlpark Emfuleni South Africa (2009). https://doi.org/10.1145/1632149.1632166.

20. De Silva, D., Alahakoon, D.: An artificial intelligence life cycle: from conception to production. Patterns 3(6), 100489 (2022). https://doi.org/10.1016/j.patter.2022.100489

21. Desmond, M., et al.: Increasing the speed and accuracy of data labeling through an AI assisted interface. In: 26th International Conference on Intelligent User Interfaces, pp. 392–401. ACM, College Station TX USA (2021). https://doi.org/10.1145/3397481.3450698.

22. Díaz-Oreiro, I., et al.: Standardized questionnaires for user experience evaluation: a systematic literature review. Proceedings 31, 14 (2019).

23. Din, E.: Ergonomics of human-system interaction - Part 110: Interaction principles (ISO 9241–110:2020) (2020).

24. Felzmann, H., et al.: Transparency you can trust: transparency requirements for artificial intelligence between legal norms and contextual concerns. Big Data Soc. 6(1), 205395171986054 (2019). https://doi.org/10.1177/2053951719860542

25. Ferrario, A., et al.: In AI we trust incrementally: a multi-layer model of trust to analyze human-artificial intelligence interactions. Philos. Technol. 33(3), 523–539 (2020). https://doi.org/10.1007/s13347-019-00378-3

26. Fischer, G., et al.: Critics: an emerging approach to knowledge-based human-computer interaction. Int. J. Man Mach. Stud. 35(5), 695–721 (1991). https://doi.org/10.1016/S0020-7373(05)80184-1

27. Forlizzi, J., Battarbee, K.: Understanding experience in interactive systems. In: Proceedings of the 5th Conference on Designing Interactive Systems: Processes, Practices, Methods, and Techniques, pp. 261–268. ACM, Cambridge MA USA (2004). https://doi.org/10.1145/1013115.1013152.

28. Gurcan, F., et al.: Mapping human-computer interaction research themes and trends from its existence to today: a topic modeling-based review of past 60 years. Int. J. Hum. Comput. Interact.Comput. Interact. 37(3), 267–280 (2021). https://doi.org/10.1080/10447318.2020.1819668

29. Hanington, B., Martin, B.: The pocket universal methods of design: 100 ways to research complex problems, develop innovative ideas and design effective solutions. Rockport (2017).

30. Huseynov, F.: Chatbots in digital marketing: enhanced customer experience and reduced customer service costs. In: Munna, A.S., Shaikh, M.S.I., Kazi, B.U. (eds.) Contemporary Approaches of Digital Marketing and the Role of Machine Intelligence, pp. 46–72. IGI Global (2023). https://doi.org/10.4018/978-1-6684-7735-9.ch003

31. Hussain, S., Ameri Sianaki, O., Ababneh, N.: A survey on conversational agents/chatbots classification and design techniques. In: Barolli, L., Takizawa, M., Xhafa, F., Enokido, T. (eds.) WAINA 2019. AISC, vol. 927, pp. 946–956. Springer, Cham (2019). https://doi.org/10.1007/978-3-030-15035-8_93

32. Issa, T., Isaias, P.: Sustainable Design: HCI, Usability and Environmental Concerns. Springer London, London (2022). https://doi.org/10.1007/978-1-4471-7513-1

33. Issa, T., Isaias, P.: Usability and human–computer interaction (HCI). In: Issa, T., Isaias, P. (eds.) Sustainable Design: HCI, Usability and Environmental Concerns, pp. 23–40. Springer London, London (2022). https://doi.org/10.1007/978-1-4471-7513-1_2

34. Jegham, I., et al.: Vision-based human action recognition: an overview and real world challenges. Forensic Sci. Int. Digit. Invest. **32**, 200901 (2020). https://doi.org/10.1016/j.fsidi.2019.200901

35. Jiang, J., et al.: Who needs explanation and when? Juggling explainable AI and user epistemic uncertainty. Int. J. Hum. Comput. Stud.Comput. Stud. **165**, 102839 (2022). https://doi.org/10.1016/j.ijhcs.2022.102839

36. Koelle, M., et al.: Social Acceptability in HCI: a survey of methods, measures, and design strategies. In: Proceedings of the 2020 CHI Conference on Human Factors in Computing Systems, pp. 1–19. ACM, Honolulu HI USA (2020). https://doi.org/10.1145/3313831.3376162.

37. Kujala, S., Kauppinen, M.: Identifying and selecting users for user-centered design. In: Proceedings of the Third Nordic Conference on Human-Computer Interaction, pp. 297–303. ACM, Tampere Finland (2004). https://doi.org/10.1145/1028014.1028060.

38. Kulkarni, P., et al.: Conversational AI: an overview of methodologies, applications & future scope. In: 2019 5th International Conference On Computing, Communication, Control And Automation (ICCUBEA), pp. 1–7. IEEE (2019).

39. Kumar, S., et al.: Cognitive Behavior and Human Computer Interaction Based on Machine Learning Algorithms. Wiley (2021)

40. Lai, V., et al.: Towards a science of human-AI decision making: a survey of empirical studies. http://arxiv.org/abs/2112.11471 (2021).

41. Lee, K., Joshi, K.: Understanding the role of cultural context and user interaction in artificial intelligence based systems. J. Global Inf. Technol. Manage. **23**(3), 171–175 (2020). https://doi.org/10.1080/1097198X.2020.1794131

42. Lewis, J.R., Sauro, J.: Usability and user experience: design and evaluation. In: Salvendy, G., Karwowski, W. (eds.) Handbook of Human Factors and Ergonomics, pp. 972–1015. Wiley (2021). https://doi.org/10.1002/9781119636113.ch38

43. Li, Y., et al.: Artificial intelligence for HCI: a modern approach. In: Extended Abstracts of the 2020 CHI Conference on Human Factors in Computing Systems, pp. 1–8. ACM, Honolulu HI USA (2020). https://doi.org/10.1145/3334480.3375147.

44. Libório, A., et al.: Interface Design through Knowledge-Based Systems: An Approach Centered on Explanations from Problem-Solving Models. In: Proceedings of the 4th international Workshop on Task Models and Diagrams, pp. 127–134 (2005).

45. Lim, B.Y., Dey, A.K.: Investigating intelligibility for uncertain context-aware applications. In: Proceedings of the 13th international conference on Ubiquitous computing, pp. 415–424. ACM, Beijing China (2011). https://doi.org/10.1145/2030112.2030168.

46. MacKenzie, I.S.: User studies and usability evaluations: from research to products. In: Graphics Interface, pp. 1–8 (2015).

47. Malodia, S., et al.: Why do people use artificial intelligence (AI)-enabled voice assistants? IEEE Trans. Eng. Manage. **71**, 491–505 (2024). https://doi.org/10.1109/TEM.2021.3117884

48. Martínez-Fernández, S., Franch, X., Jedlitschka, A., Oriol, M., Trendowicz, A.: Developing and Operating Artificial Intelligence Models in Trustworthy Autonomous Systems. In: Cherfi, S., Perini, A., Nurcan, S. (eds.) RCIS 2021. LNBIP, vol. 415, pp. 221–229. Springer, Cham (2021). https://doi.org/10.1007/978-3-030-75018-3_14

49. Mazumder, F.K., Das, U.K.: Usability guidelines for usable user interface. Int. J. Res. Eng. Technol. **3**(9), 79–82 (2014)

50. Miraz, M., et al.: Cross-cultural usability evaluation of AI-based adaptive user interface for mobile applications. Acta Sci Technol. **44**, e61112 (2022). https://doi.org/10.4025/actascitechnol.v44i1.61112

51. Morris, M.R.: AI and accessibility. Commun. ACM. ACM **63**(6), 35–37 (2020). https://doi.org/10.1145/3356727

52. Motger, Q., et al.: Software-based dialogue systems: survey, taxonomy, and challenges. ACM Comput. Surv.Comput. Surv. **55**(5), 1–42 (2023). https://doi.org/10.1145/3527450

53. Mucha, H., et al.: Interfaces for explanations in human-AI interaction: proposing a design evaluation approach. In: Extended Abstracts of the 2021 CHI Conference on Human Factors in Computing Systems, pp. 1–6. ACM, Yokohama Japan (2021). https://doi.org/10.1145/341 1763.3451759.

54. Namoun, A., et al.: Web design scraping: enabling factors, opportunities and research directions. In: 2020 12th International Conference on Information Technology and Electrical Engineering (ICITEE), pp. 104–109. IEEE, Yogyakarta, Indonesia (2020). https://doi.org/10.1109/ICITEE49829.2020.9271770.

55. Nassar, A., Kamal, M.: Ethical dilemmas in AI-powered decision- making: a deep dive into big data-driven ethical considerations. Int. J. Responsible Artif. Intell. **11**(8), 1–11 (2021)

56. Nielsen, J.: Enhancing the explanatory power of usability heuristics. In: Proceedings of the SIGCHI conference on Human Factors in Computing Systems, pp. 152–158 (1994).

57. Nielsen, J., Molich, R.: Heuristic evaluation of user interfaces. In: Proceedings of the SIGCHI Conference on Human Factors in Computing Systems, pp. 249–256 (1990).

58. Niranjani, V., et al.: System application control based on hand gesture using deep learning. In: 2021 7th International Conference on Advanced Computing and Communication Systems (ICACCS), pp. 1644–1649. IEEE, Coimbatore, India (2021). https://doi.org/10.1109/ICACCS51430.2021.9441732.

59. Ntoutsi, E., et al.: Bias in data-driven artificial intelligence systems—an introductory survey. WIREs Data Min. Knowl. Discov. **10**(3), e1356 (2020). https://doi.org/10.1002/widm.1356

60. Petrie, H., Bevan, N.: The evaluation of accessibility, usability, and user experience. Univ. Access Handb. **1**, 1–16 (2009)

61. Portugal, I., et al.: The use of machine learning algorithms in recommender systems: a systematic review. Expert Syst. Appl. **97**, 205–227 (2018)

62. Prabhakaran, V., et al.: Cultural incongruencies in artificial intelligence. http://arxiv.org/abs/2211.13069 (2022).

63. Reinecke, K.: Automatic adaptation of user interfaces to cultural preferences. Inf. Technol. **54**(2), 96–100 (2012). https://doi.org/10.1524/itit.2012.0669

64. Ren, R., et al.: Experimentation for chatbot usability evaluation: a secondary study. IEEE Access. **10**, 12430–12464 (2022)

65. Robert, J.M., Lesage, A.: From usability to user experience with interactive systems. In: Boy, G.A. (ed.) The Handbook of Human-Machine Interaction: A Human-Centered Design Approach, pp. 303–320. CRC Press (2017). https://doi.org/10.1201/9781315557380-15

66. Ruane, E., et al.: Conversational AI: social and ethical considerations. In: AICS, pp. 104–115 (2019).

67. Ruiz, J., et al.: Unifying functional user interface design principles. Int. J. Hum. Comput. Interact.Comput. Interact. **37**(1), 47–67 (2021). https://doi.org/10.1080/10447318.2020.180 5876.

68. Saeed, W., Omlin, C.: Explainable AI (XAI): a systematic meta-survey of current challenges and future opportunities. Knowl.-Based Syst..-Based Syst. **263**, 110273 (2023). https://doi.org/10.1016/j.knosys.2023.110273

69. Sambasivan, N., et al.: "Everyone wants to do the model work, not the data work": data cascades in high-stakes AI. In: Proceedings of the 2021 CHI Conference on Human Factors in Computing Systems, pp. 1–15. ACM, Yokohama Japan (2021). https://doi.org/10.1145/3411764.3445518.

70. Sauer, J., et al.: The influence of user expertise and prototype fidelity in usability tests. Appl. Ergon. **41**(1), 130–140 (2010)

71. Sauer, J., et al.: Usability, user experience and accessibility: towards an integrative model. Ergonomics **63**(10), 1207–1220 (2020). https://doi.org/10.1080/00140139.2020.1774080

72. Liyakat, K.S.S., Liyakat, K.K.S.: Electronics with artificial intelligence creating a smarter future: a review. J. Commun. Eng. Innovations **9**, 38–42 (2023). https://doi.org/10.46610/JOCEI.2023.v09i03.005

73. Schmidt, A., et al.: Introduction to intelligent user interfaces. In: Extended Abstracts of the 2021 CHI Conference on Human Factors in Computing Systems, pp. 1–4. ACM, Yokohama Japan (2021). https://doi.org/10.1145/3411763.3445021.

74. Schmidt, P., et al.: Transparency and trust in artificial intelligence systems. J. Decis. Syst.Decis. Syst. **29**(4), 260–278 (2020)

75. Schwartz, R., et al.: Towards a Standard for Identifying and Managing Bias in Artificial Intelligence. National Institute of Standards and Technology (U.S.), Gaithersburg, MD (2022). https://doi.org/10.6028/NIST.SP.1270.

76. Sears, A.: Heuristic walkthroughs: finding the problems without the noise. Int. J. Hum. Comput. Interact.Comput. Interact. **9**(3), 213–234 (1997)

77. Serban, A., et al.: Practices for engineering trustworthy machine learning applications. In: 2021 IEEE/ACM 1st Workshop on AI Engineering - Software Engineering for AI (WAIN), pp. 97–100. IEEE, Madrid, Spain (2021). https://doi.org/10.1109/WAIN52551.2021.00021.

78. Sharma, R.S., et al.: Designing recommendation or suggestion systems: looking to the future. Electron. Markets. **31**, 243–252 (2021)

79. Shin, D., et al.: Beyond user experience: what constitutes algorithmic experiences? Int. J. Inf. Manage. **52**, 102061 (2020). https://doi.org/10.1016/j.ijinfomgt.2019.102061

80. Shin, D.: User perceptions of algorithmic decisions in the personalized AI system: perceptual evaluation of fairness, accountability, transparency, and explainability. J. Broadcast. Electron. Media **64**(4), 541–565 (2020). https://doi.org/10.1080/08838151.2020.1843357

81. Shneiderman, B.: Bridging the gap between ethics and practice: guidelines for reliable, safe, and trustworthy human-centered AI systems. ACM Trans. Interact. Intell. Syst. **10**(4), 1–31 (2020). https://doi.org/10.1145/3419764

82. Shneiderman, B., et al.: Designing the User Interface: Strategies for Effective Human-Computer Interaction. Pearson (2016).

83. Singh, S., Beniwal, H.: A survey on near-human conversational agents. J. King Saud Univ. Comput. Inf. Sci. **34**(10), 8852–8866 (2022). https://doi.org/10.1016/j.jksuci.2021.10.013

84. Singh, S., Kaur, H.: Comparative sentiment analysis through traditional and machine learning-based approach. In: Kumar, S., Raja, R., Tiwari, S., Rani, S. (eds.) Cognitive Behavior and Human Computer Interaction Based on Machine Learning Algorithm, pp. 315–338. Wiley (2021). https://doi.org/10.1002/9781119792109.ch14

85. Sivakumar, N. et al.: Design and analysis of human computer interaction using AI intelligence. In: 2023 International Conference on Disruptive Technologies (ICDT), pp. 195–198. IEEE, Greater Noida, India (2023). https://doi.org/10.1109/ICDT57929.2023.10150705.

86. Sivakumar, N., et al.: Design and analysis of human computer interaction using AI intelligence. In: 2023 International Conference on Disruptive Technologies (ICDT) (2023).

87. Song, Y., Wu, R.: Analysing human-computer interaction behaviour in human resource management system based on artificial intelligence technology. Knowl. Manage. Res. Pract. 1–10 (2021). https://doi.org/10.1080/14778238.2021.1955630.

88. Šumak, B., Brdnik, S., Pušnik, M.: Sensors and artificial intelligence methods and algorithms for human–computer intelligent interaction: a systematic mapping study. Sensors **22**(1), 20 (2021). https://doi.org/10.3390/s22010020

89. Tarafdar, M., et al.: Seeking ethical use of AI algorithms: challenges and mitigations. In: Proceedings of the 41th International Conference on Information Systems (2020).

90. Thangarasu, G., Rao Alla, K.: Investing novel interaction techniques using DeepNets to improve user engagement and usability in human-computer interfaces. In: 2023 Second International Conference on Smart Technologies for Smart Nation (SmartTechCon), pp. 1168–1172. IEEE, Singapore (2023). https://doi.org/10.1109/SmartTechCon57526.2023.10391492.

91. Tracy, S.J.: Qualitative Research Methods: Collecting Evidence, Crafting Analysis, Communicating Impact. Wiley (2019).

92. Troussas, C., et al.: Harnessing the power of user-centric artificial intelligence: customized recommendations and personalization in hybrid recommender systems. Computers **12**(5), 109 (2023)

93. Vanderdonckt, J.: Knowledge-based systems for automated user interface generation: the trident experience. In: Proceedings of the CHI (1995).

94. Varona, D., Suárez, J.L.: Discrimination, bias, fairness, and trustworthy AI. Appl. Sci. **12**(12), 5826 (2022). https://doi.org/10.3390/app12125826

95. Villegas-Ch, W., García-Ortiz, J.: Toward a comprehensive framework for ensuring security and privacy in artificial intelligence. Electronics **12**(18), 3786 (2023). https://doi.org/10.3390/electronics12183786

96. Völkel, S.T., et al.: What is "intelligent" in intelligent user interfaces? A meta-analysis of 25 years of IUI. In: Proceedings of the 25th International Conference on Intelligent User Interfaces, pp. 477–487. ACM, Cagliari Italy (2020). https://doi.org/10.1145/3377325.3377500.

97. Vössing, M., et al.: Designing transparency for effective human-AI collaboration. Inf. Syst. Front. **24**(3), 877–895 (2022). https://doi.org/10.1007/s10796-022-10284-3

98. Vultureanu-Albişi, A., Bădică, C.: Recommender systems: an explainable AI perspective. In: 2021 International Conference on INnovations in Intelligent SysTems and Applications (INISTA), pp. 1–6. IEEE (2021).

99. Smith, J.W., Furxhi, O., Torlak, M.: An FCNN-based super-resolution mmwave radar framework for contactless musical instrument interface. IEEE Trans. Multimedia **24**, 2315–2328 (2022). https://doi.org/10.1109/TMM.2021.3079695

100. Walmsley, J.: Artificial intelligence and the value of transparency. AI Soc. **36**(2), 585–595 (2021). https://doi.org/10.1007/s00146-020-01066-z

101. Xu, W., et al.: Transitioning to human interaction with AI systems: new challenges and opportunities for HCI professionals to enable human-centered AI. Int. J. Hum. Comput. Interact.Comput. Interact. **39**(3), 494–518 (2023). https://doi.org/10.1080/10447318.2022.2041900

102. Yang, Q., et al.: Re-examining whether, why, and how human-AI interaction is uniquely difficult to design. In: Proceedings of the 2020 CHI Conference on Human Factors in Computing Systems, pp. 1–13. ACM, Honolulu HI USA (2020). https://doi.org/10.1145/3313831.3376301.

103. Zhang, Q., et al.: Artificial intelligence in recommender systems. Complex Intell. Syst. **7**, 439–457 (2021)

Multimodal Interfaces for Emotion Recognition: Models, Challenges and Opportunities

Danilo Greco[1]([✉])[iD], Paola Barra[2][iD], Lorenzo D'Errico[3][iD],
and Mariacarla Staffa[2][iD]

[1] Politecnico di Milano, Milan, Italy
danilo.greco@uniparthenope.it
[2] University of Naples "Parthenope", Naples, Italy
paola.barra@uniparthenope.it, mariacarla.staffa@uniparthenope.it
[3] University of Naples "Federico II", Naples, Italy
lorenzo.derrico@unina.it

Abstract. Emotional investigation has generated remarkable fascination, resulting in meticulous research with significant implications. In contrast to more comprehensive methods, which take into account multiple channels of emotion detection, traditional techniques often struggle to accommodate complex scenarios and diverse user groups due to their narrow focus. The expanding requirement for integrated emotional evaluation strategies, drawing on disparate sensory sources, can be linked to this upsurge. A comprehensive review of the progression, available choices, and outstanding concerns about multimodal emotion understanding is offered through this research. Investigating the most frequently utilized language modes, we evaluate their capacity to transmit sentiments and any inherent restrictions. Examining methods for combining diverse modalities reveals mysterious relationships between flexibility, nuance, and output. By exploring the varied uses of multi-modal emotion analysis, we demonstrate its inherent advantage over singular techniques. After carefully analyzing the key issues associated with emotional stability, persistent oscillations, and theoretical frameworks, and interpreting meaningful discoveries, we investigate the potential for further research on multi-modal emotion identification.

Keywords: Emotion recognition · Multimodal interfaces · Affective computing · Signal processing

1 Introduction

Emotion recognition is an increasingly dynamic field focusing on the creation of machines that can naturally recognize and respond to human emotions as depicted in [5]. Sophisticated automated emotion detection has become a crucial ability for seamless communication between humans and machines, with practical applications ranging from user interfaces to medical technology to entertainment and more. Reliably inferring emotions from the multitude of behavioural,

© The Author(s), under exclusive license to Springer Nature Switzerland AG 2024
H. Degen and S. Ntoa (Eds.): HCII 2024, LNAI 14735, pp. 152–162, 2024.
https://doi.org/10.1007/978-3-031-60611-3_11

speech, textual and physiological signals humans use to convey internal state remains a difficult challenge. Initial studies centred on isolating and processing singular types of sensory inputs to identify emotional responses. Let us assume that we are discussing facial expression recognition. This technology depends on pictures or videos of facial muscle movements, skin transformations, and eye fixations to identify emotions such as happiness, depression, outrage, etc., as per [25]. Acoustic attributes are identified by the technique to ascertain the emotional state from spoken samples. This technique seeks to identify emotional tone through examination of words and language structures. Though sometimes providing useful affective information, unimodal methods suffer from several key limitations. Without the ability to integrate information through multiple senses, they struggle to address uncertainty and validate assumptions. A furrowed brow could indicate frustration, confusion, or concentration based on the integrated scenario. Unimodal systems also have consistency issues across contexts like age, gender, culture and environment. These factors make generalized emotion modelling difficult with single modalities. To overcome these limitations, there is growing interest in multimodal emotion recognition systems that fuse two or more sensory channels to enable more accurate and universal emotion understanding [18]. Multimodal interfaces commonly integrate visual, vocal, linguistic and physiological cues to better approximate the rich perceptual experience of human emotion and its expression. Each modality provides complementary information - facial expressions reveal instant affective reactions, vocal tone conveys inner feelings, word choice provides emotional valence, and physiological signals indicate arousal. Fusing these diverse signal types aims to mitigate the deficiencies of any single channel for more holistic emotion recognition. Several key research challenges arise in effectively combining disparate modalities for robust multimodal emotion recognition. Heterogeneous data types with different spatiotemporal characteristics need to be synchronized and represented in a shared feature space amenable for fusion [18]. Designing optimal neural architectures to model inter-modal dynamics and dependencies is an open area of investigation. Incorporating commonsense reasoning and contextual knowledge about how emotions arise and are displayed in varying scenarios, relationships and dialogue settings remain difficult [24]. Ensuring transparency, fairness and reliability of multimodal emotion recognition for real-world adoption, especially in sensitive applications like health care, is also crucial [20]. Rapid advances in sensing capabilities, representation learning frameworks like deep neural networks, contextual modelling techniques, and affective computing methods have opened up new opportunities for advancing multimodal emotion recognition research [24]. As interaction paradigms move beyond screens towards ambient interfaces, augmented reality, and ubiquitous computing, the ability for systems to implicitly sense and respond appropriately to human emotion through contextual multisensory understanding will become increasingly critical [17]. This survey aims to provide a comprehensive overview of the emerging field of multimodal emotion recognition. We discuss commonly used modalities and their effect encoding capabilities, analyze different fusion approaches, present key applications, and outline open research challenges. Our goal is to synthesize progress to date across this multifaceted area and highlight promising directions to inspire future interdisciplinary research towards generalizable, ethical and trustworthy multimodal emotion recognition technologies with transformative societal impact.

2 Modalities for Emotion Recognition

Here, we investigate the diverse methods by which emotions are transmitted via the senses. We consolidate each medium's emotive details and evaluate their pros and cons. The three primary modalities considered are:

- *Visual Modalities.* Facial features, posture, and hand movements serve as valuable signs for determining emotions. The Facial Action Coding System (FACS) is utilized to identify the various emotional states expressed through minuscule facial gestures and visual modifications to the skin. Spontaneous vs. posed expressions and subtle microexpressions can indicate the genuineness of detected emotions. Body posture, shoulder position and hand gestures also reveal affective states like engagement, boredom, confidence, etc. Computer vision techniques are applied to automatically analyze visual behaviour based on facial landmarks, action units, eye gaze, body pose, and motion features [20]. The integration of CNNs and deep learning algorithms has given rise to exceptional accuracy in detecting emotions and actions, as verified by [9]. Visual signs hold significant emotional significance; however, their impact can be hindered in natural settings due to individual variations in expression styles, native aptitude towards emotional expression, and local regulations. Leveraging only visual information can thus limit the applicability of AI models across diverse settings and populations;
- *Vocal Modalities.* The vocal characteristics of humans, especially when speaking, are rich in emotional indicators that can be deciphered through variations in pitch, volume, tone, and other aspects. Key elements of speech, including pitch, energy, and tempo, have been examined extensively as markers of present emotional conditions. These non-linguistic vocalizations convey emotions through their distinct sounds. Automatic emotion recognition from voice uses audio processing and machine learning on acoustic features related to prosody, spectrum, and cepstral coefficients to classify emotions. Deep neural architectures, incorporating convolutional and recurrent components, have exhibited remarkable capabilities in speech emotion recognition [4]. Limited to voice-based inputs, the emotion detection system faces constraints. Language-based limitations impact the integrity of spoken communication. Cultural and dialect variations can obscure inferences. Voluntary control and social masking of vocal expressions may hide the true underlying effect. Using only vocal analysis can therefore suffer from ambiguity in interpreting emotions;
- *Physiological Modalities.* Internal autonomic nervous system parameters, such as heart rate, breathing, skin sensitivity, brain wave activity, and hormone levels, serve as markers of emotional stimulation and importance [17]. Think

about it: elevated heart rates and increased skin conductance are connected to emotional states like anger or anxiety, whereas slower and more controlled breathing patterns point towards feelings of calmness. These cutting-edge imaging tools help uncover the neural mechanisms associated with distinct cognitive conditions, distraction or frustration. These devices provide real-time monitoring of multiple physiological markers, whose data is processed using signal analysis and machine learning to anticipate emotional responses [14,22]. To demonstrate, these two signal types have been employed in studies to measure stress levels. This innovative technology allows for continuous monitoring of mental acuity [12]. Outside forces cannot affect the automatic display of emotional responses. Even though they are there, these sensors may become frustrating and tricky to interpret, with difficulty distinguishing delicate feelings. Limiting oneself to physiological markers can curtail the accuracy of emotional detection. In summary, each modality provides useful yet incomplete information related to emotions. Visual hints expose emotional responses, vocal attributes convey feelings via spoken language, and physiological markers denote arousal - while no single medium affords a holistic perspective. Merging various inputs yields enhanced emotion recognition capabilities. Next, we discuss approaches for effectively combining modalities.

3   Multimodal Fusion

Emotion perception is paramount for smooth and intuitive human-computer interplay. Initial studies primarily explored multimodal systems by assessing the unique characteristics of visual, vocal, or physical inputs. Despite their advantages, single-modal strategies frequently encounter limitations when applied across varied situations and user groups. The fusion of various sensory inputs has improved the precision and scope of emotional intelligence detection. The study of recognizing emotions through multiple modes has been an area of intense investigation throughout the last ten years. The early survey papers included [25] discussed modalities and their various applications. Surveys conducted recently have grouped fusion strategies [2], compared data sets, and detailed future possibilities. The field has rapidly advanced with the evolution of representation learning and affective computing techniques. Initial investigations integrated modalities including audio-visual [4] and linguistic-visual [18]. More complex systems now integrate facial expressions, voice, gestures, physiology and more for comprehensive emotional understanding. The key application realms consist of healthcare, education, gaming, robotics, and HCI. Early corpora like IEMOCAP have since been joined by much larger in-the-wild collections like CMU-MOSEI in the public dataset landscape. Combining modalities creates an important obstacle for multimodal emotion classification. This section analyzes fusion methods, which can broadly be categorized into three approaches [2]:

- *Feature-level Fusion.* By combining features across modalities, a more detailed joint feature representation is created. In the next step, traditional machine learning models like SVM, logistic regression, and random forest are taught using this amalgamated vector. Considering the intersection of facial muscle movements, audio cues, and heart rate changes, we can categorize feelings. Combining diverse feature extraction techniques is facilitated by feature fusion. Despite its capabilities, the framework does not explicitly account for interactions between sensory inputs or temporal patterns. The joint feature space can also be high-dimensional with redundancy. Selecting essential features or simplifying the dimensionality can be crucial;

- *Decision-level Fusion* Decision-level fusion first builds independent classifiers for each modality using the corresponding native features. The unimodal classifier outputs, such as predicted probabilities or labels, are then combined through strategies like majority voting, weighted averaging, or learned aggregation functions to generate the final multimodal prediction. Unlike feature fusion, decision fusion allows optimized unimodal representations and can model inter-modality relationships through the fusion mechanism. It discards potentially useful feature correlations across modalities. It is also limited by the least accurate unimodal classifier. Designing optimal fusion rules requires sufficient training data encompassing diverse use cases;

- *Model-level Fusion* Jointly combining models to illustrate connections and relationships through integrated statistical approaches or neural network configurations. Context-aware fusion techniques using HMMs have been developed to combine the meaning of facial expressions, hand gestures, and spoken language. The increasing interest in DNNs stems from their remarkable potential to combine models through effective representation learning. The combination of modalities in DNN architectures has been explored through the use of CNNs, RNNs, and other hybrid approaches, as discussed in [24]. Each modality's inputs are individually processed by independent input networks, and then the resulting data is consolidated employing fusion strategies like concatenation, aggregation, or attention before being labelled according to emotional patterns [19]. These advanced networks can identify subtle relationships between multiple input sources. But they require large diverse training data and substantial tuning. Interpretability can be difficult. Depending on the particular task at hand, any of the three fusion methods might be employed. Fusing characteristics streamlines selection processes, whereas combining judgments enhances versatility. Model fusion has high representational power but less transparency. The optimal method is driven by the specific emotion recognition use case and deployment constraints;

- *Quantitative Results.* Multimodal methods consistently outperform individual modalities across emotion recognition tasks. On the IEMOCAP benchmark, bimodal systems improved accuracy over unimodal approaches by 10.2% for video and speech [10] and 8.7% for text and speech. On the AFEW dataset [21], fusing audio, video and meta-data cues increased emotion classification accuracy from 50.9% (video-only) to 58.3% [17]. For depression detection, a trimodal fusion of audio, video and EEG signals boosted F1-scores by 14% over the best individual modality [1];

- *Qualitative Analysis* Multimodal integration provides complementary information that resolves ambiguity and generalization issues in unimodal systems. Visual cues like facial expressions offer instant but ambiguous reactions, while vocal tone conveys inner feelings. Fusing the two clarifies intent - a furrowed brow with an angry tone indicates frustration vs. concentration if the tone is neutral. Physiological signals indicate arousal but cannot differentiate specific emotions. Fusing with facial actions that distinguish emotions enables precise affect sensing. Demographic factors like age and culture often confound unimodal systems. Multimodal models incorporating diverse training data improve consistency across user groups [19];
- *Discussion* A detailed analysis of earlier works conclusively demonstrates that multimodal fusion offers a marked improvement in detecting emotional cues compared to working with individual modalities. These fields demonstrate how combining different modalities can bring about remarkable advantages. While open challenges exist, the survey outlines exciting opportunities and future directions for advancing multimodal emotion recognition research towards deployable technologies with transformative societal impact The survey highlights significant progress in multimodal emotion recognition but also outlines persistent challenges around robustness, contextual modelling and transparency. Key advantages of multimodal approaches include reduced ambiguity, improved consistency and fuller representation of human affect sensing compared to individual modalities. Model complexity and interpretability must be considered alongside deployment constraints when choosing the most suitable modalities and combination methods. Future opportunities include advancing in-the-wild generalization, lightweight implementations for edge devices, temporal and contextual modelling, and explainable AI methods tailored for multimodal emotion recognition. The research indicates promising growth of multimodal affective systems towards more naturalistic and proactive HCI across diverse applications.

4   Applications of Multimodal Emotion Recognition

Across multiple industries, these interfaces have demonstrated adaptability and utility. This passage pinpoints particular segments where multimodal emotion analysis exhibits noteworthy possibilities.

- *Health Care.* A patient's periodic mood assessments serve as a key indicator of potential mental health concerns, enabling clinicians to craft individualized treatment plans. The fusion of varied modalities (including facial expression analysis, voice recognition, body language detection, and physiological measures) makes it possible to continuously monitor emotional states through both clinical settings and remote telemedicine platforms, [1,3]. Integrating visual clues, spoken language, and data from wearable sensors has been shown to augment depression evaluation when compared to analyzing these factors independently. These robots rely heavily on this technology for varied modes of expression;

– *Education*. In e-learning and intelligent tutoring systems, estimating student engagement, attention, interest, and frustration from visual and posture cues can allow personalized adaptation to enhance learning outcomes. Fusing modalities like facial expressions, eye gaze, and upper body posture improved detection of engagement vs. distraction during remote learning in one study [15]. In game-based learning, multimodal affect recognition enables emotionally adaptive games that respond to student boredom and disengagement;

– *Gaming and Virtual Reality*. In gaming, multimodal emotion recognition can enable novel affect-sensitive experiences, games that respond to player emotions, and empathetic virtual characters [8]. Fusing player input, poses, facial expressions and physiology to detect engagement vs. boredom and tune game parameters accordingly improved user experience in one study [23]. For social robots and VR avatars, multimodal expression analysis enables more natural social interactions [6]. Synchronized facial and body animation using video, motion capture and audio analysis led to increased rapport compared to unimodal avatars in one experiment;

– *Surveillance & Security*. Fusing visual, vocal and behavioural cues has increasing applications in crowd surveillance, airport screening, and forensics. Multimodal suspicious behaviour detection integrating body poses, gestures, and facial expressions improved accuracy in simulated airport screening. For forensic analysis, synchronized facial expression and thermal video analysis revealed deception cues missed in individual modes [16]. With growing amounts of multimedia data, multimodal behavioural analysis enables advanced surveillance and threat detection;

– *Human-Robot and Vehicle Interaction*. Natural interaction with robots, virtual agents, and autonomous vehicles requires the capability to sense and appropriately respond to human emotions and non-verbal cues. Multimodal interfaces decoding user expressions, tone, gestures and posture can enable robots to recognize affect and intent more reliably. Fusing facial expressions, speech tone, semantics and gestures improved a robot's ability to detect confusion in users during tutoring [11]. In autonomous vehicles, driver state and intent monitoring using multimodal analysis of posture, expression and actions can enhance safety and trust [7];

– *Human-Computer Interaction*. Affect-aware user interfaces that recognize emotion through multimodal analysis of expressions, voice and physiology can enable more empathetic, adaptive and engaging interactions on devices and conversational agents [13,17]. Applications such as personalized recommendation systems, social robots, virtual assistants [6], and empathetic chatbots have utilized multimodal emotion recognition to enhance experiences. As HCI moves beyond screens towards AR/VR and ambient computing, robust user effects understanding will be critical for natural interactions. In summary, multimodal emotion recognition has diverse applications where affective state monitoring can provide value - from health care and learning to entertainment, security and assistive technology. As sensing capabilities grow, there is expanding potential to enhance these and other domains by integrating multimodal cues to infer emotional context more reliably. Next, we discuss key challenges and opportunities to advance multimodal emotion recognition research.

5 Open Challenges and Opportunities

While the field of multimodal emotion recognition has made significant progress, there remain open research questions around robustness, contextual modelling, dynamics, and algorithmic transparency. Addressing these challenges through interdisciplinary perspectives presents exciting opportunities to advance the state-of-the-art. We highlight some promising research directions:

- *Generalizability.* A persistent challenge is achieving robustness and consistency of multimodal emotion recognition across diverse individuals, cultures, contexts, and interaction scenarios. Differences in gender, age, ethnicity, sensor noise, and environments can degrade fusion algorithms that overfit to specific conditions. Novel domain adaptation techniques for multimodal models and adversarial testing of bias and sensitivity need to be explored. Utilizing large, varied training datasets will facilitate generalizability;
- *Contextual and Commonsense Modeling.* Emotional expressions occur in rich contexts - the same facial expression may convey different emotions across situations. Multimodal fusion should incorporate contextual cues like scene, dialogue history, task, relationships, and commonsense knowledge for accurate inference. Methods from computer vision, NLP and knowledge representation can provide contextual grounding;
- *Temporal Dynamics.* Emotions are temporally complex, evolving over multiple timescales from milliseconds to days. Multimodal fusion needs to model short-term dependencies, long-term variability, and continuity versus changes in affective state over time. Potential techniques include sequence modelling, graph networks, and coarse-to-fine processing across time horizons;
- *Lightweight and Transfer Learning.* Deploying multimodal interfaces on edge devices like phones, glasses, and IoT requires efficient and compact models. Transfer learning, knowledge distillation, and network compression should be investigated for multimodal fusion models. Low-cost sensors and minimal modalities needed for robust performance on edge platforms are also an area of research;
- *Explainability and Debuggability.* Lack of model transparency and debuggability is a key barrier to real-world use, especially in sensitive applications like health care. Advancing interpretability and causality analysis for multimodal fusion models will be critical. Generating explanations grounded in human-centric semantic concepts of emotion is needed. We have outlined several promising research directions that can help overcome current limitations and enable robust real-world deployment of multimodal emotion recognition systems. Advances in representation learning, contextual modelling, time series analysis, interpretable ML, and sensor technologies will facilitate addressing these challenges. As applications continue growing across diverse domains, improving the transparency, consistency and reliability of multimodal affect recognition will have broad value for society.

6   Conclusion

This analysis examines the bleeding-edge innovations employed in emotion perception via various modalities. A thorough analysis of relevant literature unwaveringly emphasizes the advantages of multi-modal approaches to affective signal processing. These domains illustrate the benefits of employing multiple modes, which are discussed in detail. Despite existing difficulties, the survey presents hopeful forecasts and trailblazing pathways for pioneering emotion perception R&D that could have profound consequences. A thorough examination of the evolving landscape of multimodal emotional sensing was conducted in this paper. Our dialogue centred around frequently utilized modalities, including visual cues, verbal indicators, nonverbal signals, and physiological responses, exploring their emotive encoding potential and any inherent constraints. A comparison of distinct fusion techniques across feature, decision, and model levels highlighted their varying degrees of adaptability, intricacy, and performance-related compromises. Applications across industries such as medicine, learning, amusement, safety, robotics, and user experience design (HCI) were exhibited to illustrate the value of multimodal emotion recognition over single-modal methods. Despite existing obstacles, the study lays out thrilling prospects and potential pathways for innovation in multimodal emotion detection studies that may bring groundbreaking influence on society.

Acknowledgements. The work was supported by the Italian Ministry of Universities and Research-MIUR (D.D. no.861), within the PRIN 2022 research project "RESTART - Robot Enhanced Social Abilities based on Theory of Mind for Acceptance of Robot in Assistive Treatments" (CUP I53D23003780001).

References

1. Alghowinem, S., et al.: Multimodal depression detection: fusion analysis of paralinguistic, head pose and eye gaze behaviors. IEEE Trans. Affect. Comput. 9(4), 478–490 (2018). https://doi.org/10.1109/TAFFC.2016.2634527
2. Atrey, P.K., Hossain, M.A., Saddik, A.E., Kankanhalli, M.S.: Multimodal fusion for multimedia analysis: a survey. Multimedia Syst. 16(6), 345–379 (2010)
3. Barra, P., Mnasri, Z., Greco, D.: Multimodal emotion recognition from voice and video signals. In: Paper in IEEE Eurocon 2023 Conference. Torino, Italy (2023)
4. Busso, C., et al.: IEMOCAP: interactive emotional dyadic motion capture database. Lang. Resour. Eval. 42(4), 335 (2008)
5. Calvo, R.A., D'Mello, S., Gratch, J., Kappas, A.: The Oxford Handbook of Affective Computing. Oxford University Press (2015)
6. DeVault, D., et al.: Simsensei kiosk: a virtual human interviewer for healthcare decision support. In: Proceedings of the 2014 International Conference on Autonomous Agents and Multi-Agent Systems, pp. 1061–1068 (2014)

7. Eyben, F., Wöllmer, M., Schuller, B.: Openear - introducing the munich open-source emotion and affect recognition toolkit. In: 2009 3rd International Conference on Affective Computing and Intelligent Interaction and Workshops, pp. 1–6 (2009). https://doi.org/10.1109/ACII.2009.5349350

8. García-Sánchez, P.G.N.Y., Togelius, J.: Artificial intelligence and games. Genet. Program Evolvable Mach. **20**, 143–145 (2019). https://doi.org/10.1007/s10710-018-9337-0

9. Kollias, D., Schulc, A., Hajiyev, E., Zafeiriou, S.: Analysing affective behavior in the first abaw 2020 competition. In: 2020 15th IEEE International Conference on Automatic Face and Gesture Recognition (FG 2020), pp. 637–643. Buenos Aires, Argentina (2020). https://doi.org/10.1109/FG47880.2020.00126

10. Kumar, N., Guha, T., Huang, C.W., Vaz, C., Narayanan, S.S.: Novel affective features for multiscale prediction of emotion in music. In: 2016 IEEE 18th International Workshop on Multimedia Signal Processing (MMSP), pp. 1–5. Montreal, QC, Canada (2016). https://doi.org/10.1109/MMSP.2016.7813377

11. Lemaignan, S., Garcia, F., Jacq, A., Dillenbourg, P.: From real-time attention assessment to "with-me-ness" in human-robot interaction. In: 2016 11th ACM/IEEE International Conference on Human-Robot Interaction (HRI), pp. 157–164 (2016). https://doi.org/10.1109/HRI.2016.7451747

12. Lin, C., Ko, L., Chuang, Y., Su, T., Lin, C.: EEG-based drowsiness estimation for safety driving using independent component analysis. IEEE Trans. Circuits Syst. I **52**(12), 2726–2738 (2005)

13. Liu, Y., Sourina, O., Nguyen, M.K.: Real-time EEG-based emotion recognition and its applications. In: Gavrilova, M.L., Tan, C.J.K., Sourin, A., Sourina, O. (eds.) Transactions on Computational Science XII. LNCS, vol. 6670, pp. 256–277. Springer, Heidelberg (2011). https://doi.org/10.1007/978-3-642-22336-5_13

14. Staffa, M., Derrico, L., Sansalone, S., Alimardani, M.: Classifying human emotions in HRI: applying global optimization model to EEG brain signals. Front. Neurorobotics **17**, 1191127 (2023). https://doi.org/10.3389/fnbot.2023.1191127

15. Monkaresi, H., Bosch, N., Calvo, R.A., D'Mello, S.K.: Automated detection of engagement using video-based estimation of facial expressions and heart rate. IEEE Trans. Affect. Comput. **8**(1), 15–28 (2016)

16. Pavlidis, I., Levine, J.: Thermal image analysis for polygraph testing. IEEE Eng. Med. Biol. Mag. **21**(6), 56–64 (2002)

17. Picard, R.W.: Affective Computing. MIT Press (2000)

18. Poria, S., Cambria, E., Bajpai, R., Hussain, A.: A review of affective computing: from unimodal analysis to multimodal fusion. Inf. Fusion **37**, 98–125 (2017)

19. Ringeval, F., et al.: AVEC 2019 workshop and challenge: state-of-mind, detecting depression with AI, and cross-cultural affect recognition. In: Proceedings of the 9th International on Audio/Visual Emotion Challenge and Workshop, pp. 3–12 (2019)

20. Sariyanidi, E., Gunes, H., Cavallaro, A.: Automatic analysis of facial affect: a survey of registration, representation, and recognition. IEEE Trans. Pattern Anal. Mach. Intell. **37**(6), 1113–1133 (2015)

21. Savchenko, A.V.: Facial expression and attributes recognition based on multi-task learning of lightweight neural networks. In: 2021 IEEE 19th International Symposium on Intelligent Systems and Informatics (SISY), pp. 119–124. Subotica, Serbia (2021). https://doi.org/10.1109/SISY52375.2021.9582508

22. Staffa, M., D'Errico, L.: EEG-based machine learning models for emotion recognition in HRI. In: Degen, H., Ntoa, S. (eds.) International Conference on Human-Computer Interaction, pp. 285–297. Springer, Cham (2023)

23. Tijs, T., Brokken, D., IJsselsteijn, W.: Dynamic game balancing by recognizing affect. In: International Conference on Fun and Games, pp. 88–93 (2008)
24. Zadeh, A., Chen, M., Poria, S., Cambria, E., Morency, L.P.: Multimodal language analysis in the wild: CMU-MOSEI dataset and interpretable dynamic fusion graph. In: Proceedings of the 56th Annual Meeting of the Association for Computational Linguistics, pp. 2236–2246 (2018)
25. Zeng, Z., Pantic, M., Roisman, G.I., Huang, T.S.: A survey of affect recognition methods: audio, visual, and spontaneous expressions. IEEE Trans. Pattern Anal. Mach. Intell. **31**(1), 39–58 (2009)

Co-creation with AI in Car Design: A Diffusion Model Approach

Zhicheng He[1]([✉]), Jun Ma[2], and Yuanyang Zuo[1]

[1] College of Design and Innovation, Tongji University, Shanghai, China
Tallis_he@tongji.edu.cn
[2] School of Automotive Studies, Tongji University, Shanghai, China

Abstract. This study delves into the idea of AI co-creation in the car design domain by employing a unique methodology of training diffusion model to learn car design. Our primary objective is to investigate how the collaborative design process, where human designers and AI work together with the assist of pre-trained car design diffusion model, can revolutionize car design by enhancing creativity, efficiency, and overall user satisfaction. We built the car design dataset for the model training, which consists of real car photos and the design renderings together with the textual prompt of the images. And we invited the professional car designers to test the pre-trained car design diffusion model in the real design scenario. This research underscores the significance of AI co-creation in car design, showcasing the potential of AI technology to revolutionize the automotive industry. The findings suggest that collaborative AI co-creation approach had the ability to empower designers, enhance creativity, and redefine the future of car design. Project page https://automotive-design-copilot.super.site

Keywords: Co-creation · Diffusion Model · DreamBooth · Car Design

1 Introduction

Recent years, the exploration of AI and human co-creation has witnessed significant achievements [1], especially in the field of art and design. The large text-to-image models have shown the strong capability of generate the high quality images based on the text prompt written in natural language [2, 3].

Car design could be the most challenging field in the industrial design. Car designers need to do beautiful freehand sketches to convey their design ideas, bringing the key sketch into digital design renderings, and developing the design rendering into photorealistic renderings, through the traditional car design process. Currently, it takes designers months of preparation and design reviews to progress from early concept ideation and sketching through to the development of full scale models. This is often hampered by incompatible tools, data and serial workflows [4]. For the early concept development stage, normally for an experience car designer it takes at least 3 h to transfer a freehand car sketch to a sketch rendering. For a detailed high quality car rendering, it will take at least half day to finish.

© The Author(s), under exclusive license to Springer Nature Switzerland AG 2024
H. Degen and S. Ntoa (Eds.): HCII 2024, LNAI 14735, pp. 163–174, 2024.
https://doi.org/10.1007/978-3-031-60611-3_12

This paper presents a novel approach of co-creation with AI car design process based on the pre-trained diffusion model, aimed at revolutionizing the traditional car design workflow. The pre-trained diffusion model provides a unique framework for translating conceptual sketches into photorealistic renderings, thereby enhancing the efficiency and creativity in the car design process.

In order to evaluating the practical applicability of the car design diffusion model in authentic design scenarios, a comprehensive user testing was conducted. Based on the conceptual framework of the AI co-creative design workflow, an interactive interface prototype focused on car design was built. The interface aimed to seamlessly integrate AI co-creation design approach into the established design processes of car design (Figs. 1 and 2).

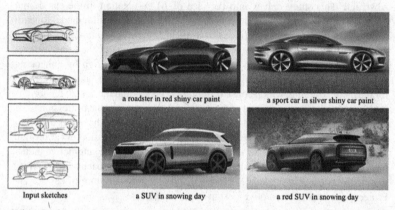

Fig. 1. With the freehand sketches input (left), the car design diffusion model we trained was able to translate car sketches into car renderings (right), keeping the proportions and the design themes.

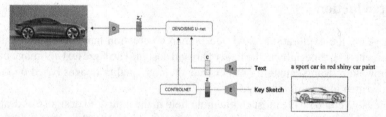

Fig. 2. Sketch to rendering. The freehand sketch input by ControlNet model [5] so that the car design diffusion model is able to generate renderings with the guiding of the sketch and prompt.

Preliminary results underscored the potential of the AI co-creative car design workflow in enhancing the design process. Most designers agree that this is a quite productive approach of generating ideas guiding AI with the input sketches, they can quickly visualize their ideas with different style by the semantic prompt. And the pre-trained car design diffusion model shows the strong capability of sketch understanding, which also encourage them to focus on exploring the design ideas by sketches.

2 Related Work

2.1 Car Design Semantic Corpus

The semantic words that people use to describe cars depends on the perception of the car body features [6]. It is not only the visible and tangible form of the car body, but also the emotional users' state in the car's perception. The existing research of summarized 85 words in the Semantic Pool [7] of automobile styling stance, which contains the most frequent using words that we describe a car design. In the semantic compass for automotive styling stance of the paper, there is 6 categories of the semantic words could be used to describe the car design, which inspired the textual prompt structure in our car design dataset.

2.2 Text-to-Image Diffusion Model

Diffusion models are probabilistic generative models that are trained to learn a data distribution by the gradual denoising of a variable sampled from a Gaussian distribution. The generative power of the diffusion model stems from a natural fit to the inductive biases of image-like data when their underlying neural backbone is implemented as a U-Net. The best generation quality is usually achieved when a reweighted objective [8] is used for training. For pre-trained diffusion model, when the textual prompt describes the content of the dataset input, the high quality image of the content will be generated [9, 10].

2.3 ControlNet

ControlNet is a neural network architecture that can enhance pre-trained image diffusion models with task-specific conditions [5]. ControlNet manipulates the input conditions of neural network blocks to further control the overall behavior of an entire neural network. Herein, a "network block" refers to a set of neural layers that are put together as a frequently used unit to build neural networks. This means the car design sketches could guide the diffusion model for car design rendering generation through the "network block".

2.4 DreamBooth Training Approach

The DreamBooth training approach [11] propose an autogenous class-specific prior preservation loss that encourages diversity and counters language drift. This allows it to generate diverse images of the class prior, as well as retain knowledge about the class prior that it can use in conjunction with knowledge about the subject instance. Once the new dictionary is embedded in the model, it can use these words to synthesize novel photorealistic images of the subject, contextualized in different scenes, while preserving their key identifying features.

3 Method

In order to teach diffusion to understand the proportions of the car body and the design theme of different design styles, a car design dataset was built for training the diffusion model. The framework of the workflow for car design co-creation with AI was structured, which is the foundation of the interactive prototype and the experiment.

3.1 Car Design Data Set

In the pursuit of advancing AI co-creation car design, a comprehensive dataset comprising 330 high-quality images of automobiles was meticulously created. These images were sourced from online database, ensuring that each photograph featured a complete main body of the car with distinct surface features. The selection criteria emphasized visual clarity to facilitate model learning.

For example, the dataset consists of 330 images of the real cars in different surroundings. In the image, the main body of the car need to be clear without losing any information, such as dead white or dead black. The surroundings also need to be simple enough without any distraction, such as other cars, or people and animals in the same image. The lighting environment of the photos need to be easy to understand, natural light and studio light is perfect, but the car in the street or in the night would lose too much information about the shape of the car body. The main principle is the visual clarity.

The augmentation of the diffusion model's capacity for car design proposal generation requires a deep understanding of the car design in semantics. For each individual photo within the created dataset, a tailored approach was employed to bridge the semantic gap between visual aesthetics and linguistic expression. Therefore, for every single photo from the dataset, a textual prompt file with the same name of the photo was compiled to match the content of the photo in the attributes of design style and structure.

The words and vocabulary we used in the textual prompt file was based on the corpus derived from the interview we had with professional car designers as well as the analysis of the existing car designs.

The pivotal step in this preprocess involved the association of these semantic words with corresponding design elements present in each car image. This alignment was orchestrated to establish a nuanced relationship between design features, stylistic elements, and their semantic representation in text [12, 13]. The dataset of car images and textual prompts facilitated the diffusion model's comprehension of intricate car design differences.

This enriched dataset not only served as a training ground for the car design diffusion model but also contributed to the interpretable prompt interaction between designer and car design diffusion model. By aligning the textual prompts in the training dataset with language commonly used by designers, the interactive process between the car design diffusion model and designers would be more interpretable and productive, fostering an intuitive co-creation with AI design approach. Therefore, the car design diffusion model would be able to generate the car design renderings to meet the expectations of the designers.

All the car images in the dataset comes from the internet, various types, colors of the car in various angle and environment were collected, and all the images were cropped by 512x512, ensuring that the car is the main image. About 10% percent of the car image is design rendering, which would teach the model to understand this image type. All the real photos of the car were captioned as "the photograph of a [car type] in [color], in [scene] background, [adj] style", all the photos of the design rendering were captioned as "the design rendering of a [car type] in [color], in [scene] background, [adj] style" (Fig. 3).

Fig. 3. Dataset. Example images of the car design dataset.

3.2 Workflow Framework

Based on the traditional car design process, we assume that the car design diffusion model could help designers visualizing and developing their design ideas. Thus, the workflow framework was designed based on the sketch ideation stage. In this stage, normally, designer would do many design sketches, then the satisfied sketches would be chosen to be developed into design rendering. Now the car design diffusion model is able to assist designers doing the sketch development. After the key sketch is chosen, designers could send the key sketch to car design diffusion model with the prompt, then the car design diffusion model would generate the design rendering based on the prompt and sketch guidance, which will improve the design efficiency and productivity significantly (Fig. 4).

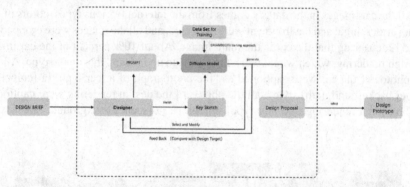

Fig. 4. Co-creation with AI in car design. This figure shows the workflow of Co-creation with AI tool in the car design scenario. It will take several rounds of generation for designers to select the satisfied generated images.

To get the satisfied generated image, designer will generate for several rounds. In each round, designer could adjust the prompt and the parameters of the generation according to the result of last round.

3.3 Training

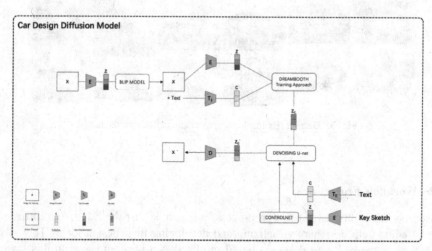

Fig. 5. The working process of the car design diffusion model.

In this section we trained the car design diffusion model with the car design dataset. The class we captioned as [car], since all the images in the dataset are different types of the cars, but in various style. The dataset aimed to teach the diffusion model what is car type, such as SUV, Sedan, Roadster, and the semantic words that describe the car design, stem from the perception of the people, like strong, delicate, luxury (Fig. 5).

The base model we chose is SD 1.5, which is quite popular used and the training requirement of the hardware is not extremely high. The training process run on Colab with the A100 graphic card, U-net training steps is 1500, learning rate is 1e-6. It takes about 2 h to complete the training process, then we loaded the model in the car design interactive prototype to run the test, based on the sketches we input, the quality of car images that generated from car design diffusion model improved significantly compared with SD 1.5 model.

3.4 Model Testing

We recruited 14 car designers to participate in the car design diffusion model test, using the interactive prototype. Designers were required to generate the car design renderings based on the prepared car sketches, the images their generated and the rounds and times it takes were recorded in the test.

Designer Recruitment. After the car design diffusion model was trained, loaded in the interactive prototype, we sent the test invitation to car designers of the main OEMs and design consultancies in China. Most car designers showed high interest in the design process co-creation with AI, especially for the car design diffusion model that we trained.

14 professional car designers from the leading OEMs in China with different working years were invited to participate the test (Table 1).

Table 1. Car designers participate the test.

OEM	Occupation	Working years
Saic	CMF Designer	5
Maxus	Exterior Designer	3
Xiaomi	Exterior Designer	2
Nio	CMF Designer	8
Xpeng	Interior Designer	3
IM	Exterior Designer	1
Changan	HMI Designer	12
Geely	Exterior Designer	1
Geely	Interior Designer	1
JLR	CMF Designer	10
GM	Advanced Exterior Designer	2
VW	Component designer	2
Pinifarina	Exterior Designer	3
Pinifarina	Exterior Designer	3

Designers of the traditional OEMs, new EV OEMs, technology company and the design consultancy are involved in the model test. 7 of them is exterior designer, 2 of them is interior designer, 3 of them is CMF designer, 1 is component designer, 1 is HMI designer.

Model Testing Process. 3 working laptop connected with the remote server with the running car design diffusion model were provided to the designers involved in the test. We rent 3 remote servers with RTX 4090 graphic card. The interactive prototypes were installed in the server before the test. For 2 images with the resolution of 960x540, it takes 28s to generate, for 4 images it takes 50s, we set 4 images for one generation round.

The task of the experiment was given, every designer provides 3 different car sketches as the input for car design diffusion model, using the prompt template we provided, only changing the car type words of the car sketches, then started to generate the rendering images. The experiment encompassed a spectrum of design scenarios, ranging from conceptual ideation to detailed refinement.

Designers were divided into 5 groups. During the model test, designers guided the model with their sketches and prompts for rendering generation. Designers input the photo of the car sketches with the prompts modified based on our prompt template, then click the generate button, one click count as one round, 4 images would be generate, for each car sketch, they were required to continue generation until their saved the satisfied generated images. Before the time recording, designers would use the interactive prototype for 10 min to get familiar with the interaction. The number of the generation rounds that designers chose their first satisfied image and the time it took were recorded during the test.

Designers were encouraged to articulate their thoughts and impressions during each interaction, providing invaluable qualitative insights into the AI co-creation car design approach. The questionnaires were garnered after the model testing and subjected to rigorous qualitative and quantitative analyses.

4   Result

4.1   Generation Rounds and Time

Most designers could get satisfied image in less than 5 generation rounds, with using less than 5 min. The designer with good freehand sketches seems to have a better generation result with less generation rounds and selection times. And when designers were getting good at co-creation with AI approach, it seems them can generate satisfied images with less rounds and less times, also there is more satisfied image in the generation result (Figs. 6 and 7, Tables 2 and 3).

The questionnaire collecting the feedback of the designers was conducted. Most designers agreed that the Co-creation with AI design approach is more creative and more efficient compared with traditional car design process. The model could understand their sketches quite well, but the images model generated lacks of a design diversity, maybe the reason is that the car image in the dataset we built lacks of style diversity. And most designers are willing to use the AI tool in their daily design work.

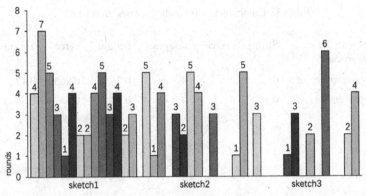

Fig. 6. The number of the generation rounds. This figure shows the generation rounds that takes for designer selecting the satisfied generated images based on the sketches that each designer input (some designers didn't have 3 car sketches, they prepared interior or component sketches, so the rounds didn't count for that sketch).

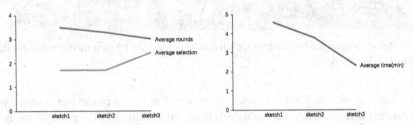

Fig. 7. Average selection rounds and time. This figure shows the average rounds it takes and the effective rounds as well as the average time it takes.

Table 2. Feedback of Co-creation with AI approach.

Co-creation with AI approach	Strong disagree	disagree	neutral	agree	Strong agree
Creativity	0	0	0.29	0.21	0.5
Style diversity	0	0	0.50	0.29	0.21
Sketch recognition	0	0	0.14	0.57	0.29
Willing to use	0	0	0.07	0.72	0.21

4.2 Comparison

We compared the result with the images generated by SD1.5 base model (Fig. 8).

Compared with SD 1.5 base model, car design diffusion model shows a strong capability of understanding the freehand car sketches. The design theme and the car proportion were kept in the generated image quite well.

Table 3. Comparison with traditional design process.

Compared with the traditional process	Strong disagree	disagree	neutral	agree	Strong agree
Creativity improvement	0	0	0.265	0.265	0.47
Speed improvement	0	0	0.13	0.53	0.34

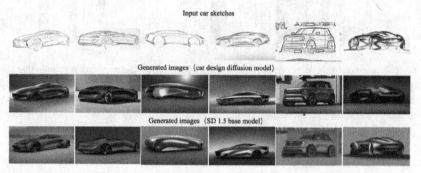

Fig. 8. Result comparison for car design diffusion model and SD 1.5 base model with same input for the SD 1.5 base model.

For the very nice detailed car sketches, car design diffusion model can generate very nice detailed images with professional rendering style while SD 1.5 generate the basic car shape, the design feature could probably be missing or misunderstood.

For the simple line work sketch, both two model could understand the shape, while car design diffusion model could visualize the sketch in a professional style.

For the rough freehand sketch, car design diffusion model gave a better result based on the understanding of the car shape and more realistic image. SD 1.5 would misunderstand some feature and generate some structure that is not shown in the sketch, the image style is not that realistic.

In general, both two models have the good understanding of the basic car shape, the pre-trained car design diffusion model show a better understanding of the freehand sketches and could visualize sketches in a professional car designer style, also the detail of the generated image is better.

5   Discussion

The ideation sketch stage is quite important in the car design process. In this stage, designers would have many freehand design ideas for the design review. The key sketches would be chosen in the design review then sent into design rendering development. In the design rendering developing process, also called sketch visualization or sketch rendering, it is very important to keep the feeling of the sketch, such as design themes, proportions and features. Normally it takes at least 3h for an experienced designer to do a quick photoshop render.

The car design diffusion model provides another solution for this, the pre-trained model could understand the freehand sketches and help designers to generate design renderings with their prompt in 5 min, which improves the sketch visualization process significantly.

5.1 Limitations

The car design dataset consists only 330 images of cars, and 10% of the image is the car design rendering, which lacks of the diversity of the design styles and the renderings styles. The car design diffusion model could understand the most car type we usually see on road, but for the style like futuristic Si-Fi vehicles, the model could not understand. Also, for car design, the interior design is also an important field, which requires a different dataset preparation, could be the future research direction.

6 Conclusion

We proposed an innovative co-creation with AI design approach based on the pre-trained car design diffusion model, and test the effectiveness in the authentic design scenario with professional car designers. The car design diffusion model demonstrates great potential of improving the efficiency in the stage of sketch visualization, which could also be the potential trend in the car design field.

This co-creation with AI design approach can also be applied in the other design field, such as product design, architecture design and so on. The application of generative AI not only enhances the efficiency of working processes for designers but also heralds a new era for the traditional design domain.

Acknowledgments. We thank all the designers in the JLR china design studio for the idea supporting, and all the designers that participated in the model test, and gave us a lot professional feedback for the future research direction. Finally, special thanks to the professor Meng Wang for his feedback, advice and support for the project.

Disclosure of Interests. The authors have no competing interests to declare that are relevant to the content of this article.

References

1. Wu, Z., Ji, D., Yu, K., Zeng, X., Wu, D., Shidujaman, M.: AI creativity and the human-AI co-creation model. In: Kurosu, M. (ed.) HCII 2021. LNCS, vol. 12762, pp. 171–190. Springer, Cham (2021). https://doi.org/10.1007/978-3-030-78462-1_13
2. Rombach, R., Blattmann, A., Lorenz, D., Esser, P., Ommer, B.: High-resolution image synthesis with latent diffusion models. In: Proceedings of the IEEE/CVF Conference on Computer Vision and Pattern Recognition, pp. 10684–10695 (2022)
3. Sohn, K., et al.: StyleDrop: text-to-image generation in any style. arXiv preprint arXiv:2306.00983 (2023)

4. Nvidia Blog page. https://blogs.nvidia.com/blog/generative-ai-auto-industry. Accessed 25 Jan 2024
5. Zhang, L., Rao, A., Agrawala, M.: Adding conditional control to text-to-image diffusion models. In: Proceedings of the IEEE/CVF International Conference on Computer Vision, pp. 3836–3847 (2023)
6. Catalanoc, E., Giannini, F., Monti, M.: Towards an automatic semantic annotation of car aesthetics. Car Aesthetics Annotation, 8–15. (2005)
7. Li, T., Li, Y., Rampino, L.: Construction of semantic pool and acquisition of semantic categories for automobile styling stance: a domain knowledge perspective. Adv. Eng. Inform. **56**, 101995 (2023)
8. Li, D., Li, J., Hoi, S.C.: Blip-diffusion: pre-trained subject representation for controllable text-to-image generation and editing. arXiv preprint arXiv:2305.14720 (2023)
9. Choi, J., Choi, Y., Kim, Y., Kim, J., Yoon, S.: Custom-edit: text-guided image editing with customized diffusion models. arXiv preprint arXiv:2305.15779 (2023)
10. Lee, S., et al.: Diffusion Explainer: visual explanation for text-to-image stable diffusion. arXiv preprint arXiv:2305.03509 (2023)
11. Ruiz, N., Li, Y., Jampani, V., Pritch, Y., Rubinstein, M., Aberman, K.: Dreambooth: fine tuning text-to-image diffusion models for subject-driven generation. In: Proceedings of the IEEE/CVF Conference on Computer Vision and Pattern Recognition, pp. 22500–22510 (2023)
12. Gong, R., Danelljan, M., Sun, H., Mangas, J.D., Van Gool, L.: Prompting diffusion representations for cross-domain semantic segmentation. arXiv preprint arXiv:2307.02138 (2023)
13. Tian, J., Aggarwal, L., Colaco, A., Kira, Z., Gonzalez-Franco, M.: Diffuse, attend, and segment: Unsupervised zero-shot segmentation using stable diffusion. arXiv preprint arXiv:2308. 12469 (2023)
14. Stiny, G.: Introduction to shape and shape grammars. Environ. Plann. B. Plann. Des.Plann. B. Plann. Des. **7**(3), 343–351 (1980)
15. Xue, Z., et al.: Raphael: text-to-image generation via large mixture of diffusion paths. arXiv preprint arXiv:2305.18295 (2023)
16. Hedlin, E., et al.: Unsupervised semantic correspondence using stable diffusion. arXiv preprint arXiv:2305.15581 (2023)
17. Radford, A., et al.: Learning transferable visual models from natural language supervision. In: International conference on machine learning, pp. 8748–8763. PMLR (2021)
18. Zhang, Y., et al.: Recognize anything: a strong image tagging model. arXiv preprint arXiv: 2306.03514 (2023)
19. Liu, N., Du, Y., Li, S., Tenenbaum, J.B., Torralba, A.: Unsupervised compositional concepts discovery with text-to-image generative models. arXiv preprint arXiv:2306.05357 (2023)
20. Avrahami, O., Aberman, K., Fried, O., Cohen-Or, D., Lischinski, D.: Break-a-scene: extracting multiple concepts from a single image. arXiv preprint arXiv:2305.16311 (2023)
21. Kim, B.K., Song, H.K., Castells, T., Choi, S.: On architectural compression of text-to-image diffusion models. arXiv preprint arXiv:2305.15798 (2023)
22. Chan, C.S.: Can style be measured? Des. Stud. **21**(3), 277–291 (2000)

A Study on the Application of Generative AI Tools in Assisting the User Experience Design Process

Hsiu-Ling Hsiao(✉) [iD] and Hsien-Hui Tang [iD]

National Taiwan University of Science and Technology, Taipei 106335, Taiwan
sharinehsiao@gmail.com, drhhtang@gapps.ntust.edu.tw

Abstract. Despite its emergent stage, Generative AI has already started to significantly influence the various aspects of user experience (UX) design, introducing both challenges and opportunities for designers. This study employs the case of a mobile banking application by a Taiwanese bank to understand the design process of UX facilitated by Generative AI, aiming to evaluate the advantages and disadvantages of incorporating Generative AI into UX design processes. To achieve this research goal, three objectives are proposed: (1) Analyze the benefits and limitations of Generative AI assistance in the UX design process; (2) Provide recommendations for designers to incorporate Generative AI into the design process; (3) Suggest improvements for Generative AI tools to better meet the needs of designers. The research results show that Generative AI tools significantly reduce the time spent by designers on context analysis and the integration of inspiration in the early stages of their projects, allowing for a greater emphasis on creative and strategic tasks. However, the specialized skills of designers remain crucial for improving AI-generated solutions. UX designers adept in strategic questioning and critical thinking demonstrate a significant advantage in working with Generative AI tools.

Keywords: Generative AI · User Experience · Design process

1 Introduction

Since the beginning of the Industrial Revolution 1.0, the focus of design has been on how to make machines interact easily with humans. Moving into the era of Industrial Revolution 4.0, the challenge was how to integrate various internet services to create a good UX. The upcoming Industrial Era 5.0 will concentrate on using research and innovation to develop in a sustainable, human-centric, and resilient direction (Breque et al., 2021). In this process, the rise of AI has not only reshaped the way humans interact with machines but has also introduced new urgent demands for UX (Nielsen, 2023a).

Among many AI technologies, Generative Artificial Intelligence (Generative AI) possesses powerful generative capabilities, providing a wealth of resources and inspiration for designers' creative ideas. Although Generative AI is in its early stages, it has

© The Author(s), under exclusive license to Springer Nature Switzerland AG 2024
H. Degen and S. Ntoa (Eds.): HCII 2024, LNAI 14735, pp. 175–189, 2024.
https://doi.org/10.1007/978-3-031-60611-3_13

already been widely applied across various sectors (McKinsey, 2023). With the development of AI, Shneiderman (2020) proposed adhering to Human-Centered AI principles (HCAI), emphasizing that AI should focus more on human needs and values. These trends have continually evolved and expanded the roles and responsibilities of designers, while also presenting new challenges to their roles. Although it is unlikely that designers will be completely replaced by AI, collaboration with AI has become a necessary trend.

Therefore, this study will utilize the case of a well-known Taiwanese mobile banking app to practice the process of using Generative AI to assist UX, explore the impact of Generative AI on UX design, analyze the benefits and limitations of Generative AI assistance in the UX process, and propose suggestions for designers on using Generative AI in their design process. This research will help designers better face the challenges of rapidly advancing technology.

2   The Impact of AI on UX Design

AI technology has the potential to modify the traditionally labor-intensive and time-consuming design process. Machine learning models identify complex data patterns, aiding decision-making in design (Ghajargar et al., 2020). In UX design, AI not only streamlines processes and enhances efficiency but also deepens exploration into user behavior, needs, and expectations, presenting new design innovation avenues (Stige et al., 2023; Chanchamnan, 2023). Verganti et al. (2020) highlighted how AI's automation capabilities convert the traditional design process into a Problem-Solving Loop, collecting real-time user interaction data to guide design, enabling the automatic creation of personalized solutions without manual input, leading to more efficient and individualized designs. AI's problem-solving ability automates complex UX functionalities like virtual assistants and personalized recommendation systems (Virvou, 2023).

The evolution of AI poses new opportunities and challenges for UX designers, such as collaborating with algorithm engineers, understanding AI deeply (Stige et al., 2023), communicating effectively in human-AI collaborations (Virvou, 2023), and studying machine learning (Dove, 2017). These challenges significantly test designers' abilities. Designers must consider probabilistic outcomes, envision all scenarios presented by new AI products, and integrate these probabilities into their design concepts (Kliman-Silver et al., 2020). Moreover, designers and developers must ensure AI decisions are transparent, explainable, and ethically aligned with human autonomy (Chanchamnan, 2023), ensuring data collection and usage comply with ethical norms and legal standards to build user trust in AI (Stige et al., 2023; Virvou, 2023).

Despite AI's automation capabilities, direct interaction between designers and users remains crucial for understanding genuine needs, a current limitation of AI, suggesting AI will not fully replace human designers (Stige et al., 2023). As AI induces significant shifts, to stay competitive, designers must thoroughly grasp AI, continuously adapt, and innovate, with their innovative thinking and ethical awareness shaping the future of human-technology interactions.

3   Method

To explore the pros and cons of Generative AI applications in the UX design process, this study utilized a case study of CUBE App, a mobile banking application in Taiwan's financial sector, following the Three Diamond Design Process (Wang et al., 2022). The design process of the CUBE App was be divided into three stages: Problem distillation, prototype design, and design validation, comprising seven key work items: (1) Competitive analysis; (2) Preliminary research interviews; (3) Usability pre-testing; (4) Functional flow planning; (5) Sketching; (6) Interface drawing; (7) Usability post-testing. Various Generative AI tools were appropriately integrated to facilitate each task, thereby examining the impact of Generative AI on the UX design process. The contents of each stage are detailed below:

1. Problem Distillation Stage
   This stage is divided into two parts. Firstly, it involves a comparative analysis of the differences in competitive analysis outcomes between human designers and ChatGPT. Secondly, Generative AI tools such as ChatGPT, Vocal AI, and Typeform are utilized to assist designers in planning preliminary research interviews and usability testing. Based on these results, a collaborative analysis of user pain points is conducted. Finally, the process of collaboration between humans and AI is reflected upon, leading to the development of recommendations for designers on the use of Generative AI in research.
2. Prototype Design Stage
   Based on the results of the problem distillation stage, this stage proposes improvements to the prototype design of the CUBE App. This includes planning functional flows, sketching, and interface drawing, where the researchers document each AI-generated outcome and discovery. Different Generative AI design tools, including Figma FigJam AI, Figma Wireframe Designer, Uizard, Midjourney, and the GPT-4 DALL·E version of ChatGPT, are used and be evaluated for their utility and limitations in the prototype design stage, providing recommendations for future collaborations between designers and AI in interface design.
3. Design Validation Stage
   In this stage, we utilized AI tools, such as ChatGPT, Good Tape, and Typeform, to compile usability testing results and gather user feedback on the CUBE App's improved UX. We compared these results with initial usability testing findings to validate the effectiveness of our collaborative design process between human designers and Generative AI. An integrated analysis was then conducted to explore the benefits and limitations of using Generative AI tools in the design process.

4   Results

4.1   Problem Distillation Stage

To evaluate the effectiveness of Generative AI in assisting the problem distillation stage, an initial comparative analysis was conducted between human designers and ChatGPT in competitive analysis. Subsequently, Generative AI tools such as ChatGPT, Vocal AI, and Typeform were utilized to support designers in the preliminary planning and subsequent synthesis of results within the processes of preliminary research interviews and usability testing. This collaborative process involved jointly analyzing user pain points and defining objectives for product enhancement.

Human designers and Generative AI exhibited distinct advantages and limitations during competitive analysis. While designers were slower in data analysis, they were adept at ensuring data practicality. On the other hand, ChatGPT faced limitations in in-depth filtering and understanding strategic contexts but excelled in data processing speed and efficiency. These findings emphasize the importance of human-machine collaboration, where designers can utilize ChatGPT's rapid search and compilation abilities to assist in data collection for competitive analysis. By integrating human expertise in industry, understanding user needs, and analytical capabilities, designers can better grasp market trends and promptly develop initial product improvement strategies.

For effective interaction between humans and Generative AI, it is crucial for designers to clearly define the expected direction of response and use specific prompts to direct Generative AI in providing the required information. To ensure alignment with ChatGPT's understanding, it is advisable to first inquire about its methodology for performing tasks, such as asking about its approach to coding classification. If necessary, adjustments can be made to facilitate the establishment of a common foundation for collaboration.

Given ChatGPT's potential decrease in accuracy when processing large amounts of data, it is recommended to process data in batches or break datasets into smaller, more specific segments. Using brief prompts to ask questions in a more frequent question-and-answer format can result in more comprehensive responses. Additionally, designers should establish the order of priority in problem-solving, prioritizing the most important aspects. Open-ended questions in the initial data collection phase allow AI more freedom to explore various perspectives. In contrast, delving into specific issues requires more detailed and specific instructions to obtain the most valuable information.

To enhance the transparency and credibility of AI analysis, designers should request AI to clarify the foundations and reasons for its analyses, and then apply their own professional knowledge to audit and correct the responses generated by AI. Using prompts such as "Please provide the sources of this information" ensures data verification and filters relevant data. Appropriate questions to ask include "Why analyze it this way?" "Is there any other data available?" This allows for a thorough exploration and enhancement of the insights provided by Generative AI, thereby providing a more comprehensive and reliable analysis.

While Generative AI could furnish valuable insights and analyses, it is more suitable for providing initial assessments and perspectives. Ideally, responses generated by AI should complement data from other sources and be verified by human experts to make final judgments and decisions. This collaborative approach between humans and machines enables designers to conduct more effective analyses of user needs and enhance the quality of design strategies.

4.2 Prototype Design Stage

In this stage, human designers and Generative AI collaboratively engaged in redesigning the prototype of the CUBE App (Fig. 1), based on the findings from the previous stage of problem distillation. The stage was divided into two parts: functional flow planning and interface drawing. Researchers documented the results and findings of each action, assessing various Generative AI design tools for their assistance and constraints in prototype design.

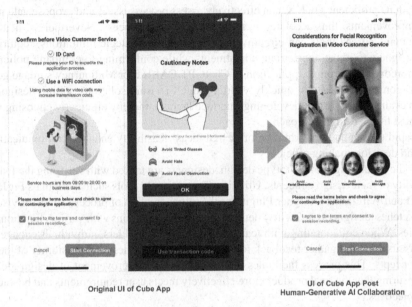

Original UI of Cube App   UI of Cube App Post Human-Generative AI Collaboration

Fig. 1. Before and After Comparison of Prototype Design

Following the findings of the problem distillation stage, proposed improvements were made to the prototype design of the CUBE App. This process included functional flow planning, sketching, and interface drawing, using various Generative AI tools for assistance and evaluating their effectiveness and limitations. This provides insights for future collaborations between designers and AI in interface design. Reflections on the collaboration between researchers and Generative AI during the prototype design stage include:

1. Accelerating the Transition from Abstract Concepts to Concrete Images

During the initial stages of the design process, ideas and concepts are often abstract. However, Generative AI tools can translate these abstract concepts into concrete visual images. Tools such as the Figma Wireframe Designer Plugin, Uizard AI, and ChatGPT DALL·E were used to assist in creating wireframe sketches. Although they require manual correction and are not directly usable for interface design, their ability to visualize abstract concepts facilitates quicker and easier understanding and discussion of design concepts. Considering the diverse sketching necessities inherent to each stage of a project, designers can select the optimal tool tailored to the particular requisites of the project, work objectives, and stakeholders' expectations. This enhances the presentation of design concepts during proposal stages or team communication.

2. Rapid Iteration of Design Ideas

   Generative AI tools can swiftly generate a variety of design alternatives, expediting the exploration and iteration within the design process. For instance, designers can transform the functional processes that require improvement in the product into textual descriptions for analysis by ChatGPT. Despite unidentified user pain points, ChatGPT, with its proficiency in UX, can effectively assess process issues and propose valuable improvements, thus accelerating the iterative design process. Nevertheless, neither humans nor AI tools can circumvent organizational strategic limitations, requiring designers to make appropriate adjustments while conforming to company policies. Moreover, the prompt application of ChatGPT DALL·E or Midjourney's image generation capabilities can quickly yield a range of visual solutions, aiding designers in evaluating style and developing interface layouts, thereby efficiently choosing the most fitting design approach.

3. Rapid testing and confirmation of design ideas' feasibility enhance communication and decision-making efficiency

   In the initial stages of prototype design, designers are tasked with verifying the feasibility of their design concepts. Utilizing Generative AI tools such as Figma's FigJam AI and Wireframe Designer Plugin for the initial creation of process charts or visual sketches, designers can swiftly demonstrate user interactions with various functionalities. When collaborating with team members or stakeholders, individuals engage in discussions and gather feedback to validate the effectiveness and feasibility of these concepts. This process facilitates the refinement and improvement of design ideas, ensuring that the final product more effectively meets user requirements and business objectives.

4. AI-Generated Contextual Images, Enhancing Interface Presentation Realism

   For instance, when designing the video customer service interface for the CUBE App, realistic human images were generated using Midjourney. These images not only enhanced the interface's professionalism and realism, bolstering user trust in financial products but also improved UX and visual appeal. Such delicate visual representations are crucial for enhancing UX and establishing brand image.

5. The Critical Role of Human Designers in Prototype Design

   Generative AI tools efficiently produced initial concepts and visual sketches, helping teams to quickly brainstorm and assess ideas in the early stages of product development. Nevertheless, current Generative AI cannot independently complete interface design, and professional expertise, creative thinking, and nuanced judgment of designers play an important role in shaping the final design's details and optimization. Designers need to synthesize, adjust, and enhance AI-generated sketches to achieve high-quality design results. Therefore, in collaboration with AI, designers remain irreplaceable in handling UX design and visual design details.

   Generative AI tools have introduced new opportunities and challenges in the prototype design process. They expand design possibilities while emphasizing the core role of human designers in deep thinking, creative ideation, and design optimization. As AI tools persist in their evolution, they will furnish increased assistance to designers, who, in turn, must consistently augment their competencies to harness these cutting-edge technologies to their fullest extent.

4.3 Design Validation Stage

To evaluate the effectiveness of Generative AI in enhancing the UX of the CUBE App, this study conducted post-usability testing on the high-fidelity prototype collaboratively developed by Generative AI and human designers. The aim was to gain a deeper understanding of the usability and efficiency of the prototype after optimization with Generative AI assistance. In this research phase, ChatGPT (based on the GPT-4 architecture, ChatGPT November 6 Version) was used to assist in planning the testing process, along with the Good Tape tool for organizing interview content, and utilizing ChatGPT was employed to expedite the production of final reports. The diversified use of Generative AI tools has not only enhanced the efficiency of data organization but also provided human designers with broader perspectives.

User testing results suggested that Generative AI had a noticeable effect on the prototype design stage. With improvement suggestions on functional planning from ChatGPT and contextual images generated by Midjourney, users found the revised process flow to be smooth and efficient, deeming the design clear and functional. However, it was also noted that some user pain points could not be resolved by AI and needed to be addressed at the strategic level of the bank. Therefore, current AI tools in the design process still necessitate the deep involvement of human designers to ensure the quality of design outcomes and user satisfaction.

4.4 Summary of Research Findings

In the process of improving the UX design of the CUBE App, the application of Generative AI not only enhanced the efficiency of the design process but also stimulated innovative thinking among designers, particularly in competitive analysis, user research, and the realization of abstract concepts. This also introduced new challenges and opportunities to the design process.

However, the limitations of Generative AI in handling complex functional structures and contextual adaptability mean that designers should not overly rely on suggestions from Generative AI. To maximize the benefits of ChatGPT, designers need to ensure that ChatGPT's knowledge aligns with their understanding and make appropriate adjustments and guidance. Additionally, strategic questioning is key to enhancing the effectiveness of Generative AI applications, including providing clear examples and constraints, segmenting large data for more accurate analysis, and flexibly using open-ended and goal-oriented strategies in question design. When summarizing data, pose open-ended questions; for in-depth analysis of specific issues, direct ChatGPT to follow certain viewpoints or adhere to specific constraints.

The responses provided by Generative AI should be considered as part of creative ideation, not as the basis for final decisions. Designers can combine these responses with other data sources and form final design strategies through professional verification processes. For instance, in the prototype design stage, while Generative AI can rapidly provide visual sketches, the final stages of decision-making and fine-tuning still rely on the professional knowledge and experience of designers.

Designers who collaborate with Generative AI must continuously develop their professional skills to more effectively leverage these advanced technologies. In response to the continuous evolution of AI technology, designers must adapt to these changes and integrate new technologies into traditional design processes to better meet user needs and product objectives.

5 Discussion

5.1 The Benefits and Limitations of Generative AI Assistance in the UX Design Process

Literature suggests AI in design boosts process efficiency and automation (Virvou, 2023; Stige et al., 2023). Generative AI notably enhances designers' creativity, elevating design quality and productivity (Chiou et al., 2023; Nielsen, 2023b). This study highlights Generative AI's key advantage as providing a starting point for design tasks. ChatGPT, for example, automatically crafts initial user interview questions, streamlining the design process by eliminating the need to start from zero and facilitating deeper inquiry. Hence, Generative AI tools significantly reduce preliminary planning time for designers.

However, this also indicates that currently, Generative AI can only assist in the initial stages of design work, with its outputs still requiring manual review and correction. AI-generated texts may lack depth, prompting additional verification for accuracy. Similarly, AI struggles to fully meet specific design needs in image creation, often as a conceptual guide. For example, Figma's FigJam AI feature can produce a functional flowchart for face recognition verification in the CUBE App within a minute. However, due to data limitations, it cannot comprehend processes beyond standard face recognition functionalities, such as video customer service, requiring designers to supple the output for practical application. Therefore, when discussing non-generic topics like special product features or data-intensive information with AI tools, designers should pay extra attention to the usability of generated results, engaging in extensive questioning and direction to achieve optimal outcomes.

Additionally, this research currently finds that ChatGPT is the most widely applied and user-friendly Generative AI tool for assisting in UX design. With its large transformer architecture, ChatGPT can effectively process and analyze extensive textual data. Moreover, ChatGPT's DALL·E image generation model transforms textual descriptions into corresponding images. Its unique and user-friendly interface allows users to interact with AI in a conversational manner akin to human interaction. These advantages make ChatGPT an invaluable aid in various aspects of the design process, such as user research, interview compilation, process improvement, and sketch generation.

Additionally, ChatGPT currently stands out as a versatile and accessible Generative AI tool for UX design, proficient in processing vast text data and transforming descriptions into images. Its intuitive interface fosters a natural dialogue with users, making it a comprehensive aid across design process. Conversely, Midjourney distinguishes itself in generating visually diverse and high-quality images, superior in creating detailed interface designs or persona scenarios compared to ChatGPT's DALL·E. Although it requires more nuanced commands, a challenge mitigated by using ChatGPT for prompt generation.

Therefore, choosing the appropriate AI tool for various design tasks can effectively enhance the efficiency and quality of the overall design process. UX design tasks can be broadly categorized into three types: text-based tasks, image-based tasks, and flowchart or wireframe-based tasks. Based on current AI capabilities, for text-based tasks such as competitive analysis and interview data compilation in the problem distillation stage of the Three Diamond Design Process (Wang et al., 2022), or usability testing in the validation stage, designers can opt for Generative AI tools capable of interactive discussion, data retrieval, creative brainstorming, and analysis and synthesis, like discussing market trends or planning product goals with ChatGPT.

For image-based tasks, including persona creation and interface design during problem distillation and design iteration stages, designers can choose image-generating AI tools like Midjourney or ChatGPT's DALL·E. For tasks centered on flowcharts or wireframes, such as creating flowcharts and wireframe sketches, designers might opt for AI tools specialized in UX design, like Figma. However, these approaches are based on current Generative AI tool capabilities, which could expand and adjust their application areas with future updates.

On the other hand, due to AI's limitations in understanding human queries and handling large volumes of data, designers must employ appropriate questioning techniques based on different usage scenarios to obtain practical responses. For data integration tasks like online searches or summaries, concise questioning can help AI to converge information broadly; for data verification, such as asking about data sources or analysis methods, a questioning approach may be used; and for in-depth analysis or strategic proposals, such as generating insight reports, designers should specify the AI's analysis angle and direction. Additionally, in the realm of image generation, particularly when creating interface images, prompts should primarily describe key functionalities. Details of the functionality can be progressively incorporated through multiple iterations of questioning and answers, or by employing image-to-image generation techniques to produce similar interfaces or visual styles.

While collaboration between designers and Generative AI tools requires an initial period of adjustment, it reduces the manpower demand for design tasks and enhances the independent operational capabilities of designers. At present, Generative AI cannot fully automate the design process and only serves merely as an auxiliary tool. Therefore, when employing AI to assist in design tasks, designers must combine strategic questioning and critical thinking to fully leverage the potential of AI, while simultaneously ensuring the quality of design outcomes.

5.2 Potential Applications of Generative AI Across Different Design Fields

An analysis of the UX Design Model and the Three Diamond Design Process reveals significant similarities across UX design, service design, and product design. Despite differences in media application, the essence of design in these fields involves a continual process of divergence and convergence (Tang, 2020). This study finds that Generative AI tools effectively assist the UX design process, and it is conjectured that similar benefits could be extended to product and service design.

Human-centered design thinking is pivotal in the design process. Under the Three Diamond Model framework, regardless of the design field, there is a uniform emphasis on the problem distillation stage. Therefore, employing Generative AI tools for competitive analysis, user research planning, and integration can effectively clarify the design direction across various design domains.

During the design iteration stage, appropriate AI tools can be selected based on the unique prototype needs of each field. In product design, the focus is mainly on the form design and usability evaluation of the product. Hence, image-generating AI tools such as ChatGPT's DALL·E, Midjourney, Stable Diffusion could facilitate early-stage inspiration and conceptual innovation (Derevyanko & Zalevska, 2023). On the other hand, service design emphasizes a multi-dimensional approach to customer experience processes (Gibbons, 2017), often requiring a blend of abstract and concrete representations in prototype design, making AI tools capable of generating both text and images, like ChatGPT, more suitable.

In UX design, prototype design concentrates on interface display within products, emphasizing usability in digital interactions. According to the UX Design Model (Garrett, 2011), prototype design can be understood in various layers, each benefiting from different Generative AI tools. For instance, in the structure layer, Figma's FigJam AI can be used for drawing functional flowcharts. In the skeleton layer, Figma plugins facilitate interface wireframe drafting. The surface layer can employ ChatGPT's DALL·E or Midjourney for inspiration in detailing interface elements.

For the design validation stage, AI tools can also assist in planning tasks and organizing test data, generating insights and recommendations. However, AI collaboration may vary in response to different validation methods in design domains. In industrial design, the focus during the validation phase is on the physical and functional aspects of tangible products, where ChatGPT could assist in establishing design standards, such as ergonomic design criteria or test plans. In contrast, in UX and service design, which both emphasize user interaction and experience, ChatGPT can help draft preliminary scripts and surveys for testing, enabling designers to start testing more quickly and subsequently assist in integrating relevant data to accelerate improvement planning and design iteration.

While the specific application of Generative AI in service and industrial design still requires further empirical research, the design process in each domain is similar - from problem distillation to design iteration and effectiveness evaluation in the validation stage. Generative AI has the potential to significantly enhance the efficiency and overall quality of the design process in each field. Current trends and research indicate that Generative AI may play a vital role in future design domains, introducing innovative work methods and thought processes for designers.

5.3   How Generative AI May Reshape the Future of UX Designers

Since the advent of Generative AI technology, there has been a divergence of opinions in the field of experience design. While some speculate that AI might replace humans, others view it as a partner aiding human progress (Stige et al., 2023). This study, implementing Generative AI in the UX design process, demonstrates that Generative AI accelerates design iterations, enhances efficiency, and aids designers in ideation. Designers can utilize AI to automatically generate user personas (Salminen et al., 2019) and ease the transition from sketches to design prototypes (Suleri et al., 2019). Moreover, AI's role in data analysis and user behavior prediction allows products to more accurately meet user needs (Virvou, 2023).

However, the automation of traditionally human-executed tasks has reduced the demand for human designers, potentially leading to fewer job opportunities in the design sector, causing anxiety about future career prospects (Oh, 2019). Despite this, human behavior remains unpredictable, and AI cannot precisely forecast user actions (Nielsen, 2023b), nor fully comprehend human emotions and deeply understand user needs (Stige et al., 2023), making the designer's role indispensable (Kaiser, 2019).

Semi-structured interviews in this study revealed varied perceptions of AI among experience designers of different seniorities. Senior designers expressed concern about job reductions due to AI, whereas younger designers were optimistic about AI's development. A department head in experience design shared how tools like ChatGPT and Midjourney enabled rapid data collection and preliminary design proposals, quickly setting the team's direction, reducing meeting frequency, and decision-making time. Design inspiration now extends beyond traditional image databases and data collection to deep interaction and collaboration with AI. However, the increased efficiency in design work due to AI applications raises concerns among designers about formulaic tasks being replaced and a potential decline in demand for designers.

These findings underscore the importance of collaboration between designers and AI, especially for experts with UX knowledge, such as senior designers, who play a pivotal role in human-AI collaborative design processes. With deeper experience, professional judgment, and strategic capabilities, senior designers are more adept at assessing the practicality and accuracy of AI-generated data (Nielsen, 2023b). Conversely, junior designers may face challenges and must critically evaluate AI-generated content to avoid being misled, possibly requiring further data verification or expert consultation.

With the widespread application of AI technology, designers confront the challenge of continuously adapting to new technologies and learning to collaborate with AI, a future trend. This includes understanding AI's operational principles and data processing mechanisms and discerning which design tasks are suitable for automation. It is vital to balance human needs with automated tasks, ensuring technological advancement does not diminish user expectations while maintaining human values.

This new interactive mode allows designers to explore a wide range of design possibilities in shorter timeframes, finding more creative solutions to multifaceted design challenges. While designers are unlikely to be completely replaced by AI, they might be superseded by those who master AI skills. Regardless of experience level, UX designers should deepen their knowledge and adeptly use various AI tools to adapt to the rapidly evolving AI landscape, maximizing their potential as designers.

5.4   Research Limitations and Future Research Directions

This study delved deeply into the application of Generative AI in the field of UX design, revealing certain limitations in its scope and offering new directions for future research. While the current study is based on the latest AI versions available during the design process, upcoming releases of new versions and improvements in AI tools could impact the findings of this study.

Given that the research focused specifically on the CUBE App case and was constrained by time, it did not involve multiple iterations of the design process, which may limit the applicability of the results to all areas of experience design. Future research could expand on the application of Generative AI in various types of digital products and design fields. For example, exploring the potential role of AI in the development of new products, website design, and in fields like service and industrial design could be fruitful.

Additionally, this study discussed results primarily from the perspective of designers. To enhance the potential of AI applications, future research could consider different product development team perspectives. This would involve examining how AI is effectively used throughout the process, its impact on team decision-making, and even the development of new team collaboration models. Such research could bring a more comprehensive perspective to product development, helping teams to be more creative and innovative in the rapidly evolving era of AI.

6 Conclusions and Future Works

6.1 Generative AI Efficiently Streamlines Early-Stage Design Processes, Enabling a Greater Focus on Creativity and Strategy

This study finds that the use of Generative AI tools in the UX design process offers an effective starting point for each design task, accelerating the iterative planning process and facilitating the development of design solutions. This transformation extends the role of designers to more closely resemble data analysts and strategists, indicating a shift from traditional human-centered design processes to data-driven, technology-oriented methodologies. Consequently, the integration of Generative AI tools within the Three Diamond Design Process has birthed a new Generative AI-Enhanced User Experience Design Process (Fig. 2).

Fig. 2. Generative AI-Enhanced User Experience Design Process

Generative AI-Enhanced Problem Distillation Stage. The application of Generative AI tools aids designers in rapidly analyzing and understanding complex data to uncover potential user needs and market trends. Utilizing Generative AI tools equipped with capabilities for interactive discussion, data retrieval, integration, and analysis supports tasks such as competitive analysis, goal setting, and the compilation of interview data. This collaborative effort facilitates the swift and effective generation of insight reports, enabling the rapid and efficient proposal of design solutions that address user issues.

Generative AI-Enhanced Design Iteration Stage. At this stage, Generative AI swiftly transforms abstract concepts into tangible, visualized functionalities. For tasks represented primarily by flowcharts or wireframes, designers can opt for AI tools specialized in UX design. For tasks requiring visual representation, image-generating AI tools are preferred. Rapid testing and validation of design ideas ensure that the final product better meets user needs and business objectives.

Generative AI-Enhanced Field Validation Stage. To verify the effectiveness of design solutions, Generative AI's data analysis capabilities can plan user testing and product performance evaluation, generating insights more quickly for necessary product adjustments and optimization.

These advancements provide design teams with new tools for faster and more efficient product development and iteration, opening new possibilities for future design innovation.

6.2 Generative AI Should Offer Clear Decision-Making Processes to Facilitate Precise Questioning by Designers

Interviews with designers highlighted challenges in using Generative AI, such as repeated adjustments to prompts to achieve desired outcomes, adding complexity and time to tasks. To improve usability and interaction smoothness, Generative AI tools should adopt Human-Centered AI principles (Shneiderman, 2020) and UX design thinking, addressing two main issues: unclear AI data generation processes from keywords, leading to unpredictable responses, and distrust in AI-generated results. Enhancing interpretability, demystifying the AI "black box," and clarifying AI decision-making processes are essential (Garrett, 2011).

Strategy Plane. The focus should be on solving human problems and enhancing abilities, fostering mutual understanding between human designers and AI, and ensuring tools are user-friendly.

Scope Plane. Collecting user data helps AI understand users better. AI must process extensive human-provided data, continuously update, and incorporate domain-specific information to refine design solutions. Also, AI should offer detailed generation processes and simplify querying for easier designer understanding.

Structure and Skeleton Plane. Explaining data sources can facilitate precise communication. Clarifying which results stem from human data versus AI model data, offering a prompt library, and a result collection area can aid in easier querying and record searching. Generative AI that automatically verifies interface designs against design system principles can save designers time in review.

Surface Plane. The unclear button layout in image-generating tools like Midjourney causes confusion. Midjourney should improve its interface layout and provide clear instructions. These strategies can enhance collaboration between designers and Generative AI tools, optimize UX, and lower the barrier to usage.

To sum up, the context of integration, UX designers leveraging Generative AI tools, combined with their expertise in strategic questioning and critical thinking, significantly enhance their design efficiency and creativity. This study highlights the importance of proficiency in Generative AI among designers, showcasing how it accelerates data processing and analysis, thereby allowing for a more focused approach to creative solutions and meeting user expectations effectively. The case of the CUBE App illustrates that skilled designers can utilize Generative AI to streamline the design process, enabling rapid iterations and improving the user experience of the final product.

Therefore, designers must enhance their problem-solving skills, engage effectively with AI tools, and critically evaluate AI-generated solutions to remain competitive. Embracing AI's capabilities for intelligent interaction and personalized experiences, designers have the opportunity to craft more engaging user experiences. Generative AI not only boosts the design process efficiency but also elevates designers' industry competitiveness. In the evolving technological landscape, it's crucial for UX designers to adeptly navigate and integrate AI technology, ensuring they stay at the forefront of the design industry (Nielsen, 2023b).

Disclosure of Interests. The authors have no competing interests to declare that are relevant to the content of this article.

References

Breque, M., Petridis, A., Nul, L.D.: Industry 5.0 - Towards a Sustainable, Human-Centric and Resilient European Industry (2021, May 1). https://research-and-innovation.ec.europa.eu/kno wledge-publications-tools-and-data/publications/all-publications/industry-50-towards-sustai nable-human-centric-and-resilient-european-industry_en

Chanchamnan, P., San, S., Ho, C.: Design in the age of Artificial Intelligence: a literature review on the enhancement of User Experience Design with AI (2023). https://doi.org/10.13140/RG. 2.2.33028.91523

Chiou, L., Hung, P., Liang, R., Wang, C.: Designing with AI: an exploration of co-ideation with image generators. In: Proceedings of the 2023 ACM Designing Interactive Systems Conference (DIS 2023), 1941–1954 (2023). https://doi.org/10.1145/3563657.3596001

Derevyanko, N., Zalevska, O.: Comparative analysis of neural networks Midjourney, Stable Diffusion, and DALL-E and ways of their implementation in the educational process of students of design specialities. Scientific Bullet. Mukachevo State Univ. Ser. "Pedag. Psychol." 9(3), 36–44 (2023). https://doi.org/10.52534/msu-pp3.2023.36

Dove, G., Halskov, K., Forlizzi, J., Zimmerman, J.: UX Design Innovation: Challenges for Working with Machine Learning as a Design Material (2017). https://doi.org/10.1145/3025453.3025739

Garrett, J.J.: The Elements of User Experience: User-Centered Design for the Web and Beyond. New Riders, Berkeley (2011)

Ghajargar, M., Persson, J., Bardzell, J., Holmberg, L., Tegen, A.: The UX of Interactive. Mach. Learn. (2020). https://doi.org/10.1145/3419249.3421236

Kaiser, Z.: Creativity as computation: teaching design in the age of automation. Des. Cult. 11(2), 173–192 (2019). https://doi.org/10.1080/17547075.2019.1609279

Kliman-Silver, C., Siy, O., Awadalla, K., Lentz, A., Convertino, G., Churchill, E.: Adapting User Experience Research Methods for AI-Driven Experiences (2020)

Mckinsey. Exploring Opportunities in the Generative AI Value Chain (2023, April 26). https://www.mckinsey.com/capabilities/quantumblack/our-insights/exploring-opportunities-in-the-generative-ai-value-chain

Nielsen, J.: UX Needs a Sense of Urgency About AI. Jakob Nielsen on UX (2023, June 15). https://jakobnielsenphd.substack.com/p/ux-needs-a-sense-of-urgency-about

Nielsen, J.: Getting Started with AI for UX. Jakob Nielsen on UX (2023, October 18). https://jakobnielsenphd.substack.com/p/get-started-ai-for-ux

Salminen, J., Sengün, S., Jung, S., Jansen, B.J.: Design issues in automatically generated persona profiles: a qualitative analysis from 38 think-aloud transcripts. In: Proceedings of the 2019 Conference on Human Information Interaction and Retrieval, pp. 225–229 (2019). https://doi.org/10.1145/3295750.3298942

Shneiderman, B.: Human-centered artificial intelligence: three fresh ideas. AIS Trans. Hum. Comput. Interact. 109–124 (2020). https://doi.org/10.17705/1thci.00131

Stige, Å., Zamani, E.D., Mikalef, P., Zhu, Y.: Artificial intelligence (AI) for user experience (UX) design: a systematic literature review and future research agenda. Inf. Technol. People (2023). https://doi.org/10.1108/itp-07-2022-0519

Suleri, S., Sermuga Pandian, V.P., Shishkovets, S., Jarke, M.: Eve: a sketch-based software prototyping workbench. In: Extended Abstracts of the 2019 CHI Conference on Human Factors in Computing Systems, pp. 1–6 (2019). https://doi.org/10.1145/3290607.3312994

Tang, H.H.: On the Genuine Relationship Between Design and Business. Medium (2020, November 6). https://pse.is/5knzrg

Verganti, R., Vendraminelli, L., Iansiti, M.: Innovation and design in the age of artificial intelligence. J. Prod. Innov. Manag. 37(3), 212–227 (2020)

Virvou, M.: Artificial intelligence and user experience in reciprocity: contributions and state of the art. Intell. Decis. Technol. 17, 73–125 (2023). https://doi.org/10.3233/IDT-230092

Wang, D., Hsieh, W.-A., Chen, S.-Y., Tang, H.-H.: The Complexities of Transport Service Design for Visually Impaired People: Lessons from a Bus Commuting Service (2022)

Estimating Reliability of Speech Recognition Results Using Recognition Results Change Degree When Minute Changes to Speech Waveform

Atsuteru Iida[✉], Hikaru Nishida, and Yumi Wakita

Osaka Institute of Technology, Osaka, Japan
atsu.iida@i.softbank.jp, yumi.wakita@oit.ac.jp

Abstract. Speech recognition technology has made remarkable progress in recent years, but 100% of speech recognition results are not guaranteed to be recognized due to the nature of the speech recognition mechanism. From the standpoint of developing applications that incorporate such speech recognition software, it is necessary to know how many misrecognition errors are included in the recognition results for the speech input as this will affect the application's performance. In this paper, we propose a method to estimate a reliability of speech recognition results by observing how they change when slight modifications are intentionally applied to the input waveform. Specifically, the two types of minute change are processed to waveform. One is to slightly shift the start points of speech parts. Another is to add slight white noise to the speech waveform. By analyzing recognition results before and after these modifications, we find a correlation between the recognition results changing degrees and the words error rate (WER). This suggests that the recognition result change rate is an effective index for estimating the reliability of output speech recognition results.

Keywords: Speech Recognition Results Reliability · minute change of recognition results · Recognition error rate · Regression Analysis

1 Introduction

Although speech recognition technology has made remarkable progress in recent years, frequent misrecognition occurs in speech recognition in daily conversation. The reasons for misrecognition in daily conversation are many: the fact that the variation of recognition parameters is large even for the same word as speaking style varies greatly depending on the conversation content and speaker's emotion; the increase in nonverbal vocalizations, such as laughter utterance; and the relatively frequent use of unknown words not found in the dictionary, such as abbreviations and appellations. Efforts are being made to improve recognition by using daily conversation speech itself for training. However, 100% of speech recognition results are not guaranteed to be recognized due to the nature of the speech recognition mechanism. From the standpoint of developing

© The Author(s), under exclusive license to Springer Nature Switzerland AG 2024
H. Degen and S. Ntoa (Eds.): HCII 2024, LNAI 14735, pp. 190–201, 2024.
https://doi.org/10.1007/978-3-031-60611-3_14

applications that incorporate such speech recognition software, it is necessary to know how many misrecognition errors are included in the recognition results for the speech input as this will affect the application's performance. In other words, the ability to evaluate the recognition results' reliability is critical.

Various methods to evaluate recognition reliability have been proposed. For example, a method for determining the reliability of the recognition results using the difference between the recognition result score and the second or lower candidate scores has been widely used [1]. Another method estimates the confidence score of recognition results using speech information other than the acoustic features used for recognition, such as the prosody information of utterances [2]. However, almost studies adopting this method have focused on speech dialogue or speech translation systems, which are based on the assumption that people and systems engage in conversational exchanges and not in daily conversation, in which people chat without constraints.

Utterances in daily conversation often lack syllables completely, which should be uttered due to instability in utterance speed or ambiguity. In [3], these have been reported as the cause of misrecognition specific to daily conversation. Such examples cannot be correctly estimated by the conventional confidence estimation method described above, unless a mechanism determines that a part of the syllables forming a word is correct even if it is missing in its entirety; however, it is especially difficult to completely compensate for a syllable that is missing in its entirety. A new method of judging the reliability of speech recognition that accommodates the unstable utterances found in daily conversation is needed.

2   Analysis of Speech Recognition Errors in Daily Conversation

2.1   Speech Recognition System

A transformer-based speech recognition system, Whisper [6, 7] was used for speech recognition. Its acoustic analysis specifications were a sampling frequency of 16,000 Hz, frame window length of 25 ms, frame shift of 10 ms, and log magnitude Mel spectrogram order of 80. The 680,000 h of speech data were used for training—a feature that allows to use large amounts of data and high accuracy without fine-tuning. Although the size models are various, in this study, a "medium model", which parameter size is 769 M, was selected for the experiments.

2.2   Conversation Database

Several daily conversations were recorded, five of which were used in this study. Speakers were six university students (five men and one woman) aged 21–23 and one female teacher (*indicates teacher). No restrictions were placed on the content of the conversations, and the speakers were allowed to speak freely. Conversation-A involved three speakers, and conversations B–F involved two speakers. Two reading utterances were also recorded for comparison: two women were asked to read the text taken from a newspaper article. Each recording lasted approximately 20 s. Table 1 shows the specifications of the conversation database used.

Table 1. Conversation conditions

Conversation symbol	Speech Style	Number of speakers	Conversation lengths
A	Daily conversation	3 (2 Men, 1 Woman*)	91 s
B	Daily conversation	2 (2 Men)	182 s
C	Daily conversation	2 (1 Man, 1 Woman*)	182 s
D	Daily conversation	2 (1 Man, 1 Woman*)	187 s
E	Daily conversation	2 (2 Men)	186 s
F	Reading aloud	1 (1 Woman)	23 s
F	Reading aloud	1 (1 Woman)	23 s

2.3 Speech Recognition Results

The word error rates (WER) for each conversation are shown in Fig. 1, where the recognition rates of daily conversation are considerably lower than that of reading speech. The difference in the average misrecognition rate between the two was 33%. The recognition rates of daily conversation also varied greatly depending on the conversation, ranging from 36% for the best performing conversation to 59% for the worst, with more than half of the words being misrecognized in the worst case. These results indicate that it is difficult to trust the speech recognition results of daily conversations as they are; however, not all daily conversations are difficult, and reliability varies greatly from conversation to conversation.

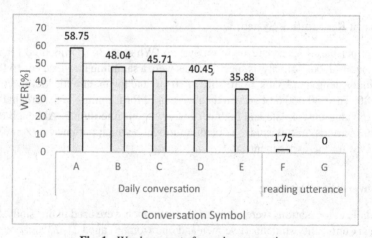

Fig. 1. Word error rate for each conversation

To confirm that the above trend in recognition results is not unique to "whisper," as described in Sect. 2.1, we conducted speech recognition experiments with other speech recognition tools using the conversation database shown in Table 1. As a speech recognition tool, we used the one included in the Azure AI Service provided by the Microsoft

Azure cloud platform. Table 2 shows the WER of each conversation in the recognition experiments with "Whisper" and "Azure."

In the recognition results for "Azure", the recognition performance of the daily conversation speech was considerably worse than that of the read speech, and the difference in recognition rates for each daily conversation was significant. This tendency is the same as that of the "Whisper" speech recognition results shown in Fig. 1. Furthermore, conversations with poor recognition rates using "Whisper" (e.g., Conversation-A, Conversation-B, etc.) also showed poor recognition rates using "Azure." Conversely, conversations with good recognition rates using "Whisper" (e.g., conversation-D, conversation-E, etc.) had good recognition rates using "Azure." This suggests that recognition performance is not dependent on the recognition tool but on the conversation.

Table 2. The word error rates when using two different recognition tools

Conversation symbol	Daily conversation					Reading speech	
	A	B	C	D	E	F	G
By Whisper	58.75	48.04	45.71	40.45	35.88	1.75	0
By Azure	54.23	42.02	37.8	36.97	27.1	17.54	7.69

The difference in recognition performance between recited speech and everyday conversation is confirmed by comparing the transcribed sentences and recognition result sentences. Table 3 shows typical examples of errors in both conversations.

The left side of the table shows the transcriptions, and the right side shows the recognition results. The red letters indicate the part of recognition errors. The parentheses "()" indicate that the entire sentence on the left side is missing from the recognition results.

Table 3. Comparison between transcriptions and recognition results

Reading speech	Mutenka no shabon **d**ama Jikan **mo** kakari masu	Mutenka no shabon **n**ama Jikan **o** ka**w**ari masu
Daily conversation	**Etto desu ne** Yatte miyo nanode Yatte **miyo nanode na** **Iida** san **sa**, kore ha mo keshi temo daijobu?	() Yatte miyo nanode Yatto () **Izawa** san san, kore ha mo keshi temo daijobu?

The transcribed and recognized speech showed no difference in the number of words and no errors in which whole words were missing. In many cases of misrecognition, some phonemes in a word were mistaken for other phonemes. In a few cases, a vowel was mistaken for another vowel. In daily speech, however, consecutive phonemes were frequently mistaken for completely different phonemes or dropped entirely. The sentence

"*Yatte miyo nanode*" in Table 3 was uttered twice by the same speaker for the exact same content; one was recognized correctly, but the second half of the utterance was not. The same frequently happened with proper nouns: the Japanese name "Iida" was misrecognized as "Izawa" in the example in Table 3, but it was misrecognized as "Ida" or correctly recognized as "Iida" in other places.

3   The Reliability Estimation Method of Speech Recognition Result by Processing Slight Changes to Input Speech Data

The results of Sect. 2 showed that daily conversational utterances, which are prone to speech recognition errors, tend to misrecognize completely different phonemes or phoneme sequences, even if they are vowels; they also tend to output different recognition results for the same word or sentence or drop whole words or word sequences. These results suggest that utterances that frequently cause misrecognition to have a greater variation in the parameter values for recognition, even if the vocalizations' content is the same. We thought that, in the case of unstable vocalizations such as those described above, deliberately making only a small change in the acoustic characteristics of the utterances would facilitate a different recognition result.

If the input speech waveform is subjected to a slight change in processing that we do not notice when we listen, the recognition result will not change if the original input speech has many stable characteristics. However, if the original speech has many unstable characteristics, the speech recognition result may change before and after the slight change processing. By observing the degree of change in recognition results when slight changes are intentionally made, we attempt to estimate the reliability of recognition results. Figure 2 shows the process of estimating the reliability of speech recognition results.

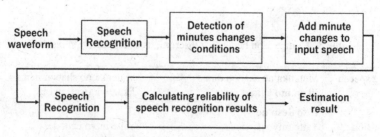

Fig. 2. Process of recognition result reliability estimation

After the speech recognition process has been completed, the input speech waveform is slightly changed, and the speech recognition is processed again. The waveform is changed in two ways.

The first one is by slightly shifting the start points of the speech parts. The speech recognition results are compared between the waveform before and after shifting, and if the number of words whose recognition results have changed is large, the reliability of the recognition results for this utterance is considered low. When calculating the recognition parameters, the waveform is divided into frames, and one vector of recognition parameters is obtained for each frame. Therefore, by shifting the start points of the speech parts, the waveform delimitation changes, and the recognition parameters of different values are calculated. This is a modification process that changes the temporal characteristics in minute increments.

Another change process involves adding slight white noise to the speech waveform, which results in a minute change in the frequency response. The speech recognition results of the waveforms before and after the noise is added are compared; if the number of words whose recognition results have changed is large, the reliability of the recognition results for this utterance is considered low.

4 Relationship Between Speech Recognition Performance and Recognition Result Change Rate

We confirmed whether the change degree in the recognition results when slight changes are made to the speech waveform file described in Sect. 2 is effective in estimating misrecognized speech utterances. The recognition rate differs greatly between a speech of manuscript reading and a daily conversation among several friends. Therefore, we confirmed the relationship between the recognition rate of each conversation and the change degree of recognition words by using two change processing—"slightly shift the start points of the speech parts" and "adding slight white noise"—using conversation databases shown in Table 1.

Figure 3 shows the WER for each conversation database as a bar graph (the same as the WER values in Fig. 1). The percentage of words that changed compared to the original recognition result (recognition result change rate) when the waveform with the speech-start portion shaved off for 0.001 s is recognized is indicated by a gray circle, " ●," and the recognition result change rate when white noise is added is indicated by a gray triangle, " ▲." The noise pressure level is 9 dB, and the average signal-to-noise ratio is 52.33 dB. Black squares (■) overlay the sum of the two types of recognition result change rates.

In conversations with a high word misrecognition rate, the total recognition result change rate is also high, and in conversations with a low word misrecognition rate, the total recognition result change rate is also low. The results suggest that recognition performance may be estimated using the recognition result change rate after the waveform is subjected to minor processing such as "slightly shift the start points of the speech parts" and "adding slight white noise."

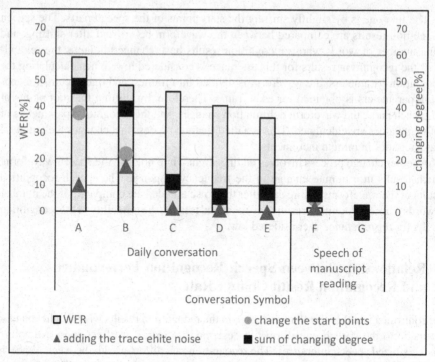

Fig. 3. Relation between word recognition rate and changing degree of recognition words (using Whisper)

Two types of processing were applied to the waveforms, and we examined whether the trend of recognition result changes differed with each processing. The results showed that words containing plosive sounds such as "pa" and "ta" changed more frequently when the "slightly shift the start points of the speech parts" processing was used, accounting for 67.4% of the changed parts. When white noise was added to the processing, plosive sounds did not change significantly, and a wide range of phonemes—including broken sounds, nasal sounds, and vowels—were changed in a rambling manner.

A similar experiment was conducted using another speech recognition tool, "Azure." The results are shown in Fig. 4, which confirms that, as with "Whisper," the total rate of change of recognition results tends to be proportional to the WER when two types of slight changes are made. These results suggest that the degree of change in the recognition result would be effective to estimate WER, even if the recognition tools are different.

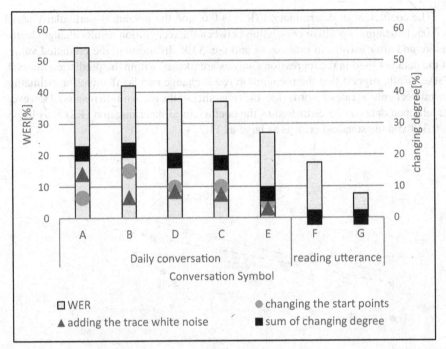

Fig. 4. Relation between word recognition rate and changing degree of recognition words (using Recognition tool from AZURU)

5 Evaluation of Reliability Estimation Performance of Speech Recognition Results

To confirm that the rate of change of speech recognition results due to waveform change processing shown in Sect. 4 is effective in estimating the reliability of the recognition results, we conducted a regression analysis with the word misrecognition rate as the objective variable and the rate of change of recognition results as the explanatory variable. In addition to the speech data used in Sect. 2, we used 24 daily conversations of 2–6 min in length and seven conversations read aloud, for a total of 38 speech data. Of the 38 data shown on the left, we used 30 (18 daily conversations and five read-aloud voices) in the regression analysis. Figure 5 shows the results of the analysis. The dotted line in the center indicates the regression line; the outer two dotted lines above and below the regression line indicate the 95% prediction interval, and the inner small, dotted line indicates the 95% confidence interval. The black circles indicate the eight-speech data not used in the regression analysis, and the triangles indicate the speech data used in the regression analysis. The horizontal axis is the sum [%] of the percent change in voice recognition results due to the two types of processing, and the vertical axis is the WER [%] for each voice.

The coefficient of determination (R2) is 0.6, and the p-value is particularly small at 0.05, indicating a positive correlation between the recognition results change degree before and after waveform processing and the WER. In addition, the predicted values of the data not used in the regression analysis are located within the prediction interval. These results suggest that the recognition result change rate is effective for estimating the misrecognition rate of words (i.e., the reliability of the recognition results). However, not all open data can be estimated as the coefficient of determination (R2) is as heavy as 0.361 and the standard error is as large as 11.774.

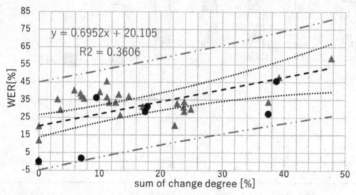

Fig. 5. Evaluating the performance of recognition results reliability estimation using the regression analysis method (when using "Whisper")

The same analysis was performed using the recognition result change rate through the Azure speech recognition tool to confirm that the proposed estimation method for recognition result reliability can be applied independently of the speech recognition tool. We observed the same trend in the Azure system. Figure 6 shows the results using the speech recognition function of Azure.

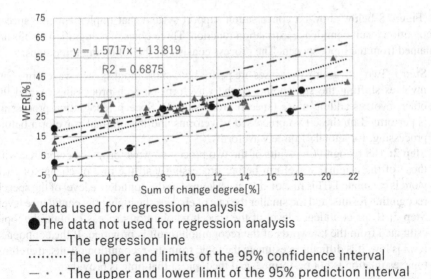

Fig. 6. Evaluating the performance of recognition results reliability estimation using the regression analysis method (when using "Azure")

6 Applications Examples Using the Recognition Result Reliability Estimation Method

We have shown the possibility of estimating speech recognition results reliability using the recognition result change degree. In this section, we explain the process of actually implementing this, using a conversation support system that we are developing separately as an example. To support smooth conversation with others, we are developing a conversation support system that provides appropriate topics when the speaker cannot immediately think of one. Figure 7 shows the structure of our conversation support system, in which the topic provided to the speaker is selected by considering the previous topics of conversation.

First, the input speech is recognized, and some content words are extracted from the recognition results. If the similarity value among recognized content words exceeds a predefined threshold value, the topic of conversation is considered to have been estimated, and topics containing many words that exceed the threshold value are selected.

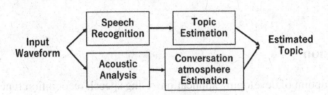

Fig. 7. The Conversation support system using speech recognition

Figure 8 below shows a conversation support system that implements the speech recognition result confidence estimation function. Three types of recognition results are obtained from the input speech. The process consists of the following three steps:

- **Step 1**: Two processing processes are performed on the input speech waveform. One involves shifting the start points of the waveform (speech processing 1), and the other involves adding noise (speech processing 2). Speech recognition processing is performed on these two processed waveforms and the original waveform before processing, for a total of three waveforms.
- **Step 2:** The recognition results of the two processed waveforms are compared with those of the original waveform before processing, and the rate of change of each word is calculated. This rate of change is defined as the confidence level of the speech recognition results, and the smaller the rate of change, the higher the confidence level.
- **Step 3:** If the confidence level of the speech recognition process is high, the topic estimated from the keywords of the recognition result is provided. If the confidence level is low, it is difficult to estimate the topic from the recognition results; therefore, topic estimation is not performed, and the topic at that time is provided.

Through this process, it is possible to provide a conversation support system that avoids unnatural conversation using topics that are appropriate for the time and outside the conversation.

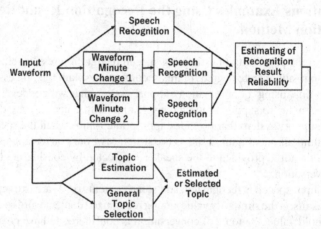

Fig. 8. The conversation support system using the proposed recognition results reliability estimation

7   Conclusion

From the standpoint of developing applications using speech recognition functions, it is important to determine the reliability of the output speech recognition results. Therefore, we proposed a method to estimate the reliability of these recognition results by observing the extent to which they change when slight changes are intentionally made to the input waveform. Two types of waveform processing were used as the changes to be given: slightly shifting the start points of speech and adding slight white noise to the speech waveform.

Even with recent high-performance speech recognition systems, frequent misrecognition occurs when daily conversation is input. We performed the above two types of processing on the waveform of daily conversation and checked the change rate of recognition results before and after each processing. As a result, the change rate of recognition results with a low word misrecognition rate was small, whereas the change rate of recognition results with a high word misrecognition rate was large. The correlation between the two was confirmed by regression analysis. This suggests that the recognition result change rate is an effective index for estimating the reliability of output speech recognition results.

The speech specifications of daily conversation are likely to vary greatly depending on the speaker's age, the place where the conversation takes place, and the human relationship between the speaker and the other party. In the future, we would like to determine the range of applicability of the proposed method for estimating the reliability of speech recognition results using a wider variety of conversational data.

Acknowledgment. This work is supported by JSPS KAKENHI Grant Number 22K04626.

References

1. Lee, A., Shikano, K., Kawahara, T.: Real-time word confidence scoring using local posterior probabilities on tree trellis search. In: Proceedings of the IEEE International Conference on Acoustics, Speech, and Signal Processing (ICASSP2004), vol. 1, pp. 793–796 (2004)
2. Hirschberg, J., Litman, D., Swerts, M.: Prosodic and other cues to speech recognition failures. Speech Commun. **43**, 155–175 (2004)
3. Nishida, H., Iida, Y., Wakita, Y.: Misrecognized utterance identification in support systems for everyday human-to-human conversations. In: Proceedings of 25th International conference on HCII, vol.14051, pp.126–134 (2023)
4. OpenAi. Introducing Whisper. https://openai.com/research/whisper. Accessed 5 Jan 2024
5. Radford, A., Kim, J.W., Xu, T., Brockman, G., McLeavey, C., Sutskever, I.: Robust Speech Recognition via Large-Scale Weak Supervision. https://cdn.openai.com/papers/whisper.pdf. Accessed 3 Jan 2024
6. Microsoft. Overview of Speech-to-Text Conversion. https://learn.microsoft.com/ja-jp/azure/ai-services/speech-service/speech-to-text. Accessed 3 Jan 2024

Emotion Detection from Facial Expression in Online Learning Through Using Synthetic Image Generation

Md Rayhan Kabir, M. Ali Akber Dewan$^{(\boxtimes)}$ (iD), and Fuhua Lin (iD)

School of Computing and Information Systems, Faculty of Science and Technology,
Athabasca University, Edmonton, Canada
{rkabir,adewan,oscarl}@athabascau.ca

Abstract. Understanding students' educational emotion is important for learning process, however, it is challenging to detect in an online learning environment. Deep learning architectures show excellent performance for emotion detection from facial expressions; however, their complexity and computational requirements limit their deployment on students' edge devices. Additionally, the availability and the size of the datasets for detecting educational emotions are scarce. In this study, we propose a lightweight deep learning model based on *MobileNet* architecture which is deployable in students' edge devices for educational emotion detection. We also propose a generative adversarial network based synthetic image generation technique to address the challenges of scarcity of the dataset. This framework is compared with the state-of-the-art models, where it demonstrated competitive performance while making it suitable for the edge devices for the educational emotion detection, and additionally, the use of the synthetic dataset further contributes to improve the performance of the proposed model.

Keywords: Educational emotion detection · lightweight architecture · online learning · facial expression recognition · neural network

1 Introduction

With the advancement of technologies and the shift in the learning methodologies, online learning has gained popularity over time (Zhang, et al., 2023). A major advantage of online education is its capacity to be pursued from any geographical location with the flexibility of the learner's time. Recent advancements in machine learning models have made it feasible to develop smart learning environments to facilitate online learners. These environments can discern various factors, such as a student's level of knowledge, learning pace, emotions, and more. As a result, they can tailor a personalized educational setting to optimize the students' knowledge acquisition. As educational institutions and learners see greater use of online learning platforms, they also recognize the significance of personalized and intelligent learning platforms. Enhancing various aspects of intelligent learning platforms is crucial to improve system efficiency and enhance user experiences. One such aspect involves the ability to detect students' emotions and

© The Author(s), under exclusive license to Springer Nature Switzerland AG 2024
H. Degen and S. Ntoa (Eds.): HCII 2024, LNAI 14735, pp. 202–216, 2024.
https://doi.org/10.1007/978-3-031-60611-3_15

improve students' engagement to their learning sessions (Dewan, et al., 2019). In a physical classroom setting, instructors can rely on visual cues such as facial expressions to gauge students' emotions and respond appropriately. For example, if students appear confused, instructors can provide additional examples to alleviate their confusion. However, in online learning platforms, instructors cannot readily observe these emotions. Nevertheless, online learning opens new possibilities. It allows for the development of machine learning models capable of detecting students' emotions through facial expressions and offering tailored feedback or suggesting alternative course materials. This personalized feedback and guidance are often unattainable in traditional classrooms. Emotion detection from facial expressions in online education has the potential to increase student engagement in learning activities, thereby ensuring maximum learning gains for students.

In detecting emotion from facial expression, deep learning models have shown promising performance (Li, et al., 2023). However, the deep-learning models require a large volume of training data. There are several benchmark datasets for detecting emotion from facial expression but most of them are not created to detect educational emotions. Few datasets created to detect educational emotions are not large enough to train a deep- learning model adequately. Another issue with the deep learning models for educational emotion detection is that the deep learning models are heavy weight and require high computation power which is often not feasible for the students' edge devices, such as laptops, tablets, or cell phones (Boulanger, et al., 2021). A possible solution to this problem could be to deploy the model on a server and stream video data from students' device to the server for further processing. However, this strategy may require high bandwidth and it may also raise privacy concerns for the students. For these reasons, building and deploying a lightweight model on the students' edge devices could be an effective solution in detecting educational emotion and providing real time feedback to the students. To address the above issues, this study intends to make the following two key contributions in this paper:

1. A lightweight deep learning model has been proposed based on *MobileNet* (Howard, et al., 2017) architecture which can be deployed on students' edge devices because of its smaller number of parameters while attaining a competitive performance to the state-of-the-art deep learning models for educational emotion detection.
2. A synthetic image generation technique has been proposed based on generative adversarial network (Goodfellow, et al., 2020) to address the issues with the data scarcity for educational emotion detection.

The rest of the paper is organized as follows: Sect. 2 discusses the related work, Sect. 3 provides the detail of our proposed model, Sect. 4 presents evaluation results of the proposed model in contrast to other state-of-the-art models, and finally, Sect. 5 provides our concluding remarks and future research directions.

2 Related Work

In any learning process, students engagement plays a vital role in their success. Students typically show three types of engagement in education: affective, behavioral, and cognitive (Dewan, et al., 2019). The emotional engagement of a student towards a topic during a learning process is defined as affective engagement (Bian, et al., 2019). The participation of a student in the classroom is defined as behavioral engagement and the effort the students make to learn complex ideas is the cognitive engagement (Anderson, et al., 2004). In this study, we focus on detecting affective engagement, more specifically students' educational emotion from their facial expression. This emotion detection process can help both the student and the instructor to increase their engagement in the learning activities. Much work on emotion detection from facial expression can be found in the literature, however, not much work on educational emotion detection in an academic setting are available in the literature.

A highly optimized GPU implementation for emotion detection from facial expression is proposed by Krizhevsky et al. (Krizhevsky, et al., 2017). In this approach, authors used a large CNN model with an optimization technique. This method achieved state-of-the-art results on ImageNet Large-Scale Visual Recognition Challenge (ILSVRC) dataset. Singh and Nasoz (Singh, et al., 2020) proposed a CNN based model for emotion detection, where the authors discussed the challenges with max-pooling and dropping out. Thai et al. (Thai, et al., 2007), Murthy et al. (Murthy, et al., 2007), and Aung et al. (Aung, et al., 2012) also used different versions of the CNN model and optimized their performance. Several other deep learning models showed high performance in emotion detection from facial expression namely ResNet50 (He, et al., 2016), Inception-v3 (Szegedy, et al., 2016), SqueezeNet (Iandola, et al., 2016), and Exception (Chollet, 2017). Although these models show high performance, these are complex, computationally extensive, and not suitable to use on low resource edge devices.

Lightweight deep learning models have the potential to use on edge devices, however, not many research studies could be found on this for educational emotion detection from facial expression. Boulanger et al. (Boulanger, et al., 2021) proposed a lightweight model for the detection of engagement of the students in online learning. Their study focused on the explainability of the model and showed how the model takes the decision on determining the emotion of the students from their facial expression. Li et al. (Li, et al., 2018) proposed a CNN model with an attention mechanism to deal with the occlusion problem while detecting facial emotion. The authors of this study collected a dataset from a real time video stream in a learning session. Their work provides an insight into considering different postures in emotion detection as while studying in-front of camera, students can sit in different posture. Inspired by these work we aim to design a lightweight deep learning model for emotion detection in an online learning environment.

Scarcity of data is another major issue with training a CNN model. Most of the datasets are not large enough for proper training of the model which inspires us to propose a model to generate synthetic images for facial expression in the setting of online learning. To generate synthetic images, Generative Adaptive Network (GAN) proposed by Goodfellow et al. (Goodfellow, et al., 2020) is widely used Liu, et al., 2015. Being inspired by the success of GAN, many researchers came forward with different versions of GAN such as Conditional Generative Adversarial Network (CGAN) (Deng, et al., 2019), StackGAN (Zhang, et al., 2017), and energy-based GAN (EBGAN) (Zhao, et al., 2016). These models show high performance in generating facial synthetic images. Being inspired by the success of the work, we used a CGAN based model to generate synthetic images for educational emotion detection.

3   Framework for Educational Emotion Detection

The proposed framework for student's engagement detection has two phases. In the first phase, synthetic facial images are generated using CGAN (Deng, et al., 2019). Then the synthetic data is used to train a lightweight CNN model to detect emotion from facial expression. We train and test the model using synthetic images combined with the original images. The processing steps of these two phases are explained in detail in the sections below. The overall architecture of the proposed framework is shown in Fig. 1.

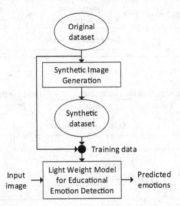

Fig. 1. The proposed educational emotion detection framework

3.1   Synthetic Image Generation

For the synthetic image generation, we used CGAN (Deng, et al., 2019). The synthetic image generation phase has three main modules: generative, enhancement, and discriminator. In the generative module, the first layer takes input about the random noise, categorical labels, and facial images. A series of transposed convolutional layers are then applied in the generator for up sampling the image and merging them with the embedded label. The output layer generates the synthesized images. The enhancement module, a high pass filter within a convolution layer is used to enhance the edges. However, sharpening the edges alone sometimes distorts some useful image features as well. This is why we also introduced a blur filter. In the blurring process, we used the Gaussian blur mechanism to make the overall images smoother. This process helped us to get better synthetic images.

The *discriminator* module differentiates a real image and a generated image. The discriminator takes an image as input and the categorical label of that image. In this layer the label is embedded to the embedding layer and reshaped to match the spatial dimensions of the image. The discriminator then applies a series of convolutional layers to extract relevant features, followed by flattening and dropout regularization. The output layer of the *discriminator* module produces a binary classification which indicates whether the input is real or fake. In this process, the *generative* module generates synthetic image, and the *discriminator* module tries to correctly classify whether the image is real or fake. Here after the *discriminator* module identifies an image as real or fake, we update the *generative* module accordingly. The goal is to generate an image that the *discriminator* model cannot identify as synthetic image. The workflow of the synthetic image generation is shown in Fig. 2.

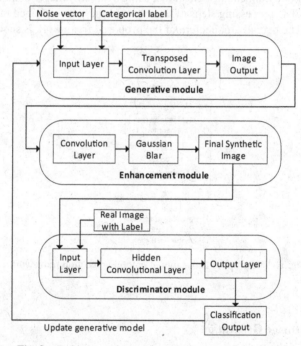

Fig. 2. Architecture for synthetic image generation model

3.2 A Lightweight Model for Educational Emotion Detection

As we mentioned earlier, very few works have been done on developing lightweight models for educational emotion detection so that the models could be deployed on student's low resource edge devices, such as mobile phones, tablets, and laptops. Also, there is a scarcity of dataset that can be used to train a deep learning model for educational emotion detection. We addressed the issue related to the scarcity of datasets using synthetic image generation (see Sect. 3.1). For the lightweight model, we used a *MobileNet* (Howard, et al., 2017) based deep learning architecture, which can detect educational emotions, such as fatigue, enjoyment, destruction, neutral and confusion. The architecture for the lightweight model is shown in Fig. 3. In the lightweight architecture, at the base, we used a pre-trained *MobileNet* model followed by a global average pooling layer, dense layer and softmax layers for feature extraction and emotion prediction. We trained our model using *adam* optimizer and *cross-entropy* loss.

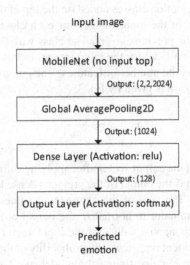

Fig. 3. Proposed model for educational emotion detection

As we mentioned, for the lightweight model, we used a pretrained *MobileNet* architecture, where we removed the top (fully connected) layer. Removing the top layer gave us the flexibility of changing the output layer according to our need and provided the advantage of reducing the model size further. For the top layer, we tested a global average pooling 2D layer and a max pooling layer, and empirically chose the global average pooling for its better performance in our application. This layer takes the spatial dimension into consideration and computes the average value of each feature map into spatial dimension. Let x be the input vector of size $H \times W \times C$, where H is the height, W is the width, and C is the number of channels. The output feature map y after applying global average pooling 2D is given by Eq. 1:

$$y_c = \frac{1}{H \times W} \sum_i^H \sum_j^w x_{ijc} \tag{1}$$

where x_{ijc} represents the value of the cth channel at the (i, j) position in the input feature map. We further added a fully connected dense layer with 128 units and ReLU activation function on top of the global average pooling layer. We added this layer to serve as a bottleneck layer that learns a compact representation from the features extracted from the input images by the base model. This modified top layer is tuned to detect five educational emotions for our application, which are fatigue, distraction, enjoyment, neutral, and confusion. At this layer, let x be the input vector of size N, where N is the number of features. The output vector y after applying the dense layer with 128 units and ReLU activation function is given by Eq. 2:

$$y_i = max(0, w_i.x + b_i) \tag{2}$$

where w_i is the weight associated with the ith unit and b_i is the bias associated with the ith unit.

The final layer is a softmax activation layer with 5 units as we have the facial images with five different emotion classes added on the top of dense layer. In this layer, the probability distribution of the input images for each class is calculated based on the learned features from the previous layers. The class with the highest probability is predicted as the final emotion label for the input image. In this layer, let x be the input vector of size N, where N is the number of features. The output vector y after applying the softmax activation function is given by Eq. 3:

$$y_i = \frac{e^{x_i}}{\sum_{j=1}^{5} e^{x_i}} \tag{3}$$

where y_i is the ith element of the output vector after applying softmax, x_i is the i_{th} element of the input vector x, which is the output of the previous dense layer with 128 units and ReLU activation function. The sum of the exponential values of all the elements in x is computed in the denominator to normalize the output probabilities. The softmax function normalizes the exponential values of the input vector to obtain a probability distribution, where each element represents the probability of the input image belonging to a specific emotion class. For fine tuning the model, we used adam optimizer and we selected categorical cross entropy as loss function as this is commonly used for multi-class classification problems.

4   Experiments and Results

4.1 Dataset

As we intended to analyze academic emotion from facial expression, we used a dataset for academic emotion inference in online learning (Bian, et al., 2019) (Anderson, et al., 2004). This dataset contains images captured during some online learning sessions. In total, 82 students participated in this dataset, where 29 were male students and 53 were female students. Their age range was from 17 years to 26 years. For the captures, webcams of the individual students were used. The webcam recorded the videos at 30 frames/s, where the capturing resolution was 720×1080. The students were not informed about the goal of the study beforehand, and they participated in a natural environment with different illumination and occlusions settings. The recording of the expression was taken for a duration of 10 to 60 min. After capturing the videos, the students were informed about the goal of the study, and they were asked to label their images with specified emotions. External raters also classified the images among the same set of emotions. More details about the dataset could be found in (Bian, et al., 2019). A total of 30,184 images were extracted from the videos which were labeled with five educational emotions: confusion, distraction, enjoyment, neutrality, and fatigue. In our experiments, we applied Viola and Jone's face detection algorithm (Viola & Jones, 2001) to detect facial region of interests (ROIs) and converted the ROIs into 64 × 64 for the further processing. Some sample ROIs with different emotions are shown in Fig. 4.

Fig. 4. A portion of the dataset where each row shows images from class labels of confusion, distraction, enjoyment, neutrality, and fatigue.

4.2 Experiment Setup

As we mentioned earlier, in addition to the real dataset, we generated synthetic images to improve training of the deep learning model. We used a CGAN based model for synthetic image generation, where we trained a generator model, a discriminator model and a combined CGAN model. During training, the function iterates 100 epochs. In each epoch, a batch of real sample images were explored, and their corresponding labels were selected from the original dataset. These original images were used to train the discriminator model. The aim of this training is to minimize the discriminator's loss by correctly classifying the real samples as real. After this step, we trained with synthetic samples. Here a batch of synthetic samples and their corresponding labels were generated using the generator model. These synthetic images and labels were used to train the discriminator model on this batch of synthetic samples and labels. Finally, we combined both the models together, and we set the goal as to train the generator model to generate samples that the discriminator would classify as real.

In synthetic image generation, we took the categorical labels from the original label of the dataset and the random noise with dimension 100. In the generator, the label was embedded and reshaped. The noise vector was passed through a dense layer after reshaping so that the image matches the desired image dimensions. While generating the images, we recorded the D1 and D2 loss for the discriminator and the G loss for the generator part. The role of D1 is to evaluate and discriminate between real and fake images. D1 receives real images from the dataset and fake images generated by the generator (G) as input. It tries to distinguish between these two types of images and outputs a probability that a given image is real. D2 acts as an additional discriminator introduced for image-to-image translation during the discriminator phase where the goal is to map images from real image domain to synthetic image domain. D2 evaluates the quality of the generated images to ensure they look realistic and adhere to the desired characteristics of the target domain. The Generator is the other primary component of our generative network. The purpose is to generate images that are realistic enough to fool D1 and D2. Over time, as D1 and D2 become better at discriminating real from fake images, G improves its ability to create more convincing and realistic images. The generator's goal is to produce images that are close to real ones. We plot the different losses in Fig. 5(a), where we can see a downward trend of the loss over the epochs. This indicates that the discriminator model gets better in discriminating the real image from the synthetic image over time. At the same time, the G loss also shows a downward trend reflecting the improvement in the generator's ability to produce realistic samples. Figure 5(b) shows some synthetic images generated by the synthetic image generation module.

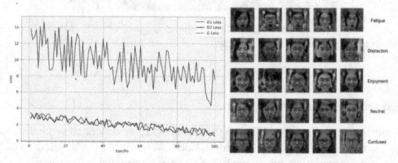

Fig. 5. (a) D1, D2, and D3 losses; (b) Generated synthetic images.

After generating the synthetic images, we appended the synthetic images with the original images and trained the lightweight emotion detection model. As we mentioned earlier, in the original dataset, we had 30,184 images. With synthetic image generation, we generated another 70,000 images. By incorporating synthetic images into the original dataset, the augmented dataset now comprises 100,184 images. We used 80% of the augmented dataset for training and 20% for testing. We further split the training data into training and validation at 80:20 ratio. To compare the performance of the lightweight model, we selected 5 other models which include Inception V3, Exception, Inception-ResNet, SqueezeNet, and MobileNet. In all the experiments, we first generated synthetic images using the original dataset. Then we augmented the generated dataset with the original dataset. We used this augmented dataset to train and test all the models.

4.3 Results and Discussion

The training vs validation accuracy and training vs validation loss of the proposed lightweight model over 100 epochs are shown in Fig. 6(a) and 6(b), respectively. Although the validation accuracy is low and the validation loss is high at the beginning, over time the accuracy increases and the loss decreases, which indicates the model fits to the dataset.

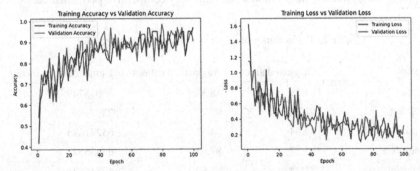

Fig. 6. Validation accuracy and loss of the lightweight model; (a) Training vs validation accuracy; (b) Training vs validation loss.

The model is compared with some other state-of-the-art models, which include *Inceptionv3, Exception, Inception-ResNet, SqeezeNet,* and the original *MobileNet* architectures. We compared the performance of the models using original dataset and the augmented dataset. We provided a comparison of training loss and validation loss of the proposed model with the other models in Table 1.

Table 1. Training and validation loss

Models	Training loss		Validation loss	
	Original	Augmented	Original	Augmented
Inception V3	0.3345	0.3075	0.5045	0.5214
Exception	0.3416	0.3118	0.3219	0.3056
Inception-ResNet	0.6845	0.6471	0.5524	0.5286
SqueezeNet	0.3055	0.2872	0.4843	0.4822
MobileNet	0.1874	0.1496	0.3268	0.2845
Proposed Lightweight Model	0.1542	0.1522	0.2044	0.2188

Table 2 shows the performance of the models in terms of accuracy and the size of the models (number of parameter). From this Table, we can see that, with the augmented dataset, the accuracy for the most models (five out of six models) improves significantly. This improvement in performance could be attributed to the availability of more data in the augmented dataset. Table 2 also shows that the proposed lightweight model achieved a high accuracy in augmented dataset with a lower number of parameters than the other models. We can observe that the proposed model has the least number of parameters, which is almost half of Exception model which shows slightly better performance than our model. Our model also has almost half parameter in comparison to SqeezeNet model. The other models, e.g., Inception V3 and Inception-ResNet have almost 100 times more parameters than the proposed model. This confirms that our model is lightweight compared to the state-of-the-art models and has very competitive performance.

Table 2. Performance of the model in terms of test accuracy

Models	Original dataset	Augmented dataset	Number of parameters
Inception V3	84.19	88.37	55915749
Exception	92.71	90.22	7392389
Inception-ResNet	83.64	84.52	65271845
SqueezeNet	85.37	87.62	6343557
MobileNet	81.22	85.89	4751582
Proposed Lightweight Model	90.47	92.58	3146126

Table 3 shows the performance comparison of the models in terms of Precision, Recall and F1 score by using the original and the augmented datasets. In Table 3, we can see that, in most cases, the precision, recall and F1 score were high when using the augmented dataset. Several factors contributed to this improved performance. Generating and augmenting synthetic data reduces the class imbalance in the augmented dataset. The synthetic dataset also increases the variation in the training data by generating images of a wide range of variation within each class. This increased diversity also helps the

Table 3. Comparison on Precision, Recall and F1 score (testing)

Models	Precision		Recall		F1 Score	
	Original	Augmented	Original	Augmented	Original	Augmented
Inception V3	0.7991	0.8233	0.7955	0.7563	0.7973	0.7884
Exception	0.8395	0.8647	0.8277	0.8474	0.8336	0.856
Inception-ResNet	0.8692	0.8316	0.7157	0.6393	0.785	0.7229
SqueezeNet	0.7583	0.6162	0.7321	0.7945	0.745	0.6941
MobileNet	0,8032	0.8472	0.6018	0.7509	0.6881	0.7961
Proposed Lightweight Model	0.8854	0.9126	0.7462	0.8128	0.8016	0.8614

model generalization and thereby improving the ability to correctly classify instances with higher accuracy.

Figure 7 shows the confusion matrix over the test dataset. From the confusion matrix we can see most of the data are classified correctly by the model. In the case of *Neutrality*, *Distraction*, and *Fatigue*, more than 90% of the test data are classified correctly by the model. In case of detecting *Confusion*, the proposed lightweight model shows lower performance. The model misclassifies many of the instances of *Confusion* class as *Fatigue* class. The rate is also high in misclassifying the data of *Confusion* class as *Enjoyment* class. Further analysis is required to understand the cause of this performance.

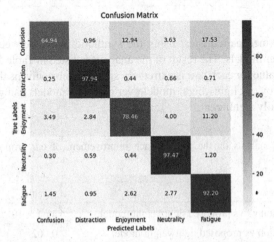

Fig. 7. Confusion matrix for the lightweight model

4.4 Statistical Analysis

We performed a statistical significance test to understand whether the improvement in accuracy by the synthetic image generation is significant or not. We performed a paired t-test (Hsu & Lachenbruch, 2014) with a null hypothesis that the improvement in the accuracy of our method is not significant. We ran the whole experiment 40 times and recorded the accuracies for each model. The difference δ in the accuracy in each pair is calculated by Eq. 4:

$$\delta = M_{augmented}(test\ data) - M_{original}(test\ data) \tag{4}$$

where $M_{augmented}$ is the accuracy by the images from augmented dataset and $M_{original}$ is by the images from original dataset. Running the models on test data provides the accuracy of the models and δ is the difference in the accuracy. From Table 4, we can see the *p-value* for each pair is less than the threshold alpha (0.05) except for *Exception* model. The *Exception* model showed better performance with the original dataset. For the other models, the improvement in accuracy using augmented dataset is significant.

Table 4. Statistical analysis on the performance improvement by synthetic images

Models	p-value
Inception v3	0.0003
Exception	0.0718
Inception-ResNet	0.0048
Squeezenet	0.0017
MobileNet	0.0041
Proposed lightweight model	0.0085

We also performed paired *t-test* using the synthetic image between our proposed model and the other models. The result of the analysis is listed in Table 5. From Table 5, we can see the p-value for each pair is extremely small which confirms that the improvement on accuracy by our lightweight model over the other models using the augmented dataset is statistically significant.

Table 5. Statistical analysis on the performance improvement of our proposed model using synthetic images.

Models	p-value
Inception v3 vs proposed lightweight model	4.64×10^{-17}
Exception vs proposed lightweight model	0.002
Inception-ResNet vs proposed lightweight model	1.67×10^{-12}
Squeezenet vs proposed lightweight model	3.55×10^{-07}
MobileNet vs proposed lightweight model	9.48×10^{-21}

5 Conclusion and Future Work

In this study, we used a generative adversarial network to generate synthetic facial images for educational emotion detection. We also proposed a lightweight model based on *MobileNet* to detect educational emotions of the students from facial expression to support online learners. By augmenting synthetic image data with the original data, we created an augmented dataset which increased the performance of the state-of-the-art model as well as the proposed lightweight model. In addition to that, being very lightweight compared to state-of-the-art models, our proposed classification model shows competitive performance in terms of accuracy, precision, recall and F1 score metrics. From the performance analysis, we found our model successfully predicted the emotion of the students with 90% accuracy using the original dataset and 91% accuracy with the augmented dataset. As the proposed model is lightweight and high performing, it can be deployed for real time emotion detection using students' edge devices.

From our experiment, we found that our generative model still produces high G-loss. Further analysis is needed to reduce this G-loss to increase the performance of the generative model. In our study, to generate synthetic images, we trained the generative model with the whole dataset and then generated images for each class. In future, we can train the generative model with data from each class individually. This might further improve the quality of the generated images. We also want to tune the hyper-parameters of the emotion detection module to see if we can further improve the performance of the model.

Acknowledgements. We acknowledge the support of the Natural Sciences and Engineering Research Council of Canada (NSERC) and Alberta Innovates, Canada.

References

Zhang, Z., Maeda, Y., Newby, T.: Individual differences in preservice teachers' online self-regulated learning capacity: a multilevel analysis. Comput. Educ. **207**, 1–13 (2023)

Dewan, M.A.A., Murshed, M., Lin, F.: Engagement detection in online learning: a review. Smart · Learn. Environ. **6**(1), 1–20 (2019)

Li, T., Chan, K.-L., Tjahjadi, T.: Multi-Scale correlation module for video-based facial expression recognition in the wild. Pattern Recogn. **142**, 1–10 (2023)

Boulanger, D., Dewan, M.A.A., Kumar, V.S., Lin, F.: Lightweight and interpretable detection of affective engagement for online learners. In: Proceedings of IEEE PICom 2021, pp. 176–184 (2021)

Howard, A.G., et al.: Mobilenets: efficient convolutional neural networks for mobile vision applications, pp. 1–9. arXiv preprint arXiv:1704.04861 (2017)

Goodfellow, I., et al.: Generative adversarial networks. Commun. ACM **63**(11), 139–144 (2020)

Bian, C., Zhang, Y., Yang, F., Bi, W., Lu, W.: Spontaneous facial expression database for academic emotion inference in online learning. IET Comput. Vision **13**, 329–337 (2019)

Anderson, A.R., Christenson, S.L., Sinclair, M.F., Lehr, C.A.: Check and connect: the importance of relationships for promoting engagement with school. J. School Psychol. **42**, 95–113 (2004)

Krizhevsky, A., Sutskever, I., Hinton, G.E.: Imagenet classification with deep convolutional neural networks. Commun. ACM **60**(6), 84–90 (2017)

Singh, S., Nasoz, F.: Facial expression recognition with convolutional neural networks. In: Annual Computing and Communication Workshop and Conference, pp. 324–328. Las Vegas, USA (2020)

Thai, L.H., Nguyen, N.D.T., Hai, T.S.: A facial expression classification system integrating canny, principal component analysis and artificial neural network. Int. J. Mach. Learn. Comput. **1**(4), 388–393 (2011)

Murthy, G.R.S., Jadon, R.S.: Recognizing facial expressions using eigenspaces. In: IEEE International Conference on Computational Intelligence and Multimedia Applications, Sivakasi, India (2007)

Aung, D.M., Aye, N.: Facial expression classification using histogram based method. In: Proceedings of the International Conference on Signal Processing Systems (2012)

He, K., Zhang, X., Ren, S., Sun, J.: Deep residual learning for image recognition. In: Proceedings of the IEEE Conference on Computer Vision and Pattern Recognition, pp. 770–778 (2016)

Szegedy, C., Vanhoucke, V., Ioffe, S., Shlens, J., Wojna, Z.: Rethinking the inception architecture for computer vision. In: Proceedings of the IEEE Conference on Computer Vision and Pattern Recognition, pp. 2818–2826 (2016)

Iandola, F.N., et al.: SqueezeNet: AlexNet-level accuracy with 50x fewer parameters and <0.5 MB model size. arXiv preprint arXiv:1602.07360 (2016)

Chollet, F.: Xception: deep learning with depthwise separable convolutions. In: Proceedings of the IEEE Conference on Computer Vision and Pattern Recognition, pp. 1251–1258 (2017)

Li, Y., Zeng, J., Shan, S., Chen, X.: Occlusion aware facial expression recognition using CNN with attention mechanism. IEEE Trans. Image Process. 28(5), 2439–2450 (2018)

Liu, Z., Luo, P., Wang, X., Tang, X.: Deep learning face attributes in the wild. In: Proceedings of the IEEE International Conference on Computer Vision, pp. 3730–3738 (2015)

Rana, S.P., Dey, M., Siarry, P.: Boosting content based image retrieval performance through integration of parametric & nonparametric approaches. J. Vis. Commun. Image Represent. 58, 205–219 (2019)

Deng, J., Pang, G., Zhang, Z., Pang, Z., Yang, H., Yang, G.: cGAN based facial expression recognition for human-robot interaction. IEEE Access 7, 9848–9859 (2019)

Zhang, H., et al.: Stackgan: text to photo-realistic image synthesis with stacked generative adversarial networks. In: Proceedings of the IEEE International Conference on Computer Vision, pp. 5908–5916 (2017)

Zhao, J., Mathieu, M., LeCun, Y.: Energy-based generative adversarial network. arXiv preprint arXiv:1609.03126 (2016)

Viola, P., Jones, M.: Rapid object detection using a boosted cascade of simple features. In: Computer Vision and Pattern Recognition (2001)

Hsu, H., Lachenbruch, P.A.: Paired t-test. In: Wiley StatsRef: Statistics (2014)

Design Method of AI Composing Smart Speaker Based on Humming Behavior

Bojia Li, Chuliang Cui, and Jing Luo(✉)

College of Art and Design, Division of Art, Shenzhen University, Shenzhen, Guangdong, China
luojing@szu.edu.cn

Abstract. This study examines the correlation between product functions that echo human behavior habits and the human-computer interaction experience of smart speakers, based on the theoretical basis of human behavior psychology. Additionally, a design method for AI composing music smart speakers based on humming behavior is proposed. Literature analysis was conducted to list the theoretical framework. A behavior-function interaction evaluation model was constructed to evaluate the conceptual design. Reliability and validity tests were carried out to further test the feasibility of the conceptual design scheme. The conceptual design scheme was further deepened and optimized using product design techniques.

Keywords: smart speaker · artificial intelligence composing music · humming behavior · music generation · smart home · human-computer interaction

1 Introduction

There are numerous types of speakers available that meet most people's requirements for music quality and appearance. The field of speaker design has expanded beyond simple audio playback due to the integration of science and technology with humanistic care. The development of smart concepts has led to increased competition and demand in this industry, making smart speakers more accessible to the masses than ever before [1]. Meanwhile, they have also expanded beyond the realm of technology and into the realm of emotional care, in keeping with current trends. For instance, Apple's 2020 release, the HomePod Mini, is equipped with the Siri intelligent voice assistant and functions as a control center for the smart home ecosystem. In addition to meeting users' daily music-listening needs, it also provides the convenience of a smart home ecosystem [2]. The rapid development of artificial intelligence has brought about revolutionary changes in various industries. As a result, users' demand for new experiences is also increasing. In this era, the field of smart speaker design should focus on new ways of human-computer interaction.

At present, some scholars believe that innovative features that meet the development trend of artificial intelligence will meet consumer demand. Qiu Yongzheng and other scholars of Fujian Engineering Institute based on the KANO model and AHP method into the innovation design method of iNPD, realizing the user's full participation in the

© The Author(s), under exclusive license to Springer Nature Switzerland AG 2024
H. Degen and S. Ntoa (Eds.): HCII 2024, LNAI 14735, pp. 217–229, 2024.
https://doi.org/10.1007/978-3-031-60611-3_16

design and decision-making in the development of smart speaker products, improving the scientific and rationality of the innovative product development of smart speaker, and enhance the feasibility and validity of the design scheme, which can provide a reference path for the innovative design of similar products [3], and in its conceptual design mention the innovation of smart home control, intercom function, humanized response and other functions. In the research of Shen Haohao et al. from the School of Design and Art of Lanzhou University of Technology, it is stated that the functional experience of smart speaker products affects the behavioral intention of users [4], and designers should focus on the design to effectively improve the perceived ease of use and enhance the behavioral intention of users [4].The aforementioned functional experiences have become increasingly prevalent in the context of rapid social development, but are gradually failing to meet the needs of consumers. Therefore, it is necessary to draw inspiration from other categories of product design to discover new approaches.

The aforementioned functional experiences have become increasingly prevalent in the context of rapid social development and are gradually failing to meet consumer needs. It is necessary to draw from other categories of product design to discover new approaches. In the field of stress-relieving products, Hao Lili suggested applying behavioral psychology to product design [5], which inspired this study. Therefore, this study proposes a method for designing AI-composed smart speakers based on humming behavior. The aim is to enhance the human-computer interaction experience between users and smart speakers by utilizing human humming behavior habits. The proposed method provides design inspiration and reference paths for human-computer interaction innovation in this field. A questionnaire is designed to investigate the correlation between humming behavior and smart speaker functions, and the validity of the data is tested using questionnaire reliability and validity. Accordingly, the design style orientation is carried out and the smart speaker conceptual design scheme is proposed.

2 Related Concept

Human-Computer Interaction. Human-computer interaction (HCI) is the exchange of information between a person and a computer using a specific dialogue language and interactive method to accomplish a task [6]. The cross-field combination between product design and human-computer interaction has given birth to many innovative and revolutionary industrial design works that meet the basic demands of human-computer interaction experience. This development is a result of the joint efforts of outstanding designers and the advancement of science and technology in modern society.

Behavioral Psychology. Behavioral psychology was founded by American psychologist John Watson in the early 20th century to study the relationship between human behavior and psychological activities. It is a science that focuses on the study of human behavior and the exploration of the relationship and laws between human psychological activities and body behaviors. The emphasis is on the study of human behavior rather than human consciousness [7]. Behavior refers to the physical responses, both internal and external, that an organism makes to adapt to changes in its environment. Behavioral psychology studies the physical responses of organisms to environmental changes in order to understand the relationship between stimulus and response, predict and control human behavior [8]. Based on psychology, this field studies the psychological state of human behavior, particularly the psychology of demand as it relates to design. The application of behavioral psychology in the design process is primarily to identify the fundamental ideas and needs of users.

Humming Behavior. Humming behavior is a phenomenon in behavioral psychology. It is an external expression of people's subconscious need to balance their internal needs [9]. Humming usually reflects a desire to be surrounded by music and expresses the inner need of the hummer to relax and relieve pressure.

Artificial Intelligence Music. Artificial Intelligence Music (AI music) refers to the technology of composing music through algorithms generated automatically by computers [10]. Since 1951, programmer Christopher Strachey created the first monophonic music using Alan Mathison Turing's large-scale computing mechanism. In 1987, American composer David Cope developed Experiments in Musical Intelligence, which can extract the creative commonalities of a large database of music and perform algorithmic compositions in specific musical styles. Artificial intelligence has greatly improved the amount of data collected and the way it analyzes music, lyrics, and other data.

3   Method and Design Process

3.1   Behavior-Function Intersection Evaluation Model

Behavior-Function Intersection Evaluation Model. A model was developed to evaluate the interaction between behavior and function. The model lists subconscious behaviors and habits that may be relevant to research and innovative functions. The results are combined into multiple conceptual designs with innovative functions. The Harris Profile Rating Chart was used to score critical design requirements. The requirements were filtered based on their degree of adaptation to different needs.

Humming is an external expression of people's inner need for pleasure. It is a subconscious behavior that has common contact points with the voice of smart speakers in various human behaviors and habits. The concept design of innovative smart speakers is produced by functional interaction with innovative function AI composition, rhythm atmosphere lamp, and aromatherapy machine. To evaluate design success factors, we drew a Harris Profile Rating Chart [11, 12]. The success factors can be categorized into functional fit, product effectiveness, product ease of use, product innovation, product fun, response speed, and perceived usefulness. By scoring these seven dimensions, the most suitable concept features for smart speakers can be selected, (see Fig. 1).

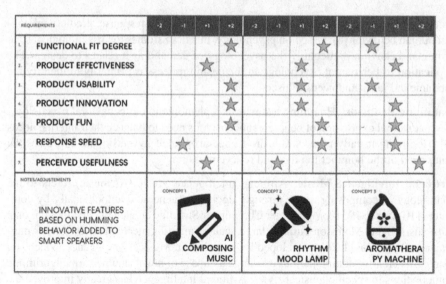

REQUIREMENTS	-2	-1	+1	+2	-2	-1	+1	+2	-2	-1	+1	+2
1. FUNCTIONAL FIT DEGREE				★				★	★			
2. PRODUCT EFFECTIVENESS		★					★				★	
3. PRODUCT USABILITY			★				★			★		
4. PRODUCT INNOVATION			★				★					★
5. PRODUCT FUN			★			★						★
6. RESPONSE SPEED	★							★				★
7. PERCEIVED USEFULNESS		★				★						★

NOTES/ADJUSTEMENTS	CONCEPT 1	CONCEPT 2	CONCEPT 3
INNOVATIVE FEATURES BASED ON HUMMING BEHAVIOR ADDED TO SMART SPEAKERS	AI COMPOSING MUSIC	RHYTHM MOOD LAMP	AROMATHERAPY MACHINE

Fig. 1. A Harris profile chart shows the score of each concept design

Based on the data presented in Fig. 1, it can be concluded that the composition function Ai, which is based on humming behavior, received the highest score. This suggests that the concept has potential for further design.

3.2 Questionnaire Design

The paper's questionnaire design comprises three parts. The first part presents prompt information, including an introduction to the questionnaire content, its purpose, and a privacy protection statement. The second part collects basic information about the respondents, such as their gender, age, and occupation. The third part constitutes the main body of the questionnaire, which includes four variables: music therapy, humming habit, smart speaker, and AI composition. The scale questions were scored on a 5-point Likert scale, ranging from strongly disagree to strongly agree.

3.3 Questionnaire Reliability and Validity Test

Reliability Test. A reliability test assesses the consistency, stability, and reliability of questionnaire results. It determines whether the measurement results accurately reflect the true characteristics of the participants' consistency and stability. A higher reliability coefficient indicates that the questionnaire results better reflect the true characteristics of the participants' consistency and stability. Cronbach α coefficient is the most commonly used reliability coefficient to evaluate the consistency of scores of each question in the questionnaire. It is an internal consistency reliability coefficient, where k is the number of questions in the survey results, S_i^2 is the variance of the score of question i, and S_T^2 is the variance of the total score.

$$\alpha = \frac{k}{k-1}\left(1 - \frac{\sum_{i=1}^{k} S_i^2}{S_T^2}\right)$$

Table 1. Reliability test table

Latent variable	The number of measurable variables	Cronbach's α coefficient
Music therapy	6	0.883
Humming behavior	6	0.885
Smart speaker	7	0.877
Totality	19	0.912

Table 1 shows that the Cronbach's α coefficient of the total questionnaire was 0.912, indicating good consistency and stability. The questionnaire's design and structure are scientific and reasonable, making it suitable for further analysis.

Furthermore, Table 1 displays the reliability test results for the three latent variables in the questionnaire. The table indicates that the Cronbach's α coefficient for all three scales is above 0.7, demonstrating the high reliability of this scale.

Validity Test. Validity test is to test the validity of the questionnaire, refers to the degree to which the means or instrument of measurement can accurately measure things, the more the test results are in line with the examination questions, the higher the validity, otherwise the lower the validity. Structural validity refers to the extent to which the structure of the questionnaire corresponds to the measured values as demonstrated in the test results. Structural validity can be assessed through statistical analyses such as structural equations, factor analysis, and correlation analysis. Factor analysis is the most commonly used statistical method. Factor analysis was used to extract several common factors from the questionnaire. Each common factor is highly correlated with specific variables that represent the basic structure of the questionnaire. It is important to conduct Bartlett's sphericity test and sampling adequacy test before performing factor analysis. A higher value of Bartlett's sphericity test indicates greater independence of each variable and lower probability of shared common factors in each item, making the questionnaire more suitable for factor analysis. The sum of squares indicates the strength of correlation between variables and the suitability of questionnaire variables for factor analysis.

To analyze the data using SPSS, it is necessary to determine the significance and KMO value. If the significance is less than 0.05, it indicates that the questionnaire data is suitable for factor analysis. Check the KMO value. A value higher than 0.8 indicates high validity, between 0.7 and 0.8 indicates good validity, between 0.6 and 0.7 indicates acceptable validity, and less than 0.6 indicates poor validity.

Table 2. Validity test table

KMO Sample Appropriateness Measure		0.922
Bartlett Sphericity Test	Approximate Chi-square	1878.490
	Degree Of Freedom	171
	Significance	0.000

Table 2 shows the test results: the p-value of the Bartlett test is less than 0.05, indicating that the questionnaire data can be factor analyzed. The KMO value was 0.922, which indicates high validity. Therefore, there is a correlation between the original variables.

4   AI Composing Smart Speaker Based on Humming Behavior

4.1   Design Style Orientation

By analyzing reports on the development of the smart speaker industry, it is positioned for specific target user groups based on their needs. These groups include young fashion music workers, middle school students, high-end business workers, and science and technology workers. The design style is flexibly matched to the unique aesthetic preferences and functional demands of each identity. Style positioning is determined by the combination of the following four key population needs:

1. Young fashion music worker. The music worker is young and fashionable and prefers a simple design style. This style is characterized by simplicity, smoothness, and modernity, with a fresh and natural interface that avoids unnecessary decorative elements. Emphasis should be placed on functionality and user experience, ensuring that the product not only meets the user's needs for listening to music but also provides comfort and pleasure.
2. Middle school students. Middle school students tend to prefer a fresh and charming design style characterized by pastel colors, cute icons, and a warm atmosphere. It is important to maintain the product's appeal while also enhancing its relatability to middle school students, allowing them to enjoy the music while also experiencing the product's warmth and kindness.
3. High-end business workers. High-end business workers prefer an atmospheric design style that is based on high-quality materials, fine detail design, and a sense of luxury. It is important to prioritize the quality and high-end feel of the product so that users can showcase their taste and style while enjoying the music.
4. Science and technology workers. Science and technology workers prefer a futuristic design style that features abstract graphics, cool special effects, and a sense of technology. It is important to maintain both the sense of science and technology and the sense of the future while also prioritizing the practicality and ease of use of products. This will allow science and technology workers to fully immerse themselves in the world of music.

To summarize, we prioritize achieving a positive user experience and functional design while also maintaining a visually appealing product style. We combine the product design style with the brand image to create a unique aesthetic. Our design style focuses on simplicity, modernity, delicacy, and natural freshness, incorporating abstract elements.

4.2 AI Composition

To implement the AI composition function on the smart speaker, it is necessary to first understand the working principle of AI composition and design interaction methods based on this technology.

Generative Adversarial Networks (GAN). The GAN model is a neural network model based on game theory, composed of a generator and a discriminator [13]. The generator and discriminator are trained alternately, optimizing the objective function using the gradient descent algorithm. This process gradually improves the generator's ability to produce realistic music samples and the discriminator's ability to accurately identify generated samples [14].

Music Generation Technology Based on GAN Model. Music generation technology based on GAN models is an innovative method for automatically generating music through machine learning. The technique establishes an adversarial training process between the generator and the discriminator, enabling the generator to produce realistic, diverse, and creative musical compositions [15].

The music generation technology is based on the basic structure of the GAN model. The generator produces music samples from random noise, while the discriminator distinguishes between the generated and real music samples. Through an iterative training process, the generator and discriminator engage in games and learn from each other. This gradually enhances the quality of the generator's ability to produce music samples and the discriminator's ability to accurately evaluate generated samples. The GAN model is used for music generation (see Fig. 2).

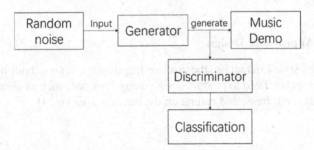

Fig. 2. GAN model diagram for music generation

It takes random noise as input and undergoes a series of hierarchical transformations through neural networks. Figure 2 illustrates the process by which the generator produces music samples. The discriminator then distinguishes between the generated and real music samples through discrimination and classification [16].

4.3 Human-Computer Interaction Process

Design the human-computer interaction process for music generation based on the technical basis described above and conforming to the GAN model working logic, (see Fig. 3).

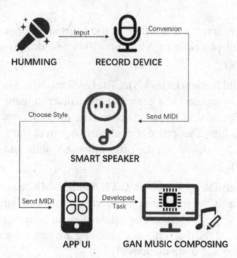

Fig. 3. The human-computer interaction flow diagram of the humming AI composition function of the smart speaker

When humming is used as input, the frequency analysis search algorithm is optimized to reduce the error rate of combining or splitting notes. The resulting MIDI file is then generated and sent to the music generation database of the smart speaker. The music style can be selected using the App, and GAN generates music based on the MIDI and the chosen style.

4.4 Product Appearance Design

Based on design style orientation, the creative inspiration map was built by searching for abstract elements related to product design using keywords such as simple, smooth, modern, delicate, soft, fresh, and natural on the Internet, (see Fig. 4).

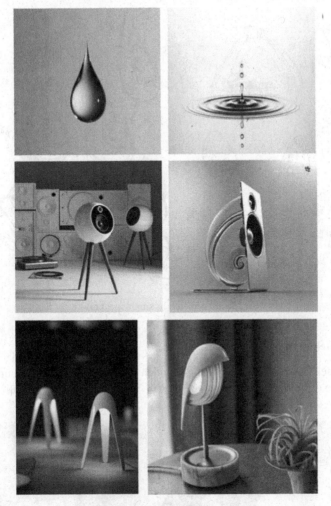

Fig. 4. Creative inspiration map

4.5 Idea Sketch

Create idea sketches based on the inspiration board. The shape of the speaker refers to the shape of water droplets, implying that the humming fragments converge into a sea of music like water droplets, (see Fig. 5).

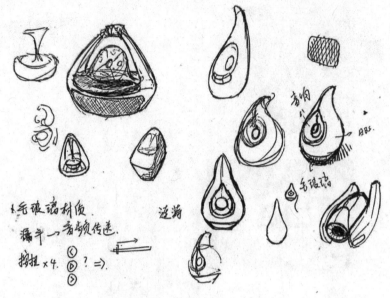

Fig. 5. Idea sketch of smart speaker.

4.6   3D Modeling

This 3D model was created using Rhino, which can provide a more accurate visual representation of product concepts, (see Fig. 6).

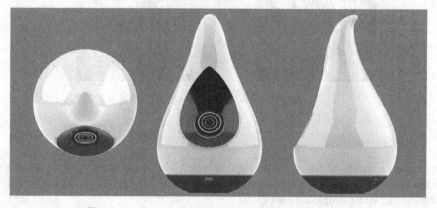

Fig. 6. Product three-view drawing. Modeled by Rhino.

4.7   Product Introduction

A brief introduction to the operating interface, recording equipment, and the use of AI composition functions, (see Fig. 7).

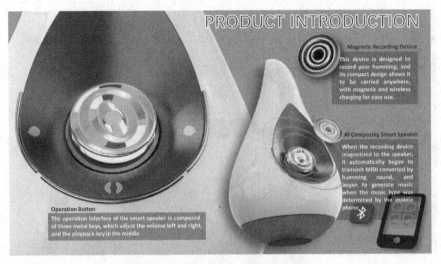

Fig. 7. Smart speaker product manual.

4.8 App UI Design

Design of user interface for the mobile client, which is responsible for the selection of music styles to be generated. From left to right: Wait to connect interface, Music therapy interface, Creator mode interface, Speaker playing interface, (see Fig. 8).

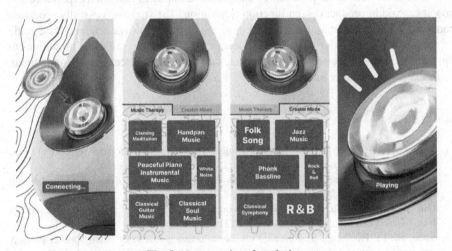

Fig. 8. App user interface design.

4.9 Product Scene Renderings

The product scene is rendered using rending software Keyshot to showcase its visual impact in real-life scenarios, (see Fig. 9).

Fig. 9. Product Scene Renderings

5 Conclusion

This study proposes a method for designing smart speakers based on humming behavior and generated music using AI composition technology. It explores the correlation between human behavioral psychology and human-computer interaction experience and how it can aid in product design function innovation. The study successfully produced conceptual design schemes using this method, which can serve as a reference and guide for the development of the smart speaker design field. There are still some limitations to this method, but it is worthwhile to prioritize customer experience research and human factor data analysis after product launch.

References

1. Shen, H., Li, F., Zhang, S.: Research on the influence factors of functional experience of smart speaker products on user behavior intention. Design **36**(7), 100–103 (2023)
2. Chen, S., Lu, D., Zhang, C.: Research on knowledge graph analysis of domestic sound design field based on CITESPACE. Design **36**(11), 83–87 (2019)
3. Qiu, Y., Zeng, X., Wu, Z., et al.: Research on innovative design of smart speaker products based on iNPD. Packag. Eng. **44**(08), 123–131 (2023)
4. Shen, H., Li, F., Zhang, S.: Research on the influencing factors of smart speaker product functional experience on users' behavioral intention. Design **36**(07), 100–103 (2023)
5. Hao, L.: Research on the application of behavioral psychology in the design of stress-relieving products. Design **36**(21), 22–24 (2023)
6. Dong, S.: Progress and challenges of human-computer interaction. J. Comput. Aided Design Graph. **1**, 1–13 (2004)
7. Sun, K., Li, J.: Behavioral Psychology. China Electric Power Press, Beijing (2011)
8. Hou, X., Wang, Y.: Research on subconscious behavioral interaction design based on product usability. Design **07**, 42–43 (2018)

9. Goldman, J., Goldman, A.: The Humming Effect: Sound Healing for Health and Happiness (2017)

10. Liu, A.Z., Han, B.: Development status and challenges of artificial intelligence music. Music People **09**, 74–77 (2020)

11. Harris, J.S.: The Product Profile Chart: A Graphical Means of Appraising and Selecting New Products (1961)

12. Roozenburg, N.F.M., Eekels, J.: Product Design: Fundamentals and Methods. Wiley, Chichester (1995)

13. Wang, W., Li, Z.: Research progress of generative adversarial networks. J. Commun. **39**(2), 135–148 (2018)

14. Wang, K., Gou, C., Duan, Y., et al.: Research progress and prospect of generative adversarial networks GAN. Acta Automat. Sinica **43**(3), 321–332 (2017)

15. Qiu, Z., et al.: Mind Band: A Crossmedia AI Music Composing Platform. Proceedings of the 27th ACM International Conference on Multimedia (2019)

16. Chen, T.: Application of artificial intelligence in music creation. Inf. Comput. (Theor. Edn.) **35**(12), 177–179 (2023)

Leveraging Generative AI Concepts with Uncertainty of Information Concept

Adrienne Raglin[✉]

DEVCOM Army Research Laboratory, Adelphi, MD 20783, USA
`adrienne.raglin2.civ@army.mil`

Abstract. The rapidly growing area of artificial intelligence (AI) that is used to create new content using machine learning is referred to as generative AI. The neural network transformer architecture and unsupervised as well as supervised learning have created the backbone of these generative models. These transformer-based large foundation models that can handle different modalities of data are the core building blocks of the generative AI concept. One requirement is data, ideally large, quality, unbiased data sets. With this data, these generative models learn patterns to form new content with characteristics of the original data. The Uncertainty of Information (UoI) concept is motivated by the fact that data is not ideal, is not perfect. Moreover, UoI considers the challenge of both capturing and communicating uncertainty associated with data. Given that generative AI, like other techniques, requires significant data, tying together these two concepts may uncover new capabilities. This paper will explore how these concepts can be leveraged, possible benefits, and challenges.

Keywords: Uncertainty of Information · Artificial Reasoning · Generative AI

1 Introduction

1.1 Generative AI, Large Language Models, Foundation Models

Artificial intelligence (AI) is a field that address many different problems by enabling computers, other machines, or software to perform intelligently. Founded in 1956 it has gone thru multiple periods of high interest. The main goals for AI research have included reasoning, knowledge representation, planning, learning and others. Recently, generative AI (GAI) is an area of artificial intelligence that can create output of different modalities based on the input. In general, GAI use prompts to obtain results from the available, accessible data. A major source of data for generative AI comes from the vast amount of data that can be obtained via the internet, publicly available datasets, crowdsourcing, and synthetic data generation. Under the broad category of generative AI are large language models (LLMs). LLMs model language to generate digital representations. Generative pertained transformers are a type of LLM. Also, considered a main technique for expanding generative AI or to describe generative AI models is foundation models. Foundation models adapt to generate bases for other things. Foundation models can be used for a variety of application by training on a set of unlabeled data.

© The Author(s), under exclusive license to Springer Nature Switzerland AG 2024
H. Degen and S. Ntoa (Eds.): HCII 2024, LNAI 14735, pp. 230–238, 2024.
https://doi.org/10.1007/978-3-031-60611-3_17

As with any technique there are pros and cons to generative AI. The lack transparency is an issue of GAI, particularly when the model performs unexpectedly. In these cases, it is extremely difficult to determine how the model works and understand why the model performs unexpectedly. The results generated can be incorrect. These results can be completely fabricated responses. They may have biases and may be vulnerable to malicious attacks. However, useful content can be obtained. This content can support creation of written material, help with discovering answers to questions, and sort through data for different use cases.

Generative AI more specifically is a type of machine learning. It trains software models to take data and make predictions without explicit programming. "They learn to identify underlying patters in the dataset based on a probability distribution and when given a prompt create similar patterns" [1]. Generative AI train the software models via huge amount of data. They are neural networks that are considered deep learning networks that are able to handle complex patters without supervision or intervention.

1.2 Type of Models

There are several types of models under GAI, they include diffusion models, generative adversarial networks (GANs), variational autoencoders (VAEs). Diffusion models have three main components: a forward process, a reverse process, and a sampling procedure. In the forward process, noise is applied to the data. In the reverse process the noise is transformed to a sample of the target data distribution. After adding the noise these models learn to recover the data by reversing that noise process.

GANs are two neural network that basically compete so that one gains and the other losses, a zero-sum game. One network, the generator tries to minimize a function. While the other network, the discriminator tried to maximize a function. This objective function represents the optimal or best solution to the problem. The output of the generator should create output that has the same distribution as the original or reference data. The discriminator will set an output value of one when the output of the generator matches the reference. If the value is set to zero then the generated content is detected. This generating of candidates and evaluating of the candidates is the competition that happens between these networks.

VAEs have two neural network components, encoders and decoders. The encoder maps "input variable to a latent space" [2]. The latent space is an embedding of items where those that resemble each other are closer together in a map space. The encoder produces multiple different samples from a single distribution. The decoder maps from the latent space to the input space, producing data points. The output of the decoder should be similar to the input.

1.3 Data

Like other methods generative AI methods require data for various steps. These models need data for training as well as input and contextual data for testing [3]. These models also need specific data for finetuning. These models also need data, prompts, to enable the models to solve specific tasks. The data, examples are given to the model. Then the model predicts the result [4]. After the model has been trained on general data, data for finetuning adapts model parameters based on that specific data.

However, all data is not equal. There are many ways to describe and discuss data. There are the five Vs, variety, volume, velocity, veracity, value. Variety refers to the different data sources. Volume refers to the amount of data. Velocity refers to the speed that data flows. Veracity refers to the accuracy. Value refers to the importance of the data. There are also the five Ds, distributed, disparate, dinky, dynamic, deceptive. Distributed refers to data that may be scattered or shared across multiple sources. Disparate refers to the diversity of data available. Dinky refers to limited data. Dynamic refers to data that changes rapidly. Deceptive refers to false or misleading data [5]. In addition, data can be discussed by it's limitations, the fact that no data is perfect and data may contain some level of uncertainty. This is motivation for the uncertainty of information (UoI) concept.

In this paper, we discuss how generative AI can complement and support uncertainty of information or vice versa. The following sections will discuss the UoI concept in more detail and present ideas where GAI and UoI have synergy.

2   Uncertainty of Information Concept

2.1   A Subsection Sample

The overall objective of the UoI concept is to aid in representing and communicating uncertainty about any information to a decision maker. In general, the decision maker may be a human or a non-human agent. Whether the decision maker is human or not, the UoI concept considers what we have called the human loop (HL) paradiagm. The human loop parafigm represents the shifts in roles between human and non-human agents as capabilities of the non-human agent increases. There are five stages in the human loop paradigm. The HL paradigm is shown in Fig. 1.

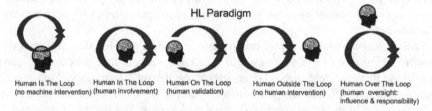

Fig. 1 Human Loop (HL) Paradigm.

First, is where the human is the loop, where all decisions, actions, and behaviors are carried out by the human. Second, the familiar human in the loop, where human and non-human agent work together to make decisions and carry out actions. Third, human on the loop, where the human moves to a more advisory role and the non-human agent makes the initial decisions. Fourth, human outside the loop, where the non-human agent performs behaviors, actions, and decisions, without direct intervention of the human.

Fifth, human over the loop, this may be the most important, where the human remains in the role of oversight as the non-human agent performs with greater autonomy. In the fifth stage the human maintains the responsibility regardless of the agent's ability to perform without human intervention or supervision. The fifth stage would be even more critical as the complexity and the impact of decisions, actions and behaviors are more critical and have greater impact. The fifth stage encapsulates the roles of the other stages, at any time the roles can shift. Moreover, the fifth stage highlights the synergy that human and intelligent systems require across different tasks.

The UoI concept supports both the human and intelligent system or non-human agent regardless of the roles, their dependence or interdependence to accomplish a task. Fundamental to the UoI concept is the fact that the information used by the human, intelligent system or both may have some type or level of uncertainty. Thus, the behaviors, actions, and decisions are greatly impacted by the UoI. For the discussion in this paper, we will take the perspective that the human loop paradigm may augment how the UoI is utilized as well as highlight the importance of the ideas around the UoI.

The UoI concept can be expressed generally and modified to the tasks as well as other factors. In general, the UoI would apply to data across various data sources. Currently, there are several board categories for the data source represented in the computational expression for UoI. The data source can be data directly from humans, data from different sensor modalities (text, images, sound, etc....), data about the device itself, data about the network, and data from visualization systems. Data sources can be added if needed or further subdivided as needed. An uncertainty category or set of categories is associated with each data source. The categories can be weights modulating the data, but more importantly they are descriptors that communicate the cause or type of uncertainty the data source may have. These categories were inspired by Gershon's work on the imperfect nature of information and have become the taxonomy for the UoI model. Currently the descriptors selected are inaccurate, questionable, incomplete, corrupt, disjoint, imperfect, inconsistent, and inappropriate. The descriptors as well as data sources can be extended or modified. The computational expression for UoI for this discussion is as follows:

$$UoI = G * S$$

In this expression, G would be a matrix of values for descriptors in the taxonomy and S would be a matrix of values for the data sources. The values for G can be binary to indicate there is a specific type of uncertainty for that descriptor. Alternatively, the values for G can indicate how much uncertainty. For example, a low uncertainty associated with a data source could be 1 or 2; while a high uncertainty could be 9 or 10.

3 Generative Uncertainty of Information

3.1 First G_UoI Idea

There are several ways to consider what we are calling the topic of generative uncertainty of information. One can be how imperfect data impacts GAI, another is how data generated by GAI can impact decisions.

First, link the uncertainty of information associated with the data used to train the GAI. As mentioned in the introduction section, generative models make predictions based on the input data. Generative models can (1) capture the underlying distribution of the data (2) "use deep learning with statistical inference for representing a data point in a latent space" (3) "are trained by maximizing training data likelihood where likelihood-based methods go through the curse of dimensionality in many data sets". For GANs, the "model learns to generate samples similar to the samples from the real data." In this case, identifying any uncertainty in the input data using the UoI concept could be helpful in highlighting potential weaknesses that could occur in results.

Moreover, a challenge for GANs is when they are unable to generate new data, when they "suffer from the limitations of generating samples with little diversity". GANs may also have problems where they do "not focus on the whole data distribution". This mode collapse issues can be of type (1) where "most of the modes from the input data are absent from the generated data" (2) only a subset of particular modes is leaned". Also "basic GANs cannot generate diverse samples in case of limited data availability". For image data, GANs have problems generating "diverse images with sufficient details" [6].

For this case, it may be helpful to note the data that will be used with different categories from UoI. For example, if the dataset is limited, knowing that there is incomplete data can be a tag that would communicate that limitation. Then the analysis of the GAN could be performed with this in mind. Determining how the UoI categories can identify or mark when limited modes as well as when limited data details occur as metadata may be possible. If this is possible then results could be adapted using the UoI categories as triggers to automate refinement of the GAN to compensate for these limitations.

3.2 Second G_UoI Idea

In [7] we are reminded that GAI are "solutions trained on massive amounts of data to produce output based on user prompts." A risk comes from the dependency on historical data which may lead to biases. Here, it may be helpful to use UoI to label and quantify when there is only smaller amount of data are available. The UoI categories could also be used to trigger the prompts from the user. This may require use of language models and assessments made that are associated with the UoI categories.

3.3 Third G_UoI Idea

In the introduction we mentioned transformers. A strength of transformers is in the "handling variable length sequences and context awareness" [8]. Thus, one idea is to embed a thread that holds UoI information in that sequence. Then a specialized self-attention mechanism could allow the model to attend to the UoI within the input sequence. If the encoder tags the input sequence so that it is added to the generated hidden representation, then the decoder could use that thread in the hidden representation to generate the output sequence retaining the UoI.

3.4 Fourth G_UoI Idea

Within reinforcement learning there is the human feedback pipeline of pre-training, reward learning, and fine-tuning. The discussion is where can UoI augment any of these steps. For example, in the reward step could the model include the preferences of the user to rely on data with lower UoI in specified categories for individual data sources. Then when there is data from a specific source for a UoI category that is marked. When new data that the model has not been trained on the UoI category for inconsistent is marked so that results would be tagged and that communicated to the decision maker. Thus, the decision maker would know the model is adjusting to new data or data not consistent with previous data.

3.5 Fifth G_UoI Idea

For this idea the question is how could UoI be used in the inverse mapping within GANs? As data is projected back into the latent space then the UoI becomes a "useful feature representation" for the task, such as decision making. The generated image may be difficult for a human to interpret but may not be for the computer to interpret.

In addition, UoI could be infused into information driven generative adversarial networks (IDGANs) [9]. The technique is based on steganography which is the practice of concealing messages or information within other nonsecret text or data (dictionary). In general, steganography can be divided into transform and spatial domain. "Transform domain steganography improves the detection-resistant ability of steganographic images by modifying the cover images". "Spatial domain techniques are those in which message bits are directly embedded into pixel values like least significant substitution methods" [10]. As this field advanced neural networks were used to learn where the optimal position to embed data in the cover. This created new images where the secret cover was visually imperceptible. In [9] paper he summarizes the work by Baluja to embed a color secret image. In this approach a preprocessing network was used with a cover image. They were encoded to generate the secret image that resembled the cover. Similar work has been done with grey secret images. Zhang's paper proposes a model that uses GANs for coverless steganography. Coverless techniques do not use a "designated cover image for embedding secret data but directly transforms secret information through its own properties" [11].

Thus one idea for a covered approach is to generate the UoI data as a matrix, then that image matrix becomes the cover. For a coverless approach augmenting the host image with its associated UoI may be possible. Another option could be to use the GAN to generate new imagery where the UoI is apart of that new image. Some combination of these ideas are in Fig. 2.

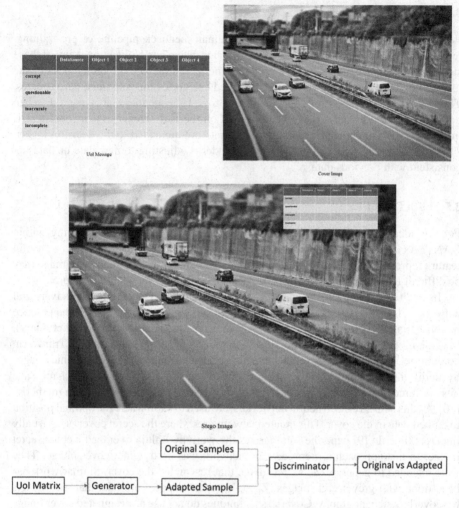

Fig. 2 UoI within images using GANs.

3.6 Sixth G_UoI Idea

This idea focuses on vectorization for G_UoI. The thread throughout the ideas for this generative uncertainty of information focuses on the data and the categories. As mentioned in a previous section one and another strength of GAI is the vectorization of data. This vectorization and vectorized databases is that strength. "In mathematics, a vector incorporates a position in coordinate space and a direction" [12]. in the context of data a vector is a way of representing multidimensional data" "Vectorized data or vectorized embedding is an ordered array of numbers that record measures of proximity and similarity as well as the data itself" "It is this similarity that really makes generative AI work." "You can vectorize any type of data – text, images, media, sensor data, and so on," Graph databases or other types of databases can be used not necessarily vector databases" Data is passed to a neural network to create vectorized representation for each element. The neural network then looks for patterns and other types of connections. If the UoI along with the raw format of the data was converted into the vector, then the UoI is treated as a feature which can be extracted from the vectorization. Now, how do we leverage this in similar ways. One approach could be the frequency across particular data sources and UoI categories. The formulas might be:

$$Term\ Frequency = \frac{Frequency\ of\ UoI\ category\ winthin\ a\ datasource}{Total\ number\ of\ UoI\ categoires\ with\ that\ datasource}$$

$$Datasource\ Frequency = \frac{Datasources\ containing\ UoI\ category}{Total\ number\ of\ datasources}$$

$$Inverse\ Datasource\ Frequency = log(\frac{Total\ number\ of\ datasources}{Datasources\ containing\ UoI\ category})$$

Thus, the more common UoI categories across the data sources the more important it is in the data source (which is the reverse for inverse document frequency).

4 Conclusion

The field of generative AI is rapidly growing. It successes to date makes it intriguing to explore new uses but also modify existing topics in new ways. This was the motivation of this idea paper. In this paper, several ideas are presented that might bridge the area of generative AI with a concept we call uncertainty of information. With one of the primary focuses of UoI being aiding the presentation and communication of uncertainty through the use of an uncertainty taxonomy, associating this UoI concept taxonomy to generative AI is clear. Providing additional information on where and what type of uncertainty is associated with data used within generative AI models can help with explaining limitations within results.

In addition to this idea the two additional ideas centered around vectorization and inverse mapping from steganography may also help identify and highlight uncertainty within data. In future work we hope to expand on these ideas and extend them to potential research directions.

References

1. Bell, E.: Generative AI: How It Works, History, and Pros and Cons. Generative AI: How It Works, History, and Pros and Cons (investopedia.com) (2023)
2. Variational autoencoder Variational autoencoder - Wikipedia
3. Re, C., Arora, S.: Foundation Models are Entering their Data-Centric Era Foundation Models are Entering their Data-Centric Era. Foundation Models are Entering their Data-Centric Era Hazy Research (stanford.edu) (2022)
4. Pai, A.: All You Need to Know About Foundation Models. All You Need to Know About Foundation Models - Analytics Vidhya (2023)
5. Raglin, A., Hoffman, H., Mittrick, M., Zheng, H., Caylor, J.: Artificial Reasoning Toward Goal-Oriented Adaptive Arrays of Sensors. In: 2021 IEEE Third International Conference on Cognitive Machine Intelligence (CogMI), pp. 197–203 (2021)

6. Saxena, D., Cao, J.: Generative Adversarial Networks (GANs): Challenges, Solutions, and Future Directions. Association for Computing Machinery (2022)
7. Saetra, H.: Generative AI: Here to Stay, But for Good? Technology in Society, vol. 75 (2023)
8. Turing, Understanding Transformer Nerual Network Model in Deep Learning and NLP, The Ultimate Guide to Transformer Deep Learning (turing.com)
9. Zhang, C., et al.: IDGAN: information-driven generative adversarial networks of coverless image steganography. Electronics **12**(13), 2881 (2023)
10. Singh, J., Gexh, M., Kue, G.: Review of spatial and frequency domain steganographic approaches. Int. J. Eng. Res. Technol. **4**(6) (2015)
11. Qin, J., et al.: Coverless image steganography: a survey. IEEE Access **7**, 171372–171394 (2019)
12. Kobielus, J.: Vector Databases and What They Mean to Generative AI, Vector Databases and What They Mean to Generative AI|Transforming Data with Intelligence (tdwi.org) (2023)

Cybersickness Detection Through Head Movement Patterns: A Promising Approach

Masoud Salehi[✉], Nikoo Javadpour, Brietta Beisner, Mohammadamin Sanaei, and Stephen B. Gilbert

Iowa State University, Ames, IA 50011, USA
{msalehi,nikoojap}@iastate.edu

Abstract. Despite the widespread adoption of Virtual Reality (VR) technology, cybersickness remains a barrier for some users. This research investigates head movement patterns as a novel physiological marker for cybersickness detection. Unlike traditional markers, head movements provide a continuous, non-invasive measure that can be easily captured through the sensors embedded in all commercial VR headsets.

We used a publicly available dataset from a VR experiment involving 75 participants and analyzed head movements across six axes (up/down, left/right, forward/backward, and rotational movements). An extensive feature extraction process was then performed on the head movement dataset and its derivatives, including velocity, acceleration, and jerk. Three categories of features were extracted, encompassing statistical, temporal, and spectral features. Subsequently, we employed the Recursive Feature Elimination method to select the most important and effective features.

In a series of experiments, we trained a variety of machine learning algorithms. The results demonstrate a 76% accuracy and 83% precision in predicting cybersickness in the subjects based on the head movements. This study's contribution to the cybersickness literature lies in offering a preliminary analysis of a new source of data and providing insight into the relationship of head movements and cybersickness.

Keywords: Cybersickness · Machine Learning · Postural Sway · Head Movements · Windowing · Fourier Transform · Wavelet Transform · Recursive Feature Elimination · Time Series

1 Introduction

In recent years, virtual reality (VR) has gained popularity as a technology that can provide users with immersive, interactive experiences. Various fields, such as entertainment [1], education [2], training [3], and healthcare [4], have found applications in virtual reality due to its ability to simulate realistic environments and provide a sense of presence. Despite the benefits of VR, it has some limitations including the experience of

---

M. Salehi and N. Javadpour—These authors contributed equally to this work.

© The Author(s), under exclusive license to Springer Nature Switzerland AG 2024
H. Degen and S. Ntoa (Eds.): HCII 2024, LNAI 14735, pp. 239–254, 2024.
https://doi.org/10.1007/978-3-031-60611-3_18

cybersickness, a form of motion sickness, that may occur in virtual environments [5, 6]. Cybersickness prevents people from widely embracing and enjoying VR experiences due to symptoms such as nausea, dizziness, disorientation, and fatigue [7]. Additionally, research has shown differences between VR and face-to-face (F2F) conditions across various parameters, highlighting the importance of understanding these distinctions in optimizing user experiences [8–11].

Cybersickness can be caused by a variety of factors, including those from hardware [12], software [13, 14], users' individual differences, and the user's task [5, 15, 16]. While the exact mechanism is not yet fully modelled, it includes factors such cue conflict (when the sensory cues received by the brain from the virtual environment contradict the cues from the body's own senses) [17] and postural instability (how well a person can maintain balance) [1, 18]. This present research focuses on a specific form of postural sway which is head movements. Research shows that individuals who experience dizziness and patients with a vestibular deficiency show different patterns of head movements [19, 33]. Therefore, in this research we aim to use the head movements signals as a potential identifier for cybersickness. Head movements data can be a reliable, cheap, and easy to access source of data coming from accelerometer and gyroscope sensors embedded in all commercial VR headsets.

Several researchers have explored methods of predicting cybersickness using machine learning [19], which has shown promising results. By identifying patterns and appropriate identifiers extracted from physiological data; machine learning models can be trained to predict cybersickness [20, 21]. However, to the best of our knowledge, there has not been a study that utilizes and processes head movements data to train a machine learning model to make predictions for cybersickness.

This study develops a predictive model that provides predictive capability for cyber-sickness symptoms. This approach uses head movements data and its derivatives: velocity, acceleration, and jerk. Extensive feature extraction techniques are then applied to extract a wide range of statistical features, temporal features (time domain), and spectral features (frequency domain). To mitigate the problem of having a relatively small data sample, a feature selection technique called Recursive Feature Elimination [22] was used to choose only the most useful features in each experiment. A variety of machine learning models were run based on these features to test against a hold-out test set.

The next section of this paper provides an overview of related work on machine learning to identify cybersickness. The experimental methodology for the preprocessing, and extraction of features from this Polhemus dataset is described in [23]. A Polhemus is a 3D tracking device worn by the participants of the study that captured the dataset. The machine learning algorithms used for prediction are described, as well as their strengths and weaknesses. The paper then assesses the performance of the predictive model and discusses the implications of our findings, potential applications, and future research directions.

2 Related Work

Many researchers have explored methods of measuring cybersickness. While SSQ [24] has frequently been used as a subjective measure, self-reported by participants, researchers have widely explored the possibility of objective physiological measures, including EEG [25]; EDA [26]; heart rate, heart rate variability, blood pressure [27, 28], and respiration [27]. Unfortunately, results have been mixed. Since sensors for these methods can be expensive and feel invasive, popular headsets are not equipped with them. On the other hand, movement accelerometers are already included in most VR headsets. Previous research in the field has attempted to use postural or head movement data collected by the headset to identify cybersickness [20], but results have been inconsistent.

Various machine learning methods have been employed to predict cybersickness, and these approaches incorporated different kind of variables into their models. Certain studies have focused on internal physiological measurements, including factors such as heart rate [9], and muscle activity [28]. In addition, some investigations emphasize eye-related variables, including measures such as eye blinks and tracking eye movements [29, 32, 33]. Also, a subset of research concentrates on neural activities, employing electroencephalogram (EEG) data to drive their models [28]. Studies utilizing EEG data have reported promising results [34].

Among factors influencing cybersickness, body posture could be a significant contributor [1]. A sensory mismatch between what the eyes see and what the body feels in terms of balance and movement can disrupt the sensory integration process, causing the symptoms of cybersickness [35, 36]. Several studies have focused on this connection indicating that individuals with greater postural instability are more prone to experiencing severe cybersickness [1]. For example, adopting a standing posture, characterized by decreased stability, has been associated with a higher likelihood of severe sickness compared to a sitting posture. Also, regarding the locomotion methods, when the body movement is not well aligned with the movement in the VR environment, it can lead to cybersickness.

Early investigations by researchers like [37] and [1] highlighted a potential link, suggesting that both increases and decreases in body sway could be indicators of how individuals react to VR environments. These studies put forward the idea that monitoring our body's adjustments in VR could be key to predicting occurrences of cybersickness, highlighting the significance of postural changes in understanding our interactions with virtual spaces.

Contrasting viewpoints from studies such as those by [20] and [21] introduced a layer of skepticism, questioning the straightforward relationship between postural sway and cybersickness. These pieces of research pointed out instances where posture changes did not consistently match up with cybersickness episodes, raising doubts about the reliability of postural data as a catch-all predictor for VR-induced discomfort.

The debate extends further when focusing on specific movements, like those of the neck and back, with some researchers proposing a strong connection to cybersickness. However, findings from [38] countered this by showing that detailed analyses on these body parts failed to conclusively link them to cybersickness, illustrating the complexity of establishing a direct correlation. This diversity in research outcomes underscores the challenge in achieving a unified understanding of how our physical responses are intertwined with our virtual experiences.

The discussion around postural sway and cybersickness has focused mainly on using tools like force plates or analyzing overall body movements to measure postural stability.

These approaches have provided valuable insights but also reveal a gap in our understanding of how specific parts of the body, particularly the head, contribute to the experience of cybersickness in virtual reality (VR) environments. Until now, the specific impact of head movements on cybersickness has not been extensively explored in the realm of cybersickness research.

This research introduces a novel perspective by specifically examining head movement data to understand its role in predicting cybersickness. This approach diverges from previous studies that have not fully considered the potential of head movements as a predictive measure for VR-induced discomfort. By shifting the focus to the head, we aim to uncover new insights into how the orientation and motion of the head could be closely linked with the onset of cybersickness. This novel approach not only fills a significant gap in the current research landscape but also opens up new avenues for developing more effective predictive models of cybersickness, potentially leading to improved VR design and user experiences.

3   Method

Figure 1 provides an overall view of the methods and approach in this study. Section 3.1 describes the dataset used in this research and discusses some details about the collection process and the experiment. Section 3.2 describes different forms of kinematics data that are calculated from the raw movement data and discusses the logic for incorporating these forms of signals. Section 3.3 explains the approach in windowing the data and discuss the benefits provided by it for our modeling performance. Section 3.4 discusses the feature extraction approach and explain the logic for choosing the wide range of features. And finally, Sect. 3.5 describes the modelling pipeline.

3.1   Dataset

This study uses a secondary, publicly available dataset titled "APAL 2019: Postural Data, Game Performance, and Subjective Responses of Cybersickness in Virtual Reality Head-Mounted Displays" published by [16]. It encompasses data from 79 participants (41 women and 38 men) aged between 18 to 49, with an average height of 1.72 m and weight of 71.58 kg. The study utilized the Simulator Sickness Questionnaire (SSQ) for assessing motion sickness, categorizing participants into "Well" or "Sick" groups based on their responses. The recorded variables include positional data (X, Y, Z in centimeters) and attitude data (pitch, roll, yaw in degrees) for the head. Due to the variability of SSQ data and its subjective nature, a different variable was chosen as dependent variable in our study. The last 10s of the movement signals of the participants who either indicated they were sick at the end of the experiment or chose to stop the experiment early because of severe sickness served as the "Sick" labeled samples. The first 10 s of all participants served as "not Sick" samples. Using this approach, the modeling task become a binary classification task. For more details about the dataset, please take a look at [16].

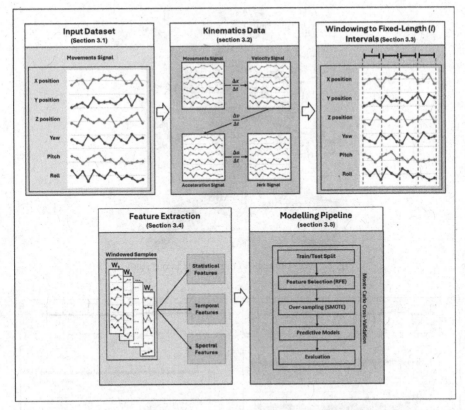

Fig. 1. Overall view of the study with representative diagrams of data; these are not real data.

3.2 Kinematics Data

The recorded head movements signal in this study records six variables. It includes head disposition in centimeter along the X, Y, and Z axes and head rotations in degrees along three axes; pitch (flexion/extension), roll (lateral flexion), and yaw (axial rotation) (see Fig. 2).

In addition to the movements data, in the study of biomechanics and postural sway, researchers also consider the velocity and acceleration of the movements signal when doing kinematic analysis [39, 40].

Jerk has also been used in several research as an indicator of postural sway smoothness, and postural instability [41, 42]. Jerk describes how smoothly or abruptly a movement changes in terms of acceleration. Higher values of jerk indicate more abrupt, and lower values of jerk indicate smoother movements (Fig. 3).

3.3 Windowing the Signals

As the first step to start processing the data, we perform a signal windowing task using a sliding window. Sliding window is a popular technique when dealing with time-series

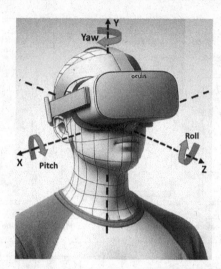

Fig. 2. Axes of the head movements in our study

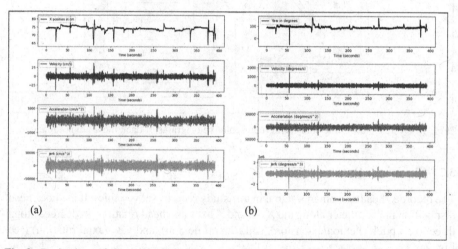

(a)   (b)

Fig. 3. Derivatives of the original signals. (a) X position and its derivatives: Velocity (cm/s), Acceleration (cm/s^2), and Jerk (cm/s^3). (b) Yaw in degrees and its derivatives: Velocity (cm/s), Acceleration (cm/s^2), and Jerk (cm/s^3).

data. In this technique, the signals are divided into fixed length intervals, chosen by the user. This technique provided several benefits in the context of our research.

First, it provides practicality. Participants have participated in a 15-min study. If one had chosen to use of the whole data to train the sickness detection model, the model could have made predictions only after at least after 15 min of observation, limiting the practicality and near-real time use cases of the model. Windowing the data into smaller lengths (1s, 2s, 3s, 5s, etc.) resulted in a model that made estimations of the sickness more frequently.

Second, windowing helps reduce the dimensionality and increasing a smaller sample size. When using machine learning algorithms, a large number of features and small number of samples can lead the model into issues like overfitting and poor generalization. In this present context, the original signal was a 15-min time series of six variables recorded with 60 Hz sampling, resulting a dimensionality of 324,000 (15 min × 60s × 60 Hz × 6 variables) for only 75 observations. When considering a window size like 1s, the dimensionality would be reduced to 360 and number of observations would increase to 67,500.

Third, windowing improves the quality of the feature extraction methods. In this context, participants' movement signals, including temporal trend trajectories and spectral characteristics, may change over time, which is associated with the transition of the postural sway from a healthy state to the sickness state. By segmenting the signal into smaller, temporally localized intervals, windowing not only facilitates a more granular analysis of time-varying trends, but also significantly enhances frequency resolution.

3.4 Feature Extraction

Handling time series data in machine learning can be challenging as there are not any explicit feature coming with the raw data. As a result, a meticulous feature extraction process is needed to identify a set of appropriate features. In the literature of postural sway and Center of Position analysis using force plate data, researchers have put forward a vast set of variables that can be extracted from the data [43–46]. These features can be mainly categorized in to three categories: statistical, temporal (time domain), and spectral (frequency domain).

While these lists are extensive and have been shown to be very effective in measuring a subjects' postural stability and balance, they are not directly applicable to the context of head movement data. To the best of our knowledge, there is only a limited body of literature discussing the processing and feature extraction of head movements data. These papers usually focus on a set of simple statistical features such as average acceleration, average velocity, and frequency of movements [39, 47]. As a result of the lack of literature in head movements signal processing, in this paper, a brute force approach was used. Influenced by postural sway literature, a large number of features in the three statistical, temporal, and spectral domains were used for the four types of kinematic data mentioned in Sect. 3.2.

It should be noted that while these features are statistically and mathematically meaningful, not all of them are good predictors of cybersickness. In addition, having a large number of these features can reduce the performance of our machine learning model. Therefore, we employ a feature selection technique, we select a handful of most meaningful features to train our model.

Statistical Features. When analyzing head movement data for detecting cybersickness, it was crucial to extract features that capture the complexity and nuances of such movements across different domains. Statistical features like kurtosis, skewness, mean, standard deviation, and histogram are fundamental as they provide insights into the distribution and variability of head movement data, enabling the identification of outliers or patterns indicative of cybersickness. These features help in understanding the basic structure and dispersion of the data, which are essential in distinguishing normal head movements from those affected by cybersickness.

Temporal Features. Time domain features, including autocorrelation, zero crossing rate, and mean absolute difference, were vital for capturing the temporal characteristics of head movements. These features allow for the analysis of how head movement changes over time, identifying specific patterns or irregularities that occur during episodes of cybersickness. For instance, autocorrelation helps in understanding the periodicity of movements, while neighborhood peaks can indicate sudden changes in movement direction or speed, which are common in cybersickness episodes.

Spectral Features. Time series data may include spectral and frequency information. A common method to look into spectral domain of the data employed by researchers in the study of Center of Position (COP) and postural sway is Fast Fourier Transform (FFT) [48, 49]. We note that applying FFT in the context of postural sway should be done with caution, as the postural sway and COP signals usually demonstrate nonstationary characteristics [49, 50]. However, windowing the data into smaller intervals can make the data closer to the stationary assumption.

In addition to Fourier transform techniques, the literature on postural sway analysis also recommends employing wavelet analysis for its distinct advantages. Wavelet transforms offer a more fitting approach for analyzing non-stationary signals due to their capability to capture intermittent, time-localized dynamics. This attribute makes them particularly effective for examining nonlinear systems that exhibit time delays [50].

Table 1 shows a list of all of the extracted features. We used a time series analysis Python package TSFEL to compute these features for each window [51].

Table 1. List of extracted features

Feature Category	List of Features
Statistical Features	Absolute energy, Average power, ECDF, ECDF Percentile, ECDF Percentile Count, Entropy, Histogram, Interquartile range, Kurtosis, Max, Mean, Mean absolute deviation, Median, Median absolute deviation, Min, Peak to peak distance, Root mean square, Skewness, Standard deviation, Variance
Temporal Features	Area under the curve, Autocorrelation, Centroid, Mean absolute diff, Mean diff, Median absolute diff, Median diff, Negative turning points, Neighborhood peaks, Positive turning points, Signal distance, Slope, Sum absolute diff, Zero crossing rate
Spectral Features	FFT mean coefficient, Fundamental frequency, Wavelet absolute mean, Wavelet energy, Wavelet entropy, Wavelet standard deviation, Wavelet variance, Human range energy, LPCC, MFCC, Max power spectrum, Maximum frequency, Median frequency, Power bandwidth, Spectral centroid, Spectral decrease, Spectral distance, Spectral entropy, Spectral kurtosis, Spectral positive turning points, Spectral roll-off, Spectral roll-on, Spectral skewness, Spectral slope, Spectral spread, Spectral variation

3.5 Modeling

The modeling process began by dividing the dataset into training and testing sets. To prevent data leakage from the training set to the test set, the participants were segregated into training and test groups before shuffling all windowed data. This approach guaranteed that no participant's data appears in both training and test sets, thus avoiding the potential for the model to learn participant-specific movement patterns. A stratified random sampling method [52] for the train/test split to maintain the proportionality of different classes in both sets.

In the second step, we used Recursive Feature Elimination [53] to identify the top 50 most informative and relevant features from our original dataset, which may contain up to 984 features per kinematic signal (i.e., 984, 1968, 2,952, or 3,936 features in each of the four experimental setting). RFE systematically assesses the importance of each feature, removing those with minimal contribution to the model's predictive accuracy. Given the small sample size in this study, RFE was particularly beneficial as it reduces model complexity and improves the performance [22, 53]. We trained a random forest-based RFE model on the training dataset and applied the same feature selection process to the test set.

In the third phase, the class imbalance issue was addressed within the training set using the Synthetic Minority Over-sampling Technique (SMOTE) [54] This method mitigates model bias towards the majority class by artificially augmenting the minority class.

Finally, to ensure the robustness and reliability of our results, a Monte Carlo Cross-Validation method [55] was used, repeating each experiment 50 times. This approach helps mitigate potential biases arising from random train/test splits, ensuring the stability and generalizability of our findings.

4 Results

Six machine learning models were trained on the processed training data and evaluated against the test set. These models include Logistic Regression, Random Forest, SVM, K-nearest Neighbors, Decision Tree, and an ensemble model Gradient Boosting. The modeling pipeline was tested in four settings, adding kinematics signals one by one. Table 2 shows the average results of the 50 repetitions of Monte Carlo cross validation experiments. Numbers in parentheses reflect the standard deviations. In all settings, Gradient Boosting outperformed other models in terms of accuracy, precision, and F1 Score.

Comparing different settings' results uncovered an interesting pattern. The performance of the best predictive model increased when more variations of the original movement signal were provided to the pipeline. Since all of the models in all the settings used the same number of 50 features selected by RFE, it could be assumed that the RFE choice of the most useful features should be different in different settings. Table 3 shows evaluation of this assumption. Also, it was observed that the standard deviation of the results decreased when more kinematic signals were added into our base feature set.

Table 2. Mean Results of Monte Carlo CV (50 repetition)

Experiment	Models	Accuracy (SD)	Precision (SD)	Recall (SD)	F1 Score (SD)
Movement	Logistic Regression	54.3% (8.6%)	53.1% (11.3%)	48.5% (19.2%)	49.8% (14.7%)
	Random Forest	58.0% (9.6%)	64.0% (19.4%)	30.5% (18.3%)	39.7% (19.2%)
	Gradient Boosting	**63.4% (9.3%)**	**69.5% (13.2%)**	44.6% (18.6%)	**58.0% (16.7%)**
	SVM	58.8% (8.0%)	60.3% (9.6%)	47.7% (17.2%)	52.2% (13.3%)
	K-Nearest Neighbors	59.6% (7.9%)	60.1% (9.0%)	**54.0% (16.7%)**	56.0% (12.6%)
	Decision Tree	61.5% (7.1%)	64.9% (11.0%)	47.0% (14.8%)	53.8% (13.1%)
Movement + Velocity	Logistic Regression	53.3% (9.3%)	51.4% (14.2%)	47.4% (20.1%)	48.4% (16.7%)
	Random Forest	64.7% (8.8%)	76.6% (14.2%)	41.6% (14.8%)	52.9% (14.9%)
	Gradient Boosting	**72.7% (7.8%)**	**80.8% (9.9%)**	**60.1% (13.9%)**	**68.0% (10.9%)**
	SVM	59.5% (8.0%)	61.8% (12.6%)	45.8% (15.3%)	51.9% (13.7%)
	K-Nearest Neighbors	56.3% (6.3%)	55.3% (5.7%)	64.8% (13.6%)	59.2% (8.3%)
	Decision Tree	62.1% (6.8%)	65.1% (11.9%)	48.6% (13.2%)	55.2% (12.7%)
Movement + Velocity + Acceleration	Logistic Regression	54.3% (8.0%)	53.7% (10.5%)	44.0% (18.2%)	47.4% (14.6%)
	Random Forest	66.1% (7.9%)	77.7% (11.0%)	44.3% (14.6%)	55.4% (13.8%)
	Gradient Boosting	**74.5% (6.6%)**	**81.5% (7.0%)**	63.6% (12.6%)	**70.8% (9.4%)**
	SVM	60.5% (7.7%)	65.5% (10.6%)	42.1% (16.5%)	50.0% (14.2%)
	K-Nearest Neighbors	56.9% (6.1%)	55.4% (5.1%)	**67.5% (14.0%)**	60.5% (8.3%)

(*continued*)

Table 2. (*continued*)

Experiment	Models	Accuracy (SD)	Precision (SD)	Recall (SD)	F1 Score (SD)
	Decision Tree	63.2% (6.5%)	66.7% (7.2%)	51.3% (13.1%)	57.4% (10.5%)
Movement + Velocity + Acceleration + Jerk	Logistic Regression	55.6% (9.0%)	55.0% (12.3%)	46.6% (18.0%)	49.6% (15.3%)
	Random Forest	68.2% (8.1%)	80.2% (10.5%)	47.9% (14.6%)	59.1% (13.5%)
	Gradient Boosting	**76.0% (5.9%)**	**82.7% (6.9%)**	66.3% (11.5%)	**73.0% (8.1%)**
	SVM	62.0% (7.7%)	66.5% (10.8%)	46.3% (16.2%)	53.5% (14.1%)
	K-Nearest Neighbors	58.3% (5.6%)	56.3% (5.1%)	**72.0% (13.0%)**	62.8% (8.1%)
	Decision Tree	64.3% (6.7%)	67.4% (7.3%)	54.0% (12.9%)	59.5% (10.7%)

To examine the validity of our assumption that "RFE choice of the most useful features should be different in different settings" we look into the importance of the features of gradient boosting model which was the best model. Looking at the Table 3, we can see that indeed the RFE model is picking different set of features in different experiments when presented with additional, possibly more informative set of features.

Table 3. Results

Experiment	Features Importance
Movement	('movement_Roll _Neighborhood peaks', 0.101), ('movement_Roll _Fundamental frequency', 0.065), ('movement_Roll _Entropy', 0.062), ('movement_Roll _ECDF Percentile_1', 0.032), ('movement_Z _ECDF Percentile_1', 0.03), ('movement_X _Max', 0.03), ('movement_Z _ECDF Percentile_0', 0.0241), ('movement_Yaw _Neighbourhood peaks', 0.0199), ('movement_Z _Median', 0.016), ('movement_X _ECDF Percentile_1', 0.015), ('movement_Z _FFT mean coefficient_0', 0.013), ('movement_Roll _Mean', 0.013), ('movement_Roll _Max', 0.011), ('movement_Pitch _Spectral distance', 0.011), ('movement_Pitch _Wavelet standard deviation_6', 0.011), ('movement_Z _Mean', 0.01), ('movement_Y _Spectral distance', 0.01022Mean absolute diff', 0.0014), ('movement_Yaw _Autocorrelation', 0.0013), ('movement_Roll _Wavelet variance_3', 0.0004), ('movement_Y _Spectral entropy', 0.00041)

(*continued*)

Table 3. (*continued*)

Experiment	Features Importance
Movement + Velocity	('Velocity_Z _Histogram_6', 0.0783), ('movement_Roll _Fundamental frequency', 0.0737), ('movement_Roll _Neighbourhood peaks', 0.0439), ('Velocity_Pitch _Histogram_6', 0.0255), ('movement_Roll _ECDF Percentile_1', 0.0228), ('movement_X _Max', 0.0201), ('movement_Z _ECDF Percentile_1', 0.017994609145126163), ('movement_Roll _Entropy', 0.0179), ('movement_Z _ECDF Percentile_0', 0.0170), ('movement_Pitch _Wavelet variance_6', 0.0146), ('movement_Z _Median', 0.0145), ('Velocity_Z _Histogram_8', 0.0110), ('Velocity_Z _Histogram_4', 0.0107), ('movement_Z _Absolute energy', 0.0104), ('movement_Z _FFT mean coefficient_0', 0.0102), ('Velocity_Roll _Histogram_9', 0.0102), ('movement_Pitch _Wavelet standard deviation_6', 0.0098), ('Velocity_Pitch _Histogram_4', 0.0097), ('Velocity_Pitch _Spectral roll-on', 0.0091), ('movement_X _ECDF Percentile_1', 0.0089), ('Velocity_Roll _Histogram_0', 0.0085)
Movement + Velocity + Acceleration	'movement_Roll _Fundamental frequency', 0.0726), ('Velocity_Z _Histogram_6', 0.057), ('movement_Roll _Entropy', 0.0440), ('movement_Roll _Neighbourhood peaks', 0.037), ('acceleration_X _Neighbourhood peaks', 0.0313), ('acceleration_Z _Entropy', 0.0309), ('Velocity_Pitch _Spectral roll-on', 0.0273), ('movement_Roll _ECDF Percentile_1', 0.021), ('movement_Z _ECDF Percentile_1', 0.0157), ('movement_X _Max', 0.0125), ('movement_Yaw _Fundamental frequency', 0.0112), ('movement_Pitch _Wavelet standard deviation_6', 0.0108), ('acceleration_Pitch _Power bandwidth', 0.0105), ('movement_Roll _Max power spectrum', 0.0101), ('movement_Z _Median', 0.0098), ('movement_X _ECDF Percentile_1', 0.0097), ('movement_Z _ECDF Percentile_0', 0.0096), ('Velocity_Z _Histogram_4', 0.0094), ('movement_Pitch _Wavelet variance_6', 0.0087), ('Velocity_Yaw _Spectral roll-on', 0.0086), ('movement_Y _Power bandwidth', 0.0085), ('Velocity_Pitch _Histogram_1', 0.0084)
Movement + Velocity + Acceleratio + Jerk	('movement_Roll _Fundamental frequency', 0.0870), ('Velocity_Z _Histogram_6', 0.0518), ('movement_Roll _Neighbourhood peaks', 0.0423), ('acceleration_Z _Entropy', 0.0276), ('Velocity_Pitch _Spectral roll-on', 0.0275), ('movement_Roll _Entropy', 0.0213), ('jerk__Y _Neighbourhood peaks', 0.0181), ('acceleration_X _Neighbourhood peaks', 0.01690), ('jerk__X _Neighbourhood peaks', 0.0157), ('movement_Roll _ECDF Percentile_1', 0.0151), ('movement_Yaw _Fundamental frequency', 0.0148), ('movement_Z _ECDF Percentile_1', 0.0141), ('movement_X _Max', 0.0130), ('movement_Z _Average power', 0.0128), ('movement_Pitch _Wavelet standard deviation_5', 0.0107), ('movement_Z _Median', 0.0106), ('acceleration_Z _Neighbourhood peaks', 0.0103), ('movement_Y _Power bandwidth', 0.0102), ('movement_Roll _Max power spectrum', 0.0097)

5   Discussion

This study has introduced a novel approach to addressing the persistent issue of cyber-sickness in Virtual Reality (VR) environments. While cybersickness has been extensively studied through traditional physiological markers, this research focused on the analysis of head movement patterns as a promising marker for cybersickness detection. The study leveraged a publicly available dataset from a VR experiment involving 75 participants [23] and meticulously analyzed head movements and their derivatives across multiple axes and extracted statistical, temporal, and spectral features. Results included 76% accuracy and 83% precision in predicting cybersickness, showcasing the potential effectiveness of head movement patterns as an essential contributor to the understanding and mitigation of cybersickness in VR applications.

This study contributes to the field of cybersickness by providing an analysis of a new source of physiological marker that can be used as an indicator of cybersickness. The results also identify most valuable set of head movement features that are worth being extracted. The authors hope that future work can include further exploration of head movement data, combined with eye movement data to create real-time cybersickness detection systems.

References

1. Arcioni, B., Palmisano, S., Apthorp, D., Kim, J.: Postural stability predicts the likelihood of cybersickness in active HMD-based virtual reality. Displays **58**, 3–11 (2019). https://doi.org/10.1016/j.displa.2018.07.001
2. Lee, H., Hwang, Y.: Technology-enhanced education through VR-making and metaverse-linking to foster teacher readiness and sustainable learning. Sustainability **14**(8), 4786 (2022). https://doi.org/10.3390/su14084786
3. Huang, D., Wang, X., Liu, J., Li, J., Tang, W.: Virtual reality safety training using deep EEG-net and physiology data. Vis. Comput.Comput. **38**(4), 1195–1207 (2022). https://doi.org/10.1007/s00371-021-02140-3
4. Van Der Kruk, S.R., Zielinski, R., MacDougall, H., Hughes-Barton, D., Gunn, K.M.: Virtual reality as a patient education tool in healthcare: a scoping review. Patient Educ. Couns.Couns. **105**(7), 1928–1942 (2022). https://doi.org/10.1016/j.pec.2022.02.005
5. Gilbert, S.B., Jasper, A., Sepich, N.C., Doty, T.A., Kelly, J.W., Dorneich, M.C.: Individual differences & task attention in cybersickness: a call for a standardized approach to data sharing. In: 2021 IEEE Conference on Virtual Reality and 3D User Interfaces Abstracts and Workshops (VRW), Lisbon, Portugal, pp. 161–164. IEEE (2021). https://doi.org/10.1109/VRW52623.2021.00037
6. Lackner, J.R.: Motion sickness: more than nausea and vomiting. Exp. Brain Res. **232**(8), 2493–2510 (2014). https://doi.org/10.1007/s00221-014-4008-8
7. Kennedy, R.S., Drexler, J., Kennedy, R.C.: Research in visually induced motion sickness. Appl. Ergon. **41**(4), 494–503 (2010). https://doi.org/10.1016/j.apergo.2009.11.006
8. Sanaei, M., Machacek, M., Eubanks, J.C., Wu, P., Oliver, J., Gilbert, S.B.: The effect of training communication medium on the social constructs co-presence, engagement, rapport, and trust: explaining how training communication medium affects the social constructs co-presence, engagement, rapport, and trust. In: Proceedings of the 28th ACM Symposium on Virtual Reality Software and Technology, Tsukuba Japan, pp. 1–3. ACM (2022). https://doi.org/10.1145/3562939.3565686
9. Sanaei, M., Machacek, M., Gilbert, S., Eubanks, C., Wu, P., Oliver, J.: The impact of embodiment on training effectiveness. In: 2023 11th International Conference on Information and Education Technology (ICIET), Fujisawa, Japan, pp. 44–50. IEEE (2023). https://doi.org/10.1109/ICIET56899.2023.10111344
10. Calfa, B.A., Wu, P., Sanaei, M., Gilbert, S., Radlbeck, A., Israelsen, B.: Combining natural language and machine learning for predicting survey responses of social constructs in a dyad. In: 2022 IEEE 2nd International Conference on Intelligent Reality (ICIR), Piscataway, NJ, USA, pp. 58–61. IEEE (2022). https://doi.org/10.1109/ICIR55739.2022.00028
11. Sanaei, M., Machacek, M., Gilbert, S.B., Wu, P., Oliver, J.: Comparing perceptions of performance across virtual reality, video conferencing, and face-to-face collaborations. In: 2023 IEEE International Conference on Systems, Man, and Cybernetics (SMC), Honolulu, Oahu, HI, USA, pp. 4556–4561. IEEE (2023). https://doi.org/10.1109/SMC53992.2023.10394218
12. Hughes, C.L., Fidopiastis, C., Stanney, K.M., Bailey, P.S., Ruiz, E.: The psychometrics of cybersickness in augmented reality. Front. Virtual Real. **1**, 602954 (2020). https://doi.org/10.3389/frvir.2020.602954
13. University of Zagreb, Faculty of Graphic Arts, Croatia et al.: The impact of different navigation speeds on cybersickness and stress level in VR. J. Graph. Eng. Des. **11**(1), 5–11 (2020). https://doi.org/10.24867/JGED-2020-1-005
14. Sanaei, M., Perron, A.J., Gilbert, S.B.: Pendulum chair: a research platform for cybersickness. Proc. Hum. Factors Ergon. Soc. Annu. Meet. **67**(1), 1837–1843 (2023). https://doi.org/10.1177/21695067231192456

15. Sepich, N.C., Jasper, A., Fieffer, S., Gilbert, S.B., Dorneich, M.C., Kelly, J.W.: The impact of task workload on cybersickness. Front. Virtual Real. **3**, 943409 (2022). https://doi.org/10.3389/frvir.2022.943409

16. Venkatakrishnan, R., et al.: The effects of auditory, visual, and cognitive distractions on cybersickness in virtual reality. IEEE Trans. Vis. Comput. Graph. 1–16 (2023). https://doi.org/10.1109/TVCG.2023.3293405

17. Ng, A.K.T., Chan, L.K.Y., Lau, H.Y.K.: A study of cybersickness and sensory conflict theory using a motion-coupled virtual reality system. Displays **61**, 101922 (2020). https://doi.org/10.1016/j.displa.2019.08.004

18. Qi, R.-R., et al.: Profiling of cybersickness and balance disturbance induced by virtual ship motion immersion combined with galvanic vestibular stimulation. Appl. Ergon. **92**, 103312 (2021). https://doi.org/10.1016/j.apergo.2020.103312

19. Gasteiger, N., Van Der Veer, S.N., Wilson, P., Dowding, D.: Virtual reality and augmented reality smartphone applications for upskilling care home workers in hand hygiene: a realist multi-site feasibility, usability, acceptability, and efficacy study. J. Am. Med. Inform. Assoc. **31**(1), 45–60 (2023). https://doi.org/10.1093/jamia/ocad200

20. Dennison, M.S., D'Zmura, M.: Cybersickness without the wobble: experimental results speak against postural instability theory. Appl. Ergon. **58**, 215–223 (2017). https://doi.org/10.1016/j.apergo.2016.06.014

21. Widdowson, C., Becerra, I., Merrill, C., Wang, R.F., LaValle, S.: Assessing postural instability and cybersickness through linear and angular displacement. Hum. Factors J. Hum. Factors Ergon. Soc. **63**(2), 296–311 (2021). https://doi.org/10.1177/0018720819881254

22. Chen, X., Jeong, J.C.: Enhanced recursive feature elimination. In: Sixth International Conference on Machine Learning and Applications (ICMLA 2007), Cincinnati, OH, USA, pp. 429–435. IEEE (2007). https://doi.org/10.1109/ICMLA.2007.35

23. Curry, C., Li, R., Peterson, N., Stoffregen, T.: APAL 2019: postural data, game performance, and subjective responses of cybersickness in virtual reality head-mounted displays. Data Repository for the University of Minnesota (DRUM) (2019). https://doi.org/10.13020/A9W0-8K04

24. Kennedy, R.S., Lane, N.E., Berbaum, K.S., Lilienthal, M.G.: Simulator sickness questionnaire: an enhanced method for quantifying simulator sickness. Int. J. Aviat. Psychol.Aviat. Psychol. **3**(3), 203–220 (1993). https://doi.org/10.1207/s15327108ijap0303_3

25. Nam, Y. H., Kim, Y.Y., Kim, H.T., Ko, H.D., Park, K.S.: Automatic detection of nausea using bio-signals during immersion in a virtual reality environment. In: 2001 Conference Proceedings of the 23rd Annual International Conference of the IEEE Engineering in Medicine and Biology Society, Istanbul, Turkey, pp. 2013–2015. IEEE (2001). https://doi.org/10.1109/IEMBS.2001.1020626

26. Martin, N., Mathieu, N., Pallamin, N., Ragot, M., Diverrez, J.-M.: Virtual reality sickness detection: an approach based on physiological signals and machine learning. In: 2020 IEEE International Symposium on Mixed and Augmented Reality (ISMAR), Porto de Galinhas, Brazil, pp. 387–399. IEEE (2020). https://doi.org/10.1109/ISMAR50242.2020.00065

27. Oh, S., Kim, D.-K.: Machine–deep–ensemble learning model for classifying cybersickness caused by virtual reality immersion. Cyberpsychology Behav. Soc. Netw. **24**(11), 729–736 (2021). https://doi.org/10.1089/cyber.2020.0613

28. Recenti, M., et al.: Toward predicting motion sickness using virtual reality and a moving platform assessing brain, muscles, and heart signals. Front. Bioeng. Biotechnol. **9**, 635661 (2021). https://doi.org/10.3389/fbioe.2021.635661

29. Garcia-Agundez, A., et al.: Development of a classifier to determine factors causing cybersickness in virtual reality environments. Games Health J. **8**(6), 439–444 (2019). https://doi.org/10.1089/g4h.2019.0045

30. Islam, R., Lee, Y., Jaloli, M., Muhammad, I., Zhu, D., Quarles, J.: Automatic detection of cybersickness from physiological signal in a virtual roller coaster simulation. In: 2020 IEEE Conference on Virtual Reality and 3D User Interfaces Abstracts and Workshops (VRW), Atlanta, GA, USA, pp. 648–649. IEEE (2020). https://doi.org/10.1109/VRW50115.2020.00175

31. Islam, R., et al.: Automatic detection and prediction of cybersickness severity using deep neural networks from user's physiological signals. In: 2020 IEEE International Symposium on Mixed and Augmented Reality (ISMAR), Porto de Galinhas, Brazil, pp. 400–411. IEEE (2020). https://doi.org/10.1109/ISMAR50242.2020.00066

32. Dennison, M.S., Wisti, A.Z., D'Zmura, M.: Use of physiological signals to predict cybersickness. Displays 44, 42–52 (2016). https://doi.org/10.1016/j.displa.2016.07.002

33. Dennison, M.S., D'Zmura, M., Harrison, A.V., Lee, M., Raglin, A.J.: Improving motion sickness severity classification through multi-modal data fusion. In: Pham, T. (ed.) Artificial Intelligence and Machine Learning for Multi-Domain Operations Applications, Baltimore, United States, p. 27. SPIE (2019). https://doi.org/10.1117/12.2519085

34. Yildirim, C.: A review of deep learning approaches to EEG-based classification of cybersickness in virtual reality. In: 2020 IEEE International Conference on Artificial Intelligence and Virtual Reality (AIVR), Utrecht, Netherlands, pp. 351–357. IEEE (2020). https://doi.org/10.1109/AIVR50618.2020.00072

35. Hale, K.S., Stanney, K.M.: Technology management and user acceptance of virtual environment technology. In: Handbook of Virtual Environments, pp. 523–534. CRC Press (2014). https://doi.org/10.1201/b17360-29

36. Lawson, B.: Motion sickness symptomatology and origins. In: Hale, K.S., Stanney, K. (eds.) Handbook of Virtual Environments: Design, Implementation, and Applications, 2nd edn, pp. 531–600. CRC Press (2014)

37. Chardonnet, J.-R., Mirzaei, M.A., Mérienne, F.: Features of the postural sway signal as indicators to estimate and predict visually induced motion sickness in virtual reality. Int. J. Human-Computer Interact. 33(10), 771–785 (2017). https://doi.org/10.1080/10447318.2017.1286767

38. Hadadi, A., Guillet, C., Chardonnet, J.-R., Langovoy, M., Wang, Y., Ovtcharova, J.: Prediction of cybersickness in virtual environments using topological data analysis and machine learning. Front. Virtual Real. 3, 973236 (2022). https://doi.org/10.3389/frvir.2022.973236

39. Mijovic, T., Carriot, J., Zeitouni, A., Cullen, K.E.: Head movements in patients with vestibular lesion: a novel approach to functional assessment in daily life setting. Otol. Neurotol.Neurotol. 35(10), e348–e357 (2014). https://doi.org/10.1097/MAO.0000000000000608

40. Lubetzky, A.V., Hujsak, B.D.: A virtual reality head stability test for patients with vestibular dysfunction. J. Vestib. Res.Vestib. Res. 28(5–6), 393–400 (2019). https://doi.org/10.3233/VES-190650

41. Mancini, M., Horak, F.B., Zampieri, C., Carlson-Kuhta, P., Nutt, J.G., Chiari, L.: Trunk accelerometry reveals postural instability in untreated Parkinson's disease. Parkinsonism Relat. Disord.Relat. Disord. 17(7), 557–562 (2011). https://doi.org/10.1016/j.parkreldis.2011.05.010

42. Mancini, M., Carlson-Kuhta, P., Zampieri, C., Nutt, J.G., Chiari, L., Horak, F.B.: Postural sway as a marker of progression in Parkinson's disease: a pilot longitudinal study. Gait Posture 36(3), 471–476 (2012). https://doi.org/10.1016/j.gaitpost.2012.04.010

43. Baratto, L., Morasso, P.G., Re, C., Spada, G.: A new look at posturographic analysis in the clinical context: sway-density versus other parameterization techniques. Mot. Control 6(3), 246–270 (2002). https://doi.org/10.1123/mcj.6.3.246

44. Han, T.R., Paik, N.J., Im, M.S.: Quantification of the path of center of pressure (COP) using an F-scan in-shoe transducer. Gait Posture 10(3), 248–254 (1999). https://doi.org/10.1016/S0966-6362(99)00040-5

45. Paillard, T., Noé, F.: Techniques and methods for testing the postural function in healthy and pathological subjects. BioMed Res. Int. **2015**, 1–15 (2015). https://doi.org/10.1155/2015/891390

46. Arzanipour, A., Olafsson, S.: Evaluating Imputation in a Two-Way Table of Means for Training Data Construction. SSRN, preprint (2023). https://doi.org/10.2139/ssrn.4476272

47. Werner, P., Al-Hamadi, A., Limbrecht-Ecklundt, K., Walter, S., Traue, H.C.: Head movements and postures as pain behavior. PLoS ONE **13**(2), e0192767 (2018). https://doi.org/10.1371/journal.pone.0192767

48. Duarte, M., Freitas, S.M.S.F.: Revisão sobre posturografia baseada em plataforma de força para avaliação do equilíbrio. Rev. Bras. Fisioter.Fisioter. **14**(3), 183–192 (2010). https://doi.org/10.1590/S1413-35552010000300003

49. Pachori, R.B., Hewson, D.J., Snoussi, H., Duchene, J.: Analysis of center of pressure signals using empirical mode decomposition and fourier-bessel expansion. In: TENCON 2008 - 2008 IEEE Region 10 Conference, Hyderabad, India, pp. 1–6. IEEE (2008). https://doi.org/10.1109/TENCON.2008.4766596

50. Chagdes, J.R., et al.: Multiple timescales in postural dynamics associated with vision and a secondary task are revealed by wavelet analysis. Exp. Brain Res. **197**(3), 297–310 (2009). https://doi.org/10.1007/s00221-009-1915-1

51. Barandas, M., et al.: TSFEL: time series feature extraction library. SoftwareX **11**, 100456 (2020). https://doi.org/10.1016/j.softx.2020.100456

52. Cochran, W.G.: Relative accuracy of systematic and stratified random samples for a certain class of populations. Ann. Math. Stat. **17**(2), 164–177 (1946). https://doi.org/10.1214/aoms/1177730978

53. Guyon, I., Weston, J., Barnhill, S., Vapnik, V.: No title found. Mach. Learn. **46**(1/3), 389–422 (2002). https://doi.org/10.1023/A:1012487302797

54. Chawla, N.V., Bowyer, K.W., Hall, L.O., Kegelmeyer, W.P.: SMOTE: synthetic minority over-sampling technique. J. Artif. Intell. Res.Artif. Intell. Res. **16**, 321–357 (2002). https://doi.org/10.1613/jair.953

55. Xu, Q.-S., Liang, Y.-Z.: Monte Carlo cross validation. Chemom. Intell. Lab. Syst.. Intell. Lab. Syst. **56**(1), 1–11 (2001). https://doi.org/10.1016/S0169-7439(00)00122-2

Paleo-Games: Using AI and Gamification to Generate an Unguided Tour of an Open World Virtual Environment for STEM Education

Harman Singh[1], Sarah Saad[1], Chencheng Zhang[1], Thomas Palazzolo[1],
Jessee Horton[1], Robert Reynolds[1,2(✉)], John O'Shea[2], Ashley Lemke[3],
and Cailen O'Shea[4]

[1] Wayne State University, Detroit, MI 48201, USA
robert.reynolds@wayne.edu
[2] University of Michigan, Ann Arbor, MI 48109, USA
[3] University of Wisconsin-Milwaukee, Milwaukee, WI 53201, USA
[4] North Dakota State University, Fargo, ND 58105, USA

Abstract. This paper discusses a novel addition to Virtual Reality-based Learning Environments (VRLEs). Guiding user actions in these virtual models has been an obstacle in their usability in a classroom timeframe. This study focuses on the introduction of audio and visual cues as a method of indirect influence on user pathfinding through an open world virtual exhibit. This project utilizes a Virtual Reality simulation of an ancient Paleolithic environment now submerged underneath Lake Huron. The simulation was originally designed to help predict the location of ancient occupational remains of Ancient Paleo-Indians. The system has been repurposed to provide a more immersive cultural and anthropological experience for High School Stem Education. The impact of this methodology on the pathfinding efficiency of a sample group of students is analyzed with qualitative and quantitative metrics. These metrics include aspects of user engagement, immersion, and ease of navigation. The previous efforts in this area are then discussed and compared with the results produced here. The paper concludes with a brief discussion of potential new directions for the use of VR for STEM educational use.

Keywords: Virtual Reality · STEM · Indirect Control · Point of Interest · Virtual Reality for Education · Archeology · Gamification · Game Audio · Artificial Intelligence · Simulation · AI-based Games

1 Introduction

1.1 The Advent of Virtual Reality

Please Following Morton Heilig's "Sensorama" in 1962, virtual reality has been an evolving field with a consistent core idea - To create an immersive virtual world, for the purposes of exploration, and understanding [1]. The first true head mounted virtual-reality display to execute this idea, the "Sword of Damocles," debuted in 1967. Over the

© The Author(s), under exclusive license to Springer Nature Switzerland AG 2024
H. Degen and S. Ntoa (Eds.): HCII 2024, LNAI 14735, pp. 255–277, 2024.
https://doi.org/10.1007/978-3-031-60611-3_19

next thirty years, Virtual Reality was largely used in one field, training, and education. Teachers and mentors from the fields of automobile engineering, military training, and aeronautics identified the potential of simulating situations that were too dangerous or too costly to test practically [2]. Around the beginning of the 21st century, Game companies, such as Atari, SEGA, and Nintendo adopted VR technology and began to develop video games for the medium. In the decade that followed, the public was not yet swayed by the new technology. For a variety of reasons including cost and comfort. But in 2010, the Oculus Rift was released to significant acclaim. Ever since, with strides in headset innovation by Vive, SteamVR, Oculus Quest VR, and PlayStationVR2, the virtual reality market has grown and developed stronger displays of immersion and interaction [3].

Whilst virtual reality technology has grown significantly through the consumer-fueled field of video games, its initial applications have not been forgotten. Thanks to these advances, exploring immersive environments and learning from these experiences has never been more impactful. As our proficiency with technology improves, we have been able to develop alien worlds, unseen worlds, even predictive worlds such as how the earth may appear in the past or future. This is the application this project would like to focus on, teaching students about the past through these virtual environments. A large number of studies have been conducted on the potential for VR's use in educational spaces (VRE). Some studies cite the most significant obstacles being expense and realism [4, 5]. Other studies cite the difficulty for teachers to integrate the tool into their lessons, i.e. VRE-based pedagogy [6–8]. There have been quite a few experiments over the years that have attempted to determine the potential applications of VR in the classroom [9, 10]. Most practical attempts have focused on "scene-based" learning. That is to say, the VR environments were typically smaller, constrained areas whose value lay purely in the interactivity of the artifacts within a closed environment [11, 12]. There was one case in which the VR experience was so constrained it was limited to picking pinpoints on the map and viewing 360-degree images of the locations [13]. There are few examples of open world exhibits in which students and instructors can move about in unrestricted fashion, with some notable exceptions such as the Egyptian Temple educational environment developed by Jacobsen and Holden which is explored later in the paper. In contrast to these, this paper attempts to introduce the "Open-World" environment to improve engagement and to better leverage the strengths of virtual reality. The question that this paper aims to answer is "How can Open-World virtual environments be used as an engaging, time-efficient educational tool, and can we as developers influence the users to improve these parameters?".

1.2 Walking the Way of the Caribou

The Deep Dive Virtual Reality system was originally developed to reproduce a portion of North America occupied by Paleo-Indians from 10,000 to 8,000 B.P. for the purpose of Archaeological site prediction. [14]. The region of interest, the Land Bridge, was an isthmus of land that connected what is now Amberley in Canada to what is now Alpena, Michigan in the USA. During the Ice Age the region was semi-arctic, and the bridge was above lake levels for the time period. Archaeologist from the University of Michigan led by Dr. John O'Shea postulated that since it was above water for such a lengthy period that it could be used as a migration pathway for caribou. Dr. Reynolds and his team from Wayne State University were recruited to use Artificial Intelligence to reproduce the ancient environment in Virtual Reality for use in the prediction of ancient sites that are now currently underwater [20].

As stated by Millington, while Artificial Intelligence is ubiquitous in games today, rarely is it used to produce a holistic game ecosystem replete with food chains and population models [15]. To undertake such a task here, Artificial Intelligence and Machine learning techniques were used to recreate the ancient ecosystem and to generate AI based models of herd behavior with the idea that where caribou go hunters will follow. This tool was successfully employed to suggest locations for underwater site exploration [16]. In the process of doing that it was observed that the system can also be repurposed to be a learning tool for STEM based high school education classes. That is, students can be given the opportunity to explore the land bridge and make predictions about how it was used in the past by Paleo-Indians. However, since the bridge itself was 80 miles long and 8 miles wide, it was an expansive open world. As a result, students often wandered about without ever getting a complete and holistic understanding of the ecosystem.

It was then proposed to "gamify" the system to provide students with a more holistic approach to the environment in terms of the flora, fauna, geology, and hydrology of the biomes that make up the land bridge. The key to the approach is that an Evolutionary Learning model of optimal herd foraging, Cultural Algorithms, was used to generate optimal paths based on aspects of caribou herd behavior taken from the research. Taking inspiration from Isaac Newton who stated that, "If I have seen further, it is by standing on the shoulders of Giants," the idea was to use these optimal pathways to indirectly guide their explorations on the Land Bridge in a way that would insure a more holistic and balanced view of the landscape as experienced by the caribou. Here, the student is invited to experience the way of the caribou indirectly by explicitly walking along their path.

This is done here through the development of a "scavenger hunt" game similar to those found in *Genshin Impact* or the *Sonic* franchise. Scavenger hunt-style games work by creating a series of collection tasks revolving around the exploration of an environment and the acquisition of target objects. This method of game design was found to be highly effective in the context of education [17–19]. The idea is to position points of interest (POI) strategically along example caribou pathways as they pass through various biomes during their crossing. Since the landscape itself does not have many visual features to act as beacons it was felt that associating the POI with both visual and audio cues that could attract a student's attention indirectly and will give them a feeling of freedom. At the same time, it would provide them with an immersive experience akin to that of a migrating caribou. Future work can install POI that reflect the hunting and foraging behavior of Paleo Indians as well. Optimal paths produced by Pathfinder are then used in the VR subsystem to generate paths followed by caribou in the virtual world.

The basic hypothesis to be tested in the VR prototype here is what information is necessary in the POI to allow students to follow desired movement patterns without reducing the immersive quality of the game. Two basic versions will be constructed and compared. They are:

1. Visual cues associated with the POI but with no audio.

2. Visual cues plus audio that change linearly relative to the user's position associated with POI.

The paths of students in each of the two scenarios can be tracked and compared statistically with each other. While each version can potentially provide more information to the student, the improvement in a student's understanding can be evidenced by their movements on the bridge relative to the hypothesized paths. The versions will then be compared with each other in terms of the paths generated along with students' responses to follow up questionnaires about what they have learned in their explorations.

The remainder of the paper is structured as follows. The Deep Dive VR project is described in Sect. 2. The Point of Interest approach for indirect control of student movement is presented in Sect. 3. Section 4 gives the experimental framework used to test the POI prototype here. The quantitative and qualitative results of the experiments are given in Sect. 5. Section 6 provides a summary of the results and suggestions for future work.

2 The Deep Dive Land Bridge Simulation Project

2.1 Overview of Project

In order to understand this experiment, it is important to understand its foundation. In 2022, a team led by Dr. Robert Reynolds developed an immersive simulation of the Alpena-Amberley Ridge Land Bridge. This land bridge (Fig. 1), now submerged, once stretched across Lake Huron between 10,000 and 7000 BP.

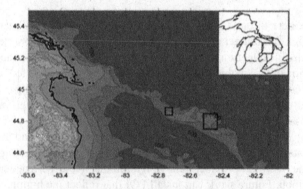

Fig. 1. The Alpena-Amberley Ridge Land Bridge

The initial objective of this virtual asset was to discover prehistoric sites located underwater and refer these locations to interested archaeologists. The DEEPDIVE virtual world system was utilized to develop a virtual reality representation of this land bridge.

Figure 2 gives an overview of the overall Deep Dive system. It has three basic components: The Pathfinder MAP Simulation system; the Graphical User Interface (GUI) for the simulation system; and the Virtual Reality system.

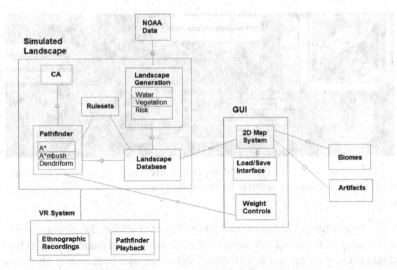

Fig. 2. The Overall Organization of the Deep Dive system.

The topographic data acquired from the National Oceanographic and Atmospheric database (*NOAA*) of the area was fed into the AI pipeline to *Generate* AI content via the Landscape database. The created content includes the water level of various cells of the landscape to identify which areas of the Land Bridge were above the current water level or not for a given year between 10,000 and 8,000 B.P. For any given year height map data for those portions of the landscape was calculated along with derived slope. Hydrological information including the location of ponds, swamps, and rivers that are present in the location were then calculated. Given the location, water content, slope and sun angle the AI pipeline can predict the cells potential vegetation at each location on the Land Bridge. This information is stored in the *Landscape Database* for use by the Pathfinder system.

"Pathfinder," is an artificial intelligence-based multi-agent planner. Pathfinder was comprised of three similar pathfinding heuristics: A*-Single Agent, A*mbush, and Den-driformA*. A* is a search-based algorithm that can be used to generate optimal path plans. In its initial form it was restricted to the herd following a single agent. The next version, dubbed A*mbush, took A*'s parameter-based pathfinding and applied it to a wave of agents as opposed to a single agent. This helped demonstrate the movement of separate sub-herds of animals interacting with and consuming their environment. The third version, DendriformA*, allowed the splitting and merging of a wave into sub-waves. This allowed the algorithm to model situations such as parting ways around an obstacle or large boulder field. Cultural Algorithms were employed as a meta-heuristic to optimize the parameters for each of the three algorithms for a given herd size and Lake Level.

The Pathfinding simulation system then communicates with the GUI in two basic ways. First, the user interface displays a series of tabs through which the user may navigate to a given data set or select an experiment to run as shown in Fig. 3. Maps can be viewed in a variety of data styles, such as biome data, topographical data, archaeological

Fig. 3. The Current Deep Dive GUI. The upper left gives the path produced by an algotihm. Bottom left gives the 4 basic parameters for the optimization.

points of interest, ruleset hotspots, and so on. Pictured above, the user has selected to run six iterations of the A*mbush pathfinder, each wave being made up of 1000 caribou. The weight priority wheel on the bottom left allows the user to manually set the weights for Effort, Risk, Nutrition, and Time in the performance function. The priority weights control what will be important to the caribou in the current run. The green segment denoted by a "N" is the nutrition this will have caribou prioritize situations which will lead to an increase in calorie or food intake. The blue segment is effort ("E"). An increase in this priority will cause the caribou to avoid scenarios that lead to excess calories being spent, for example going up a steep incline. The red segment is risk ("R") which influences caribou to avoid scenarios that lead to a higher percentage of deaths. The last weight denoted by yellow is time ("T"). This parameter prioritizes the amount of time it would take to cross the entirety of the portion of the land bridge simulated.

The resultant paths were stored and then passed to the Virtual Reality system and used to guide the movement of caribou there as shown in Fig. 4. The knowledge represented by these paths can be used in another way. Specifically, it could be used to provide information about the experience of the agents, both caribou and hunters, as they move across the landscape. This became clear when the team travelled to Alaska and interviewed traditional hunters from the Native Village of Kotzebue to explore the virtual land bridge. The hunters shared their experiences and observations as they explored the virtual world and spoke at length about their interpretations of the environment. This collaboration helped combine traditional ecological knowledge with the procedurally generated content that made up the majority of the project's assets.

Fig. 4. A caribou herd moving across the Land Bridge.

To capitalize on this idea, during the spring of 2022 the DeepDive tool was integrated into the STEM curriculum of high school students in Alpena, as they attempted to identify these ancient hunting sites via the virtual environment. The students spent two weeks with the system and their experiences provided valuable insight into the potential of open-world VR in education. This experiment was the first foray into the Land Bridge's application as an educational tool. This project attempts to build on that experience by enriching the Land Bridge environment with knowledge that can be collected by users as they are influenced indirectly by information about the environment and its past usage.

Although future work will involve placement of POIs to reflect human and animal behavior on the Landbridge the goal of this work is to demonstrate the feasibility by constructing an indirect path that serves as a literal cooks tour of all of the known biomes that comprise the land bridge. It is a variation on the classic travelling salesman problem I, n the Computer Science literature. In fact, it was viewed to be more complex than those generated for the caribou since migrating animals are likely to visit only a subset of these biomes as they move across the landscape. However, it can be viewed as a way to introduce students to the breadth of the land bridge environment. They can then use that knowledge as they further explore the environment based upon generated migration pathways.

3   The Point of Interest System

3.1   Motivation: User Immersion in VRE

The Alpena High School demonstrations opened the doorway for the Land Bridge's use as an educational tool [20]. The curiosity and enthusiasm of the students as they interacted with the Land Bridge simulation contrasted with the blank stares and inattention that characterize the classrooms of today. As children are brought up in a world filled with technology and interactivity, it's important that teaching methods should evolve similarly to retain their effectiveness. In 2020 Liu, Wei, Lei, Wang, and Ren carried out an experiment to determine the improvement, if any, of integrating immersive VR (IVR) into a classroom setting. The experiment, which consisted of 90 students split into experimental and control groups, revealed that the experimental group underwent significant improvement in the academic and engagement scores. Liu, Wei, Lei, Wang, and Ren determined that "the students who engaged in the IVRC [the name of their virtual environment education system] had significantly higher academic achievement and better engagement (cognitive, behavioral, emotional and social) compared to those who learned through traditional teaching methods in a normal classroom [21]." This finding appeared consistent with other research done on the topic, namely by Parong and Meyer in 2018 [22], and Jitmahantakuli and Chenrai in 2019 [23]. These latter two papers describe similar approaches to applying virtual reality to classrooms, one to the field of biology and the other in geoscience. Although prior studies had reached positive conclusions regarding the benefits of VR in the classroom, a question that has yet to be answered is the time efficiency of "open world" virtual environments in the classroom, more importantly, the extent by which developers can shape VR environments to help direct students to learn in the most time efficient manner whilst retaining its vital immersive qualities. To give an example, in Fig. 5, the experiment conducted by Liu, Wei, Lei, Wang, and Ren centered around "fixed location" learning, akin to a museum.

Fig. 5. Image of the virtual environment designed by Liu et al. [21].

There, the animal models were all clearly presented to the students, and students would interact with each to learn. This is a highly efficient method of conveying information as quickly as possible, with the added novelty of being in Virtual Reality. However, the Land Bridge project does not present itself in a similar way. Instead, it provides an "open world" for students to explore. This is closer to the environment created by Jacobsen and Holden [24]. Their Egyptian temple model accurately depicts the environment in a way that the focus was more on the environment, rather than simply artifacts within the environment. Similarly, the Land Bridge project attempts to focus on the environment using behavioral artifacts such as migration pathways to influencing pathfinding by students through principles of indirect control.

3.2   The Role of Sound in Decision-Making

Indirect control in game development is the idea that the game developer subtly influences the player to act in certain ways without needing to overtly instruct the player on what to do. This is achieved in multiple ways depending on the objective of the developer. Millington states that user perception of their environment can be expressed in terms of the five basic senses: sight, sound, touch, smell, and taste. The first three senses are the most frequently employed in video games to support immersion. For example, audio cues in games often prime players on how to act in a given situation. Happy upbeat music influences players to relax and enjoy the scenery. In contrast, tense, suspenseful music primes players to look for aggressive encounters and to be vigilant of danger [25]. Slight changes in the camera angle when approaching an important objective can also help alert players to scrutinize the scene before them more closely. Each of these are examples of how a developer can influence a player to act in a certain way. For the experiments here the focus will be on the first two senses, sight and sound as sources for indirect control of user movements in the open world.

It was decided to focus on the combination of audio and visual cues to make the developers' influence less overt. Although not as direct as vision, sound plays an important role in pathfinding and decision-making [26–29]. Many studies have endorsed this relationship, and some have even attempted to illustrate the different effects that different audio types had on VR users [30]. In this project two levels of indirect control are represented: indirect control with visual cues only; and indirect control with both video and audio cues together. The idea is to determine the additional levels of control produced with the new layer. The first step in this endeavor was to identify the method to be used. It was important to first research the different types of audio available, and which would suit the purposes of the study.

The three available types of audio available for this study were mono, stereo, and 3D audio. In Brinkman's experiments on the effect of audio on immersion in a virtual environment, the participants reported significant differences between the same environments with or without sound [31]. This experiment entailed simulating a 3D wasp near the user through both visual and audio methods. However, these same subjects reported no significant difference between 3D sound environments and stereo sound environments. While this implies that the effect of directed sound and 3D soundscapes would be an unnecessary development, it's important to note that the intent of the Brinkman's experiment did not rely on the agency of the user, but instead treated them purely as a physiological reactor. That is to say that the objective of the Virtual environment may factor into the effect that 3D sound has on the user vs stereo sound. If the objective was to avoid the wasp, then 3D sound would be considerably more useful information than mono sound.

Within this project, the overall objective is to utilize audio to focus student trajectories toward specific regions, while providing them with a time-efficient tool to explore each unique biome of the Land Bridge simulation. With this objective in mind, it can be hypothesized that the audio cues will indirectly affect the pathfinding conducted by the user. In an open world the visual cues are too varied to suggest a single path. The lack of dominant visual cues is pertinent as it removes one of the easiest and most direct tools for influencing choices. If every artifact was clearly visible from a distance, through direct visual cues, not only would it detract from the immersive experience by introducing an alien element, but it would also remove the feeling of agency and control the user has that is vital to an open world environment. Therefore, it is sound that is being utilized, which not only helps provide a method of guidance towards objectives, but also serves to enhance the overall ambience, rather than clash with it.

3.3 The Point of Interest System: POI

The point of interest system (POI) was developed to create an incentive to influence players to remain on a more structured route, as opposed to wandering off and exploring the entire map. It was inspired by the Memorial Quest designed by Volkmar et al. [32] The POIs for the land bridge project are based on the type of fauna that would live in each of the seven different biomes present assuming a semi-artic environment like that of Alaska today. There is only limited knowledge about the plant and animal content on the Land Bridge in the time between 10,000 and 8,000 B.P. on the land bridge so the use of flora and fauna from present day semi-artic environments is the best guess now.

There are three POIs per animal, and ten total animals. The fauna utilized for this exercise included the boreal toad (Anaxyrus boreas boreas), the arctic ground squirrel (Urocitellus parryii), trumpeter swans (Cygnus buccinator), caribou (Rangifer tarandus), polar bears (Ursus maritimus), wolves (Canis lupus), the snowy owl (bufo scandiacus), the bald eagle (Haliaeetus leucocephalus), the osprey (Pandion haliaetus) and the brown bear (Ursus arctos). Each POI is composed of two main components: A collider and an auditory clue. The auditory clue is the sound of the animal in question, and the collider triggers a gameObject destruction, causing the POI to be recorded as "claimed" when the user gets close enough to "see" the object. An example of the collider setting associated with Polar Bear POI is given in Fig. 6.

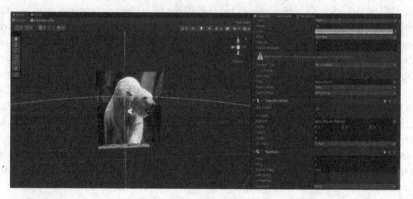

Fig. 6. The Capsule Collider and RigidBody Settings of the Polar Bear POI

In addition to the main two components, the POI is comprised of two more sub-components: A minor visual cue, and the associated information. The minor visual cue (pictured in Fig. 7) is a light green point light that serves to help locate the Points of Interest without sound. By design, this point light is not especially bright. This is done in order to ensure that the point of interest's visual presence does not significantly reduce the immersive environmental quality of the Land Bridge project. Instead, the light is visible when the user is close enough and indicates the presence of a visual POI at that location.

Each POI is fitted with code to display an image of the animal and one of three facts about it. Its name, both cultural and scientific, its height and weight, and a fact unique to the animal itself is provided for each. This is meant to educate the players in an engaging matter. First by finding the animal based on their cries, and then by learning about them. These POIs are not randomly scattered, but instead follow an intentional path, leading the players through each of the biomes to become acquainted with their residents. Some fauna, such as Trumpeter Swans are less ubiquitous across the land bridge and so therefore are more concentrated in one or two locations, making it slightly easier to obtain information about them as shown in Fig. 8.

However, these POI generally follow a consistent path across the Land Bridge save for a slight loop in the middle so that the sandy beach biome can be explored as well. These POI provide the incentive used to influence the user's decision-making about

Fig. 7. Polar Bear POI situated near an artifact. The green light surrounding the POI denotes its presence and can be seen as the user gets close enough, even though the POI itself is not yet visible.

Fig. 8. Two out of three of the Trumpeter Swan points can be found in the Lake Biome.

where to go. Without these POI, the users have no real guidance, and theoretically can travel everywhere eventually. By influencing user decision-making with POIs, the experience should produce a more holistic perception of the Land Bridge ecosystem.

3.4 Designing the Narrative Route

Ultimately the goal of the POI is to indirectly highlight a caribou path(s) generated by pathfinder and followed by caribou in the virtual world. To facilitate a holistic environmental experience, it was deemed important that each of the different biomes should be visited. These biomes represented different environments that could be found along this land bridge. Despite the Land Bridge representing a stretch of land between Alpena Michigan and Amberly, Ontario, the biomes were based on the subarctic region of Alaska as these environments best represented the environment of the Land Bridge several thousand years ago. The biomes for this land bridge included the following: boulder fields, cliffs, sandy beaches, tundra plains, swamp marshes, lakes, lakeside marshes, and landmarks known as eskers.

Figure 9 illustrates the different biomes, represented here by different colors. The tundra is the majority, represented by the color white. The lake biome is light blue, the lakeside marsh is dark blue, the eskers as red, the swamp marsh as green, the boulder

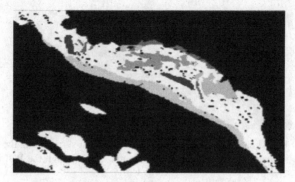

Fig. 9. The Biome distribution on the Land Bridge

field is orange, and the cliffs are gray. A list of fauna was compiled that inhabit each of these biomes such that no one biome would appear too sparse, despite some being generally inhospitable for common kinds of life. For instance, the sandy beach is rarely home to the kinds of animals that emit sounds, with the exception of birds. Each of these animals' calls were recorded into sound files that would be emitted from each POI when the environment was initialized. An important factor involved in the design was the sound's volume in relation to distance [33].

By giving sound a linear roll off up to a range of 200 m, users can determine their relative distance from the point of interest. Given the number and intended distribution of these POI, the effect was intended to make the virtual simulation appear more alive and more immersive, by appealing to an additional sense other than sight.

The example route itself was designed to provide the user with an overview of the overall landscape and its occupants in a time efficient sequence whilst retaining fidelity to the occupants' natural biomes. A rendition of this idea can be found in Fig. 10.

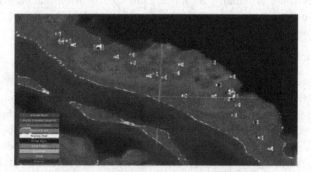

Fig. 10. Example path through the biomes.

This path would pass through each of the available biomes, allowing the user to theoretically experience every unique environment this virtual world has to offer. The path generated above approximately represents the estimated most efficient path through the POI on the Landbridge. Combined with the scavenger hunt nature of the POI system, it can be theorized that the trial participants would be highly incentivized to follow this route. An additional unintended incentive is that the Land Bridge has few topographic features to serve as beacons of movement, except for trees and differences in slope. Therefore, it is believed that auditory stimulus would be weighted more heavily than the somewhat lacking visual stimulus.

4 Trials: The Effects of Indirect Control

4.1 The Hypothesis

Hypothetically, it is assumed that the introduction of sound as variable in an Open World for pathfinding should lead to a more focused and predictable route for the users. By manipulating the placement of Points of Interest on the Land Bridge, developers can indirectly influence the pathfinding and decision-making of the users, guiding them in a more focused, time efficient tour of the simulation. As an educational tool, this interactive approach should lead to better engagement and retention by students, especially when compared to an Open World with no audio, and only minimal visual cues to mark the locations of these POI.

4.2 Experimental Framework

The experimental setup was consistent with previous ones associated with the grants approved by the Universities IRB. Students were volunteers from Dr. Reynolds Game Programming courses along with other students in the Computer Science program familiar with the research. Each participant gave their informed consent. The results were then anonymized and pooled for the generation of the statistical results.

In the experiments represented here each user was given 15 min to collect as many of the POIs as they can. Fifteen minutes was set as a baseline since one of the designers of the VR landscape was able to collect all objects in 15 min. It was not expected that those unfamiliar with the landscape would be able to achieve that level of performance. In addition, fifteen minutes also served the hypothesis well as it was a relatively short amount of time, and in a hypothetical educational scenario, it would allow multiple students to run the simulation within a single class period. This would in turn, allow the school to purchase the VR equipment to share between students, instead of expecting each student to buy their own.

The spawn point was selected near the far northeast side of the Land Bridge due to being the default spawn point for viewing the caribou due to its elevation. Its location was near the spawn point used for the Alaskan interviews. The space north of the point was used to allow a choice for the user to travel further north or south with the intent of hiding a handful of points in the northernmost biome. Theoretically, users would be less likely to visit that set of points in the audio-free version due to the natural logic of there being more to discover in the vast expanse of land south of the spawn point. The weather chosen was the default clear weather, and the time of Fall was selected so that weather played a less impactful role in this experience to minimize extraneous information.

4.3 · Trial Design

The trials were originally intended to consist of two main groups: The experimental audio group, and the audio-free control group. The audio-free control group would enter the Land Bridge without the sounds enabled, but still employ the visual features and the voiced facts. The experimental group will engage the Land Bridge with the sounds intact. An opportunistic sampling of 14 volunteers was employed. Approximately one half of the subjects were students in Dr. Reynolds Game Design and Artificial Intelligence classes. The remainder were known to members of the development team and were for the most part college age young adults.

These volunteers would first enter the soundless iteration of the Landbridge and attempt to find the 30 points scattered across the map. This group would then get a short break to fill out a survey and to recover from any VR fatigue, and then enter the sounds-enabled version. The data gathered consisted of two types: measured, and self-reported. With regards to the measured data, the simulation would chronologically log the POIs gathered, and the timestamp for each collection.

```
Congratulations! Here are the points collected!
Polar Bear POI
Found at 5.44 seconds
Toad POI (2)
Found at 146.68 seconds
Wolf POI (1)
Found at 221.17 seconds
CaribouPOI
Found at 301.48 seconds
Squirrel POI (2)
Found at 407.17 seconds
CaribouPOI (1)
Found at 507.35 seconds
Wolf POI (2)
Found at 532.47 seconds
```

Fig. 11. Example of the Log file generated from a run.

This text file would serve as the raw data that would later be charted to compare the performances of the players. In the case of the self-reported data, a questionnaire was presented to the player, as shown in Fig. 13. The questions concerned the number of points they were able to collect, their ability to collect all 30 points if they had chosen to do so, their initial interest in the experiment, their immersion in the experiment, their favorite animal to search for and the easiest animal to find. These questions would be common between the two different environments (Soundless vs sound), but the Sound version would contain an additional question regarding the effectiveness of the cue for locating the POI.

Since the subjects had already been exposed to the Land Bridge in the previous run, they should do at least as well as before unless audio was a hindrance rather than an aid. However, one expects that the audio group will do at least as well as the visual only group since they had already become somewhat familiar with the land bridge in the previous run with no audio. Yet, in terms of performance there was much room for improvement since the average subject collected about half of the available POIs. If there was an improvement with audio it would likely be a result of increased emergence and understanding on the part of the users.

5 Trial Results

5.1 Objective Data

In this section the performance of the 14 users in the open world with and without the audio is examined (Fig. 12).

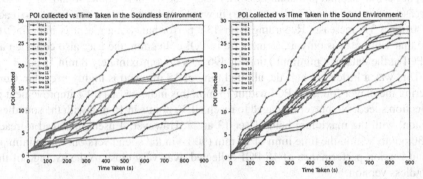

Fig. 12. The results of all 14 test subjects in the soundless environment (left) and the sound environment (right)

In Fig. 14 the number of items acquired is plotted against the time taken. Notice that there is broader spread in the learning curve for the no audio version versus the audio version. The overall slope of the learning is increased for the audio phase as well. The fact that the learning curves are much more uniform with the audio suggests that the user experience is more uniform and immersive when sound is added. Overall, players performed consistently better in the sound environment. They gathered, on average, 9.0 more POIs than their soundless environment runs. The average improvement from soundless to sound environment was 74%. An example of player improvement can be seen in Fig. 13 below.

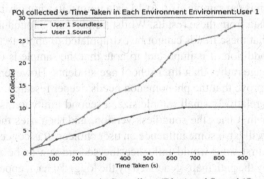

Fig. 13. User 1's performance over time in Soundless (Blue) and Sound (Orange) versions. (Color figure online)

User 1's performance comparison is not completely indicative of all users when it comes to discussing aspects such as the number of points collected over time by users. Due to the different and creative methods players use to reach POI, the exact movements could not be recorded, and only the approximation via POI collection data could be generated. However, it does hold true that without exception, every player performed better in the sound version, although the improvement margin did vary. The highest margin between sound and soundless was User 1 at 18 more points found, or a 280% increase in performance. The lowest margin was User 13 at 1 extra point found (to reach 30/30) or a 3% increase. Regarding User 13's performance margin, it is important to note that while it was only a 3% increase in POI collection, the user also collected all 30 POI at the dataset's minimum time of 496.69 s or approximately 8 min 16 s.

This was a little over half the allotted time of 15 min and is highly irregular. Considering the player found 29 POI within 15 min, this indicates a 44.9% improvement in collection speed. No player managed to reach all 30 points in 15 min with the soundless version, with the maximum being User 13 at 29. However, 4 users managed to reach all 30 points within the time limit of 15 min (900s) in the sound version. The minimum sound version performance of 15 POI collected, was very close to the average of the soundless version.

```
soundless = [10,12,10,20,23,7,16,17,7,21,22,21,29,14]
sound = [28,19,15,30,30,16,28,26,23,27,28,30,30,25]
print(np.mean(soundless))
print(np.mean(sound))
16.357142857142858
25.357142857142858
```

Fig. 14. Calculating the averages of the Sound and Soundless Collections

The average number of points gathered in the environment without audio was ~ 16.36/30, and the average number of points gathered in the environment with audio was ~ 25.36/30. This is a significant improvement and would seem to support the hypothesis. However, this is a good time to address the limitations of this experiment. The largest elephant in the room is the sample size. At 14 data points, it is impossible to draw statistically significant data from these results. Whilst trends can be found and analyzed, it's important to note that these trends cannot be extrapolated to apply to the greater population of users. In addition, it is important to note that the sample is opportunistic and consists of college age rather than high school age students. However, the consistency of this data should prove that the phenomenon needs deeper research.

In addition to a relatively small sample size, a second limitation is user familiarity. Given that the user first tries the soundless version, and then tries the sound version, residual memories will have some influence on user choices. It is conceivable that doing something for the first time would influence the second run to be more successful. However, judging by the path maps generated by the logged data, it appears far less likely than initially determined. Almost consistently, players followed completely different paths from their original soundless runs, and their sound runs mapped very similarly to the example path displayed in Fig. 11. Although the strict order was different, the general path was noticeably similar. An example of this difference in behavior can be shown in Fig. 15.

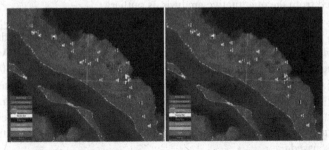

Fig. 15. The approximated path taken by User 1 during the Soundless (Left) and Sound (Right) iterations.

As shown in Fig. 15, the path taken by User 1 during the sound run proceeds in the completely opposite direction than the soundless iteration. This not only supports the idea that sound cues affect user pathfinding, but also implies that the influence of the sound cues are more impactful to the user than their residual memories. This trend holds true for Users 2,4,6,7,9,10,12,13, and 14. Users 3,5,8, and 11 did not exhibit as much variance in their paths, largely due to either their low performance in the soundless iteration, leading to a difficult comparison, or that they were already moving along the intended path as depicted in Fig. 11. It is important to note that the first three points are placed very intentionally relative to the spawn point. A Polar Bear is placed directly in the field of view of the player as they spawn. This was done in an effort to immediately inform the player about what it is that they are looking for. During the initial testing of this prototype, it was observed that users spent a considerable amount of early time unsure about what they were looking for. To address this, the Polar Bear point was placed directly in front of the spawn point in the 2.0 version of the product, and the early testers of version 1.0 had their data unused for this experiment in the service of consistency. In addition to this, the two closest points, Snowy Owl 1 and 2, are placed approximately equidistant from the Polar bear point – so much so that the sound version has both of their cries playing at equal volume in equal directions. It is very interesting to note that most players chose to move northwest towards Snowy Owl 1 instead of Snow Owl 2. In many cases, players who moved towards Snowy Owl 2 in the Soundless version opted to move towards Snowy Owl 1 in the Sound version, whilst it was rarely the same vice versa. This can be seen in Fig. 15 as well. User 1 travelled southeast towards Snowy Owl 2 in the Soundless version but opted to move northwards towards Snowy Owl 1 in the Sound version. This is precisely the movement the initial map describes in Fig. 11.

5.2 Subjective Data

As discussed previously, the second portion of this project's data was self-reported results via a questionnaire. The results of the questionnaire are listed below. While each of the fourteen dual-environment users participated in this survey, an additional 2 users participated in the soundless test only, and 5 additional users participated in the sound test only. These seven users participated before the Objective data log feature was added to the build, and the new dual-environment testing format was established, and therefore were excluded from the quantitative analysis as outliers.

In total 21 users tested the system but only those that participated in the dual trials were used to produce the quantitative data. However, it was decided not to discount the experience of the 7 other individuals who tested just one of the systems. Two subjects tested just the visual POI system only, while five tested the audio version. Their observations were therefore included here for the sake of completeness. Sixteen assessments are recorded for the sound free and nineteen for the sound enabled portion. The additional subjects can easily be removed from the displays in the future, but their presence provides a wider variety of experience that will be useful in designing the future version as will be discussed later.

From Fig. 16 it is clear people were interested in the sound version. It did produce high ratings. It is shown quite clearly in Fig. 17 that the audio cues heightened the users' sense of immersion. Not only were the majority of users rating the soundless version a 2 before even trying the sound version, most users rated the sound version far more highly. It is important to note that only one of the "2" ratings were from a 'sound only' tester, meaning 4/5 'sound only' testers rated the experience a 4 or a 5, without even experiencing the control group. If this were not the case, it would have been much more concerning, as the evidence would then suggest that the users may have rated the sound version as highly due to comparison with the control group soundless version. However, the '2' ratings were split evenly between one 'sound only' user and user 13 who completed the entire course within 8 min and 16s. Evidently, they considered the sounds produced a less immersive experience for them, despite their incredible performance when compared to their soundless run. It is very interesting to note that despite users rating the sound version very highly in terms of immersion, they all followed very similar paths. This supports the idea that game developers can indirectly influence players to

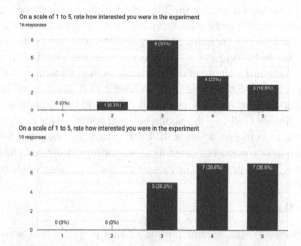

Fig. 16. The self-reported initial interest level in the soundless (top) and sound (bottom) iterations

follow a certain path, without having the influence affect the user's immersion, but instead enhancing it. In the case of these users, the audio cues lent themselves towards completing the gameplay fantasy of the simulation, as opposed to breaking it. Yet it also succeeded at its primary task of guiding players through each of the biomes in a time-efficient manner. They were guided towards the POI, making sure their time was well spent, while still allowing them enough agency to decide the specifics of their path in an order that appealed to them.

Figure 18 records how the users perceived the ease by which they could acquire the POIs. As is shown in Fig. 18, approximately half of the soundless users considered the POIs quite difficult to locate, with a lesser percentage of users on either end of the scale rating the points either average or considerably difficult to locate. This stands in stark contrast to the response of those who viewed both versions in the duo experiments, where almost three quarters of the testers considered the POIs relatively easy to find, with the exception of a single tester. This trend suggests that users have a markedly positive impression of the immersive quality of the experimental version, and that they attributed the improvement of their performances to the audio cues as shown in Fig. 17.

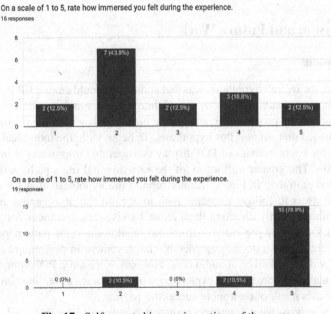

Fig. 17. Self-reported immersion ratings of the users.

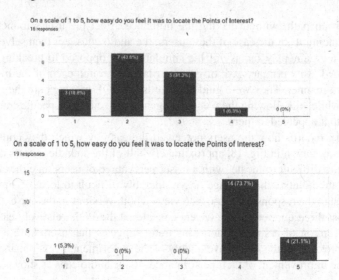

Fig. 18. Ease of Access for soundless (top) and sound (bottom).

6   Conclusion and Future Work

6.1   Conclusions

In conclusion, the overall hypothesis was that audio cues could enable VR developers to influence their users' pathfinding activity and time efficiency and provide a more immersive experience in the process. There are some clear trends within the measurable data that was collected that support this hypothesis. To begin with, the individual path maps representing the users' pursuit of POI display considerable improvement in collection and navigation. The greater uniformity of the experimental run's paths and similarity to the intended path map in Fig. 11 further support the hypothesis that VR developers can influence users to follow a specific path to accomplish an objective or series of objectives without overtly directing them either by visual environment designs (roads, arrows, trails, etc.) or by pre-entry instructions. In addition to the path maps, the User Comparison charts illustrate the considerable improvement in performance that users experienced with the addition of audio cues. Not only were more POIs found, but most users also managed to traverse and explore each of the biomes as outlined on the biome map in Fig. 9 as a result of their more successful pursuit.

In terms of improvement, four users managed to gather all 30 points, while the majority of the other users managed to get within ~ 5 POI of the goal. On the qualitative side of the experiment, the audio experience was rated highly. These self-reported statistics compose an important facet of support for the hypothesis by indicating that the audio cues did not break the immersion or feel manipulative, but rather led to deeper immersion within the VR world. Overall, this experiment yielded several very illuminating pieces of evidence that point to VR environments, such as this Land Bridge, becoming valuable supplements to STEM education.

6.2 Future Extensions of the Experimental Framework

These investigations have just touched on the potential of this gamification. The distribution of POIs in this work focuses on a path that allows the student a more holistic view of the environment by visiting all the biomes. However, the framework has the potential to provide a rich spectrum of user experiences. Some possible extensions of the framework are as follows:

1. Information Content: The path can be constructed to reflect what a caribou observes as it follows an optimal path produced by one of the herd movement algorithms. It can also reflect paths taken by hunters as they move through the open world.
2. Distribution Control: The current distribution of POIs is static but can change over time depending on the season, for example.
3. Spawn Point Distribution: Currently students are spawned at the same location in the virtual world. In the future other spawn points, static or random can be used.
4. Temporal context: The contents of the POIs are currently static but can also be seasonally dynamic.
5. Artificially intelligent POI: The POI are currently static, but they could be allowed to move within the boundaries of their biome to allow for a more dynamic experience.
6. Participant Interaction: Currently a student has limited ability to interact with a POI. Alternatively, users can have more tactile and conversational interaction and be exposed to biological, geological, and cultural information through interaction with the POI.

In summary, through gamification of the open world VR, a whole host of new and novel hypotheses can be tested in the future.

References

1. Chalmers, A., Zányi, E.: Real Virtuality: emerging technology for virtually recreating reality. Becta (2009). http://www.becta.org.uk
2. Christou, C.: Virtual reality in education. Affective, Interactive and Cognitive Methods for E-Learning Design, pp. 228–243 (2010). https://doi.org/10.4018/978-1-60566-940-3.ch012
3. Brown, J., White, E., Boopalan, A.: Looking for the ultimate display: A brief history of virtual reality. Boundaries of Self and Reality Online (2017). https://www.sciencedirect.com/science/article/abs/pii/B9780128041574000128
4. Huang, H.-M., Rauch, U., Liaw, S.-S.: Investigating learners' attitudes toward virtual reality learning environments: Based on a constructivist approach. Comput. Educ. 55(3), 1171–1182 (2010). https://doi.org/10.1016/j.compedu.2010.05.014
5. Kavanagh, S., Luxton-Reilly, A., Wuensche, B., Plimmer, B.: A systematic review of virtual reality in Education. Themes in Science and Technology Education (2017). https://www.learntechlib.org/p/182115/
6. Alfalah, S.F.: Perceptions toward adopting virtual reality as a teaching aid in information technology. Educ. Inf. Technol. 23(6), 2633–2653 (2018). https://doi.org/10.1007/s10639-018-9734-2
7. Lege, R., Bonner, E.: Virtual reality in education: the promise, progress, and challenge. JALT CALL J. 16(3), 167–180 (2020). https://doi.org/10.29140/jaltcall.v16n3.388
8. Velev, D., Zlateva, P.: Virtual reality challenges in education and training. Int. J. Learn. Teach. (2017). https://doi.org/10.18178/ijlt.3.1.33-37

9. Merchant, Z., Goetz, E.T., Cifuentes, L., Keeney-Kennicutt, W., Davis, T.J.: Effectiveness of virtual reality-based instruction on students' learning outcomes in K-12 and higher education: a meta-analysis. Comput. Educ. **70**, 29–40 (2014). https://doi.org/10.1016/j.compedu.2013.07.033

10. Mikropoulos, T.A., Natsis, A.: Educational virtual environments: a ten-year review of empirical research (1999–2009). Comput. Educ. **56**(3), 769–780 (2011). https://doi.org/10.1016/j.compedu.2010.10.020

11. Moro, C., Štromberga, Z., Stirling, A.: Virtualisation devices for student learning: comparison between desktop-based (Oculus Rift) and mobile-based (Gear VR) virtual reality in medical and health science education. Australas. J. Educ. Technol. **33**(6) (2017). https://doi.org/10.14742/ajet.3840

12. Cecil, J., Ramanathan, P., Mwavita, M.: Virtual learning environments in engineering and STEM education. In: 2013 IEEE Frontiers in Education Conference (FIE) (2013). https://doi.org/10.1109/fie.2013.6684874

13. Cho, D., Chun, B.A.: Virtual reality as a new opportunity in geography education. In: Proceedings of the 2019 5th International Conference on Education and Training Technologies (2019). https://doi.org/10.1145/3337682.3337701

14. Saad, S., et al.: Incorporating the dynamics of climate change into the deep dive virtual reality underwater site prediction system. In: Degen, H., Ntoa, S. (eds.) Artificial Intelligence in HCI. HCII 2023. LNCS, vol. 14051, pp. 554–573. Springer, Cham (2023). https://doi.org/10.1007/978-3-031-35894-4_41

15. Millington, I.: AI for Games, 3rd edn. CRC Press (2019)

16. O'Shea, J.M., Lemke, A.K., Sonnenburg, E.P., Reynolds, R.G., Abbott, B.D.: A 9,000-year-old caribou hunting structure beneath Lake Huron. Proc. Natl. Acad. Sci. **111**(19), 6911–6915 (2014). https://doi.org/10.1073/pnas.1404404111

17. Bellotti, F., Berta, R., De Gloria, A., D'ursi, A., Fiore, V.: A serious game model for cultural heritage. J. Comput. Cult. Heritage **5**(4), 1–27 (2012). https://doi.org/10.1145/2399180.2399185

18. Lu, Y., Chao, J.T., Parker, K.: HUNT: Scavenger hunt with augmented reality. Interdisc. J. Inf. Knowl. Manag. **10**, 21–35 (2015). http://www.ijikm.org/Volume10/IJIKMv10p021-035Lu1580.pdf

19. Schell, J.: The Art of Game Design: A Book of Lenses. CRC Press, Taylor & Francis Group (2020)

20. Reynolds, R.G., Palazzolo, T., Lemke, A., O'Shea, J., Saad, S., Zhang, C.: Deepdive: the use of virtual worlds to create ethnographies of ancient civilizations. In: Human Computer Interaction International Conference, Washington D.C. (2021)

21. Liu, R., Wang, L., Lei, J., Wang, Q., Ren, Y.: Effects of an immersive virtual reality-based classroom on students' learning performance in science lessons. Br. J. Edu. Technol. **51**(6), 2034–2049 (2020). https://doi.org/10.1111/bjet.13028

22. Parong, J., Mayer, R.E.: Learning science in immersive virtual reality. J. Educ. Psychol. **110**(6), 785–797 (2018). https://doi.org/10.1037/edu0000241

23. Chenrai, P., Jitmahantakul, S.: Applying virtual reality technology to Geoscience Classrooms. Review of International Geographical Education Online, pp. 577–590 (2019). https://doi.org/10.33403/rigeo.592771

24. Jacobson, J., Holden, L.: Virtual heritage. Techné Res. Philos. Technol. **10**(3), 55–61 (2007). https://doi.org/10.5840/techne200710312

25. Lin, J.-H.: Fear in virtual reality (VR): fear elements, coping reactions, immediate and next-day fright responses toward a survival horror zombie virtual reality game. Comput. Hum. Behav. **72**, 350–361 (2017). https://doi.org/10.1016/j.chb.2017.02.057

26. Byun, J., Loh, C.S.: Audial engagement: effects of game sound on learner engagement in digital game-based learning environments. Comput. Hum. Behav. **46**, 129–138 (2015). https://doi.org/10.1016/j.chb.2014.12.052

27. Danevičius, E., Stief, F., Matynia, K., Larsen, M.L., Kraus, M.: 3D localisation of sound sources in virtual reality. In: Brooks, A., Brooks, E.I., Jonathan, D. (eds.) ArtsIT 2020. LNICSSITE, vol. 367, pp. 307–319. Springer, Cham (2021). https://doi.org/10.1007/978-3-030-73426-8_18

28. Ekman, I.: Meaningful noise: understanding sound effects in computer games. In: Proceedings of Digital Arts and Cultures (2005)

29. Lindquist, M., et al.: The effect of audio fidelity and virtual reality on the perception of virtual greenspace. Landsc. Urban Plan. **202**, 103884 (2020). https://doi.org/10.1016/j.landurbplan.2020.103884

30. Meghanathan, R.N., et al.: Spatial sound in a 3D virtual environment: all bark and no bite? Big Data Cogn. Comput. **5**(4), 79–95 (2021). https://doi.org/10.3390/bdcc5040079

31. Brinkman, W.-P., Hoekstra, A., Vanegmond, R.: The effect of 3D audio and other audio techniques on virtual reality experience. Stud. Health Technol. Informat. **219** (2015). https://doi.org/10.3233/978-1-61499-595-1-44

32. Volkmar, G., Wenig, N., Malaka, R.: Memorial quest - a location-based serious game for cultural heritage preservation. In: Proceedings of the 2018 Annual Symposium on Computer-Human Interaction in Play Companion Extended Abstracts (2018). https://doi.org/10.1145/3270316.3271517

33. McArthur, A., et al.: Distance in audio for VR. In: Proceedings of the 12th International Audio Mostly Conference on Augmented and Participatory Sound and Music Experiences (2017). https://doi.org/10.1145/3123514.3123530

Enhancing Product Design Efficiency Through Artificial Intelligence-Generated Content: A Case Study of a Home Office Desk

Xiaoying Tang ⓘ, Silu Zheng⁽⊠⁾ ⓘ, and Zitao Liu ⓘ

Guangdong University of Technology, No. 729 Dongfeng Road, Yuexiu District, Guangzhou, Guangdong, China
msms.silu@qq.com

Abstract. With the rapid development of technology, Artificial Intelligence Generated Content (AIGC) tools have attracted a lot of attention and brought unprecedented opportunities to the design field. Based on the "Design Thinking" theory, this study explores how AIGC tools can enhance creative stimulation and efficiency in product design, using the home office desk as a case study. The research team used the AI text generation tool to assist users in the empathy stage to identify and create an interview outline and in the problem definition stage to transform the interview information into questions and needs. In the conceptualization phase, the AIGC tool helped stimulate creativity and transform user needs into concrete design solutions. The design prototype phase uses AI image generation tools to visualize the design solution. The testing and validation phase verifies the feasibility of the AIGC tool in design practice through a user satisfaction questionnaire, demonstrating its potential to improve design efficiency. The study aims to inspire researchers in the field of product design and encourage the application of AIGC tools to future product design and development processes to meet the changing market demands.

Keywords: Generative AI · Artificial Intelligence Generated Content · Product design · Home Office Desk · Design Efficiency · ChatGPT · Midjourney

1 Introduction

With the development of science and technology and the intensification of market competition, product design needs to be constantly innovated to meet the needs of consumers [1]. How to effectively stimulate product design creativity and improve the speed of product updating to meet user needs has become a key issue [2]. The traditional product design process usually relies on methods such as competitive product analysis and market research to ensure the design process is consistent with user needs and market demands. In the fast-changing market environment, relying only on traditional product design methods often makes it difficult to approach diversified user needs quickly. Therefore, introducing AIGC technology tools has become a promising direction to enhance the efficiency of product design creativity explosion.

© The Author(s), under exclusive license to Springer Nature Switzerland AG 2024
H. Degen and S. Ntoa (Eds.): HCII 2024, LNAI 14735, pp. 278–292, 2024.
https://doi.org/10.1007/978-3-031-60611-3_20

This research aims to explore how AIGC tools can be used to inspire product design ideas. This research aims to apply AIGC tools to product design by analyzing user needs, generating novel and practical design points, and transforming them into visualized design outcomes. Through this research, we aim to solve the challenges in the idea generation and iteration process in product design and improve design efficiency and quality. In the following, this project will detail the application of the AIGC tool, the design methodology, and the analysis of experimental results to demonstrate its practical application value in product design creativity. By integrating AI with design, this topic is expected to bring more innovations and breakthroughs in product design and improve design speed and user satisfaction.

2 Related Work

2.1 Current Status of AIGC Development and Application

The Web 3.0 era has arrived and is booming [3], and generative AI is one of the important developing technologies [4]. Artificial Intelligence Generated Content (AIGC) leverages AI techniques such as Generative Adversarial Networks (GANs) and other large-scale pre-trained models to learn and make sense of existing data with appropriate generalization capabilities to create appropriate content [5]. The ability to generate real and novel data has a huge impact in several industries, such as entertainment, healthcare, and finance. Generative AI opens new avenues for applications such as image synthesis, text generation, music composition, and even human-like chatbots [6, 7].

OpenAI's GPT family [8] is an important archetypal product for generative AI, which improves the fluency and complexity of AI dialog scenarios, enabling complex authoring tasks such as programming and writing articles, a new way of deep interaction that is rapidly gaining widespread popularity on the Web. After its launch on November 30, 2022, the rapid public acceptance and widespread use of ChatGPT was phenomenal. Within just 100 days of its release, it became a global hit. By the end of January 2023, ChatGPT had surpassed 100 million monthly active users, leapfrogging it to become the fastest-growing app in history in terms of users [9, 10]. Data from the World of Engineering can provide a reference-. -Twitter, Meta (formerly known as Facebook), and Instagram took five years, 4.5 years, and 2.5 years to reach 100 million monthly active users, respectively [11]. In addition to the text generation field, the image generation field is another important development of AIGC. As a typical AI image generation program, Midjourney outperforms OpenAI in image generation. The user inputs simple and concise keywords, and the platform outputs highly lifelike photos without the need to spend a lot of time on tedious image editing.

These products of generative AI have broad transformative power to undercut costs, increase efficiency, and help people become more productive. About 30% of new code is generated within the tech industry through AI assistance through tools like Chat-GPT and GitHub's Copilot [9]. The arts [12], advertising [13], and education industries [14] have also embraced it as a productivity gas pedal. The continued advancement and widespread adoption of AIGC technology highlight AI's immense potential in creative content generation. It has attracted widespread attention from various sectors, including entrepreneurs, investors, academics, and the public [3]. Industries are also coming to recognize the value of AI tools and expect to employ them to improve efficiency, foster innovation, and enhance quality. This trend presents unprecedented opportunities for the design field, including generating all types of content, such as text, images, slides, etc. [15]. This trend has provided new tools and resources for design thinking methodologies, making innovation easier to realize. Designers and related researchers are actively exploring paths to fully utilize AIGC tools in design practice to stimulate innovation and improve design efficiency.

2.2 Study Case Selection

Product design refers to creating and developing new products or improving existing products to meet specific goals and user needs [16]. The traditional product design process results from various factors, including user needs, market trends, technological limitations, and designer creativity. Product design encourages engineers and designers to think creatively, embrace emerging technologies, and develop cutting-edge solutions by exploring novel design approaches and anticipating future trends [16, 17]. The introduction of AIGC tools can be viewed as an extension and enhancement that further helps designers mine creative inspirations from a large amount of information while accelerating the design iteration process. These tools can provide new creative perspectives and be supplemented with additional design options and creative stimulation based on the designer's experience or market research.

In the post-pandemic era, working from home has become a common work pattern in modern daily life. A study by Dingle and Neyman found that during the 2019 coronavirus disease pandemic, 37% of work could be done from home, for example. Managers, educators, and people working in the computer, finance, and legal fields could mostly work from home [18, 19]. This is a broader group of users, and it is evident that research on home office desk design is directly related to many people's daily work and life experiences. With the popularization of the home office model, people's expectations of the home office environment are also evolving. Home office desk design needs to consider the different needs of users in terms of work efficiency, comfort, and space utilization, making the study case more representative and able to cover a wide range of user expectations. In addition, the home office desk is not only a basic working tool but can also introduce elements such as multifunctional design and space optimization through creative design [20]. This provides researchers with a wealth of creative and design possibilities, making using AIGC tools more interesting and challenging in terms of product design creativity. Considering the above factors, using the home office desk as a research case can provide a concrete and valuable demonstration of the AIGC tool in product design creativity and closer to user needs in practical application, providing useful insights for innovation in the design field.

3 Empathize

"Design Thinking is the process of understanding users, challenging assumptions, and reframing problems in an attempt to identify solutions, and there are many variations of the design thinking process currently used in the design industry [21]. This study explores the five-stage design thinking model proposed by the Hasso-Plattner Institute at Stanford University [22], which focuses on five aspects of design thinking: Empathize - Define - Ideate - Prototype - Test. Test", we discussed how to utilize the AIGC (Artificial Intelligence Generated Content) tool to inspire design ideas for home office desks.

During the empathy phase, this project chose semi-structured user interviews as the primary methodology to gain an in-depth understanding of the needs and contexts of users of home office desks. This decision was based on the strength of user interviews' ability to provide in-depth user insights, enabling the research team to better understand users' actual experiences and expectations.

3.1 Interview Preparation

ChatGPT version 3.5 was chosen as the main AIGC tool to assist in the preparation of the interviews.

Identify Respondents. On ChatGPT 3.5, we output the instruction "How should I categorize users of home office desks to conduct interviews? " To determine the types of respondents, the main home office workers were told to be telecommuting business people, higher education faculty, students, and self-publishing workers. Interviewees were selected from each type of home office group through purposive sampling. Inclusion criteria for the sample included (1) a minimum of 2 years of home office experience, (2) a separate desk in their home that they have and are using, and (3) a willingness to voluntarily participate in this study after being informed of the content and purpose of the study. Ultimately, a total of 20 interviewees were included in this study, including three telecommuters, four higher education faculty members, eight students, and five self-publishers.

Initial Development of Interview Outlines. In the first step, on ChatGPT, we enter the initial instruction in the format of "Background description (self-positioning + research purpose + research content + research object) plus "AI identity positioning (user researcher senior expert)," i.e., "I am a user researcher in the research team of a product design company. I am a user researcher in the research team of a product design company, and I need to complete the user research work of using the home office desk and gain insights into user needs through user interviews, but I don't have experience in this area. You are a senior expert in this user research; I would like to ask you some questions; please try to answer them professionally and in detail." In the second step, output the requirement instruction for the required AI help, i.e., "I want to do a user interview exploring the home desk design needs of office workers. Please help me create an in-depth interview outline. "The third step is to manually evaluate the interview outline produced in the previous step and input detailed adjustment instructions, such as "Propose the optimization direction of the total time: "Please control the total time within 20 min", "Please summarize the questions from the perspective of exploring the design requirements. ". In the end, we obtained a preliminary outline of the interviews, which included aspects including workspace configuration, daily tasks and activities, comfort, and preference needs.

Pre-interviews to Determine the Outline of the Interview. Pre-interviews were conducted to verify and optimize the accuracy and validity of the outline. Role-playing through ChatGPT simulated a real-life interview scenario to confirm the practical feasibility of the outline. In the first step, the role-playing instructions were inputted, including "Define the target audience, the purpose of the consultation, target actions, and division of labor," i.e., "This is my first time to do a user interview, and I am worried that the outline is not perfect, so I would like to do a practice exercise first. Let's play a role-playing game: I'll play the role of a user researcher, and you play the role of a "teacher-user in higher vocational colleges and universities," so please cooperate with me in the interview, I'll ask you questions, and you have to cooperate with me to answer the questions just like a real user." The second step is to communicate all the relevant questions with the AI tool step by step. In the third step, the interview outline was updated based on the results of the preventive interviews, and the final interview outline was finalized. This outline mainly contains the following open-ended questions:

1. Style and aesthetics: what kind of style and aesthetics do you consider when choosing a desk for your home office?
2. Space Configuration: What kind of space configuration do you think an ideal home office desk should have?
3. Storage and organization: Do you need a desk with storage for documents, stationery, and other items needed for work? What are your expectations for desk storage and organization?
4. Device Integration: What electronic devices do you typically use to work? How would you like your desk to integrate these devices?
5. Day-to-day experience: Do you have any day-to-day experiences, questions, or suggestions about using the desk?

3.2 Interview Process

This study was implemented in May-June 2023, and the interviews were simultaneously audio-recorded to ensure data integrity. Before conducting the formal interviews, the purpose and significance of the interviews were explained to the interviewees, and a commitment was made to handle all data in an anonymous manner to ensure the privacy of the interviewees. Interviews include face-to-face interviews, video interviews, and telephone interviews, and the length of each interview is limited to 20 min or less to ensure the focus and comfort of the interviewee. During the interview, we will ask questions based on a pre-determined interview outline and encourage interviewees to fully express their views and feelings. We will pay attention to recording the tone and expression of the interviewees to enhance the richness and accuracy of the data.

3.3 Advantages of Using the AIGC Tool During the Empathize Phase

We chose ChatGPT as the primary AIGC tool to increase efficiency during the interview prep phase. This was more flexible and time-saving compared to the traditional approach. ChatGPT played a key role in providing interview outlines and pre-interviews, which supported the smooth conduct of the interviews. During the implementation of the interviews, we still used traditional face-to-face, video, and telephone methods to ensure depth and authenticity. The combination of AIGC tools and traditional methods provided more comprehensive and efficient support for user interviews.

4   Define

4.1 Interview Data Organization

After the interviews, we will use the Flying Book tool to transcribe the audio data into text form and verify it with what was recorded during the interviews. To process this data further, we have chosen to use ChatGPT to assist in the distillation, generalization, and conceptualization of the data. The process consisted of the following steps:

Organizing First-Order Data. The interview results were organized according to the five themes of the interview outline (style and aesthetics, space configuration, storage, device integration, and daily experience), which constitute the first-order data.

Refinement to Second-Order Data. Use ChatGPT (AIGC text tool) to refine and simplify the interview results for each theme to generate second-order data. Taking style aesthetics as an example, the text compiled by ChatGPT is as follows: "When choosing a home office desk, I will consider several factors. First, I will consider whether the style of the desk harmonizes with my home environment. I want the desk to blend into the overall style of my home, which will make the office area look more unified and comfortable. Secondly, I would also look at the practicality and functionality of the desk. The desk needs to have enough space for my computer, files, stationery, and other office supplies. I usually choose a desk with drawers or storage space so that I can better manage and organize the items I need for my office. Aesthetics is also one of the important factors I consider. I would choose a simple and fresh design and avoid overly complicated or fancy styles because I think a tidy office environment helps to improve productivity and concentration. Also, the quality of the desk is crucial. I tend to choose desks made of durable materials, which will ensure that the desk remains in good condition after a long period of use. Overall, my choices will combine style, practicality, aesthetics, and quality to create a comfortable office area for work."

Organize as a Table. Use ChatGPT (AIGC text tool) to organize the second-order data into a table and make corrections based on the data verification results, and finally form a table of design requirements for the home office desk, as shown in Table 1 for the third-order data.

Table 1. Home Office Desk Design Requirement Sheet

Dimensions	Design Requirements
Style and Aesthetics	1. Practicality and functionality; 2. Simple, refreshing design; 3. Good product quality
Space Configuration	1. Moderate size, not occupying too much space; 2. Hidden cable design
Storage Solutions	1. Adequate storage space for files, stationery, etc.; 2. Includes drawers and open storage areas
Device Compatibility	1. Spacious desktop to accommodate a computer and monitor; 2. Designated space for keyboard and mouse
Daily Experience	1. Preferable placement for green plants; 2. Easy to clean and maintain hygiene

4.2 Advantages of Using the AIGC Tool in the Problem Definition Phase

The use of the Flying Book tool and ChatGPT to assist in the process of organizing the interview data increased efficiency and accuracy and greatly reduced the workload. The Flying Book tool helped to transcribe the audio recordings into text, while ChatGPT assisted in distilling and summarizing the data, which could have been more time-consuming and labor-intensive than the traditional approach. In contrast to traditional methods, which can be more time-consuming and labor-intensive, AIGC tools have the advantage of intelligent word-processing capabilities that enable them to handle large amounts of data more quickly and ensure the quality of the data. In addition, they can help us organize data into tables and understand user needs in a more systematic way so as to define the problem better.

5 Ideate

5.1 Programmatic Diffusion

Based on meeting the user's needs, we had ChatGPT design a desk that combined practicality, aesthetics, and ergonomics. Table 2 shows the specific solutions for each design requirement as reported by the AIGC tool.

These solutions synthesize the actual needs of users in pursuit of creating a practical, aesthetically pleasing, comfortable, and efficient desktop experience in a work or study environment. By adopting strategies such as multi-functional design, hiding cables, and making full use of storage space, this topic seeks to maximize the user's needs within a limited space. These recommendations will provide users with a functional, clean, and organized desk to enhance the daily work and study experience Table 3.

Table 2. Table of design options

Dimensions	Design Requirements	design options
Style and Aesthetics	1. Practicality and functionality; 2. Simple, refreshing design; 3. Good product quality	- Designed with multifunctional table tops such as adjustable height and foldable extension area - Ensure product quality by using simple lines and bright colors
Space Configuration	1. Moderate size, not occupying too much space; 2. Hidden cable design	- Design the right size tabletop; consider folding legs or a removable table - An integrated cable management system is used to hide power and data cables
Storage Solutions	1. Adequate storage space for files, stationery, etc.; 2. Includes drawers and open storage areas	- Design tables with drawers and open storage for document and stationery storage needs - Sliding drawer units are provided underneath the table
Device Compatibility	1. Spacious desktop to accommodate a computer and monitor; 2. Designated space for keyboard and mouse	- Designed with a spacious desktop to accommodate computers, monitors, and other devices - Integrated keyboard and mouse storage location for ergonomic use
Daily Experience	1. Preferable placement for green plants; 2. Easy to clean and maintain hygiene	- Allow a special place in the tabletop design for small green plants - Designed with a simple structure for easy cleanup of the tabletop and surrounding area

Table 3. Table of design options

Title	Title Score	Overall Satisfaction Score
Style and Aesthetics	4.3	4.14
Space Configuration	4.2	4.14
Storage Solutions	3.8	4.14
Device Compatibility	4.25	4.14
Daily Experience	4.3	4.14

5.2   Advantages of Using the AIGC Tool at the Conceptualization Stage

In the conceptualization stage, the comparison between the use of AIGC tools and the traditional way mainly focuses on the dispersion and depth of the creative ideas of the solutions. The use of AIGC tools can quickly generate creative suggestions by inputting keywords, problems, or scenarios, which can rapidly broaden the ideas and realize rapid creative dispersion; at the same time, it can also provide real-time intelligent solutions for specific problems, which can effectively help researchers to It can also provide real-time intelligent solutions to specific problems, effectively helping researchers to obtain information about solutions more quickly and improve work efficiency.

But here, we must recognize the advantages of the traditional way; the traditional way is more likely to lead team members to in-depth discussion and thinking through face-to-face exchanges, brainstorming, and some other ways to form more complex and specific solutions. The traditional way of teamwork can establish a closer collaborative atmosphere in the group and promote the exchange of information and creative collision between members, thus promoting more creative results.

In actual design practice, the R&D team should make comprehensive use of AIGC tools and traditional methods according to the specific situation so as to maximize the advantages of speed and intelligence of AIGC tools in the idea dissemination stage and to realize deeper communication and cooperation through traditional methods in the in-depth discussion and specific solution formulation stage. This integrated approach helps to effectively improve the quality and comprehensiveness of program design.

6   Prototype

6.1   AIGC Tool Selection

DALL-E, Midjourney, and Stable Diffusion are currently the dominant AIGC tools for generating images from AI text, and Fabian Stelzerd's research has shown that Midjourney generates images that are more creative and artistic [23], which is very much in line with the goals of this project --The use of AIGC tools to accomplish the inspiration of product design ideas. Therefore, we chose Midjourney, an AI image generator, for our design practice.

6.2   Generate Product Design Drawings Through Midjourney

The research team translated the design solution into keyword descriptions for Midjourney, for example, "A home desk with drawers, modernist, can put documents, books, stationery, mouse, display, keyboard, built-in storage, hidden cable design. Keyboard, built-in storage, hidden cable design. Ultra HD picture quality, studio lighting". The keywords "Ultra HD picture quality" and "studio lighting" were added to ensure the high definition of the generated images. Modernism is a style school summarized by combining the results of user research.

Next, we entered these keywords into Midjourney's IMAGE function box and obtained four images (see Fig. 1). Since Midjourney generates keywords from the screen descriptions, the generated images may not exactly match our expectations of the product to some extent. Therefore, the designer needs to select the product image that best meets the expectations based on the design requirements among the multiple randomly generated images. In this example, we have chosen the 2nd image. If you need to change the detailed design of the selected product image, you can use the Vary (subtle) function to spread your mind; see Fig. 2.

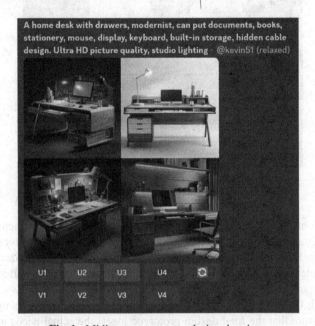

Fig. 1. Midjourney generates design drawings.

6.3 Characteristics of Using AIGC Tools in the Prototyping Phase of Design

First, the AIGC tool can generate creative and diverse design prototypes through keyword descriptions, providing novel design inspiration for design teams and realizing creative inspiration; second, it can generate multiple design solutions quickly, accelerating the design process and improving efficiency, especially more obvious under the demand of large-scale design generation, achieving high efficiency; third, the design prototypes generated by the AIGC tool may cover a variety of styles and elements, providing more choices for the design team and helping to explore different design directions and achieve diversity. However, we must recognize that the images generated by the AIGC tool may not fully meet the needs of the actual project, requiring designers to make choices and adjustments to the generated images. In addition, AIGC tool generation is limited by its algorithms and training data, which may make it difficult to meet specific design detail requirements and lack flexibility.

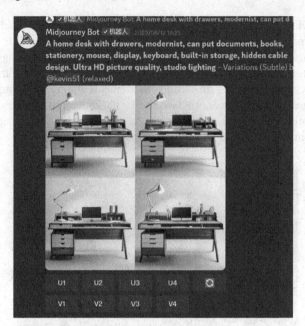

Fig. 2. Midjourney generates design drawings.

The traditional approach allows designers to intuitively make adjustments and modifications with greater flexibility to meet specific design goals more accurately. However, it requires more human and material resources, more time and effort to handcraft prototypes, and is relatively costly. Especially in large-scale projects, it may affect the design schedule. The suggestion here is that after the visualization scheme is generated by the AIGC tool, further refinement and adjustment can be carried out using traditional methods to ensure that the final design prototype meets the actual needs and is highly professional.

7 Test

To confirm that the generated product design drawings meet the users' needs, a questionnaire was used to collect users' satisfaction feedback on the product design to verify the validity of the methodology of this project. The research team distributed a satisfaction questionnaire to 20 participating users, which focused on four aspects of satisfaction selection: the style and aesthetics of the product design drawings (see Fig. 3), the space configuration, the storage and storage capacity, and the daily use experience. Finally, after successfully collecting and organizing the 20 valid questionnaires, the research team analyzed the data in detail, which resulted in a detailed table of the results of the survey on user satisfaction with the design drawings of the home office desk (see Table 2 for details).

Based on the tabular data and analyzed with the help of statistical tools, we learned that the average user satisfaction score for the home office desk design drawing was 4.14, with a satisfaction index of 85%. This satisfaction rating clearly confirms that the product design drawings generated using the AIGC tool have some market value, enabling the research team to gain a better understanding of their commercial potential. In addition, the questionnaire also collected direct feedback from users about the design drawings, such as "there is a little less space for files or books" and "the organization could be more concise." With this information, we can better understand the users' needs and optimize our product design accordingly.

Fig. 3. Selected Home Office Desk Designs

8 Discussions

Two tools, ChatGPT and Midjourney, were selected for practice in this study. It is important to note that it is not necessary to choose these two AIGC tools in a similar design practice process. As long as the intended purpose can be achieved, it is just as fine to choose text-generating AI tools such as Claude and NewBing or other image-generating tools such as Stable Diffusion.

Imaging tools such as Midjourney exhibit a certain amount of randomness in their use. While this uncertainty can help to inspire more innovative design ideas, it can also cause some distress in terms of moving the project forward in depth. For example, it may be difficult to accurately capture the intended design intent of the subject or to gain a deeper understanding of specific details. In addition, image generation tools generate images through keywords, so keywords play a crucial role in the whole process. However, in practice, it is often difficult to perfectly translate design points obtained from research into keyword descriptions, which is one of the main problems faced by industries using AIGC tools. When initially selecting the generated design drawings, the research team currently has to rely on the experience of the designers and the information from the preliminary research to select the most relevant design drawings for the project, which has some limitations.

We also recognize that over-reliance on the AIGC tools is undesirable in the completion of a design project. For example, while these tools can assist the research team in developing an outline for interviews, true user feedback is still key to obtaining design requirements and requires direct interaction with users. Meanwhile, although AIGC's image-based tools facilitate innovative thinking, product realization usually involves many other factors, including ergonomics, material selection, and production processes [24, 25], which are areas not covered by AIGC tools. Although the practice results are not perfect, this project found that these tools significantly enhance the dispersion of innovative thinking, especially in the iterative process of product styling, and they effectively improve work efficiency.

9 Conclusion

Difficult problems are starting to become easier to solve thanks to technological developments. In particular, the emergence of Artificial Intelligence Image Generators (AIGC) has provided the design industry with new ways to reform innovative workflows. Although the current phase of AIGC tools still exhibits some shortcomings in practice, there is reason to believe that their performance will continue to improve. Many innovations in history, such as the automobile, have also performed less well than their predecessors at the beginning of their existence but eventually became mainstream transportation, replacing the horse-drawn carriage. Looking to the future, we can envision a time span in which product designers will be able to conveniently generate detailed design drawings through simple text input, and these images will be able to be fed directly into factories for production. This is not only possible, it is expected. The purpose of this study is to provide new perspectives and insights for product designers and other professionals in related fields. We believe that AIGC tools will grow rapidly in the coming years and be widely used in a wide range of industries.

Acknowledgments. This study was funded by 2023 General Program of the National Social Science Foundation of China in Art (23BC048); Ministry of Education Industry-University Cooperation Collaborative Breeding Program (220900316224726); Ministry of Education Industry-University Cooperation Collaborative Education Program (202102199034).

Disclosure of Interests. The authors have no competing interests to declare that are relevant to the content of this article.

References

1. Veryzer, R.W., Borja, B., de Mozota,: The impact of user-oriented design on new product development: an examination of fundamental relationships. J. Prod. Innov. Manage **22**(2), 128–143 (2005). https://doi.org/10.1111/j.0737-6782.2005.00110.x
2. Kumpe, T., Bolwijn, P.T.: Toward the innovative firm—challenge for R&D management. Res. Technol. Manag. **37**, 38–44 (1994). https://doi.org/10.1080/08956308.1994.11670953
3. Wu, J., Gan, W., Chen, Z., Wan, S., Lin, H.: AI-Generated Content (AIGC): A Survey. http://arxiv.org/abs/2304.06632 (2023)
4. Gan, W., Ye, Z., Wan, S., Yu, P.S.: Web 3.0: The Future of Internet. http://arxiv.org/abs/2304.06032 (2023)
5. Shao, L., Chen, B., Zhang, Z., Zhang, Z., Chen, X.: Artificial intelligence generated content (AIGC) in medicine: a narrative review. MBE. **21**, 1672–1711 (2024). https://doi.org/10.3934/mbe.2024073
6. Bandi, A., Adapa, P.V.S.R., Kuchi, Y.E.V.P.K.: The power of generative AI: a review of requirements, models, input–output formats, evaluation metrics, and challenges. Future Internet **15**(8), 260 (2023). https://doi.org/10.3390/fi15080260
7. Zhang, C., et al.: A Complete Survey on Generative AI (AIGC): Is ChatGPT from GPT-4 to GPT-5 All You Need? (2023). https://doi.org/10.13140/RG.2.2.29980.16001
8. Brown, T.B., et al.: Language models are few-shot learners, http://arxiv.org/abs/2005.14165, (2020). https://doi.org/10.48550/arXiv.2005.14165Https://doi.org/10.48550/arxiv.2005.14165
9. Camill, J. (PZCE 156): ChatGPT: Unlocking the Potential of Large Language Models
10. Hu, K., Hu, K.: ChatGPT sets record for fastest-growing user base - analyst note, https://www.reuters.com/technology/chatgpt-sets-record-fastest-growing-user-base-analyst-note-2023-02-01/ (2023)
11. World of Engineering:"Time it took to reach 100 million users worldwide: Telephone: 75 years Mobile phone: 16 years World Wide Web: 7 years iTunes: 6.5 [@engineers_feed]: years Facebook: 4.5 years WhatsApp: 3.5 years Instagram: 2.5 years Apple App Store: 2 years ChatGPT: 2 months, https://twitter.com/engineers_feed/status/1621226994670125057 Accessed 23 Jan 2024
12. Anantrasirichai, N., Bull, D.: Artificial intelligence in the creative industries: a review. Artif. Intell. Rev. **55**, 589–656 (2022). https://doi.org/10.1007/s10462-021-10039-7
13. Kietzmann, J., Paschen, J., Treen, E.: Artificial intelligence in advertising: how marketers can leverage artificial intelligence along the consumer journey. J. Advert. Res. **58**, 263–267 (2018). https://doi.org/10.2501/JAR-2018-035
14. Kandlhofer, M., Steinbauer, G., Hirschmugl-Gaisch, S., Huber, P.: Artificial intelligence and computer science in education: From kindergarten to university. In: 2016 IEEE Frontiers in Education Conference (FIE), pp. 1–9 (2016). https://doi.org/10.1109/FIE.2016.7757570
15. Foo, L.G., Rahmani, H., Liu, J.: AI-Generated Content (AIGC) for Various Data Modalities: A Survey (2023)
16. Ivanov, V., Pavlenko, I., Evtuhov, A., Trojanowska, J.: Product Design. In: Ivanov, V., Pavlenko, I., Evtuhov, A., Trojanowska, J. (eds.) Augmented Reality for Engineering Graphics, pp. 13–20. Springer Nature Switzerland, Cham (2024). https://doi.org/10.1007/978-3-031-44641-2_2

17. Horváth, D., Zs, R., Szabó,: Driving forces and barriers of Industry 4.0: Do multinational and small and medium-sized companies have equal opportunities? Technol. Forecast. Social Change **146**, 119–132 (2019). https://doi.org/10.1016/j.techfore.2019.05.021

18. Dingel, J.I., Neiman, B.: How many jobs can be done at home? J. Public Econ. **189**, 104235 (2020). https://doi.org/10.1016/j.jpubeco.2020.104235

19. Vyas, L., Butakhieo, N.: The impact of working from home during COVID-19 on work and life domains: an exploratory study on Hong Kong. Policy Design and Practice. **4**, 59–76 (2021). https://doi.org/10.1080/25741292.2020.1863560

20. Davis, K.G., Kotowski, S.E., Daniel, D., Gerding, T., Naylor, J., Syck, M.: The home office: ergonomic lessons from the "new normal." Ergonomics in Design. **28**, 4 (2020). https://doi.org/10.1177/1064804620937907

21. Dam, R., Siang, T.: What is Design Thinking and Why Is It So Popular?

22. Brown, T.: Design thinking (2008)

23. AI Image Generators Compared Side-By-Side Reveals Stark Differences | PetaPixel. https://petapixel.com/2022/08/22/ai-image-generators-compared-side-by-side-reveals-stark-differences/. Accessed 12 Oct 2023

24. Stoffels, P., Kaspar, J., Bähre, D., Vielhaber, M.: Integrated product and production engineering approach – a tool-based method for a holistic sustainable design. Process Material Selection. Procedia Manufact. **21**, 790–797 (2018). https://doi.org/10.1016/j.promfg.2018.02.185

25. Zare, M., Croq, M., Hossein-Arabi, F., Brunet, R., Roquelaure, Y.: Does ergonomics improve product quality and reduce costs? a review article. Human Factors Ergonom. Manufact. Serv. Indust. **26**, 205–223 (2016). https://doi.org/10.1002/hfm.20623

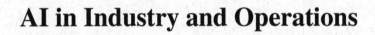

AI in Industry and Operations

Redefining Interaction in a Digital Twin Laboratory with Mixed Reality

Paola Barra[1]([⊠])(iD), Marco Giammetti[2](iD), Augusto Tortora[3](iD), and Attilio Della Greca[2](iD)

[1] Parthenope University of Naples, 80133 Naples, Italy
paola.barra@uniparthenope.it
[2] University of Salerno, 84084 Fisciano, Italy
{mgiammetti,adellagreca}@unisa.it
[3] University of Naples Federico II, 80133 Naples, Italy
augusto.tortora@unina.it

Abstract. In the era of Industry 4.0, Digital Twin (DT) emerges as a pivotal tool for enhancing competitiveness and reaping economic benefits across various sectors. Originating in aerospace, DT is poised to revolutionize multiple industries, facilitating advancements in design, optimization, maintenance, security, decision support, remote access, and training. By seamlessly connecting the physical and virtual realms in real-time, DT enables a comprehensive understanding of unforeseen scenarios, thus fostering efficiency and productivity. This study introduces and analyzes a DT model of a laboratory integrated into Virtual and Augmented Reality platforms. The digital laboratory, merging virtual representations with real-time data collection and analysis, offers new avenues for research, training, and technological advancement. Through immersive collaboration and remote learning opportunities, it adapts to evolving lifestyle habits and aligns with the future of laboratory work. The integration of Oculus Quest 3 with digital twin labs is a significant achievement in post-pandemic interactions, offering personalized and engaging working experiences. Moreover, the audio detection capabilities of the Quest 3's integrated microphone have the potential to enhance user trust and satisfaction, adding another layer of immersion and usability to the experience. This research aims to deepen understanding of DT and its applications in virtual and augmented laboratories, providing insights for future advancements.

Keywords: digital twin · extended reality · virtual reality

1 Introduction

In the era of Industry 4.0, with multiple sectors undergoing a digital transformation, the concept of Digital Twin (DT) represents a central element for gaining a competitive advantage and obtaining economic benefits over competitors. Initially developed in aerospace, DT is expected to revolutionize other industries

© The Author(s), under exclusive license to Springer Nature Switzerland AG 2024
H. Degen and S. Ntoa (Eds.): HCII 2024, LNAI 14735, pp. 295–307, 2024.
https://doi.org/10.1007/978-3-031-60611-3_21

[26]. The main application areas of DT include design, optimization, maintenance, security, decision support, remote access and training, among others. This tool can significantly encourage the growth of businesses, improving their competitiveness, productivity and efficiency [9]. DT allows us to connect the physical world with the virtual one in real-time, allowing for a more accurate and complete representation of unexpected and unpredictable scenarios [28]. The contribution of DT to any sector, through the reduction of time to market, the optimization of operations, the reduction of maintenance costs, the increase in user interaction and the integration of technological information, is undeniable [26].

Virtual reality (VR) has already enabled the creation of virtual spaces for multi-user interactions for training [1], safety, or entertainment purposes. With the integration of augmented reality (AR), the adoption of digital twin (DT) emerges as an innovative approach for managing complex systems within both virtual and real environments. The objective of this study is to introduce and analyze a DT model of a laboratory, seamlessly integrated into Virtual and Augmented Reality platforms.

The concept of a digital laboratory, which merges the virtual representation of a physical environment with real-time data collection and analysis, opens up new avenues for research, training, and technological advancement. Specifically, the DT of the laboratory enables experiments, simulations, and analyses to be conducted within a secure and controlled environment, both locally and remotely. This study will delve into the technical, architectural, and functional aspects of the laboratory's DT, along with its potential implications and benefits in education, scientific research, and industrial development.

The integration of Oculus Quest 3 and digital twin labs is a significant milestone in the redefinition of post-pandemic interactions. This innovative system not only accommodates emerging lifestyle habits but also acts as a precursor to the future of laboratory work. By seamlessly combining the tangible and the virtual, it introduces avant-garde possibilities personalised and engaging work experiences. Key Features and Implications:

- Immersive Collaboration: The integration of a real laboratory with its digital twin creates an immersive collaborative environment. Users, whether physically present or remote, can engage in seamless interactions, fostering teamwork and knowledge sharing. Furthermore, there is the possibility of complete and absolute interaction both only in the Real World and only in the Virtual one.
- Remote Learning Opportunities: The system opens avenues for remote learning by allowing users to participate in laboratory exercises and educational activities virtually. This is especially valuable for individuals who prefer or need to access educational resources from the comfort of their homes.
- Adaptability to Changing Lifestyles: Our integrated system proves adaptable and future-oriented as the world adapts to evolving lifestyle habits. It accommodates the increasing preference for remote interactions and aligns with the growing significance of virtual experiences.

Through this research endeavor, our aim is to enhance the understanding and dissemination of knowledge surrounding DT and its applications in virtual and augmented laboratories, thereby providing valuable insights for further exploration and future advancements in the field of applied virtual and augmented reality.

The article starts with the Background section, where we provide context on Digital Twin concepts and review previous applications, including those related to digital twin labs. Section 3 exposes the tools used for the digital twin under study. Section 4 illustrates the proposed digital twin laboratory, with a focus on its representation in both virtual and augmented reality. Finally, in Sect. 5 the conclusions are presented.

2 Background

In this section, key concepts related to the Digital Twin and their applications in the context of virtual and augmented laboratories are presented.

2.1 The Concept of Digital Twin

The Digital Twin is an emerging concept in systems engineering, which refers to the creation of a digital replica of a real physical system. This digital replica is interconnected with its physical counterpart through sensors and other monitoring technologies, allowing real-time data collection and simulation of scenarios and behaviors [21].

Essentially, a Digital Twin mirrors the real-time state of its physical counterpart, and vice versa. Its applications encompass real-time monitoring, design/planning, optimization, maintenance, and remote access and much more. A Digital Twin concept entails constructing a digital simulation within an information platform, enabling predictive analytics, optimization, monitoring, control, and real-time decision-making enhancements, as well as facilitating performance improvements, predictive maintenance, and training. This is achieved by integrating physical feedback data and incorporating it with Artificial Intelligence (AI), machine learning, and software analytics. Researchers worldwide have conducted extensive research across various domains, including air, land, and sea [6,12,27].

For instance, in [11], the authors integrated data from multiple sensor locations, using this amalgamated information as input for the Digital Twin system, and coupled it with simulation data to assess structural performance.

Additionally, Staffa et al. developed the Digital Twin of a marine drone to manage all sensors, simulate its operations, predict potential malfunctions, and analyze extensive datasets [22].

2.2 Applications and Technology of Digital Twins

Digital Twins are utilized across different industrial sectors, including manufacturing [17], energy [19], transportation [4], and healthcare [24], offering significant advantages such as enabling virtual experiments and simulations, real-time operational optimization, and enhanced preventative maintenance.

Despite the potential benefits, the adoption of Digital Twins faces challenges due to a lack of clear understanding of its value and a deficiency in technical and practical knowledge. Additionally, the absence of successful case studies or business models implementing digital twins and realistic cost estimations further hinders progress [20].

Digital Twin technology relies on the convergence of various technologies, including 3D simulations, IoT/IIoT [14], AI, big data, machine learning, and cloud computing. However, the long and complex development phases of these underlying technologies hinder the evolution of Digital Twins. Improvements in infrastructure, such as High-Performance Computing (HPC), machine learning, real-time virtual-real interactive technology, and intelligent perception and connection technology, are essential for effective implementation [25].

Furthermore, the availability of supporting software adds complexity to the adoption process. Numerous software packages, such as Predix by General Electric, Azure Digital Twin by Microsoft, and Digital Enterprise Suite by Siemens, among others, offer Digital Twin solutions, making it challenging for industries to select the most suitable platform for their specific needs [2].

2.3 DTL: Digital Twin Laboratory

In the context of virtual and augmented laboratories, the digital twin takes on a critical role in providing an accurate and dynamic representation of a physical laboratory environment. Virtual and augmented reality technologies allow users to interact with the digital twin in an immersive and interactive way, making it easier to run experiments and analyze data.

In recent years, virtual laboratories have played a significant role in education by offering well-designed computer simulations that enhance student learning across various contexts. The typical setup of a virtual laboratory mimics the environment of a physical university lab, enabling students to explore physical phenomena safely. Moreover, virtual labs offer advantages such as access to information not otherwise available and incorporating visual cues or alternative representations that are inaccessible in traditional labs, such as visualizing emergent molecular interactions [16].

The concept of Digital Twins (DTs) is expounded upon in various papers. According to [18], DTs are software representations of physical entities, operating via application program interfaces (APIs) to interact with and potentially control the physical devices they monitor.

DTs can be dynamically controlled and programmed in real-time from computer interfaces, with the ability to enact operational adjustments on the physical object if required, [10,13]. This reciprocal exchange between the digital and physical realms enables the physical twin to leverage insights from its digital counterpart to enhance its functionalities.

The DT serves as a valuable tool for conducting safety training simulations. Virtual Reality facilitates lifelike training for emergency scenarios that are challenging to replicate in real-world settings. As shown by the authors in [7], leveraging Digital Twins enables real-time, hands-on learning experiences, eliminating the need to physically enter manufacturing facilities. Use case demonstrations underscore that virtual training is immersive, collaborative, and interactive, accommodating various scenarios, from general safety protocols to specific tasks within manufacturing cells.

Authors in [5] explore the utilization of DT within eXtended Reality (XR) environments, focusing on Supervisory Control and Data Acquisition (SCADA) applications. The research aims to enhance industrial training and control systems by integrating XR and DT technologies. Through real-time experiments with physical objects and their digital counterparts, the effectiveness of the prototype is validated, affirming its potential for practical applications. Additionally, the study includes a thorough literature review, laying the groundwork for this research endeavor. Future investigations will involve refining Interface (UI) elements for improved intuitiveness and informativeness, further advancing the integration of XR and DT in industrial settings.

Previously, the use of a digital twin office was adopted to control social proximity in order to contain COVID-19 infections [15]. Our work is in a similar direction, but with different aims, focusing on the implementation of a digital twin laboratory.

3   Planning and Modeling

This section provides an overview of the hardware and software tools used for laboratory model development with Digital Twin.

3.1   Blender

Blender[1] is a 3D graphics open-source software allowing the modelling and rendering of images in three dimensions using a professional work environment. It is a constantly evolving and updating program and is increasingly adopted in gaming, cinema, advertising, and architectural design.

Among other advantages, Blender offers native tools for creating animations and animated videos of projects, now increasingly in demand even in interior design and architectural design. It is important to underline the possibility of inserting sounds, interactive paths and animated characters into the scene videos.

3.2   Unity

Unity game engine[2] is a framework offering possibilities to import visual model files in various formats, create scenes based on these model files and apply logical functionalities into these scenes[3] According to Sim et al. [23], Unity is the most widely used game engine with a wide developer support network.

---

[1] https://www.blender.org/.

[2] Unity Technologies, San Francisco, USA, https://unity.com/.

[3] "Game engines - how do they work?" accessed 20 May 2020. [Online]. Available: https://unity3d.com/what-is-a-game-engine.

3.3   Meta Quest 3

Most of the studies presented in Sect. 2 show experiments done with the HTC Vive which has been the most used headset in research for many years. Since its release in October 2023, the Meta Quest immediately entered the world of research thanks to its ease of use, development and integration with a true extended reality system thanks to the front cameras. Furthermore, unlike the HTC Vive, it can be used standalone. In Fig. 1 we can see a preview of the environment within Unity; compared to that shown in the interface through the headset, we can see the colliders and physical objects highlighted.

Fig. 1. Meta Quest 3

The Meta Quest 3 is equipped with Qualcomm Snapdragon XR2 Gen 2 System On a Chip (SOC), designed with a 4nm production process for AR, VR, and MR applications. The SOC is built on Armv8.2-A (64-bit) architecture, enabling energy consumption optimization. It features 6 CPU cores with 6 threads each, operating at frequencies ranging from 1.38 to 2.36 GHz. For AR and VR applications, as well as communication between the two worlds, adequate graphic power is necessary, which is provided by the integrated Qualcomm Adreno 740 GPU within the SOC. It comprises 5 GPU Execution Units, enabling a maximum display resolution of 3K x 3K. Regarding image and environmental reality acquisition, the Meta Quest 3 is equipped with a system of 3 groups of cameras mounted on the front of the headset. Each group consists of two 4MP cameras. This arrangement allows for optimal image and video capture in pass-through mode and enables hand motion detection in space in AR and MR modes.

4   Laboratory Digital Twin

Essentially, a Digital Twin (DT) encompasses three primary components: (a) tangible items in the physical realm, (b) intangible representations in a digital environment, and (c) the data and insights facilitating the connection between these physical and digital counterparts, as we can see in Fig. 2. That we can think of as the real environment in augmented reality, the virtual environment and the data and acquisitions that we can analyze. Grieves [20] illustrated the flow of DT as a continuous cycle between physical and digital realms (referred to as twinning), where data moves from the physical to the digital, while information and processes move from the digital to the physical domains.

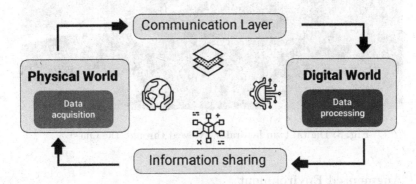

Fig. 2. The Digital Twin circle.

Grieves and Vickers [3] delineate two types of Digital Twins (DTs) based on their development timing within the product lifecycle: Digital Twin Prototypes (DTPs) and Digital Twin Instances (DTIs).

Digital Twin Prototype (DTP): DTPs are virtual representations containing essential data for creating physical copies. They facilitate testing, including potentially destructive trials, before physical production. DTPs help anticipate and prevent unforeseen issues, ensuring the quality of the physical twin aligns with the virtual model.

Digital Twin Instance (DTI): DTIs are counterparts linked to physical systems throughout their lifecycle, initiated during production. They enable real-time monitoring and predictive analysis by transferring data between physical and virtual domains. Any alterations in one realm are mirrored in the other, aiding in identifying and rectifying deviations from expected behavior. A grouping of DTIs forms a Digital Twin Aggregate (DTA).

4.1 Virtual Environment

The virtual environment, denoted in Fig. 3, can be accessed both in-person at the physical laboratory and remotely. It was designed to provide users with the perception of work continuity from the environment he or she is used to, but without the need to travel to the presence. Therefore, this allows the user to behave normally and facilitates data acquisition.

Fig. 3. Digital twin laboratory viewed through the Quest 3.

4.2   Augmented Environment

In the context of the real environment, a depth scan can be performed using the Quest 3's LIDAR sensors. This technology allows not only the detection of walls but also the identification of obstacles present in the real environment, maintaining synchronization with the corresponding virtual representation. In our laboratory, the LIDAR scan corresponds with the colliders created in the virtual environment to guarantee an authentic experience also in the perception of the spaces and objects of the room, Figs. 6. Such synchronization offers an integrated understanding of spaces, both real and virtual. Augmented reality allows virtual objects to be well mixed with the real context; for example, in Fig. 4, we see two cups, one virtual (left) and one real (right). We can potentially consider inserting a clock, a planner, a whiteboard or any virtual insert that can personalize the user experience (Fig. 5).

4.3   Data Gathering and Analysis

The Oculus Quest 3 represents a significant step in integrating virtual reality (VR) and augmented reality (AR), allowing users to explore a hybrid environment that combines digital and physical elements. This platform offers the ability to seamlessly transition between viewing virtual content overlaid on real-world viewing and participating in remote laboratory experiences, regardless of the user's geographic location.

Fig. 4. Reproduction of a virtual cup in augmented reality, alongside its real version.

Fig. 5. Photo of the real laboratory for the digital twin laboratory reproduction.

Thanks to the ability to track movements in space in both virtual and physical environments, the Quest 3 allows precise monitoring of users' position in the room, taking advantage of the headset's localization technology.

Hand tracking in both environments eliminates the reliance on traditional controllers, allowing users to interact with virtual objects naturally and intuitively.

The "digital twin" allows us to acquire and analyse data, also obtained through a series of sensors that can be positioned both in the real environment and on the user himself. This data, including biometric sensors such as ECG and EEG, allows for an in-depth understanding of your activities and surrounding environment.

Fig. 6. Digital twin laboratory within Unity, it is possible to identify colliders that correspond to objects and obstacles in the environment.

The Fig. 6 illustrates the representation of collider objects within the Unity Engine development environment. This aspect is crucial to guarantee users a correct perception of obstacles present in the real world, thus facilitating interaction with virtual objects. A practical example of this interaction is the visualization of a virtual cup, which allows users to simulate physical interaction with a real object in both the virtual and physical environments.

Furthermore, utilizing the audio detection capabilities of the Quest 3's integrated microphone has the potential to enhance user comfort, trust and satisfaction. This can be achieved by utilizing voice analysis to recognize emotions or incorporating voice commands to interact with a virtual assistant, as evidenced by past research in this domain [8].

5 Conclusions

This study provided a comprehensive overview of digital twins (DTs), exploring digital twin laboratories and presenting a prototype of a university laboratory's digital twin.

While the concept of DT has existed for decades, its profound impact has only recently been realized. The digital market is witnessing continuous growth as industries increasingly adopt DT technology to reduce operational costs and time, enhance productivity, improve maintenance practices, ensure accessibility, promote workplace safety, and explore new possibilities. When integrated with technologies like AR/VR, mixed reality, additive manufacturing, and 3D printing, DTs unlock new applications and potentials, despite encountering challenges.

This paper classified different types of DTs to refine our understanding and establish consensus on their definitions and limitations. Recognizing and harnessing the potential of DT in various sectors, coupled with appropriate DT types, facilitates the development of Industry 4.0 tools offering simulation, prediction, record-keeping, and troubleshooting capabilities. By highlighting the advantages and challenges of DT implementation, this paper emphasized cost reduction, increased outputs, remote accessibility, and streamlined operations without additional material or investment costs.

Looking ahead, future challenges lie in the thorough analysis of extracted data, including biometric data such as EEG, ECG, or movement data derived from the positioning of the headset in space. Additionally, leveraging microphone capabilities for emotion detection or interaction with intelligent virtual agents presents yet another avenue for exploration and innovation in the realm of digital twins.

References

1. Barra, P., et al.: Metacux: social interaction and collaboration in the metaverse. In: Abdelnour Nocera, J., Kristín Lárusdóttir, M., Petrie, H., Piccinno, A., Winckler, M. (eds.) INTERACT 2023. LNCS, vol. 14145, pp. 528–532. Springer, Cham (2023). https://doi.org/10.1007/978-3-031-42293-5_67
2. Bulygina, I.: Product owner talks: 20 digital twins solution providers (2019). https://wwwdashdevs.com/blog/product-owner-talks-20-digital-twins-service-companies
3. Grieves, M., Vickers, J.: Digital twin: mitigating unpredictable, undesirable emergent behavior in complex systems. In: Kahlen, J., Flumerfelt, S., Alves, A. (eds.) Transdisciplinary Perspectives on Complex Systems, pp. 85–113. Springer, Cham (2017). https://doi.org/10.1007/978-3-319-38756-7_4
4. Jafari, M., Kavousi-Fard, A., Chen, T., Karimi, M.: A review on digital twin technology in smart grid, transportation system and smart city: challenges and future. IEEE Access 11, 17471–17484 (2023)
5. Jeršov, S., Tepljakov, A.: Digital twins in extended reality for control system applications. In: 2020 43rd International Conference on Telecommunications and Signal Processing (TSP), pp. 274–279 (2020). https://doi.org/10.1109/TSP49548.2020.9163557
6. Jin, B., Gao, J., Yan, W.: Pseudo control hedging-based adaptive neural network attitude control of underwater gliders. In: OCEANS 2017 - Aberdeen, pp. 1–5 (2017). https://doi.org/10.1109/OCEANSE.2017.8084963
7. Kaarlela, T., Pieskä, S., Pitkäaho, T.: Digital twin and virtual reality for safety training. In: 2020 11th IEEE International Conference on Cognitive Infocommunications (CogInfoCom), pp. 000115–000120 (2020). https://doi.org/10.1109/CogInfoCom50765.2020.9237812
8. Kim, K., Boelling, L., Haesler, S., Bailenson, J., Bruder, G., Welch, G.F.: Does a digital assistant need a body? The influence of visual embodiment and social behavior on the perception of intelligent virtual agents in ar. In: 2018 IEEE International Symposium on Mixed and Augmented Reality (ISMAR), pp. 105–114 (2018). https://doi.org/10.1109/ISMAR.2018.00039
9. Kritzinger, W., Karner, M., Traar, G., Henjes, J., Sihn, W.: Digital twin in manufacturing: a categorical literature review and classification. IFAC-PapersOnLine 51(11), 1016–1022 (2018). https://doi.org/10.1016/j.ifacol.2018.08.474. https://www.sciencedirect.com/science/article/pii/S2405896318316021 16th IFAC Symposium on Information Control Problems in Manufacturing INCOM 2018

10. Kuts, V., Otto, T., Tähemaa, T., Bondarenko, Y.: Digital twin based synchronised control and simulation of the industrial robotic cell using virtual reality. J. Mach. Eng. **19**, 128–144 (2019). https://doi.org/10.5604/01.3001.0013.0464

11. Lai, X., Wang, S., Guo, Z., Zhang, C., Sun, W., Song, X.: Designing a shape-performance integrated digital twin based on multiple models and dynamic data: a boom crane example. J. Mech. Des. **143**(7), 071703 (2021). https://doi.org/10.1115/1.4049861

12. Liu, Z., Chen, W., Zhang, C., Yang, C., Cheng, Q.: Intelligent scheduling of a feature-process-machine tool supernetwork based on digital twin workshop. J. Manufact. Syst. **58**, 157–167 (2021). https://doi.org/10.1016/j.jmsy.2020.07.016. https://www.sciencedirect.com/science/article/pii/S0278612520301266

13. Makarov, V., Frolov, Y., Parshina, I.S., Ushakova, M.: The design concept of digital twin. In: 2019 Twelfth International Conference "Management of Large-Scale System Development" (MLSD), pp. 1–4 (2019). https://doi.org/10.1109/MLSD.2019.8911091

14. Minerva, R., Lee, G.M., Crespi, N.: Digital twin in the IoT context: a survey on technical features, scenarios, and architectural models. Proc. IEEE **108**(10), 1785–1824 (2020)

15. Mukhopadhyay, A., et al.: Virtual-reality-based digital twin of office spaces with social distance measurement feature. Virtual Reality Intell. Hardware **4**(1), 55–75 (2022). https://doi.org/10.1016/j.vrih.2022.01.004. https://www.sciencedirect.com/science/article/pii/S2096579622000043

16. Nolen, S.B., Koretsky, M.D.: Affordances of virtual and physical laboratory projects for instructional design: impacts on student engagement. IEEE Trans. Educ. **61**(3), 226–233 (2018). https://doi.org/10.1109/TE.2018.2791445

17. Psarommatis, F., May, G.: A literature review and design methodology for digital twins in the era of zero defect manufacturing. Int. J. Prod. Res. **61**(16), 5723–5743 (2023)

18. Scheibmeir, J., Malaiya, Y.: An API development model for digital twins. In: 2019 IEEE 19th International Conference on Software Quality, Reliability and Security Companion (QRS-C), pp. 518–519 (2019). https://doi.org/10.1109/QRS-C.2019.00103

19. Semeraro, C., et al.: Digital twin application in energy storage: trends and challenges. J. Energy Storage **58**, 106347 (2023)

20. Simchenko, N., Tsohla, S., Chyvatkin, P.: IoT & digital twins concept integration effects on supply chain strategy: challenges and effect. Int. J. Supply Chain Manag. **8**(6), 803–808 (2019)

21. Singh, M., Fuenmayor, E., Hinchy, E.P., Qiao, Y., Murray, N., Devine, D.: Digital twin: origin to future. Appl. Syst. Innov. **4**(2) (2021). https://doi.org/10.3390/asi4020036. https://www.mdpi.com/2571-5577/4/2/36

22. Staffa, M., Izzo, E., Barra, P.: Leveraging the robomaker service on AWS cloud platform for marine drone digital twin construction. In: Ali, A.A., et al. (eds.) ICSR 2023. LNCS, vol. 14453, pp. 22–32. Springer, Singapore (2024). https://doi.org/10.1007/978-981-99-8715-3_3

23. Stefan, H., Mortimer, M., Horan, B.: Evaluating the effectiveness of virtual reality for safety-relevant training: a systematic review. Virtual Reality **27**(4), 2839–2869 (2023)

24. Sun, T., He, X., Li, Z.: Digital twin in healthcare: recent updates and challenges. Digital Health **9**, 20552076221149652 (2023)

25. Tao, F., Cheng, J., Qi, Q., Zhang, M., Zhang, H., Sui, F.: Digital twin-driven product design, manufacturing and service with big data. Int. J. Adv. Manufact. Technol. **94**, 3563–3576 (2018)
26. Tao, F., Zhang, M., Nee, A.Y.C.: Digital Twin Driven Smart Manufacturing. Academic Press (2019)
27. Wang, Y., Kang, X., Chen, Z.: A survey of digital twin techniques in smart manufacturing and management of energy applications. Green Energy Intell. Transp. **1**(2), 100014 (2022). https://doi.org/10.1016/j.geits.2022.100014. https://www.sciencedirect.com/science/article/pii/S2773153722000147
28. Warshaw, L.: Industry 4.0 and the digital twin: manufacturing meets its match (2017). Accessed 23 January 2019

Challenges of Machine Failure Prediction with Product Data - A Case Study

Dominik Buhl[(✉)] and Carsten Lanquillon

Heilbronn University of Applied Sciences, 74076 Heilbronn, Germany
dbuhl.info@gmail.com, carsten.lanquillon@hs-heilbronn.de

Abstract. Predictive maintenance aims to minimize downtime and component costs by predicting machine failures. However, the implementation of such a failure prediction system poses several challenges. In this study, a case study is conducted using time series data from a real machine. The time series data of the dataset was recorded at irregular intervals due to product data and machine characteristics. This poses a challenge when using deep learning methods for failure prediction, as they require a coherent fixed latent space. Since non-equidistant time series cannot provide this property, one solution is to convert the time series into an equidistant time series. The objectives of this publication are to present the options for converting non-equidistant time series. Additionally, it will explore the utilization of product data for failure prediction. Subsequently, the failure prediction will be tested using selected methods in a case study. In total, seven conversion possibilities were identified, and the failures were predicted using the product data. This study shows that the deep learning model developed can reduce downtime costs by 10% based on product data.

Keywords: Predictive Maintenance · Failure Prediction · Deep Learning · Case Study · Product Data · Irregular Time Series

1 Introduction

The connectivity of components in the industry enables the collection of data for well-founded decisions and process optimizations [17]. Especially in maintenance, which is an essential part of production, data unlocks new potentials [46]. Predictive maintenance (PdM) uses data to anticipate potential faults before a machine fails. This can save costs by minimizing downtime [5, 32].

Due to the cost-saving potential, an industrial company has decided to integrate PdM through a case study using the collected data. For the company, the primary purpose of introducing PdM was to assist machine operators and maintenance personnel. Typically, experienced personnel (maintenance or operators) will recognize when a machine is about to fail by monitoring the products the machine produces or noticing a particular chain of fault events in a machine. Artificial Intelligence (AI) methods can help these people detect errors before they occur,

© The Author(s), under exclusive license to Springer Nature Switzerland AG 2024
H. Degen and S. Ntoa (Eds.): HCII 2024, LNAI 14735, pp. 308–322, 2024.
https://doi.org/10.1007/978-3-031-60611-3_22

and repair the machine before it fails. The AI approaches are using data from the machine to predict when it will fail. In such a system, this results in information about the time the machine is failing. With that information, it can be reacted to an upcoming fault by fixing it before the machine stands still [43,46]. However, implementing such a system for failure prediction poses several challenges and problems. These problems include limits on data sources, machine repair activities, finances, and organization. Data poses a particular challenge as it forms the basis for PdM [1]. The primary challenge in the field of data is the availability of relevant and accurate data. This can be due to issues with sensor data acquisition, offline data, inconsistent data storage structures, or other factors [1,35]. Despite these challenges, PdM should still be carried out using the available data. Any gaps or issues with the data can then be identified and addressed [35]. The dataset of the company presents issues with the data source. Specifically, it lacks sensor data from the machine and instead includes data from the produced parts. This presents two problems. Firstly, the time series resulting from production has irregular intervals between data points. This can cause issues when using deep learning (DL) approaches as they require a fixed-dimensional feature space. Non-equidistant time series cannot provide such a feature space due to their properties, as they have variable sets of observations, different temporal dimensions, and different distances between the observations [38]. Secondly, due to the low correlation between the machine and parts, the data may not contain enough information about defects. Despite these challenges, the goal remains to predict machine defects. These factors motivate the main research question: *How is it possible to predict machine failures from product data?*

The goal of this work is to demonstrate how machine failures can be predicted using a real-world dataset. The two problems of the dataset are illustrated and possible solutions are presented. Furthermore, a prototype is developed to predict failures based on the dataset. The prototype should provide maintenance staff and operators with valuable information in the form of warnings before machine failure.

The first part of this paper explains the challenges of the dataset in detail and presents possible solutions. In the second part, the approaches will be implemented in a case study. During the development of the prototype, a fault prediction artifact is created using a goal-oriented design science research (DSR) approach, as described by [29]. The goal identification phase involves a content analysis of internal documents to determine the objectives such PdM artifact. The artifact is created during the design phase as part of prototyping [30]. Following the development phase, the prototype's functionality is tested in a combined demonstration and evaluation phase.

2   Background

2.1   Predictive Maintenance and Failure Prediction

In the production environment, maintenance is focused on ensuring the functionality of machines. This is accomplished through three main tasks: maintenance, inspection, and repair [4]. These tasks are achieved through various maintenance strategies, which can be divided into three categories. Run-to-failure maintenance involves maintenance only when a fault occurs, resulting in high costs, particularly due to downtime. Preventive maintenance involves replacing critical components of a machine in a fixed cycle, resulting in high component costs [45, 46]. PdM aims to minimize downtimes and component costs by predicting machine failures based on data from the most important components. Two methods of predicting downtime exist, including the Remaining Useful Lifetime (RUL), which estimates the amount of productive time remaining before a machine component becomes defective. Fault prediction is the process of determining the likelihood of a fault occurring within a specified time window [44]. This entails categorizing faults into groups, distinguishing between "fault" and "no fault" [23]. While the RUL predicts far into the future, fault prediction only considers a short period of time [2]. The main difference between the two methods is the underlying dataset. To determine the RUL, the dataset must include sensor data that can identify component degradation. To predict faults, the dataset must be labeled and include both sensor data and specific faults [9, 40].

2.2   Irregular Time Series

Time series can be defined "[. . .] as a set of quantitative observations arranged in chronological order" [22]. These observations are quantitative and are recorded at defined points in time, resulting in a series of values with various properties. Time series can be classified as either continuous or discrete [6]. Additionally, the distance between observations can be either equidistant or at irregular intervals [10, 37]. Time series with equal intervals exist when data is retrieved and stored at a fixed interval. Non-equidistant time series are data with unequal intervals between the observations [39]. Time series can also be differentiated by their dimensionality. Univariate time series exist if there is one variable in the time series. Multivariate time series contain more than one variable that is recorded at the same observation time [11, 28].

2.3   Industrial Data

Industrial data is the information collected during the manufacturing process of a machine, production line, or factory. It can be divided into two categories. The first type relates to direct, man-made influences, such as regulating the specific temperature required for a particular manufacturing process. The second type refers to data that originates from inspection or measurement activities during the production process [13]. This data can originate from various sources. The publication by [34] presents a total of ten sources. Some of these sources are discussed in more detail below. Product data is generated throughout the entire product life cycle and originates from interactions between products, people, and the environment [12]. This includes the processes used to produce the product [12, 41]. Examples of product data include quality values during production, product names, or assembly instructions. Machine operation data refers to the data collected from the sensors of a machine's control system, including vibration and temperature readings. Monitoring data, on the other hand, records when a machine experiences a breakdown and provides information on the system status of various components, such as the power supply unit and repairs needed [34].

3 Related Work

Numerous articles discuss failure prediction in PdM, which can be achieved through various methods. One widely used approach to predict component degradation is to estimate the RUL. In their publication, [7] determine the failure of the system based on the degradation and derive maintenance actions from this. The time until failure is then specified in either seconds [16] or cycles [24]. Another method uses the RUL in conjunction with a limit. The authors of [26] use a machine indicator, such as speed, and define the time until failure as the duration from when the speed falls below a limit until the machine stops. [8] employ a similar method by calculating a "Degradation Energy Indicator" and combining it with limits to determine the remaining time.

In addition to the aforementioned methods, there are alternative approaches that do not rely on component degradation. [7] utilizes machine component images to predict time to failure, treating the prediction as a regression task. The defined time to failure is given in units of time, such as minutes [3]. It is crucial to maintain objectivity and avoid subjective evaluations unless marked as such. It is important to note that this method is also based on generic values but specifies a probability of failure within a given time frame. In this context, failure prediction is approached as a classification task [31]. The DL model specifies the probability of different classes, which can include time intervals such as five hours, twelve hours, one day, two days, and one week, as described by [47]. The model determines the class and predicts when an error will occur.

4 Challenges with Product Data and Irregular Time Series

This section provides a detailed description of the limitations of using product data to predict machine faults with DL methods. Section 4.1 explains the challenges associated with using product data for error prediction, while Sect. 4.2 focuses on the irregularities in the time series.

4.1 Product Data

The most suitable data for predicting machine failures is machine data that originates from different machine components, such as vibration sensors, heat sensors, or acoustic sensors [15]. Anomalies in the sensor data, such as a decreasing trend, an outlier, or the absence of data, can be checked historically if a key component of the machine fails, causing the machine to come to a standstill. Anomalies in the data may indicate an emerging error [27]. When predicting failures using machine data, the correlation with the machine is strong, and anomalies can only have one source. However, when predicting failure using product data, the anomalies can have several sources, making it difficult to assign a clear trend due to the origin of the product data. The anomalies may be triggered by the product itself or an entire batch of the current product. Alternatively, the machine may trigger the anomaly if a sensor is faulty, which can have an effect on quality tests and cause the values to continue to decrease. However, to predict machine errors, product data can be combined with monitoring data, such as machine downtimes [12]. This enables the determination of the next error in the production time windows and the identification of anomalies in the previous time series that may be linked to the error. For example, repeated outliers in voltage tests could indicate a faulty power supply unit. There are various methods for predicting machine faults using the data, whether based on outliers or component degradation. As explained in Sect. 3, there are several methods for predicting failures that change depending on the data.

4.2   Irregular Time Series

The non-uniform time distances between data points are a result of the product data and machine type. For example when a machine is manually triggered, causing variations in the distances between individual products. A data point is created and saved after each stapling. This results in different time gaps between the data points. DL architectures have a limited ability to handle irregularities, which can result in problems like missing information or models with bad performance [38]. DL approaches require a coherent and fixed-dimensional feature space. The feature space cannot be effectively established in non-equidistant time series because of their inherent characteristics, including varying sets of observations, distinct temporal dimensions, and dissimilar distances between observations [38]. In the field of DL, some models have been developed that can handle non-equidistant time series [38]. However, it has been found that the performance of these models is worse when compared to training processes with equidistant time series [21]. If non-equidistant time series are transformed into regular time series, both statistical and DL models can be applied [14]. [38] proposes solutions for dealing with irregular time series. The literature analysis of [38] revealed a total of six methods for dealing with irregular time series. These approaches include the following:

Temporal discretization is the process of converting non-equidistant time series into equidistant time series by using a grid. The first step is to create grids at regular intervals. The values are then summarised within the grids. If a grid does not contain any value, imputation methods can be used to determine individual values, resulting in a regular time series [38]. *Interpolation* involves calculating a function using discrete data points from a time series, which can be equidistant or irregular. Equidistant points can be obtained through rasterization, which converts the time series into regular time intervals [38]. *Recurrence* can be used to transform irregular time series into equidistant ones by considering not only the sequence during processing but also the time intervals through adjusting internal weights [38]. *Neural differential equations (NODEs)* are neural networks that utilize ordinary differential equations to model the internal processes and dynamics of the system. The continuous latent space of NODEs allows for predictions to be made at any point in time, regardless of the temporal distance between the points [38]. *Attention* considers the distances between data points by assigning weights, allowing for the inclusion of irregular time series structures [38]. *Structural invariance* refers to the removal of temporal context from a time series dataset. This means that the data is viewed as a set of data points without any temporal structure [38]. Another method is the *delta method*, which creates an extra feature by calculating the delta between the data points. This removes the irregularity caused by the attribute with the date, which can then be removed [20, 42].

5   Case Study

The following chapters describe the case study using the goal-oriented DSR [29] approach. The case study was conducted in an industrial company. The data source originates from a machine that produces components for an electric motor. The subsequent chapters are structured as follows. Firstly, the objectives of the artifact are presented, followed by the architecture. The last chapter demonstrates and evaluates the artifact's functionality.

5.1   Objectives of the Artifact

The artifact aims to develop an AI model that predicts the failure of a production machine. The company is required to make a statement about whether a fault will occur in the next 30 min. This value is interesting in two ways. On the one hand, it supports the maintenance engineer who can react early and repair a fault before the machine reaches a fault state. On the other hand, it is possible to prepare another machine or find another task for the person working on the machine when the machine is at a standstill. This makes it possible to keep the person busy without interruption. The lead time allows the necessary steps to be taken to either alert a maintenance person or prepare another machine. Failures must be predicted to allow a lead time. Failure prediction is performed using DL methods in the form of a classification task. The achievement of the goal is determined by two measurable values. One is the performance of the model and the other is the downtime saved by the model.

5.2   Design and Development of the Artifact

This section focuses on the development of the artifact. Firstly, the data basis is described, followed by the development of a pipeline for data preparation. Finally, the prediction models used are presented.

Dataset Description. The product dataset comprises 96 columns and 53452 rows, with each row representing a produced product. The columns can be divided into three classes. The product specification data provides information about the product, including its name and dimensions. Quality data presents test results and indicates whether the product is free of defects. Process data describes the manufacturing process, including cycle times per station.

Figure 1 shows the error sequence of fault 324. The sequence contains 71 products, corresponding to one failure after 71 manufactured products. There are a total of 581 error sequences in the data. The median sequence length is 80 and the median sequence time is 2777 s. Upon analysis of the individual sequences, no degradation or anomalies in the timing of the outliers are found.

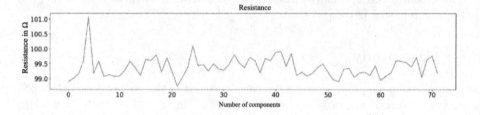

Fig. 1. Example of error sequence (own illustration)

In addition to the visual findings, various statistical methods are used to describe the dataset. The correlation matrix indicates no correlations between the target variable and other variables. To develop a reliable forecasting model, a stationary time series is necessary. The Augmented Dickey-Fuller method can be used to determine whether a time series is stationary, taking into account autocorrelation and trend [22,25]. Based on the test results, it can be concluded that the dataset comprises stationary time series, except for four columns. No measures, such as removing trends or seasonality, are taken, as three of the four columns are not relevant to the subsequent training. One column is slightly above the limit for seasonality, so it is rechecked by examining the trend, which does not show any significant changes.

Data Preparation. In the first step, features are selected based on their relevance. First, those features that are identified as not relevant based on the exploratory analysis, such as columns containing only zeros or columns consisting of only one value (such as threshold values), are removed. Additionally, a Principal Component Analysis is performed to aid in the selection process based on statistical and visual information. The method extracts the significant features by analyzing the correlation between the principal components and the features, as described in [19].

After the feature selection new features are created. In this step, the method for handling the irregular time series is applied. The method used is delta which involves recording distances as variables and considering the order of the data. Discretization, attention mechanisms, interpolation, and neural differential equations assume the continuity of the time series. It is assumed that there is further unrecognized data between the recorded data points. However, this does not apply to the dataset used, as no other components were produced between the recorded data points. Due to the large gaps in the data, generating a large amount of data would distort the results. The method of structural invariance describes the removal of all sequences or dependencies. However, this is not used because the information on the sequence is necessary for error prediction. To assess the effectiveness of the selected method, the models were trained without applying any methods. To achieve this, irregularities were ignored and the time series was treated as equidistant. The results of this comparison are discussed in Sect. 5.4.

To predict the time to failure, two new features are engineered. Firstly, the distance between the data points is calculated and added as a new feature. The time interval between the data points is calculated by finding the delta of the date between points t and t-1. Afterward, the date feature can be removed, which eliminates the irregularity of the time series. Secondly, the Time to Error (TTE) is calculated based on the monitoring data. This is done by measuring the time interval between each data point and the previous one. If the distance is greater than 1.5 times the cycle time per component, the time between the data points is defined as a standstill. For each standstill, the operating data is checked to determine if an error occurred during this time. If an error did occur, the standstill is classified as a fault. This provides a measure of pure productive time and allows for the prediction of how much productive time remains.

In the step of outlier handling the outliers are treated based on the z-score. All values outside the interval -3 and 3 are identified as outliers. In total, there are 32 columns with outliers. Different procedures are used to deal with the outliers. In the first procedure, the outliers are not changed as they are not outliers after checking the features. The second procedure consists of limiting the outlier values [33] by replacing the outlier values, identified as such by the z-score, by the mean, to which four times the standard deviation is added. To use the non-numerical values in the subsequent model, they need to be converted. This is done by "label encoding". Finally, the data are standardized. After the data preparation, the dataset consists of 27 features and 53452 rows.

5.3 Architecture of the Models

Five fault prediction models are developed for the failure prediction task. Two types of models are created: one without feature extraction and one with feature extraction. The structure of the basic model, including hyperparameters, connections, number of layers, and activation function, remains consistent across both variants.

The initial layer of the base model comprises a neural network layer, which is variable and is substituted by a feedforward neural network (FNN), long short-term memory (LSTM), or bidirectional-LSTM (BiLSTSM) in the experiments.

This layer consists of 64 neurons, followed by a dropout layer with a factor of 0.3. These values are selected as they provided the best performance in the artifact development experiments. Another combination of a neural network layer with half the neurons and another dropout layer is then implemented. The model includes additional layers, such as another neural network layer with 16 neurons, before the final FNN layer. The activation function used is the sigmoid function, which is well-suited for classification tasks [36]. The optimizer implemented is RMSprop, which has demonstrated the best performance in artifact development tests. For the loss function, binary crossentropy is used, as it performs well in classification tasks [18]. In the models without feature extraction, different approaches (FNN, BiLSTM and LSTM) are compared for the neural network layers, swapping the respective blocks.

In models with feature extraction, a layer is added to the base model to learn the structures of the features and extract the relevant ones. A BiLSTM is used for the neural network layers, which is useful for additional feature extraction. The first variant for feature extraction includes a one-dimensional CNN with 64 neurons using the "relu" activation function. This function is well-suited for hidden layers and is commonly used [36]. The second option is to position an attention layer in front of the base model. The attention layer comprises a "dot-product-attention layer" that computes a scalar product of vectors. The vectors are generated from the input, taking into account the significant elements of the input. The sliding window method processes the data used as input. The windows are passed to the models as a two-dimensional array of size $b x f$, where b is the width of the selected window and f is the number of features. In the training process several widths are chosen (see Fig. 2).

5.4 Demonstration and Evaluation

This chapter demonstrates and evaluates the model. The pipeline and dataset are used to train the model, which is then evaluated using different metrics. The results are subsequently discussed.

Demonstration. The model was trained for a total of 500 epochs using a batch size of 32. Early stopping was implemented with a patience of five, which halts the training if the loss fails to decrease for five consecutive times. This low patience value was chosen to prevent overfitting and limit the training time. The dataset was divided into three parts: 60% for training, 20% for testing, and 20% for validation. The models are trained by varying the window width b between 1 and 80. The limit for error prediction is set at 1800 s, because of the artifact's objective of predicting an error 30 min before it occurs. The method involves training five different models with five window widths, resulting in a total of 25 models for comparison. The evaluation metrics used are accuracy, F1 score, recall, precision, and area under the curve (AUC). These metrics are chosen because it is crucial for production to accurately predict defects. Failures that are not detected or are not recognized as failures lead to unnecessary downtime.

Model	Metric	Window size									
		Delta method for handling irregularities					Ignored irregularities				
		1	10	30	50	70	1	10	30	50	70
LSTM	Accuracy	0,61	0,60	0,54	0,61	0,68	0,61	0,65	0,59	0,66	0,66
	F1-Score	0,75	0,71	0,65	0,73	0,81	0,76	0,78	0,71	0,78	0,80
	Precision	0,61	0,67	0,67	0,68	0,68	0,61	0,66	0,69	0,70	0,67
	Recall	0,98	0,77	0,64	0,80	1,00	0,99	0,93	0,73	0,89	0,98
	AUC	0,51	0,53	0,48	0,50	0,51	0,51	0,53	0,50	0,53	0,50
BiLSTM	Accuracy	0,61	0,65	0,52	0,66	0,60	0,62	0,60	0,43	0,64	0,64
	F1-Score	0,75	0,77	0,62	0,78	0,73	0,75	0,71	0,48	0,76	0,76
	Precision	0,61	0,67	0,68	0,70	0,68	0,62	0,66	0,64	0,70	0,69
	Recall	0,98	0,90	0,57	0,87	0,79	0,96	0,77	0,38	0,82	0,85
	AUC	0,51	0,54	0,50	0,54	0,50	0,53	0,53	0,45	0,54	0,52
FNN	Accuracy	0,61	0,64	0,68	0,66	0,67	0,61	0,64	0,68	0,65	0,67
	F1-Score	0,75	0,78	**0,81**	0,79	0,80	0,75	0,78	0,81	0,78	0,80
	Precision	0,61·	0,65	0,68	0,68	0,67	0,61	0,65	0,68	0,69	0,67
	Recall	0,97	0,98	0,99	0,94	0,99	0,98	0,98	0,98	0,91	0,99
	AUC	0,50	0,50	0,50	0,50	0,50	0,50	0,50	0,50	0,51	0,50
CNN-BiLSTM	Accuracy	0,61	0,65	0,65	0,68	0,67	0,61	0,65	0,68	0,68	0,67
	F1-Score	0,76	0,79	0,78	**0,81**	0,80	0,76	0,78	0,81	0,81	0,80
	Precision	0,61	0,65	0,69	0,68	0,67	0,61	0,65	0,68	0,68	0,67
	Recall	0,99	1,00	0,90	0,99	0,99	0,99	0,99	0,99	0,99	0,99
	AUC	0,51	0,50	0,50	0,50	0,50	0,51	0,50	0,50	0,50	0,50
Attention-BiLSTM	Accuracy	0,61	0,66	0,64	0,65	0,65	0,61	0,62	0,63	0,70	0,67
	F1-Score	0,75	0,78	0,74	0,76	0,78	0,76	0,74	0,76	0,81	0,77
	Precision	0,61	0,66	**0,73**	0,71	0,68	0,61	0,66	0,69	0,72	0,72
	Recall	0,98	0,94	0,74	0,83	0,91	0,99	0,86	0,85	0,93	0,84
	AUC	0,51	0,54	**0,58**	0,55	0,52	0,51	0,52	0,50	0,57	0,57
Decision Tree	Accuracy	0,59	0,62	0,69	0,71	0,74	0,57	0,60	0,67	0,68	0,72
	F1-Score	0,59	0,61	0,67	0,70	0,74	0,56	0,59	0,65	0,68	0,72
	Precision	0,59	0,61	0,67	0,70	0,74	0,57	0,58	0,65	0,68	0,72
	Recall	0,59	0,61	0,68	0,70	0,74	0,57	0,59	0,66	0,68	0,72
	AUC	0,59	0,62	0,68	0,71	0,75	0,58	0,60	0,65	0,69	0,72

Fig. 2. Results of the failure prediction for 1800 s limit (own illustration)

Figure 2 presents the metrics achieved for each model with different window widths. In addition to the five models, a decision tree is trained as a comparison model with default settings. The left side of the table shows the results of models trained with the handled irregularities with the delta method. On the right side of the table are the results of training the model while ignoring the irregularities.

Identifying the best model in the table is challenging since the metrics of the models differ by only a few percentage points. Therefore, a detailed analysis of the left side of the table is provided below. Upon analyzing the accuracy, the CNN-BiLSTM model with a window width of 40 is the best, achieving an accuracy of 69%. According to the F1 score, the FNN model with a window width of 30 and the CNN-BiLSTM model with a window width of 50 are the best, reaching an F1 score of 81%. The Attention-BiLSTM model with a window width of 30 achieves the highest precision at 73%. Notably, the recall values are high and the variance is large. The best models, identified by precision and F1 score, achieve a recall of approximately 99%. Other models perform at over 90%, with some ranging from 48% to 88%. To critically evaluate this behavior, refer to Fig. 3 for the confusion matrix of the FNN model with a window width of 30. The figure illustrates that the model classifies more than 99% of the cases as positive. As positive, resulting in a high recall due to the correct classification of almost all positive cases. However, this comes at the expense of negative cases, resulting in low accuracy due to the prevalence of false negatives.

| | | Prediction | |
		„Error" (1)	„No Error" (0)
True Class	„Error" (1)	4888	60
	„No Error" (0)	2256	21

Fig. 3. Confusion matrix of the FNN model with window width 30 (own illustration)

It can be inferred from this that models with high recall may not learn the structures and dependencies. There could be two reasons for this. Firstly, the architecture of the models may not be suitable for learning the structures and dependencies. Secondly, the data may lack the necessary information. Models with such high recall are not necessarily the best result. However, to determine the best model, we consider the AUC metric, which indicates the model's ability to distinguish between classes. The metric is generally low, with the Attention-BiLSTM model with a window width of 30 achieving the highest value at 58% in the AUC metric. Figure 4 displays the model's confusion matrix.

| | | Prediction | |
		„Error" (1)	„No Error" (0)
True Class	„Error" (1)	3667	1281
	„No Error" (0)	1336	941

Fig. 4. Confusion matrix of the Attention-BiLSTM model with window width 30 (own illustration)

The model attempts to assign classes and has learned structures, as shown in the confusion matrix. This model achieves the highest precision value of 73%, which makes it the best performing. However, the metrics are relatively inadequate, with only a 74% F1 score, 64% accuracy, and 58% AUC. Based on the training and evaluation, the Attention-BiLSTM model with a window width of 30 is considered the best option for the reasons mentioned above.

To evaluate the chosen approach's efficacy, the models underwent training without the application of any techniques. This involved disregarding irregularities and treating the time series as uniformly spaced. The results are presented on the right-hand side of the table in Fig. 2. A slight difference between the delta method and ignoring the irregularities was observed. The differences were only a few percentage points, with the delta method achieving better values for the BiLSTM and Attention-BiLSTM models. In the LSTM models, ignoring the irregularities was found to be better. The FNN and CNN-BiLSTM models do not differ in their approach to handling irregularities. It can be demonstrated that the delta method is the most effective model. In general, the performance of the DL model is dependent on the method chosen to handle irregularities.

Evaluation. The purpose of this section is to evaluate whether the artifact meets the objectives and is justified from an economic perspective. The initial objective assesses whether the model outperforms the baseline model. The attention-BiLSTM model, with a window width of 30, achieves a higher F1 score, along with associated precision and recall, than the decision tree with the same window width. However, the decision tree outperforms the model in terms of accuracy and AUC. Since the F1 score is considered the most important metric and is higher in the developed model, the effort put into developing the DL model can be justified.

The second important factor to consider is the time saved in downtime due to fault prediction. This is based on the average downtime after a fault, which is 5.6 h for the machine. According to [43], PdM can reduce downtime by 35% to 50%. For this paper, it is assumed that the downtime can be reduced by 35%, which reduces the machine downtime to 3.6 h. To justify the use of the model with this performance, we use the confusion matrix from Fig. 3 to calculate the absolute downtime. The confusion matrix shows a total of 4948 true faults. Multiplying this number by the downtime before the introduction of PdM results in a total downtime of 27708.8 h for all faults. After the introduction of PdM, there are four possible scenarios:

- TP: A fault is detected before it occurs, and the machine is stopped for a maximum of 3.6 h.
- FN: A fault occurs which is not detected, and the machine stops for 5.6 h.
- FP: The model detects a fault, but there is no fault, so the machine stops for 3.6 h. As the system only checks to see if there is a fault, this case may result in a shorter downtime.
- TN: No fault is detected and there is no fault, so the machine does not stop.

The confusion matrix evaluation indicates an optimized downtime of 25185.2 h for the 4948 faults. It is important to note that this value is based on average values and may vary significantly in individual cases. The calculation was performed using the averages for an initial assessment. Despite the moderate performance of the model, time savings can still be achieved, with approximately 10% downtime potentially saved.

6 Discussion

The first part of this paper illustrates the problems and challenges of using product data as a basis for failure prediction. The challenges are discussed, and solutions are provided based on the literature. The first challenge is the missing correlation of the product data with the machine. One possibility to fix this is to combine the product data with the monitoring data of the machine. For the irregular time series, several methods can be used to learn from this data. The paper's second part outlines the development of a fault prediction model using an existing machine dataset through a goal-oriented DSR approach. The challenges and solutions encountered during the development of the model were also considered. The results show that fault prediction is possible despite the low performance, and the requirement to predict whether an error will occur in the next 30 min was met. Additionally, the two defined objectives were achieved. The superior model outperforms the base model in the F1 metric. Additionally, using the superior model can reduce machine downtime by 10%. It was demonstrated that the selected method for converting the non-equidistant time series has a significant impact on the models' performance.

Regarding the results, it is important to note that higher performance may be achieved with different hyperparameters and architecture. Additionally, different results may be obtained by splitting the data into test, validation, and training sets differently. It is critical to evaluate the generalization of the results through further applications of fault prediction.

Future research could expand on this study by generalizing the difficulties and devising established solutions. To investigate the specific case in the company, sensor data could be gathered, enabling the models to be trained with more relevant data and potentially achieve higher performance.

References

1. Achouch, M., et al.: On predictive maintenance in industry 4.0: overview, models, and challenges. Appl. Sci. **12**(16), 8081 (2022)
2. Aggarwal, K., Atan, O., Farahat, A.K., Zhang, C., Ristovski, K., Gupta, C.: Two birds with one network: unifying failure event prediction and time-to-failure modeling. In: Proceedings - 2018 IEEE International Conference on Big Data, Big Data 2018, pp. 1308–1317 (1 2019). https://doi.org/10.1109/BIGDATA.2018.8622431
3. Ahmad, M.W., Akram, M.U., Ahmad, R., Hameed, K., Hassan, A.: Intelligent framework for automated failure prediction, detection, and classification of mission critical autonomous flights. ISA Trans. **129**, 355–371 (2022)
4. Biedermann, H.: Instandhaltung. Ersatzteil management, pp. 9–28 (2008)
5. Bink, R., Zschech, P.: Predictive maintenance in der industriellen praxis. HMD Praxis der Wirtschaftsinformatik **55**(3), 552–565 (2017)
6. Brockwell, P.J., Davis, R.A.: Introduction to Time Series and Forecasting. Springer Cham (2016). https://doi.org/10.1007/978-3-319-29854-2
7. Chen, C., Shi, J., Shen, M., Feng, L., Tao, G.: A predictive maintenance strategy using deep learning quantile regression and kernel density estimation for failure prediction. IEEE Trans. Instrum. Meas. **72**, 1–12 (2023)

8. Cheng, C., et al.: A deep learning-based remaining useful life prediction approach for bearings. IEEE/ASME Trans. Mechatron. **25**, 1243–1254 (2018)
9. Davari, N., Veloso, B., de Assis Costa, G., Pereira, P.M., Ribeiro, R.P., Gama, J.: A survey on data-driven predictive maintenance for the railway industry. Sensors (Basel, Switzerland) **21** (2021). https://doi.org/10.3390/S21175739
10. Eckner, A.: A framework for the analysis of unevenly spaced time series data (2014)
11. Eckstein, P.P.: Zeitreihenanalyse. Statistik für Wirtschaftswissenschaftler (2012)
12. Feng, Y., Zhao, Y., Zheng, H., Li, Z., Tan, J.: Data-driven product design toward intelligent manufacturing: a review. Int. J. Adv. Rob. Syst. **17**(2), 172988142091125 (2020)
13. Grzegorzewski, P., Kochanski, A.: Data and modeling in industrial manufacturing. In: Grzegorzewski, P., Kochanski, A., Kacprzyk, J. (eds.) Soft Modeling in Industrial Manufacturing. SSDC, vol. 183, pp. 3–13. Springer, Cham (2019). https://doi.org/10.1007/978-3-030-03201-2_1
14. Hasan, M.K., Alam, M.A., Roy, S., Dutta, A., Jawad, M.T., Das, S.: Missing value imputation affects the performance of machine learning: a review and analysis of the literature (2010–2021). Inform. Med. Unlocked **27**, 100799 (2021)
15. Hashemian, H.M.: State-of-the-art predictive maintenance techniques. IEEE Trans. Instrum. Meas. **60**, 226–236 (2011)
16. Hsu, C.Y., Lu, Y.W., Yan, J.H.: Temporal convolution-based long-short term memory network with attention mechanism for remaining useful life prediction. IEEE Trans. Semicond. Manuf. **35**, 220–228 (2022)
17. Hänisch, T.: Grundlagen industrie 4.0. Industrie 4.0, pp. 9–31 (2017)
18. Janocha, K., Czarnecki, W.M.: On loss functions for deep neural networks in classification. Schedae Informaticae **25**, 49–59 (2017)
19. Jollife, I.T., Cadima, J.: Principal component analysis: a review and recent developments. Philos. Trans. Royal Soc. A Math. Phys. Eng. Sci. **374** (2016). https://doi.org/10.1098/RSTA.2015.0202
20. Kim, Y.J., Ausin, M.S., Chi, M.: Multi-temporal abstraction with time-aware deep q-learning for septic shock prevention. In: Proceedings - 2021 IEEE International Conference on Big Data, Big Data 2021, pp. 1657–1663 (2021)
21. Kim, Y.J., Chi, M.: Temporal belief memory: imputing missing data during RNN training (2018)
22. Kirchgässner, G., Wolters, J.: Introduction to Modern Time Series Analysis, pp. 1–274. Springer, Heidelberg (2007). https://doi.org/10.1007/978-3-540-73291-4
23. Leukel, J., González, J., Riekert, M.: Machine learning-based failure prediction in industrial maintenance: improving performance by sliding window selection. Int. J. Qual. Reliab. Manag. **ahead-of-print** (2022)
24. Li, H., Zhao, W., Zhang, Y., Zio, E.: Remaining useful life prediction using multi-scale deep convolutional neural network. Appl. Soft Comput. **89**, 106113 (2020)
25. Livieris, I.E., Stavroyiannis, S., Pintelas, E., Pintelas, P.: A novel validation framework to enhance deep learning models in time-series forecasting. Neural Comput. Appl. **32**, 17149–17167 (2020)
26. Lu, H., Barzegar, V., Nemani, V.P., Hu, C., Laflamme, S., Zimmerman, A.T.: GAN-LSTM predictor for failure prognostics of rolling element bearings. In: 2021 IEEE International Conference on Prognostics and Health Management, ICPHM 2021, June 2021. https://doi.org/10.1109/ICPHM51084.2021.9486650
27. Nunes, P., Santos, J., Rocha, E.: Challenges in predictive maintenance - a review. CIRP J. Manuf. Sci. Technol. **40**, 53–67 (2023)
28. Pedrycz, W., Chen, S.M.: Time series analysis, modeling and applications: a computational intelligence perspective. Intell. Syst. Ref. Libr. **47** (2013)

29. Peffers, K., Tuunanen, T., Rothenberger, M.A., Chatterjee, S.: A design science research methodology for information systems research **24**, 45–77 (2014)
30. Pomberger, G., Pree, W., Stritzinger, A.: Methoden und werkzeuge für das prototyping und ihre integration. Inform. Forsch. Entwickl. **7**(2), 49–61 (1992)
31. Rahman, M.M., et al.: Real-time cavity fault prediction in CEBAF using deep learning. In: NAPAC 2022: Proceedings of the North American Particle Accelerator Conference, January 2022
32. Ran, Y., Zhou, X., Lin, P., Wen, Y., Deng, R.: A survey of predictive maintenance: systems, purposes and approaches. IEEE Commun. Surv. Tutor. **XX** (2019)
33. Runkler, T.A.: Datenvorverarbeitung. Data Mining, pp. 21–34 (2010)
34. Sang, G.M., Xu, L., de Vrieze, P., Bai, Y., Pan, F.: Predictive maintenance in industry 4.0. In: Proceedings of the 10th International Conference on Information Systems and Technologies, ICIST 2020. ACM, June 2020
35. Serradilla, O., Zugasti, E., Rodriguez, J., Zurutuza, U.: Deep learning models for predictive maintenance: a survey, comparison, challenges and prospect. Appl. Intell. **52**, 10934–10964 (2020). https://doi.org/10.48550/arxiv.2010.03207
36. Sharma, S., Sharma, S., Athaiya, A.: Activation functions in neural networks. Towards Data Sci. **6**(12), 310–316 (2017)
37. Shukla, S.N., Marlin, B.M.: Interpolation-prediction networks for irregularly sampled time series. In: 7th International Conference on Learning Representations, ICLR 2019, September 2019. https://doi.org/10.48550/arxiv.1909.07782
38. Shukla, S.N., Marlin, B.M.: A survey on principles, models and methods for learning from irregularly sampled time series (2020)
39. Shukla, S.N., Marlin, B.M.: Multi-time attention networks for irregularly sampled time series, January 2021. https://doi.org/10.48550/arxiv.2101.10318
40. Si, X.S., Wang, W., Hu, C.H., Zhou, D.H.: Remaining useful life estimation - a review on the statistical data driven approaches. Eur. J. Oper. Res. **213**, 1–14 (2011). https://doi.org/10.1016/J.EJOR.2010.11.018
41. Stark, J.: Product Lifecycle Management (Volume 2). Springer, Cham (2016). https://doi.org/10.1007/978-3-319-24436-5
42. Tang, H., Yin, Y.: Forecast position for ship in port based on irregular time series. In: Proceedings - 2022 International Symposium on Electrical, Electronics and Information Engineering, ISEEIE 2022, pp. 135–138 (2022)
43. Van, T.T., Chan, H.L., Parthasarathi, S., Lim, C.P., Chua, Y.Q.: IoT and machine learning enable predictive maintenance for manufacturing systems: a use-case of laser welding machine implementation. SSRN Electron. J. (2022)
44. Wang, Q., Zheng, S., Farahat, A., Serita, S., Gupta, C.: Remaining useful life estimation using functional data analysis. In: 2019 IEEE International Conference on Prognostics and Health Management, ICPHM 2019, April 2019
45. Zhang, W., Yang, D., Wang, H.: Data-driven methods for predictive maintenance of industrial equipment: a survey. IEEE Syst. J. **13**, 2213–2227 (2019)
46. Zonta, T., da Costa, C.A., da Rosa Righi, R., de Lima, M.J., da Trindade, E.S., Li, G.P.: Predictive maintenance in the industry 4.0: a systematic literature review. Comput. Ind. Eng. **150**, 106889 (2020)
47. Züfle, M., Agne, J., Grohmann, J., Dörtoluk, I., Kounev, S.: A predictive maintenance methodology: predicting the time-to-failure of machines in industry 4.0. In: IEEE International Conference on Industrial Informatics (INDIN) (2021)

Predictive Maintenance of an Archeological Park: An IoT and Digital Twin Based Approach

Liliana Cecere[1] , Francesco Colace[1] , Angelo Lorusso[1(✉)] ,
and Domenico Santaniello[2]

[1] DIIn, University of Salerno, Fisciano, SA, Italy
{lcecere,fcolace,alorusso}@unisa.it
[2] DiSPaC, University of Salerno, Fisciano, SA, Italy
dsantaniello@unisa.it

Abstract. The preservation of cultural heritage is one of the main goals that a nation must pursue since it represents an important resource, both economically and for the historical memory it holds. Thanks to the spread of new technologies, the possibility of applying innovative approaches to historical heritage is becoming increasingly real, in order to monitor in real time the progressive damage of structures or intercept any sudden risk situations. In this scenario, a significant contribution is made by the paradigm of the Internet of Things, which enables the collection in real time, of data from sensors installed on the structures to be monitored, and the concept of the Digital Twin, which represents a digital copy of reality, and can be utilized for practical purposes, such as simulations and tests. To make the Digital Twin even more effective, it is possible to link it to the real structure through HBIM, which is a process that aims not only at the mere restitution of the tridimensional model but at the creation of so-called "smart models", in which all the components are parametric objects with well-defined semantics and capable of containing all the information useful for understanding the artifact. The paper, therefore, presents a methodology to consider HBIM models as Digital Twins enriched with data from real-time IoT devices placed on the structures to be monitored. The proposed methodology was applied to a real case study within the Velia Archaeological Park: Porta Rosa, which is the oldest known example of a round arch in Italy. The first results of the experiment are more than satisfactory.

Keywords: Digital Twin · Predictive Maintenance · IoT · Cultural Heritage

1 Introduction

The preservation of cultural heritage constitutes one of our most important missions, since it includes historic buildings and archaeological parks that rap-present a piece of our still-living history. Every ancient artifact or area is to be considered heritage, since every stone of it, even the oldest, still witnesses its past. Simply put, ancient structures constitute a common asset that, as such, must be maintained and protected in order to be enjoyed by future generations as well [1]. The structural management of such assets therefore translates into constant care and strategic attention that must be given to them

© The Author(s), under exclusive license to Springer Nature Switzerland AG 2024
H. Degen and S. Ntoa (Eds.): HCII 2024, LNAI 14735, pp. 323–341, 2024.
https://doi.org/10.1007/978-3-031-60611-3_23

over time. Within this discussion, modern preservation practices are considered optimal because they are characterized by a proactive vision for implementing systems that
can monitor structures on an ongoing basis so that necessary maintenance is proactive
and not "reactive" [2]. In recent years, technology has increasingly evolved bringing
about significant changes in various disciplines, particularly in the area of ICT with
the advent of the Internet of Things (IoT) paradigm. Another significant change that
is playing an increasingly important role in this rapid evolution lies in the concept of
Heritage Building Information Modeling (H-BIM), which is an extension of Building
Information Modeling (BIM) particularized, however, to the field of historic buildings
[3]. Thanks to a 3D visualization of the element, H-BIM allows for a detailed management of information related to historic assets, taking into account the entire life cycle
of the element itself, including precedent maintenance and/or restoration phases, while
also considering both textural and historical information; in short, it is possible to use
an HBIM model as a repository of data and information for a better understanding of
the artifacts under consideration [4]. At this stage, the concept of HBIM is joined by
that of IoT, giving rise to an example of Digital Twin (DT), which, by integrating sensor
data and Edge computing in real time, enables continuous, predictive and more reliable
monitoring of buildings [5–7]. Thus, the static information in a BIM model becomes
dynamic from the moment a digital model is connected to IoT devices such as sensors. To obtain a geometrically reliable digital model, however, requires an extensive
research and development phase through the use of live surveying techniques such as, for
example, Terrestrial Laser Scanner (TLS), photogrammetry and aero-photogrammetry
(drones) and then obtain a point cloud, and thus obtain a Heritage Digital Twin (HDT).
These surveying techniques allow us to obtain very high reliability, since they allow us to
derive not only metric information but also information about materials and their related
textures and plots [8]. In some particularly complex cases, the possibility of combining
different surveying techniques makes it possible to obtain a starting model that is even
more detailed and closer to the real thing visually [8]. Equally important is phase of
data acquisition from the sensors: this process of information integration is fundamental
because it allows us a better characterization of the various monitored elements. The
introduction of ICT and especially IoT within various disciplines has radically revolutionized their traditional approach [3]. In particular, IoT has seen one of its greatest
uses precisely in the area of continuous monitoring of systems, such as in the industrial,
medical and construction fields, given its ability to adapt to different scenarios, thus
the versatility and cost-effectiveness of connected devices [7]. In addition, through the
analysis of data collected by IoT devices, it is possible to have a kind of snapshot of the
health condition of a building both from a structural and predictive monitoring point of
view. For this very reason, the use of H-BIM and the more advanced HDT in the field
of predictive maintenance is increasingly relevant and applicable [9]. Having a virtual
replica of a physical entity facilitates both the analysis and decision-making phases for
insiders such as maintainers and restorers. Through the integration of advanced sensing,
big data analytics, artificial intelligence and machine learning, DT offers new opportunities for monitoring, diagnosis and optimization of maintenance operations. Nowadays,
the cultural heritage sector is also proving to be increasingly interested in predictive
maintenance, i.e., maintenance that is based on the analysis of the actual conditions of

the artifact, which is why it is necessary to explore new proposals for best practices and effective workflows in order to have guidelines that are applicable to the different scenarios that may arise taking into account the history and the various peculiarities that each asset brings with it [9].

For the preventive maintenance of cultural property, monitoring of environmental and climatic variables with the aim of preventing long-term damage caused by factors such as changes in temperature and humidity, exposure to light, vibration, and air pollution is essential [10]. So, in this study, an active monitoring method is proposed through a multidisciplinary approach that takes into account the different professional sensitivities in the field. The proposed methodology utilizes innovative technologies to predict problems and reduce downtime and extend the lifespan of structures, and was then applied to a real-life case study to verify its effectiveness and any improvable aspects in order to demonstrate that the proposed approach, and continuous monitoring in general, is crucial for effective conservation of our priceless cultural heritage.

2 Related Works

Technological development in recent years has enabled increasing application of the IoT paradigm in various fields of work and life. Despite the great-recognized potential, research on the integration of BIM and IoT is still in its infancy, and most of the studies in the literature are purely theoretical, with few applications in the practical field.

One of the earliest articles that can be referred to is [11] in which a comprehensive study of this methodology is addressed from an application perspective. The authors identify areas of application of the methodology, make a review of current limitations and predictions about future research directions. Various integration methods that use the API of BIM tools and transform the latter into a database of data are summarized. Generalizing, it can be said that the potential of connecting BIM and IoT-based data sources lies in representing two complementary visions of the project, providing one a solution to the limitations of the other, through three main components of the integration process. The integration and fusion of data between BIM and IoT, represents a focal point of the methodology that is not easy and straightforward to solve; in particular, it is important to identify how data from BIM and IoT information systems could be coupled to develop a fusion framework between them and facilitate their processing flow for various applications. As clarified in the article [12], the characteristic problems of the data fusion process include the following three aspects: representation of observations or phenomena under uncertainty; combination of non-commensurate information; and application of a method to the association and interpretation of multi-source observations. From this perspective, the main considerations on generic data fusion problems should be: how to acquire data, how to make them commensurable, and how to analyze the paired data. In this regard, a general model was proposed in the article [13] divided into four main stages that identify the general flow of BIM and IoT data processing and interaction from source to application. An in-depth discussion of what the digital twin is about, in general terms, however, is developed in the article [14], in which the concept of a "digital twin" is clarified by exploring the advantage of its use in building lifecycle management. Wireless sensor network (WSN) integration and data analysis are two necessary components for the creation of a digital twin, the visualization of which can be based on a 3D CAD model extracted from the BIM or a customized 3D model of the building. As elucidated in [15], the use of sensors in ordinary buildings has become widespread in various applications due to their flexibility and benefits. This includes cultural heritage buildings with their critical issues with respect to the preservation of the artifacts and environments in which they are located, such as the case of museums. One example is the application of HBIM to existing historic buildings, which extends the potential of the BIM method by creating models considered not only as digital representations of their geometry, but as dynamic models, enriched by different levels of real-time information derived from sensors and IoT technologies, allowing for better management and preservation [16]. In the case of cultural heritage assets, the construction of the digital twin, i.e., the HDT, necessarily involves an additional step concerning the survey and modeling of the state of the asset. The workflow of the methodology, therefore, becomes even more complicated, having to involve on-site surveying operations for the generation of point clouds from which to build the 3D model. Also in the case of metric surveying, technological progress offers great advantages over traditional surveying methods; in particular, the Laser Scanner technique and Photogrammetric surveying, representing the most widely used methods in this field, allow minimizing geometric error by providing much more reliable data for analysis and knowledge purposes [17]. This phase allows the acquisition of semantic and spatial data essential for the development of a high-precision 3D model, to be integrated with the information provided by the monitoring performed by sensors. Thanks to the IoT paradigm, therefore, the management of the built heritage is also becoming increasingly dynamic and direct, with the possibility of both monitoring the state of affairs in real time, but also performing performance simulations, considering different scenarios, real or theoretical, thanks to the availability of HDTs. As specified in [18], it is precisely on the basis of the analysis and simulations of data, acquired from on-site sensors, that threats to site integrity and corresponding preventive actions can be predicted. In particular, an HBIM-based methodology is analyzed to support the realization of a digital twin consisting of three components: physical element, monitored through sensors, data and information collected, and the corresponding virtual element. Several case studies have been addressed through this approach, including the digitization of the Church of St. Francis of Assisi for space exploration through AI [18].

For cultural heritage, there is increasing talk of preventive conservation (PC) which, in the context of restoration and conservation, can be defined as the complexity of behaviours aimed at avoiding and diminishing possible material loss and damage to tangible cultural heritage, implemented with respect to the context in which the object or element is located [4]. The development of IoT and HBIM are significant in achieving these goals. The possibility of storing and processing, even remotely, data on the climatic conditions of architectural spaces is a very effective tool for the conservation of the built heritage. An example of preventive conservation is the case study proposed in [4] that sees the application on the former Farina tobacco factory in Battipaglia, Italy, of a methodology for monitoring and visualising data from sensors within a BIM model. The monitoring phase of the environmental parameters was implemented through a remote control system by installing digital sensors inside the structure and was managed through a Digital Twin, based on an HBIM model, integrated on a data management platform called ThingsBoard. An active control of the climatic conditions of the rooms inside the building undergoing renovation was then validated in order to preserve the masonry parts, plasters and wooden elements. A similar approach was applied to an external wall element of the urban villa 'Praedia di Giulia Felice' at the archaeological site of Pompeii [9]. The aim of the research was to demonstrate the possibility of using predictive maintenance tools, based on Deep Learning, to predict rising damp in masonry with sensors. The methodology was also effective in studying the correlation that is established between weather conditions, soil moisture and moisture in the masonry element. In addition, it is also possible to use the derived model to simulate different environmental conditions and verify the responses of the structure. Further studies in the literature have also focused on the possibility of exploiting IoT and HBIM integration for the management of equipment designed to control environmental parameters, as well as the active monitoring of the latter. This is the case of the St. Paul's catacombs, a UNESCO site in Malta [19], The aim of the work is to develop a mechanism for the conservation of the site that allows daily environmental monitoring, operation and maintenance of ventilation equipment and emergency response. In conclusion, one can highlight the evident progress in the integration of IoT and HBIM and its potential contribution in active environmental monitoring for cultural heritage assets, as an effective example of a DT concept for predictive maintenance to support expert users.

3   Methodology

As part of this research work, an innovative methodology for data integration and management in the context of cultural heritage preservation is introduced, taking advantage of advanced IoT and HBIM technologies. This methodological approach is designed to address the challenges posed by the need for accurate and continuous monitoring of cultural heritage assets, while providing a tool for their conservation and predictive maintenance. The methodology is based on the use of leading-edge technologies in the fields of computer and architectural engineering, integrating data from different sources to obtain a comprehensive and up-to-date picture of the state of cultural property. This integration makes it possible to overcome the limitations of traditional preservation techniques, providing a dynamic and interactive view of cultural heritage that continuously adapts to environmental conditions and maintenance needs. The main elements of the methodology include collecting data through IoT sensors, creating a detailed digital twin using laser scanning and BIM modeling, and integrating this data into a dynamic and interactive environment. The role of advanced software, such as Dynamo and Autodesk Revit, is crucial in this process, enabling data to be processed, visualized, and updated efficiently. In this way, the proposed methodology opens the way to new possibilities for cultural heritage management by combining the accuracy of modern surveying and modeling techniques with the power of real-time data processing and communication. This innovative combination of technologies not only improves the preservation of cultural heritage, but also provides valuable tools for its analysis and understanding.

The architecture on which the proposed work is based consists of four layers: the first layer is the Data Collection layer, the second and third layers are the Data Processing and Data Visualization layers, and finally a centralized Hub Cloud, which connects the previous layers, with the task of storing information and interchange between the layers of the proposed architecture. Data Ingestion is layer of the architecture that deals with the collection of raw data from the sensors placed on the structure being monitored (temperature, acceleration, humidity, etc.). The collected data are sent to the central layer, Hub; which is responsible for recording and organizing the data (Time Series). Next is the data processing phase: the raw data recorded in the Hub are processed to produce new information useful for predictive analysis of the monitored element. At this very stage, data are taken from the Hub through internal APIs; these are connected and integrated with data from the HBIM model. At this point, a prediction engine will use all this information to make future projections from the current state of the analyzed structure. Finally, the results obtained will be sent to the Hub. The interface with the end user is through the Data Visualization layer, this layer provides a structured data visualization interface through the use of different modules: Real-time Dashboards allow visualization of raw data from sensors in the form of graphs; through 3D models it is possible to visualize the placement of sensors and related data; real-time alert systems allow intuitive and rapid identification of any anomaly situations, including and especially with regard to the damage prediction module and related maintenance. Finally, external APIs allow external systems to access the data (see Fig. 1). ThingsBoard, an open-source cloud platform reserved for IoT sensor management, was used as the cloud hub to collect and exchange data between layers. With the platform, it is possible to communicate with devices in real time through various protocols, including MQTT used to connect structural monitoring sensors to the platform. In addition, ThingsBoard gives the ability to view real-time data values through useful Dashboards, which can be customized and extended according to user needs. These capabilities were then used to develop the visualization layer of the proposed architecture. Specifically, time sequences, alarms, and a widget developed ad hoc to visualize the data on a three-dimensional model. Finally, parametric modeling information and related values were implemented through the marriage of Revit and Dynamo.

3.1 IoT Communication and Dynamo Software

The "IoT and Dynamo Software Communication" phase represents a critical aspect of the proposed methodology, featuring a sophisticated system of interaction between IoT devices and Dynamo software. This methodological segment is critical to establish a continuous and reliable flow of data from the monitored cultural heritage. IoT Sensor System: In this phase, advanced sensors are installed on the artifact or surrounding area to collect a variety of environmental and structural data. These sensors are designed to operate in real time, capturing critical information such as temperature, humidity, structural movement, and other vital parameters for assessing the condition of cultural heritage assets. Data Transmission and IoT Platform: Data collected by the sensors are transmitted to a centralized IoT platform. This platform acts as a hub for data collection and processing, ensuring that it is transmitted securely and efficiently to Dynamo software. The IoT platform is designed to handle large volumes of data, ensuring that information is transferred without interruption or loss. Integration with Dynamo Software: Dynamo, an advanced pro-engineering and parametric modeling tool, receives data from the IoT platform. The software is configured to interpret this data and integrate it into the HBIM

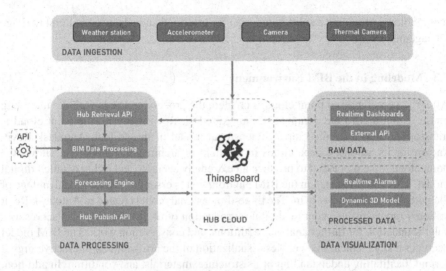

Fig. 1. Proposed architecture

model. Dynamo automatically updates the model with the new information, ensuring that the artifact representations are always current and accurate. Dynamic HBIM Model Update: The result of this phase is an HBIM model that reflects the status of the artifact in real time, thanks to the continuous updates provided by IoT sensors through Dynamo. This dynamic interaction between sensors, IoT platform, and Dynamo software allows preservation professionals to access an up-to-date HBIM model that provides a detailed and up-to-date view of the condition of the cultural heritage.

3.2 Creation of a Digital Twin

The creation of a digital twin of the artifact represents a crucial step in the proposed methodology, beginning with an accurate survey of the artifact using laser scanner technology. This tool, known for its accuracy, makes detailed scans of the physical structure, capturing every geometric and structural aspect of the artifact. The result is an in-depth analysis that includes identification of architectural details, structural conditions, and material characteristics, providing an accurate basis for subsequent modeling. From the scans taken, a georeferenced point cloud is obtained, in which each point represents a precise datum in space. This point cloud is essential for building an accurate three-dimensional digital model of the artifact. Georeferencing ensures that the digital model is perfectly aligned with its actual location in the physical world, ensuring a faithful representation of the real object. The final step sees the transformation of the point cloud into a detailed digital twin of the artifact. This digital model becomes an exact representation of the artifact in its current state, incorporating all the information gathered during the survey. The digital twin becomes a fundamental element of the methodology, serving as the basis for IoT data integration and further analysis and conservation interventions. In summary, the process of creating the digital twin is essential to the success of the methodology, providing a solid foundation for informed and advanced cultural heritage management.

3.3 Modeling in the BIM Environment

After the georeferenced point cloud is created, the process proceeds with the modeling phase within a BIM environment. Using Autodesk Revit software, the point cloud is transformed into a detailed three-dimensional model of the artifact. Autodesk Revit, known for its advanced capabilities in the field of architectural modeling, allows the point cloud to be processed to produce an extremely accurate and richly detailed digital model. This modeling step in the BIM environment is essential to take full advantage of the potential of the digital twin. The three-dimensional model created in Autodesk Revit not only represents an accurate digital reproduction of the artifact, but also serves as a solid foundation for further analysis, additions, and conservation work. The BIM model becomes a key element that enables visualization of the artifact in an interactive digital format, facilitating understanding of its structure, materials, and condition. In addition, modeling in a BIM environment paves the way for a range of advanced analyses, such as scenario simulation, structural analysis, and conservation optimization. The BIM model can be further enriched and updated with data from IoT sensors, creating an integrated system that combines the accuracy of architectural modeling with the innovation of real-time data. This process represents a qualitative leap forward in cultural heritage management and preservation, offering a versatile and powerful platform for proactive monitoring and intervention.

3.4 Data Collection from Sensors on ThingsBoard

Data collection from IoT sensors is a crucial step in the methodology, carried out through ThingsBoard, an advanced and specialized IoT platform. ThingsBoard serves as a central hub for collecting, processing and managing data from sensors placed on or near the artifact. The platform is designed to handle a wide variety of data, which can include not only physical measurements such as temperature, humidity and pressure, but also environmental information such as lighting levels, air quality and other parameters relevant to the condition and preservation of the artifact. This data collection phase is critical to providing a continuous flow of up-to-date and accurate information about the condition of the artifact. The ThingsBoard platform makes it possible not only to collect this data in real time, but also to organize and visualize it in an intuitive way, facilitating analysis and interpretation. The ability to collect and analyze data in real time brings a significant advantage in the management of cultural property, enabling timely interventions and detailed information for preservation and maintenance. In addition, data collection on ThingsBoard allows environmental and physical information to be integrated with the HBIM digital model, enriching the digital twin with up-to-date and dynamic data. This level of data integration significantly improves the ability to monitor the condition of the artifact, providing a solid basis for informed decisions and effective conservation strategies.

3.5 Integration of Data with the HBIM Model via Dynamo

The integration of data collected from IoT sensors into the HBIM model using Dynamo software is a complex and fundamental process of the proposed methodology. Dynamo, an advanced parametric design software, receives data from the IoT ThingsBoard platform and processes it, allowing complex data to be manipulated and converted into a format that can be used within the HBIM model. This data processing is crucial to ensure that it aligns perfectly with existing model elements, thus adding a dynamic layer of information to the digital twin. Once the data has been processed and integrated into the HBIM model, Dynamo makes it easy to understand and navigate through its intuitive interface and visualization capabilities. Operators can view variations and trends directly in the digital model, which makes areas of interest or concern immediately obvious. This dynamic visualization in the HBIM model not only improves preservation accuracy and effectiveness, but also provides a new perspective in understanding and interacting with cultural heritage. In addition, the integration of data provides crucial support in decisions regarding conservation and maintenance. Up-to-date information makes it possible to plan targeted interventions, evaluate the effectiveness of conservation measures, and optimize predictive maintenance. The ability to simulate future scenarios and analyze the long-term condition of the artifact results in more informed and proactive management of the cultural heritage. In summary, data integration through Dynamo transforms the HBIM model into a comprehensive and versatile tool for cultural heritage management, combining the accuracy of architectural modeling with the innovation of real-time data.

The proposed methodology represents an innovative and integrated approach for cultural heritage management and conservation, combining advanced IoT technologies with HBIM through the use of Dynamo software. This approach offers a holistic solution for cultural heritage monitoring, visualization, and analysis, providing a detailed and dynamic digital representation that integrates real-time data from IoT sensors. The methodology begins with a precise survey of the artifact using laser scanner technology, followed by the creation of an accurate three-dimensional model within a BIM environment. Data collected from IoT sensors are then integrated into the HBIM model through Dynamo, allowing for an interactive and up-to-date visualization of the condition of the artifact. This process not only improves the conservation and maintenance of cultural property, but also provides a valuable tool for its analysis and understanding. So, the proposed methodology represents a significant step toward advanced cultural heritage management, leveraging the integration of cutting-edge technologies to create a comprehensive and dynamic information system that can effectively respond to conservation needs in an ever-changing context.

4   Case Study

The methodology just described, as mentioned, can be applied to a variety of areas of work: among them, the preservation of cultural and historical heritage. For this reason, one possible application could be related to the monitoring and management of archaeological parks. The case study that we want to examine in this paper, in fact, refers precisely to the archaeological park of Velia, in the province of Salerno, within which we want to study, specifically, the Porta Rosa located within the archaeological area.

Dating back to the fourth century B.C., the Porta Rosa is a monumental work that is part of the Archaeological Park of the ancient city of Velia, in the municipality of Ascea within the Cilento and Vallo di Diano National Park. It is the oldest known example of a round-arched vault in Italy and, as such, should be properly preserved so that future generations can enjoy it to the fullest. Although it is known by the appellation "gate," it was actually a viaduct within the wall passage that separated the southern side of the city from the northern, as well as also serving as a containment for the walls of the gorge in which it is located.

The purpose of this work is to provide the described artifact with an intelligent monitoring system, with the aim of ensuring its good preservation through a predictive maintenance approach. For the purpose of monitoring, several sensing sensors, cameras, and thermal imaging cameras were installed (see Table 1). In particular, a Sainlogic WS3500 model weather station was installed, which integrates several different sensors inside. It is designed to integrate a wide range of weather information in real time, using high-quality sensors to collect accurate and reliable data, while also offering the ability to record it over time. The installed weather station's sensors enable it to clearly measure parameters such as temperature, humidity, atmospheric pressure, and wind speed and direction.

Specifically, the sensors with which the station is equipped are:

- BME680: is a four-in-one digital sensor capable of detecting various environmental parameters such as: temperature, humidity, barometric pressure and volatile organic compounds (VOCs). The operating temperature is between -40 °C and 85 °C, with a range of maximum accuracy between 0 °C and 60 °C. Under these conditions, the sensor can achieve a detection accuracy of $\pm 3\%$ for relative humidity, ± 1.0 hPa for pressure, and ± 0.5 °C for temperature. For air quality measurement, the BME680 works through the presence of a small MOX (Metal - Oxide) sensor: metal oxide is heated by changing the resistance according to the Volatile Organic Compounds (VOCs) in the air.
- SI1145: is a digital sensor with a light detection algorithm calibrated to calculate the UV index. It does not contain an actual UV detection element, but approximates the index based on visible and IR light from the sun. Despite this, however, as studies have shown, the data derived from it are very accurate. The operating temperature must be between -40 °C and 85 °C; the IR sensor possesses a spectrum wavelength of 550 nm–1000 nm (centered on 800), that of visible light, on the other hand, 400 nm–800 nm (centered on 530).
- PMSA003: is a sensor that is responsible for monitoring air quality and is in fact used to detect contaminants in the air, including particles, pollutants, and harmful gases that are harmful to health. This sensor uses laser scattering to irradiate airborne particles, then collects the scattering light to obtain the scattering light change curve over time. The microprocessor calculates the equivalent particle diameter and the number of particles with different diameters per unit volume. The data stream updates once per second, obtaining the concentration of PM1.0, PM2.5 and PM10.0 particulate matter in both standard and ambient units.
- Rain gauge: is a device used to measure the amount of rain that falls in a given period of time. It consists of a collecting cylinder or funnel that captures rainwater and a

measuring mechanism that records the amount of water collected. It is part of the main equipment of a common weather station. The rain gauge, in order to properly record rainfall levels, must be in-stalled in an open place free of obstacles.
- Wind Speed: a sensor for measuring wind speed, that is, a device designed to detect and measure the speed of moving air. This sensor uses an ultrasonic anemometer to detect and measure wind speed in real time. The WS3500 ultrasonic anemometer uses high-frequency sound waves to determine time-of-flight and calculate speed. The data collected by this sensor are shown on the weather station display and can be recorded for later analysis.
- Wind Direction: a device that uses an internal magnetic sensor that detects changes in the direction of the Earth's magnetic field caused by wind. This data is then processed and translated into a numerical reading or angular value indicating the wind direction.

 Also installed were:

- ADXL345: is a sensor capable of detecting and/or measuring acceleration, specifically detecting and measuring changes in linear velocity along one or more axes. It generally works by converting physical acceleration into a measurable electrical signal, which can be read and interpreted by a microcontroller or data processing device.
- Raspberry Pi High Quality HQ Camera: installing a camera allows the current state of the cultural property to be visually recorded and documented, making it easier to identify any changes or damage over time. The images can be used as a reference for future comparisons, enabling the identification of changes, deterioration, or the need for restoration work.
- MLX90640 Thermal Camera: a device that detects and measures thermal radiation emitted by objects to create images based on temperature difference. This technology uses a thermal sensor to capture the infrared radiation emitted by objects, converting it into a visible image that represents temperature changes through colors: each color corresponds to a specific temperature range.

4.1 Phase 1 - Survey

The survey of the artifact was based on Laser Scanner data acquisition, which was divided into three phases: survey, processing and data return.

The first phase of surveying essentially involved the practical operations of surveying, in which includes, for example, identification of the area of interest, selection of the optimal gripping station position, i.e. scanner location, installation and configuration of surveying instruments, etc. The actual survey, in our case, was carried out by laser scanner method, using the so-called "range based" technique. This is an advanced method of capturing the physical dimensions and shape of an object or artifact in a precise and detailed manner. The technique is based on active optical sensors that, through laser technology, acquire information about the spatial position of points (including depth) and return digitized surfaces. The great advantage of its use is the ability to capture a large amount and density of data with good accuracy in a short time. The laser scanner chosen for surveying the artifact is of type FARO FOCUS 3D X 330, and it was used statically,

Table 1. Measured parameters and related sensors.

Parameters	Sensors
Relative humidity, barometric pressure, ambient temperature and gas (VOC)	BME680 Breakout (Adafruit Industries, New York, NY, USA)
Outdoor air quality	PMSA003 (Adafruit Industries, New York, NY, USA)
UV index with IR sensors and visible light	SI1145 (Adafruit Industries, New York, NY, USA)
Weather Station	Sainlogic WS3500 (SparkFun Electronics, Niwot, Colorado, USA)
Temperatures of the manufact	MLX90640 24x32 IR Thermal Camera Breakout - 110° FoV (Adafruit Industries, New York, NY, USA)
Peak ground acceleration	ADXL345 (Adafruit Industries, New York, NY, USA)
Structural and material alterations	Raspberry Pi High Quality HQ Camera – 12 MP (Adafruit Industries, New York, NY, USA)

that is, placing it at an initial point, and then changing its position from time to time so as to ensure maximum coverage. The raw data, once acquired from the scanner, were processed with Faro Scene, a software program that allows processing and management of even large three-dimensional point clouds, enabling their visualization, registration and export. The workflow in Faro Scene is an "obligatory" path, divided into processing, registration, point cloud generation and georeferencing, which allows each step to be completed only if the previous one has been concluded. In the procedure performed, 24 scans were first imported and processed, from which the scan cloud was derived. In the next registration phase, the surfaces, which at first appear to be offset, are aligned first automatically, and then manually, bringing the scan cloud to a common coordinate system: prior to this phase each scan has a reference system independent of the others, each identified by the individual scanner position at the time the individual scan was acquired, which is why alignment plays a key role. After alignment, we proceed to the cloud optimization phase, which allows minimizing the average error in point placement, and at the end of which we obtain the point cloud, which must then be georeferenced. Georeferencing is done through control points, with known coordinates, obtained from an aero photogrammetric survey of the entire area of the Velia archaeological park. The coordinates of the control points were tabulated on a cvs file in Microsoft Excel and imported as references into the Faro Scene workspace. The end of this first phase, therefore, concluded with the return of the survey data in the form of a georeferenced point cloud (see Fig. 2). The latter was first exported from Faro Scene and then displayed in Autodesk Recap, to allow its import into Autodesk Revit.

4.2   Step 2 - HBIM Model Return

As mentioned, digital modeling is carried out through Autodesk Revit software following a workflow that involves first importing the point cloud generated during the survey phase into the program, then modeling the architectural elements and, finally, defining the so-called design parameters. The shapes are modeled directly on the point cloud, considering both the different geometries of the elements and the stratigraphies that make up the masonry of the building, in particular identifying the materials and different construction techniques. After that, the textures to be assigned to the various elements are defined to achieve a graphic rendering that is as effective and close to reality as possible. However, it is important to emphasize that the model is always defined as a simplification of reality, and its main characteristic must be the simplicity of management and visualization of the space to allow, later, the reading of the data. Once the structure of the artifact has been created, the design parameters are defined that will be needed in the next steps to visualize the data from the sensors in the BIM environment. The design parameters to be created are instance parameters, which will therefore allow the properties of only the element they refer to to be changed. In particular, those that are created must correspond to the sensors actually installed on the artifact, so each real sensor, will have its respective "virtual" sensor in the digital model, which will in turn be linked to the corresponding reference instance.

4.3   Step 3 - Data Acquisition

The third phase involved capturing and then collecting data on an IoT platform. Specifically, in our case, ThingsBoard was chosen: an open source, IoT-based platform that provides advanced functionality for data management and monitoring of connected devices. The platform offers an intuitive interface for device management and data collection, as well as allows the creation of custom dashboards, with thirty different widgets available, to display data in real time. The chosen platform enables not only visualization, but also secure monitoring and control of data and archiving of data from the last telemetry performed surviving network and hardware failures. Thanks to its flexible and modular architecture, ThingsBoard can be adapted to the specific needs of any IoT project, allowing developers to focus on implementing the desired functionality without having to start from scratch. Once logged in via an ad hoc authentication token, which does not allow unauthorized access, data from the sensors can be read and displayed: each sensor, in fact, has its own identification ID and an access token that allows it to send data and be recognized by the platform: the Raspberry takes and collects data from the sensor and then sends it to the platform, which, thanks to an identification token, is able to recognize that data from the virtual sensor that has been connected. The basis of the system is the presence of the Raspberry Pi: it is a single motherboard, a complete, low-cost minicomputer that includes processor, memory, USB input/output ports, network connectivity and more. In the present case, a Raspberry Pi 4 was used, which is the physical hub of the system, i.e., the data sorting node. The Raspberry, then, acts as a link between all the sensors: thanks to an identification token, it recognizes data from the sensors, collects it and interacts with the cloud system, sending it to the platform. At this point, as mentioned, the data can be stored in ThingsBoard, read and then visualized through the relevant dashboards. In fact, the dashboard allows the data to be visualized in an easy and intuitive way, enabling the user to analyze and interpret the data captured by the device.

Fig. 2. Point cloud

4.4   Step 4 – Data Visualization

The next step was to visualize, automatically and in real time, data from ThingsBoard directly in the BIM environment, via Dynamo. Dynamo allows us to create and edit elements within a Revit model: it comes with a visual modeling tool that allows us to create custom visual scripts for controlling model parameters, managing data, building complex geometry, and more, allowing us to automate the Revit workflow. With libraries of predefined nodes, you can easily and automatically connect, combine and modify model inputs and outputs. The creation of nodes within the software, therefore, is an essential process for automating tasks and workflow; the connection between ThigsBoard and Dynamo is precisely through a series of nodes with inputs and outputs.

The first node to be used, which is necessary to configure ThingsBoard, is "ThingsBoard.TBConfig", which has as both input and output strings, which can be collections of text or manipulatable alphanumeric characters, commonly used to represent textual information such as names, addresses, etc.. This node returns as output the platform authentication token, confirming that ThingsBoard has been accessed. Next, the "ThingsBoard.TBLastTelemetry" node allows us to detect the last telemetry, i.e., the last data that arrived on the platform and needs to be read into Dynamo. The output in this case is returned to us in the form of a dictionary, i.e., a list in which all the parameters that are being analyzed by the sensor and their respective values appear; for example, in the case of the BME680 sensor, a dictionary is displayed for the humidity, pressure, air quality and temperature parameters measured by the sensor. For the complete display of parameter values, it is necessary to implement links by inserting additional nodes, especially in order to individually display values recorded by sensors capable of detecting several parameters simultaneously.

The next step is the crux of this phase: building the node connection that allows the data to be read automatically in the BIM environment as well. The ultimate goal is to be able to display on a particular instance in Autodesk Revit, the value of the parameters measured by the sensor to which it refers. With the "Select Model Element" node, the instance on which we are interested in working is selected, specifically the architectural element on which the sensor is installed, and with the "Element.Parameters" node, a query is performed on all the parameters of the selected mass, and then all the parameters of both type and instance are displayed in the form of a list. To make the actual connection, then, the "Element.SetParameterByName" node is used, which has three inputs and one output. The inputs are Element, which is the element to which the value will be assigned, ParameterName where the name of the parameter will be entered, and finally Value, which is the value obtained from the previous connections. At this point, running the program actually displays, on the 3D model, the values measured and in automatic update (see Fig. 3).

By simply selecting the reference instance of the generic sensor, it is possible to enter the properties panel and read the values for individual parameters, based on the reference sensor. This step, of course, is effective for all installed sensors.

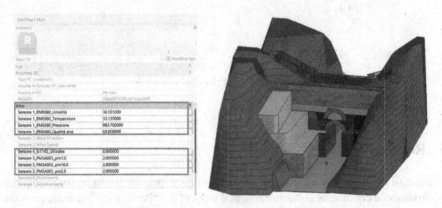

Fig. 3. Data visualization on Revit

4.5 Step 5 – RULE CHAIN

At this point in the workflow, further potentialities of the Thingsboard platform were explored, including that concerning the possibility of creating "alerts" through so-called rule chain. The Rule Chain is a function that allows the creation of a logical sequence of interconnected rule nodes to manage the flow of data and monitor events, and for this reason it can be used in various contexts, especially in management or automation systems. For example, in our research, a rule chain was generated such as to send an "alert," in the form of a warning, when the temperature exceeds a certain value set as a maximum (see Fig. 4). For the creation of this rule chain, a "script" node was chosen that can filter incoming messages according to the function that the user configures. Rules are generally structured in a logical series in which the output can influence the execution of subsequent rules. So, the "script" node filters the data based on the condition processed and returns output information: output "TRUE" if the threshold value is exceeded, which reports to an "alarm" action node, and output "FALSE" instead if there is no exceedance. Rules can be supplemented with additional information in a way that filters the data more accurately as needed, making the rule sequence more complex. For example, Rule Chains can be generated such that alerts can be sent, in different modes, when the temperature exceeds a certain threshold value for ten (or more) consecutive days with a particularly low level of humidity: such an alert can be useful for monitoring drought in the area in order to predict possible damaging events generated by fires in the warmer months.

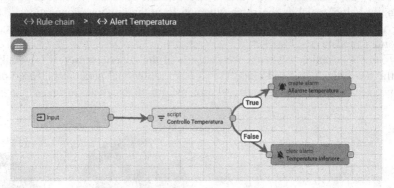

Fig. 4. Example of the used rule chain

5   Results

The aim of the present work, as mentioned above, is to provide a system for monitoring environmental conditions at the monumental work of the "Porta Rosa", in order to enable the implementation of an effective predictive maintenance methodology. This type of maintenance requires continuous analysis of conditions and events, as it is based on the possibility of timely intervention on the structure, before potential damage occurs. For this reason, the proposed methodology is based precisely on the application of the IoT paradigm, which allows a real-time visualization of environmental parameters of interest through DT, the use of sensors and appropriate connections.

The validity of the proposed methodology can be demonstrated through the ability to visualize data in real time, not only in the BIM environment, but also on ThingsBoard, thanks to specially created Dashboards. Each Dashboard provides information that can be visualized numerically through average, maximum and minimum measured values, and through graphs that are explanatory of parameter trends over time.

In the case of the BME680 sensor, for example, the use of data such as temperature and humidity can be very useful in the maintenance of masonry elements to monitor the state of preservation of buildings, identifying any forms of deterioration caused by factors such as excessive water or temperature changes. It is possible to prevent, in this way, the formation of mold or other masonry pathologies, intervening promptly with preventive or corrective actions, so as to ensure greater durability and strength of the structures, preventing greater damage and reducing long-term maintenance costs. In the case of the Porta Rosa of Velia, it is important to monitor that excessive temperatures (above 30–35 °C) are not reached, which can cause the masonry mortars to crack and, likewise, excessive humidity (above 75–80%), which causes the development of mold and mildew, the cause of the disintegration of the material and the formation of cracks or holes in the masonry.

Another example is related to the monitoring of atmospheric particles: atmospheric particulate matter can be very harmful to masonry, since this is a porous material and therefore easily attacked by small particles. In particular, in fact, with the PMSA003 sensor what we want to keep under control is the presence in the air of small particles, less than 10 microns (PM10), since these are the ones that, precisely because of their small size, have the greatest chance of penetrating inside porous materials. In the present case, the ability to monitor the presence of harmful particles in the environment surrounding the Porta Rosa over time may allow for the timely introduction of measures such as regulation of vehicular traffic, reduction of industrial emission, and control of emissions from combustion processes. The benefit is even more appreciable when one considers that the area housing the archaeological park has often been subject to frequent fires: the ability to monitor air quality will, over time, allow one to assess how and to what extent these episodes may affect the health of the facility.

Another parameter that plays a key role in the preservation of the artifact concerns the values recorded by the accelerometer, which allow any vibrations and movements to be kept under control. These can cause structural damage or alterations to the artifact, especially considering the fragile nature of the materials of which it is made. In general, the maximum allowable acceleration limit for masonry buildings is 1.47 m/s2, but for the type of asset under consideration, it is intuitive to conclude that the maximum values of the bearable acceleration will be even lower and, moreover, will depend on its condition of preservation and the type of vibrational event that affects it; the range within which it can be considered to be in a safe state must therefore be assessed through more in-depth structural investigations. Once the latter is established, however, through the system of analysis proposed in this paper, subsequent monitoring steps will certainly be facilitated.

It is evident how, by having up-to-date data in real time, general monitoring of the structure can be achieved, which is basic to introducing appropriate predictive maintenance strategies. The use of sensors allows for accurate and timely environmental and structural measurements and assessments, enabling immediate interventions to be fielded if necessary.

6 Conclusion and Future Outcomes

In conclusion, downstream of the work carried out, the results obtained can be considered satisfactory: the initial objective was to propose a methodology for the control of the Porta Rosa such as to allow the analysis and visualization of environmental parameters in real time, which would be preparatory to the creation of a monitoring system as part of the predictive maintenance of the artifact. This purpose was pursued through the use of IoT paradigm, which, through the use of high-reliability sensors, made possible the creation of a DT on which to visualize changes in environmental conditions in real time. So, through the integration of HBIM-IoT technologies, it was possible to arrive at the creation of a DT that could potentially be used in a variety of application fields, foremost among them predictive maintenance. The further potentiality of this methodology lies in its versatility: the same workflow can be used, for example, in the life cycle of nonheritage structures to make assessments of living comfort but also as support in the design or decommissioning phases. From the methodology presented, the scope for development is very promising. Already in recent years, predictive maintenance has been affected by great strides precisely because of the introduction of technologies that, integrated with the IoT, have made it possible to optimize and make the processes of control and preservation of cultural property increasingly reliable. Continued research in this field, however, will make it possible to make the system even more accurate and reliable. It will be possible, for example, to integrate the system with Machine Learning techniques, which will allow machines to learn from data, draw conclusions or make predictions without the need for them to be given a specific set of instructions. It will be possible to create neural networks, train them through the data made available by the weather station sensors, and use them to genre images that are able to predict trends in environmental parameters and structure conditions. The model, therefore, can be used to simulate future environmental conditions and verify the response of the artifact under study. The latter, moreover, can also be integrated with an automated automated warning system such that it automatically identifies critical thresholds that could lead to damaging scenarios, thus representing a valuable support for all supervision and monitoring operations that would otherwise have to be done manually.

References

1. Cheng, J.C.P., Chen, W., Chen, K., Wang, Q.: Data-driven predictive maintenance planning framework for MEP components based on BIM and IoT using machine learning algorithms. Autom. Constr. **112**, 103087 (2020). https://doi.org/10.1016/j.autcon.2020.103087
2. Di Benedetto, A., Fiani, M.: Integration of LiDAR data into a regional topographic database for the generation of a 3D city model, pp. 193–208 (2022). https://doi.org/10.1007/978-3-031-17439-1_14
3. De Simone, M.C., Lorusso, A., Santaniello, D.: Predictive maintenance and Structural Health Monitoring via IoT system. In: 2022 IEEE Workshop on Complexity in Engineering (COMPENG), pp. 1–4. IEEE (2022). https://doi.org/10.1109/COMPENG50184.2022.9905441
4. Casillo, M., Guida, C.G., Lombardi, M., Lorusso, A., Marongiu, F., Santaniello, D.: Predictive preservation of historic buildings through IoT-based system. In: 2022 IEEE 21st Mediterranean Electrotechnical Conference (MELECON), pp. 1194–1198. IEEE (2022). https://doi.org/10.1109/MELECON53508.2022.9842965
5. Wong, J.K.W., Zhou, J.: Enhancing environmental sustainability over building life cycles through green BIM: a review. Autom. Constr. **57**, 156–165 (2015). https://doi.org/10.1016/j.autcon.2015.06.003
6. Santos, R., Costa, A.A., Silvestre, J.D., Pyl, L.: Integration of LCA and LCC analysis within a BIM-based environment. Autom. Constr. **103**, 127–149 (2019). https://doi.org/10.1016/j.autcon.2019.02.011

7. Lorusso, A., Celenta, G.: Internet of Things in the construction industry: a general overview. In: Karabegovic, I., Kovačević, A., Mandzuka, S. (eds.) New Technologies, Development and Application VI: Volume 1, pp. 577–584. Springer, Cham (2023). https://doi.org/10.1007/978-3-031-31066-9_65

8. Barba, S., di Filippo, A., Limongiello, M., Messina, B.: Integration of active sensors for geometric analysis of the chapel of the holy shroud. In: The International Archives of the Photogrammetry, Remote Sensing and Spatial Information Sciences, vol. XLII-2/W15, pp.149–156 (2019). https://doi.org/10.5194/isprs-archives-XLII-2-W15-149-2019

9. Casillo, M., Colace, F., Gupta, B.B., Lorusso, A., Marongiu, F., Santaniello, D.: A deep learning approach to protecting cultural heritage buildings through IoT-based systems. In: 2022 IEEE International Conference on Smart Computing (SMARTCOMP), pp. 252–256. IEEE (2022). https://doi.org/10.1109/SMARTCOMP55677.2022.00063

10. Lorusso, A., Guida, D.: IoT system for structural monitoring. In: Karabegović, I., Kovačević, A., Mandžuka, S. (eds.) New Technologies, Development and Application V, pp. 599–606. Springer, Cham (2022). https://doi.org/10.1007/978-3-031-05230-9_72

11. Tang, S., Shelden, D.R., Eastman, C.M., Pishdad-Bozorgi, P., Gao, X.: A review of building information modeling (BIM) and the internet of things (IoT) devices integration: present status and future trends. Autom. Constr. **101**, 127–139 (2019). https://doi.org/10.1016/j.autcon.2019.01.020

12. Madakam, S., Ramaswamy, R., Tripathi, S.: Internet of Things (IoT): a literature review. J. Comput. Commun. **03**, 164–173 (2015). https://doi.org/10.4236/jcc.2015.35021

13. Huang, X., Liu, Y., Huang, L., Onstein, E., Merschbrock, C.: BIM and IoT data fusion: the data process model perspective. Autom. Constr. **149**, 104792 (2023). https://doi.org/10.1016/j.autcon.2023.104792

14. Khajavi, S.H., Motlagh, N.H., Jaribion, A., Werner, L.C., Holmstrom, J.: Digital twin: vision, benefits, boundaries, and creation for buildings. IEEE Access **7**, 147406–147419 (2019). https://doi.org/10.1109/ACCESS.2019.2946515

15. Jutraž, A., et al.: Monitoring Environmental and Health Impact Data in BIM Models to Assure Healthy Living Environments, pp. 287–94 (2019). https://doi.org/10.52842/conf.ecaade.2019.2.287

16. Saricaoglu, T., Saygi, G.: Data-driven conservation actions of heritage places curated with HBIM. Virt. Archaeol. Rev. **13**, 17–32 (2022). https://doi.org/10.4995/var.2022.17370

17. Marra, A., Gerbino, S., Greco, A., Fabbrocino, G.: Combining integrated informative system and historical digital twin for maintenance and preservation of artistic assets. Sensors **21**, 5956 (2021). https://doi.org/10.3390/s21175956

18. Jouan, P., Hallot, P.: Digital twin: a Hbim-based methodology to support preventive conservation of historic assets through heritage significance awareness. In: The International Archives of the Photogrammetry, Remote Sensing and Spatial Information Sciences, vol. XLII-2/W15, pp. 609–615 (2019). https://doi.org/10.5194/isprs-archives-XLII-2-W15-609-2019

19. Zhang, J., Kwok, H.H.L., Luo, H., Tong, J.C.K., Cheng, J.C.P.: Automatic relative humidity optimization in underground heritage sites through ventilation system based on digital twins. Build. Environ. **216**, 108999 (2022). https://doi.org/10.1016/j.buildenv.2022.108999

FAUNO: A Machine Learning-Based Methodology for Monitoring and Predictive Maintenance of Structures in Archaeological Parks Through Image Analysis

Francesco Colace[1], Massimo De Santo[1], Rosario Gaeta[1(✉)], Rocco Loffredo[1], and Luigi Petti[2]

[1] Dipartimento di Ingegneria Industriale, DIIN, Università degli Studi di Salerno, Fisciano, Italy
{fcolace,desanto,rgaeta,rloffredo}@unisa.it
[2] Dipartimento di Ingegneria Civile, DICIV, Università degli Studi di Salerno, Fisciano, Italy
petti@unisa.it

Abstract. Archaeological parks represent one of the most important cultural resources for a nation. Archaeological parks safeguard, conserve, manage, and defend their archaeological, architectural, environmental, and landscape heritage. An Archaeological Park experiences very complex operational dynamics: for example, visitors often come into direct contact with artistic artifacts and, even unintentionally, can damage them. In addition, Archaeological Parks are usually outdoors; therefore, their cultural assets are subjected to environmental influences such as rain, wind, sun, and weeds. New technologies can effectively support monitoring activities. This paper will present an approach that aims to identify and classify potential critical issues within an Archaeological Park in an automated manner and to communicate these issues to the various actors in the reference scenarios. The reference scenario for this activity is the Archaeological Park of Pompeii, which cyclically produces high-definition images of its artistic resources using aerial drones. In particular, on a fortnightly basis, high-definition orthophotos of the park and its artistic artifacts are produced. It is understood that the entire operation is time-consuming and does not allow for Real-Time maintenance. Therefore, the research's objective is to automate this process by introducing Machine Learning techniques for automatically identifying and classifying problems in the image and implementing a mechanism for notifying park personnel. The methodology is based on using deep learning systems capable of identifying and classifying potential issues. The YoloV7 library was used to detect the issues in the images.

Keywords: Consumer and industrial application domains · Deep Learning · Image Processing · Predictive Maintenance

© The Author(s), under exclusive license to Springer Nature Switzerland AG 2024
H. Degen and S. Ntoa (Eds.): HCII 2024, LNAI 14735, pp. 342–359, 2024.
https://doi.org/10.1007/978-3-031-60611-3_24

1 Introduction

Protecting cultural and artistic properties is a challenging issue that affects, especially, all those countries that, for historical reasons, are endowed with an extensive and interesting heritage. In particular, the Italian national territory is famous for its significant archaeological remains, historical landscape, and artistic and cultural movable and immovable properties. The purpose of archaeological parks is, in particular, to safeguard, conserve, and manage all this heritage. Actions related to safeguarding and maintaining the archaeological heritage represent one of the most critical aspects of a park's daily activities, especially when it has to monitor many cultural resources or large areas. In the past, all those activities carried out to safeguard the cultural heritage had to be done manually, employing many human resources to identify and adjust any problems in the park and to make decisions about the management of the park.

Artificial Intelligence (AI) and Machine Learning enable a new asset management approach involving deep and rapid data analysis aimed at identifying potential problems and formulating preventive strategies. Using these technologies in any field enables rapid intervention to solve problems immediately after they occur in a way that prevents problems from worsening and new ones from arising.

Applying Machine Learning algorithms and predictive models powered by Artificial Intelligence provides unprecedented decision support. By analyzing complex data from various sources, these tools identify patterns, trends, and areas of concern, enabling the managers of entities and institutions in any field to make informed preservation decisions and tailor strategies to the specific needs of each site.

The evolution in the approaches for collecting and storing large amounts of data and in artificial intelligence, data science, and machine learning techniques has opened up new possibilities for preservation and maintenance purposes in the context of artistic and cultural heritage. Such approaches can be coupled with IoT paradigms that allow the usage of sensors and devices to collect much helpful information regarding cultural properties: for example, the data can be analysed using machine and deep learning approaches in order to preserve such [1], integrating for example data of images and sensors [2].

In particular, the recent impressive advancement in the field of computer vision techniques, both in classification, regression and object detection problems in media broke new ground in the world of identifying issues from images and photos, in particular for the detection of defects and problems into images in cultural heritage context, regarding artworks, monuments and sites: **Sizyakin R. et al.** [3] and **Yuan Q. et al.** [4] propose techniques for detection and segmentation of cracks in painting. Other works are focused on damage and problems identification on buildings like **Wang N. et al.** [5] and **Choi W. et al.** [6]. **Altaweel M. et al.** [7] uses deep learning techniques for the detection of looting on cultural heritage site using RGB images taken from Unmanned aerial vehicles (UAVs), in order to monitor and protect the heritage site.

In such a context, identifying problems within archaeological parks is critical. Typically, archaeological parks are characterized by an extensive area extending hundreds of square kilometres and various structures and buildings requiring periodic inspections and constant maintenance. Indeed, the structures inside archaeological parks are often subjected to rapid deterioration, both for human and natural causes:

- Archaeological parks are visited by hundreds or even thousands of people every days which can damage buildings, structures and artifacts also unintentionally;
- Archaeological parks are outdoors, for this reason they are subject to natural and weather phenomena, like rain, sun, wind and weedy vegetation.

Typical defects and issues caused by such problems must be detected and solved quickly to allow maintenance to fix such problems and avoid more severe problems. However, this is a challenging problem, especially in big archaeological parks, where minor problems can be difficult to detect and solve.

We propose a drone-based system for monitoring and maintaining archaeological parks in such a context.

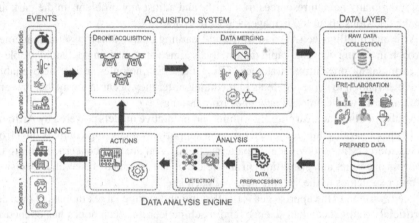

Fig. 1. Archeological Park Monitoring System UAV-Based

In such a system, which can be seen in Fig. 1, the archaeological park is equipped with a series of drones that can be used for aerial surveys, inspection, and monitoring of the area to identify issues in the park. These drones are typically in resting or recharging stations, and they can be activated in their monitoring action at periodic intervals, by sensor events, or by human operators requiring a flyover of the environment. When the drones start their surveys, they make a routine or preset route for collecting photos in a way that covers the entire area of interest. Such images are sent and stored in a database with contextual information coming from sensors and API. All this data from the drones must be collected in a database: the entire chain that allows such collection represents the acquisition part of the system. The data collected in such a way can help infer new knowledge about the state of the park and the issues to be solved. However, during the acquisition phase, the data received may be affected by issues that make their use only recommended with appropriate correction. For example, sensor acquisition can fail and lead to missing or error data in the dataset. Therefore, Preprocessing operations should be carried out to solve or limit these problems. Such operations can be:

- **Data Cleaning:** schema-level or instance-level techniques designed to ensure compliance with a certain Quality of Data (QoD) that must be defined based on the specific problem;

- **Data Integration:** techniques for integrating data of a heterogeneous nature or from various sources;
- **Data Reduction:** techniques for reducing or compressing redundant data;
- **Data Transformation:** aggregation or normalization techniques that often need to be applied for proper use of the predictive models that are fed with these data;
- **Data Imputation:** techniques that aim to reconstruct missing data within datasets or databases. Such reconstruction can be done with rule-based data mining algorithms, statistical techniques, machine learning, or hybrid approaches.

Since, in our case, drones acquire a series of images that can be analysed to find flaws. Also, the addition of geo-referential information can be helpful. After such operation, data are stored and ready to be analysed and used.

The previously acquired and prepared images and contextual data can feed the analysis layer. In particular, the data can be pre-processed to optimize the inference phase: working with aerial images like that of the archaeological park, image equalization, value and orient normalization, super-resolution, and image cleaning operations can be helpful. After such operations, images are given in input to pattern recognition, machine, and deep learning techniques to detect possible issues in the park. Detection aims to identify the typology and position of issues in the park. Since the system works on georeferenced images, the detection is finalized to discover and rapidly solve issues in the ambient. Once the issues are detected, the information coming from the analysis module can be used to perform various actions:

- New surveys can be launched to identify new problem in the area or to better investigate the issues founded;
- The system can automatically activate rovers or actuators to solve a problem identified;
- The system can generate a detailed report of the situation and send it to human operators to go in the place interested by the flaws and prompt solve the problems.

The case study that led to the writing of this paper concerns the archaeological park of Pompeii: Such site, located in the Campania region, with its excavated surface of 44 hectares and 1500 buildings discovered, is one of the biggest and most important archaeological parks in the world.

Such sites use an air drone equipped with a high-definition RGB camera for taking photos of the area. The operators of the sites can fly over the place to take aerial images, which can be very useful in identifying various problems in the park: such an operation typically takes around 15 days to photograph the entire park. After this, the various photos are merged and geometrically corrected ("orthorectified") to create one or two giant photos of the area of the size of the order of various GBs. Obviously, such a process may generate some defects in the photo, which present blurs and low-resolution texture in the zone in which the images are merged and corrected. In the new orthophoto, the scale is uniform, so it can be used to measure accurate distances. After the orthorectification process, the photo is georeferenced: taking three well-known points of reference, each pixel of the area is associated with a coordinate in the Monte Mario 2 reference system: when two photos of the area are created, typically there is a specific grade of overlapping between them.

Given the excellent definition of the original photos, the orthophoto allows us to appreciate the area's features in excellent detail. For this reason, nowadays, such orthophotos are used by the Pompeii site operators to identify problems in the park, manually checking the presence of issues scrolling the entire orthophoto: such operations averagely last 12–15 days, with a detection that is subjected to error. The problem is that identifying such problems is finalized to their fixation, hence the need to have georeferenced photos so operators can repair each issue. However, a problem needs much time to be fixed. In that case, the risk worsens the problem itself or causes more severe problems (for example, if a roof remains broken for too long, adverse weather events such as rain or hail could ruin frescoes of great cultural and artistic value).

For this reason, a system capable of detecting such problems automatically could increase performance and a higher speed in problem identification, intervening faster and being more functional. In such a context, detection means identifying the problem's position in the image and the type of the problem. In particular, the experts in the domain have identified five problems:

- **Water Mounds:** typically basins carved by water on floor or roofs and that generate infiltrations;
- **Weedy Vegetation:** vegetation defacing and ruining structures in the park;
- **Damaged Conduits:** ruined conduits on flat roofs that must be repaired;
- **Fallen Elements:** breakage and rubble falling from park structures;
- **Disconnected Elements:** typically tiles and roofs breaks of various material and type.

So, in such a context, our work aims to detect these problems in the vast aerial images. In our context, some difficulties in detection are characterized by the fact that any techniques we apply must work on images of enormous dimensions (nowadays, there are no machine learning techniques or neural networks capable of operating on images on the order of various gigabytes). Also, the problems to be identified are heterogeneous and typically cannot be identified as objects because they are characterized by pixel patterns that do not have a fixed shape and pixel patterns that can be identified as a problem only in some contexts (for example, vegetation is a problem only on some context). Moreover, aerial images are typically affected by shades and light conditions that vary widely.

2 Related Works

As described in Introduction, the developing of artificial intelligence and learning methods allowed many applications also in the cultural heritage context. In particular, in the context of archaeological parks, literature goes in direction of the discovery of sites, historical buildings, structures and other entities [8, 9] or of the identifications of issues, like crack segmentation [10] or looting detection [7].

However, from our analysis, the literature is lacking in terms of identifying issues in cultural heritage context from RGB images. Since in an Archaeological Park the problems that can be detected are of various nature, the approaches that can be followed can be specific for a certain problem. For this reason, starting from the 5 classes of problems which have been identified based on the classes defined by the experts of the site. we define the state of the art of detection approaches applied to each of the problem identified:

2.1 Water Mounds

Considering the papers which analyses issues detection in archaeological park, nothing of these considers the detection of water accumulations or mounds in such type of sites. Despite this, there are some papers which propose methods for the detection of water mounds in ground and agricultural context, which is very similar to the problems which can occur in an archaeological park. In particular, **Bouachir et al.** [11] proposes a supervised system for counting mounds in plantation performing detection based on an object proposal and a CNN model for classification which processes aerial multispectral images obtained to an altitude of 100 m; after the work group together with other authors proposes another system [12] uses YoloV3 detector trained on objects present in six orthomosaics divided in batches and annotated with 9661 mounds.

2.2 Weedy Vegetation

Weedy vegetation and alien plant invasions is a problem that is addressed in various context: **Dvorak et al.** [13] uses UAV images for a fast and efficient monitoring of alien plant testing various detection and classification approach object and pixel based. **Yadav et al.** [14] uses an approach for greenery region detection for smart cities which performs color and texture (Gray-Level Co-Occurrence Matrix (GLCM) and LBP) feature extraction, followed by a logistic regression model and boundary extraction methods. **Wang et al.** [15] propose a deep learning segmentation method for the detection of alien plant invasion, in particular *Solanum rostratum*. They processes images acquired by an UAV with a network based on U-Net convolutional neural network, named DeepSolanum-Net.

2.3 Damaged Conduits

In the context of identification of damaged flat roof, **Yudin et al.** [16] proposed a deep learning neural network based system for the segmentation of flat roof defect in aerial image: they categorize also the type of defect as "hollows", "swelling", "folds", "patches" and "breaks" and work on 6400. They perform segmentation comparing U-NetMCT, DeepLabV3+ and HRNet+OCR. The work of **Pi et al.** [17] performs detection and semantic segmentation of images of roofs after disasters. They uses two architecture of convolutional neural network for semantic segmentation, performing data augmentation to preserve data balance.

2.4 Disconnected Elements

Disconnected elements is a class which refers in general to damaged tiles and roofs. In the context of cultural heritage such problem has not been yet considered. However such problem is one of the most critical because if some roof is broken, rain wind and other weather phenomenon can damage frescoes and other cultural properties. The problem of damaged roofs and tiles is instead actively considered in the context of post disaster damage identification, which is a very similar problem. **Jing et al.** [18] uses YoloV5 for the identification of damaged roofs and houses after earthquake event: in particular they train YoloV5 with 400 image samples with 860 damaged houses in various conditions (houses collapsed, partially collapsed or with roofs cracks). **Pi et al.** [19] uses a CNN based on YOLO trained on Volan2018 dataset (65,580 frames of aerial videos taken by UAVs) to detect post disaster effect, included damaged and undamaged roofs.

2.5 Fallen Elements

This classes considers are broken bricks, stone pieces of wall and other types of debris fallen on the grounds that must be detected to be removed or fixed. In our knowledge, such types of issue in cultural heritage and aerial images context have not been addressed yet, however similar problems have been considered.

Bak et al. [20] uses UAV and deep learning for the detection and monitoring of beach litter and debris: they propose a case of study in Heungnam beach in which they use SegNet, developed by the University of Cambridge, to perform litter detection on image acquired by a MAVIC 2 PRO equipped with a 20 MP camera. In particular after the acquisition of images by the UAV an orthoimage is obtained and divided in 224 × 224 patches size which are after processed by the neural network. **Alam et al.** [21] uses deep learning for the detection of debris on the road using UAV images. They use faster R-CNN for object detection on images video acquired with DJI Mavic Mini equipped with a 12 MP camera. **Munyer et al.** [22] performs Foreign object debris detection on airport pavements. The deep learning model is trained using images collected in an airport by a Unmanned aerial system (UAS). They uses an autoencoder to perform localization segmentation and obtain bounding boxes of the detected object. Than a supervised classification architecture is used.

3 Proposed Methodology

With this paper we are particular interested in the developing of the Data Analysis Engine and, in particular, in a methodology for identifying issues in an Orthophoto of an archaeological site.

The approach we designed in Fig. 2 takes into input a georeferenced orthophoto of the archaeological park: such an orthophoto can represent the whole site or only a single section. Since such orthophotos typically have a considerable size (thousands of pixels in width and height), there are no detection algorithms capable of processing such images. For this reason, a Batch Generator module is proposed. Such a module takes the entire orthophoto in input and divides this orthophoto into smaller images, applying a sliding window on the original photo in X and Y coordinates. The images must be split with a specific grade of overlap both in X and Y directions to be sure that the border objects are not lost because they are divided into two different images: both size and grade of overlap must be chosen by the implementers. Each image obtained by the split must be georeferenced like the original orthophoto. At this point the dataset with all the images is created and such images are given to a preprocessing module. Such module focus on increasing the quality of the images, removing defect eventually present and to make easier for a deep learning algorithm to detect some problems. In the context of our work useful approach can be to use techniques capable of remove various type of noise from the images (Gaussian and Blur Noise), techniques for dark zone and shadow removal like histogram equalization, and super resolution techniques to improve the resolution of the images.

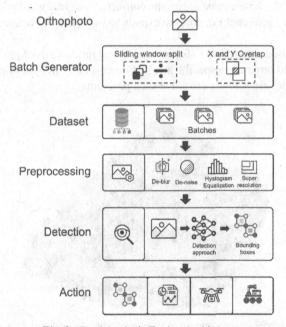

Fig. 2. Data Analysis Engine Architecture

After the images are given in input to one or more object detection models. The main objective of a detector is to identify the position of some object or entity inside the image and classify them. To do this such a detector will attempt to identify a bounding box for each object or entity inside the photo (this will give the position of the object inside the image), and for each bounding box the class of belonging is identified. In this architecture, the technique to be used could be traditional, based, for example, on feature extraction, or deep learning two-shot or single shot detectors.

Once all the images have been processed and all the objects have been identified the coordinates, of the bounding box are converted from the image coordinate system into the coordinate system of the real world in which the orthophoto has been georeferenced.

In this way such information is usable to identify where the problems is located inside the park.

The last module is the action module which uses the information and bounding boxes in the images to generate all the action necessary for the maintenance of the park. This module gives in output an orthophoto with all the bounding boxes which identify the issues found in all the area considered by the orthophoto.

In addition, a report is generated which can be consulted by the human operators of the park in order to fix the issues. For this reason the report must contain all the information useful for the operators to reach the problems and solve it. The report will have a general introduction which summarize the issues detected in the park and a section for each class of the problem. Each problem detected will have an image of the problem, so as the operators can assess the problem, and the coordinates of the problem, also in the form of a google maps or street view link detected. For such reasons the object that were detected in the image must always be converted into real word coordinate (Monte Mario 2 system of reference) in order to explain to the operators where they must go to do their job.

The information inferred can also be used to trigger new overflights of the area but more detailed and targeted to specific areas of interest (also in light of problems noted) or to trigger automatic actuators to solve such problems.

Fig. 3. Orthophoto of a portion of Pompeii Archaeological park in April 2022

4   Case of Study

In this article we bring the case of the archaeological park of Pompeii as an example of application of the designed system to a real archaeological site. This step will describe the available dataset and a demonstrator of the system described in Sect. 3.

4.1 Dataset

The dataset considered has been collected inside the area of the archaeological park of Pompeii. In particular, a series of recon flights has been performed using an UAV equipped with a camera in order to collect images of the site.

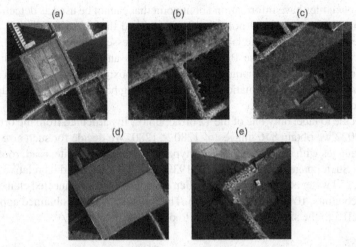

Fig. 4. Type of problems identified: (a) damaged conduits, (b) weedy vegetation, (c) water mounds, (d) disconnected elements, (e) fallen elements

Flights are conducted monthly and from each flight an orthophoto of the entire area scanned is taken, typically each month two orthophotos are produced with a certain grade of overlap. As part of this work we were provided with 6 pairs of orthophotos, for April (Fig. 3), July August, September and two pairs for November (one before and one after an event that was held in the park, in such a way as to survey the damage caused by that event).

For each image, the expert of the domain have identified 5 problems Fig. 4:

- **Water Accumulation:** typically basins carved by water on floor or roofs and that generate infiltrations;
- **Weedy Vegetation:** vegetation defacing and ruining structures in the park;
- **Damaged Conduits:** ruined conduits on flat roofs that must be repaired;
- **Fallen Elements:** breakage and rubble falling from park structures;
- **Disconnected Elements:** typically breaks on tiles and roofs of various material and type.

Since our objective is to train a deep learning-based object detector to identify the issues in the park, we need as many images as possible to create a representative dataset of the problems under consideration. The images of the dataset must be in a dimension that is processable by an algorithm; for this reason, to create a dataset usable in the training and test phase, we must split the orthophoto into smaller images. Such images must be labeled in a format usable by a detector, i.e., a bounding box characterized by top-left and bottom-right vertices or top-left vertex plus the width and height of the box together with the class of the object inside the bounding box. The UAV users labeled the issues inside the photo with points positioned in the issue area using QGIS, creating a.gpkg file with a series of information regarding the position (in Monte-Mario 2 coordinate) and the zone in which the problem is. QGIS has also been used for the georeferencing process.

Such *.gpkg* files have information about point that cannot be used as detection label, because in detection we need bounding boxes around the object to identify. For this reason the orthophotos and the labels have been processed in order to create a dataset usable in this context. We use Python with *Rasterio* and *Gdal* library to divide the orthophotos and convert each point into a bounding box: each images is than given in input to *labelme* and the automatic generated bounding boxes are manually adjusted to fit the object considered.

We decide to label only one of the 12 orthophotos: in particular, from the orthophoto of April 2022 we obtain 846 images of 1280 × 1280. We decide for such size in order to obtain images with an evidence of each type of structure in the site, road, roofs, green space etc.. Such images are labelled with 1939 bounding boxes and its relative class. In particular, 224 water accumulation, 304 fallen elements, 100 disconnected elements, 310 damaged conduits, 1001 weedy vegetation. The images have been obtained applying an overlap of 0.5 to the sliding window used to obtain the batches.

4.2   Data Augmentation

Since we typically have a couple of thousands of images, we decided to operate data augmentation to increase the number of examples given to our model. In particular, during the training phase, we use Yolo data augmentation to apply a series of modifications to the image to avoid overfitting as much as possible and to make the model stronger to any variation the images can have during the acquisition.

We use color-oriented data augmentation based on an edit of hue saturation or/and the value of an image to make the network more robust and more reliable when there are changes in light intensity and color [23] during UAV surveys.

We also randomly apply an image translation of 20% and a rotation of ±90° and a scaling in the images with a gain of 0.5.

Left and right flipping is also applied with a probability of 50%.

Also a mosaic based augmentation with a probability of 0.5.

Such augmentation approaches are randomly applied for the network training to give images that are as different as possible during epochs and thus give as many examples to the network as possible. In the end, such an approach can give a network with a high grade of robustness if it is used to predict results in a configuration that is different from the one in which it is trained.

4.3 Experimental Phase

With this paper we are particular interested in the developing of a system capable of performing the automatic detection of issues in an archaeological park based on the classes of issues described in the dataset. For this reason we propose a demonstrator of an issues detector obtained from the single shot object detector Yolo training [24]. In particular, we have used the state of the art YoloV7 model [25] to train an issues detector capable of identifying the problem in the archaeological park. YoloV7 is made available as a GitHub library together with a series of declination of such model and weights obtained training such model on the MS Coco dataset [26]. We use pretrained *YoloV7-tiny* model and with a fine tuning approach we decide to train this model on our problem. We choose this architecture for its lightness and simplicity compared to other V7 model fit very well our case in which we do not have many data to fine tune a complex deep learning architecture. We train the network with 1280×1280 size images.

The network used for the proposed demonstrator has been trained using an Adam Optimizer with a beta1 momentum based of 0.90 an initial learning rate 0 ($lr0$) of 0.001 and a learning rate final of 0.05. The final learning rate at the end of a cycle will be ($lr0 \cdot lrf$). The network have been trained with a *weight_decay* of 0.0005 and an initial *warmup momentum* of 0.8. A *warmup initial bias learning rate* of 0.1 was used.

For the training phase we train our network for 500 epochs using the 80% of the images described in the dataset section. The remain 20% has been divided in 50% validation and 50% test.

During the training phase, data augmentation described in sub Sect. 4.2 is applied, since in each epoch some or all the augmentation techniques can be applied randomly to the images used to feed the network. In Fig. 5 two training images are shown in which data augmentation has been applied, in particular mosaic, color based and translation data augmentation.

Fig. 5. Example of training images with data augmentation

After the training phase, we have a model that can predict the issues in an orthophoto. The idea is to use this model to predict the archaeological park's problems automatically. Once an orthophoto of the archaeological park is created after an aerial survey of the UAV squad, such orthophoto can be given in input to the analysis system, which divides the orthophoto into various images that, after a preprocessing phase, are analyzed by the trained model. Such a model processes each image and outputs a bounding box for each detected issue together with a class of membership and with the confidence of the model in such class.

In Fig. 6 an example of a test image elaborated by the network is given. The network successfully identifies a damaged conduit and a weedy vegetation in such cases. In a case like this, the system we propose would be handy because such type of elaboration and detection is performed on georeferenced images, so a report of the position of such a problem could be presented to the maintainers of the site to help them fix such problem right away. Without a system like this, these problems must be searched manually in aerial images or with periodic inspections, significantly slowing the identification of problems. This highlights the great utility that a system we are proposing can have.

Fig. 6. Example of test image elaborated by the network

However, it can also be noticed that in the same picture, less severe damaged conduits are not detected and that the problems identified are identified with low confidence. In our case, low confidence is not a big problem since our system is thought of as a system in which humans are at the center of the loop. Once the system has detected the problem, it must assess its actual presence and its severity to decide how to intervene. In addition, we are interested in a system with high recall, even at a cost of relatively low precision.

By the way, the poor performance at the detection level and low confidence can be attributed to the fact that we have a small dataset and a strong unbalance in the label classes. Such problems can be thus reduced with the proper arrangement.

In Fig. 7 an example of images with detected weedy vegetation issues is shown. As can be seen, a series of weedy vegetation samples are correctly detected. Indeed, from a qualitative analysis of the test dataset, we notice that the system behaves quite well, compared with the other problems, in detecting the weedy vegetation class. This result does not surprise us as it is the class with the highest presence. Even with damaged conduits, the network performs quite well while it struggles in the remaining classes.

In Fig. 8 an example of water mounds detected and fallen elements is given, showing how the network can detect various issues. However, from our analysis, we notice how the network often misses this type of class and also disconnected elements. Since these problems are mainly with the least present classes, i.e., water accumulations and disconnected elements, these problems most likely can be caused by a lack of data from these classes.

From our analysis we notice that the network is strongly influenced by shadows, which can be interpreted as wrong issues (especially in case of water mounds).

Fig. 7. Examples of images with detected weedy vegetation

Fig. 8. Examples of images with water mounds and fallen elements

In Fig. 9 a confusion matrix of the test set is created. As can be seen, the model give correct prediction rates of 88% for weedy vegetation, 82 for fallen elements, 94 for disconnected elements, 100 for water mounds and 86 for damaged conduit. The remaining percentage of sample for each class is not detected by the model. From the confusion matrix we see that many real background object are considered weedy vegetation: indeed, analysing the test set we notice that actually some alien plants were not labelled in the dataset.

As can be seen, the results given by the network are encouraging, considering the small dataset. The network behaved excellently in many cases, even identifying details (especially in the case of climbing vegetation and water accumulation) that had not been labelled in the dataset but were present. However, often the network is confused by shadows and misses many issues: this can due to the small dataset and poor number of samples in the training set. So, although the method needs refinement and more investigation, the results bode well for future improvements and applicability.

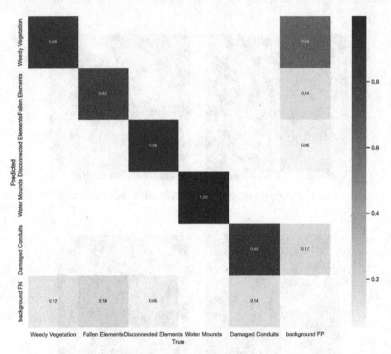

Fig. 9. Confusion Matrix on the test set

5   Conclusions

In this paper, we propose a system for managing and safeguarding an archaeological park, one of Italy's most critical cultural heritage resources. We propose a drone-based architecture composed of a module capable of acquiring images and information about the park periodically or on the base of some event (triggered by other systems or humans). The information acquired can be used by a second module, which analyzes the data coming from the acquisition phase to find automatically issues in the park. Such information is then helpful to act in feedback on the acquisition module to launch new drone surveys, trigger automatic actions by actuators, or generate reports useful for maintainers to troubleshoot park problems.

After we focus on the definition of a general architecture for the analysis module, which divides the orthophoto of the park that must be given in input, and after a preprocess, use traditional or deep learning techniques in order to detect some problems in the park, determining the position and classes of issues in the images of the park.

We describe our case study based on the archaeological park of Pompeii. We used a dataset of images acquired by a UAV that collected photos of the whole park of Pompeii, and we labeled, with the support of some experts, five classes of issues in the park. Such a dataset has been used to train and test a YoloV7 model to detect issues in the park in an automatic way. Data augmentation has been performed to obtain a model characterized by better robustness and less subject to overfitting.

However, although results give hope for the applicability of an automatic method based on deep learning for identifying issues in images of archaeological parks, only a preliminary attempt at experimentation has been made so far, and the method has been shown to need further refinement.

For future development, we aim to label a larger dataset from the remaining orthophotos of the Pompeii archaeological park that we have available. More will be done on the preprocessing techniques to be adopted to optimize the images in such a way as to clean them of shadows and defects in georeferencing and merging.

The results of various detection models, will be analytically evaluated, and the chosen method will be incorporated into a larger system that will represent the implementation of the Data Analysis Engine architecture presented in Fig. 2.

We found the results obtained so far encouraging for continuing the research in this area, considering also the vital interest of park operators in our proposed system.

Acknowledgments. The authors would like to thank the archaeological park of Pompeii for their precious collaboration, for the images from which the dataset was obtained and the material provided that allowed the writing of this work.

References

1. Colace, F., Elia, C., Guida, C.G., Lorusso, A., Marongiu, F., Santaniello, D.: An IoT-based framework to protect cultural heritage buildings. In: Proceedings - 2021 IEEE International Conference on Smart Computing, SMARTCOMP 2021, Institute of Electrical and Electronics Engineers Inc., August 2021, pp. 377–382 (2021). https://doi.org/10.1109/SMARTCOMP52413.2021.00076

2. Casillo, M., Colace, F., Gupta, B.B., Lorusso, A., Marongiu, F., Santaniello, D.: A deep learning approach to protecting cultural heritage buildings through IoT-based systems. In: Proceedings - 2022 IEEE International Conference on Smart Computing, SMARTCOMP 2022, Institute of Electrical and Electronics Engineers Inc., pp. 252–256 (2022). https://doi.org/10.1109/SMARTCOMP55677.2022.00063

3. Sizyakin, R., Cornelis, B., Meeus, L., Voronin, V., Pizurica, A.: A two-stream neural network architecture for the detection and analysis of cracks in panel paintings (2020). https://doi.org/10.1117/12.2555857

4. Yuan, Q., He, X., Han, X., Guo, H.: Automatic recognition of craquelure and paint loss on polychrome paintings of the Palace Museum using improved U-Net. Herit. Sci. **11**(1) (2023). https://doi.org/10.1186/s40494-023-00895-7

5. Wang, N., Zhao, X., Wang, L., Zou, Z.: Novel system for rapid investigation and damage detection in cultural heritage conservation based on deep learning. J. Infrastruct. Syst. **25**(3) (2019). https://doi.org/10.1061/(asce)is.1943-555x.0000499

6. Choi, W.Y., Park, J.W., Lee, S.Y.: GAN based deep learning model for detecting damage and displacement of cultural asset. In: 2021 IEEE International Conference on Consumer Electronics-Asia, ICCE-Asia 2021 (2021). https://doi.org/10.1109/ICCE-Asia53811.2021.9641996

7. Altaweel, M., Khelifi, A., Shana'ah, M.M.: Monitoring looting at cultural heritage sites: applying deep learning on optical unmanned aerial vehicles data as a solution. Soc. Sci. Comput. Rev. (2023). https://doi.org/10.1177/08944393231188471

8. Trier, Ø.D., Reksten, J.H., Løseth, K.: Automated mapping of cultural heritage in Norway from airborne lidar data using faster R-CNN. Int. J. Appl. Earth Observ. Geoinf. **95** (2021). https://doi.org/10.1016/j.jag.2020.102241

9. Anttiroiko, N., et al.: Detecting the archaeological traces of tar production kilns in the northern boreal forests based on airborne laser scanning and deep learning. Remote Sens. (Basel) **15**(7) (2023). https://doi.org/10.3390/rs15071799

10. Zhang, Y., Zhang, Z., Zhao, W., Li, Q.: Crack segmentation on earthen heritage site surfaces. Appl. Sci. (Switzerland) **12**(24) (2022). https://doi.org/10.3390/app122412830

11. Bouachir, W., Ihou, K.E., Gueziri, H.E., Bouguila, N., Belanger, N.: Computer vision system for automatic counting of planting microsites using UAV imagery. IEEE Access **7** (2019). https://doi.org/10.1109/ACCESS.2019.2923765

12. Zgaren, A., Bouachir, W., Bouguila, N.: Automatic counting of planting microsites via local visual detection and global count estimation. IEEE Trans. Emerg. Top Comput. Intell. **7**(6) (2023). https://doi.org/10.1109/TETCI.2023.3272004

13. Dvořák, P., Müllerová, J., Bartaloš, T., Brůna, J.: Unmanned aerial vehicles for alien plant species detection and monitoring. In: International Archives of the Photogrammetry, Remote Sensing and Spatial Information Sciences - ISPRS Archives (2015). https://doi.org/10.5194/isprsarchives-XL-1-W4-83-2015

14. Yadav, D., Choksi, M., Zaveri, M.A.: Supervised Learning based Greenery region detection using Unnamed Aerial Vehicle for Smart City Application. In: 2019 10th International Conference on Computing, Communication and Networking Technologies, ICCCNT 2019 (2019). https://doi.org/10.1109/ICCCNT45670.2019.8944548

15. Wang, Q., et al.: An image segmentation method based on deep learning for damage assessment of the invasive weed Solanum rostratum Dunal. Comput. Electron. Agric. **188** (2021). https://doi.org/10.1016/j.compag.2021.106320

16. Yudin, D.A., Adeshkin, V., Dolzhenko, A.V., Polyakov, A., Naumov, A.E.: Roof defect segmentation on aerial images using neural networks. Stud. Comput. Intell. (2021). https://doi.org/10.1007/978-3-030-60577-3_20

17. Pi, Y., Nath, N.D., Behzadan, A.H.: Detection and semantic segmentation of disaster damage in UAV footage. J. Comput. Civil Eng. **35**(2) (2021). https://doi.org/10.1061/(asce)cp.1943-5487.0000947

18. Jing, Y., Ren, Y., Liu, Y., Wang, D., Yu, L.: Automatic extraction of damaged houses by earthquake based on improved YOLOv5: a case study in Yangbi. Remote Sens. (Basel) **14**(2) (2022). https://doi.org/10.3390/rs14020382

19. Pi, Y., Nath, N.D., Behzadan, A.H.: Convolutional neural networks for object detection in aerial imagery for disaster response and recovery. Adv. Eng. Inform. **43** (2020). https://doi.org/10.1016/j.aei.2019.101009

20. Bak, S.H., Hwang, D.H., Kim, H.M., Yoon, H.J.: Detection and monitoring of beach litter using UAV image and deep neural network. In: International Archives of the Photogrammetry, Remote Sensing and Spatial Information Sciences - ISPRS Archives (2019). https://doi.org/10.5194/isprs-archives-XLII-3-W8-55-2019

21. Alam, H., Valles, D.: Debris object detection caused by vehicle accidents using UAV and deep learning techniques. In: 2021 IEEE 12th Annual Information Technology, Electronics and Mobile Communication Conference, IEMCON 2021 (2021). https://doi.org/10.1109/IEMCON53756.2021.9623110

22. Munyer, T., Brinkman, D., Zhong, X., Huang, C., Konstantzos, I.: Foreign object debris detection for airport pavement images based on self-supervised localization and vision transformer. In: Proceedings - 2022 International Conference on Computational Science and Computational Intelligence, CSCI 2022 (2022). https://doi.org/10.1109/CSCI58124.2022.00249

23. Qiu, Z., Rong, S., Ye, L.: YOLF-ShipPnet: improved RetinaNet with pyramid vision transformer. Int. J. Comput. Intell. Syst. **16**(1) (2023). https://doi.org/10.1007/s44196-023-00235-4

24. Redmon, J., Divvala, S., Girshick, R., Farhadi, A.: You only look once: unified, real-time object detection. In: Proceedings of the IEEE Computer Society Conference on Computer Vision and Pattern Recognition (2016). https://doi.org/10.1109/CVPR.2016.91

25. Wang, C.-Y., Bochkovskiy, A., Liao, H.-Y.M.: YOLOv7: Trainable Bag-of-Freebies Sets New State-of-the-Art for Real-Time Object Detectors (2023). https://doi.org/10.1109/cvpr52729.2023.00721

26. Lin, T.-Y., et al.: Microsoft COCO: common objects in context. In: Fleet, D., Pajdla, T., Schiele, B., Tuytelaars, T. (eds.) ECCV 2014. LNCS, vol. 8693, pp. 740–755. Springer, Cham (2014). https://doi.org/10.1007/978-3-319-10602-1_48

ChatLsc: Agents for Live Streaming Commerce

Chengjie Dai[1], Ke Fang[1], Pufeng Hua[1], and Wai Kin (Victor) Chan[2(✉)]

[1] Interactive Media Design and Technology Center, Shenzhen International Graduate School, Tsinghua University, Shenzhen, China
dcj21@mails.tsinghua.edu.cn
[2] Tsinghua-Berkeley Shenzhen Institute, Shenzhen International Graduate School, Tsinghua University, Shenzhen, China
chanw@sz.tsinghua.edu.cn

Abstract. Live-streaming commerce refers to a form of e-commerce that uses live streaming as a channel to achieve marketing objectives, a product of the bidirectional integration of live streaming and commerce in the digital era. However, utilizing large language models for sales in live-streaming commerce faces the challenge of low interaction quality. In this paper, we introduce ChatLsc, a Vtuber designed for live-streaming commerce. Drawing inspiration from leadership behaviors in human societies, we assign different identities and capabilities to agents and encourage their collaboration. In the preparation phase, leaders plan and prepare for the upcoming broadcast based on initial information received from humans. During the live streaming phase, ChatLsc perceives audience comments in real-time through the collaboration of observers, creators, broadcasters, and leaders, combining these with past live streaming activities to generate visual and auditory feedback for the audience. We demonstrate how to use LLMs to interact with audiences in real-time live-streaming commerce, revealing the potential of LLMs for new commercial applications.

Keywords: Human-AI Interaction · Agents · Large language models · Live-streaming

1 Introduction

Live-streaming commerce (LSC) refers to a form of online commerce that utilizes live streaming as a channel to achieve marketing objectives. It is a product of the integration between live streaming and commerce in the context of the digital era. With the advent of the 5G era, live streaming technology has been widely applied, and the prevalence of mobile devices has enabled consumers to watch live broadcasts anytime and anywhere. A statistic from China Internet Network Information Center shows that, by June 2023, 48.8% of Chinese Internet users, 526 million people, had participated in LSC [3].

Compared to traditional commerce, live-streaming commerce offers greater interactivity. As illustrated in Fig. 1, consumers can ask the broadcaster

© The Author(s), under exclusive license to Springer Nature Switzerland AG 2024
H. Degen and S. Ntoa (Eds.): HCII 2024, LNAI 14735, pp. 360–372, 2024.
https://doi.org/10.1007/978-3-031-60611-3_25

Fig. 1. ChatLsc, a vtuber designed for live-streaming commerce. With the initial information about the live session, ChatLsc can adequately prepare for the broadcast and engage in real-time interaction with the audience during the live stream.

questions in real time, gain information about products, and receive immediate feedback. For consumers, there is an increasing demand each year. The traditional e-commerce model has become relatively limited, with consumers desiring to purchase higher-quality products in a shorter time span. From the perspective of the e-commerce industry, factors such as the COVID-19 pandemic have brought about significant changes to online retail. The surge in consumer demand has provided new traffic and consumption outlets for businesses and platforms.

In recent years, large language models (LLMs) have achieved significant accomplishments in the field of natural language processing and have demonstrated commendable performance in a wide range of downstream tasks, such as context-based question answering, text translation, and code generation. Additionally, in social scenarios, large language models have also shown exemplary performance. Similar to simulations of human life, intelligent agents driven by large language models exhibit unique personalities and develop through interactions with the environment and other agents [9,10] (Fig. 2). However, in real-time complex social contexts like live-streaming commerce, agents powered by large language models still face several challenges, such as inconsistencies in interactions over extended live sessions.

To address these challenges, we introduce ChatLsc, a vtuber designed for live-streaming commerce. During both the preparation and live streaming phases, ChatLsc employs multiple agents to play different roles, such as leaders, observers, creators, and broadcasters, to complete specific tasks in different periods. Leadership provides a better pathway for all agents to cooperate, thereby maintaining consistency and continuity during the live stream. In the

Fig. 2. Examples of vtubers for live streaming commerce.

preparation phase, ChatLsc receives initial information from humans and uses it to plan and prepare for the upcoming live stream. During the live streaming phase, ChatLsc employs an interactive framework to facilitate collaboration among leaders, observers, creators, and broadcasters. This framework is designed to perceive audience comments, assess the quality of interactions, and generate visual and auditory feedback for the audience. Preliminary experiments indicate that our approach contributes to the creation of credible, high-quality real-time live streaming interactions.

Our contributions can be summarized as follows:

- We propose ChatLsc, a vtuber designed for live-streaming commerce. With the initial information about the live session, ChatLsc can adequately prepare for the broadcast and engage in real-time interaction with the audience during the live stream.
- We have developed a leadership system and an interaction value assessment to ensure consistency and stability in ChatLsc's live stream, and to enhance the quality of live-streaming interactions.
- Our experiments demonstrate that through leadership and collaboration among agents, ChatLsc is capable of generating credible and high-quality real-time live-streaming interactions.

2   Related Work

Live-Streaming Commerce. Live-streaming commerce is an online retail model that integrates live streaming technology with electronic commerce functions. It allows sellers to showcase products to audiences via live video broadcasts and provides instant purchasing options. This model breaks the boundaries of traditional commerce, offering consumers an immersive shopping experience and fostering more personal relationships [5,20]. Research related to live streaming predominantly focuses on the characteristics of live streaming and the motivations behind consumer participation [2,18,24]. Based on the Stimulus-Organism-Response (SOR) model, the perceived value of live shopping acts as a stimulus, influencing consumer trust in products and merchants, thereby encouraging greater participation in live streams [21]. The personalization, authenticity, and reciprocity brought about by real-time interaction have been proven to positively impact the engagement level in live-streaming commerce, suggesting that merchants can enhance sales effectiveness through real-time interaction [22]. Our work has enhanced the capabilities of vtubers for intelligent real-time interaction, thereby improving the effectiveness of ChatLsc's live-streaming commerce.

LLM-Based Agent. Agents possess four core attributes: autonomy, reactivity, proactivity, and sociability. First, leveraging the powerful natural language capabilities of large language models, agents can perceive their environment and take appropriate actions based on changes. Second, large language models enable agents to engage in autonomous exploration and decision-making through creative natural language generation, accomplishing tasks without the need for human intervention and guidance [4,25]. Third, existing research indicates that with technologies like thought chains, large language models demonstrate exceptional reasoning and planning abilities. This facilitates task decomposition and the adjustment of strategies according to the environment [16,17,19]. Lastly, agents based on large language models exhibit social behaviors such as cooperation and competition, effectively enhancing task efficiency [12]. Additionally, large language models can also perform role-playing, simulating social phenomena in the real world [13]. Therefore, our work employs an LLM-based agent as the core to simulate real human interactive behaviors in live-streaming activities.

Multi-agents Coordination. Multi-agents coordination Based on the natural language capabilities of large language models, communication between agents has become more elegant and easier to understand, leading to a significant leap in interaction efficiency. With specialized division of labor and efficient collaboration, multiple agents can complete a larger workload compared to non-specialized scenarios, significantly improving the overall system's efficiency and output quality [1,6,14,15,23]. Specifically, interactions among agents involve both cooperative and adversarial methods [7,8,11]. In cooperative interactions, agents actively seek collaborative actions and information sharing, with CAMEL being a successful implementation of orderly assistance [12]. In the CAMEL role-playing communication framework, two agents play the roles of an AI user issuing commands and an AI assistant providing solutions. They engage in natural language dialogues in turns, autonomously collaborating to fulfill user commands. In our work, agents are assigned different roles, and they cooperate with each other to fulfill their responsibilities and tasks.

3   Methodology

We focus on how to realize human-like commerce Vtubers through multi-agent systems. Currently, the interaction quality of commerce Vtubers is subpar, possibly due to delayed, unintelligent responses, or even incorrect information, negatively impacting the overall live-streaming experience. To address these shortcomings, we studied real-world live-streaming commerce scenarios and introduced a Vtuber-ChatLsc. As shown in Fig. 3, ChatLsc comprises agents with different responsibilities and authorities, such as leaders, observers, creators, and broadcasters. When ChatLsc conducts live-streaming activities, these agents collaborate to perceive audience comments and generate visual and auditory feedback for the audience. ChatLsc utilizes large language models as its decision-making core, enabling the agents to simulate human live-streaming broadcasters in real-time activities without the need for fine-tuning the model.

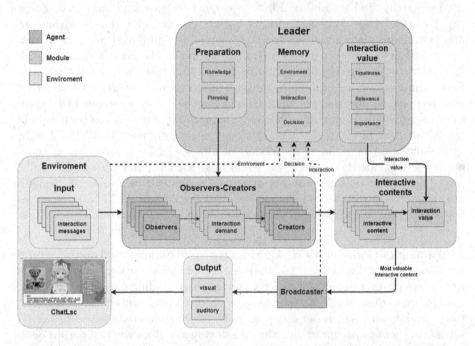

Fig. 3. ChatLsc is composed of agents with different responsibilities and authorities, such as leaders, observers, creators, and broadcasters. During a live broadcast, observers monitor various interaction information throughout the process, creators generate live broadcast content text based on the broadcast plan and audience interaction, broadcasters primarily transform text content into visual and auditory information, while leaders oversee the overall situation, outline the direction and plan of work, and coordinate cooperation among other agents.

3.1 Leadership

Based on the operational mode of human broadcasters, ChatLsc adopts a work-flow similar to real-life broadcasters. Real-time interaction with audience comments during a live broadcast requires firstly perceiving the audience's comments. Subsequently, it involves generating interactive texts with the audience by combining the current status of the live event, and finally producing visual and auditory feedback for the audience. Each action necessitates real-time, consistent communication among the agents. However, in the long-term operation of live broadcasting, ChatLsc faces challenges such as hallucinations and inconsistencies produced by large language models.

To resolve these issues, we introduced a leadership system, assigning different levels of authority to various agents, and using higher-level agents to lead lower-level agents in completing different tasks at different stages. This inspiration comes from the division of labor and collaboration in human groups. Humans do not always participate equally in all tasks; instead, more experienced leaders oversee the big picture, outlining the direction and planning of the work, while younger, more energetic individuals execute the specific tasks.

Specifically, Fig. 3 depicts an instance of leadership. In the preparation phase, leaders prepare detailed product knowledge and plans for the live broadcast. Then, during the live broadcast phase, leaders synchronize the transmission of product information and broadcasting plans with observers, creators, and other agents. Leadership provides a better pathway for all agents to cooperate, thereby promoting consistency and continuity among all agents during the live broadcast, enhancing the live broadcasting effectiveness of ChatLsc in live activities.

3.2 Preparation Phase

During the preparation phase, ChatLsc receives initial information from humans. This information includes details about the products for sale, the character settings of the broadcaster, the time of the live broadcast, and other relevant live-streaming information. ChatLsc is required to use this initial information to plan and prepare for the upcoming live broadcast comprehensively. As the overall planning and preparation are overview-type tasks, they are handled by leaders with higher authority levels.

Knowledge. One major reason for hallucinations in large language models is the lack of specialized domain knowledge. To mitigate this, the leader, before the official live broadcast phase, constructs a specialized knowledge base for the current live session and synchronizes it with observers, creators, and broadcasters to ensure the accuracy and consistency of the information received by all agents. The knowledge base includes specialized domain knowledge relevant to the current live session. Specifically, it covers details about the products and live broadcast information involved in the live stream, including product names, functions, prices, and details of promotional activities during the live broadcast.

Planning. Adequate live broadcast planning not only prevents content repetition and looping but also enhances the coherence and interactive quality of the broadcast. Without unified planning, ChatLsc's live broadcast might fall into content loops, such as repeating user questions from earlier in the broadcast. Therefore, the leader undertakes detailed and flexible planning of the live broadcast process. The live broadcast plan includes the theme, focus, and structure of the broadcast and allows for adjustments based on audience interaction and feedback during the live stream.

3.3   Live Streaming Phase

During the live streaming phase, ChatLsc engages in real-time interaction. Through the collaborative efforts of the observer, creator, broadcaster, and leader, ChatLsc continuously perceives audience comments, integrates them with the recent live streaming activities, and generates visual and auditory information to provide feedback to the audience (Fig. 4).

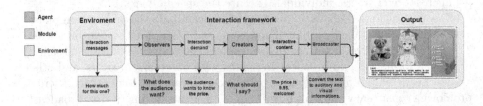

Fig. 4. An example of an observer, creator, and broadcaster collaborating in an orderly manner.

Interaction Framework. In the interaction framework of ChatLsc, the primary roles include the observer, creator, and broadcaster. These roles collaborate in an orderly manner to form the basis of real-time interaction capabilities.

The observer monitors various interactive information during the live broadcast, including audience reactions and comments. Since the broadcaster is the central figure in the live streaming context and receives much more interaction and information than the audience perceives, it is essential to first comprehensively consider and filter interaction information in the broadcast. This involves identifying hidden needs in valuable information to provide decision support for subsequent content creation.

The creator's main responsibility is to generate live broadcast content text based on the live broadcast plan and audience interaction information. Content creation is the most fundamental and crucial ability of the broadcaster and is the core responsibility of this system. With support from other roles, the creator provides the audience with realistic and engaging product promotional content, as well as socially and personally tailored interactive content for specific viewers.

The broadcaster's primary responsibility is to convert textual content into visual and auditory information and transmit it to the audience via streaming media. Serving as a bridge between the creator and the audience, the broadcaster must ensure the accuracy and vivid expression of the information, presenting the interactive content provided by the creator to the audience in front of the screen.

Memory. Memory retains the agents' previous dialogue records, past environmental information in the live broadcasting context, and historical interaction behaviors with the audience. Formally, an agent's conversation at time t is denoted as C_t, the environmental information in the live broadcasting context as S_t, the interaction with the audience as I_t, and the live broadcast planning and knowledge base as K. Equation 1 represents the memory set at time t:

$$M_t = \{(C_1, S_1, I_1), (C_2, S_2, I_2), ..., (C_t, S_t, I_t), K\} \quad I_t \leftarrow \psi(C_t, S_t, K) \quad (1)$$

In the subsequent time step $t + 1$, ChatLsc uses historical information, the latest environmental information S_{t+1}, and live broadcast planning and knowledge base K to obtain C_{t+1} and I_{t+1} through new conversations.

$$C_{t+1} = S(M_t, S_{t+1}, K) \quad I_{t+1} = C(M_t, C_{t+1}, S_{t+1}, K) \quad (2)$$

Finally, according to Eq. 3, all information in the memory is updated:

$$M_{t+1} = M_t \cup (C_{t+1}, S_{t+1}, I_{t+1}) \quad (3)$$

Through the above memory operation mechanism, ChatLsc can maintain coherence and consistency during the live broadcast.

Parallel Action. In the dynamic environment of live broadcasting, the broadcaster's ability to react in real-time is evidently crucial. However, the inference speed of large language models in complex social scenarios is often slower than the speed at which humans perform social behaviors, posing higher demands on the real-time capabilities of ChatLsc. Unlike the sequential action pattern of humans, multiple agents can act concurrently, compensating for the slower inference speed of large language models. Specifically, within ChatLsc, there are multiple observers and creators to support simultaneous responses to interactions initiated by multiple viewers. Whenever a viewer initiates an interaction, ChatLsc immediately dispatches an available observer to analyze and creatively respond to the viewer's interaction, thus reducing the latency in ChatLsc's content creation.

Interactive Value. During the live streaming process, not all interactions initiated by the audience are valuable. To better facilitate live streaming interaction, this section introduces the metric of 'interaction value', evaluating the effectiveness of live streaming interactions from three dimensions: timeliness, relevance, and importance.

Timeliness involves the timing of the interaction, used to assess the sense of participation and interactivity with the current live stream. The shorter the time of interaction occurrence, the stronger the sense of participation and interactivity in the live stream, hence a higher score for timeliness.

Relevance refers to the degree of association between the content of the interaction and the theme of the live broadcast. It assesses whether the content of the interaction is closely related to the core topic of the live broadcast and whether it can provide value to other viewers. Interactions with high relevance can promote in-depth discussion of the topic, enrich the content of the live broadcast, and increase the participation of other viewers. In contrast, interactions lacking relevance may distract the audience and affect the overall quality of the live stream.

Importance evaluates the contribution of an interaction to the overall value of the live broadcast. This includes the richness of information in the interaction, audience response, and potential long-term impact. For instance, insightful questions or positive comments that inspire important discussions are beneficial for achieving the goals of the live broadcast and therefore possess higher importance. On the other hand, superficial or routine interactions may have only limited impact. By comprehensively assessing interaction value through these three dimensions, it becomes possible to more effectively identify and utilize valuable interactions, thereby enhancing the quality of live streaming interaction.

4   Experiments and Results

Our experimental setup utilized the gpt-3.5-turbo version as the large language model for ChatLsc. The temperature was set to 0.3 to balance the stability and creativity of the live broadcast. In addition, we conducted live streaming on the Bilibili platform and used VSeeFace to drive the vtuber, along with text-to-speech services provided by Tencent Cloud.

4.1   Qualitative Analysis

For qualitative analysis, we removed each component of ChatLsc and discussed how it would impact the generation of interactions.

- Interaction framework: The interaction framework consists of observers, creators, and broadcasters. Evidently, we cannot do without them, as they are the foundation of ChatLsc's normal operation. Without them, ChatLsc would be unable to perceive audience information and generate and output interactive content.
- Memory: Memory is a detailed record of information over a past period. When we remove memory, the large language model can only generate interactions based on current information. In experiments, this sometimes leads to ChatLsc falling into a loop of repetitive interactions, such as continuously greeting viewers in the live room, unable to proceed with subsequent live broadcasting activities.

- Parallel action: Parallel action refers to the ability of observers and creators to respond simultaneously to comments from different viewers. If we remove the capability for parallel action by observers and creators, the interaction speed of ChatLsc will rapidly decrease. When ChatLsc can only interact sequentially with two users per minute, other users may become impatient and leave the live room.
- Interactive value: Interactive value is a method for evaluating the effectiveness of interactions generated by ChatLsc. Without interactive value assessment, ChatLsc cannot discern which of the many audience comments is more helpful for the live broadcast. In this case, ChatLsc can only reply to audience comments in actual order or randomly, leading to a decline in its interactive capability.
- Leadership: Leadership refers to the method of mutual leadership among agents. Through leadership, agents can more efficiently divide and cooperate, thus completing their respective tasks. If leadership is removed, the cooperation among agents will be hindered. For example, a creator might notify the leader of erroneous information, who records and disseminates it to other agents, eventually leading to the prevalence of incorrect information throughout the system.
- Knowledge: The knowledge is a collection of specialized domain knowledge made by the leader. If the knowledge base is removed, agents will lack detailed information about products and live broadcasting. When LLMs lack specialized domain knowledge, they are more likely to produce hallucinations, leading to unreliable interactions. In fact, without the knowledge base, agents relying only on limited initial information often generate incorrect information.
- Planning: Live broadcast planning is the planning made by the leader during the preparation phase. Adequate live broadcast planning prevents content repetition and looping. When we remove live broadcast planning, the broadcast may enter meaningless loops, severely reducing the coherence and quality of live broadcast interaction.

4.2 Qualitative Analysis

For quantitative analysis, to assess the performance of ChatLsc, we utilized a GPT-4 evaluation. We randomly selected 100 interactions from ChatLsc's real-time live broadcast records and generated single interactions using the GPT-3.5 model in the exact same environmental conditions to create a control group. Subsequently, we used GPT-4 to evaluate the interactions generated by ChatLsc and GPT-3.5. Specifically, we had GPT-4 score the two interactions generated under the same environmental conditions to determine which one was superior. Additionally, after removing some modules, we manually assessed whether the interactions generated by the system were credible. Some non-credible interactions could be due to discrepancies with basic information or contradictions.

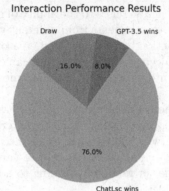

Fig. 5. Quality of interactions by ChatLsc vs GPT-3.5.

Figure 5 lists the comparative results of interactions directly generated by ChatLsc and GPT-3.5. The data indicates that ChatLsc is superior in the vast majority of cases compared to using GPT-3.5 directly.

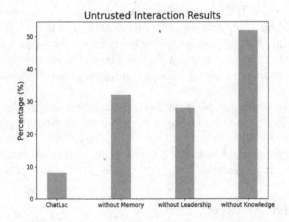

Fig. 6. Percentage of untrusted interaction outputs.

Figure 6 demonstrates that ChatLsc generates more credible live streaming interactions compared to any variant with a removed component. This proves that every part of our method is essential.

5   Conclusion and Future Work

In this paper, we designed ChatLsc, a virtual broadcaster for live streaming commerce powered by large language models. ChatLsc employs multiple agents to perform different roles, such as leaders, observers, creators, and broadcasters, to accomplish specific tasks at different stages. With just the initial information about the live session, ChatLsc can adequately prepare for the broadcast and engage in real-time interaction with the audience. Additionally, we introduced methods such as a leadership system and an interaction value assessment to help ChatLsc maintain consistency and stability during tasks and to promote the generation of high-quality live streaming interactions. Experiments show that through the leadership and cooperation among agents, ChatLsc can generate credible and high-quality real-time live streaming interactions.

However, our study also has certain limitations. First, our interaction quality assessment is far from perfect due to the potential errors in the GPT-4 jury evaluation. We plan to conduct more detailed manual evaluations in the future. Second, our method consumes a significant number of tokens, which represents a non-negligible cost in live streaming activities. We plan to explore more efficient methods of interaction generation in the future to balance the high token consumption with good interaction quality.

References

1. Balaji, P.G., Srinivasan, D.: An introduction to multi-agent systems. In: Srinivasan, D., Jain, L.C. (eds.) Innovations in Multi-agent Systems and Applications-1, vol. 310, pp. 1–27. Springer, Heidelberg (2010). https://doi.org/10.1007/978-3-642-14435-6_1

2. Chen, C.C., Lin, Y.C.: What drives live-stream usage intention? The perspectives of flow, entertainment, social interaction, and endorsement. Telematics Inform. **35**(1), 293–303 (2018)

3. China Internet Network Information Center: The 52th China statistical report on internet development. Report, China Internet Network Information Center (CINIC) (2023). https://www.cnnic.cn/NMediaFile/2023/0908/MAIN1694151810549M3LV0UWOAV.pdf

4. Gravitas, S.: Auto-GPT: an autonomous GPT-4 experiment (2023)

5. Haimson, O.L., Tang, J.C.: What makes live events engaging on Facebook live, periscope, and snapchat. In: Proceedings of the 2017 CHI Conference on Human Factors in Computing Systems, pp. 48–60 (2017)

6. Hao, R., Hu, L., Qi, W., Wu, Q., Zhang, Y., Nie, L.: ChatLLM network: more brains, more intelligence. arXiv preprint arXiv:2304.12998 (2023)

7. Hassan, M.M., Knipper, A., Santu, S.K.K.: ChatGPT as your personal data scientist. arXiv preprint arXiv:2305.13657 (2023)

8. Irving, G., Christiano, P., Amodei, D.: AI safety via debate. arXiv preprint arXiv:1805.00899 (2018)

9. Jiang, G., Xu, M., Zhu, S.C., Han, W., Zhang, C., Zhu, Y.: MPI: evaluating and inducing personality in pre-trained language models. arXiv preprint arXiv:2206.07550 (2022)

10. Kosinski, M.: Theory of mind may have spontaneously emerged in large language models. arXiv preprint arXiv:2302.02083 (2023)

11. Lewis, M., Yarats, D., Dauphin, Y.N., Parikh, D., Batra, D.: Deal or no deal? End-to-end learning for negotiation dialogues. arXiv preprint arXiv:1706.05125 (2017)

12. Li, G., Hammoud, H.A.A.K., Itani, H., Khizbullin, D., Ghanem, B.: CAMEL: communicative agents for "mind" exploration of large scale language model society. arXiv preprint arXiv:2303.17760 (2023)

13. Liang, T., et al.: Encouraging divergent thinking in large language models through multi-agent debate. arXiv preprint arXiv:2305.19118 (2023)

14. Lin, B.Y., et al.: SwiftSage: a generative agent with fast and slow thinking for complex interactive tasks. arXiv preprint arXiv:2305.17390 (2023)

15. Mandi, Z., Jain, S., Song, S.: RoCo: dialectic multi-robot collaboration with large language models. arXiv preprint arXiv:2307.04738 (2023)

16. Radford, A., Jozefowicz, R., Sutskever, I.: Learning to generate reviews and discovering sentiment. arXiv preprint arXiv:1704.01444 (2017)

17. Shinn, N., Labash, B., Gopinath, A.: Reflexion: an autonomous agent with dynamic memory and self-reflection. arXiv preprint arXiv:2303.11366 (2023)

18. Sjöblom, M., Hamari, J.: Why do people watch others play video games? An empirical study on the motivations of twitch users. Comput. Hum. Behav. **75**, 985–996 (2017)

19. Wei, J., et al.: Chain-of-thought prompting elicits reasoning in large language models. Adv. Neural. Inf. Process. Syst. **35**, 24824–24837 (2022)

20. Wohn, D.Y., Freeman, G., McLaughlin, C.: Explaining viewers' emotional, instrumental, and financial support provision for live streamers. In: Proceedings of the 2018 CHI Conference on Human Factors in Computing Systems, pp. 1–13 (2018)

21. Wongkitrungrueng, A., Assarut, N.: The role of live streaming in building consumer trust and engagement with social commerce sellers. J. Bus. Res. **117**, 543–556 (2020)

22. Xue, J., Liang, X., Xie, T., Wang, H.: See now, act now: how to interact with customers to enhance social commerce engagement? Inf. Manag. **57**(6), 103324 (2020)

23. Yang, Y., Wang, J.: An overview of multi-agent reinforcement learning from game theoretical perspective. arXiv preprint arXiv:2011.00583 (2020)

24. Zhao, K., Hu, Y., Hong, Y., Westland, J.C.: Understanding characteristics of popular streamers on live streaming platforms: evidence from twitch. tv. J. Assoc. Inf. Syst. (2019, Forthcoming)

25. Zhu, D., Chen, J., Shen, X., Li, X., Elhoseiny, M.: MiniGPT-4: enhancing vision-language understanding with advanced large language models. arXiv preprint arXiv:2304.10592 (2023)

Knowledge Transfer Reinvented: A Comprehensive Exploration of Heilbronn University's Virtual AI Laboratory and Its Impact on Interdisciplinary Collaboration

Valeria Kinitzki, Ana Ramos Wittek, and Nicolaj C. Stache[✉]

Heilbronn University, Max-Planck-Strasse 39, 74081 Heilbronn, Germany
{valeria.kinitzki,ana.ramoswittek,
nicolaj.stache}@hs-heilbronn.de

Abstract. In the age of rapidly advancing technology, knowledge sharing and access to expertise are crucial drivers of innovation. Heilbronn University of Applied Sciences has successfully undertaken a project to address this need by creating an accessible virtual platform for public knowledge transfer. This initiative aims to bridge the knowledge gap, offering valuable insights into cutting-edge fields like Artificial Intelligence (AI) to local businesses and individuals.

The virtual environment, designed for user-friendly exploration, facilitates more frequent presentation of results compared to traditional formats. Accessible round-the-clock from any internet-enabled device, the platform showcases physical demonstrators of Heilbronn University, creating a seamless connection to the real world.

Technically, the virtual AI Laboratory has been constructed with all buildings and content presented as 3D models in Blender, a free 3D graphics software. This allows for content modification and expansion. In a virtual tour software, such as 3D Vista Virtual Tour, 360° panoramic images are enhanced with waypoints and information icons, where additional content can then be incorporated through HTML in popup windows.

The primary evaluation conducted after the initial launch of the virtual AI Laboratory has yielded valuable insights. It became evident that language is a pivotal consideration. The second key insight derived from the evaluation is related to user behavior we could collect by tracking the order of selected waypoints within the virtual platform. This behavior indicates that individual users possess varying levels of knowledge and familiarity with AI concepts.

Looking towards the future, it can be affirmed that the virtual AI Laboratory has already garnered significant interest. Through collaborations and partnerships with additional institutes, this expansion will provide visitors with an even broader range of AI-based topics, consistently presented in a didactic manner.

The virtual AI laboratory is freely accessible via this link: https://www.hs-heilbronn.de/ki-labor

Keywords: Virtual AI Laboratory · AI Demonstrators · Knowledge Transfer Platform

© The Author(s), under exclusive license to Springer Nature Switzerland AG 2024
H. Degen and S. Ntoa (Eds.): HCII 2024, LNAI 14735, pp. 373–386, 2024.
https://doi.org/10.1007/978-3-031-60611-3_26

1 Introduction

The need for further education and digitization in companies has been steadily increasing since globalization, and especially since the pandemic in 2019, it has become clear that a transformation is necessary. It became evident that small and medium-sized regional businesses across all industries often struggle to keep up with current developments, despite being essential drivers for economic growth and development. (Philbin et al. 2022) The challenge arises not from a deficit in determination or resources but from the absence of tailored strategies designed for the unique characteristics of the organization in question. (Gouveia and Mamede 2022).

This project, undertaken by Heilbronn University of Applied Sciences, has developed 'an accessible platform for public knowledge transfer, with a primary focus on serving small and medium-sized enterprises (SMEs) in the region. The goal is to bridge the knowledge gap and provide local businesses and individuals with valuable insights into cutting-edge fields such as Artificial Intelligence (AI). In this process, the research findings and insights of the university are transferred to the companies to support them in their digitization efforts.

The profound shift in work culture during the pandemic, with numerous offices vacant as employees embraced remote work, mandated a reassessment of the conventional results presentation process. Adaptations were crucial to accommodate the evolving dynamics, ensuring effective communication and collaboration in the new era of decentralized work environments. So the focus of this work was placed on an online platform to meet the demands of current global events. While physical buildings primarily foster contact and communication during a local meeting, virtual buildings provide easy access to information. Thus, especially during times of contact restrictions, significant added value is created in this regard. The design of the virtual AI lab will be further discussed later in the course of the paper.

2 Background

2.1 State of the Art

At the beginning of the project, the market was searched for potential platforms for designing the virtual AI Laboratory. Some museums offer virtual tours in which physical exhibition objects are digitally presented. In the German Museum, virtual visitors have the opportunity to freely navigate through the museum, look around, and zoom in on exhibits within the browser. A map is provided for orientation, allowing users to view selected objects and navigate to specific exhibitions. (Reimann 2020) While at the German Museum, the tour was measured in three dimensions using laser technology and simultaneously captured by multiple 360° cameras, individual areas of the National Gallery London were created through modeling of the space (Gallery 2024) followed by visualization by Moyosa Media BV. (HQ 2024).

Unity provides a platform for the creation and operation of interactive real-time 3D content for game developers, architects, or filmmakers. (Technologies, Unity Technologies 2024) With free tutorials, users can learn the structure of the C# programming language used in Unity, and the software itself is also provided free of charge to new developers, making Unity the most widely used game development platform in the world. (Technologies, Unity Technologies 2024) Typically, with Unity, a three-dimensional environment would be developed, allowing visitors to navigate freely throughout the entire area using specific keys.

The next evolutionary stage of social networking and the successor to today's mobile internet is promised by the metaverse of Meta Platforms. (Meta, Meta, 2024) After the era of social media, Meta aims to overcome the limits of two-dimensionality and promote immersive experiences with Augmented, Virtual, and Mixed Reality (AR, VR, MR) to contribute to the advancement of social technologies. In addition to various commercially available VR devices, Meta also offers the so-called Meta Horizon, which provides a platform for creating virtual content. This platform runs on the Unity game engine mentioned earlier. What makes it special is its structure as a social network, allowing users to create and share common spaces and locations through a software toolkit. (Meta, Meta, 2024).

The characteristics of the three platforms are compared as followed (Tables 1, 2 and 3).

Table 1. Comparison of platforms – 3D Vista Virtual Tour

Item	3D Vista Virtual Tour
Target group	Museum tours, real estate presentation
Creation of the environment	Taken with a camera or freely modeled
Getting around	Freely in space or via fixed waypoints
Presentation of additional content	Pop-up window afterwards
Performance	Very good in the web browser because of small file size
Support	Numerous tutorials freely available
Costs	Chargeable, license already available for university
Actuality	Graphics dependent on rendered images

Table 2. Comparison of platforms - Unity

Item	Unity
Target group	Game development, simulation and rendering
Creation of the environment	Modeling within software
Getting around	Freely in space
Presentation of additional content	Extended Reality within the 3D environment
Performance	Displaying 3D content with WebGL in the web browser
Support	English tutorials freely available
Costs	Free software, paid subscriptions depending on configuration
Actuality	Modern game graphics

Table 3. Comparison of platforms – Meta Horizon

Item	Meta Horizon
Target group	Game developers as well as "everyone"
Creation of the environment	Using VR devices
Getting around	Using VR devices
Presentation of additional content	Extended Reality within the 3D environment
Performance	Within the Meta Horizon social network
Support	Low, as it is very new
Costs	Costs for VR devices and in-app purchases
Actuality	Abstracted 3D graphics

After thoughtful deliberation, the team dismissed the option of Unity or Meta Horizon, given the complexity for visitors. Concerns about security and productivity arose due to blocked websites on work computers. Opting for wider accessibility, the decision favored using Blender and 3D Vista Virtual Tour to craft the virtual AI Laboratory.

2.2 Promotion of Knowledge Transfer by Government

As part of the measures for AI in small and medium-sized enterprises, the Ministry of Economic Affairs, Labor, and Tourism of Baden-Württemberg, Germany, provided 4.2 million euros for the promotion of regional AI labs until the end of 2024. (Ministerium für Wirtschaft, Arbeit und Tourismus Baden-Württemberg, n.d.) Artificial intelligence as a key technology is crucial for the value creation and competitiveness of the economy in the country.

There was already a successful initial pilot project with 19 regional AI labs between 2019 and 2022. During this period, Heilbronn University was already among the first participants in the funding program. (Ministerium für Wirtschaft, Arbeit und Tourismus Baden-Württemberg, n.d.) The regional AI labs aim to advance artificial intelligence across the state of Baden-Württemberg. These labs serve as spaces for information exchange, networking, testing, and experimentation for companies, particularly for small and medium-sized enterprises (SMEs).

With the reissue of the call for proposals for regional AI labs, the primary goal is to disseminate knowledge about the economic potentials of AI solutions for small and medium-sized enterprises (SMEs). In addition to further establishing AI labs in the region, the current funding call places increased emphasis on climate protection. This call specifically focuses on sustainable AI solutions, aiming to showcase environmentally friendly AI solutions through regional AI labs and demonstrate potential resource savings achievable through AI applications.

Heilbronn University established a Center for Machine Learning, overseeing the AI Laboratory to integrate findings from various domains. Designed as a 3D campus, the AI Laboratory facilitates prompt dissemination of research outcomes, serving as an accessible entry point to AI for diverse stakeholders in the era of rapid progress.

3   Our Work

The AI Laboratory was initially conceived as a knowledge transfer platform. The presentation of research findings and the initial point of contact for businesses have been complemented by cross-institutional activities, now also serving internal knowledge transfer and exchange within the university. This results in a platform that encompasses content spanning both specific programs and faculties for the staff.

The description of the platform's development will now be outlined. Special emphasis will be placed on the advantages of virtual design over physical design. The technical approach for emulation will be explained as well.

3.1   Added Value of the Virtual AI Laboratory

Throughout the project, the virtual AI Laboratory underwent multiple iterative expansions and adjustments to meet evolving needs and requirements. This iterative development process resulted in substantial added value, which is detailed in the following table for comprehensive insight into the project's advancements and enhancements. The following site plan serves to enhance the understanding of the structure of the virtual campus (Fig. 1).

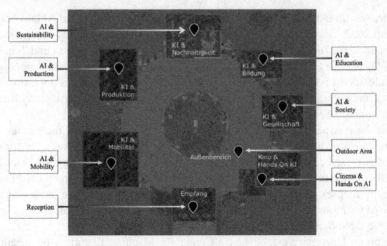

Fig. 1. Layout of virtual AI Laboratory

Table 4. Added value of the virtual AI Laboratory

Item	Value
Dedicated virtual buildings	Structured as a campus, the virtual AI Laboratory features dedicated buildings for themes such as Mobility, Production, Sustainability, Education, and Society based on the physically available conditions The arrangement of the independent buildings allows the campus to be easily expanded and additional content added
Seamless connection to the real-world	By virtually showcasing physical demonstrators from Heilbronn University, a seamless connection to the real-world is established. Plus, the presentation of research results takes place in a playful and appealing manner Avatars representing university staff, created with 3D scanning, enhance the connection to reality. Attendees can interact with these avatars, receiving video greetings in corresponding buildings or engaging in theme-based dialogues (e.g., elucidating requirements for companies implementing AI)

(continued)

Table 4. (*continued*)

Item	Value
Cinema	The cinema provides an opportunity for conference attendees to delve deeper into AI through comprehensive video materials. Additionally, detailed videos are presented for a deeper understanding. This allows for an entertaining experience in other areas of the virtual campus
Hands On AI	This designated area allows visitors to assess their programming skills in AI using Jupyter Notebooks with hands-on examples. Tailored for interactive learning, visitors can modify provided programming codes, fostering a dynamic and engaging environment for honing their abilities in AI programming through practical experimentation
Free access	Offering free, round-the-clock access from any internet-enabled device, the user-friendly design encourages exploration, making complex concepts accessible Both the unlimited visit to the virtual AI Laboratory and the advice from the university are free
Fast research dissemination	The virtual environment allows for more frequent presentation of results compared to physical formats: The 3D campus is accessible on the internet without limitations and is designed to be inviting with an appealing layout and engaging content presentation. This promotes a significantly faster dissemination of research compared to, for example, time-limited consultation sessions with physical tours at the university
Ecological advantage	The advantages over physical structures are apparent. Swift adaptation to changes aligns with the agile nature of the topic. Accessibility in virtual or digital form is inherently more achievable. Moreover, the initiative promotes ecological considerations by eliminating the need for travel to exhibitions and the consumption of physical space and materials. Furthermore, a virtual building requires neither maintenance nor heating
Planning aid	The virtual AI Laboratory extends its utility as a planning aid for tangible structures in the physical world, offering practical applications beyond the digital realm

(*continued*)

Table 4. (*continued*)

Item	Value
Connection with customers	The contact with companies or interested parties is maintained through newsletters. Regular updates and information shared via newsletters foster ongoing engagement, ensuring a continuous and informed connection that keeps stakeholders abreast of relevant developments and activities within the community

3.2 Technical Approach

At the beginning of the project, it was decided to model the spaces using the free software Blender. To align with the goal of making an ecological contribution, the virtual spaces were designed to be modern (Scurati et al. 2021), incorporating sustainable construction practices such as green roofing and a nature-inspired layout using renewable materials into the design. (Wu et al. 2020) (Yazici and Tanacan 2020).

In the first iteration, an initial building with multiple rooms was designed, but it quickly became evident that the content scope was too extensive for this layout. Consequently, a virtual campus with separate spaces was created to accommodate the breadth of research findings from Heilbronn University adequately.

In several iterations, elements such as windows, materials, and objects were added to the virtual framework. License-free content (reserved, kein Datum) was utilized throughout to ensure project milestones were consistently met without wasting time on irrelevant details. The modeling phase concluded with the integration of existing 3D models of demonstrators.

In the next step, virtual cameras were strategically placed on the virtual campus to render 360° panoramic images. The rendering duration depended on the size of the image, maintaining a constant aspect ratio of 1:2 (e.g., 2000px x 4000px or 3000px x 6000px). These images were essential for creating the virtual tour using 3D Vista Virtual Pro software. The university already possessed licenses for this software, streamlining the decision-making process. Additionally, positive past experiences with using this software for creating virtual tours of physical spaces at Heilbronn University influenced the choice.

Using the 3D Vista Virtual Tour Pro software, the rendered 360° panoramic images were seamlessly combined into a cohesive tour. Waypoints were placed at locations where cameras were positioned during the 3D modeling, allowing the creation of paths within the campus. Moreover, this software facilitated the integration of content in the form of images, text, or videos through popup windows in the form of action points. This method of content integration was employed for rendered objects like demonstrators or screens. Content in the form of boards or posters had to be rendered directly into the panoramic image in Blender such as in the following figure (Fig. 2).

Fig. 2. Rendered content on a board

To maintain a tidy virtual tour while ensuring clear and organized presentation of popup windows containing text, images, and videos, HTML was used for their integration (as shown in Fig. 3).

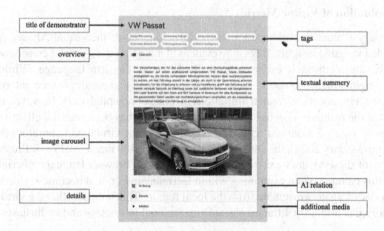

Fig. 3. Popup window showing accordion structure

This format of information display was predominantly employed for demonstrators. A consistent accordion structure was established for all demonstrators, featuring a brief content summary initially. Additional expandable fields provided AI relevance, details, and media. Tags facilitated in-depth exploration and linkage to other demonstrators. Presenting content in popup windows with HTML pages as separate URLs allowed swift integration and simplified the update process in case of changes, making it the third chosen building block (Fig. 4).

The virtual tour is uploaded to the university's web space after integrating the previously uploaded HTML pages as URLs in popup windows and exporting the tour from the 3D Vista Virtual Pro software. Subsequently, the virtual tour is made available to visitors.

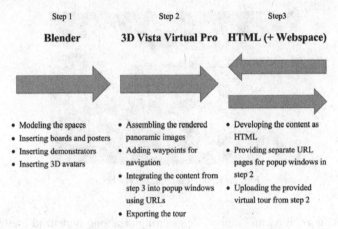

| Step 1 | Step 2 | Step3 |
| Blender | 3D Vista Virtual Pro | HTML (+ Webspace) |

- Modeling the spaces
- Inserting boards and posters
- Inserting demonstrators
- Inserting 3D avatars

- Assembling the rendered panoramic images
- Adding waypoints for navigation
- Integrating the content from step 3 into popup windows using URLs
- Exporting the tour

- Developing the content as HTML
- Providing separate URL pages for popup windows in step 2
- Uploading the provided virtual tour from step 2

Fig. 4. Three-stage construction of the virtual tour

4   Conclusion

4.1   Evaluation of Visitor Metrics

The primary evaluation conducted after the initial launch of the virtual AI Laboratory has yielded valuable insights. It became evident that language is a pivotal consideration. Currently, the platform is exclusively available in the German language. While this was the original intention due to its focus on local small and medium-sized enterprises (SMEs) in Germany, it has created limitations in terms of potential users. However, it also means that the primary objective of serving local SMEs has been realized effectively.

Approximately 3 months after the official launch of the virtual AI Laboratory (October 2023 to January 2024), the site has been visited over 400 times. As Fig. 5. Illustrates, over 95% of these visitors are from Germany. The web browser language distribution mirrors this pattern. When examining within Germany in Fig. 6, it becomes evident that the majority of visitors originate from the local region. This indicates that the virtual AI Laboratory has primarily attracted visits from regional businesses and enthusiasts.

486 visits

Fig. 5. Distribution of visitors by country of origin

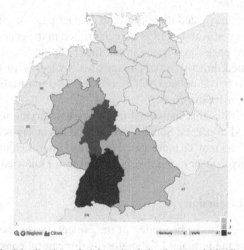

Fig. 6. Distribution of visitors by federal state within Germany

The 486 visitors collectively visited 1,263 pages within the virtual AI Laboratory. The average duration of their stay was 3 min and 49 s. With an average of 2.8 actions, the highest number of actions performed by a visitor was 21 times, as illustrated in Fig. 7.

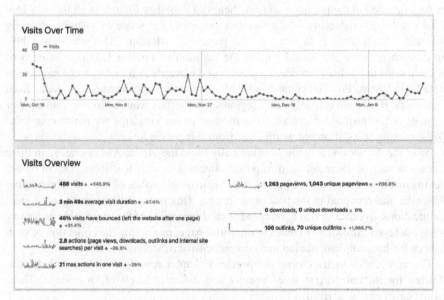

Fig. 7. Visits overview

The second key insight derived from the evaluation is related to user behavior we could collect by tracking the order of selected waypoints within the virtual platform.

12% of the visitors navigated directly to the contact page to initiate an inquiry or subscribe to the newsletter. Another 18% were interested in the genesis of the virtual AI Laboratory. These two pages are located in the first building, the reception area. 20% of the visitors navigated directly to the cinema area, with 54% of these subsequently clicking directly to the hands-on area. All other pages (demonstrators or outdoor area) were visited in less than 10% of cases.

This behavior indicates that individual users possess varying levels of knowledge and familiarity with AI concepts. Some users may be beginners seeking foundational information, while others may be more experienced and interested in applied examples. The platform's capacity to cater to this diverse range of user knowledge levels is pivotal.

4.2 Summary and Discussion

As described in Sect. 2.1 at the beginning of the project, the market was explored for potential platforms for the virtual AI Laboratory. After careful consideration, the team rejected the solution with Unity or even Meta Horizon, as the operation by visitors would have been much more complex. Additionally, many websites on a work computer are blocked, which would compromise security and productivity. In contrast, a website displaying discrete images with popup windows would be more widely accessible. Therefore, the decision was made to use the software Blender and 3D Vista Virtual Tour for creating the virtual AI Laboratory.

As explained in the previous section, there is a language limitation on the site. Due to the exclusive availability of the German language, the scope of visitors is locally restricted. The three-step structure of the page with Blender, 3D Vista Virtual Pro, and content presentation would require the addition of another language in each of the three steps individually: rendering posters and placards in Blender, menu navigation in 3D Vista Virtual Pro, and content in HTML. Since the supplementary guidance from Hochschule Heilbronn can only occur regionally, the effort required to integrate another language is not justified. German is the most effective language for addressing local SMEs, making translation not worthwhile from this perspective.

After the decision was made to structurally build the virtual AI Laboratory in three stages, a certain obstacle emerged: If posters and boards were to display content before clicking on the action point (see Fig. 1), they had to be incorporated into the 3D modeling in Blender and rendered in the panoramic image. This posed difficulties in subsequent modifications, as changes had to be made in all three stages of the setup. This necessary process delayed immediate updates to the entire page, prompting the collection of such changes for later implementation in a comprehensive rendering pass.

The analysis of metrics from the previous chapter reveals diverse user behavior, allowing for the categorization of visitors into different levels of knowledge. Three distinct cases can be derived:

- The first group of visitors aims to establish contact with the university, with about 40% abandoning the tour at this point. No information about their knowledge of artificial intelligence can be ascertained.
- The second group of visitors explores multiple pages of the virtual tour without a specific goal, requiring no prior knowledge of artificial intelligence.

- The third group of visitors navigates directly to the Hands-On area to test their advanced programming skills and knowledge of AI.

Currently, the size distribution of these three visitor groups is balanced, and the virtual AI Laboratory can serve all three equally. However, there is potential for the virtual AI Laboratory to evolve and focus more on a specific group in the future.

4.3 Further Work

Looking at the project plan, it becomes apparent that additional content will be added to the virtual AI Laboratory over the course of the current year. The topic of AI and sustainability needs to be further developed in accordance with project requirements. Several sub-projects are already being worked on by university staff and students. For example, projects include the resource-efficient cultivation of strawberries using AI or ecologically sustainable weed control in monoculture fields. Additional demonstrators in the production domain can also be added, as discussions are already underway with other faculties at the university.

Feedback from numerous visitors has led to discussions about potential improvements in the user-friendliness of the virtual tour. If not already done, these enhancements will be incorporated with the next major update to continuously improve the quality of the virtual AI Laboratory.

Enabling use by students would be desirable, as inquiries from teachers and student classes have already been received. One idea is to integrate a feature for playful exploration of content, such as a scavenger hunt or rally. Overall, the field of AI and education is intended to be further expanded through online courses.

Seeking marketing opportunities for the AI Laboratory through additional collaborations with regional partners and exhibitions would help enhance its visibility. Finally, the question remains of how to sustain the virtual AI Laboratory without government funding.

Looking towards the future it can be affirmed that the virtual AI Laboratory has already garnered significant interest. Through collaborations and partnerships with additional institutes, it will benefit in content and steadily expand. This expansion will provide visitors with an even broader range of AI-based topics, consistently presented in a didactic manner.

You are welcome to try out the AI lab yourself: https://www.hs-heilbronn.de/ki-labor.

4.4 The AI Laboratory is Supported by the Ministry of Economic Affairs, Labor, and Tourism

We express our gratitude for the support of the AI lab by the Ministry of Economic Affairs, Labor, and Tourism of Baden-Württemberg (Fig. 8).

Fig. 8. Logos of the sponsor

References

Gallery, T.N.: The national gallery (2024). Accessed 24 Jan 2024. https://www.nationalgallery.org.uk/visiting/virtual-tours

Gouveia, F.D., Mamede, J.H.: Digital transformation for SMES in the retail industry. Procedia Comput. Sci. **204**, 671–681 (2022)

HQ, G.: Moyosa Media (2024). Accessed 24 Jan 2024. https://moyosamedia.com

Meta. (2024). Meta. Accessed 25 Jan 2024. https://about.meta.com/de/what-is-the-metaverse/

Meta. (2024). Meta. Accessed 25 Jan 2024. https://www.meta.com/de-de/help/quest/articles/horizon/explore-horizon-worlds/

Ministerium für Wirtschaft, Arbeit und Tourismus Baden-Württemberg. (n.d.). wm. baden-wuerttemberg.de. Accessed 15 Jan 2024. https://wm.baden-wuerttemberg.de/de/service/presse-und-oeffentlichkeitsarbeit/pressemitteilung/pid/neuer-foerderaufruf-fuer-regionale-ki-labs-startet/

Ministerium für Wirtschaft, Arbeit und Tourismus Baden-Württemberg. (n.d.). wm. baden-wuerttemberg.de. Accessed 15 Jan 2024. https://wm.baden-wuerttemberg.de/de/service/presse-und-oeffentlichkeitsarbeit/pressemitteilung/pid/wirtschaftsministerium-foerdert-aufbau-regionaler-ki-labs-mit-23-millionen-euro

Philbin, S., Viswanathan, R., Telukdarie, A.: Understanding how digital transformation can enable SMEs to achieve sustainable development: a systematic literature review. Small Bus. Int. Rev. **6**(1) (2022)

Reimann, M.: Deutsches museum. Accessed 24 Jan 2024 (2020). https://blog.deutsches-museum.de/2020/06/19/der-neue-virtuelle-rundgang-durch-das-deutsche-museum

reserved, B. A. (n.d.). BlenderKit. Accessed 18 Jan 2024. https://www.blenderkit.com

Scurati, G., Graziosi, S., Bertoni, M., Ferrise, F.: Exploring the use of virtual reality to support environmentally sustainable behavior: a framework to design experiences. Design to Drive Behavior Change for Sustainability and Circular Economy, 18 Jan 2021

Technologies, U.: Unity Technologies (2024). Accessed 25 Jan 2024. https://unity.com/de/learn/get-started

Technologies, U.: Unity Technologies (2024). Accessed 25 Jan 2024. https://unity.com/de/how-to/beginner-game-coding-resources

Wu, Y., et al.: Design with nature and eco-city design. Ecosystem Health Sustain. **6**(1), 1781549 (2020)

Yazici, S., Tanacan, L.: Material-based computational design (MCD) in sustainable architecture. J. Build. Eng. **32**, 101543 (2020)

Human-AI Teaming: Following the IMOI Framework

Styliani Kleanthous[⊠]

Fairness and Ethics in AI - Human Interaction (fAIre) Research Group, CYENS CoE,
Nicosia, Cyprus
s.kleanthous@cyens.org.cy

Abstract. Human-AI teams are becoming more and more important in
decision making (DM). In this work we propose approaching Human-AI
teams in DM in a similar way that we approach Human-only teams. In
this respect, processes that proved to be important for the functioning of
human-only teams, need to be understood in these diverse socio-technical
Human-AI settings. Following research in organizational psychology, we
propose examining the work that has been done in Human-AI teams
following the Input - Mediator - Output - Input framework. In this paper,
we reviewed related work on DM in Human-AI teams, to demonstrate
that by taking this perspective we can identify aspects, important for
the successful functioning of Human-AI teams. Potential future work in
the area is then highlighted.

Keywords: Human-AI Teaming · Human-AI Interaction · Decision
Making · Human-Centered AI

1 Introduction

Research in the area of human-centered AI advocates that the next evolution of
AI is not going to be only technological, but also humanistic. In this endeavor,
work has already made a shift into a more ethical, inclusive, responsible, human
centered approach for Human - Artificial Intelligence (HAI) interaction, acknowledging the role that cognitive and social process, are playing in this context
[51]. HAI teams are becoming very popular in the context of decision making (DM) [76,110]. These socio-technical entities are demonstrating intelligent
behavior and are consisting of humans and AI systems that are working together
achieving both their individual and collective goals [62]. For example, a group
of human experts (coming from different scientific/professional areas) are gathered together and take decisions. They are aided by a decision support system
(DSS) that provides additional information, according to the scenario at hand
and help the experts make an informed decision. Team members can either adopt
the system's prediction/recommendation or ignore it.

Although, there was a lot of discussion in the academia and the press about
the potential biases that might be inherited in AI DSS (e.g., in the recruitment industry), there were also a lot of successful collaborative efforts between

© The Author(s), under exclusive license to Springer Nature Switzerland AG 2024
H. Degen and S. Ntoa (Eds.): HCII 2024, LNAI 14735, pp. 387–406, 2024.
https://doi.org/10.1007/978-3-031-60611-3_27

humans and AI systems [96,104,116]. There is an increasing interest in understanding technical approaches for supporting HAI teams in DM [76]. Hence, it is important to understand the processes involved during the interaction between humans and AI, and how can these be supported especially when they might have serious social implications. According to organizational research, there are specific processes that characterize effectiveness and efficiency in the functioning of teams and groups. Two review papers provide an overview of the area from the organizational psychology perspective [57,67].

Building on the results of [76], who are calling for *"Bridging AI and other communities (e.g., HCI, psychology, and economics) to mutually shape human-AI decision making"*, we approach HAI interaction in teams by following human centered processes (e.g., context understanding, collaboration, diversity, etc.). This, provides us with a new perspective into HAI teaming [59]. Effective communication and collaboration between Humans and AI are paramount for developing useful, usable, trustworthy and diversity-aware AI for supporting socio-technical teams. Therefore, in HAI collaboration the system can be considered as a "member" of the team.

Hence, we follow [57] who proposed the Input - Mediator - Output - Input framework (I-M-O-I) that characterizes the research around teams in organizations. I-M-O-I framework consists of three stages defined as - Forming (i.e., the IM Phase), Functioning (i.e., the MO phase) and Finishing (i.e., the OI phase). This work contributes in HAI interaction by: i) Providing an overview of the recent work in HAI team interaction; ii) Demonstrating that recent work in the area of HAI teams is acknowledging the importance of organizational processes that need to be supported in socio-technical HAI settings; and iii) By taking the perspective, of the I-M-O-I, we identified processes important to be supported in HAI teams and highlighted future work.

2   Methodology

A systematic literature review has been performed in the areas of DM, HAI teams, HCI, Collective Intelligence and Human - Agent Interaction, to identify relevant papers and categorize them based on the I-M-O-I framework. It was expected that relevant research will be published at different disciplines, thus we have searched the major digital libraries of ACM, Springer, IEEE, AAAI, as well as Google Scholar using the phrases "Human - AI teams", "Human - AI Collective Intelligence", "Human - Agent Collaboration", "Human - AI Collaboration" and "Human - AI teaming". We aimed at collecting papers that were describing theoretical frameworks and/or empirical studies where humans were collaborating and/or interacting with AI enabled systems. 186 papers have been collected and reviewed at the first stage for their suitability. 95 papers have been excluded due to not satisfying the relevance criteria (e.g., no collaboration was described between the system and the human, only algorithmic performance discussed), thus a total of 91 papers have been analysed and thematically categorized based on the I-M-O-I stages: Forming, Functioning, Finishing.

3   Forming

Trusting
Trust has been extensively discussed in many studies as an important element for the success of human-only teams. This stage is where the members learn to work together, trust each other and each others' intentions, discover how efficient they are together and identify where knowledge and information is located in the team. In the I-M-O-I framework, trust has been discussed in relation to *Potency* and *Safety*. Team members need to trust their team and provide valid information for making a decision [101]. Similarly, research in HAI interaction (Table 1) vows that the acceptance of AI, in almost any context, depends heavily on human trust in the decision provided by the AI [55,109,113]. Trust has mainly been examined, as a self-reported parameter [1,6,46,103] taking different forms (e.g., Acceptance of model recommendations [31,82,87], confidence in the model [6,75], perceived accuracy [71,100]).

Potency refers to the team's belief that they can be effective together. In human teams potency has been associated to self and collective efficacy, self rating of the member's effectiveness as well as the management's evaluations of the team. In addition, communication was proven as important and correlated to collective efficacy and team performance. In HAI teams system's confidence score and uncertainty predictions can be used as indications of the system's self efficacy in contributing to the team's DM process [54,77,78]. Communication of the system through explanations (local and global) have been used in different studies aiming at helping in the development of potency between humans and systems [68,79,100,106,106]. The efficacy of systems has been evaluated in the form of the accuracy of the system's decisions, predictions and recommendations. Feedback can be provided by team members as an indication on the system's success rates (e.g., how many times the system's predictions contributed to a successful or not successful decision respectively [28,33,54]).

Safety related to trust, is dealing with team members trusting other members' intentions and actions. Related work has examined psychological safety [35] - the shared belief that the team is safe for interpersonal risk taking - in relation to the team's efficacy and performance. System response time can contribute to the potential development of psychological safety [20]. Buçinca et. al. looked into cognitive forcing functions and found that it moderates the effectiveness of explainable AI solutions that could promote safety in the team. The systems performance and quality of proposed decision can also be taken into account for increasing the sense of safety among HAI teams [37,92,100]. Similarly to how we either trust or distrust other people based on their punctuality and the reliability of their response, systems are judged based on their response time and quality of this response [2,28,43,107,115]. This can be in the form of their speed in completing a request, etc. Similarly, the transparency of the system, especially in black-box setups is contributing to the increase of the sense of safety and consequently trust in the AI decision support [7,39,69]. However, inconclusive results have been drawn from several studies on whether techniques such as explainability (see below) improve trust in AI DSS [7,36,37,75,77].

Planning

This stage is considered as a ground setting step. The team is identifying relevant information and knowledge sources that are available through its members and the DSS. As part of Planning *Gathering Information*, including communication of information within the team and identifying other sources of information, as well as to develop a *Strategy* for completing the required task, are discussed.

Gathering Information that is useful for the task at hand is very crucial for a team for achieving its goal [34]. Functional diversity of the team members has been proven to be very important, particularly for information sharing in DM, and has been positively correlated to team performance [23]. In HAI teams, human members, should provide the system with any relevant information, so the system can update its task model. The system is usually providing additional projections to the team to help them in reaching a decision. Information are then shared accompanied by an explanation. Explanations can take different forms, for example in the form of natural language [15], visualizations [4], uncertainty of the model decision (e.g., confidence) [21], by providing examples [41], etc. Explanations should be informative and easy to be interpreted by a specific audience. As discussed above, information can also be shared by the system with respect to the training dataset used for training the model to enhance the team's understanding [9,54,93,102].

Developing Strategy. Usually decisions, especially in high risk scenarios are taken in multiple stages before reaching the final output. Relevant work on HAI teams found that DM strategies impact the efficacy of the team as well as the participation approaches of team members [91]. Specifically, in [32] HAI teams found it more difficult to plan, adapt and anticipate the needs of team members', compared to all-human teams. In addition, early coordination among team members and task delegation between human members and AI proved to be beneficial and improves the perception of humans towards the AI system [56].

Structuring

The rules, norms, and roles need to be defined in teams, and in HAI teams these need to also include the system. Research in organizations focused on two main constructs, *Shared Mental Models (SMM)* and *Transactive Memory (TM)*.

SMM have been one of the most researched constructs in the organization, groups, teams and communities, research areas. Work in the area explored how explanations affected the user's mental model for trusting the system [15] and their perception of the impact of their decision to either follow or not the system's suggestion [12,13,75]. The interaction behaviour of an agent was examined in [11], where the speed of the agent response was used as a cue for developing a mental model of the system. Others looked into SMM in human only and in hybrid teams, to found that when humans were working with agents, they had significantly inconsistent levels of team mental models when compared to human only teams [98]. However, developing mental models when interacting with an AI system may not always be trivia for the user [58] and it has been proven to be context and condition dependant [14]. There are controversial results on whether the accuracy of the user's mental model about the system would improve the performance of the team, with some positive (e.g., [12]) and some negative (e.g., [58]) associations.

In HAI teaming, it is not only important for the human members to form an accurate mental model about the system, but also for the system to be human aware and have a "mental" model of the team [8,32,64,65,112]. The team's and the system's mental models should be aligned in the sense of having an understanding of the shared and individual goals, information needs, and capabilities. There are many challenges in eliciting, measuring and implementing HAI SMM [8]. Most earlier work looked into defining and measuring SMM in such teams, emphasizing the importance of similarity, over accuracy, of the models that are developed between team members [61]. More recently, research explored SMM in a collaboration scenario between humans and intelligent agents to find that the development of SMM impacts trust in the agent's decision, team performance and communication [53]. Others proposed keeping personalized models of how the human has approached a shared task, following reinforcement learning algorithms and maintaining it through human interaction [65]. An architecture for HAI interaction with emphasis given to the models developed in relation to how the HAI team is approaching the task was proposed in [64].

Transactive Memory has also been highly investigated in team functioning. TM deals with knowing what, and where, relevant information, skills etc., are located within the team, so a member can access it when needed [83,84]. It is a resemblance to using the memory of each other as an extension of their own.

HAI teams could benefit from developing a TM system. On one hand, the human members need to be aware of the relevant information and cababilities that the system can provide to the team. On the other hand, the system should communicate information about the model. Hence, different approaches have been followed for providing information of the model predictions. Information about how and why a prediction was given helps the team in understanding the value of the system in the DM process, for providing useful input and decide on how much weight should the team give to the information they will receive. Thus, by understanding how and with what information the system could contribute to the team's effort, members can start building a TM system. However, the system should be able to "know" what the other team members know. Consequently, personalized user models and a personalized team model is needed, where information about the user and the overall team and task can be stored. Furthermore, research demonstrates how the system needs to develop and maintain a model about the task and the users in order to be able to communicate relevant information and collaborate effectively [63]. Similarly, in [64] symbolic representation is used for facilitating HAI interaction, by keeping and updating a symbolic representation of the users and their interaction with the AI enabled system. Scrutability has been identified as an approach for allowing the user to view and modify their own user models e.g., [66]. When interacting with AI users can provide feedback or view and change the personalization model that the system developed for them [74,100]. In [60] they proposed a framework for context-aware HAI collaboration, where the scrutability of the user model allows the system and the users to mutually evolve.

Table 1. Forming and Functioning stages processes and relevant work

Forming Processes	Relevant Work
Trusting:	$[1,6,21,31,46,55,103,109,113]$
	$[71,75,82,87,100]$
Potency	$[28,33,54,68,77\text{--}79,100,106]$
Safety	$[2,20,28,35,43,92,100,107,115]$
	$[7,36,37,39,69,75,77]$
Planning:	
Gathering Information	$[4,9,15,21,36,41,52,54,93,102]$
Developing Strategy	$[32,56,91]$
Structuring:	$[15,19,31,47,50,87,106,111]$
Shared Mental Models	$[11\text{--}15,29,43,63,90,91,98]$
	$[8,32,53,58,61,64,65,75,112]$
Transactive Memory	$[60,63,64,66,73,74,100]$
Functioning Processes	Relevant Work
Bonding:	$[44,110]$
Managing diversity of membership	$[22,30,40,42,45,49,89,93,97,99]$
Managing conflict among team members	$[10,19,20,87,106,109,110]$
Adapting:	$[60,108,114]$
Performance routine vs novel conditions	$[25,72,81,114]$
Helping and Workload sharing	$[13\text{--}15,38,88,95,109]$
Learning:	$[74,87,95,100]$
Learning from Minority team members	$[16,24,26,74,80,113]$
Learning from the team's best member	$[86]$

3.1 Research Challenges at Forming Stage

Trusting: It is clear based on both organization, and HCI research that trust has a fundamental role in forming a functional relationship between humans and AI. **Potency** needs to be supported further to help humans develop trust towards the system's decisions. We need to understand how the technical solutions discussed above are perceived by humans, how their usefulness and effectiveness varies in different contexts and how these should be delivered to the humans in order to be more understandable. **Safety** is also highly associated with developing trust. More approaches are needed for communicating clearly the intentions of the system to the team, how the information that the team is sharing with the system are being handled, for what purpose is the system storing information about the team, the task, and other contextual data. Several studies in the past few years have discovered that training datasets may potentially result in biased and discriminatory decisions [9,93,102], which contributes to human distrust towards the system. Thus, having information about the dataset based on which the system is trained, could improve the sense of safety in black-box systems.

Planning: Gathering Information about the task and sharing this between the team and the system is very important. The system should be able to develop models for all the entities involved and provide any inferred information to the team. Explanations need to accompany this information in a contextually relevant form [85]. Research has employed different methods (e.g., [4,15]), for delivering and explaining information that the system holds, however, we need to further understand how the information shared by the system, affect the overall DM process; Are different delivery forms more suitable than others in a team environment?; Does the system need to be 'sensing' and delivering this information temporally for improved team efficiency or for not biasing the team? **Strategy** development is closely related to temporal releasing of information. Although, we have discussed above a small number of approaches related to strategic planning in HAI teams, from what we have seen there is not a coordinated effort in understanding how strategy development can be supported in socio-technical teams. This is an area that needs to be further developed, technologically and scientifically in the areas of organizational psychology and computer science related fields.

Structuring: A big part of the research in HAI teams is concerned with the development of **SMM**. Currently, there is not a substantial amount of empirical work in understanding how to design, develop and maintain SMM of the team and the system, or how to evaluate SMM between humans and the machine to ensure that these have been developed. Additionally, work in **TM** systems in the HAI teams need to start investigating how context aware team models (about the team members, the task and the information available), will be developed, maintained, and allow the team members to interact with it. Research in user modeling has developed several approaches over the years for extracting, maintaining and utilizing individual and group user model (e.g., [66,86]). Research in HAI teams needs to adopt relevant techniques from this area to develop models where the system will store information about the team members, their abilities, skills and knowledge so it can utilize those when needed.

4   Functioning

Bonding

Bonding denotes that team members have a strong connection with each other and they are willing to continue working together even when the current task finishes [57]. Bonding among team members can be achieved in the long term and not at the initial stages the team's lifetime. It includes emotional and affective attachments between team members [17]. Research in HAI interaction discussed how humans are developing bonds with robots and other AI enabled artifacts similar to how they express the need for developing attachments to other humans [44]. Studies focused on two main parameters that are considered as important for achieving bonding, the management of, *the diversity of members in the team* and *the conflict that might occur among them.*

Managing Diversity of Membership has been associated to the performance of human teams. Diversity itself is a complex construct to capture and has been studied by researchers in several disciplines who tried to understand the attributes that relate to diversity [94]. Demographic/surface diversity (age, gender, culture), functional diversity (cognitive, experience/ knowledge), Subjective/deep diversity (values, beliefs, motivations, experience), are affecting collaboration negatively or positively [3]. In AI-enabled technologies, particularly in those that operate in social spaces, diversity-aware algorithms can play a crucial role in reducing bias and minimizing the perpetuation of social stereotypes [40,45]. Managing diversity is becoming even more important when we are dealing with HAI teams due to the complexity of the interaction and collaboration processes involved [30]. To manage the different types of diversity of human team members, we need the AI system to be able to "understand" and accommodate for this when the team is interacting.

Managing conflict among team members has been for a long time an area of research in the collaboration and interpersonal relationships research [27]. In HAI teams, conflicts between human members might occur due to trust or distrust towards the AI, where subgroups can be created within the team. However, the role of the leader and how the rules that the team has agreed on at the beginning are being reinforced, is paramount for resolving potential conflicts [110]. In addition, in HAI teaming it is important to manage conflict between human and AI decisions/predictions. For example, when the system provides a different decision from the one selected by members, mechanisms should be in place to resolve this. In [87] authors found that humans are using different heuristics including their own confidence when deciding when to rely on a system's decision, while in [20] they suggest that engaging the user with the system's decision leads to better performance and less over-reliance to the AI. Similarly, explanation types are contributing differently in enhancing or reducing trust and reliance to the AI predictions [106] and are affecting in extend the bonding relationship between humans and AI [109]. The directionality of communication between humans and AI has been investigated by [10] showing that human expectations and communication differ when they believe they are interacting with another human, compared to when they think they are interacting with AI [19].

Adapting

In [57] adaptation refers to the ability of the team to *perform in novel vs routine situations* and how team members are *helping and workload sharing* with each other. Humans are well known for their abilities in adapting to the environment [108], however, a mutual adaptation is required in HAI teams. Mutual Adaptation has been studied in the context of human - agent collaborative interaction [108] where the system and the human are collaborating towards a common goal, and they can work independently on a specific part of the task according to the information available. The authors show that both the agent and the human are at some point changing their behaviour to adapt to each other and to the changing conditions during their collaboration. More recent work has looked into the adaptation of the system to either the user [114] or the context [60].

Performance in Routine vs Novel Conditions. In HAI, the team should be able to perform in conditions that are different from what the team is accustomed to [25]. This means that the system should be able to adapt in the changing context and also recognise and adapt to the human team, which in its turn should be able to adapt to the new conditions [114]. In order for the AI system to adapt to a certain condition, it first need to be able to make a relevant detection (e.g., the goal of the user, or the team), and try to adapt its behavior accordingly [72,81]. AI systems in DM today are mostly fine tuned to assist in a specific task, under certain conditions. However, in dynamic HAI collaboration scenarios the system should be able to detect, or have a mechanism of allowing emerging information to be loaded to the system and transform its behaviour accordingly. Most of the current work focuses primarily on algorithmic and sensory techniques of improving the system's adaptation to the user/team.

Helping and Workload Sharing. Like in every type of team, in HAI teams, understanding who is your teammate, what can be their role and how workload can be most efficiently allocated, can be very beneficial but challenging at the same time [88]. It is evident that AI systems can perform better than humans in certain tasks, while in others, human input or human only action is preferred [14]. It is important for the team to be able to understand and recognize how the AI system could be best utilized and how task allocation should be performed between the human members [38]. This goes back to trust and self-efficacy. Humans involved in HAI teams, need to trust the system in tasks that the system is performing better [13,15,109], while also understanding how they can be more effective together [67]. In [95] the authors have taken an organization view on HAI collaboration, discussing possible workload sharing models between the human and the system, where for example each one is working on a specialized task (e.g., the system performs quantitative analysis on a dataset while the human performs qualitative analysis on the same data).

Learning

Learning has been an important cognitive process that requires understanding the needs of the team, and be able to attend to those. Focusing primarily on "knowledge", learning is studied under two main themes: *Learning from Minority and Dissenting team members* and *Learning from teams best member* [57]. In [67] they have also looked into the importance of the member's centrality or peripherality, finding correlation in how others in the team are learning from those members and how it affects the DM efficiency of the team. In [95] they proposed learning configurations in HAI collaborative DM, taking an organization approach, where learning can be achieved collaboratively or independently depending on the context and task at hand. In HAI socio-technical context, learning can take different forms. For example, AI systems are learning through training data [87], but they are also learning when the user is updating a model that the system has developed about the user or the world [74,100]. In HAI teams, learning is not just in terms of training data. Based on the organizational perspective, the system and humans are learning from each other.

Learning from Minority team members has been very important for human only teams [57]. In the context of HAI teams, minority members, in terms of personal and cultural characteristics (gender, ethnicity) or knowledge, can provide a different perspective and unique information to the rest of the team. There is a lot of work discussing biases in AI enabled systems and how the closed loop approach that black box systems follow, does not provide opportunities for improvement [16,24]. By allowing a minority or peripheral member to input information, provide feedback or update a model created by the system, can be a way towards minimizing biased DM and allowing the system to learn for future tasks [74,113]. For example, in [26] allowed participants to denote the important points in an image that the system should be looking for when performing future tasks with similar images. Similarly, in [80] they allowed users to override the system's decision on food splits between students improves fairness perception.

Learning from the teams best member is also an important aspect, but in order to take advantage of this, the skills and knowledge of the team members need to be available to all. Research in organizations shows that it is even more important to rely on the most knowledgeable person when the difficulty of the task is higher [18]. Taking the system's angle, we have discussed earlier how user models developed by the system can allow the system to "understand" who are the members of the team, their skills, expertise, knowledge and information they hold. This can be helpful for the system in developing a team mental model, but it can also be helpful for the human members when they need to refer to members with unique skills or are more knowledgeable than others in specific areas. For example, in [86] the authors have looked into how cognitive centrality [67] can be extracted based on knowledge sharing patterns and used in benefiting the whole knowledge-sharing community to function more efficiently.

4.1 Research Challenges at the Functioning Stage

Bonding: Managing Diversity of Membership is one of the major challenges in AI systems primarily because diversity has been very difficult to be captured and quantified. Integrating diversity awareness in the context of collaboration between humans and AI is still an open issue that needs to be investigated by future work. Given the user models, approaches should be developed particularly for "measuring" diversity within the team and between members (e.g., [22]), to allow the system to "understand" the potential differences between people in the team, and communicate with them accordingly. **Managing Conflict** is another area that can be explored further in HAI teams. Approaches have been examined that will enable AI systems to turn down directives from humans when it is needed [19]. Studying theoretical work on conflict resolution in teams (e.g., [5]) will allow better understanding how conflict resolution can be implemented and managed in HAI teams.

Adapting: One of the most challenging aspects in HAI teams is for the humans and the system, to be able to adapt to the various situations in the environment and to capture the dynamics within the team. For example, in **Performance routine vs novel conditions** most of the work so far has focused primarily on technology approaches (e.g., algorithmic, sensory) for enabling the system's adaptation to the individual user or the team. Future work should investigate how context dynamics can be taken into account, what parameters (e.g., cognitive, emotional, social) need to be considered, what changes within the team, or about the task at hand need to be measured for understanding the ability of the team to adapt in different conditions and how does the system influences this adaptation. Furthermore, regarding **Helping and Workload sharing**, we need to understand how task allocation and workload sharing is changing with the introduction of a system as part of the team. Future work needs to investigate through experimental methods how the models are changing with the introduction of a system as part of the team, how the relationships between humans within the team change in terms of task and workload sharing, taking into account the delegation of work to the AI system, and how do they manage low-performing systems in certain conditions.

Learning: Collaborative learning approaches have been proposed e.g., [95], following different configurations. **Learning from Minority and Dissenting team members** can be very important in this socio-technical context. Future work needs to examine the benefits of encouraging minority or peripheral members to interact with the system and their team (e.g., input information, provide feedback, update a model) for improving the learning process within the team and as an approach for addressing and minimizing biases in the DM process. Similarly, **Learning from the teams best member** can be achieved as long as the system and the rest of the team have an understanding of who is holding important information for the task at hand. Although, research has looked into the central or best members in terms of the knowledge and information they hold, future work should also investigate, how cognitive processes might affect the functioning of a HAI team.

5   Finishing

Finally the team enters into the **Finishing** stage. At this stage the team has reached its goal successfully or not. Important knowledge that was shared within the team is kept by team members, and transferred to other teams or to the future tasks. Groups and teams in organizational contexts disband for many reasons, however they might as well continue working together in a different project. The knowledge, trust, etc., that were developed through their collaboration and interaction, would be useful for the future. In HAI teams, the humans are developing a mental model of the system and they have adjusted their expectations from, and trust to, the system based on their experiences, successes and failures by utilizing the system during their DM process. The system should store information about the HAI interaction for each member and for the team, tasks and context, in different personalized models and use those as a starting point in their future collaborations.

5.1 Research Challenges at the Finishing Stage

Through theoretical and empirical studies we need to investigate how the processes, models, experiences that have been developed through a team's life-cycle could be exploited. The knowledge developed during the collaboration of a HAI team can be used as an input for both the system and the human members for improving the functioning and performance of future HAI teams. Furthermore, the models and data that the system keeps for each member of the team, could be loaded into a different system and used in a future project, so we can avoid the well known "cold start problem". Similarly, the system's performance and mental model will be known to the human members involved in the current HAI team and this will allow for future "collaboration" between the same team members to be more efficient.

6   Conclusion

Research work in HAI teams in DM scenarios is growing fast [48, 70, 104, 105, 108]. Processes like trust, development of mental models, communication and collaboration are acknowledged and explored by the research community. Understanding how the human mental models developed by the humans about a system, affects their interaction and adoption of the systems recommendation [13] is considered very important. Human expectations of how they will interact with the system affects how they will perceive the system's output.

Facilitating the collaboration in socio-technical teams is not just a technological challenge but also social and psychological. For successfully building and facilitating the functioning of HAI teams we need to inform AI systems with theories and processes from organizational research. In this work, we have proposed understanding HAI teams following the Input - Mediator - Output - Input framework (I-M-O-I). We reviewed relevant work on DM in HAI teams, for demonstrating that by taking this perspective we can identify processes, important for the successful functioning of HAI collaboration. Future work needs to be done in the area for successful HAI teaming.

References

1. Abdul, A., von der Weth, C., Kankanhalli, M., Lim, B.Y.: COGAM: measuring and moderating cognitive load in machine learning model explanations. In: Proceedings of the 2020 CHI Conference, pp. 1–14 (2020)

2. Abdul, A., von der Weth, C., Kankanhalli, M., Lim, B.Y.: Cogam: Measuring and moderating cognitive load in machine learning model explanations. In: Proceedings of the 2020 CHI Conference, CHI 2020, pp. 1-14. ACM, New York, NY, USA (2020). https://doi.org/10.1145/3313831.3376615

3. Aggarwal, I., Woolley, A.W., Chabris, C.F., Malone, T.W.: The impact of cognitive style diversity on implicit learning in teams. Front. Psychol. **10** (2019). https://doi.org/10.3389/fpsyg.2019.00112

4. Alicioglu, G., Sun, B.: A survey of visual analytics for explainable artificial intelligence methods. Comput. Graph. **102**, 502–520 (2022). https://doi.org/10.1016/j.cag.2021.09.002

5. Alper, S., Tjosvold, D., Law, K.S.: Conflict management, efficacy, and performance in organizational teams. Pers. Psychol. **53**(3), 625–642 (2000)

6. Alqaraawi, A., Schuessler, M., Weiß, P., Costanza, E., Berthouze, N.: Evaluating saliency map explanations for convolutional neural networks: a user study. In: Proceedings of the 25th International Conference on IUI, IUI 2020, pp. 275-285. ACM, New York, NY, USA (2020). https://doi.org/10.1145/3377325.3377519

7. Alufaisan, Y., Marusich, L.R., Bakdash, J.Z., Zhou, Y., Kantarcioglu, M.: Does explainable artificial intelligence improve human decision-making? Proc. AAAI Conf. AI **35**(8), 6618–6626 (2021). https://doi.org/10.1609/aaai.v35i8.16819

8. Andrews, R.W., Lilly, J.M., Srivastava, D., Feigh, K.M.: The role of shared mental models in human-AI teams: a theoretical review. Theor. Issues Ergon. Sci. **24**(2), 129–175 (2023). https://doi.org/10.1080/1463922X.2022.2061080

9. Arnold, M., et al.: Factsheets: increasing trust in AI services through supplier's declarations of conformity. IBM J. Res. Dev. **63**(4/5), 6:1–6:13 (2019). https://doi.org/10.1147/JRD.2019.2942288

10. Ashktorab, Z., et al.: Effects of communication directionality and AI agent differences in human-AI interaction. In: Proceedings of the 2021 CHI Conference on Human Factors in Computing Systems, CHI 2021, ACM, New York, NY, USA (2021). https://doi.org/10.1145/3411764.3445256

11. Ashktorab, Z., et al.: Human-AI collaboration in a cooperative game setting: measuring social perception and outcomes. Proc. ACM Hum.-Comput. Interact. **4**(CSCW2) (2020). https://doi.org/10.1145/3415167

12. Bansal, G., Nushi, B., Kamar, E., Horvitz, E., Weld, D.S.: Is the most accurate AI the best teammate? optimizing AI for teamwork. Proc. AAAI Conf. AI **35**(13), 11405–11414 (2021). https://doi.org/10.1609/aaai.v35i13.17359

13. Bansal, G., Nushi, B., Kamar, E., Lasecki, W.S., Weld, D.S., Horvitz, E.: Beyond accuracy: the role of mental models in human-AI team performance. In: Proceedings of the AAAI HCOMP Conference, vol. 7, pp. 2–11 (2019)

14. Bansal, G., Nushi, B., Kamar, E., Weld, D.S., Lasecki, W.S., Horvitz, E.: Updates in human-AI teams: understanding and addressing the performance/compatibility tradeoff. Proc. AAAI Conf. AI **33**(01), 2429–2437 (2019). https://doi.org/10.1609/aaai.v33i01.33012429

15. Bansal, G., et al.: Does the whole exceed its parts? the effect of AI explanations on complementary team performance. In: Proceedings of the 2021 CHI Conference, CHI 2021, ACM, New York, NY, USA (2021). https://doi.org/10.1145/3411764.3445717

16. Barlas, P., Kyriakou, K., Guest, O., Kleanthous, S., Otterbacher, J.: To see is to stereotype: image tagging algorithms, gender recognition, and the accuracy-fairness trade-off. Proc. ACM Hum.-Comput. Interact. **4**(CSCW3) (2021). https://doi.org/10.1145/3432931

17. Bishop, J.W., Scott, K.D.: An examination of organizational and team commitment in a self-directed team environment. J. Appl. Psychol. **85**(3), 439–450 (2000). https://doi.org/10.1037/0021-9010.85.3.439

18. Bonner, B.L., Baumann, M.R., Dalal, R.S.: The effects of member expertise on group decision-making and performance. Organ. Behav. Hum. Decis. Process. **88**(2), 719–736 (2002). https://doi.org/10.1016/S0749-5978(02)00010-9

19. Briggs, G.M., Scheutz, M.: Sorry, i can't do that': developing mechanisms to appropriately reject directives in human-robot interactions. In: 2015 AAAI fall symposium series (2015)

20. Buçinca, Z., Malaya, M.B., Gajos, K.Z.: To trust or to think: cognitive forcing functions can reduce overreliance on AI in AI-assisted decision-making. Proc. ACM Hum.-Comput. Interact. **5**(CSCW1) (2021). https://doi.org/10.1145/3449287

21. Buçinca, Z., Malaya, M.B., Gajos, K.Z.: To trust or to think: cognitive forcing functions can reduce overreliance on AI in AI-assisted decision-making. Proc. ACM on Hum.-Comput. Interact. **5**(CSCW1), 1–21 (2021)

22. Budescu, D.V., Budescu, M.: How to measure diversity when you must. Psychol. Methods **17**(2), 215–227 (2012). https://doi.org/10.1037/a0027129

23. Bunderson, J.S., Sutcliffe, K.M.: Comparing alternative conceptualizations of functional diversity in management teams: process and performance effects. Acad. Manage. J. **45**(5), 875–893 (2002). https://doi.org/10.5465/3069319

24. Buolamwini, J., Gebru, T.: Gender shades: intersectional accuracy disparities in commercial gender classification. In: Friedler, S.A., Wilson, C. (eds.) Proceedings of the 1st Conference on Fairness, Accountability and Transparency. Proceedings of Machine Learning Research, vol. 81, pp. 77–91. PMLR, 23–24 February 2018

25. Burke, C.S., Stagl, K.C., Salas, E., Pierce, L., Kendall, D.: Understanding team adaptation: a conceptual analysis and model. J. Appl. Psychol. **91**(6), 1189–1207 (2006)

26. Cai, C.J., et al.: Human-centered tools for coping with imperfect algorithms during medical decision-making. In: Proceedings of the 2019 CHI Conference, CHI 2019, pp. 1–14. ACM, New York, NY, USA (2019). https://doi.org/10.1145/3290605.3300234

27. Carnevale, P.J., Pruitt, D.G.: Negotiation and mediation. Ann. Rev. Psychol. **43**(1), 531–582 (1992). https://doi.org/10.1146/annurev.ps.43.020192.002531

28. Carton, S., Mei, Q., Resnick, P.: Feature-based explanations don't help people detect misclassifications of online toxicity. Proc. Int. AAAI Conf. Web Soc. Media **14**(1), 95–106 (2020). https://doi.org/10.1609/icwsm.v14i1.7282

29. Cila, N.: Designing human-agent collaborations: Commitment, responsiveness, and support. In: CHI Conference, pp. 1–18 (2022)

30. De-Arteaga, M., Fazelpour, S.: Diversity in sociotechnical machine learning systems. Big Data Soc. **9**(1) (2022). https://doi.org/10.1177/20539517221082027

31. De-Arteaga, M., Fogliato, R., Chouldechova, A.: A case for humans-in-the-loop: decisions in the presence of erroneous algorithmic scores. In: Proceedings of the 2020 CHI Conference, CHI 2020, pp. 1–12. ACM, New York, NY, USA (2020).https://doi.org/10.1145/3313831.3376638

32. Demir, M., McNeese, N.J., Cooke, N.J.: The impact of perceived autonomous agents on dynamic team behaviors. IEEE Trans. Emerg. Top. Comput. Intell. **2**(4), 258–267 (2018). https://doi.org/10.1109/TETCI.2018.2829985

33. Dressel, J., Farid, H.: The accuracy, fairness, and limits of predicting recidivism. Sci. Adv. **4**(1), eaao5580 (2018). https://doi.org/10.1126/sciadv.aao5580

34. Durham, C.C., Locke, E.A., Poon, J.M.L., McLeod, P.L.: Effects of group goals and time pressure on group efficacy, information-seeking strategy, and performance. Hum. Perform. **13**(2), 115–138 (2000). https://doi.org/10.1207/s15327043hup1302_1

35. Edmondson, A.: Psychological safety and learning behavior in work teams. Adm. Sci. Quart. **44**(2), 350–383 (1999). http://www.jstor.org/stable/2666999

36. Edwards, L., Veale, M.: Slave to the algorithm: why a right to an explanation is probably not the remedy you are looking for. Duke L. Tech. Rev. **16**, 18 (2017)

37. Ehrlich, K., Kirk, S.E., Patterson, J., Rasmussen, J.C., Ross, S.I., Gruen, D.M.: Taking advice from intelligent systems: the double-edged sword of explanations. In: Proceedings of the 16th International Conference on IUI, IUI 2011, pp. 125-134. ACM, New York, NY, USA (2011). https://doi.org/10.1145/1943403.1943424

38. Endsley, M.R.: Supporting human-AI teams: transparency, explainability, and situation awareness. Comput. Hum. Behav. **140**, 107574 (2023). https://doi.org/10.1016/j.chb.2022.107574

39. von Eschenbach, W.J.: Transparency and the black box problem: why we do not trust AI. Philos. Technol. **34**(4), 1607–1622 (2021)

40. Fan, S., Barlas, P., Christoforou, E., Otterbacher, J., Sadiq, S., Demartini, G.: Socio-economic diversity in human annotations. In: Proceedings of the 14th ACM WebSci Conference 2022, WebSci 2022, pp. 98–109. ACM, New York, NY, USA (2022). https://doi.org/10.1145/3501247.3531588

41. Feng, S., Boyd-Graber, J.: What can AI do for me? evaluating machine learning interpretations in cooperative play. In: Proceedings of the 24th International Conference IUI, IUI 2019, pp. 229–239. ACM, New York, NY, USA (2019). https://doi.org/10.1145/3301275.3302265

42. Flathmann, C., Schelble, B.G., Zhang, R., McNeese, N.J.: Modeling and guiding the creation of ethical human-AI teams. In: Proceedings of the 2021 AAAI/ACM Conference on AIES, AIES 2021, pp. 469-479. ACM, New York, NY, USA (2021). https://doi.org/10.1145/3461702.3462573

43. Gero, K.I., et al.: Mental models of AI agents in a cooperative game setting. In: Proceedings of the 2020 CHI Conference on Human Factors in Computing Systems, CHI 2020, pp. 1–12. ACM, New York, NY, USA (2020). https://doi.org/10.1145/3313831.3376316

44. Gillath, O., Ai, T., Branicky, M.S., Keshmiri, S., Davison, R.B., Spaulding, R.: Attachment and trust in artificial intelligence. Comput. Hum. Behav. **115**, 106607 (2021). https://doi.org/10.1016/j.chb.2020.106607

45. Giunchiglia, F., Kleanthous, S., Otterbacher, J., Draws, T.: Transparency paths - documenting the diversity of user perceptions. In: Adjunct Proceedings of the 29th ACM UMAP Conference, UMAP 2021, pp. 415–420. ACM, New York, NY, USA (2021). https://doi.org/10.1145/3450614.3463292

46. Green, B., Chen, Y.: The principles and limits of algorithm-in-the-loop decision making. Proc. ACM Hum.-Comput. Interact. **3**(CSCW) (2019). https://doi.org/10.1145/3359152

47. Grgić-Hlača, N., Engel, C., Gummadi, K.P.: Human decision making with machine assistance: an experiment on bailing and jailing. Proc. ACM Hum.-Comput. Interact. **3**(CSCW) (2019). https://doi.org/10.1145/3359280

48. Groh, M., Epstein, Z., Firestone, C., Picard, R.: Deepfake detection by human crowds, machines, and machine-informed crowds. Proc. Natl. Acad. Sci. **119**(1), e2110013119 (2022)

49. Grother, P., Ngan, M., Hanaoka, K.: Face recognition vendor test part 3: demographic effects (2019-12-19 2019). https://doi.org/10.6028/NIST.IR.8280

50. Günther, M., Kasirzadeh, A.: Algorithmic and human decision making: For a double standard of transparency. AI Soc. **37**(1), 375–381 (2022). https://doi.org/10.1007/s00146-021-01200-5

51. Haesevoets, T., De Cremer, D., Dierckx, K., Van Hiel, A.: Human-machine collaboration in managerial decision making. Comput. Hum. Behav. **119**, 106730 (2021). https://doi.org/10.1016/j.chb.2021.106730

52. Hancox-Li, L.: Robustness in machine learning explanations: does it matter? In: Proceedings of the 2020 Conference on Fairness, Accountability, and Transparency, FAT* 2020, pp. 640–647. ACM, New York, NY, USA (2020). https://doi.org/10.1145/3351095.3372836

53. Hanna, N., Richards, D.: The impact of multimodal communication on a shared mental model, trust, and commitment in human-intelligent virtual agent teams. Multimodal Technologies and Interaction **2**(3) (2018). https://doi.org/10.3390/mti2030048, https://www.mdpi.com/2414-4088/2/3/48

54. Harrison, G., Hanson, J., Jacinto, C., Ramirez, J., Ur, B.: An empirical study on the perceived fairness of realistic, imperfect machine learning models. In: Proceedings of the 2020 Conference on Fairness, Accountability, and Transparency, FAT* 2020, pp. 392-402. ACM, New York, NY, USA (2020). https://doi.org/10.1145/3351095.3372831

55. Hauptman, A.I., Duan, W., Mcneese, N.J.: The components of trust for collaborating with AI colleagues. In: Companion Publication of the 2022 Conference on Computer Supported Cooperative Work and Social Computing, CSCW'22 Companion, pp. 72-75. ACM, New York, NY, USA (2022). https://doi.org/10.1145/3500868.3559450

56. Hemmer, P., Westphal, M., Schemmer, M., Vetter, S., Vössing, M., Satzger, G.: Human-AI collaboration: the effect of AI delegation on human task performance and task satisfaction. In: Proceedings of the 28th International Conference on Intelligent User Interfaces, IUI 2023, pp. 453-463. ACM, New York, NY, USA (2023). https://doi.org/10.1145/3581641.3584052

57. Ilgen, D.R., Hollenbeck, J.R., Johnson, M., Jundt, D.: Teams in organizations: from input-process-output models to IMOI models. Annu. Rev. Psychol. **56**, 517–543 (2005)

58. Inkpen, K., et al.: Advancing human-AI complementarity: the impact of user expertise and algorithmic tuning on joint decision making (2022)

59. Jennings, N.R., et al.: Human-agent collectives. Commun. ACM **57**(12), 80–88 (2014). https://doi.org/10.1145/2629559

60. Jiang, N., Liu, X., Liu, H., Lim, E., Tan, C.W., Gu, J.: Beyond AI-powered context-aware services: the role of human-AI collaboration. Ind. Manage. Data Syst. (2022). https://doi.org/10.1108/IMDS-03-2022-0152, epub ahead of print. Published online: 9 December 2022

61. Jonker, C.M., van Riemsdijk, M.B., Vermeulen, B.: Shared mental models. In: De Vos, M., Fornara, N., Pitt, J.V., Vouros, G. (eds.) Coordination, Organizations, Institutions, and Norms in Agent Systems VI, pp. 132–151. Springer, Heidelberg (2011)

62. Kamar, E.: Directions in hybrid intelligence: complementing AI systems with human intelligence. In: Proceedings of the Twenty-Fifth International Joint Conference on Artificial Intelligence, IJCAI 2016, pp. 4070–4073. AAAI Press (2016)

63. Kambhampati, S.: Challenges of human-aware AI systems: AAAI presidential address. AI Mag. **41**(3), 3–17 (2020). https://doi.org/10.1609/aimag.v41i3.5257

64. Kambhampati, S., Sreedharan, S., Verma, M., Zha, Y., Guan, L.: Symbols as a lingua franca for bridging human-AI chasm for explainable and advisable AI systems. In: Proceedings of the AAAI Conference on Artificial Intelligence, vol. 36, pp. 12262–12267 (2022)
65. Kaur, H.: Building shared mental models between humans and AI for effective collaboration (2019)
66. Kay, J., Kummerfeld, B.: Creating personalized systems that people can scrutinize and control: Drivers, principles and experience. ACM Trans. Interact. Intell. Syst. **2**(4) (2013). https://doi.org/10.1145/2395123.2395129
67. Kerr, N.L., Tindale, R.S.: Group performance and decision making. Annu. Rev. Psychol. **55**, 623–655 (2004)
68. Kiani, A., et al.: Impact of a deep learning assistant on the histopathologic classification of liver cancer. NPJ Digit. Med. **3**(1), 23 (2020)
69. Kleanthous, S., Kasinidou, M., Barlas, P., Otterbacher, J.: Perception of fairness in algorithmic decisions: future developers' perspective. Patterns **3**(1), 100380 (2022). https://doi.org/10.1016/j.patter.2021.100380
70. Kleinberg, J., Lakkaraju, H., Leskovec, J., Ludwig, J., Mullainathan, S.: Human decisions and machine predictions. Q. J. Econ. **133**(1), 237–293 (2018)
71. Kocielnik, R., Amershi, S., Bennett, P.N.: Will you accept an imperfect AI? exploring designs for adjusting end-user expectations of AI systems. In: Proceedings of the 2019 CHI Conference on Human Factors in Computing Systems, CHI 2019, pp. 1-14. ACM, New York, NY, USA (2019). https://doi.org/10.1145/3290605.3300641
72. Koert, D., Pajarinen, J., Schotschneider, A., Trick, S., Rothkopf, C., Peters, J.: Learning intention aware online adaptation of movement primitives. IEEE Robot. Autom. Lett. **4**(4), 3719–3726 (2019). https://doi.org/10.1109/LRA.2019.2928760
73. Koh, P.W., Liang, P.: Understanding black-box predictions via influence functions. In: International conference on ML, pp. 1885–1894. PMLR (2017)
74. Kulesza, T., Stumpf, S., Burnett, M., Kwan, I.: Tell me more? the effects of mental model soundness on personalizing an intelligent agent. In: Proceedings of the SIGCHI Conference on Human Factors in Computing Systems, CHI 2012, pp. 1-10. ACM, New York, NY, USA (2012). https://doi.org/10.1145/2207676.2207678
75. Kulesza, T., Stumpf, S., Burnett, M., Yang, S., Kwan, I., Wong, W.K.: Too much, too little, or just right? ways explanations impact end users' mental models. In: 2013 IEEE Symposium on Visual Languages and Human Centric Computing, pp. 3–10 (2013). https://doi.org/10.1109/VLHCC.2013.6645235
76. Lai, V., Chen, C., Smith-Renner, A., Liao, Q.V., Tan, C.: Towards a science of human-AI decision making: An overview of design space in empirical human-subject studies. In: Proceedings of the 2023 ACM FACCT Conference, FAccT 2023, pp. 1369-1385. ACM, New York, NY, USA (2023). https://doi.org/10.1145/3593013.3594087
77. Lai, V., Liu, H., Tan, C.: why is 'chicago' deceptive? towards building model-driven tutorials for humans. In: Proceedings of the 2020 CHI Conference on Human Factors in Computing Systems, CHI 2020, pp. 1–13. ACM, New York, NY, USA (2020). https://doi.org/10.1145/3313831.3376873
78. Lai, V., Tan, C.: On human predictions with explanations and predictions of machine learning models: a case study on deception detection. In: Proceedings of the Conference on Fairness, Accountability, and Transparency, FAT* 2019, pp. 29–38. ACM, New York, NY, USA (2019). https://doi.org/10.1145/3287560.3287590

79. Lee, M.H., Siewiorek, D.P., Smailagic, A., Bernardino, A., Bermúdez i Badia, S.: Co-design and evaluation of an intelligent decision support system for stroke rehabilitation assessment. Proc. ACM Hum.-Comput. Interact. **4**(CSCW2) (2020). https://doi.org/10.1145/3415227

80. Lee, M.K., Jain, A., Cha, H.J., Ojha, S., Kusbit, D.: Procedural justice in algorithmic fairness: leveraging transparency and outcome control for fair algorithmic mediation. Proc. ACM Hum.-Comput. Interact. **3**(CSCW) (2019). https://doi.org/10.1145/3359284

81. Levine, S.J., Williams, B.C.: Watching and acting together: concurrent plan recognition and adaptation for human-robot teams. J. Artif. Intell. Res. **63**, 281–359 (2018)

82. Levy, A., Agrawal, M., Satyanarayan, A., Sontag, D.: Assessing the impact of automated suggestions on decision making: domain experts mediate model errors but take less initiative. In: Proceedings of the 2021 CHI Conference on Human Factors in Computing Systems, CHI 2021, ACM, New York, NY, USA (2021). https://doi.org/10.1145/3411764.3445522

83. Lewis, K.: Measuring transactive memory systems in the field: scale development and validation. J. Appl. Psychol. **88**(4), 587 (2003)

84. Lewis, K.: Knowledge and performance in knowledge-worker teams: a longitudinal study of transactive memory systems. Manage. Sci. **50**(11), 1519–1533 (2004). https://doi.org/10.1287/mnsc.1040.0257

85. Liu, H., Lai, V., Tan, C.: Understanding the effect of out-of-distribution examples and interactive explanations on human-AI decision making. Proc. ACM Hum.-Comput. Interact. **5**(CSCW2) (2021). https://doi.org/10.1145/3479552

86. Loizou, S.K., Dimitrova, V.: Adaptive notifications to support knowledge sharing in close-knit virtual communities. In: UMUAI (2013)

87. Lu, Z., Yin, M.: Human reliance on machine learning models when performance feedback is limited: heuristics and risks. In: Proceedings of the 2021 CHI Conference on Human Factors in Computing Systems, CHI 2021, ACM, New York, NY, USA (2021). https://doi.org/10.1145/3411764.3445562

88. McNeese, N.J., Schelble, B.G., Canonico, L.B., Demir, M.: Who/what is my teammate? team composition considerations in human-AI teaming. IEEE Trans. Hum.-Mach. Syst. **51**(4), 288–299 (2021). https://doi.org/10.1109/THMS.2021.3086018

89. Mitchell, M., et al.: Diversity and inclusion metrics in subset selection. In: Proceedings of the AAAI/ACM Conference on AI, Ethics, and Society, AIES 2020, pp. 117-123. ACM, New York, NY, USA (2020). https://doi.org/10.1145/3375627.3375832

90. Mucha, H., Robert, S., Breitschwerdt, R., Fellmann, M.: Interfaces for explanations in human-AI interaction: Proposing a design evaluation approach. In: Extended Abstracts of the 2021 CHI Conference on Human Factors in Computing Systems, CHI EA 2021, ACM, New York, NY, USA (2021). https://doi.org/10.1145/3411763.3451759

91. Munyaka, I., Ashktorab, Z., Dugan, C., Johnson, J., Pan, Q.: Decision making strategies and team efficacy in human-AI teams. Proc. ACM Hum.-Comput. Interact. **7**(CSCW1) (2023), https://doi.org/10.1145/3579476

92. Nourani, M., et al.: Anchoring bias affects mental model formation and user reliance in explainable AI systems. In: 26th International Conference on Intelligent User Interfaces, IUI 2021, pp. 340–350. ACM, New York, NY, USA (2021). https://doi.org/10.1145/3397481.3450639

93. Orphanou, K., et al.: Mitigating bias in algorithmic systems-a fish-eye view. ACM Comput. Surv. **55**(5) (2022). https://doi.org/10.1145/3527152

94. Phillips, K., O'Reilly, C.: Demography and diversity in organizations: a review of 40 years of research, vol. 20, pp. 77–140, January 1998

95. Puranam, P.: Human-AI collaborative decision-making as an organization design problem. J. Organ. Des. **10**(2), 75–80 (2021)

96. Ramchurn, S.D., et al.: A disaster response system based on human-agent collectives. J. AI Res. **57**, 661–708 (2016)

97. Recchiuto, C., Sgorbissa, A.: Diversity-aware social robots meet people: beyond context-aware embodied AI (2022)

98. Schelble, B.G., Flathmann, C., McNeese, N.J., Freeman, G., Mallick, R.: Let's think together! assessing shared mental models, performance, and trust in human-agent teams. Proc. ACM Hum.-Comput. Interact. **6**(GROUP), 1–29 (2022)

99. Schelenz, L., et al.: The theory, practice, and ethical challenges of designing a diversity-aware platform for social relations. In: Proceedings of the 2021 AAAI/ACM Conference on AI, Ethics, and Society, AIES 2021, pp. 905–915. ACM, New York, NY, USA (2021). https://doi.org/10.1145/3461702.3462595

100. Smith-Renner, A., et al.: No explainability without accountability: an empirical study of explanations and feedback in interactive ml. In: Proceedings of the 2020 CHI Conference, CHI 2020, pp. 1–13. ACM, New York, NY, USA (2020). https://doi.org/10.1145/3313831.3376624

101. Spears, R.: Social influence and group identity. Annu. Rev. Psychol. **72**(1), 367–390 (2021). https://doi.org/10.1146/annurev-psych-070620-111818

102. Toreini, E., Aitken, M., Coopamootoo, K., Elliott, K., Zelaya, C.G., van Moorsel, A.: The relationship between trust in AI and trustworthy machine learning technologies. In: Proceedings of the 2020 FAT* Conference, FAT* 2020, pp. 272–283. ACM, New York, NY, USA (2020). https://doi.org/10.1145/3351095.3372834

103. Tsai, C.H., You, Y., Gui, X., Kou, Y., Carroll, J.M.: Exploring and promoting diagnostic transparency and explainability in online symptom checkers. In: Proceedings of the 2021 CHI Conference on Human Factors in Computing Systems, CHI 2021, ACM, New York, NY, USA (2021). https://doi.org/10.1145/3411764.3445101

104. Tschandl, P., et al.: Human-computer collaboration for skin cancer recognition. Nat. Med. **26**(8), 1229–1234 (2020)

105. Vaccaro, M., Waldo, J.: The effects of mixing machine learning and human judgment. Commun. ACM **62**(11), 104–110 (2019)

106. Wang, X., Yin, M.: Are explanations helpful? a comparative study of the effects of explanations in AI-assisted decision-making. In: 26th International IUI Conference, IUI 2021, pp. 318–328. ACM, New York, NY, USA (2021). https://doi.org/10.1145/3397481.3450650

107. Wu, S., Dong, Z.: An auxiliary decision-making system for electric power intelligent customer service based on hadoop. Scientific Programming, pp. 1–11 (2022)

108. Xu, Y., et al.: Formation conditions of mutual adaptation in human-agent collaborative interaction. Appl. Intell. **36**(1), 208–228 (2012). https://doi.org/10.1007/s10489-010-0255-y

109. Yin, M., Wortman Vaughan, J., Wallach, H.: Understanding the effect of accuracy on trust in machine learning models. In: Proceedings of the 2019 Chi Conference on Human Factors in Computing Systems, pp. 1–12 (2019)

110. You, S., Robert, L.P.: Subgroup formation in human-robot teams: a multi-study mixed-method approach with implications for theory and practice. J. Am. Soc. Inf. Sci. **74**(3), 323–338 (2023). https://doi.org/10.1002/asi.24626

111. Zerilli, J., Knott, A., Maclaurin, J., Gavaghan, C.: Transparency in algorithmic and human decision-making: is there a double standard? Philos. Technol. **32**, 661–683 (2019)

112. Zhang, R., McNeese, N.J., Freeman, G., Musick, G.: An ideal human: expectations of AI teammates in human-AI teaming. Proc. ACM Hum.-Comput. Interact. 4(CSCW3) (2021). https://doi.org/10.1145/3432945

113. Zhang, Y., Liao, Q.V., Bellamy, R.K.E.: Effect of confidence and explanation on accuracy and trust calibration in AI-assisted decision making. In: Proceedings of the FAT* 2020 Conference, FAT* 2020, pp. 295–305. ACM, New York, NY, USA (2020). https://doi.org/10.1145/3351095.3372852

114. Zhao, M., Simmons, R., Admoni, H.: The role of adaptation in collective human-AI teaming. Top. Cogn. Sci. (2022). https://doi.org/10.1111/tops.12633

115. Zhao, Y.: Decision support system for economic management of large enterprises based on artificial intelligence. Wirel. Commun. Mob. Comput. **2022**, 1–11 (2022)

116. Zhu, J., Villareale, J., Javvaji, N., Risi, S., Löwe, M., Weigelt, R., Harteveld, C.: Player-AI interaction: what neural network games reveal about AI as play. In: Proceedings of the 2021 CHI Conference, pp. 1–17 (2021)

Through the Eyes of the Expert: Aligning Human and Machine Attention for Industrial AI

Alexander Koebler[1,2]([⊠]), Christian Greisinger[1,3], Jan Paulus[3], Ingo Thon[1], and Florian Buettner[1,2,4,5]

[1] Siemens AG, Munich, Germany
{alexander.koebler,christian.greisinger,ingo.thon,
buettner.florian}@siemens.com
[2] Goethe University Frankfurt, Frankfurt, Germany
[3] Nuremberg Institute of Technology, Nuremberg, Germany
jan.paulus@th-nuernberg.de
[4] German Cancer Research Center (DKFZ), Heidelberg, Germany
[5] German Cancer Consortium (DKTK), Frankfurt, Germany

Abstract. Human expertise and intuition are crucial in solving many tasks in expert-driven domains such as industrial manufacturing or medical diagnosis. In this work, we use the human expert's gaze information to take a step towards transferring this knowledge to a machine learning model. In this way, we are aligning the attention the machine and the human pay to solve the task. Previous works in the medical field have shown that privileged gaze information during training can increase predictive performance and reduce the label requirement of a machine learning model. We extend on the aim of those works and quantitatively evaluate the benefit of aligning human and machine attention on the quality of the model's explanations as well as its robustness - thus, its trustworthiness. We demonstrate our approach on a real-world visual quality inspection task in the multi-label setting, which is common in industrial applications. Our work illustrates the importance of incorporating human knowledge more explicitly in training machine learning models and takes a step towards enabling machine learning based systems in high-stakes applications.

Keywords: Human-Centered AI · Explainable AI · Model Robustness · Human Gaze

1 Motivation and Contribution

With the increasing demand for the use of Machine Learning (ML) in high-stakes industrial applications [27,30], the requirements for robustness and trustworthiness are increasing, with the aim of developing industrial-grade AI systems. However, frequently used deep learning models require large amounts of labeled data

---

F. Buettner—Work done for Siemens AG.

© The Author(s), under exclusive license to Springer Nature Switzerland AG 2024
H. Degen and S. Ntoa (Eds.): HCII 2024, LNAI 14735, pp. 407–423, 2024.
https://doi.org/10.1007/978-3-031-60611-3_28

and are subject to effects such as shortcut learning [6,11,15]. Once deployed, the resulting brittle models can lead to highly harmful, unexpected behavior. To tackle this, there is a strong need for the inclusion of more detailed human knowledge during training [5,26].

However, current supervised ML approaches typically rely on simple, manually generated labels as the single form of supervision. Those are unable to benefit from the complex reasoning process of the human expert. Multiple works in the medical domain [1,16,19,20,28] integrate information about the medical expert's gaze during the labeling process in the model training. The authors in [19,20] term this concept observational supervision. With the developed methods they could drastically reduce the data requirement of ML models for medical image classification tasks. The utilized gaze information is collected passively without posing any additional cognitive workload on the human annotator.

Once collected, it serves as an indicator of where the annotator paid attention to, and thereby as a low-level proxy for the human reasoning process.

We generalize this concept to the equally expert-driven industrial domain and tackle the previously unaddressed but vital task of multi-label classification [17] for a Visual Quality Inspection (VQI) use case.

The contributions of our work are given by:

- Extending the concept of observational supervision to the new setting of multi-label classification.
- Applying the proposed method to a real-world industrial use case and linking the observed benefits concerning the increase in performance and trustworthiness to the importance of human machine alignment for high stakes AI applications.
- Quantitatively evaluating the achieved increase in trustworthiness by analyzing the quality of the model's explanations as well as the model's robustness concerning input perturbations.

2   Related Work

The paradigm of utilizing additional information only available during the training process of a machine learning model is prominently introduced as Learning Using Privileged Information (LUPI) by Vapnik et al. [24,25] in the context of support vector machines. The authors hypothesize that human students are more sample efficient than learning machines concerning a given learning task because an intelligent teacher provides information besides simple semantic labels. Different works [4,14] transferred this concept to deep learning models for image classification tasks, where the privileged information is given by segmentation masks or bounding boxes containing relevant areas in the image. The knowledge about relevant image areas is either introduced in the training via targeted dropout [14] based on irrelevant areas or propagated back as the loss on a second task of generating masks enclosing relevant areas [4].

One option to obtain the relevance of a part of an input with respect to a task is given by recording the attention a human pays while completing it. This concept sparks a second research stream, where the human eye gaze is considered a proxy for the human attention. In Natural Language Processing (NLP), Hollenstein et al. [10] aim to exploit that the human gaze during reading includes information about the text's lexical and syntactic properties. Consequently, [2, 10] show that utilizing the gaze information allows significant improvements for different NLP tasks.

The concept of gaze information also carrying task relevant information in the context of vision tasks [31] leads to several works considering the benefit of including human gaze in the training of Computer Vision (CV) models. Here, applications in the medical domain attract particular interest, as the labeling requires high domain expertise and applications often face a lack of a sufficient amount of data. To include gaze information, it is often represented as heat maps where the activation indicates the time the human gaze spent on a particular area within the image. The authors in [19, 28] utilize this heat maps by comparing them with explanations based on the feature maps of the machine learning model and regularizing the model accordingly to better align with the human attention. The work by [19] shows that this approach is especially beneficial for difficult tasks which also often occur in industrial settings. In [20] the authors either fully rely on gaze information and train their model using a weakly supervised learning approach or add the gaze information as an additional task in a multitask learning framework. However, we aim to align the model's attention and thereby the explanations and reasoning with the human annotator, expecting benefits besides the predictive performance, i.e., in explanation quality and model robustness. The two approaches described in [20] do not consider these two dimensions. The authors in [1] introduce different model architectures to also be able to handle more complex data modalities for diagnosing Alzheimer's disease. Lastly, [16] directly embeds the gaze information in the architecture of a vision transformer. Thereby, the authors have shown a reduced reliance on shortcuts when including gaze information in the training of their model for a medical application.

Aside from that, the described works limit their evaluation to quantifying the increase in predictive performance of the model. However, in the context of high-stakes applications and industrial AI systems, other requirements such as trustworthiness and robustness are also in high demand. The benefit on those by including gaze information in the training of machine learning models is, to our knowledge, not yet thoroughly and quantitatively evaluated.

The authors in [23] show, that models which are stronger aligned with humans, i.e., human-understandable concepts which are similar are also in close proximity in the model's latent representation space, tend to be more robust to adversarial attacks and distribution changes. Therefore, we hypothesize that the alignment of the model's explanations with human gaze information can also positively affect the model's robustness to input perturbations.

3 Problem Setting

Assessing the quality of a product at different stages of the manufacturing process is essential to guarantee a high-quality production output. Reducing the requirement of manual inspection and still accounting for the wide variety of possible product damages is a natural task for ML-based vision approaches. However, using ML in such applications comes with several challenges. Missing defects on a product can lead to high subsequent costs, the deployed vision systems can often suffer from external interference, such as stray light, and gathering high quality labels requires significant expertise by the annotator.

3.1 Use Case

In this work, we include an expert annotator's gaze, see Fig. 1a, in the training of a ML model in the context of a real-world VQI use case depicted in Fig. 1b. Thereby, we aim to increase performance, trustworthiness, and robustness of the machine learning based system to lower the mentioned burdens faced in real-world applications. We demonstrate the benefits of gaze-enhanced supervision at the example of a product that consists of five different objects and is assembled by a robot. To reduce waste, instead of sorting out the entire product if one or multiple objects are damaged, only the damaged objects get replaced in a subsequent rework step. Therefore, the VQI system needs to classify which of the objects is damaged. This is solved by using a binary multi-label classification model, where the prediction for the input image x is given by $\hat{y} = \{\hat{y}^0, ..., \hat{y}^n\}$ with $\hat{y}^i = [0, 1]$. For the observed use case, the product consists of five different objects $n = 5$.

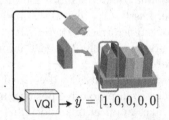

(a) Labeling procedure recording gaze information x^* while the annotator is generating label y for image x.

(b) VQI task for replacing damaged objects indicated by prediction $\hat{y}$ of the machine learning model.

Fig. 1. Setup of the considered real-world VQI use case

3.2   Human Interaction

For the labeling process the human annotator is equipped with Microsoft's HoloLense2 AR-glasses. The input images are projected into the AR-glasses and voice commands are used to proceed to the subsequent image. The system-provided eye-tracking capabilities are utilized to capture the eye movement of the expert and generate Human Attention Maps (HAM) x^* aligned with the corresponding input image x. We refer to heat maps with the intensity corresponding to the time the expert's gaze spent on the image area as HAMs. The annotator does know the use case and the different manifestations of product damages. However, he is instructed to avoid putting an artificially strong focus on the damaged areas, which would generate high-quality but unrealistic HAMs. There is no time limit for labeling one instance, such that the overall intensity of the generated HAMs varies. To guarantee that the labels y are actually in line with the HAMs, the annotator is asked to note them down in parallel.

4   Approach and Results

In the following section, we elaborate on the developed method for the described multi-label task. Further, we introduce metrics to thoroughly evaluate the method with respect to explanation quality, model robustness, and predictive performance. Lastly, we conduct various experiments with different model architectures and training set sizes.

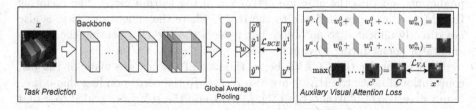

Fig. 2. Observational supervision for multi-label classification

4.1   Observational Supervision for Multi-label Classification

In order to integrate the HAMs x^* as privileged information in the training of a machine learning model, we build upon the observational supervision method introduced by Saab et al. [19]. Our resulting approach for the multi-label setting is depicted in Fig. 2. As in [19], the ML model is constrained to align its reasoning and explanations with the HAMs by introducing an auxiliary visual attention loss term $\mathcal{L}_{VA}$ alongside the binary cross-entropy classification loss $\mathcal{L}_{BCE}$

$$\mathcal{L} = \mathcal{L}_{BCE} + \lambda \mathcal{L}_{VA}. \tag{1}$$

The $\mathcal{L}_{VA}$ term evaluates the mismatch between explanations of the model expressed by Class Activation Map (CAM) [32] and the HAMs. The hyperparameter λ balances between the classification and the alignment objective. The generation of CAMs presupposes a Global Average Pooling (GAP) layer after the last convolutional layer of the fully-convolutional backbone. This allows a linear mapping between the predictions and the feature maps via the weights w of the fully-connected output layer. Different from the single-label classification case in [19], we account for the option that multiple of the labels are classified as positive by generating a CAM for every positive ground truth label, i.e., actually damaged object, according to

$$c_k^i = y^i \cdot \sum_{j=0}^{m} w_j^i \cdot f_{k,j}(x) \,, \tag{2}$$

where $f_{k,j}$ is the kth element of the jth feature map of the last convolutional layer of the model and m is the number of feature maps generated by that layer. The yield CAMs c^i indicate the important image areas for the prediction of the model with respect to label i. Subsequently, we introduce a Combined CAM (CCAM) C for the entire prediction by calculating the pixel-wise maximum of the single CAMs

$$C_k = \max_{0 \le i \le n} \bar{c}_k^i \,, \tag{3}$$

where prior to that the CAMs are min-max normalized yielding $\bar{c}^i$. This normalization maps the CAM to only positive values and allows to represent CAMs of ground truth positive predictions independent of the score of the model's prediction and thus the absolute activation of the feature maps. The resulting CCAM C is in correspondence to the HAM, where the annotator's gaze is also not directly allocated to an object but reflects the overall attention the human annotator spent during solving the task.

To account for the CCAMs being the size of the feature maps of the last convolutional layer, the HAMs are also resized to the corresponding shape (i.e., in our case 7×7). Further, both the CCAM and the HAM are scaled to a unit norm to decouple the HAM from the total observation time of the annotator resulting in different overall activations for the particular image and the CCAM from the number of positive ground truth predictions

$$\bar{C}_k = \frac{C_k}{||C||} \qquad (4) \qquad \qquad \bar{x}_k^* = \frac{x_k^*}{||x^*||} \,. \qquad (5)$$

The visual attention loss $\mathcal{L}_{VA}$ now quantifies the difference between the normalized CCAM $\bar{C}$ and HAM $\bar{x}^*$ via the Mean Squared Error (MSE) and enforces their alignment

$$\mathcal{L}_{VA}(\bar{C}, \bar{x}^*) = MSE(\bar{C}, \bar{x}^*) = \frac{1}{d} \sum_{k=1}^{d} (\bar{C}_k - \bar{x}_k^*)^2 \,, \tag{6}$$

where d reflects the number of elements in the feature maps given by the product of their height and width.

4.2   Evaluation Metrics and Experiments

We quantify the effect of including the human gaze information in the training of the machine learning model along three dimensions. First, we measure the impact on the models' predictive performance via accuracy. Second, we quantify the quality of the models' explanations and their alignment with the human reasoning utilizing three metrics derived from XAI literature and adapted to our setting. Last, we quantitatively assess how the increased alignment of the models affects their robustness concerning input perturbations.

Metrics for Quality of Explanations and Model Robustness. To assess the increase in the quality of model explanations, besides visual inspection, we use three quantitative metrics based on the implementation by Hedström et al. [8] and adapted to our setting.

First, we introduce *Alignment* derived from Attribution Localization [13] indicating the alignment between the model's and the human's attention. More precisely, *Alignment* quantifies the relative accumulation of attribution the model assigns to areas considered relevant via the human gaze

$$\mu_A(C, \tilde{x}^*) = \frac{\sum_{k=1}^{d} C_k \cdot \tilde{x}_k^*}{\sum_{k=1}^{d} C_k} \cdot \frac{\sum_{k=1}^{d} \tilde{x}_k^*}{d}, \tag{7}$$

where $\tilde{x}^* = \{0, 1\}$ is the binarized HAM x^* based on a threshold $\gamma = 0.5 \cdot \max(x^*)$ relative to the maximum activation in the respective HAM. Remember, the time the human spends and thus the overall activation in the HAM is not restricted concerning a particular data instance. d is the number of elements in the HAM. Second, *Complexity* [3] expresses the conciseness of the explanations via their entropy

$$\mu_C(C) = H\left(\frac{C}{\sum_{k=1}^{d} C_k}\right). \tag{8}$$

Explanations relying on fewer features to show the model's reasoning are more straightforward to interpret by human users, promoting a higher level of perceived trustworthiness.

However, low complexity of the explanations can also mean that the model does not capture all relevant features, e.g., only one of multiple damages on an object. Thus, a low complexity should be considered in the context of the other two explanation metrics.

The previous two metrics assess the comprehensibility of the explanations. To evaluate whether the model's predictions are actually based on those explanations, we adapted Faithfullness introduced in [3] inspired by Shift-Faithfulness

[12] to the binary multi-label setting as *BMLC-Faithfulness* (BMLC-Faith)

$$\mu_F(f, C; x, y) = \underset{S \in \binom{[d]}{|S|}}{corr} \left(\sum_{k \in S} C_k, \mathcal{L}_{BCE}\big(f(x_{[x_S = \bar{x}_S]}), y\big) - \mathcal{L}_{BCE}\big(f(x), y\big) \right). \quad (9)$$

Thereby, we are using the BCE-loss instead of the output for a single label allowing to consider the combined influence of the feature removal on all labels, i.e., outputs of the model. *BMLC-Faithfulness* quantifies the correlation between the importance of an image area assigned via the CCAMs and the influence of that area being removed from the image on the model's loss. If an explanation is faithful, removing image areas attributed high importance should lead to an increase in the model's loss. On the contrary, removing an area assigned low importance should have little effect on the model's loss if the predictions are actually based on the areas highlighted by the CCAMs. As it is common practice for images, removing is realized by substituting the respective areas with the mean of the data set.

Assessing the robustness of machine learning models is an important but also challenging endeavor, as the particular perturbations of the input data faced by a model during deployment are unknown.

However, in our experiments, we follow the prominent ImageNet-C benchmark introduced by Hendrycks and Dietterich [9] for the ImageNet data set [18] introducing synthetic perturbations reassembling a selection of plausible real world input changes. Further, we utilize the metrics introduced by the authors in [9] to measure the resilience of a model towards performance degradation given input corruption. The Corruption Error CE_ψ^f provides a relative measure for the Error Rate E_ψ^f for model f on a test set in the presence of input corruption ψ. To account for the varying difficulty of the different input perturbations with respect to the task as well as the test samples, the error rate of a reference model is used for adjustment. For this purpose, we utilize a ResNet50 model without gaze-enhanced supervision during training

$$CE_\psi^f = \frac{E_\psi^f}{E_\psi^{ResNet50}}. \quad (10)$$

Unlike the evaluation in [9] on ImageNet, we only use the first severity level of the perturbations included in the benchmark. Given the differing task and the much lower amount of training data, higher severity levels customized for ImageNet lead to very low model performances and thus to unstable evaluations in our case. Additionally to the regular CE score, we also report the relative CE (rCE) score as both metrics alone might present an incomplete impression depending on the original performance of the model on clean data

$$rCE_\psi^f = \frac{E_\psi^f - E_{clean}^f}{E_\psi^{ResNet50} - E_{clean}^{ResNet50}} \quad (11)$$

For all experiments we aggregate both metrics over a set of different perturbations Ψ as mean CE (mCE) and mean rCE ($mrCE$)

$$mCE^f = \frac{1}{|\Psi|} \sum_{\psi \in \Psi} CE_\psi^f \qquad (12) \qquad mrCE^f = \frac{1}{|\Psi|} \sum_{\psi \in \Psi} rCE_\psi^f. \qquad (13)$$

Experiment Setup. We test our approach on three widely used Convolutional Neural Network (CNN) based architectures: ResNet18, ResNet50, and VGG16. Throughout the experiments all models are pretrained on ImageNet [18]. The adaptation of the ResNets [7] for our setting is limited to replacing the output layer with originally 1000 outputs by one with 5, which is the number of objects in our task, as they are already relying on a fully convolutional architecture only extended by a GAP-layer and a single fully connected layer. This differs from the VGG16 architecture [22] that originally relies on three fully connected layers. We replaced the original max-pooling as well as the three fully connected layers with a GAP-layer and a single fully connected output layer. This architecture is denoted as VGG16 with CAM (VGG16wC). To report a potential performance decline given the accompanying reduction of model capacity, we also consider the original VGG16 architecture during our experiments concerning performance evaluation. Regarding the very low amount of data available for the considered use case, we base the experiments on a stratified 5-fold cross-validation [21]. We evaluate three training set sizes of 50, 100, and 200 images. The test sets consist of 64 samples. The single-channel greyscale images recorded by an industrial camera are extended to three channels by channel copying. All models are trained for a maximum of 200 epochs using a batch size of 32 and a learning rate of 0.01. During training, we use early stopping with a patience of 20 epochs.

Accounting for the large confidence intervals between different splits, which are caused by the low data regime of the experiments, we verify the significance of the improvement using our method by providing a p-value resulting from a paired Wilcoxon signed-rank test [29] for all results.

Experimental Results. In the first experiment, we evaluate the influence of the weight λ for the $\mathcal{L}_{VA}$ loss term on accuracy and alignment. Figure 3 shows an improvement in predictive performance as well as alignment for all three models up to $\lambda = 10^3$. At this point, the lower capacity VGG16wC model outperforms the larger original VGG16 architecture. A further increase with respect to enforcing the alignment leads to a drastic drop in the performance of all models. The reason for the drop may be that at this point the visual attention loss exceeds the task-specific BCE-loss to an extent that the task-specific objective perishes. For both ResNets the alignment stagnates at this point. In all further experiments the inclusion of gaze information is done by setting $\lambda = 10^3$.

Reflecting on one of the core aims of our work via Table 1 shows that our proposed approach allows for a highly significant improvement of the alignment between the attention the human annotator paid during the labeling process and

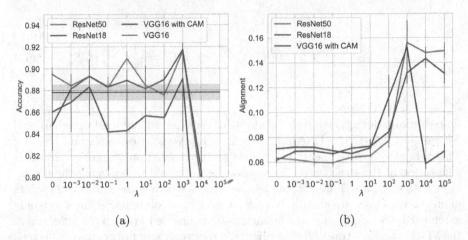

Fig. 3. Evaluation of the influence of λ on model accuracy (a) and explanations alignment (b) with 68% confidence intervals on 5-fold cross-validation.

the attention of the trained machine learning model during inference throughout all architectures and data set sizes. Similarly, the complexity of the explanations is strongly decreased. Both of these points are compellingly visually observable in Fig. 4. The image of the CCAM with gaze-enhanced supervision not only generates more concise explanations but also highlights the error on the upper edge of the third object not considered by the model without gaze information. This observation underpins our assumption about the increase in the model's robustness with respect to input perturbations. If the model does not solely rely on a single feature, given that there are more that are relevant for the prediction, it can base its predictions on other features in the absence of one of them, e.g., because of occlusion. For both ResNets also a significant increase in faithfulness of the explanations is observed. This indicates that the explanations are not only more comprehensible but actually more trustworthy. Lastly, the models' accuracy is significantly increased in those cases. Once more, we hypothesize that the observed increase in the alignment of the models' and the human annotator's reasoning, in combination with an increased faithfulness in the explanations, leads to a rise in the models' robustness concerning input perturbations. Thereby, we argue that the attention of the human annotator is focused on image areas that are actually task-relevant. The model also faithfully focusing predominantly on those areas should lead to increased resilience to changes in non-task-relevant areas counteracting a brittle behavior of the model. To verify our assumption, we apply a selection of image perturbations Ψ shown in Fig. 5 and report the

Table 1. Experimental results for different training set sizes $|D_{train}|$ with ($\lambda = 10^3$) and without ($\lambda = 0$) utilizing gaze information in the training with 95% confidence intervals on 5-fold cross-validation.

Model	$|D_{train}|$		Accuracy ↑	Alignment ↑	Complexity ↓	BMLC-Faith ↑
ResNet50	200	w/ gaze	**0.972 ± 0.016**	**0.180 ± 0.017**	**10.08 ± 0.03**	**0.021 ± 0.026**
		w/o gaze	0.970 ± 0.014	0.070 ± 0.007	10.70 ± 0.03	0.010 ± 0.028
	100	w/ gaze	**0.916 ± 0.012**	**0.156 ± 0.010**	**10.20 ± 0.13**	**0.000 ± 0.040**
		w/o gaze	0.895 ± 0.023	0.063 ± 0.010	10.72 ± 0.07	−0.026 ± 0.035
	50	w/ gaze	**0.856 ± 0.021**	**0.119 ± 0.014**	**10.50 ± 0.08**	**0.017 ± 0.069**
		w/o gaze	0.810 ± 0.031	0.054 ± 0.008	10.76 ± 0.01	−0.011 ± 0.034
	p-value		$2.1 \cdot 10^{-3}$	$3.1 \cdot 10^{-5}$	$3.1 \cdot 10^{-5}$	$6.2 \cdot 10^{-3}$
ResNet18	200	w/ gaze	**0.970 ± 0.009**	**0.167 ± 0.016**	**10.20 ± 0.06**	**0.050 ± 0.046**
		w/o gaze	0.962 ± 0.011	0.076 ± 0.007	10.65 ± 0.04	0.014 ± 0.049
	100	w/ gaze	**0.917 ± 0.040**	**0.132 ± 0.026**	**10.38 ± 0.15**	**0.040 ± 0.058**
		w/o gaze	0.847 ± 0.013	0.061 ± 0.007	10.73 ± 0.02	0.028 ± 0.030
	50	w/ gaze	**0.840 ± 0.023**	**0.108 ± 0.013**	**10.55 ± 0.08**	**0.058 ± 0.038**
		w/o gaze	0.822 ± 0.021	0.059 ± 0.007	10.74 ± 0.02	0.030 ± 0.022
	p-value		$9.4 \cdot 10^{-4}$	$3.1 \cdot 10^{-5}$	$3.1 \cdot 10^{-5}$	$4.7 \cdot 10^{-2}$
VGG16wC	200	w/ gaze	0.841 ± 0.159	**0.145 ± 0.048**	**10.29 ± 0.24**	**0.067 ± 0.052**
		w/o gaze	**0.920 ± 0.132**	0.075 ± 0.017	10.69 ± 0.10	0.053 ± 0.092
	100	w/ gaze	**0.891 ± 0.136**	**0.152 ± 0.059**	**10.23 ± 0.36**	**0.041 ± 0.114**
		w/o gaze	0.860 ± 0.1089	0.070 ± 0.012	10.73 ± 0.05	0.032 ± 0.058
	50	w/ gaze	**0.783 ± 0.081**	**0.123 ± 0.037**	**10.41 ± 0.21**	**0.052 ± 0.026**
		w/o gaze	0.762 ± 0.100	0.058 ± 0.017	10.76 ± 0.01	0.016 ± 0.076
	p-value		0.60	$3.1 \cdot 10^{-5}$	$3.1 \cdot 10^{-5}$	0.3

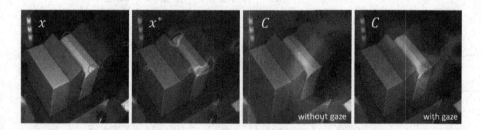

Fig. 4. Example visualization of a test image for ResNet50 models trained on 200 samples with and withouth gaze-enhanced supervision where the last three objects are damaged and correctly classified. From left to right: original image with highlighted product damages, image with HAM, image with CCAM without gaze-enhanced supervision, image with CCAM with gaze-enhanced supervision.

mCE and $mrCE$ across all models and data set sizes in Table 2. We refer to the Appendix for a detailed breakdown of the CE and rCE concerning the different perturbations ψ.

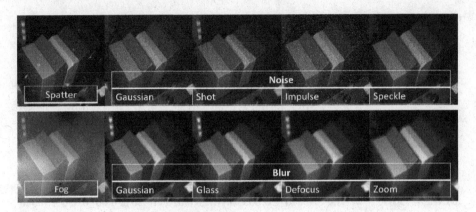

Fig. 5. Set of image perturbations based on the ImageNet-C benchmark used to assess the increase in model robustness.

Table 2. Evaluation results concerning the models' robustness towards input perturbations for different training set sizes $|D_{train}|$ using mean Corruption Error (mCE) and mean relative Corruption Error ($mrCE$) with 95% confidence intervals.

Model	$|D_{train}|$		$E_{clean} \downarrow$	$mCE \downarrow$	$mrCE \downarrow$
ResNet50	200	w/ gaze	$\mathbf{2.8 \pm 1.6}$	$\mathbf{81 \pm 10}$	$\mathbf{79 \pm 8}$
		w/o gaze	3.0 ± 1.4	100	100
	100	w/ gaze	$\mathbf{8.4 \pm 1.2}$	$\mathbf{85 \pm 10}$	$\mathbf{76 \pm 9}$
		w/o gaze	10.5 ± 2.3	100	100
	50	w/ gaze	$\mathbf{14.4 \pm 2.1}$	$\mathbf{80 \pm 11}$	$\mathbf{53 \pm 13}$
		w/o gaze	19.3 ± 3.1	100	100
	p-value			$1.5 \cdot 10^{-14}$	$4.9 \cdot 10^{-17}$
ResNet18	200	w/ gaze	$\mathbf{3.0 \pm 0.9}$	$\mathbf{79 \pm 9}$	$\mathbf{78 \pm 9}$
		w/o gaze	3.8 ± 1.1	108 ± 15	109 ± 12
	100	w/ gaze	$\mathbf{8.3 \pm 4.0}$	$\mathbf{84 \pm 13}$	$\mathbf{76 \pm 15}$
		w/o gaze	15.2 ± 1.3	103 ± 12	111 ± 15
	50	w/ gaze	$\mathbf{16.0 \pm 2.3}$	$\mathbf{79 \pm 7}$	$\mathbf{53 \pm 7}$
		w/o gaze	17.7 ± 2.1	104 ± 14	126 ± 28
	p-value			$1.3 \cdot 10^{-15}$	$3.8 \cdot 10^{-18}$
VGG16wC	200	w/ gaze	15.9 ± 15.9	$\mathbf{78 \pm 16}$	$\mathbf{77 \pm 14}$
		w/o gaze	$\mathbf{8.0 \pm 13.3}$	90 ± 14	89 ± 11
	100	w/ gaze	$\mathbf{10.9 \pm 13.6}$	$\mathbf{69 \pm 11}$	$\mathbf{58 \pm 10}$
		w/o gaze	14.0 ± 10.9	78 ± 14	74 ± 16
	50	w/ gaze	$\mathbf{21.7 \pm 8.1}$	$\mathbf{83 \pm 10}$	$\mathbf{57 \pm 11}$
		w/o gaze	23.8 ± 10.0	84 ± 11	76 ± 15
	p-value			$4.9 \cdot 10^{-4}$	$7.3 \cdot 10^{-8}$

According to both metrics, we can observe an overall highly significant improvement in the models' robustness over the set of input perturbations. This observation is particularly convincing concerning the ResNet models.

In summary, our experimental results show that incorporating human gaze information into model training using our approach can lead to significant improvements in all considered metrics across different model architectures and training set sizes. The benefits observed, particularly in the quality of the models' explanations and the increased model robustness, indicate the potential of aligning machine learning models with humans to create trustworthy AI systems for high-stakes applications beyond the evaluated use case.

5 Limitations and Future Work

The use of AR-glasses to record gaze information in our method is compelling due to their ability to generate high-quality HAMs without adding cognitive workload to the human annotator. However, this approach has some limitations. AR-glasses are still relatively expensive and can be inconvenient for extended use. Thus, to broaden the range of applications, it is also desirable to evaluate different eye-tracking approaches. Additionally, it is important to investigate how the quality of the HAMs varies between different participants and eye-tracking technologies, and what implications this has on the observed benefits with respect to the trained model. Furthermore, it should be noted that gaze information can only be considered as a proxy for a part of the entire complex human reasoning process. This prompts the investigation of alternative interfaces to incorporate higher fidelity representations of human knowledge into machine learning models while limiting the cognitive burden on the human annotator.

6 Conclusion

The way towards the use of AI systems in high stakes applications will require to include humans and their knowledge more rigorously in the training stage. In this work, we demonstrated the benefits of using a human annotator's passively recorded gaze information in a realistic industrial use case. We have shown, through an in-depth evaluation, that the method leads to significant improvements in model performance, the quality and faithfulness of the model's explanations, and the model's robustness towards perturbations of the input data.

All these factors can increase the trust of the user in the model's predictions and enable more informed decisions based on the knowledge about the model's reasoning. This contributes to an overall more trustworthy system, allowing for its use in a wider variety of applications.

Appendix

In this Appendix, we present the breakdown of all perturbations for the robustness evaluation condensed in Table 2. Table 3 shows the results for the regular Corruption Error and Table 4 for the relative Corruption Error.

Table 3. Additional results to Table 2 for Corruption Error (CE).

Model	$|D_{train}|$		E_{clean}	Weather		Noise				Blur				mCE
				Spatter	Fog	Gaussian	Shot	Impulse	Speckle	Gaussian	Glass	Defocus	Zoom	
ResNet50	200	w/ g	2.8 ± 1.6	77 ± 13	76 ± 16	73 ± 13	76 ± 15	77 ± 25	88 ± 27	105 ± 73	80 ± 11	80 ± 36	76 ± 29	81 ± 10
		w/o g	3.0 ± 1.4	100	100	100	100	100	100	100	100	100	100	100
	100	w/ g	8.4 ± 1.2	94 ± 20	69 ± 26	65 ± 15	71 ± 19	77 ± 25	91 ± 51	88 ± 42	94 ± 42	104 ± 24	97 ± 22	85 ± 10
		w/o g	10.5 ± 2.3	100	100	100	100	100	100	100	100	100	100	100
	50	w/ g	14.4 ± 2.1	84 ± 27	79 ± 17	86 ± 38	91 ± 42	77 ± 19	118 ± 55	60 ± 20	72 ± 26	69 ± 27	64 ± 29	80 ± 11
		w/o g	19.3 ± 3.1	100	100	100	100	100	**100**	100	100	100	100	100
	p-value			$6.2 \cdot 10^{-3}$	$3.1 \cdot 10^{-5}$	$2.1 \cdot 10^{-3}$	$3.3 \cdot 10^{-3}$	$3.1 \cdot 10^{-5}$	0.32	$4.7 \cdot 10^{-2}$	$7.5 \cdot 10^{-3}$	$1.7 \cdot 10^{-2}$	$4.6 \cdot 10^{-3}$	$1.5 \cdot 10^{-14}$
ResNet18	200	w/ g	3.0 ± 0.9	79 ± 29	83 ± 13	75 ± 11	77 ± 13	68 ± 15	67 ± 19	103 ± 47	71 ± 26	75 ± 19	93 ± 42	79 ± 9
		w/o g	3.8 ± 1.1	88 ± 7	88 ± 8	124 ± 48	125 ± 45	122 ± 34	111 ± 38	135 ± 80	72 ± 19	103 ± 60	114 ± 40	108 ± 15
	100	w/ g	8.3 ± 4.0	79 ± 9	86 ± 30	67 ± 14	69 ± 11	66 ± 13	75 ± 13	96 ± 62	101 ± 59	100 ± 59	96 ± 67	84 ± 13
		w/o g	15.2 ± 1.3	75 ± 20	76 ± 21	109 ± 23	107 ± 23	105 ± 11	105 ± 32	130 ± 53	91 ± 45	121 ± 52	114 ± 33	103 ± 12
	50	w/ g	16.0 ± 2.3	81 ± 11	74 ± 27	75 ± 22	81 ± 16	73 ± 14	101 ± 19	81 ± 35	73 ± 20	78 ± 29	77 ± 33	79 ± 7
		w/o g	17.7 ± 2.1	77 ± 17	70 ± 20	136 ± 45	141 ± 51	103 ± 24	124 ± 33	112 ± 52	77 ± 20	105 ± 45	98 ± 43	104 ± 14
	p-value			0.48	0.72	$3.1 \cdot 10^{-5}$	$3.1 \cdot 10^{-5}$	$3.1 \cdot 10^{-5}$	$3.1 \cdot 10^{-5}$	$1.3 \cdot 10^{-2}$	0.64	$1.5 \cdot 10^{-4}$	$1.5 \cdot 10^{-2}$	$1.3 \cdot 10^{-15}$
VGG16wC	200	w/ g	15.9 ± 15.9	79 ± 50	42 ± 18	68 ± 13	69 ± 10	97 ± 54	56 ± 13	134 ± 107	74 ± 33	76 ± 32	81 ± 47	78 ± 16
		w/o g	8.0 ± 13.3	96 ± 16	38 ± 14	80 ± 41	93 ± 53	120 ± 32	77 ± 43	108 ± 47	92 ± 6	93 ± 50	97 ± 61	90 ± 14
	100	w/ g	10.9 ± 13.6	72 ± 22	30 ± 19	65 ± 15	64 ± 12	67 ± 14	60 ± 7	90 ± 60	76 ± 39	93 ± 45	78 ± 30	69 ± 11
		w/o g	14.0 ± 10.9	90 ± 28	34 ± 14	73 ± 32	70 ± 23	122 ± 43	67 ± 13	85 ± 61	90 ± 65	84 ± 43	65 ± 37	78 ± 14
	50	w/ g	21.7 ± 8.1	99 ± 27	47 ± 9	86 ± 28	84 ± 17	125 ± 14	87 ± 20	78 ± 17	88 ± 39	71 ± 27	64 ± 16	83 ± 10
		w/o g	23.8 ± 10.0	92 ± 37	56 ± 14	88 ± 26	90 ± 24	104 ± 48	104 ± 41	89 ± 33	71 ± 37	78 ± 32	75 ± 24	84 ± 11
	p-value			0.1	0.24	$3.1 \cdot 10^{-2}$	$3.5 \cdot 10^{-2}$	$4.7 \cdot 10^{-2}$	$5.3 \cdot 10^{-3}$	0.54	0.28	0.28	0.45	$4.9 \cdot 10^{-4}$

Table 4. Additional results to Table 2 for relative Corruption Error (rCE).

Model	$|D_{train}|$		E_{clean}	Weather		Noise				Blur				mrCE
				Spatter	Fog	Gaussian	Shot	Impulse	Speckle	Gaussian	Glass	Defocus	Zoom	
ResNet50	200	w/ g	2.8 ± 1.6	76 ± 13	74 ± 16	71 ± 14	74 ± 16	75 ± 22	85 ± 28	107 ± 89	78 ± 10	78 ± 10	73 ± 34	79 ± 8
		w/o g	3.0 ± 1.4	100	100	100	100	100	100	**100**	100	100	100	100
	100	w/ g	8.4 ± 1.2	89 ± 26	59 ± 29	53 ± 17	60 ± 25	66 ± 29	84 ± 63	71 ± 60	89 ± 51	99 ± 27	97 ± 22	76 ± 9
		w/o g	10.5 ± 2.3	100	100	100	100	100	100	100	100	100	100	100
	50	w/ g	14.4 ± 2.1	63 ± 37	59 ± 24	64 ± 61	70 ± 71	50 ± 21	109 ± 111	2 ± 27	48 ± 30	38 ± 37	31 ± 42	53 ± 13
		w/o g	19.3 ± 3.1	100	100	100	100	100	**100**	100	100	100	100	100
	p-value			$1.0 \cdot 10^{-3}$	$3.1 \cdot 10^{-5}$	$7.6 \cdot 10^{-4}$	$4.2 \cdot 10^{-3}$	$3.1 \cdot 10^{-5}$	0.10	$1.8 \cdot 10^{-2}$	$2.7 \cdot 10^{-3}$	$9.0 \cdot 10^{-3}$	$3.2 \cdot 10^{-3}$	$4.9 \cdot 10^{-17}$
ResNet18	200	w/ g	3.0 ± 0.9	78 ± 31	82 ± 15	73 ± 10	75 ± 12	66 ± 15	64 ± 17	105 ± 54	69 ± 27	73 ± 22	91 ± 47	78 ± 7
		w/o g	3.8 ± 1.1	87 ± 7	88 ± 6	126 ± 52	127 ± 50	125 ± 37	112 ± 41	140 ± 90	70 ± 20	102 ± 63	114 ± 44	109 ± 12
	100	w/ g	8.3 ± 4.0	72 ± 10	80 ± 34	55 ± 15	57 ± 15	53 ± 14	65 ± 16	91 ± 126	98 ± 70	99 ± 81	95 ± 117	76 ± 15
		w/o g	15.2 ± 1.3	70 ± 24	71 ± 26	112 ± 31	109 ± 29	106 ± 15	108 ± 44	174 ± 117	91 ± 58	143 ± 93	124 ± 57	111 ± 15
	50	w/ g	16.0 ± 2.3	58 ± 14	53 ± 33	46 ± 30	53 ± 28	44 ± 18	76 ± 30	46 ± 50	50 ± 14	53 ± 49	51 ± 49	53 ± 7
		w/o g	17.7 ± 2.1	63 ± 25	55 ± 26	187 ± 110	199 ± 128	107 ± 48	162 ± 93	201 ± 277	66 ± 23	117 ± 80	104 ± 70	126 ± 28
	p-value			0.23	0.47	$3.1 \cdot 10^{-5}$	$3.1 \cdot 10^{-5}$	$3.1 \cdot 10^{-5}$	$3.1 \cdot 10^{-5}$	$7.5 \cdot 10^{-3}$	0.34	$1.5 \cdot 10^{-4}$	$1.1 \cdot 10^{-2}$	$3.8 \cdot 10^{-18}$
VGG16wC	200	w/ g	15.9 ± 15.9	78 ± 53	38 ± 19	66 ± 14	67 ± 9	97 ± 59	52 ± 12	145 ± 130	73 ± 33	74 ± 36	79 ± 53	77 ± 14
		w/o g	8.0 ± 13.3	96 ± 18	34 ± 16	80 ± 44	93 ± 57	122 ± 34	76 ± 45	108 ± 54	92 ± 7	93 ± 54	96 ± 67	89 ± 11
	100	w/ g	10.9 ± 13.6	64 ± 29	13 ± 20	53 ± 17	52 ± 16	54 ± 15	45 ± 10	80 ± 95	68 ± 45	87 ± 55	62 ± 38	58 ± 10
		w/o g	14.0 ± 10.9	87 ± 34	19 ± 15	66 ± 42	61 ± 29	129 ± 58	57 ± 18	94 ± 143	90 ± 88	86 ± 77	49 ± 52	74 ± 16
	50	w/ g	21.7 ± 8.1	85 ± 36	16 ± 16	61 ± 31	55 ± 21	123 ± 32	52 ± 35	32 ± 32	73 ± 50	41 ± 39	30 ± 27	57 ± 11
		w/o g	23.8 ± 10.0	87 ± 63	30 ± 26	80 ± 45	79 ± 43	107 ± 82	105 ± 84	95 ± 109	54 ± 55	62 ± 51	56 ± 36	76 ± 15
	p-value			$6.0 \cdot 10^{-2}$	0.19	$1.6 \cdot 10^{-3}$	$5.8 \cdot 10^{-5}$	$4.2 \cdot 10^{-2}$	$7.6 \cdot 10^{-4}$	0.34	0.13	$6.0 \cdot 10^{-2}$	0.28	$7.3 \cdot 10^{-8}$

Both tables indicate a more significant improvement in the models' robustness for the noise-based perturbations than those clustered under weather or blur.

References

1. Antunes, C., Silveira, M.: Generating attention maps from eye-gaze for the diagnosis of Alzheimer's disease. In: NeuRIPS 2022 Workshop on Gaze Meets ML (2022). https://openreview.net/forum?id=yL1qcv2Q0bC
2. Barrett, M., Bingel, J., Hollenstein, N., Rei, M., Søgaard, A.: Sequence classification with human attention. In: Korhonen, A., Titov, I. (eds.) Proceedings of the 22nd Conference on Computational Natural Language Learning, pp. 302–312. Association for Computational Linguistics, Brussels, Belgium, October 2018. https://doi.org/10.18653/v1/K18-1030, https://aclanthology.org/K18-1030
3. Bhatt, U., Weller, A., Moura, J.M.: Evaluating and aggregating feature-based model explanations. In: Proceedings of the Twenty-Ninth International Conference on International Joint Conferences on Artificial Intelligence, pp. 3016–3022 (2021)
4. Bisla, D., Choromanska, A.: VisualBackProp for learning using privileged information with CNNs. Technical Report arXiv:1805.09474, arXiv, May 2018, http://arxiv.org/abs/1805.09474, arXiv:1805.09474 [cs] type: article
5. Decker, T., Gross, R., Koebler, A., Lebacher, M., Schnitzer, R., Weber, S.H.: The thousand faces of explainable AI along the machine learning life cycle: industrial reality and current state of research. In: Degen, H., Ntoa, S. (eds.) Artificial Intelligence in HCI. HCII 2023. Lecture Notes in Computer Science, Part I, vol. 14050, pp 184–208. Springer, Cham (2023). https://doi.org/10.1007/978-3-031-35891-3_13
6. Geirhos, R., et al.: shortcut learning in deep neural networks. Nat. Mach. Intell. **2**(11), 665–673 (2020)https://doi.org/10.1038/s42256-020-00257-z, http://arxiv.org/abs/2004.07780, arXiv:2004.07780 [cs, q-bio]
7. He, K., Zhang, X., Ren, S., Sun, J.: Deep residual learning for image recognition. In: Proceedings of the IEEE Conference on Computer Vision and Pattern Recognition, pp. 770–778 (2016)
8. Hedström, A., et al.: Quantus: an explainable AI toolkit for responsible evaluation of neural network explanations and beyond. J. Mach. Learn. Res. **24**(34), 1–11 (2023). http://jmlr.org/papers/v24/22-0142.html
9. Hendrycks, D., Dietterich, T.: Benchmarking neural network robustness to common corruptions and perturbations. In: International Conference on Learning Representations (2018)
10. Hollenstein, N., Zhang, C.: Entity recognition at first sight: improving NER with eye movement information. In: Burstein, J., Doran, C., Solorio, T. (eds.) Proceedings of the 2019 Conference of the North American Chapter of the Association for Computational Linguistics: Human Language Technologies, Volume 1 (Long and Short Papers), pp. 1–10. Association for Computational Linguistics, Minneapolis, Minnesota, June 2019. https://doi.org/10.18653/v1/N19-1001, https://aclanthology.org/N19-1001
11. Kauffmann, J., Ruff, L., Montavon, G., Müller, K.R.: The clever hans effect in anomaly detection. arXiv:2006.10609 [cs, stat], June 2020. http://arxiv.org/abs/2006.10609, arXiv: 2006.10609
12. Koebler, A., Decker, T., Lebacher, M., Thon, I., Tresp, V., Buettner, F.: Towards explanatory model monitoring. In: XAI in Action: Past, Present, and Future Applications (2023). https://openreview.net/forum?id=nVGuWh4S2G
13. Kohlbrenner, M., Bauer, A., Nakajima, S., Binder, A., Samek, W., Lapuschkin, S.: Towards best practice in explaining neural network decisions with LRP. In: 2020 International Joint Conference on Neural Networks (IJCNN), pp. 1–7. IEEE (2020)

14. Lambert, J., Sener, O., Savarese, S.: Deep learning under privileged information using heteroscedastic dropout. In: Proceedings of the IEEE Conference on Computer Vision and Pattern Recognition, pp. 8886–8895 (2018)

15. Lapuschkin, S., Wäldchen, S., Binder, A., Montavon, G., Samek, W., Müller, K.R.: Unmasking clever hans predictors and assessing what machines really learn. Nat. Commun. **10**(1), 1096 (2019). https://doi.org/10.1038/s41467-019-08987-4, https://www.nature.com/articles/s41467-019-08987-4

16. Ma, C., et al.: Eye-gaze-guided vision transformer for rectifying shortcut learning. IEEE Trans. Med. Imaging **42**, 3384–3394 (2023)

17. Read, J., Perez-Cruz, F.: Deep learning for multi-label classification. arXiv preprint arXiv:1502.05988 (2014)

18. Russakovsky, O., et al.: ImageNet large scale visual recognition challenge. Int. J. Comput. Vis. **115**, 211–252 (2015)

19. Saab, K., Dunnmon, J., Ratner, A., Rubin, D., Re, C.: Improving sample complexity with observational supervision (2019). https://openreview.net/forum?id=r1gPtjcH_N

20. Saab, K., et al.: Observational supervision for medical image classification using gaze data. In: de Bruijne, M., et al. (eds.) MICCAI 2021, Part II. LNCS, vol. 12902, pp. 603–614. Springer, Cham (2021). https://doi.org/10.1007/978-3-030-87196-3_56

21. Sechidis, K., Tsoumakas, G., Vlahavas, I.: On the stratification of multi-label data. In: Gunopulos, D., Hofmann, T., Malerba, D., Vazirgiannis, M. (eds.) ECML PKDD 2011, Part III. LNCS (LNAI), vol. 6913, pp. 145–158. Springer, Heidelberg (2011). https://doi.org/10.1007/978-3-642-23808-6_10

22. Simonyan, K., Zisserman, A.: Very deep convolutional networks for large-scale image recognition. In: Bengio, Y., LeCun, Y. (eds.) 3rd International Conference on Learning Representations, ICLR 2015, San Diego, CA, USA, 7-9 May 2015, Conference Track Proceedings (2015), http://arxiv.org/abs/1409.1556

23. Sucholutsky, I., Griffiths, T.L.: Alignment with human representations supports robust few-shot learning. In: Thirty-seventh Conference on Neural Information Processing Systems (2023). https://openreview.net/forum?id=HYGnmSLBCf

24. Vapnik, V., Izmailov, R.: Learning using privileged information: similarity control and knowledge transfer. J. Mach. Learn. Res. **16**(61), 2023–2049 (2015). http://jmlr.org/papers/v16/vapnik15b.html

25. Vapnik, V., Vashist, A.: A new learning paradigm: learning using privileged information. Neural Netw. **22**(5), 544–557 (2009). https://doi.org/10.1016/j.neunet.2009.06.042 , https://www.sciencedirect.com/science/article/pii/S0893608009001130

26. Von Rueden, L., et al.: Informed machine learning-a taxonomy and survey of integrating prior knowledge into learning systems. IEEE Trans. Knowl. Data Eng. **35**(1), 614–633 (2021)

27. Wang, J., Ma, Y., Zhang, L., Gao, R.X., Wu, D.: Deep learning for smart manufacturing: methods and applications. J. Manuf. Syst. **48**, 144–156 (2018). https://doi.org/10.1016/j.jmsy.2018.01.003, https://linkinghub.elsevier.com/retrieve/pii/S0278612518300037

28. Wang, S., Ouyang, X., Liu, T., Wang, Q., Shen, D.: Follow my eye: using gaze to supervise computer-aided diagnosis. IEEE Trans. Med. Imaging **41**, 1688–1698 (2022). https://api.semanticscholar.org/CorpusID:246359652

29. Wilcoxon, F.: Individual comparisons by ranking methods. Biometrics Bull. **1**(6), 80–83 (1945). http://www.jstor.org/stable/3001968

30. Wuest, T., Weimer, D., Irgens, C., Thoben, K.D.: Machine learning in manufacturing: advantages, challenges, and applications. Prod. Manuf. Res. **4**, 23–45 (2016). https://doi.org/10.1080/21693277.2016.1192517

31. Yun, K., Peng, Y., Samaras, D., Zelinsky, G., Berg, T.: Exploring the role of gaze behavior and object detection in scene understanding. Front. Psychol. **4** (2013). https://doi.org/10.3389/fpsyg.2013.00917, https://www.frontiersin.org/articles/10.3389/fpsyg.2013.00917

32. Zhou, B., Khosla, A., Lapedriza, A., Oliva, A., Torralba, A.: Learning deep features for discriminative localization. In: Proceedings of the IEEE Conference on Computer Vision and Pattern Recognition, pp. 2921–2929 (2016)

Methodological Challenges of Multimodal Corpus Analysis of Interpreter-Mediated Conversations

Raquel Lázaro Gutiérrez(✉) ⓘ

Universidad de Alcalá, 28801 Alcalá de Henares, Madrid, Spain
raquel.lazaro@uah.es

Abstract. In this contribution we will describe methodological challenges of multimodal corpus analysis, providing the project PRAGMACOR as an example. PRAGMACOR is the acronym for Corpus pragmatics and telephone interpreting: analysis of face-threatening acts. The project runs from the 1st of September 2022 to the 31st of August 2026 with funds obtained in the national competitive Spanish Program for Scientific, Technical and Innovation Research 2021–2023. Specifically, we will focus on the corpus compilation procedure, including ethical and practical issues concerning the formalization of agreements and permissions, and challenges related to the collection and formatting of the compiled conversations. The goal of this project is to develop tools that will allow for the preparation of interpreters and the automation of different tasks within the interpretation practice, such as the documentation process and the elaboration of glossaries (prior to the assignment), the automated search of terms and multi-word expressions or the integration of real-time machine translation during the assignment. The project will thus contribute to the development of computer-assisted interpreting tools, which are at the core of the paradigm of human-machine interaction in interpreter-mediated contexts.

Keywords: Telephone Interpreting · Corpus Pragmatics · Multimodal Corpora

1 Introduction

Telephone conversations are an example of delocalized communication as opposed to face-to-face communication and, on the other hand, interpreted interactions can be considered asynchronous as a speaker's discourse is reworked before it reaches the final recipient. Some authors have already pointed to a greater presence of image attacks in both remote and indirect communication [1–3]. According to the results of previous research (see [4, 5], face-threatening acts (FTAs) constitute a frequent difficulty perceived by telephone interpreters, who point out the lack of guidelines and training to deal with the. On the other hand, after the results of previous projects [6], it was possible to establish that FTAs occurred both against service providers and end users, and against interpreters.

© The Author(s), under exclusive license to Springer Nature Switzerland AG 2024
H. Degen and S. Ntoa (Eds.): HCII 2024, LNAI 14735, pp. 424–438, 2024.
https://doi.org/10.1007/978-3-031-60611-3_29

Our starting hypothesis is that, since interpreter-mediated telephone interactions are examples of both distant and indirect communication, a high number of FTAs of various kinds are to be expected. With PRAGMACOR, we aim at describing this phenomenon and the FTAs that appear in our corpus. To achieve this objective, we have designed a methodology based on corpus pragmatics, which will be described below. The first essential step has already been taken and consists of generating agreements with companies providing telephone interpreting services in Spain. The corpus of conversations is multilingual, with English, French, German, Spanish and Chinese being the most frequent languages. It has been estimated that to meet the recommended standards for corpus size it is necessary to collect 500,000 words in each language. Based on samples from previous projects, we have calculated that we would need approximately 10,000 min of recordings in each language pair, equivalent to 700 conversations in each language pair (2,800 in total).

Research is developed according to the following steps:

1. Corpus generation, which consists of the creation and collection of electronic files [7].
2. As this is a multilingual corpus (Spanish, English, French, German, French, Chinese and Spanish), files corresponding to the languages in which calls have been received are produced. This first phase is complex and time-consuming and consists of several steps: the selection of the conversations, their anonymization, their transcription (the texts are processed semi-automatically), the verification of transcriptions and the verification of tagging.
3. Three different procedures for the analysis of FTAs are addressed. For each of them it is necessary to develop a detailed protocol that allows the simultaneous work of several researchers/annotators.
   a. First, a form-to-function analysis of those elements that can be related to FTAs is performed. For example, we search for expressions of apology, such as "sorry", or expressions of thanks, such as "thank you". This type of analysis does not retrieve all related FTAs because some do not match their typical forms.
   b. Secondly, an automatic search for surrounding elements (metacommunicative utterances, [8]) is performed. In our case, the different forms of "threaten", "request", "thank", which are verbs that announce an attack on the image, are useful.
   c. The third procedure consists of a thorough horizontal analysis in which FTAs are identified and then coded according to Brown and Levinson's [9] classification, and according to their sender (provider, user or interpreter), their receiver (provider, user or interpreter) and the effect they produce (positive, negative or neutral). Tagging is carried out by pairs of annotators and an interrater agreement criterion of 70 % is followed.
4. An interpretative analysis of the results is carried out examining the tagged multilingual data.
5. A contrastive comparison is made taking into account the different source languages on the basis that in each language and culture there are different politeness rules. For this purpose, we will follow an approach based on both intercultural pragmatics,

which analyses the interaction of people from different cultures, and cross-cultural pragmatics, which compares the pragmatic patterns of different cultures [10].

6. Finally, an analysis of the performance of the interpreters reacting towards the presence of FTAs is performed.

With the results of the analysis phase described in the previous section, we will be able to develop useful materials for the training and practice of this type of interpreting.

2 Theoretical Framework

Although most of the research on telephone interpreting consists of comparisons with onsite interpreting and has a focus on quality, in the past years, issues such as the relationship of interpreters with technology and their working environments (ergonomics, [11]) have gained momentum within the human-machine interaction paradigm. This human-machine interplay in the interpretation context in general has already been examined to account for the relationship that the different actors in interpreter-mediated interactions establish with technology [12] in different interpretation settings. On the other hand, corpus analysis has also become recognized as an appropriate methodology in interpreting studies, particularly linked to the creation of automated models for telephone communication in specific contexts [13].

Technology is intertwined with interpretating in many ways. Apart from highly technological research methodologies, the practice of interpreting is surrounded by a wide arrange of technological devices and accompanying software. For instance, interpretation is provided by means of booths, portable systems (bidule) or remotely over the phone or via video link. On the other hand, interpreters can use very varied software for the preparation phase (term tools, machine translation, CAT tools) or during the assignment (what has been termed as computer assisted interpreting or CAI tools, which may comprise automatic speech recognition (ASR), text to speech translation, automated summarizing, unit converters, recognition of named entities, etc.).

Despite the omnipresence of technology in their daily practice, interpreters feel reluctant about using it [14–17]. This might relate to a perceived difficulty in adapting to new technological advances, which sometimes imply a twist in the interpreters' abilities and an impact on working conditions and ergonomics [11, 18]. In fact, the use of CAI tools is far less frequent than that of CAT tools amongst professionals [19–22]. This might be related to the size of the interpretation industry, which addresses a reduced number of uses [23].

Back in 2005, Moser-Mercer [24] already pointed out to a better and more ergonomic adaptation of the working environment for remote interpreters. Apart from the higher cognitive load that the introduction of technology involves [25], the tools already in place fell short in the in accounting for interpreters' visual and social needs. Both Moser-Mercer [24] and more recent authors such as O'Brien [26], Spinolo [27] or Zhang et al. [28] claim for a fine-tuning of technologies and shorter shifts for interpreters who use them, to avoid premature fatigue and stress [29, 30]. As obvious as it may seem, for technology to be truly useful and used, interpreters should be included in the design of user-centered technologies [31]. The goal should be to shape interpreters' experience and interaction in a positive way, so that, instead of suffering an increase in their cognitive load, they can externalize cognitive efforts to technology.

The question remains whether the automation of interpreting is feasible, useful, and acceptable. It has already been noticed that this reluctance in the use of technologies is more prominent for consecutive (bilateral) assignments that for simultaneous ones [32]. This is, of course, because of the intrinsic and contextual characteristics of this modality of interpretation. Even when the popularization of artificial intelligence has promoted within the interpreting practice certain linguistics-based tools (machine translation, text to speech, automatic speech recognition, term extraction, etc.), most of these are only useful when interpreters perform in front of a computer. This scenario is possible in most simultaneous and remote assignments, but not so frequent for onsite bilateral interpreting or for interpretation over the phone. Although it is possible to design CAI tools or the equivalent of an artificial boothmate [22, 33, 34] for interpreters over the phone, the most challenging part involves changing frequent patterns and practices in the delivery of this kind of interpretation. Many telephone interpreters do not use any kind of technology (apart from the telephone) during their assignments [17] and are not used to work in front of a computer. Instead, they enjoy the freedom of counting on a fully and comfortably portable main tool: a smartphone, which they will carry around, allowing for accepting assignments wherever they are. This practice, which is discouraged by many trainers and telephone interpreting companies, should be targeted, and discussed as a previous step in the introduction of CAI tools for telephone interpretation. Other aspects, such as the influence of economic forces [35] or public perceptions on quality and the interpreter's role [36] also require attention.

3 The Project

According to results of previous research by the FITISPos group (see [4, 5]), in a study resulting from the collaboration between the University of Alcalá and one Spanish telephone interpreting company, the interpretation of face-threatening acts is a frequent challenge perceived by telephone interpreters, who point out the lack of guidelines and training to address it. Within the framework of the project "Design, compilation and analysis of a multilingual corpus of mediated interactions on roadside assistance" (Ref. CCGP2017-HUM002), thanks to the cooperation with another telephone interpreting company, 346 conversations in Spanish and German, Chinese, French, English, Italian and Russian, which were anonymized, transcribed, and processed with corpus tools to extract vocabulary and frequent patterns. The objective presence of face threatening acts was detected. On the other hand, thanks to the project "Analysis of face threatening acts in telephone interpretation" (Ref. CM/JIN/2019-040), which exploited this same corpus, it was possible to verify that these threats occurred both against the face of service providers and end users as against interpreters [37].

With PRAGMACOR we intend to continue within the framework of language pragmatics to analyze the prevalence and characteristics of face threatening acts in a corpus of telephone conversations in which the two main parties and the interpreter are distant, that is, in which the end user of the service calls the company or institution that offers it and, after selecting from a list of options provided by an answering machine, is connected with an interpreter and, subsequently, with the service provider. PRAGMACOR's hypothesis, already partially confirmed by previous research, is that in telephone conversations mediated by interpreters a high number of face threatening acts of different kinds occur. This would be because these are, on the one hand, interactions in which the participants relate at a distance and in an asynchronous and indirect manner. Goffman [38] argues that interaction consists of the influence that the participants in a communicative event exert on each other when they share time, space, and context. This author refers, always, to encounters that occur face to face. However, when we talk about mediated telephone conversations, the participants are distant from each other (they do not share space), they do not receive the full meaning of the other's messages immediately (they do not share time) because a third person must transform them so that they are understandable (providing, reworking, or reorganizing the context of communication). The order of interaction proposed by Goffman [39] is organized around meanings and pragmatic rituals. When the interaction undergoes modifications as important as those we have mentioned, it is logical to think that these pragmatic aspects are altered [40]. Some authors have already pointed to a greater presence of face threatening acts both in distance and indirect communication [1–3].

4 Methodology

The great complexity of face threatening acts represents a challenge when carrying out quantitative research on them. However, our research proposes a mixed, qualitative, and quantitative approach. To carry out this research, a methodology based on corpus pragmatics will be used. In this way, our study combines telephone interpretation, pragmatics, and corpus studies in a novel way.

4.1 Methodological Frameworks

PRAGMACOR is based on several pillars: pragmatics (specifically, theories of politeness and face threatening acts), interpretation and corpus analysis. The methodology designed for the project, therefore, is based on corpus pragmatics for the analysis of face threatening acts in telephone interpretation.

According to Yule [41], polite social behavior can be described within a given culture and it can be assumed that the participants in an interaction are aware of the norms and principles that govern them. Within an interaction, politeness reaches a different state and can be described as the means used to show that one is aware of the face of the other. Therefore, normally, conversation partners expect their face to be respected. However, these expectations can be threatened by verbal, paraverbal or non-verbal attacks. The face work [38, 42, 43] is developed through communicative behaviors and can have a positive, negative (threat) or neutral effect (modality, in terms of [43]) on the face of the speaker, that of the interlocutor or even that of other people, such as the interpreter (directionality, [43]).

Brown and Levinson [9] describe two types of face: negative and positive. Positive face refers to self-esteem and is related to the desire to relate positively to others. On the other hand, the negative face represents freedom from imposition and implies the right of individual action and is related to autonomy. The positive and negative aspects of face play a determining role in social interaction, and cooperation between all participants is needed to maintain everyone's face, whether through positive or negative politeness. The negative face is threatened when the freedom of action of the interlocutor is challenged. On the other hand, threats on the positive face occur when the speaker does not consider what his or her interlocutor wants.

Some researchers who have studied onsite dialogue interpreting (see, for example, [44, 45] suggest combining the theoretical framework of Brown and Levinson with other approaches, such as that of Goffman [38] or that of Kerbrat-Orecchioni [46], to better understand the performance of interpreters. We agree with Mason and Stewart [47, p. 51] in that aspects related to politeness and other pragmatic interactional variables are crucial to understand what happens in communicative events within the framework of dialogic interpretation. Therefore, with our research we intend to delve into these issues starting from the cornerstone of Brown and Levinson's Politeness Theory [9], face threatening acts, without leaving aside the specific complementary use of other theories or approaches.

Regarding the analysis of face threatening acts with corpus tools, it is worth mentioning that the nature of the pragmatic aspects of the language implies studying units that go beyond words or terms. To carry out our study, we used an approach based on corpus pragmatics, a very novel methodology both in the field of pragmatics and in the field of corpus linguistics, so much so that Romero Trillo [48, p. 2] considered them parallel, but often mutually exclusive. If studies on pragmatics were initially qualitative and focused on small sets of discourse fragments for which there was great contextual information, in the case of corpus linguistics the interest was in lexicon, grammar, morphology. And syntax, particularly in those aspects that addressed superficial manifestations of the language and that could be recovered through search algorithms [49].

In general, in interpretation studies there are not many pieces of research that have been carried out with computer-processed corpora. In the field of dialogue interpreting, the ComInDat Pilot Corpus has been developed, which is composed of two corpora of mediated conversations between doctors and patients and a corpus of interpreted judgments [50]. This corpus is processed with the EXMARaLDA software, created at the University of Hamburg in 2011 at the Center for Collaborative Research in Multilingualism. A great advantage of this software is that it allows multimodality, by being able to consult both the transcription and the audio on the same platform. It has been used successfully in the qualitative analysis of the TIPp project (Translation and Interpretation in Criminal Proceedings) of the Autonomous University of Barcelona. It is precisely this software that we will use to process our corpus.

4.2 Methods

As mentioned above, the objectives of PRAGMACOR are to detect face threatening acts in a multilingual corpus of three-way interpreter calls and classify them according to their type, directionality, effect, and impact. Considering results from previous research, we have determined the compilation of a multilingual corpus in the most frequent languages along with Spanish: English, French, German, and Chinese [6]. It is estimated that it is necessary to compile 500,000 words in each language to meet the recommended standards for corpus size. Based on samples from previous projects, we have estimated that we would need approximately 10,000 min of recordings in each language pair, which would be equivalent to 700 conversations in each language pair (2,800 in total).

For this project, we count on the collaboration of the three main companies in the provision of telephone interpretation services in Spain. To reach the desired figures, 250 conversations in each pair of languages are requested from each of the companies. These conversations are subjected to a screening and selection procedure, in which those that are unsuccessful are discarded due to their duration (they are cut off at the beginning) or appropriateness (those that are erroneous, such as a person calling an incorrect number) until reaching the established figures. Once the conversations have been extracted, they are prepared and anonymized before transcribing them. Transcription is done semi-automatically with EXMARaIDA. After verifying the transcription, the first labels corresponding to the language and gender of the speakers are assigned, which are essential to carry out contrastive analyzes and to disaggregate the data.

To analyze face threatening acts, three different procedures are carried out. Firstly, a form-to-function analysis is performed on those elements that can be related to politeness and face threatening acts. As this procedure does not recover all the forms related to the different kinds of face-threatening acts, an automated search is carried out for metacommunicative expressions that, as described by Jucker and Taavitsainen (2014) are surrounding elements that announce a face threatening act. The third procedure is an inevitable thorough horizontal analysis.

Once face threatening acts are detected, they are tagged with information about their type, directionality, effect, and impact, as shown in the following table (Table 1):

Annotation is carried out in pairs and a 70% interrater agreement criterion is followed. This information is entered into XML tags to allow automatic searches. To determine the impact of face threatening acts, an analysis of the performance of the interpreters in the face of each of its types is performed. Performance is evaluated using a Likert scale to determine whether they are satisfactory or not (1 = not at all satisfactory; 5 = completely satisfactory) when it comes to maintaining a fluent conversation, transferring information appropriately, following the ethical principles of interpretation and obtaining acceptance and satisfaction from service providers and users.

Table 1. Description of tags

Directionality	Provider (DP)	User (DU)	Interpreter (I)	
	Against the hearer		Against the speaker	
Kind	Negatve: - Orders and requests (TONP) - Suggestions, advice (TONS) - Reminders (TONR) - Threats, warnings, dares (TONA) - Offers (TONO) - Promises (TONQ) - Compliments (TONC) - Expressions of emotions (TONE)	Positive: - Disapproval, criticism, complaints, reprimands, accusations, insults (TOPA) - Contradictions, disagreements, challenges (TOPC) - Expressions of violent emotions (TOPE) - Irreverence (TOPI) - Bad news for hearer, boasting (TOPN) - Raising emotional or divisive topics (TOPT) - Blatant non-cooperation (TOPF) - Address terms (TOPS)	Negative: - Thanks (TENA) - Acceptance of thanks or apologies (TENB) - Excuses (TENE) - Acceptance of offers (TENC) - Responses to hearer's faux pas (TENR) - Unwilling promises and offers (TENP)	Positive: - Apologies (TEPD) - Acceptance of a compliment (TEPA) - Breakdown of physical control over body (TEPF) - Self-humiliation (TEPT) - Confessions (TEPC) - Emotion leakage (TEPE)
Effect	Positive (EP)	Negative (EN)	Neutral (EO)	
Impact (from 1 to 5 according to interreters' performance)	Keeps the conversation fluent (IF1–5)	Translates information properly (II1–5)	Follows ethical principles (IE1–5)	Obtains approval and satisfaction from main speakers (IS1–5)

5 Analysis Examples

The audio files are entered into EXMARaLDA and a first automatic transcription is carried out. This transcription is post-edited by the researchers to obtain a text faithful to the audio. The interface presents the audio and its transcription together, so that it is possible to listen to the turns or fragments of speech by clicking directly on them (Fig. 1).

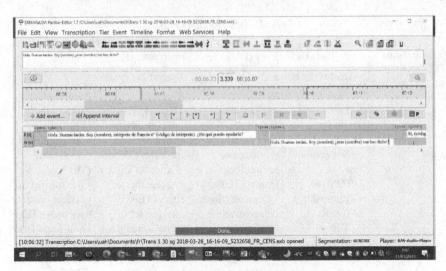

Fig. 1. Audio and text in EXMARaLDA

The EXMARaLDA interface allows to include annotations and presents results in a comfortable and visual way, as the following three figures show (Figs. 2, 3 and 4):

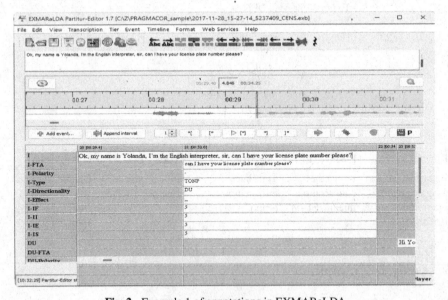

Fig. 2. Example 1 of annotations in EXMARaLDA

The recent entrance of Spain in CLARIAH (the European Research Infrastructure Consortia CLARIN and DARIAH), allows for free use of the software ELAN. Annotations have also been made in ELAN, whose use is more extended. The following figures show some examples (Figs. 5, 6 and 7):

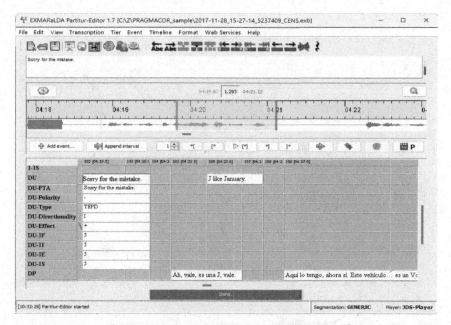

Fig. 3. Example 2 of annotation in EXMARaLDA

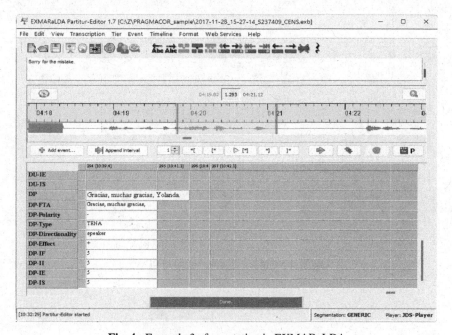

Fig. 4. Example 3 of annotation in EXMARaLDA

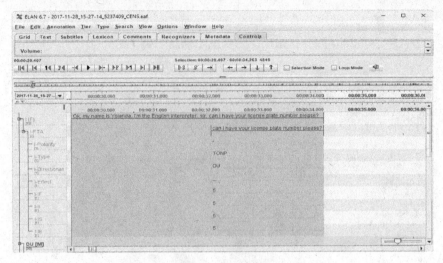

Fig. 5. Example 1 of annotations in ELAN

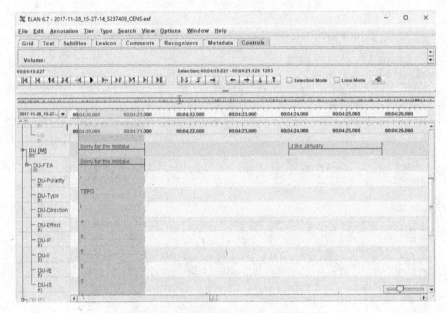

Fig. 6. Example 2 of annotations in ELAN

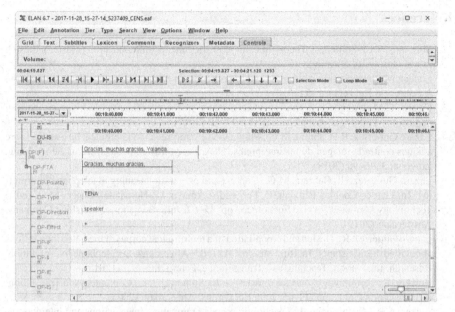

Fig. 7. Example 3 of annotations in ELAN

6 Conclusion

PRAGMACOR is work in progress and will be completed by the end of 2026. Its methodology is thorough and time-consuming, but also very innovative and worth showing. The results of PRAGMACOR will provide valuable information about a usually unexplored part of discourse and interaction. After an annotated multilingual corpus of these characteristics not only pragmatic, but also multimodal annotation can be obtained. The more elements are considered for annotation, the more complete data and the more accurate derived artificial intelligence products will be. Research with multilingual and oral corpora give way for both CAI tools that support the work of interpreters, but also products that contribute to automation or machine interpreting.

Downie [35, p. 288] claims that it is important that society stops understanding human and machine interpreting as "rivals, bidding for the same clients and the same work". Machine and human interpreting can coexist and be complementary in a wider panorama of language access and communication services. Within the human-machine interaction sphere, interpreters can use machines to augment their abilities, whereas end users might choose to communicate by means of an aseptic artificial tool.

Acknowledgments. This project receives funds from "Proyectos de generación de conocimiento" en el marco del Programa Estatal para Impulsar la Investigación Científico-Técnica y su Transferencia, del Plan Estatal de Investigación Científica, Técnica y de Innovación 2021–2023. Corpus pragmatics and telephone interpreting: analysis of face-threatening acts, Ref. PID2021-127196NA-I00).

References

1. Simmons, T.L.: Politeness Theory in Computer Mediated Communication [Master's thesis]. Aston University, Birmingham (1994)
2. Locher, M.: Introduction: politeness and impoliteness in computer-mediated communication. J. Politeness Res. **6**(1), 1–5 (2010)
3. Castro, C.M.:. Ataque a la imagen y descortesía en los comentarios de blogs en español peninsular. Philologia Hispalensis. **31**(1), 37–63 (2017)
4. Lázaro Gutiérrez, R., Cabrera, M.G.: Pragmática e interpretación telefónica: un estudio sobre ataques contra la imagen de los intérpretes (FTA, Face threatening acts). EPiC Series Lang. Linguist. **3**, 85–90 (2018)
5. Lázaro Gutiérrez, R., Cabrera, M.G.: Context and pragmatic meaning in telephone interpreting. In: Garcés-Conejos Blitvich, P., Fernández Amaya, L., Hernández-López, M.O. (eds.) Technology Mediated Service Encounters, pp. 45–67. John Benjamins Publishing Company, Amsterdam (2019)
6. Lázaro Gutiérrez, R.: Design and compilation of a multilingual corpus of mediated interactions about roadside assistance. In: Ruiz Mezcua, A., (ed.). Approaches to Telephone Interpretation. Research, Innovation, Teaching and Transference. Peter Lang, Bern (2018)
7. Bowker, L.: Terminology tools for translators. In: Somer, H. (ed.) Computers and Translation: A Translator's Guide, pp. 49–65. John Benjamins, Amsterdam (2003)
8. Jucker, A.H., Taavitsainen, I.: Diachronic corpus pragmatics: Intersections and interactions. In: Taavitsainen, I., Jucker, A.H., Tuominen, J. (eds.) Diachronic Corpus Pragmatics, pp. 3–26. John Benjamins, Amsterdam (2014)
9. Brown, P., Levinson, S.C.: Politeness: Some Universals in Language Usage. Cambridge University Press, Cambridge (1987)
10. Kecskes, I.: Cross-cultural and Intercultural pragmatics. In: Huang, Y. (ed.) The Oxford Handbook of Pragmatics, pp. 400–415. Oxford University Press, Oxford (2017)
11. Dong, J., Turner, G.: The ergonomic impact of agencies in the dynamic system of interpreting provision: an ethnographic study of backstage influences on interpreter performance. Transl. Spaces **5**(1), 97–123 (2016). https://doi.org/10.1075/ts.5.1.06don
12. Mellinger, C.D., Pokorn, N.K.: Community interpreting, translation and technology. Transl. Interpreting Stud. **13**(3), 337–341 (2018)
13. Braun, S.: Technology and interpreting. In: O'Hagan, M., (ed.) The Routledge Handbook of Translation and Technology. Routledge, New York (2019)
14. Corpas Pastor, G., Fern, L.: A Survey of Interpreters' Needs and Practices Related to Language Technology. Technical paper [FFI2012-38881-MINECO/TI-DT-2016-1] (2016)
15. Corpas, P.G.: Tools for interpreters: the challenges that lie ahead. Curr Trends Transl Teach Learn E. **5**, 157–182 (2018)
16. Mellinger, C.D., Hanson, T.A.: Interpreter traits and the relationship with technology and visibility. Transl. Interpreting Stud. **13**(3), 366–394 (2018)
17. Stengers, H., Lázaro Gutiérrez, R., Kerremans, K.: Public service interpreters' perceptions and acceptance of remote interpreting technologies in times of a pandemic. In: Corpas Pastor, G., Defrancq, B. (eds.) Interpreting Technologies – Current and Future Trends, pp. 109–141. John Benjamins Publishing Company, Amsterdam (2023)
18. Lázaro, G.R.: Remote (telephone) interpreting in healthcare settings. In: Susam-Saraeva, Ş, Spišiaková, E. (eds.) The Routledge Handbook of Translation and Health, pp. 216–231. Routledge, London (2021)
19. Tripepi-Winteringham, S.: The usefulness of ICTs in interpreting practice. Interpreters' Newslett. **15**, 87–99 (2010)
20. Drechsel, A.: The tablet interpreter. Lean Publishing, Canada (2015)

21. Pedagogy, M.-M.: In: Pöchhacker, F., Grbic, N., Mead, P., Setton, R. (eds.) Routledge Encyclopedia of Interpreting Studies, pp. 303–306. Routledge, London (2015)
22. Fantinuoli, C.: Computer-assisted preparation in conference interpreting. Transl. Interpreting. 9(2), 24–37 (2017)
23. Fantinuoli, C.: Towards AI-enhanced computer-assisted interpreting. In: Corpas Pastor, G., Defrancq, B. (eds.) Interpreting Technologies – Current and Future Trends, pp. 46–71. John Benjamins, Amsterdam (2023)
24. Moser-Mercer, B.: Remote interpreting: the crucial role of presence. Bull. VALS-ASLA. 81, 73–97 (2005)
25. Mellinger, C.D.: Computer-assisted interpreting technologies and interpreter cognition: a product and process-oriented perspective. Tradumàtica. 17, 33–44 (2019)
26. O'Brien, S.: Translation as Human-Computer Interaction. Translation Spaces. 1(1), 101–122 (2012)
27. Spinolo, N.: Remote interpreting. In: ENTI (Encyclopedia of Translation & Interpreting). AIETI (2022)
28. Zhang, J., Chen, Y., Liu, C., Niu, N., Wang, Y.: Empirical evaluation of ChatGPT on requirements information retrieval under zero-shot setting. In: 2023 International Conference on Intelligent Computing and Next Generation Networks (ICNGN), pp. 1–6 (2023)
29. Roziner, I., Shlesinger, M.: Much ado about something remote. Interpreting 12(2), 214–247 (2010)
30. Liu, J.: The impact of technology on interpreting. An interpreter and trainer's perspective. Int. J. Chin. Engl. Transl. Interpreting (IJCETI) 1, 1–8 (2022)
31. Mellinger, C.D.: Embedding, extending, and distributing interpreter cognition with technology. In: Corpas Pastor, G., Defrancq, B. (eds.) Interpreting Technologies – Current and Future Trends, pp. 195–216. John Benjamins Publishing Company, Amsterdam (2023)
32. Deysel, E.: Investigation the use of technology in the interpreting profession. In: Corpas Pastor, G.C., Defrancq, B. (eds.) Interpreting Technologies – Current and Future Trends, pp. 142–168. John Benjamins Publishing Company, Amsterdam (2023)
33. Rodriguez, S., et al.: SmarTerp: A CAI system to support simultaneous interpreters in real-time. In: Mitkov, R., Sosoni, V., Giguère, J.C., Murgolo, E., Deysel, E., (eds.). Proceedings of the Translation and Interpreting Technology Online Conference. INCOMA Ltd., pp. 102–109 (2021)
34. Fantinuoli, C., Marchesini, G., Landan, D., Horak, L.: Kudo interpreter assist: automated real-time support for remote interpretation (2022)
35. Downie, J.: Where is it all going? Technology, economic pressures and the future of interpreting. In: Corpas Pastor, G.C., Defrancq, B. (eds.) Interpreting Technologies – Current and Future Trends, pp. 277–301. John Benjamins Publishing Company, Amsterdam (2023)
36. Fantinuoli, C.: Computer-assisted interpreting: challenges and future perspectives. In: Durán, I., Corpas Pastor, G.C. (eds.) Trends, E-Tools and Resources for Translators and Interpreters, pp. 153–174. Koninklijke Brill Nv, Liden (2018)
37. Lázaro Gutiérrez, R.: Analysis of Face-Threatening Acts against Telephone Interpreters. The Interpreters' Newsletter, vol. 26 (2021)
38. Goffman, E.: Ritual de la interacción. Ensayos sobre el comportamiento cara a cara. Tiempo Contemporáneo, Buenos Aires (1967)
39. Goffman, E.: The interaction order. Am. Sociol. Rev. 48(1), 1–17 (1983)
40. Jenkins, R.: Erving goffman: a major theorist of power? J. Power. 1(2), 157–168 (2008)
41. Yule, G.: Pragmatics. Oxford University Press, Oxford (1992)
42. O'Driscoll, J.: What's in an FTA? Reflections on a chance meeting with Claudine. J. Politeness Res. 3, 237–262 (2007)
43. Hernández, F.N.: Actividad de imagen: caracterización y tipología en la interacción comunicativa. Pragmática Sociocultural/Sociocultural Pragmatics. 1(2), 175–198 (2013)

44. Merlini, R.: Changing perspectives. Politeness in cooperative multi-party interpreted talk. In: Schäffner, C., Kredens, K., Fowler, Y., (eds.). Interpreting in a Changing Landscape. Selected papers from Critical Link 6, John Benjamins, Amsterdam, pp. 267–283 (2013)

45. Vargas-Urpí, M.: Public service interpreting in educational settings: issues of politeness and interpersonal relationships. In: Tipton, R., Desilla, L. (eds.) The Routledge Handbook of Translation and Pragmatics, pp. 354–366. Routledge, New York (2019)

46. Le, K.-O.: Discours en interaction. Armand Colin, Paris (2005)

47. Mason, I., Stewart, M.: Interactional Pragmatics, Face and the Dialogue Interpreter. In: Mason, I. (ed.) Triadic Exchanges: Studies in Dialogue Interpreting, pp. 51–70. St. Jerome, Manchester and Northampton (2001)

48. Romero-Trillo, J., (ed.) Pragmatics and corpus linguistics. A mutualistic entente. Mouton de Gruyter, Berlin, New York (2008)

49. Jucker, A.H.: Introduction to part 5: Corpus pragmatics. In: Jucker, A.H., Schneider, K.P., Bublitz, W. (eds.) Methods in Pragmatics, pp. 455–466. de Gruyter, Berlin (2018)

50. Angermeyer, P., Meyer, B., Schmidt, T.: Sharing community interpreting corpora. In: Schmidt, T., Wörner, K. (eds.) Multilingual Corpora and Multilingual Corpus Analysis, pp. 275–294. John Benjamins, Amsterdam (2012)

Multi-Criteria Decision Making (MCDM) with Causal Reasoning for AI/ML Applications – A Survey

Atul Rawal[1] , Justine Rawal[2(✉)] , and Adrienne Raglin[2]

[1] Towson University, Towson, MD 21252, USA
[2] DEVCOM Army Research Laboratory, Adelphi, MD 20783, USA
justine.c.rawal.civ@army.mil

Abstract. Multi-criteria decision making (MCDM) refers to making the best possible decision out of different alternatives based on factors which can sometimes be vague. MCDM methods focus on structuring complex operations to choose the best possible decision out of the available alternatives by weighing and evaluating the different criteria. The process involves alternatives, criteria, weights, and the decision makers. It is utilized primarily for aiding in decision making with domain knowledge. However, the availability of domain knowledge for all the different alternatives can be a challenge, especially when using observational datasets. To overcome the lack of domain knowledge (sometimes the proper data) causal reasoning can be utilized to enhance the decision-making process by highlighting the hidden relationships with the data. Causal reasoning can discover the hidden relationship between the variables in observational datasets, and then provide estimates of treatment effects of the various alternatives. This study provides an overview of the causal reasoning with MCDM methods. We provide a detailed survey of MCDM and MCDM methods along with causal reasoning. We provide a detailed survey of how causal reasoning techniques have been used with MCDM methods for different applications. Finally, we highlight the challenges associated with the use of causal reasoning techniques with MCDM and provide some potential perspectives and solutions towards them.

Keywords: Causal Reasoning · Multi Criteria Decision Making · Machine Learning

1 Introduction

Decision science is the field of science that relates to decision making at both the individual and population levels. It includes decision-making based on decision analysis, risk-benefit analysis, cost analysis, optimizations and is derived from other sciences such as operations research, statistical inference, economics, cognitive/behavioral sciences, and computer sciences. Even though the field of decision-making has been around for quite a while, recent advancements in artificial intelligence and machine learning (AI/ML) have propelled the field into a new era [1–3]. Similarly, advancements in multi-criteria decision making (MCDM) and causal reasoning have also brought about progress for decision making as a whole [4, 5].

© The Author(s), under exclusive license to Springer Nature Switzerland AG 2024
H. Degen and S. Ntoa (Eds.): HCII 2024, LNAI 14735, pp. 439–448, 2024.
https://doi.org/10.1007/978-3-031-60611-3_30

Multi-criteria decision making is a vital component and process of decision making within operations research. MCDM methods rank the list of potential alternatives as the solution for the decision-making problems based on observational/experimental data. These methods have been applied in a wide array of applications such as healthcare, environmental sciences, engineering, and business/managements [6, 7]. (Fig. 1 highlights the applications of multi-criteria decision making in different fields.) The availably of a plethora of datasets and data-sources have been made available as a consequence of the explosion of applications for AI/ML. These same datasets and sources can be utilized with MCDM techniques, including the evaluation of different parameters such as subjective/objective preferences. AI/ML methods when combined with MCDM techniques can aid in defining the problem, extracting different alternative solutions, and defining the criteria for the data-driven solutions.

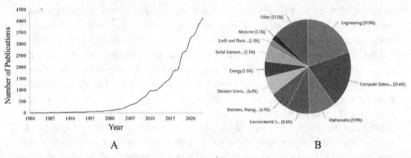

Fig. 1. (A) Number of publications for MCDM in recent years. (B) Applications of multi-criteria decision making in different fields. (Data derived from Scopus)

Causal reasoning for AI/ML applications has seen an increase in research interest in the recent years, even though the field of causality and causal reasoning have been around for quite some time. Causal reasoning allows for the derivation of causal relations between different variables in both experimental and observational datasets. Since experimental studies are not always feasible, observational datasets are commonly used in applications that require investigating causality within the data. However, observational datasets come with challenges such as the lack of ground truth or domain knowledge. When combined with MCDM methods, causal reasoning may help alleviate some of the burden of the need for ground truth or domain knowledge by identifying the cause-and-effect relations between the different features or alternatives for decision making applications. Causal reasoning can discover the hidden relationship between the variables in observational datasets, and then provide estimates of treatment effects of the various alternatives. Literature highlights a few examples of the use of causal reasoning with MCDM methods for decision making applications [5, 8, 9].

In this paper, we present a survey for decision making from observational datasets by combining muti-criteria decision making and causal reasoning for machine learning applications. The paper is organized as follows: Sect. 2 provides a brief overview of causal reasoning covering its different aspects, Sect. 3 covers an overview of multi-criteria decision making and its application for machine learning, Sect. 4 presents the ensemble framework of causal learning and multi-criteria decision making for machine learning applications, finally Sect. 5 includes concluding remarks.

2 Causal Reasoning

Causal reasoning refers to the process for establishing of the cause effect relationship across data. It aims to identify the causal relationships between different variables. For any given variable the cause describes the "why" whereas the effect describes the "what", where the cause is responsible for the effect and the effect is dependent on the cause. [10, 11]. For machine learning systems, causal reasoning refers to the leveraging of these relationships between the various features within the datasets. Generating causal relationships in observational datasets for machine learning requires these advanced systems to go beyond traditional statistical associations and correlations. While correlations within the datasets provide great insight into the behavior and trends of specific variables, causal reasoning can provide added relationship between these variables, particularly changes within the variables. In machine learning applications, causal reasoning allows for identifying relations between the features, and the degree of change in the system prediction caused by the change in a feature due to the modification/manipulation of another feature. The feature being modified is referred to as the *treatment*, whereas the feature whose degree of change is investigated is called the *outcome*. Other variables within the dataset that can cause an effect on both the outcome and the treatment are called *confounders* whereas the noise variables are referred to as the *covariates*.

Judea pearl classified the causal relationships between the treatment and outcome into three different categories known as the causal hierarchy. These categories were called association, intervention and counterfactuals [11–13]. Association refers to the statistical correlation between the variables. Intervention goes further into the causal relations by investigating the effect of treatment actions on the outcome based on the causal structure between the two. The last category is called the counterfactual, and it incorporates both association and intervention. Counterfactuals are utilized to generate causal relations underlying both the association and intervention levels to make predictions based on unknown outcomes [11, 14].

Causal relations within a dataset can be investigated via one of the two available techniques: causal discovery and causal inference [15, 16]. Causal discovery highlights the causal relations between variables in the dataset and causal inference aims to study effects to the outcome caused by the modifications on the treatment. Two formal frameworks are available to investigate causal relations via either causal discovery or causal inference: *structural causal models* (SCMs) and *potential outcome framework*. SCMs provide an inclusive view of causality with causal graphs and structural equations, whereas the potential outcome framework provides methods to quantify the causal relations between the treatment and outcome. [12, 17–19].

Even though causal reasoning has been around for quite some time, the utilization of causality with multi-criteria decision making is still relatively new. Causal learning in combination with MCDM methods can be applied to various machine learning applications. As machine learning systems are based on statistical correlations to deduce relations between the different features and make data-driven predictions, causal relations cannot be derived directly without the use of causal reasoning. Causal reasoning for machine learning can be done via a number of available open-source toolboxes and packages such as the Causal Discovery Toolbox, CausalML, and DoWHY [20]. In the field of causality for ML, there are challenges that remain. These challenges include the use of causal learning in ensemble with MCDM methods for decision-making still need to be investigated.

3   Multi-Criteria Decision Making

Multi-Criteria Decision-Making (MCDM) methods are a way to aid in the decision-making process, especially in situations that involve numerous alternatives and options to consider [21]. MCDM methods allow for the evaluation, prioritization, and selection of the most optimal alternative from a set of available ones [22]. The MCDM involve the following steps [21, 23]: 1) State or define the decisive problem, 2) Elicit criteria to be judged, 3) screen the alternatives, 4) Define evaluation criteria preferences, 5) Apply an appropriate MCDM method, and 6. Evaluate the results provided.

There are several MCDM methods that exist that have differing capabilities when it comes to evaluating the alternatives and criteria. Not all decisive problems are the same and may require different computations. Additionally, growing in popularity in research is creating a hybrid MCDM approach, which consists of the combination of two or more MCDM methods. This allows for the leverage of the strengths of the MCDM method while minimizing limitations or weaknesses [21, 24].

MCDM can be broken down into two categories: Multi-Attribute Decision-Making (MADM) or Multi-Objective Decision-Making (MODM) all dependent on the decisive problem at hand [23, 25–27]. With MADM, the decision is focused on a comparison of a finite number of alternatives [23, 28]. Popular examples of MADM methods include Weighted Sum Model (WSM), Analytical Hierarchy Process (AHP), Technique for Order Preferences by Similarity to Ideal Solutions (TOPSIS), Preference Ranking Organization Method for Enrichment Evaluations (PROMETHEE), Elimination Et Choix Traduisant la REalite´ (ELECTRE), VlseKriterijumska Optimizacija I Kompromisno Resenje (VIKOR). Whereas MODM focuses on the optimization of the multiple objectives and criteria is continuous and generally infinite or very large. Popular examples of MODM include neural networks, goal programming, and genetic algorithms.

3.1   MCDM Applications for Machine Learning and Artificial Intelligence

MCDM techniques, when used in conjunction with ML methodologies provide new insights for decision making in complex applications. MDCM techniques allow for evaluation of different predictions made by the AI/ML models, whereas ML models can aid in overcoming the shortcomings of MCDM methods such as TOPSIS and AHP. Below we present some studies that highlight the utilization of MCDM and ML together for various applications.

Costache et al. focused on using MCDM and ML for flash-flood susceptibility assessment [29]. k-Nearest Neighbor (kNN) and K-Star (KS) ML algorithms were combined with MCDM method, Analytical Hierarchy Process (AHP). This created the ensemble models kNN-AHP and KS-AHP to be used for calculating a Flash-Flood Potential Index (FFPI).

Lavate & Srivastava combined ML and MCDM for the purpose of channel allocation in wireless sensor networks [30]. The strategy of combining these two methods allow for ML to provide automation and predictive power, whereas MCDM allows for a transparent and understandable decision-making process. Their proposed methodology includes four stages: 1. Pre-processing the data, 2. Setting selection criteria, 3. TOPSIS algorithm, and 4. Fine-tune classification model. The goal of this methodology is to provide reliable and flexible allocation of wireless communication networks.

Guhathakurata et al. used ML and MCDM to evaluate fundamental factors that countries during COVID-19 and compare the death rate of South Asian Association for Regional Cooperation (SAARC) countries versus the First World Nations [31]. The research procedure consisted of 1) Selection of the attributes, 2) Weight calculations using the MCDM method AHP, 3). Attributes are labeled with weight scores, 4) Risk factor is formed combining labeled attributes, 5) Calculation of individual country risk factors using the dataset, 6) ML hierarchical clustering countries into groups (Low Risk, Medium Risk, and High Risk), and 7) analysis of SAARC countries using clustering results.

Kartal, Oztekin, Gunasekaran, and Cebi proposed integrating ML and MCDM for multi-attribute inventory analysis [32]. MCDM methods (SAW, AHP, and VIKOR) were used to determine the class for each inventory item. Then ML methods (naïve bayes, Bayesian networks, artificial neural networks (ANN) and support vector machine (SVM)) were uses for prediction of the stock item classes. The results revealed that the proposed hybrid approach is effective and applicable for inventory classification.

Musbah, Ali, Aly, and Little used MCDM and ML methods for determining the best combination of energy sources of a hybrid energy system (HES) for a case study focused on providing electricity to a specific remote area [33]. The MCDM method TOPSIS was used to generate an energy management plan. Additionally, another MCDM method AHP was used to calculate criteria weights, and was validated using Fuzzy AHP (F-AHP). A new dataset was created using TOPSIS and then ML methods (random forest (RF) and LightGBM, comparably), determined the best alternative.

4   Hybrid Causal MCDM Approach to Decision Making

As mentioned previously the focus of this paper is topresent a hybrid approach to decision making using AI/ML systems by combining causal reasoning and multi-criteria decision making to generate robust decisions that are based on causal reasoning and not just correlation. We propose using causality in conjunction with MCDM to generate fundamental cause-effect decision criteria. Here we provide a summary of the current state of the art of the use of causality with MCDM techniques.

Khorasani et. al. Used MCDM (hierarchical fuzzy TOPSIS specifically) to evaluate road safety performance indicators that are causally related to the number of crashes or to the injury consequences of a crash [REF]. They conclude that their method proved to be valuable for road safety performance evaluation as they were able to rank and prioritize indicators.

DEMATEL (Decision Making Trial and Evaluation Laboratory) is an MCDM method [34]. It allows the causal relationship of criteria to be constructed into a structural model and analyzed. It has the capability of understanding the influence levels of each element over the other, and is an effective decision-making method to identify cause and effect relations between the components of a complex system. It uses a visual structural model to identify causal relations by evaluating the dependencies between the factors involved in the decision.

Zou et. al. Used MCDM (DEMATEL specifically) to construct an influence relation structure (IRSD) and influential weight within a diagnosis-related group (DRG) system [REF]. This allows decision makers to learn what the key causal criteria were, understand the interactions between criteria, and understand their influence.

Wattahayu and Peng proposed a MCDM approach that combined Bayesian networks and influence diagrams to highlight the interactions between the variables in their data [35]. They presented influence diagrams, which can be viewed as causal graphs, where nodes represented the decision alternatives and objectives. Conditional probability tables associated with the nodes were utilized to model the connections between the nodes.

Fouladgar et al., used causal layered analysis (CLA) and MCDM method TOPSIS to evaluate the environmental policies and identify observation policies for prioritized policy making [36]. Based on causal layered analysis authors highlighted the identification of four uncertainties for four scenarios and multiple discrete scenarios.

Yang and Tzeng proposed an integrated MDCM model with DEMATEL and cluster-weighted analytic network process (ANP) method to identify causal relations and structures between different decision criteria and quantify their effect on the decision [37]. Weights of the criteria were derived in the proposed approach by calculating cluster-weighted super matrix, where the influence matrix is used as the normalization base for the super matrix to calculate ANP weights. Using the criteria weights causal diagram are created to easily visualize the problem complexity and decision.

Wang et al., presented a novel hybrid MCDM model that utilized DEMATEL to analyze the different factors that influenced the unsafe behaviors of miners in intelligent mines to prevent mining accidents [38]. They used MCDM approach of fuzzy DEMATEL amalgamated with maximum mean de-entropy (MMDE), interpretative structural modeling (ISM), and matrix of cross-impact multiplications applied to classification (MICMAC) to understand the interactions and relationships among causal factors related to miners' unsafe behaviors. The article investigated the relationship between 20 different factors such as government regulation, leadership attention, safety standards, supervision etc. The authors presented the maximum mean de-entropy (MMDE) to enhance the DEMATEL method with fuzzy theory. Using the proposed method, the authors were able to determine the causal relationship between each influencing factor.

Raut et. al. Used MCDM (AHP specifically) to ascertain the relative importance by comparing causal factors for the purpose of modeling the reasons of post-harvest losses [39]. After completing the study, they suggested using another MCDM method (DEMATEL, TOPSIS, etc.) to overcome limitations AHP may have and improve accuracy of the model. Results indicate that critical causal factors of post-harvest losses were determined using MCDM.

Hsu presented a hybrid factor analysis and DEMATEL approach for investigating the factors that affect blog design [40]. The study used factor analysis in the first phase to simplify and categorize the causal factors. In the second phase, the author utilized the DEMATEL method to evaluate the causal relationships between the different factors and visualize the connections between the different criteria for the decision-making process.

Montibeller and Belton presented a new MCDM method called Reasoning Map [8]. The method derives causal graphs to provide and evaluate multi-criteria decision alternatives. The proposed model utilizes causal maps to structure the evaluation of the alternatives to rank them qualitatively. The authors state that their method "permits the evaluation of options along complex chains of reasoning statements: from the means available to the ends that decision-makers want to achieve." It considers the limitations of decision makers to provide domain knowledge for the desired decisions to provide an evaluation of the different alternatives by aggregating qualitative data.

Teresa et al., proposed extending reasoning maps via multi-linear evaluation model structure integrated with the MACBETH MCDM method [9]. It utilizes the MACBETH method to evaluate the strength of effect for all the means-end links to capture the relations between the concepts within the map. The authors applied their method to construct a population health index by assessing the options and multi-criteria interactions for the decision problem.

Comes et al., proposed a new approach called Decision Maps for complex decision making situations to evaluate muti-criteria decision alternatives when heterogeneous uncertainty is present [41]. The approach provides solutions for decision-making when complex uncertainty is present. It integrates causal maps and attribute trees together to process relevant information for the decision and provide an evaluation of the causal reasoning with respect to various decisionaims and domain knowledge from the decision maker.

Jam et al., used causal layers in conjunction with hybrid MCDM methods such as AHP-TOPSIS, AHP-VIKOR and IIM to evaluate landslide susceptibility in Iran [42]. The authors produced landslide susceptibility maps by evaluating causal factors such as slope angle, slope aspect, rainfall. This was done by using domain knowledge from SMEs to calculate the weights for each of the causal factors using the AHP method.

Seiti et al., presented R. Graph as a new approach for variability and risk analysis to evaluate the causal effects of risk factors on different variables [43]. The model is capable of calculating the amount of change in different variables and rank them based on their importance for the decision. The authors presented a use-case study of COVID-19 on the Iranian electric industry.

Falatoonitoosi et al., presented the use of causal graphs for mapping the strategic variables in balanced scorecards that are integrated with the DEMATEL method to evaluate and rank the different strategies [44].

Yazdani et al., proposed a DEMATEL approach for supplier selection. The authors evaluated the causal relations between the customer requirements by generating a causal relation structure [45]. The level of relation between pairs of different criteria and customer requirements is identified using the quality function deployment and deriving the relationship matrix.

5 Conclusion

Multi-criteria decision making (MCDM) methods can aid AI/ML systems in the decision-making process. While there have been many studies showing the use of MCDM for ML or ML for MCDM methods, there is a lack of studies that integrate causal reasoning within the MDCM framework. Even though methods like DEMATEL and reasoning maps take into consideration causal factors to construct directed acrylic graphs (DAGs) based on Bayesian networks, they do not derive direct causal relationships from observational data without utilizing domain knowledge or decision preferences. The integration of causal reasoning with MCDM can provide a robust approach to decision making. This paper provided a brief survey of existing studies in literature that have utilized causal reasoning with MCDM methods.

Disclosure of Interests. The authors have no competing interests to declare that are relevant to the content of this article.

References

1. Elbasheer, M., et al.: Applications of ML/AI for decision-intensive tasks in production planning and control. Procedia Comput. Sci. **200**, 1903–1912 (2022)
2. Haefner, N., Morf, P.: AI for decision-making in connected business. Connected Business: Create Value in a Networked Economy, pp. 215–231 (2021)
3. Schmitt, M.: Automated machine learning: AI-driven decision making in business analytics. Intell. Syst. Appl. **18**, 200188 (2023)
4. Aruldoss, M., Lakshmi, T.M., Venkatesan, V.P.: A survey on multi criteria decision making methods and its applications. Am. J. Inf. Syst. **1**(1), 31–43 (2013)
5. Martin, T., Chang, K.-C.: A causal reasoning approach to DSA situational awareness and decision-making. In: Proceedings of the 16th International Conference on Information Fusion, IEEE (2013)
6. Sandra, M., et al.: A novel decision support system for the appraisal and selection of green warehouses. Socio-Economic Planning Sciences, 2024. **91**
7. Jain, A.K., et al.: Multi-criteria decision making to validate performance of RBC-based formulae to screen [Formula: see text]-thalassemia trait in heterogeneous haemoglobinopathies. BMC Med. Inform. Decis. Mak. **24**(1), 5 (2024)
8. Montibeller, G., Belton, V.: Qualitative operators for reasoning maps: evaluating multi-criteria options with networks of reasons. Eur. J. Oper. Res. **195**(3), 829–840 (2009)
9. Rodrigues, T.C., et al.: Modelling multicriteria value interactions with reasoning maps. Eur. J. Oper. Res. **258**(3), 1054–1071 (2017)
10. Morgan, S.L., Winship, C.: Counterfactuals and causal inference. Cambridge University Press, Cambridge (2015)
11. Pearl, J.: The seven tools of causal inference, with reflections on machine learning. Commun. ACM **62**(3), 54–60 (2019)
12. Pearl, J.: Causal inference in statistics: An overview (2009)
13. Pearl, J.: Theoretical impediments to machine learning with seven sparks from the causal revolution. arXiv preprint arXiv:1801.04016 (2018)
14. Pearl, J.: Structural and probabilistic causality. Psychol. Learn. Motiv. **34**, 393–435 (1996)
15. Gelman, A.: Causality and Statistical Learning. University of Chicago Press Chicago, IL (2011)

16. Peters, J., Janzing, D., Schölkopf, B.: Elements of Causal Inference: Foundations and Learning Algorithms. The MIT Press, Cambridge (2017)
17. Guo, R., et al.: A survey of learning causality with data: problems and methods. ACM Comput. Surv. (CSUR) 53(4), 1–37 (2020)
18. Pearl, J.: Causality. Cambridge University Press, Cambridge (2009)
19. Yao, L., et al.: A survey on causal inference. ACM Trans. Knowl. Disc. Data (TKDD) 15(5), 1–46 (2021)
20. Malinsky, D., Danks, D.: Causal discovery algorithms: a practical guide. Philos Compass 13(1), e12470 (2018)
21. Caylor, J.P., Hammell, R.J., Raglin, A.J.: Preliminary evaluation of multi-criteria decision-making methodology for emergency management. In: Nunes, I.L. (ed.) Advances in Human Factors and System Interactions, AHFE 2021, LNNS, vol. 265, pp. 11–18. Springer, Cham (2021). https://doi.org/10.1007/978-3-030-79816-1_2
22. Xu, L., Yang, J.-B.: Introduction to multi-criteria decision making and the evidential reasoning approach, Manchester School of Management Manchester, Manchester, vol. 106 (2001)
23. Singh, A., Malik, S.K.: Major MCDM techniques and their application-a review. IOSR J. Eng. 4(5), 15–25 (2014)
24. Velasquez, M., Hester, P.T.: An analysis of multi-criteria decision making methods (2013)
25. Chauhan, A., Vaish, R.: Magnetic material selection using multiple attribute decision making approach. Mater. Des. (1980–2015) 36, 1–5 (2012)
26. Mardani, A., et al.: Multiple criteria decision-making techniques and their applications–a review of the literature from 2000 to 2014. Econ. Res.-Ekonomska istraživanja 28(1), 516–571 (2015)
27. Zavadskas, E.K., Turskis, Z., Kildienė, S.: State of art surveys of overviews on MCDM/MADM methods. Technol. Econ. Dev. Econ. 20(1), 165–179 (2014)
28. Nijssen, D.: Improving spatiality in decision making for river basin management (2013). Lehrstuhl für Hydrologie, Wasserwirtschaft und Umwelttechnik, Ruhr-Univ
29. Costache, R., et al.: Flash-flood susceptibility assessment using multi-criteria decision making and machine learning supported by remote sensing and GIS techniques. Remote Sens. 12(1), 106 (2019)
30. Lavate, S.H., Srivastava, P.: Optimal channel allocation: a dual approach with MCDM and machine learning. Int. J. Intell. Syst. Appl. Eng. 12(5s), 196–206 (2024)
31. Guhathakurata, S., et al.: South Asian countries are less fatal concerning covid-19: a fact-finding procedure integrating machine learning & multiple criteria decision-making (MCDM) technique. J. Inst. Eng. (India): Ser. B 102, 1–15 (2021)
32. Kartal, H., et al.: An integrated decision analytic framework of machine learning with multi-criteria decision making for multi-attribute inventory classification. Comput. Ind. Eng. 101, 599–613 (2016)
33. Musbah, H., et al.: Energy management using multi-criteria decision making and machine learning classification algorithms for intelligent system. Electric Power Syst. Res. 203, 107645 (2022)
34. Si, S.-L., et al.: DEMATEL technique: a systematic review of the state-of-the-art literature on methodologies and applications. Math. Probl. Eng. 2018, 3696457 (2018)
35. Watthayu, W., Peng, Y.: A Bayesian network based framework for multi-criteria decision making. In: Proceedings of the 17th International Conference on Multiple Criteria Decision Analysis (2004)
36. Fouladgar, M.M., et al.: A policy prioritization framework using causal layered analysis and MCDM: case study of Iran's environmental policies. Foresight 24(6), 678–693 (2022)
37. Yang, J.L., Tzeng, G.-H.: An integrated MCDM technique combined with DEMATEL for a novel cluster-weighted with ANP method. Expert Syst. Appl. 38(3), 1417–1424 (2011)

38. Wang, X., et al.: Analysis of factors influencing miners' unsafe behaviors in intelligent mines using a novel hybrid MCDM model. Int. J. Environ. Res. Public Health **19**(12), 7368 (2022)
39. Raut, R.D., et al.: Modeling the drivers of post-harvest losses–MCDM approach. Comput. Electron. Agric. **154**, 426–433 (2018)
40. Hsu, C.-C.: Evaluation criteria for blog design and analysis of causal relationships using factor analysis and DEMATEL. Expert Syst. Appl. **39**(1), 187–193 (2012)
41. Comes, T., et al.: Decision maps: a framework for multi-criteria decision support under severe uncertainty. Decis. Support. Syst. **52**(1), 108–118 (2011)
42. Salehpour Jam, A., et al.: GIS-based landslide susceptibility mapping using hybrid MCDM models. Nat. Hazards **108**, 1025–1046 (2021)
43. Seiti, H., et al.: R. Graph: a new risk-based causal reasoning and its application to COVID-19 risk analysis. Process Saf. Environ. Prot. **159**, 585–604 (2022)
44. Falatoonitoosi, E., Leman, Z., Sorooshian, S.: Casual strategy mapping using integrated BSC and MCDM-DEMATEL. J. Am. Sci. **8**(1), 125–155 (2012)
45. Yazdani, M., et al.: Integrated QFD-MCDM framework for green supplier selection. J. Clean. Prod. **142**, 3728–3740 (2017)

Unlocking Operational Clarity: The Integration of Artificial Intelligence, Digital Twins, and Mixed Reality in Production for Enhanced User Transparency

Carsten Wittenberg[✉], Sabine Boos, Felix Harst, Carsten Lanquillon, Morris Ohrnberger, Nicholas Schloer, Fabian Schoch, and Nicolaj C. Stache

Center for Industrial Artificial Intelligence (iAI), Heilbronn University, Max-Planck-Street 39, 74081 Heilbronn, Germany

{carsten.wittenberg,sabine.boos,felix.harst,carsten.lanquillon, morris.ohrnberger,nicholas.schloer,fabian.schoch, nicolaj.stache}@hs-heilbronn.de

Abstract. The implementation of artificial intelligence (AI) methods in automated production introduces several challenges that must be addressed. Among these challenges is the need for transparency, specifically the need to clarify the decisions made by AI during a production cycle. This issue is being tackled through the use of digital twin and mixed reality approaches. Within an interdisciplinary project funded by the Carl Zeiss Foundation, these challenges are being explored, and solutions are being developed through industrial lead applications. Beyond these applications and the promised collaborations with industry, the "Center for Industrial AI" will be established at Heilbronn University as a permanent entity to ensure the sustainable dissemination of results.

Keywords: Artificial Intelligence · Predictive Maintenance · Predictive Quality · Anomaly detection · process parameter optimization · Explainable AI · Human-Computer Interaction · Mixed Reality

1 Introduction

Digitalization is the initial step towards smart production in automated industrial processes [1, 2]. The collection and evaluation of production data plays a crucial role in digitalization. The term 'smart data', which refers to the usability of the data obtained, is more relevant than 'big data'. [3].

© The Author(s), under exclusive license to Springer Nature Switzerland AG 2024
H. Degen and S. Ntoa (Eds.): HCII 2024, LNAI 14735, pp. 449–460, 2024.
https://doi.org/10.1007/978-3-031-60611-3_31

In the modern industrial era, characterized by technological innovations and a paradigm shift in the production landscape, the integration of AI plays a key role in designing and optimizing production processes. Smart production is defined by the intelligent linking of digital technologies, data analysis, and artificial intelligence in industrial production. This not only opens up new horizons for increasing efficiency and resource utilization but also fundamentally transforms the way products are designed, manufactured, and managed [4].

The consistent application of AI technologies in the production environment is at the heart of this evolutionary fusion. Smart production with AI offers a wide range of innovative possibilities, from predictive maintenance to quality optimization.

This paper outlines the initial steps required to establish operational clarity of AI in an industrial context. Auxiliary technologies, such as digital twins and mixed reality, are utilized for this purpose.

2 Currently Research Goal

Figure 1 presents an overview of the research areas and lead applications under investigation and development in the project. The user interface (UX) is the central focus of development in all areas [5, 6].

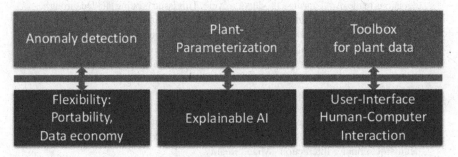

Fig. 1. Research areas and key applications [5]

' Currently, work is being done on anomaly detection with a focus on data economy and portability, as well as user experience (UX). Specifically, the team is developing the user interface for a sample system and the digital twin for the model factory [5, 6].

3 Model Factory

Heilbronn University has a testing facility for various technologies, including IIoT, automation, mixed reality, and AI [7]. The facility is used to test these technologies.

Figure 2 displays the AFB-Factory, marketed by Festo Didactic, which is a model factory that automatically fills, transports, and packages bottles through sample processes. At the end of each cycle, all components are dismantled and fed back into the system. The factory comprises multiple stations, each controlled by its own PLC.

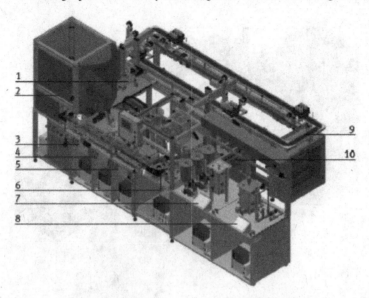

Fig. 2. Model factory at University Heilbronn

1. Station unpacking
2. Station robot recycling
3. MPS station distribute
4. MPS station processing
5. Handling MPS station
6. Filling station
7. MPS-PA station reactor (not available)
8. MPS-PA station mixing (not available)
9. Transportation station
10. Packaging station

The model factory's largest component is comprised of the AFB stations, which consist of five stations responsible for unpacking, recycling, filling, transporting, and packing the bottles. Figure 3 displays the stations, while the MPS stations and MPS-PA stations are grayed out.

3.1 MPS-PA

The Modular Production System Process Automation (MPS-PA) features a Compact Workstation that serves as a model for process automation and control technology. Figure 4 displays both the digital twin and the real module. The MPS-PA module replicates standard processes involving liquids, such as mixing and heating.

Figure 4 presents a direct comparison of the simulated system module and the real module of the model system.

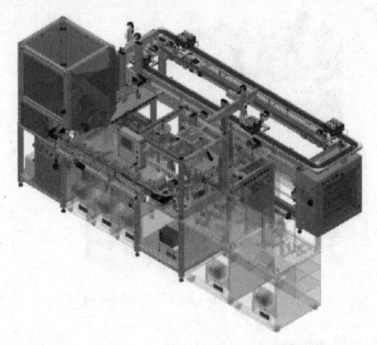

Fig. 3. Model factory without MPS-PA station at University Heilbronn

Fig. 4. Comparison of real system and simulation

4 Predictive Maintenance by Anomaly Detection with Deep Learning Methods

Determining appropriate maintenance intervals for machines and detecting faults and anomalies early, before they significantly impact the system and cause downtime or rejections, is a major challenge in mechanical engineering. To address this challenge, this project shows a deep learning method as a solution.

4.1 Process

For anomaly detection, only the sub-process of the plant, the MPS-PA station, is considered. This segment of the model factory is where the filling process takes place. Liquid is pumped to a container and the level of the container is measured and controlled. The pump is also controlled by an analog signal. When the level of the container is reached, the filling process begins. The flow rate into the container can be used as an additional measurement to detect anomalies.

4.2 Anomaly

To demonstrate the feasibility of anomaly detection in industrial plants, this study generated three synthetic anomaly cases: 1) a tank leak, 2) a partial inlet blockage, and 3) a partial outlet blockage. Figure 5 shows the normal condition (left) and an anomaly (right) in a graph over 30 s. The sampling rate has been reduced to 200 ms. The anomaly shown here is the partial blockage of the outlet. This anomaly is closest to normal. The most obvious way to identify this anomaly is the change in the shape of the flow measurement curve.

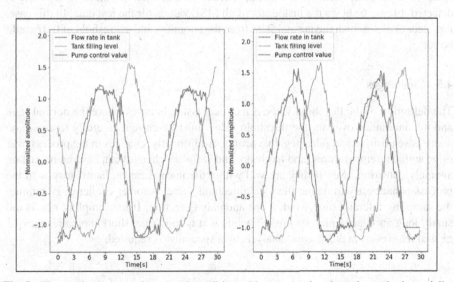

Fig. 5. The graph compares the normal condition with an anomaly where the outlet is partially blocked. The data has been normalized. The left side represents the normal condition, while the right side shows the anomaly

4.3 Anomaly Detection

The AI-based anomaly detection method in this example uses the normal state learning approach. The self-supervised model is trained using process data that represents only the normal state of the process, without any anomalies. This eliminates the need for labeled data. The model takes the flow rate into the tank and the analog control value of the pump as input variables and produces the level as output. The model takes the flow rate into the tank and the analog control value of the pump as input variables and produces the level as output. The model is designed to estimate the level based on the input variables for the normal state. The training is successful if the estimated level in the normal state deviates only slightly from the actual level, while the estimated level in the fault state deviates measurably from the actual level. The mean square error (MSE) is used as the metric. For the deep learning model, a small transformer-encoder model based on the architekture from "Attention is all you need" [8] was implemented for time series, and the following hyperparameters were chosen: The batch size is 32, the model dimension is 32, the transformer feedforward is 256, and the transformer has 4 layers and 4 heads with a drop-out rate of 0.1. The input data was summarized by a CNN into segments of size 16, with 50% overlap between segments. The model has about 200k parameters. The training time is a few minutes on an RTX 3050Ti.

4.4 Result

To detect an anomaly using the model, the first step is to perform an inference on the model. This provides an estimate of the level based on the input data as learned by the normal state. The estimate is then compared to the actual level and the mean squared error (MSE) is calculated. If the MSE deviates from a defined threshold, an anomaly is detected. Figure 6 shows the histogram of all MSE values for the test data. In this case, it is clear to distinguish the normal state from the anomaly, and a threshold of 0.07 could be set.

4.5 Challenges

The definition of the threshold value is a critical issue. In cases where the normal state and the anomalies overlap, the threshold value must be chosen carefully to avoid too many false positive and false negative results. Additionally, changes in the process over time, ambient temperatures, and hardware and software changes can have an impact on anomaly detection, even if they are still within the normal range. Familiarity with the process is necessary to define the ideal threshold value. Another challenge is defining the sampling rate and time window for anomaly detection. If the sampling rate is too small, long anomalies may be missed, while if it is too large, short anomalies may be missed. However, in either case, analysis by a specialist is required.

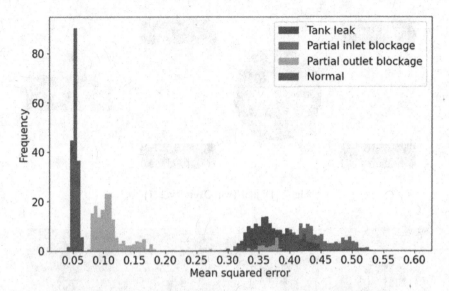

Fig. 6. Histogram of the MSE for each data point in the test data

5 Digital Twin and Mixed Reality

5.1 Digital Twin

A digital twin is a representation of a tangible or intangible object or process from the real world in the digital world. It does not matter if the counterpart already exists in the real world or will only exist in the future. In production technology, the 3D CAD model of the system is the basis for creating a digital twin. The illustration of the digital twin shows that the automation concept also serves as a basis, in addition to the CAD model. The digital twin is augmented with additional information from other sources, such as the physical model. Depending on the implementation, AI and XR data can further enhance the twin's capabilities. It serves as the central data processing hub for all components that interact with the system. [9, 10].

There are several expansion stages of the digital twin that can be considered. These include the component twin, which focuses on a single component, such as a valve in the model system; the asset twin, which combines multiple components; the system twin, which fully maps an entire system, such as a plant, and can therefore make statements about improving performance with the help of AI; and finally, the process twin, which describes the entire production and distribution process.

After generating the CAD data in the Unity game engine, the digital twin of the model system is kinematized by adding a physical model. While linear drives, grippers, and gripping are relatively easy to model, fluids pose a challenge for real-time physical modeling (Fig. 7).

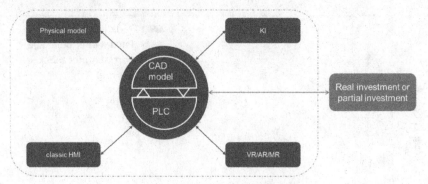

Fig. 7. Digital Twin Overview [11]

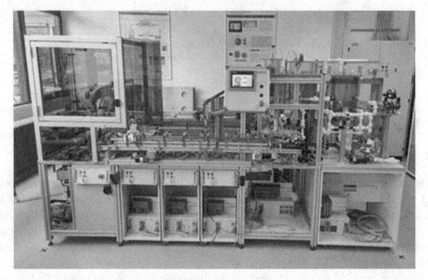

Fig. 8. Model factory

Figure 8 shows the current model system. The CAD data shown in Fig. 9 was reverse engineered from this system. This data is then provided with kinematics in the Unity game engine. There are several ways to implement the logic for this. The first option is to do this purely in Unity using the C-Shape programming language. The second way is to link Unity with the Siemens Simit software.

The MQTT protocol is used for data communication between the control unit and the digital twin. The system employs a Raspberry PI 5 as the MQTT broker, which also records data via the protocol to feed the AI. Alternatively, it is possible to retrieve this data using OPC-UA.

The accuracy of the digital twin is crucial for effective process monitoring. If the twin only approximates the system, it cannot provide reliable information about the process. However, if the twin precisely mirrors the system, including its current status, commands

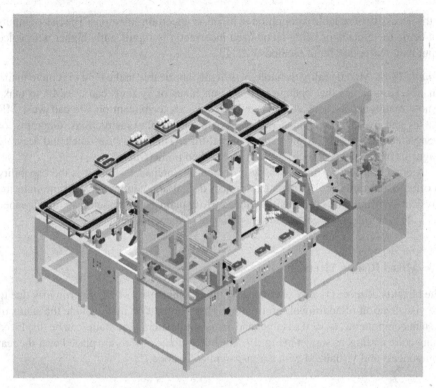

Fig. 9. Model factory as digital Twin

can be tested in the digital twin before being executed on the real system. This can prevent incorrect operation by the system operator and reduce potential damage. If the system operator accidentally opens or closes the wrong valve manually, the digital twin can check the effects on the system beforehand and, if necessary, initiate an emergency shutdown or refuse to open a valve. This overview is especially useful if the digital twin has access to various scenario results through the use of AI. In safety-critical environments, AI and digital twins can help prevent incorrect decisions with serious consequences [12].

5.2 Mixed Reality

Mixed reality is an advanced form of augmented reality that utilizes holographic elements for interaction. The primary means of user input in this concept is through gestures, which can also be used to display information. Additionally, eye tracking or voice input may be utilized. The latter is not suitable for industrial environments due to the increased auditory load on the surroundings [13].

Mixed Reality Into Industrial Area. As previously stated, voice control is not suitable for industrial systems with a certain basic volume. Therefore, we exclusively rely on intuitive gesture control for our system. This does not imply that we do not use auditory elements, but rather that we do not utilize voice control for command input. This is due to the necessity of reliable recognition of inputs in uncertain situations. The risk of inputs not being recognized or being recognized incorrectly is significantly higher with voice input than with other input methods. [2] [13].

Remote Work. Mixed reality technology is highly applicable in the field of remote maintenance. Companies that operate complex machines or systems can use MR to make remote maintenance more efficient and effective. A technician on site can wear MR glasses and use the augmented reality elements to display instructions, diagrams, or even video transmissions from experts in real-time. This allows for quick and accurate diagnosis of problems, which can then be rectified immediately.

A crucial aspect of mixed reality in remote maintenance support is the capability to offer visual guidance. Experts can project digital annotations in real-time onto the physical environment of the on-site technician to explain troubleshooting or maintenance steps. This significantly enhances the efficiency of the work performed.

5.3 Mixed Reality Meets AI

The benefits of mixed reality in enhancing the explainability of AI are primarily due to the visualization of additional information. This information may include the status of system components, as well as target and actual parameters. The status can be displayed using color coding, as shown in Fig. 10. The holographic objects are placed over the real components and visualized with a transparent color code.

Fig. 10. The status of the active pump from the MPS-PA is indicated by a green light.

6 Outlook

In principle, it is possible to access the sensors of mixed reality devices to provide the AI with additional data. For instance, quality control can be done through the visual sensors of the HoloLens or other mixed reality devices.

For the best possible monitoring of the model factory, anomaly and fault detection will be visualized with MR/VR in the future. Failure states and deviations from the normal state can be visualized directly in the VR/MR at the right place in the plant and provide the service personnel with the best possible information about the plant. Anomaly detection will be gradually extended to the entire plant. In addition, known fault classes of the sub-processes can be classified by further models to obtain direct information about the possible source of the fault.

Acknowledgments. The support of the Carls-Zeiss-Stiftung enabled us to carry out data collection, analysis and interpretation as well as to cover expenses for research materials and personnel costs. Their investment in our work has contributed significantly to the quality and impact of our research findings.

Carl Zeiss
Stiftung

Disclosure of Interests. The authors have no competing interests to declare that are relevant to the content of this article.

References

1. Kolberg, D., Zühlke, D.: Lean automation enabled by industry 4.0 technologies. IFAC-PapersOnLine **48**, 1870–1875 (2015). https://doi.org/10.1016/j.ifacol.2015.06.359
2. Wittenberg, C.: Challenges for the human-machine interaction in times of digitization, CPS & IIoT, and artificial intelligence in production systems. IFAC-PapersOnLine **55**, 114–119 (2022). https://doi.org/10.1016/j.ifacol.2022.10.241
3. Moving from big data to smart data for enhanced performance, business efficiency, and new business models. JIBM (2020). https://doi.org/10.37227/jibm-2020-02-16
4. Cioffi, R., Travaglioni, M., Piscitelli, G., Petrillo, A., de Felice, F.: Artificial intelligence and machine learning applications in smart production: progress, trends, and directions. Sustainability **12**, 492 (2020). https://doi.org/10.3390/su12020492
5. Wittenberg, C., et al.: User transparency of artificial intelligence and digital twins in production – research on lead applications and the transfer to industry. In: Degen, H., Ntoa, S. (eds.) Artificial Intelligence in HCI, LNCS, vol. 14051, pp. 322–332. Springer, Cham (2023). https://doi.org/10.1007/978-3-031-35894-4_24
6. Wittenberg, C., et al.: Künstliche Intelligenz und igitaler Zwilling in der Produktion – Forschung zu Leitanwendungen und dem Transfer in die Industrie. In: Mit Automatisierung gegen den Klimawandel. Hochschule für Technik, Wirtschaft und Kultur Leipzig (2023). https://doi.org/10.33968/2023.35

7. Rempel, W., Bauer, B., Stache, N.C., Wittenberg, C.: First steps to control a digitalized factory via augmented reality. IFAC-PapersOnLine **52**, 1–6 (2019). https://doi.org/10.1016/j.ifacol.2019.12.072
8. Singh, M., Fuenmayor, E., Hinchy, E., Qiao, Y., Murray, N., Devine, D.: Digital twin: origin to future. ASI **4**, 36 (2021). https://doi.org/10.3390/asi4020036
9. Tao, F., Xiao, B., Qi, Q., Cheng, J., Ji, P.: Digital twin modeling. J. Manuf. Syst. **64**, 372–389 (2022). https://doi.org/10.1016/j.jmsy.2022.06.015
10. Mit Automatisierung gegen den Klimawandel. Hochschule für Technik, Wirtschaft und Kultur Leipzig (2023). https://doi.org/10.33968/2023.01
11. Gursel, E., et al.: Using artificial intelligence to detect human errors in nuclear power plants: a case in operation and maintenance. Nucl. Eng. Technol. **55**, 603–622 (2023). https://doi.org/10.1016/j.net.2022.10.032
12. Wittenberg, C., Bauer, B., Stache, N.: A smart factory in a laboratory size for developing and testing innovative human-machine interaction concepts. In: Ahram, T., Falcão, C. (eds.) Advances in Usability and User Experience. Advances in Intelligent Systems and Computing, vol. 972, pp. 160–166. Springer, Cham (2020). https://doi.org/10.1007/978-3-030-19135-1_16

Author Index

© The Editor(s) (if applicable) and The Author(s), under exclusive license
to Springer Nature Switzerland AG 2024
H. Degen and S. Ntoa (Eds.): HCII 2024, LNAI 14735, pp. 461–464, 2024.
https://doi.org/10.1007/978-3-031-60611-3

Printed in the United States
by Baker & Taylor Publisher Services

Printed in the United States
by Baker & Taylor Publisher Services